"A marvelous narrative . . . As Beschloss explains, the greatest wartime presidents successfully leaven military action with moral concerns. . . . There are fascinating nuggets on virtually every page of *Presidents of War.*"

—Jay Winik, *The New York Times Book Review*

"Sparkle and bite . . . Valuable and engrossing study of how our chief executives have discharged the most significant of all their duties . . . Excellent . . . A fluent narrative that covers two centuries of national conflict."

—Richard Snow, *The Wall Street Journal*

"Filled with fascinating insights . . . A compelling work on the necessary qualities and dangers for wartime presidents."

—Albert R. Hunt, *Bloomberg*

"Beschloss sounds the alarm about the president's power to drag the nation into war. . . . Well crafted . . . Excellent."

—NPR

"In this monumental book, the incomparable Michael Beschloss tells the riveting story of how, through history, our presidents came to be so powerful and to lead Americans into waging major wars. With his new research discoveries and unerring eye for human detail, Beschloss has brought us an unforgettable narrative."

—Jon Meacham, Pulitzer Prize–winning author of *The Soul of America*

"Once again, Beschloss captures our presidents in terms both historic and human, showing that whoever holds the office will fearlessly—or fearfully—impact our world."

—Tom Hanks, author of *Uncommon Type*

"A powerful and troubling story, essential reading for our time."

—Drew Gilpin Faust, author of *This Republic of Suffering* and President Emerita and Lincoln Professor of History, Harvard University

"Michael Beschloss, our leading historian of the American presidency, presents a deeply researched and elegantly written chronicle of how presidents have handled this most daunting and important responsibility."

—Annette Gordon-Reed, Pulitzer Prize–winning author of *The Hemingses of Monticello* and Charles Warren Professor of American Legal History, Harvard Law School

"A sweeping chronicle of presidential war-making from the birth of the republic to the twenty-first century."

—David M. Kennedy, Pulitzer Prize–winning author of *Freedom from Fear* and Professor of History Emeritus, Stanford University

ALSO BY MICHAEL BESCHLOSS

Kennedy and Roosevelt: The Uneasy Alliance (1980)

Mayday: Eisenhower, Khrushchev and the U-2 Affair (1986)

The Crisis Years: Kennedy and Khrushchev, 1960–1963 (1991)

*At the Highest Levels: The Inside Story of the End of
the Cold War* (with Strobe Talbott, 1993)

Taking Charge: The Johnson White House Tapes, 1963–1964 (1997)

Reaching for Glory: Lyndon Johnson's Secret Tapes, 1964–1965 (2001)

*The Conquerors: Roosevelt, Truman and the
Destruction of Hitler's Germany* (2002)

*Presidential Courage: Brave Leaders and
How They Changed America* (2007)

Presidents of War

Michael Beschloss

B\D\W\Y

BROADWAY BOOKS

NEW YORK

Library of Congress Cataloging-in-Publication Data

Names: Beschloss, Michael R., author.
Title: Presidents of War / Michael Beschloss.
Description: First edition. | New York: Crown, [2018]
Identifiers: LCCN 2018007697| ISBN 9780307409607 (hardback) | ISBN
    9780804137010 (ebook)
Subjects: LCSH: Presidents—United States—History. | Political leadership—United
    States—History. | Executive power—United States—History. | United States—
    History, Military. | BISAC: HISTORY/Military/United States. | HISTORY/
    Military/Strategy. | HISTORY/United States/General.
Classification: LCC E176.1 .B475 2018 | DDC 355.00973—dc23
    LC record available at https://lccn.loc.gov/2018007697

ISBN 978-0-307-40961-4
Ebook ISBN 978-0-8041-3701-0

PRINTED IN THE UNITED STATES OF AMERICA

10 9 8 7 6 5 4 3 2 1

First Paperback Edition

For Afsaneh, Alex, and Cyrus

Preface

SINCE THE START of the Republic, Presidents of the United States have taken the American people into major wars roughly once in a generation. This book is about eight Presidents who did so, as well as Thomas Jefferson, who refused.* It illuminates the motivations of the war makers; how candid each was with the public; their struggles with Congress, the courts, and their critics; how they drew strength from spouses, families, and friends; their health, both physical and emotional; their respect for civil liberties (or lack of it); and whatever efforts they made to search for lessons from the American past. As a political history of Presidents who sought and waged war, the book suggests some of the most important qualities of leadership that Americans should demand when they choose a candidate for that office.

Above all, it shows how Presidents of war have dealt with political power under the Constitution. The framers of that document in 1787 knew that British and other European monarchs had abused their

---

* With the exception of the Civil War, this book covers major wars waged against foreign adversaries; thus it does not focus on the federal government's military struggles against native Americans, which lasted for more than half the life of the United States. The 2001 terrorist attacks and the wars in Afghanistan and Iraq are too recent to be written about as history, so they are treated synoptically.

absolute authority to make war: if a regime was growing unpopular, they sometimes cited or invented a foreign danger in order to launch a war that would unite their people and expand their own power and popular esteem. To reduce the risk of such offenses by an American President, the Founders created a Constitution that gave Congress the sole power to declare war, and divided the responsibility to wage war between the executive and legislative branches. As Congressman Abraham Lincoln wrote to his friend William Herndon in 1848, the early Americans resolved that "*no one man* should hold the power" to take the nation into war.

As this volume demonstrates, during the past two centuries, Presidents, step by step, have disrupted the Founders' design. With the too-frequent acquiescence of Congress, they have seized for themselves the power to launch large conflicts, almost on their own authority. It is telling that the last time a President asked Congress to declare war was 1942. Were the Founders to come back, they would probably be astonished and chagrined to discover that, in spite of their ardent strivings, the life or death of much of the human race has now come to depend on the character of the single person who happens to be the President of the United States.

Presidents of War

CONTENTS

Prologue

The Fugitive

AND SO IT had come to this. Horrified as he stood on a height above the Potomac, James Madison, the fourth President of the United States—and now, some wondered, the last?—watched his beloved Washington City as it seemed to vanish into a crimson-orange swirl of fire. It was after midnight on Wednesday, August 24, 1814, and Madison was a fugitive, escaping the Capital—first by ferry, then by galloping horse—for the dark wilderness of Virginia.

Still wearing formal knee breeches and buckled shoes, the sixty-three-year-old Madison knew that the invader-incendiaries from Great Britain were out for his capture and arrest, which might force him to be hanged. But he kept dismounting his horse to stare, with those intelligent blue eyes that "sparkled like stars," at the inferno across the Potomac. He could not help himself. As a student of the Bible since college, Madison knew that God had warned Lot's wife not to look back at burning Sodom or else become a pillar of salt. Nevertheless the beleaguered President—who stood about five feet, four inches, and weighed perhaps a hundred pounds—kept gazing at the flaming, otherworldly spectacle, the nadir of the War of 1812, which many Americans bitterly called "Mr. Madison's War."

Earlier that day, Madison's popular, shrewd, vivacious wife, Dolley, had stayed behind at the Executive Mansion while James was out reviewing the forces charged with Washington's defense. She asked her husband's enslaved body servant Paul Jennings (who once lauded the President as a man who would not "strike a slave") to bring out ale and cider in anticipation of a three o'clock White House dinner they were planning for Cabinet secretaries, "military gentlemen," and their wives.* Dolley hoped that if Washingtonians learned that the President's lady was keeping a normal schedule, they would feel more sanguine about the danger of the approaching British marauders. But she received a worried, scribbled plea from her nearby sister Anna: "Tell me for gods sake where you are. . . . We can hear nothing but what is horrible here."

From the Mansion, Dolley peered anxiously through a spyglass with "unwearied anxiety." As she wrote her other sister, Lucy, she was thinking, "Mr. Madison comes not; may God protect him!" Recoiling from the distant booms of British cannon, Dolley refused to flee until "my dear husband" was safe in her arms. But in preparation, she quickly packed letters, books, valuables, a demijohn of wine, and clothes. Determined to prevent the British from grabbing the life-sized portrait of George Washington, an irresistible battle trophy, she called out, "Save that picture! . . . If not possible, destroy it!" She ordered the painting removed from its gilded frame and taken by wagon to a "humble but safe roof," thus ensuring her place in American history. (The Declaration of Independence, Constitution, and other treasures had already been slipped into plain linen sacks and taken to a Virginia gristmill.)

Then the Madisons' freedman servant James Smith, waving his hat, cantered up with a message from the President: "Clear out! General Armstrong has ordered a retreat!"† Stuffing flatware into her handbag, Dolley and Sukey, her enslaved personal maid, were helped into

---

* The President's residence was not officially called the White House until President Theodore Roosevelt issued an executive order to this effect in 1901, but the term was occasionally used during Madison's time.

† General John Armstrong Jr. was Secretary of War.

carriages, which rushed them and their traveling companions across the Potomac to the wilds of northern Virginia, where she and James had agreed to meet. But Dolley was told that the President could not be found, and she cowered in agony and tears. Part of her fear stemmed from the fact that the British invaders were not her husband's only enemies. Furious at the invasion of their Capital and, in fact, at Madison's whole war, some of his own countrymen had vowed to commit violence against the President if he tried to flee the city. "I hear of much hostility towards him," Dolley had warned her sister Lucy. "Disaffection stalks around us." One American had threatened the President with "dagger or poison." According to Paul Jennings, when Dolley was desperately seeking safe haven that night in Virginia, one would-be hostess raged at her, "If that's you, come down and go out! Your husband has got mine out fighting and, damn you, you shan't stay in my house!"

Back across the Potomac, about 150 British soldiers—"the most hellish looking fellows that ever trod God's earth," recalled one bystander—torched the Capitol of the United States. At nine o'clock, spurred on by the British Rear Admiral George Cockburn, soon called "the harlequin of havoc," with "sun-burnt visage and his rusty gold-laced hat," the arsonists had laid siege to the limestone building—two still-unconnected wings shut down in midconstruction by the war. In the chambers of the House, Senate, and Supreme Court, the enemy soldiers piled up mahogany desks, red morocco chairs, green curtains, and books. Before they lit this tinder with rocket powder, Cockburn sat in the House Speaker's chair and mocked the democratic pretensions of Britain's ex-colonies, demanding of his brother redcoats, "Shall this harbor of Yankee 'democracy' be burned? All for it will say, 'Aye!'"

Soon the Capitol was enveloped by jagged tongues of orange flame, so searing that glass lamp shades melted. Cockburn decreed the raising of his own country's Union Jack, then, riding on a mule, ordered his redcoats to march double file down Pennsylvania Avenue. Demanding their silence, to avoid arousing Washingtonians to fight back, Cockburn shouted, "If any man speaks in the ranks, I'll put him to death!" One American yelled at Cockburn that if George Washington were still alive, "you could not have done this." The Admiral replied that George

Washington, unlike Madison, would never have "left his capital defenseless, for the purpose of making conquest abroad."

Bursting into the White House, Cockburn's soldiers sat down at the dining table—still set with crystal, gold, and silver—and feasted on the Madisons' uneaten Virginia hams and "super-excellent Madeira." Marching upstairs into the President's private dressing room, whose opened drawers betrayed a hasty departure, Cockburn seized the black bicorne military hat owned by the man he derided as "Little Jemmy Madison" and merrily stuck it on the tip of his bayonet. Stealing a seat cushion from Dolley's boudoir, Cockburn made ribald jokes about her voluptuous derriere and breasts. Other redcoats donned the President's starchy shirt and waved his ceremonial sword. Madison's guitar and pianoforte, a half-packed portmanteau, and French sofas and commodes purchased by Thomas Jefferson were all gathered and shoved into a pile in the Mansion's grand oval reception room. These and other spoils of war were lit by perhaps fifty torches, each charged with glowing coals from a nearby tavern. Soon, it was said, the Mansion was "wrapt in one entire flame." Cockburn reputedly finished his night of destruction at a nearby brothel, reveling in "the coarse luxury of lust."

James Madison, who had done so much to conceive the political institutions of Washington, DC, was reviled by many of his fellow citizens as the destroyer of their capital city. Vicious handbills appeared, demanding that the President receive a "black and bitter day of retribution" for "this foul stain on our national character." They called him a "coward" who had fled his White House command post for Virginia, "begging" shelter and bread "from door to door"—and a cad, leaving poor Dolley "to shift for herself." Such attacks stung the proud Madison. But his ordeal was more profound.

The War of 1812 was the first major conflict conducted by a President of the United States under the document of which Madison was justly revered as the "Father." During the Constitutional Convention at Philadelphia, Madison and the other Founders had debated the quandaries of war. They sought to ensure that, unlike in the Old World societies governed by sovereigns, Americans would go to war only when it was absolutely necessary—and that the decision would be made not by the

President but by the legislature. Virginia's George Mason had written that he was "ag[ainst] giving the power of war to the Executive, because [that branch was] not safely to be trusted with it." James Wilson of Pennsylvania insisted that the Constitution "will not hurry us into war; it is calculated to guard against it." Madison himself considered war "the true nurse of executive aggrandizement." As he reminded Jefferson in 1798, "The constitution supposes, what the History of all Gov[ernmen]ts demonstrates, that the Ex[ecutive] Is the branch of power most interested in war, & most prone to it. It has accordingly with studied care, vested the question of war in the Legisl[ative]."*

The 1812 conflict proved to be the first major test of the constitutional system for waging war. In Philadelphia, Madison the Founder had worried that American Presidents, like the European monarchs they execrated, might be tempted to take the nation into military confrontation without a national consensus and an immediate, overwhelming foreign danger. But with the War of 1812, Madison had, however reluctantly, succumbed to exactly that temptation. Much of the country and Congress had opposed waging war with Great Britain, and two years into this struggle, many Americans still did not fully understand why they were fighting.

By leading his country into a major war that had no absolute necessity or overwhelming support from Congress and the public, Madison, of all people, had opened the door for later Presidents to seek involvement in future conflicts that suffered from such shortcomings. Madison's fateful decision to seek this war had brought him, after midnight, to this dark Virginia forest, searching for Dolley and running for his life.

---

* Early in the process, Congress was to be given authority to "make" war, but Madison and Elbridge Gerry of Massachusetts successfully changed that word to the more specific "declare," so the record shows, "leaving to the Executive the power to repel sudden attacks."

CHAPTER ONE

"Torrent of Passion"

THE CASCADE OF hostilities that led to the War of 1812 and the burning of Washington had begun a half decade earlier, under President Thomas Jefferson, when an unexpected naval confrontation brought the United States and its estranged British parent to the edge of full-scale war. As Jefferson later mused during his retirement, in a letter to his "antient friend and classmate" James Maury, "The affair of the Chesapeake put war into my hand. I had only to open it, and let havoc loose." Had Jefferson opened his hand, the United States would have waged a War of 1807. But instead his political mastery, his refusal to enter a war unprepared, and his insistence on peace prevented his country from lurching into military conflict.

On Monday morning, June 22, 1807, all was right with the New World, or so it seemed. It was the radiant first dawn of the summer solstice, and the USS *Chesapeake* moved across the shimmering harbor off Norfolk, Virginia. It was starting a yearlong voyage to the Mediterranean, where the four-masted frigate was to relieve the wilted crew of the *Constitution* (which later became famous as "Old Ironsides"). Shambling down the *Chesapeake*'s sun-washed decks was the tall, genial, pear-shaped thirty-eight-year-old Commodore James Barron, whose swallowtail pennant snapped overhead.* Barron had a pink face, bulbous red nose, and sad, dark blue eyes, which assumed a perpetual squint. With his casual gait, Barron did not radiate command presence.†

Before his ship sailed, he had proudly received this personal request, written with quill pen, from his Commander-in-Chief:

> Th: Jefferson presents his friendly salutations to Capt. Barron and asks the favor of him to give a safe conveyance to the inclosed letter for mr Higgins at Malta. It is to ask of him to send a pipe of Marsala Medeira by any good conveyance which may occur. if Capt Barron can advise mr Higgins of any such Th: J. will be thankful to him, & he wishes him a pleasant voyage.

Later, after his ill-fated command of the *Chesapeake* wrecked his career, Barron would angrily scrawl across the obverse side of the President's message: "From that infamous Hypocrite, T. Jefferson."

* * *

I N 1794, WARY of Atlantic battles between Britain and France, Congress had grudgingly approved President George Washington's appeal to build six mighty frigates.‡ Unlike Washington and his successor, John Adams, President Jefferson treated the US Navy like an unlovable stepchild. Seeking to trim the entire federal government, he wished to minimize the nation's standing military force, which, he believed, had the

---

* Commodore was then the highest rank in the young US Navy, which eschewed the title of Admiral until 1862 because it sounded too European and aristocratic.

† Years later, Barron scrawled out some notes about himself in the third person: "He was very remarkable for never exalting himself—he had a sense of native dignity, but was never vain glorious. . . . His manners were self-possessed & gentlemanly and always gentle & kind to subordinates. . . . He was systematically a temperate man in all things—restricting himself in eating & drinking. Was always much interested in the progress & happiness of his country—deeply sensitive to its honour & glory."

‡ At Washington's behest, five of the frigates were named for an institution or a metaphor related to the US Constitution (the USS *President, Congress, Constitution, United States,* and *Constellation*). The sixth was the *Chesapeake.*

dangerous potential to draw it into unnecessary wars. When Jefferson took power in 1801, he cited the peace Adams had recently concluded with France as an excuse to halve the military's $5 million budget, including the $2.1 million annual stipend for the Navy.

Jefferson's designs against the Navy were so notorious that four men refused his request to be Secretary of the Navy before he appointed a middling Baltimore lawyer, Robert Smith.* The President ordered Smith to fire two-thirds of enlisted Navy men and mothball most US frigates in order to avoid a skirmish on the Atlantic that might draw the country into war. Some of his ideas for cutting the Navy were laughable. He hallucinated that the entire American coast, from Boston all the way down to Savannah, could be defended by two hundred cheap gunboats, manned by noble citizen volunteers. Jefferson's light, flimsy vessels—derided as the "Jeffs"—were prone to capsize when they reached the choppy Atlantic, their guns were too small, and their crews were sitting ducks for musket fire. Nevertheless he compelled his Republican majorities in Congress to finance 177 such boats for a sum that could have paid for eight new frigates.† Federalist critics chortled, "The President of the United States—*First Admiral of American Gun-Boats!*"

During his first term as President, Jefferson pursued the conflict known as the First Barbary Coast War, in which American merchant ships were protected against pirates off of North Africa. Although Congress had refused to declare war, it authorized the President to "protect our commerce and chastise their insolence—by sinking, burning or destroying their ships and vessels wherever you shall find them."‡ The conflict claimed about three dozen American lives. When it was

---

* Smith's chief qualification was that his brother Samuel was a powerful Maryland Senator.

† Members of Jefferson's Democratic-Republican Party—formed to oppose Alexander Hamilton's Federalists after the political cleavage between the two Founders during the 1790s and the lineal ancestor of today's Democratic Party—called themselves Republicans.

‡ This episode encouraged some later Presidents to engage in hostilities after seeking a lower level of authorization from the House and Senate than a war declaration. Nevertheless, in 1805, with Spanish forces threatening Louisiana, Jefferson showed his reverence for the congressional war power by writing, "Considering that Congress alone is constitutionally invested with the power of changing our condition from peace to war, I have thought it my duty to await their authority for using force." He desisted after Congress said no.

settled with the Pasha of Tripoli in 1805, Jefferson had every US frigate except the *Constitution* detained "in ordinary" at the Washington Navy Yard, where their oaken timbers rotted in the sludge of a shallow river. The Barbary hero Commodore Edward Preble wrote to James Barron, "What are we to do for a Navy, God only knows." Then in January 1807, Secretary Smith ordered Barron to sail the *Chesapeake* to Gibraltar as the new commander of the Mediterranean Squadron.

Of George Washington's original frigates, the *Chesapeake* was the runt. So many corners had been cut in its design that its architect, the renowned Joshua Humphreys, took his name off the vessel. When the *Chesapeake* was launched, a man was killed, which fueled a belief among sailors that this frigate was cursed. In May 1807, after major repairs, Barron took the *Chesapeake*'s helm for what proved to be a slow, ill-starred monthlong journey to Norfolk. The ship ran aground two miles downriver. Five crewmen were killed in freak accidents. Eighty-five others were stricken by a fast-spreading contagion. Thirteen sailors deserted. Ill-fitting cartridges and sponges, as well as faulty gunpowder and cannon, kept the ship from firing the customary sixteen-gun salute while gliding past Mount Vernon. When the *Chesapeake* arrived in Norfolk, its crew was 60 men short of its full 329. Informed that the frigate had to leave Norfolk fast, recruiters were quickly sent to New York and Philadelphia, seeking men to work the ship for $12 a month. Many of those recruited had never sailed before, let alone for a year on treacherous waters.

Barron had been knocked back on his heels to learn that the six top officers provided for his Mediterranean voyage were all protégés of Captain John Rodgers, his rival and mortal enemy. One of these, Barron's newly assigned captain (since Barron would command the whole squadron, he was not technically captain of the *Chesapeake*), would be Master Commandant Charles Gordon. Barron had tried to block Gordon's appointment, charging that the stylish Maryland patrician was "too much addicted to pleasure," but the younger man had high-level protection. Gordon's uncle by marriage was Jefferson's Treasury Secretary, Albert Gallatin, and Gordon's cousin, Baltimore Congressman

Joseph Nicholson, had worked hard for Jefferson's election. Nicholson's brother-in-law was a lawyer and casual poet called Francis Scott Key.

✳ ✳ ✳

ONCE THE *Chesapeake* made its way onto the high seas, Commodore Barron welcomed some of his most distinguished passengers to his elegant cabin.* Dr. John Bullus was the newly appointed US consul and Navy agent for the Mediterranean. The genial, handsome, young, London-born Bullus had been President Jefferson's personal physician; he was accompanied by his wife, Charlotte Jane, his children, Robert, Oscar, and Charlotte, and a "maidservant and Negro boy."

Another guest was Captain John Hall, who commanded fifty-two Marines aboard Barron's ship. In 1804, Jefferson, who was passionate about music, had sent Hall to Italy, which, he insisted, had the world's best musicians, to recruit some for the US Marine Band, which Jefferson had christened "The President's Own." After nine months of effort, Hall returned with sixteen. But people asked why Jefferson was wasting public money on musicians while starving the rest of the military. In response, the President turned his back on his Italians. One of the musicians was Gaetano Carusi, who complained that his troupe had been "lured by false and deceitful promises," then "insulted and betrayed with all the indignity of Barbarians." Thus Carusi and his sons scrambled onto the *Chesapeake,* along with most of his fellow players, all impatient to get back to Italy.

When Barron's party sat down to dinner after 2:00 p.m., his ship was seven hours out from Norfolk. Through an open porthole appeared a menacing sight—the HMS *Leopard,* a fifty-gun British ship of the line, tacking in parallel with the smaller *Chesapeake* on its windward side. Barron should have been alarmed—only a vessel with warlike intentions would pass that way—but he did not rise from his dining table.

---

* Barron could entertain lavishly because the Navy had laid on 3,900 pounds of cheese, 63,875 loaves of bread, 450 barrels of beef and pork, and 4,563 gallons of wine and spirits for this trip.

When the meal was over, the *Leopard* was only about sixty yards away. Barron walked out onto the starboard gangway. From the *Leopard,* Captain Salusbury Pryce Humphreys called through a brass trumpet megaphone that he had a message for the Commodore. Through his own trumpet, Barron shouted back that Humphreys should send a man over. Thus, at 3:39, the British Lieutenant John Meade boarded the *Chesapeake.* Taken to the Commodore's cabin, Meade handed Barron an order from Admiral George Berkeley, the British Commander-in-Chief for North America, charging that British seamen had "deserted and entered On Board the United States frigate called the *Chesapeak.*" Berkeley was demanding a search of the American frigate.*

After Meade's arrival, Barron now called in Dr. Bullus—not only for advice but no doubt also to have a high-level witness in case his behavior should later be criticized. Barron told Meade that David Erskine had conceded that the *Melampus* men were not deserters. (Knowing that Ratford had not been included in Erskine's protest, Barron did not mention him.) Unfamiliar with high diplomacy, Meade replied to Barron that he did not know who Erskine was. After consulting Bullus and Gordon, Barron sat down and, playing for time, took a half hour to draft his response to Humphreys, which said that he would never let his crew be mustered by anyone but its own officers. Meade took Barron's defiant document and climbed back into his rowboat.

Soon Barron saw a warning banner flying from the *Leopard*'s mast-

---

* Barron knew that his crew included a British sailmaker named Jenkin Ratford, who had deserted the British sloop *Halifax*. On the streets of Norfolk, Ratford (who used the alias "John Wilson") had encountered a *Chesapeake* recruiter, who offered him immediate US citizenship. Ratford accepted; the next day, parading with three dozen other new recruits, he was spotted by the *Halifax* captain, Lord James Townshend, and cried, "I will be damned if I go back! I am safe in the land of liberty!" Ratford's case was referred to the British Minister, David Montagu Erskine, who was told that the *Chesapeake*'s crew included four other deserters from the British frigate *Melampus*. Deeming such problems a "trifling" waste of his time, Erskine sent a protest about the four *Melampus* deserters to Secretary of State James Madison but did not add Ratford's name. Consulted about Erskine's protest, Barron had responded that one of the *Melampus* crewmen had vanished and the other three were native-born Americans. Berkeley had dropped his demand for the *Melampus* quartet but complained that there were still "about ten thousand British seamen in United States employ."

head and that the tompions had been removed from the British guns. Phlegmatic about the *Chesapeake's* immediate peril, the Commodore told Gordon, "You had better get your gundeck clear, as their intentions appear serious." But as both men knew, the *Chesapeake* was grossly unprepared for battle. Strewn across its decks, obstructing guns and passageways, were tall wooden secretaries and steamer trunks belonging to the Bulluses and Halls, an armorer's forge, empty casks, a large grindstone, planks of lumber, pork barrels, cases of claret, and chicken coops. Lying on hammocks, strung across gunbarrels, were dozens of men groaning from the illness that had decimated the *Chesapeake's* crew.

Barron asked Gordon to bring his men to quarters, but quietly, so that the British could not "charge us with making the first hostile show." (This made little sense, because the *Leopard* was so close that its crew could see the US preparations for battle.) Then, by mistake, the *Chesapeake's* drummer performed a drumroll. Barron cried out for silence, and Gordon struck the drummer with the flat of his sword. Some of the crewmen mistakenly presumed that the drummer's sudden silence meant they should stand down. Hall and Bullus sent their wives and the Bullus children down to hide in the ship's steaming cockpit.

From the *Leopard,* sailing even closer, Humphreys shouted at Barron through his megaphone that he had been ordered to remove the British deserters. Risking the chance that the British would think he was stalling (which they did and he was), Barron bellowed back with a fib: "I do not understand what you say!" While his crewmen yanked bulky anchor cable away from the *Chesapeake's* guns, Barron and everyone on his ship heard the *Leopard,* now side by side with the *Chesapeake,* fire a warning shot across his bow. Then, after perhaps two minutes, came a ferocious, full-scale broadside that tore through the frigate's sails and masts.

Through flame and black smoke, Barron, yelling through his trumpet, tried to hail Humphreys in hopes of working things out, but it was too late. Two more broadsides crashed into the *Chesapeake's* hull.

One US crewman's heart was struck by a twenty-four-pound ball, which killed him instantly. Others were wounded, including Barron. With his legs bleeding from flying splinters, he shouted at Gordon, "For God's sake, fire one gun for the honor of the flag!" But how could the *Chesapeake* return the *Leopard*'s fire? Most of the fifty-four powder horns required to prime their ship's guns were empty. Nor were there matches at hand. Some of the crewmen fled from their battle stations, refusing to "be shot at like so many sheep." The hapless Barron cried out, "For God's sake, gentlemen, will nobody do their duty?"

Taking matters into his own hands, Gordon raced to the ship's magazine, snatched two filled powder horns from a seaman, ran back down the gun deck, and threw the horns to Lieutenant William Henry Allen, who had three guns primed. But the only available loggerhead was too cool to ignite them. Allen rushed to the galley stove, grabbed a red-hot coal and brought it back.* Thanks to Allen, one American gun finally sounded, whereupon Barron bawled, "Stop firing, stop firing! We have struck!" The *Leopard* fired once more. Then, with a handkerchief stanching his bloody leg, Barron hauled down the *Chesapeake*'s flag.

Three Americans were dead, eight gravely wounded. Barron sent Lieutenant Sidney Smith by rowboat to the *Leopard* with a message for Humphreys: "Sir, I consider the frigate *Chesapeake* your prize, and am ready to deliver her to any officer authorized to receive her." Even now, the *Chesapeake* was surrounded by its ship-of-fools aura: as its gig was lowered into the water, someone caught his finger in the pulley. Suffering from his wounds and mortification, Barron stumbled to his cabin and collapsed.† The British victors quickly found the recruited Jenkin

---

* Some grammar school history books later had it that the stalwart Allen bravely carried the coal in his bare hands, searing his own flesh, but more likely he carried it by cup or ladle.

† According to the questionable, much-later recollection of Charlotte Bullus, one member of the *Leopard*'s boarding party conveyed Humphreys's invitation to her British-born husband to escape the *Chesapeake* and enjoy, along with his family, the comforts of his motherland's ship. Mrs. Bullus claimed that her husband so harshly dismissed the offer—his "patriotism and indignation" had been "sternly aroused"—that he and the Briton took up swords for a moment of "cut and thrust" before a bystander's "speedy interposition" foreclosed more violence.

Ratford crouching in the *Chesapeake*'s coalhole, and clamped him, along with the renegades from the HMS *Melampus*, in irons.* Shaking his head aboard the *Leopard*, Humphreys pocketed the American instrument of surrender and deplored the carnage.

As the sun descended, the *Chesapeake*'s seamen scattered sand across the bloody decks of their ship. Barron called Bullus, Gordon, and other high officers to his cabin and proposed that they all share responsibility for the day's mistakes. He felt that while he may have been indecisive, bracing the ship against battle had been Gordon's job. Barron also noted that Bullus had helped him draft the response to the démarche from the *Leopard*. Thus weren't they all in this together? Dubious from the start about Barron, the other officers did not agree. Gordon brashly told him, "I regret we had not gone to quarters and returned the *Leopard*'s fire. . . . A few more broadsides would have been to our credit." Lieutenant William Crane agreed: "Better if the *Chesapeake* were blown from under us than to be thus dishonored!"

The next day, under heavy squalls, the tragic ship that was now funereally called "the late U.S. frigate *Chesapeake*" returned to Norfolk. Its sails and riggings were ravaged and its deck under three feet of water. After hopping off the frigate, Gordon and Bullus boarded a pilot boat, bound upriver for the nation's capital, where they intended to inform President Jefferson and his Cabinet that Barron should be blamed for the *Chesapeake* disaster.

✻ ✻ ✻

IN THAT AGE when news fanned out slowly, by dint of gazettes and wax-sealed letters delivered on horseback, citizens of Norfolk were the first to learn of the *Chesapeake*'s assault. As surgeons cared for the wounded in that city's Marine Hospital, a frenzied throng outside, called the largest in Norfolk's history, demanded "revenge" for the

---

* The British later hanged Ratford and severely whipped the three other deserters before sending them to prison. They were offered a choice between death or rejoining the Royal Navy.

"unprovoked, piratical, savage and assassin-like attack" and destroyed hundreds of hogsheads of water destined for a British schooner. The *Norfolk Gazette and Publick Ledger* cried, "The blood of our countrymen has been shed by the hand of violence, and the honour and independence of our nation insulted." In Virginia's capital of Richmond, someone roared, "The first blow of war has been struck!"

As the fury spread, the *Massachusetts Spy* announced, "THE NATION INSULTED." In Washington, DC, Mayor Robert Brent asked citizens to appear "in your full strength at the Theatre with souls indignant but calm" to denounce the "perfidious and pusylanimous enemy." Baltimore's *American* called the British "desperately mad." In Philadelphia, the *Democratic Press* asserted that the "savage outrage" had "no precedent in naval annals," adding darkly, "If we do go to war, it will be with the united energies of a whole people." Philadelphia's *Aurora* called Americans to arms:

> The time is now arrived, which leaves us but *one choice;* either to submit to the galling yoke of *British slavery;* or firmly resent the numerous insults we daily receive from that nation. Already have your citizens been seized, and forced on board ships of war. . . . Already have the banners of your country been repeatedly and grossly insulted, not only by a set of unprincipled *villains,* but even under the absolute orders of a *British commodore.* . . . The various public prints have informed you of the particulars of the most *cowardly* and *damnable* outrage committed on the frigate Chesapeake, by which many of your fellow citizens have been *inhumanly murdered.* . . . ROUSE my countrymen and avenge the death of your slaughtered citizens . . . and if *they will not* punish their officers, for these unwarrantable outrages on a friendly nation, *let us do ourselves justice.*

The reason why the confrontation between the *Chesapeake* and the *Leopard* now threatened war was that, twenty-four years after winning their independence, Americans still felt affronted and besieged by England. In 1794, to avert a military rematch that he knew America might lose, President Washington had sent Chief Justice John Jay to London, where Jay hammered out a treaty sufficiently weighted with American concessions that an angry US House of Representatives nearly refused to pay for it. In that compact, Britain pledged to pull its garrisons out of forts in the Northwest Territory, discuss the disputed US border with British Canada, and repay America for hundreds of merchant ships it had peremptorily seized. But American hearts still burned with grievance.

Some of the problem was psychological. As a Kentucky paper observed, "Britain never has treated the Americans as an independent nation, and has only acknowledged it in words." Many British leaders did not bother to conceal their view that the union of what they deprecated as their "quondam colonies" was a short-lived, radical experiment, an impulsive child on the world stage who could be bullied without serious penalty, especially as Jefferson shrank the US Navy. Tensions grew in 1803 when British leaders feared that their empire was in jeopardy from Napoleon. Overwhelmed by their sense of emergency, Britons were furious at the United States for staying neutral in the struggle and moved to hamper America's ability to help the French. In the 1805 *Essex* decision, British courts ruled that the Royal Navy could lawfully capture US ships that took cargo between France and its colonies. Ignoring Secretary Madison's protests against this "new and shameful depredation," the British Navy seized and sometimes fired upon hundreds of US trading vessels.

Great Britain also escalated its strong-arm practice of impressment. The Royal Navy would overtake another country's merchant ship, search its crew for British subjects (or crewmen they claimed as British), and drag the suspects away for maritime service.* No weapon of British oppression rankled Americans more than impressment. Philadelphia's *Democratic Press* complained, "George the Third is thus maintained *king of the impressed Americans and sovereign of our flag!!*" The journal asked, "Have they an indisputable right to impress and hold in

---

* Many of the seamen thus detained on US vessels were certified American citizens, but the British refused to grant such status for anyone who had been a British subject as late as 1783, when Americans won their Revolutionary War. "Once a subject," Britons liked to say, "always a subject."

bondage our Fathers our Children and our Citizens? . . . Why will the spirit of '76 permit the sea robbers of Britain, the tyrants of the ocean, to insult with impunity, the flag of our country?" For Thomas Jefferson, impressment was a test of the human rights cause that was so deep in his heart.

* * *

WATCHING THE *Chesapeake* furor from the Executive Mansion, Jefferson wrote a friend, "Never since the battle of Lexington, have I seen this country in such a state of exasperation as at present. And even that did not produce such unanimity." But the President knew that, especially after his drive to cut the military, the United States was in no shape to fight England. Jefferson hated war, which, to him, would introduce more federal spending, centralize political power, and strengthen the "monied classes," all prospects that he abhorred. He had been disgusted when in 1798 President Adams had allowed fellow Federalists to goad him toward what Jefferson considered to be an unnecessary war with France, designed, at least in part, to bolster their party's sagging political fortunes. But in the aftermath of the *Chesapeake,* Jefferson understood that he must now do something to satisfy the nation's rising calls for revenge.

Arriving in Washington on Thursday, June 25, 1807, Gordon and Dr. Bullus handed the President and Secretary Smith an account of the *Chesapeake* debacle written by Barron, no doubt adding their own oral recitation of the Commodore's errors. Jarred by what he heard, at 5:20 p.m., Jefferson urgently summoned the five members of his Cabinet: "I am sincerely sorry that I am obliged to ask your attendance here without a moment's avoidable delay." Told that Gallatin and Henry Dearborn, his Secretary of War, had already decamped the swampy, overheated "Seat of Government"—infamous for yellow fever and other summer afflictions—for cooler respites in Maine and New York, the President deferred the meeting. He wrote his friend William Cabell, the Governor of Virginia, that when his Cabinet convened, "we shall then determine on the course which the exigency & our constitutional powers call for." He went on to say that "whether the outrage is a proper cause of war" was an issue that belonged "exclusively to Congress." He hoped the Senate and House would conclude that, "having taught so many other useful lessons to Europe," the United States should show the British "that there are peaceable means of repressing injustice."

As Dolley Madison noticed, Jefferson had been recently suffering from "a sick headake every day," with the pain forcing him to "retire to a dark room" at nine in the mornings. The danger of a new military confrontation with England was unlikely to help. On Wednesday, July 1, Jefferson had his full Cabinet to dinner on the state floor of the Executive Mansion. The secretaries approved his intention to issue a proclamation barring British warships from US waters, in order to stop "future insults within our harbors." The President would not exclude the possibility that the *Chesapeake* affair would lead to active hostilities but deliberately put roadblocks on the path to war. He said he would first ask the British for "honorable reparation" for the *Leopard*'s attack. While he did not say so aloud, this would effectively impose a pause of at least four months while his demand crossed the Atlantic, British leaders considered the matter, and their reply was brought back. Jefferson also rejected advice to call Congress into emergency session. His excuse was that he first had to know how the British would respond to his letter. But deferring a "Convention of Congress" until at least October would also purchase time for the national war fever to dissipate. Showing respect for the Constitution, he reminded his Cabinet that a war declaration was the sole prerogative of Congress. So he, in the meantime, "should do no act committing them to war."

Assigned to draft the President's proclamation, James Madison was eager to align it with the public's rage against England. The Secretary of State had a special motive to get the politics of the statement right: he hoped to run for President himself in 1808 as Jefferson's legatee. He gave his chief a draft that—at least from the pinched, mild-tempered Madison—was brimstone and fire. He wanted Jefferson to say, "The public sensibility has at length been brought to a serious crisis by an act transcending all former outrages," and that the *Chesapeake* had been "trusting to a state of peace, and therefore unprepared for defence." When Jefferson read Madison's draft, however, he softened its martial tone, fearing that it might escalate the antagonism between Britain and America. He conceded that his new version might not be belligerent enough to satisfy "the ardor of our fellow citizens." He shrewdly scratched out Madison's assertion that the *Chesapeake* had been "unprepared." Using that word would have handed a spiked club to Jefferson haters, who, once the spell of national unity was gone, were likely to condemn him anew for having shortchanged the military.*

When the President's proclamation was published, the semiofficial, pro-Jefferson paper the *National Intelligencer* provided a barbed reminder to "the unreflecting part of our countrymen": "From the government we have a right to expect decisions tempered by calmness, even on the eve of certain war, and much more so at a period when the occurrence of such an event is uncertain." Although most Americans were willing to back their President, however grudgingly, for at least this one patriotic moment, Jefferson was right to be pessimistic. Irate about the *Chesapeake,* many were longing for a President who had more of a stomach for war. The Federalist *Courier* of Charleston, South Carolina, cried, "O! for a Washington or an Adams to wield the sword of state!"

✳ ✳ ✳

---

* In one little-noticed aspect of the President's proclamation, Jefferson and Madison, though slaveholders themselves, unwittingly established a modest precedent for better treatment of African Americans in the country's future. Two of the *Melampus* deserters were enslaved; the mother of the third was a slave. In more generous language than was usually employed at the time to describe the enslaved, the President referred to the three men hauled off by the *Leopard* as "natives of the United States." Madison even publicly referred to the trio as "citizens," as did a committee of the House of Representatives. In 1857, when the Supreme Court ruled in its infamous *Dred Scott* decision that descendants of Africans brought to America as slaves could never be US citizens, the abolitionist Charles Francis Adams of Massachusetts, grandson of President John Adams and later a Congressman, denounced the *Dred Scott* ruling by noting that even the slavemaster Jefferson had argued that the men of African blood removed from the *Chesapeake* should enjoy constitutional protection against kidnapping by the Royal Navy.

I F JEFFERSON FEARED that his critics would blame the *Chesapeake* mess on his seemingly cavalier indifference, as the "King of Economy," to national defense, he knew that Exhibit A would be the two commanders who had presided over this worst humiliation ever suffered by the fledgling US Navy—Commodore Barron, accused of vacillating when the *Leopard* challenged his ship and then surrendering too hastily, and Captain Gordon, who had clearly botched his responsibility to prepare the *Chesapeake* for any skirmish. Likely to be dragged into this political morass was the courtly Dr. Bullus, who was known to be the President's ex-physician and social friend.

In his report to Secretary Smith, Barron had noted "your anxiety that the ship should sail with all possible dispatch," thus offending Smith with an insinuation that his pressure to leave Norfolk quickly had led to the *Chesapeake* fiasco. While admitting his own errors, Barron criticized Gordon for the frigate's dishevelment:

> Captn Gordon immediately gave the orders to the officers and men to go to quarters and have all things in readiness but before a match cou'd be lighted or . . . the Lumber on the Gun Deck such as sails Cables &c cou'd be clear'd the Commander of the Leopard hail'd. . . . It is distressing to me to acknowledge that I found from the advantage they had gain'd over our unprepared and unsuspicious state did not Warrant a longer opposition nor shou'd I have exposed this ship and crew to so galling a fire, had it not been with a hope of getting the Gun Deck clear so as to have made a more formidable defence consequently our resistance was but feeble—in about 20 minutes after I ordered the Colours to be struck.

Barron also accused Bullus, describing how the doctor had stood by his side and counseled him on how to respond to the *Leopard*'s attacks.

Were Barron not so simple and maladroit, he would have known it was dangerous for him to cast himself as the accuser-scourge of Smith, Gordon, and Bullus, all of whom had close ties to the Jefferson establishment. Despite his genteel and diffident exterior, this President could be ferally self-protective, and, though he liked to style himself as the champion of the underdog, in fact both his bloodlines and earliest instincts connected him to the elite. Jefferson was not likely to let himself be made into a ritual human sacrifice for the benefit of Barron, a little-known, ill-read Navy man. Thus from Jefferson's point of view, if anyone was to take the primary blame in the *Chesapeake* affair, it was going to be Commodore Barron.

In July 1807, the President sent Bullus to London on a Navy schooner, ominously called the *Revenge,* with his written terms for healing the Anglo-American rupture: the British must disavow the *Leopard*'s attack, restore the four detained seamen to the *Chesapeake,* and stop all impressments against US ships. It made sense for the British-born Bullus, who had heard the howls of the *Chesapeake*'s wounded and dying, to present the British with Jefferson's demands. Also, during the early investigation of the *Chesapeake* episode, it was in the President's interest for Bullus to be far away from North America and unavailable for interrogation about the ship's unreadiness.

While waiting for the British to respond to his stipulations, Jefferson tried to strengthen the nation's ability to wage war against England, should it come to that. He wanted to protect himself against the charge of being pathologically unwilling to fight. He realized that the British might be more conciliatory if they felt some fear of American military power. And he could not be certain that even his own political skills could prevent the slide toward war.

With his affinity for new, exotic gadgetry (he was, of course, a kinetic inventor himself), the President studied Robert Fulton's novel experiments in military technology. Fulton was known to latter-day schoolchildren as the cheerful creator of the steamboat, but his more lasting contribution to Western civilization was a murderous, far more potentially lucrative device, which he marketed in 1807 as "FULTON'S ARTIFICIAL TORPEDO, FOR DESTROYING SHIPS." In 1803, although his country was at loggerheads with Britain, Fulton, eager to make a fortune, had quietly offered to sell the British exclusive rights to his torpedo, which was essentially a floating mine. (He had already peddled it to Napoleon, who turned him down.) When the British refused, he threatened to give his technology to every country on earth, which, as Fulton knew, would pose a serious danger to the Royal Navy. Fulton's extortion sufficiently unnerved the British to pay him £40,000 to desist.

In the summer of 1807, just after the *Chesapeake* was attacked, Fulton offered his torpedo to Secretary Dearborn for use against British vessels. Knowing that such deployment would provoke the British into out-and-out war, Dearborn wrote Madison with weary humor, "I think we may as well let Fulton try some experiments upon them—if he could blow up one of their largest Ships, I doubt whether any others would trouble us again."

Hoping that public indignation over the *Chesapeake* would stimulate public demand for his torpedoes, Fulton craftily scheduled a demonstration for New York Harbor on a Sunday (to attract a larger crowd) in July 1807. With a showman's panache, he had a wrecked old two-hundred-ton brig towed into position between Governors and Ellis Islands. After his first effort fizzled (causing much of the audience, craning their necks from the Battery's wharves, to depart disenchanted), he ordered another torpedo placed close to the old vessel's hull. Fulton later boasted to Jefferson, by letter, that the brig "was rent in two, and went to the bottom in 20 seconds."

Addressing the President as a fellow inventor, Fulton used diagrams to show how his underwater weapon could be propelled by cables shot from harpoons mounted on—Fulton was not stupid, so what else?—Jefferson's beloved gunboats: "500 men in a Ship of the line would be certain of annihilation if harpooned by only two Boats." Playing to the President's signature frugality (at least with government money), Fulton asked him, "Is there any mode of defence so cheap so easy of practice so fitted to common understandings?" Fulton also pandered to Jefferson's well-known affection for peace: "One vessel of an enemy blown up with such engines would give the peace you might think it proper to demand and if the fear of the torpedoes produced peace the same fear would make the peace eternal."

From Monticello, Jefferson wrote Fulton that putting such a device on his lightweight, open gunboats might let them be too easily attacked, but he was intrigued by the torpedo's possibilities:

> Not that I go the whole length (as I believe you do) of considering them as solely to be relied on. Neither a nation, nor those entrusted with its affairs, could be justifiable, however sanguine their expectations, in trusting solely to an engine not yet sufficiently tried, under all the circumstances which may occur, & against which we know not as yet what means of parrying may be devised. If, indeed, the mode of attaching them to the cable of a ship be the only one proposed, modes of prevention cannot be difficult: but I have ever looked to the submarine boat as most to be depended on for attaching them. . . . I should wish to see a corps of young men trained to this service.

While musing about futuristic weapons like submarines and torpedoes, Jefferson asked his Secretary of War to consider the imminent possibility of military conflict. Shown new reports that the British were conspiring against the United States with the Indians in Canada, he wrote Dearborn, "We should immediately prepare for war in that quarter, & at the same time redouble our efforts for peace." Jefferson told Secretary Smith that if British warships entered Virginia's Elizabeth River or passed a certain point near New York City—"perhaps the narrows"—the proximate US captain should "attack them with all his force," which, as the President knew, would mean war with England. As summer turned to fall, Jefferson was anxious that the public's warlike mood would cause Americans to demand excessive spending on the Navy. But he remained obsessed by his favorite military innovation, insisting to Thomas Paine, his friend from the Revolution, "Gunboats are the only *water* defence which can be useful to us, & protect us from the ruinous folly of a Navy."

★ ★ ★

IN OCTOBER 1807, Gallatin, Jefferson's wise, Swiss-born Treasury Secretary, read an early draft of the President's annual written message to Congress—partly composed by Madison—and warned him that it sounded like "a manifesto against Great Britain on the eve of a war" that might "incite" the British to a speedy declaration of war."* Gallatin reminded his chief that

> recommendations or incitements to war should not, under our Constitution, be given by the Executive, without much caution. . . . Great Britain will prefer actual war to any system of retaliation short of war which we might select. . . . We will be universally justified in the eyes of the world, & unanimously supported by the Nation, if the ground of war be England's refusal to disavow or to make satisfaction for the outrage on the Chesapeak. But I am confident that we will meet with a most formidable opposition, should England do justice on that point, and we should still declare war, because she refuses to make the prepared arrangement respecting seamen.

Gallatin advised Jefferson that the US military was so ill prepared that any fighting must be postponed for at least a few months. He presumed that if Congress declared war, the United States would want to attack British Canada: there would be a greater chance for success if it waited until the winter or spring anyway. If war came, he wrote, Britain would attempt "the capture of our vessels, attacks on our most exposed seaports & defence of Canada." Since the US Navy was so underdeveloped, "unable either to protect our commerce or to meet their fleet, our

---

* Allergic to royal trappings, Jefferson had stopped the Washington-Adams practice of reading the annual message aloud to Congress, which reminded him of the British monarch's speech from the throne. Federalists had retorted that sending a written statement by messenger was even more imperious, like some "Turkish Bashaw" dispersing royal favors. But Jefferson had established a tradition that prevailed until 1913, when Woodrow Wilson, eager to promote his legislative program and strengthen presidential authority, gave his annual message in person.

offensive operations must by sea be confined to privateers: and we must, as soon as practicable, draw in those vessels we cannot defend, place our ports in a situation to repel mere naval aggressions, organize our militia for occasional defence, raise troops & volunteers for permanent garrisons or attack." The Treasury Secretary cautioned Jefferson that if the British expected their reply to his démarche to provoke war, they might assault New York before winter: "Great would be the disgrace attaching to such a disaster." Gallatin's bottom line was this: "I feel strongly impressed with the propriety of preparing to the utmost for war & carrying it with vigor if it cannot be ultimately avoided, but in the mean while of preserving in that caution of language & action which may give us some more time."

In the final version of his message to Congress on October 27, Jefferson said that on the "outrage" of the *Chesapeake*, "no commentaries are necessary. Its character has been pronounced by the indignant voice of our citizens with an emphasis and unanimity never exceeded." The British were "remaining within our waters in defiance of the authority of the country, by habitual violations of its jurisdiction, and at length by putting to death one of the persons whom they had forcibly taken from on board the Chesapeake." Because Charleston, New York, and New Orleans were "most likely first to need protection," he had moved many of the gunboats to the latter two cities and the Chesapeake Bay, which would require new moneys for defense. The President told Congress, "When a regular Army is to be raised, and to what extent" would depend on the nature of the reply he shortly expected from London. "In the meantime I have called on the States for quotas of militia, to be in readiness for present defense, and have, moreover, encouraged the acceptance of volunteers; and I am happy to inform you that these have offered themselves with great alacrity in every part of the Union." These would be trained to be "ready at a moment's warning." Congress gave him $850,000 to build 188 new gunboats and restore three of the Navy's biggest warships for the war against England that might be soon to come.

In mid-December 1807, just before the *Revenge* reached New York City after a rocky voyage from England—the Atlantic twice washed the schooner's captain overboard—Dr. Bullus climbed down its side into a hired boat and sailed off "with all possible speed" to present Jefferson with Britain's answer to his demands to settle the *Chesapeake* affair. This was a letter from Foreign Secretary George Canning: the President observed that Canning's surname combined the words "canny" and "cunning." As it happened, the President had already obtained a copy from the British Minister, David Erskine. "Unfriendly, proud and harsh," Jefferson sniffed, noting "little concern to avoid war." Canning's letter disowned the *Leopard*'s attack and offered a special British envoy to discuss reparations. But on the crucial issue of impressment, Great Britain refused to budge an inch.

Jefferson sputtered that Canning's "haughty" message would leave Americans' tranquillity to the mercy of British sea captains, "whose interest and wish is war with all mankind." Back in July, the President had managed to tamp down the American people's eagerness for a fistfight. Now, even though Britain had coldly dismissed his central condition for peace, Jefferson knew that Canning's offer of talks and reparations would make it difficult for him, even if he wished, to generate any mass enthusiasm for war. It was one thing to make war over an assaulted US ship, another to do it over a principle of maritime law that would strike many Americans, especially those far from the Eastern Seaboard, as abstract. One pro-Jefferson columnist complained that Americans had already become "as abject and as obsequious as asses to the mulester," while "the blood of the Chesapeake smokes unexpiated."

Disinclined to make war, Jefferson opted for another tactic. He would ratchet up the pressure against both England and France to improve their behavior toward US ships by asking Congress for an embargo against imported goods, while "keeping our ships and seamen out of harm's way." Enthusiastically backed by Madison, who had a naive faith in the power of economic sanctions, Jefferson claimed that depriving British merchants and factory bosses of their profitable American market would push England into an economic slump that would force it to start treating Americans with respect. Gallatin warned the President that his scheme would not work—the chief victims, he said, would be the Americans—but Jefferson persuaded his House and Senate majorities to give him his embargo, and it proved to be the most disastrous decision of his presidency.

* * *

SOON AFTER NEW Year's 1808, Americans opened their broadsheets to read about the court-martial of Commodore Barron. Not long after the damaged *Chesapeake* had returned to Norfolk, Secretary Smith had received a letter from a half dozen of the frigate's officers demanding Barron's immediate arrest. Rather than censure the men for leapfrogging the Navy's chain of command by writing him directly, Smith stripped Barron of his *Chesapeake* command and leaked stories to friendly journalists, charging the Commodore with shameful negligence, cowardice, and ineptitude.

Devastated by his public vilification and suffering from his injuries, Barron lay painfully on his side at home near Norfolk (his neighborhood was called Little England). Unable to spot the hidden motives of other people, Barron foolishly asked Dr. Bullus to help him clear his name. He wrote Bullus that he had received

> so many darts in the heart and them shot by my Country men without knowing the Merits of my Case. . . . The Conduct of the British was Cruel in the extreme it is certainly infamous in every Point of View, but the manner in Which the Government has acted and is about to act towards me does not fall far Short of it, Knowing as they do the Situation of the Ship Lumbers in every Quarter more like a transport than a Man of War . . . the gunners Worthless Cowardly and trifling in the Extreme. . . . Never did I Set Sail in a Ship so totally unprepared for defense in all my Life. . . . Believe me, that there was no order of mine executed with one hundreth Part of the Alacrity that this was after the Ensign was hauled down which was only done on the order to Strike the Colours.

Not long afterward, Barron received a letter from "an anonymous friend," warning that Bullus, with his "sycophancy" toward the powerful, would soon be exposed as his "decided enemy."

Secretary Smith knew that if a court of inquiry focused on the *Chesapeake*'s unpreparedness, it might get out of control and put his and Jefferson's neglect of the whole Navy on trial. He made certain therefore that the obloquy would fall on the lonely Barron, not on Captain Gordon, who was linked to the President. To chair the inquiry, Smith shamelessly chose one of Gordon's cousins, Commodore Alexander Murray, who could be expected to ignore any spoken testimony that might jeopardize his relative. In case Murray needed an excuse for doing so, he could cite the fact that a loud cannon explosion during the Revolutionary War had left him nearly deaf. During the hearings, Gordon claimed that Barron had never intended any response to the *Leopard*'s attack, except "fire a few guns and surrender the ship."* Smith ordered the court-martial of both Barron and Gordon—as well as Captain Hall and the ship's gunner, William Hook—but made certain that the proceedings were stacked against Barron. Presiding over the trial would be two of Barron's fiercest enemies—Commodores John Rodgers and Stephen Decatur, both heroes of the Barbary War.†

Opening in January 1808, the court-martial was staged in frigid Norfolk aboard the ice-encrusted wreck of the *Chesapeake,* a macabre setting. Gordon repeatedly declined to discuss evidence of his own responsibility for the *Chesapeake*'s sloppiness, including a report he had sent Barron before sailing, which claimed that both frigate and armaments were ready. Gordon insisted that the "stain" on the *Chesapeake*'s flag came not from any errors made by him. In a closing plea read aloud by his lawyer,

---

* At the hearings' end, Murray spared Secretary Smith—whose job it was to decide Barron's fate—the trouble of wading through what he called the "prolix and elaborate" transcript by sending him his own personal summary, which included twenty-eight accusations against Barron and did not even mention Gordon.

† When the principled Decatur, who had replaced Barron as Commodore of the *Chesapeake*'s squadron, tried to beg off, warning that he was "prejudiced" against Barron, Smith ordered him to serve anyway. Eager to settle his own scores with Barron, Rodgers refused to admit his own similar conflict of interest.

Barron testified that Gordon's sworn charges against him were lies: "My condemnation is the pledge of his acquittal." In the end, Gordon not only got off almost without penalty but was even asked to remain captain of the *Chesapeake!*[*]

Barron received no such mercy. For failure to prepare his ship against imminent attack, the Navy suspended him for five years without pay. This harsh verdict hinged on the notion that Captain Humphreys's written demand had alerted Barron that the *Leopard*'s cannon would soon fire. Barron's defense lawyer had asked the court to summon Dr. Bullus, who could have cleared the Commodore by confessing that he too had failed to interpret Humphreys's letter as a sign of immediate attack. But Smith kept Bullus from testifying by approving the doctor's "earnest entreaties" that he could not attend because he had to support his family. This claim was a howler, since Bullus's wife, Charlotte, was well known to be rich.

Jefferson had much reason to be grateful to Bullus, whose silence had helped to keep the *Chesapeake* debacle from tarnishing the President. He made his old doctor the US Navy's official agent in New York—a plum position that landed the Bulluses on the city's social A-list (they bought a Greenwich Village mansion suitable for grand entertaining) and helped him to launch a lucrative gunpowder company in partnership with Stephen Decatur's brother. (For a top Navy man to give official contracts to his own firm was not deemed unethical in those days.) Bullus died in 1818 at forty-three, but Charlotte survived through the Civil War and beyond. When she died, the *New York Herald* saluted her as the last key witness to the *Chesapeake* attack, "one of the dastardly outrages perpetrated upon the honor of the then young and comparatively weak republic." The *Leopard*'s cannon fire and cries of dying seamen were so graven upon their son Oscar's memory that he joined the Navy himself.

Other lives were also changed by the *Chesapeake*. The personal effects of the musical Carusis had been knocked overboard during the cross fire

---

[*] For the single offense of forgetting to demand written assessments of the *Chesapeake*'s gunnery, Gordon received a private reprimand from Secretary Smith. The jurors later insisted that they would have preferred to impose an even milder sentence on Gordon, had one existed.

between the *Chesapeake* and *Leopard,* and the family never made it back home to Italy. (In 1831, Gaetano appealed to Congress for a compensatory $1,000 but was turned down.) Resigned to stay in Washington, the old maestro and his sons ran the much-loved "Carusi's Saloon," which attracted Presidents to its galas, balls, and concerts.*

Despite his courtroom victory, Captain Gordon found no rest. Responding to a rebuke from the Capital's anti-Jefferson *Federal Republican,* he challenged the editor, Alexander Contee Hanson, in 1810, to a duel, and was gravely wounded in the abdomen, which aborted his Navy career and finally killed him at thirty-eight. As Gordon wrote Dr. Bullus, he felt cursed by the *Chesapeake*—"that unfortunate, unhappy ship on board which all my wretchedness and misery commenced."

And there was poor Commodore Barron, who staggered out of his court-martial crying, "God only knows what I am to witness in a world of torment!" Hard up for money, the old tar sold his house near Norfolk and worked on a vessel in Brazil before traveling to Copenhagen to command a tiny trading boat, the *Portia.* Sidelined in Denmark during the War of 1812, Barron lived on charity and mailed his salary back to his daughters and sick wife. Returning to Norfolk in 1818, he asked the Navy for reassignment, but was confronted with a "treasonous" charge that he had not resisted the *Leopard* because he thought the *Chesapeake* was guilty of harboring British deserters.†

The chief, self-appointed obstacle to Barron's return to the Navy was Stephen Decatur, one of the most honored heroes of the War of 1812. Using prize money from his military exploits, Decatur had built a grand red brick Federal house for himself and his adoring wife, Susan, on the northwest corner of the "President's Park," later called Lafayette Square. After his blistering personal attacks on Barron, Decatur accepted his rival's demand for a duel. On the chosen day in March 1820, at the

---

* During World War II, Eugene Carusi, Gaetano's great-great-grandson, won a Purple Heart for heroism on D-Day at Normandy. He became an influential lawyer in Washington and played poker at the White House with President Harry Truman.

† Barron had supposedly claimed that since Jefferson knew that deserters were aboard, the President must have conspiratorially sent out the *Chesapeake* in order to deliberately "embroil" Great Britain in war.

oft-used dueling ground of Bladensburg, Maryland, Barron told his opponent that "when we meet in another world," he hoped "we shall be better friends." Decatur claimed, "I have never been your enemy, sir." Pistols were fired, and Decatur, struck in the groin, cried out, "Oh, Lord, I am a dead man!"

Thenceforth James Barron was best known as the man who had killed the glorious Decatur. The Navy let him manage shipyards in Philadelphia and Norfolk, but never to command another vessel of war. About his fate Barron was bitter, but he finally had the satisfaction of outliving every other principal in the *Chesapeake* affair. When Barron died at eighty-two, in 1851, the *New Orleans Times-Picayune* recalled that the attack on the *Chesapeake,* "more than any other single incident previous to the war, roused a flame of excitement against Great Britain."

* * *

Thomas Jefferson had been lucky. Had the House or Senate of 1808 been dominated by hostile Federalists, enjoying powers of subpoena, he might have had to fend off an ugly, freewheeling election-year inquest into the *Chesapeake* designed to ridicule him for neglecting the military. But by the fall of 1808, the President had far more serious trouble. Even his own Republicans realized that Jefferson's embargo was a catastrophe.

As Gallatin had warned him, the halt of foreign commerce had brought deep suffering to American farmers, fishermen, mechanics, merchants, and day laborers. A Boston paper complained that the British were getting "all the trade of the world to themselves . . . while we are starving and our produce rotting at home." A Norfolk banker had "never seen more gloomy times." Since Great Britain made up for losing the US market by developing other sources of trade, especially in Latin America, the British people were not demanding—at least, not yet—that their government cave in to the Americans on impressment. Foreign Secretary Canning gibed that perhaps England should help Jefferson end his embargo, since it was so clearly "inconvenient" for

Americans. Showing that he had the upper hand, Canning made sure that when his special envoy, George Rose, arrived in Washington, as promised, to discuss a settlement of the *Chesapeake* affair, the latter's attaché case was almost empty.

The embargo's intense unpopularity among normally Republican voters in the Southern and middle states injected a fillip of new life into the frail Federalist Party. Timothy Pickering, the arch-Federalist Senator from Massachusetts, asked, "Are our sixty thousand seamen and fishermen to be deprived of employment, and, with their families, reduced to want and beggary?" "We are destroying our farmers and every thing by this Embargo," said Alexander Hamilton's old *New York Evening Post*. "Did Washington & Adams & the Federalists ever bring us to such a pass as this?" Sarcastically the *Luzerne Federalist* of Pennsylvania asked, "Are the people happy? Do they prosper? Is money plenty? Is business lively? Does harmony reign among us?" Deriding Jefferson's plan to raise a standing Army of six thousand regulars and twenty-four thousand volunteers, the latter to be paid and trained for only three months every year, a *Providence Gazette* columnist scoffed,

I can tell him it will require *three* men to drag *one* volunteer from his home in these parts. . . . To be dragged up and down the country, heaven knows whither—and some say, he intends marching them out to sea, either with or without gun-boats, after British men of war! . . . They say he has got this embargo partly to deprive poor men of their labour, and to starve them, so that he may get them into the Army for little or nothing.

Hatred of Jefferson was spreading. "You Infernal Villain," John Lane Jones of Boston wrote the President. "How much longer are you going to keep this damned Embargo on to starve us poor people?" For many, the embargo seemed to prove the longtime accusation that Jefferson was, above all, a self-intoxicated philosopher-king, whose silly dreams ran roughshod over reality.

Jefferson's critics had a point. One of the President's worst qualities was his eccentric, inflexible commitment to certain doctrines, long past the time real life had proven him wrong. Why else, on the brink of a war against the largest Navy on earth, would this President still be imploring Congress to spend scarce public money on still more useless little gunboats? Refusing to concede the futility of his embargo, Jefferson angrily claimed that his scheme was being undermined by American smugglers of foreign goods, committing "treason" and "parricide" against their own country. He demanded that some of his gunboats be diverted to patrol the American coast against such violations.

Much worse, Jefferson was so determined to make his embargo a success that he asked Congress for stringent new methods of enforcement that violated his most profound political beliefs by expanding federal government power and stamping on the people's liberties. Angry Bostonians dispensed flyers, signed by "A Descendant of the Pilgrims":

> *The constitution gone!!* . . . If *such* an act as this . . . had been received in New-England prior to 1776, the newspapers in which it should be inserted, would have been clad in Mourning. . . . It *subjects* us to domiciliary and nocturnal visits, by . . . military hirelings. . . . It *subjects* the whole people to the will of the Executive, authorizing him to make a *secret code of laws*. . . . It *establishes* a ruinous and corrupting system of espionage, and encourages pimps, spies and informers, who are always the basest of mankind.

James Madison, who had once imagined riding easily to victory in 1808 on Jefferson's coattails, was instead blamed for "the awful crisis in our public affairs: impending war, internal broils, the defenceless state of our country." That September, Gallatin sadly wrote Madison from New York, "You have heard that New England is lost. If there was an election tomorrow here it would I think, be no better." Madison managed to win the presidency (he did carry New York), but only after pledging to shut down Jefferson's embargo.

Anguished to have to leave the problem of England to his successor and condemned for his embargo—especially by members of his own party who lost their seats in Congress over it—Jefferson felt despondent as his presidency ground to its inauspicious end. He wrote a friend about the "scenes of rural retirement after which my soul is panting." To get his embargo passed, Jefferson had promised members of Congress that if it failed, the next step would be war. But that pledge was almost certainly hollow. This President detested the notion of another military conflict. During his final year in office, he confided to his fellow revolutionary John Langdon of New Hampshire, who had helped to write the Constitution, "I think one war enough for the life of one man, and you and I have gone through one which at least may lessen our impatience to embark on another."

Jefferson had made mistakes in dealing with Britain—not only the embargo and his neglect of national defense, which emboldened England and France, but his toothless ultimatum to George Canning, who could have called Jefferson's bluff and launched a war that America was unready to fight. Nevertheless the country's third President was supremely accomplished in restraining the national outrage over the *Chesapeake* from pushing Congress toward declaration of war. Jefferson was absolutely correct when he recalled to James Maury in 1812 that the *Chesapeake* assault had put full-scale conflict into his hand. He wrote his friend,

> But if ever I was gratified with the possession of power, and of the confidence of those who had entrusted me with it, it was on that occasion when I was enabled to use both for the prevention of war, towards which the torrent of passion here was directed almost irresistibly, and when not another person in the United States, less supported by authority and favor, could have resisted it.

A leader less wily and contrarian than Jefferson, or one more avid for military glory, might have joined the national frenzy against Great Britain, but this leader said no. Especially in contrast with some of the pugnacious Presidents of the American future, Jefferson's success in keeping the nation out of war deserves respect. Sadly for the United States, Jefferson's achievement was not equaled by his well-intentioned but often bumbling successor, James Madison, who could not halt, and ultimately abetted, the spiraling of Anglo-American antagonisms into the War of 1812.

CHAPTER TWO

"Man of Straw"

F OR A SINGLE, misbegotten moment in April 1809, it seemed like a
time for celebration. After only a month as President, James Madison had suddenly unveiled what appeared to be a settlement of America's principal differences with England, ensuring that his countrymen
would not have to die in war. As the result of hurried secret bargaining
with the British Minister in Washington, David Erskine, Britain would
cancel its hated Orders in Council. The two nations would resume trading and live in peace.*

"GLORIOUS NEWS!" exclaimed the *Bee* of Hudson, New York. "Renewal of Intercourse with Great-Britain!" said the *New-England
Palladium.* "Probably no event since the peace which secured our independence has diffused a joy so general as the restoration of harmony
between this country and Great Britain," asserted the *Gazette* of Alexandria, Virginia. Along the Eastern Seaboard, church bells rang,
grand illuminations whitened the night skies, bands played patriotic
hymns, and soldiers and militiamen paraded. In South Carolina, the
HMS *Liberty,* anchored on Charleston's harbor, fired off a royal salute.
In New York City, cannons boomed from federal forts and the frigate

---

* Congress had replaced Jefferson's embargo with a ban on US commerce with Britain and France.

Constitution, which had been poised for war. The *Newburyport Herald* of Massachusetts hoped "that through Mr. Madison, the wounds of our country, from party spirit, may be healed."

From Monticello, Thomas Jefferson wrote his successor, "I sincerely congratulate you on the change it has produced in our situation. . . . I rejoice in it as the triumph of our forbearing and yet persevering system." Jefferson predicted that Madison's achievement would "lighten your anxieties," allow "the compleat extinguishment of our public debt," and "give us peace during your time."*

There was, however, a slight difficulty with all of this jubilation: Erskine's chief, Foreign Secretary Canning, had never authorized his deal with the Americans. Unbeknownst to Madison, the young British diplomat had acted—with spectacular, reckless temerity—on his own.

* * *

ERSKINE'S APPOINTMENT TO Washington had been a bad idea from the start. At age thirty, he had only received this plum job because his father, the first Baron Erskine, Britain's Lord Chancellor, had persuaded the Foreign Secretary at the time, Charles James Fox, to appoint the son as a favor, despite the fact that, as the *Anti-Jacobin Review* complained, the callow Erskine was "without talents or experience."† The new Minister also suffered from a notable conflict of interest. His father had invested the preponderance of his family fortune in the United States, which gave David a powerful motive to forestall an Anglo-American war that might endanger their wealth.

The fey, social Minister Erskine was enchanted by the United

---

* Ignoring Madison, some of Jefferson's fans claimed it was their hero's toughness toward England, including the embargo, that had now compelled "the British Lion to crouch to the American Eagle." The Federalist *Palladium* responded, "England has done now just what she promised us before we hectored and blustered, and in undertaking to ruin her trade, half ruined ourselves."

† By contrast, Lord Erskine, although of noble birth, as the grandson of the Earl of Buchan, had fought his way up from an Edinburgh slum to earn a small fortune and was called "the greatest lawyer England ever knew."

States. His American wife, Frances, daughter of the Revolutionary War General John Cadwalader of Philadelphia, was called "one of the remarkable beauties of her time" and a favorite of the Madisons. The Erskines gave their son Thomas the middle name "Americus." David had also formed a close relationship with President Jefferson, who appreciated his informality. One of Erskine's aides groused that the Minister, wearing country apparel, would "drive up constantly" to the President's Mansion "in a dirty Hack without a servant." For a time, Erskine grew his fingernails to a bizarre, eye-catching length, which provoked his appalled father to write him, "For God's sake remember NAILS."

Soon after Madison's inauguration, Erskine had started private talks with the new Secretary of State, Robert Smith, who had moved over from the Navy.* The Minister was so desperate for an agreement that he refused to insist on three conditions that Foreign Secretary Canning had ordered him to demand from the Americans before the Orders in Council were scrapped.† Back in London, when Canning discovered that Erskine had signed a compact that ignored his three provisos, he complained that the Minister had "acted in direct contradiction to his instructions, and had deviated from their letter and from their spirit." Canning demanded a special meeting of King George III's Cabinet, which, at Canning's behest, canceled Erskine's deal and approved a new Order in Council calling for harassment of American ships.

When the new British order was announced, the peace with America popped like a soap bubble, and Federalist journals denounced Madison as a fool. "WHO'S THE DUPE?" asked the *Reporter* of Lexington, Kentucky. "*Not the British.*" The *New York Gazette* charged that Madison had been "*bribed by* BRITISH GOLD!!" Republican papers put the blame

---

* Madison was not wild about the pedestrian Smith—who had campaigned for the job with help from his brother Samuel—but chose him after judging that there was too much opposition to the man he really wanted, Albert Gallatin.

† The stipulations were that America welcome British trading vessels but keep banning the French; accept the Rule of 1756, which authorized England to seize neutral ships—including America's—that traded with its enemies during wartime; and let the Royal Navy seize any US vessels found violating the American ban on trade with France, which would place the US in the humiliating posture of granting England two forms of carte blanche to oppress its own ships.

not on Madison but the British. The *Courier* of Charleston, South Carolina, decried "the shameful and treacherous manner in which the good faith and honesty of our government have been abused. . . . Behold! as we were about to take a full draught of the proferred bliss, the cup is dashed from our lips, and we are tantalized, vexed and disappointed!" Another journal asked, "Is there any government upon Earth so barefacedly corrupt, except England, as to practice such dishonorable tricks upon a friendly power?" The *Virginia Gazette* reminded the British that "when a nation loses its honor, it loses everything." It warned, "The AMERICAN PEOPLE are now on *tip-toe*—patient—waiting events—ready to ACT! Britain has it now in her power to keep us *all friends* with her—her conduct must be more than a mere profession—if it is not, then we shall 'hurl the weapon back upon the foe.'"

At the moment Madison learned of the British betrayal, he had already started fulfilling his side of the bargain with Erskine, allowing nearly six hundred US ships to sail to England and the shipment of American goods to British shops and warehouses. The bewildered President now wrote to Jefferson that England's sleight of hand had been "crooked." Jefferson responded that the British "tricks," which he found "so strange," would probably renew the war fever on both sides of the Atlantic. He wrote Madison that he had "never doubted the chicanery of the Anglomen. . . . In general their administrations are so changeable, and they are obliged to descend to such tricks to keep themselves in place, that nothing like honor or morality can ever be counted on in transactions with them." Madison's brother-in-law, Congressman John G. Jackson of Virginia, loyally informed him, "My blood boils at the recital of Mr. Canning's intolerable insults." The new Navy Secretary, Paul Hamilton of South Carolina, assured Madison, with a feeling of "affliction and indignation" (and some false bravado), that if they had to wage war against England, "we shall have no cause to be fearful."

Despite his convoluted efforts to explain himself, Minister Erskine was ordered back to London and drummed out of the diplomatic service for sixteen years, when he was finally rehabilitated as Minister to Stuttgart. By then, he badly needed the government salary and pension. Frances had borne him twelve children, and his father had become a heavy drinker—Baron Erskine was thought to be suffering from mental illness—and lost all of the family's wealth.

* * *

GREAT BRITAIN'S CHOICE for Erskine's successor made it clear that London was in no hurry to patch things up. Francis James "Copenhagen" Jackson had gained his nickname in 1807, while serving as England's special envoy to Denmark, when he masterminded the burning of the Danish capital, which killed two hundred civilians, to seize that country's coveted fleet. After kissing his monarch's knuckles, Jackson sailed in the frigate l'Africaine to the United States. Several American towns burned him in effigy. Others demanded that "the bloody bully of Copenhagen" be tarred and feathered. Madison's Attorney General, Caesar Rodney, advised him that since Jackson's record showed he was "personally obnoxious," perhaps the British should be told that the United States would not deal "with a minister from whose personal character we could expect no favorable result." Madison grumbled that Jackson was clearly a "worthy instrument" of the ill-motivated Canning.

On their arrival in Washington, Jackson and his haughty wife, Elizabeth, once a Prussian baroness, scarcely bothered to conceal their image of America as a jungle of crude gaucherie. They insisted on staying at the Capital's finest inn until the "ruin and dirt" of the Erskines' former residence was removed; Jackson muttered that he was not surprised to find poor housekeeping in an abode occupied by an American woman and a Scot. When the new Minister read Erskine's letters and dispatches, he scoffed at the "mass of folly and stupidity," concluding that his predecessor was "really a greater fool" than he had imagined: How could Erskine have tolerated listening to Madison speak, when "every third word was a declaration of war"?

Invited for dinner at the White House in October 1809, Jackson and his wife alighted in an elegant barouche landau, which, he was certain, "astonishes the natives." He found President Madison, in person, to be "a plain and rather mean-looking little man." Elizabeth felt that Dolley was "without distinction either in manners or appearance, but, to be just, she is also without pretentions." Jackson observed that the President's wife, although now "fat and forty," must have been "a comely person when she served out the liquor" at the tavern owned by her father. (Dolley's Quaker father did not own a tavern.) But the Madisons were so gracious that by the end of the evening even the malicious Jackson had to confess he had probably never "had more civility and attention shown me."

When Secretary Smith received Jackson, he demanded an explanation of Erskine's folly in making a deal that his superiors would not stand behind. By the President's instruction, Smith told Jackson that all future exchanges between them must be written down, so that they could be cleared with Canning, in order to avoid "misconceptions" like those that stemmed from Erskine's freelancing. Jackson complained that such an insulting requirement would defy diplomatic tradition. Letting his arrogance show, he told Smith he did not need to explain why His Majesty had repudiated Erskine: any British diplomat could be overruled by the King. With this statement, Jackson had just confessed that the United States should place no more faith in his assurances than Erskine's. He went on to claim that in any case, Madison and Smith must have been aware that Erskine was violating Canning's instructions when they made their pact with him—a base slander against the good character of the President and Secretary of State.

With customary understatement, Madison later told Smith that he had absorbed Jackson's "gross insinuation" with "no small degree of surprise." Advised that the Minister had refused to retract his charge, which suggested that Britain felt free to insult any American it wanted—even the President—Madison issued Jackson's diplomatic death warrant, ordering him informed "that no further communications will be received from you, and that the necessity of this determination will, without delay, be made known to your Government." Copenhagen Jackson's tenure as a functioning envoy in Washington had lasted a minuscule thirty-six days.

The *National Intelligencer*, which was close to Madison, reported that Jackson had been jettisoned because he had "insulted the personal feelings of the members of the administration, & the character and dignity of the nation generally." It explained that "Jackson, like the Devil in Paradise, attempts delusion in a variety of shapes; but he was not, like Satan, eventually successful." A Richmond paper denounced the British envoy as "a political monster": "Were we to expect the olive from the hand which had wielded the torch at Copenhagen? . . . The day of retribution will yet arrive."

In his annual message of November 1809, Madison revealed to Congress that Jackson had not even made "a reference" to the still-unresolved matter of a settlement for Britain's "murderous aggression" against the *Chesapeake.* Showing that America would not be knocked around, the President stressed "the importance of giving to our militia, the great bulwark of our security and resource of our power, an organization best adapted to eventual situations for which the United States ought to be prepared." Writing more bluntly in the *National Intelligencer* was "Publius," which may have been Madison himself. (In 1787 and 1788, along with Alexander Hamilton and John Jay, he had employed this nom de plume while writing for *The Federalist.*) "Must war be prepared for?" asked Publius. "Congress alone can decide the question." The writer insisted that he was a "friend of peace . . . but would blush to discourage a war in a pre-eminently just cause. . . . If we do strike, let us strike where we can be felt."

Told by the US government he was no longer welcome, a more decent human being than Copenhagen Jackson would have taken the first available boat back to England. Instead, backed by his superiors, he treated himself and his wife to a garish, spiteful tour of revenge, cruising up the Eastern Seaboard aboard the British sloop *Experiment,* spraying poison against James Madison and praising Federalist aspirants for public office. Feted in the ballrooms and parlors of wealthy Federalists (opponents called them "the British party in America"), Jackson invited them to overturn the spirit or even the fact of their Revolution. But not all Americans were so welcoming. When Jackson and his wife arrived at Mr. Gregory's inn of Albany, New York, they were confronted by a straw-stuffed effigy of Jackson, which was hanged and set aflame on the doorstep. Several American journals warned Jackson not to spend His Majesty's cash to corrupt their nation's yeomanry. The *American Mercury* reminded Jackson that he was in a country "where the *Chesapeake* had been assailed by privileged pirates" and whose sons were "suffering torture in the British Navy."

* * *

B Y THE SPRING of 1810, even Madison, with his faith in sanctions, had to concede that commercial retaliation was not restraining Britain or France from persecuting American ships. At his request, the House and Senate passed "Macon's Bill #2"—drafted by Secretary Gallatin and sponsored by the North Carolina Congressman Nathaniel Macon—which lifted trade restrictions on both countries but pledged to renew them for either one if the other stopped harassing American ships.

Critics charged that Macon's approach was both surrender and bribery, which "held up the honor and character of this nation to the highest bidder." Governor John Tyler Sr. of Virginia, the father of a future President, complained to Jefferson, "We have lost our resentment for the severest Injuries a Nation ever suffer[e]d, because of their being so often repeated, and all we have done has been to quarrel with each other about which Government injur[e]d us most." The British consul in Norfolk assured London that the Macon measure was negligible: "After the Hurricane of Passion in which the Congress opened their Session, it is truly laughable to witness the miserable, feeble, Puff, in which they evaporated. . . . With every disposition to injure Great Britain, they have found themselves totally unable to do so."

During the haggling over Macon's Bill, Henry Clay, a little-known, thirty-two-year-old Kentuckian with a towering career ahead of him, stepped onto the Senate floor and delivered an impassioned early argument for an American war against England. "No man in the nation," Clay insisted, "desires peace more than I. But I prefer the troubled ocean of war, demanded by the honor and independence of the country, with all its calamities and desolations, to the tranquil, putrescent pool of ignominious peace." Clay argued that if America had to fight, the enemy should be clear: "Britain stands preeminent, in her outrage on us, by her violation of the sacred personal rights of American freemen, in the arbitrary and lawless impressment of our seamen—the attack on the *Chesapeake*—the murder, Sir." Waging war would injure the British adversary and benefit the American nation: "The conquest of Canada is in your power. . . . I verily believe that the militia of Kentucky are alone competent to place Montreal and Upper Canada at your feet." America had the chance to seize "the last of the immense North American possessions" held by England and "acquire the entire fur trade connected with that country."

Clay asserted that a war against England could renew "a martial spirit amongst us" that was "essential to the protection of the country." He noted that soon the giants of the Revolution would all be gone. "Their deeds of glory and renown will then be felt only through the cold medium of the historic page." The country needed "a new race of heroes." But the fundamental issue was British tyranny. "If we surrender without a struggle to maintain our rights, we forfeit the respect of the world, and what is infinitely worse, of ourselves," he explained. "I protest against the castigation of our colonial infancy being applied in the independent manhood of America. . . . Let those who attempt to molest us, take to themselves the consequences of their own violence."

While Macon's Bill was pending, Napoleon wrote a fiendish letter asking his Foreign Minister, the Duke of Cadore, successor to the amoral Talleyrand, to assure Washington that his decrees against US ships "will not have any effect after November first" if Americans "shall cause their rights to be respected by the English" by renewing their commercial ban against Great Britain. Federalists cautioned that the French emperor's offer was vague and that he would never fulfill it—they correctly noted that Napoleon's "bait does not half cover the hook"—but, even after having been embarrassed by his hastiness with Erskine, Madison took the bait, announcing that France's edicts against the United States had been "revoked." He told Attorney General Rodney, with obvious relief, that the Cadore letter would free him from having to consider "a war with both the great belligerents." He wrote Jefferson that the Cadore letter would let Americans have "but one contest on our hands at a time."

Appalled, Chief Justice John Marshall found Madison's faith in Cadore's message to be "one of the most astonishing instances of national credulity . . . in political history." He wondered whether the President could have actually been so gullible as to believe that the Cadore letter was a genuine breakthrough for peace. Madison hoped that if there should be a French-American rapprochement, the British might repeal their Orders in Council. Thus he persuaded Congress to let him restrict trade with England until the British orders were revoked. Before long, French behavior made it clear that the Cadore letter was meaningless. But Madison continued to maintain that the document could be relied upon. Publicly humiliated by his naive mistake of vouching for the Erskine agreement, he could not easily afford to confess that he had also been duped by the French, which might give weight to the Federalists' hoary charges that Madison and his "ventriloquist" Jefferson were in bed with France.

After the President made his stand against Copenhagen Jackson, the new British Foreign Secretary, the Marquess of Wellesley, took almost two months to respond. Madison took the delay as another British insult, but his envoy in London assured him that Wellesley was just "indolent." When Wellesley finally expressed himself, he not only defended Jackson's insolence but informed Secretary Smith that he would reduce England's level of representation in America by leaving its business to a mere chargé d'affaires. This showed Madison how little the British feared the United States. As for canceling the Orders in Council, Wellesley told the Americans to forget it.

These rebuffs by Britain and France allowed Madison's foes to charge that, in contrast with the brilliant political philosopher who had worked on the Constitution, Madison the President was someone whose diplomacy was too often idle posturing. The Federalist Congressman Samuel Taggart, of western Massachusetts, told a friend that Madison, that "old clucking hen," had proven himself "little better than a man of straw."

More dangerous for Madison, the newly elected Twelfth Congress, although still controlled by his Republicans, included a number of politicians who were growing impatient with the President's failure to ensure

American self-respect. Soon they were dubbed the "War Hawks"—a term originally invented by then–Vice President Jefferson in 1798 to describe Federalist rabble-rousers against the French. Their leader was Henry Clay, who, after deciding that the House was a more suitable venue for his oratorical and organizing skills, had relinquished what he called the "solemn stillness" of the Senate to seek election as a Congressman. After his victory, he was immediately elected Speaker of the House, a job that he quickly infused with new power. Clay exploited his Speakership to goad Madison to be more aggressive toward England, loading the House Foreign Affairs Committee with three newly elected War Hawks. During a debate on rechartering the Bank of the United States, Clay complained that Great Britain owned seven-tenths of the institution's capital: "Has it released from galling and ignominious bondage one solitary American seaman, bleeding under British oppression? Did it prevent the unmanly attack upon the *Chesapeake*? . . . Are not the two nations brought to the very brink of war?"

Anxious to win a second term in 1812, Madison wished to avoid an intraparty battle for the Republican presidential nomination, so he persuaded his most dangerous conceivable rival, James Monroe, who had just been elected Governor of Virginia, to set aside their personal rivalry and become his Secretary of State. Monroe took a while to consent—he worried that so close a connection with Madison's stumbling leadership might damage his own future prospects.*

Creating a place for Monroe required removing Smith from the State Department. Smith would not go quietly, although the President offered him an appointment to Russia. "His overthrow is my object," Smith wrote his brother Samuel about Madison, "and most assuredly I will effect it." Seeking "vindication," the fired Smith published an anti-Madison diatribe, charging that the President lacked the "energetick mind" needed to resist the tricky diplomacy of Erskine and the Duke of Cadore. He urged Americans to elect in 1812 someone more "sagacious

---

* One French diplomat, perhaps projecting his own country's practices onto America's politics, claimed that Monroe had only agreed to serve Madison after obtaining a financial bribe.

in discerning the rights of our much injured and insulted country." One of Madison's partisans called the ousted Secretary's rant "one of the rare instances of a man's giving the finishing stroke to his own character, in his eagerness to ruin his enemy." Dolley Madison had worried that Smith's pamphlet might open *"the eyes of the world on all our sins."* She wrote her sister Anna that "Mr. M" laughed at Smith's literary assault, "but I did not."

* * *

MADISON HAD ALLOWED the nation's fleet to remain so under-developed that US ships had little capacity to patrol the nation's shoreline any farther than a few miles into the Atlantic. On May 1, 1811, off Sandy Hook, New Jersey, the frigate *Guerriere,* one of four British cruisers dogging the American coast, halted the American brig *Spitfire* and impressed a young apprentice named John Diggio into the Royal Navy.*

The incident generated new outrage at the President from both Federalists and Republicans. In Richmond, the normally pro-Madison *Enquirer* asked why Madison "does not *expel* the British ships of war from the waters and the jurisdiction of the United States?" Deriding the President's "pitiful imbecility," the *New York Evening Post* predicted that Madison would timidly issue a formal protest and deploy some of Jefferson's tiny gunboats against other British frigates, which amounted to doing "nothing." Samuel Smith, already furious at Madison over his brother's dismissal, wrote, "Indeed the impressments can no longer be tolerated. Pusyllanimity has been Charged on the president."

Madison responded by sending the forty-four-gun *President,* commanded by Commodore John Rodgers, to guard the East Coast, creating at least the impression that he was finally getting belligerent about impressments. On May 16, Rodgers's frigate was sailing off the Virginia capes, toward New York City, when one of his lookouts told him he

---

* The British had disregarded the insistence of the *Spitfire*'s Captain Neil that Diggio was not only an American but lived in Neil's own house.

had seen the *Guerriere* moving to the east. Rodgers ordered the vessel pursued. What his crew had actually seen was a twenty-gun sloop of war called the *Little Belt.** Peering through his telescope, in the dwindling sunlight, Rodgers realized that the other ship was not the *Guerriere* but could not see that it was a small corvette, with only a single tier of guns.

After dark, the two ships were just a hundred yards apart. Rodgers and the other vessel's captain, Arthur Bingham, signaled each other for identification. As Rodgers later testified, "before I had time to take the trumpet from my mouth," he "was answered by 32-pound shot and canister." In a fiery, brief exchange, the *President* easily prevailed, pummeling the weaker *Little Belt* and killing nine of its crew. Suffering little more than a damaged mainmast, the *President* emerged with but a single casualty—a gunner's boy had lost his arm.† Which ship fired the first shot was uncertain. The next morning, Rodgers was disturbed to find that Britain's ship was "a vessel of her inferiour force." He sent a lieutenant, John Creighton, to the *Little Belt* with regrets for the "unfortunate affair." As Rodgers later explained, he had refused to be "a passive spectator of insult to the flag of my country" but had a "humane & generous heart" and would never stop feeling remorse.

With his militant new stance toward British ships off the East Coast, Madison let it be known that Rodgers's conduct enjoyed his "approbation." Secretary Hamilton told Rodgers that he wished to take the poor armless young crewman and "hug him to my bosom (whatever may be his condition, or circumstance in life), while I made him an officer in the American Navy." Hamilton backed Rodgers by ordering him to take the *President* promptly back to sea, but warned him to be careful, since he would be a natural target "for British vengeance."

Federalist leaders demanded to know why Rodgers had overreacted to a small British ship. After Senator Pickering insisted that the

---

* Formerly the *Lillebælt,* the vessel had been Denmark's before the Danish fleet was seized for Great Britain by Copenhagen Jackson.

† The *National Intelligencer* later reported that the wounded boy had begged the surgeon's mate to let him go back on deck, saying, "If I can do no more, I can at least be shot at."

Commodore's behavior had been an illegal act of war, the President wrote Jefferson with disgust that Pickering was "so conspicuous in the British service." The pro-Madison *Farmer's Repository* asked, "What can be thought of a party which blames the commander of a national ship for resisting an outrage and repelling an attack?" "Will these federalists ever cease to regard Britain as their mother country?" inquired New York's *Columbian.*

Britain finally sent a new minister to Washington, the foppish, thirty-year-old Augustus John Foster, who arrived on the HMS *Minerva.* Foster joked about the Americans who peed into their fireplaces and spat out the caviar he gave them when they discovered it was not jam. Madison was so eager to make a deal with England that he had Secretary Monroe inform the new Minister that if the British wished to fully reopen trade with the United States, all they had to do was issue a "conditional and ambiguous" pledge to cancel the Orders in Council. But Foster refused. In frustration, Monroe told a British friend, "War, dreadful as the alternative is, could not do us any more injury than the present state of things, and it would certainly be more honorable to the nation, and gratifying to the publick feelings."

* * *

DURING THE SUMMER of 1811, the President and Dolley took a holiday at their Virginia estate, Montpelier. As Mrs. Madison wrote friends, "We passed two Months on our Mountain in health & peace." But there were new threats to the nation's tranquillity. As the *New-Jersey Journal* reported, "The Indians on our frontiers have very recently committed several murders and robberies, and are taking the attitude of war, and are receiving fire arms and ammunition from a British fort." The Governor of the Indiana Territory, William Henry Harrison, warned Secretary of War William Eustis that he was about to face an Indian attack, aided by furtive British operatives from Fort Malden in Canada.

After losing the Revolutionary War, Great Britain had clung to some of its fortresses on American soil. Not averse to making trouble for the victors, the British favored the native Americans with food, weapons, and ammunition. Early in his presidency, George Washington moved against the danger to his nation's sovereignty over the new, lush, fertile lands of the West. In 1794, General "Mad Anthony" Wayne launched what he conceived as the decisive struggle. Starting from Fort Washington in Ohio, 4,600 men of the "Legion of the United States" marched north, building a line of defense (Forts Deposit, Recovery, Loramie, Adams, Randolph, St. Marys, Defiance). From a camp near the Maumee River, in the Battle of Fallen Timbers, Wayne's soldiers raised their bayonets and sent cavalry against an onrushing wave of Ojibwas, Potawatomis, Mingos, Wyandots, Delawares, Miamis, and Shawnees. The native Americans fled to Britain's Fort Miami, but the fort commanders had been ordered to avoid provoking the Americans and thus shut them out.

By signing Jay's Treaty in 1795, the British agreed to relinquish six of their remaining forts in America, but they continued to abet the Indians from Fort Malden in Amherstburg, Ontario, only eighteen miles from Detroit. That same year, General Wayne and ten Indian tribes concluded the Treaty of Greenville, which gave them farm animals, implements, and blankets, as well as an annual stipend, in exchange for the native Americans' pledge not to contest US ownership of land in Ohio or territory that would later include Chicago and Detroit. But there was a significant holdout from the Greenville compact. Tecumseh ("Shooting Star" or "Flying Panther") was an ambitious, unyielding Shawnee leader born in 1788, who was disgusted by what he considered to be the greedy, self-abasing tribal chieftains caving in to the white Americans, whom he called the "Long Knives." Since he believed that no tribal leader had the right to give up ancient, sacred native American land without the consent of all the chiefs, he refused to recognize the existing treaties.

For Tecumseh, the embodiment of the Long Knives was the patrician Governor Harrison, whose father had signed the Declaration of Independence. From his arrival in 1800 at the old French city of Vincennes, in what is now Indiana, Harrison had patiently acquired piece after piece of terrain from the native Americans. Attuned to signs of

British instigation of Indian attacks and other indignities, Harrison had warned his legislature that even the *Leopard*'s attack on the *Chesapeake* had been connected to British subversion on the frontier: "Who does not know that the tomahawk and scalping knife of the savage are always employed as the instruments of British vengeance?" Harrison grimly reminded friends that around Tecumseh's neck hung a medallion of King George III.

Tecumseh's brother Tenskwatawa ("the Prophet") demanded that Indian people keep themselves apart from the Long Knives and embrace age-old customs and values. Harrison considered him, like Tecumseh, "a tool of British fears or British avarice."* He sent a warning to the two brothers that they could expect only disappointment from England, and offered to finance a visit by them to President Madison in Washington, but they declined. Moving to Vincennes in August 1810, Tecumseh and four hundred armed men were warned by Harrison that the United States would enforce its land treaties, if necessary, by violence. The Governor wrote Secretary Eustis that it was time to quash the conspiracy between the Indians and Britain. Petitioners in Vincennes wrote President Madison that "this Banditti is now prepared to be let loose upon us, and nothing but vigorous measures will prevent it."

In November 1811 came the Battle of Tippecanoe. Harrison sent a small brigade—about 250 US infantry, hundreds of members of his own militia, and perhaps 50 volunteers from Kentucky—up the Wabash River in canoes, poised for battle. Before dawn on November 7, the Long Knives began firing on the Prophet's town. By noon, having exhausted their bullets and arrows against the enemy, the native Americans retreated as the federal forces burned their village to the ground, earning Harrison a victory. (In 1840, he would use the nickname "Tippecanoe" to win the presidency.) This preemptive strike had been waged by Harrison's Army and there was little evidence of British involvement, but many Americans blamed London. Some citizens of

---

* One hundred and eighty miles up the Tippecanoe River from Harrison's headquarters, Tecumseh's brother founded a settlement called the Prophet's town, raising the hackles of the Governor, who viewed it as a launching pad for attacks by British and Indian coconspirators.

Vincennes concluded that the "real *murderers*" of the thirty dead Americans were "the BRITISH," with "the Indians only hired assassins."

Tales of Tippecanoe spread fresh anger against Great Britain throughout the United States. *"Behold the effects of British Influence!"* shouted the *Albany Register.* "The British agents have at length succeeded in stimulating the Indians to shed the blood of our brave countrymen on the frontiers. But thanks be to God, American intrepidity has triumphed over the SAVAGES. . . . If Congress do their duty, the blood of these martyrs will ere long be avenged on the plains of Abraham." The *Reporter* of Lexington, Kentucky, asked whether Congress planned to treat Britain's role in Indian aggression against "the citizens of the *Western country*" with the same indifference with which it regarded impressment on the high seas.

"The crisis is at hand," warned the *Baltimore Sun,* "and we hope that when once the scabbard is thrown away, the sword will never be sheathed until Britain relinquishes her sovereignty to every foot of land on the American continent." Philadelphia's *Aurora* proclaimed, "War has been begun with British arms and by the Indians instigated by British emissaries. The blood of American citizens have already been shed in actual war, begun undeclared." The Republican Congressman Matthew Lyon of Kentucky wrote Madison, "I would advise the immediate Extermination of every Nation who have aided in the Attack on our Troops."

Madison declined to wrap himself in Harrison's victory cloak. He did not wish to antagonize the many tribal chiefs who were cooperating with the US government (leaders like Negro Legs, Stone Eater, and Little Otter, whom both Jefferson and Madison addressed, at the Indians' request, as "My Children"). Even the warlike Speaker Clay conceded in the fall of 1811 that "it will certainly add to our embarrassments if we have to carry on a war with them, as well as their good friends, the English."

But many Americans were eager to attack what seemed to be the staging ground of the threat—the crescent of British territory above the Great Lakes then known as "Upper Canada." Some sought invasion of Canada in order to steal the British fur trade, virgin land, and new markets during an economic slump. Abolitionists hoped that annexing Canadian territory would tip the balance against the curse of slavery. But the most basic urge of many who wished to assault Canada was that it was the only place within easy striking distance where Americans could injure the British. The *Liberty Hall* of Cincinnati warned that if England did not shape up, "the most valuable of all her colonies will be torn from her grasp, & thus she will accelerate her own destruction."

✻ ✻ ✻

A S MADISON PREPARED his annual message to Congress for November 1811, the Republican *Reporter* of Lexington, Kentucky, warned him not to be "a mere stock, or block, or statue" on the subject of war with Great Britain, which would demonstrate "we have a *British agent*, a *monarchist*, or *federalist* for president."

The President did not need the advice. He told the House and Senate that there had been more "scenes" on American coasts and harbors "derogatory to the dearest of our national rights," as well as "murders and depredations committed by Indians." He suggested that in light of Britain's "hostile inflexibility in trampling on rights which no independent nation can relinquish, Congress will feel the duty of putting the United States into an armor and an attitude demanded by the crisis, and corresponding with the national spirit and expectations." Despite these martial words in public, however, Madison still hoped for some quiet diplomatic maneuver that would stop the slide toward war with England. He sent Minister Foster a private message that if Britain wished to avert war, it did not need to permanently revoke the Orders in Council, merely to stop harassing American ships for the time being.

When the Twelfth Congress reassembled in January 1812, Madison asked it for ten thousand new Army soldiers—a piddling force, if the President was really contemplating war, but Madison did not want to demand new taxes in an election year. The War Hawks ensured that twenty-five thousand were authorized instead. House Republicans, including some War Hawks, rejected a bill to create twenty new frigates and a dozen ships, largely because they disdained the Navy as a

Federalist bastion. Madison wrote Jefferson that "the mixture of good & bad, avowed & disguised motives accounting for these things is curious." Minister Foster and his superiors in London took these contradictory actions as new evidence that Madison's threats about war were not serious.

In March, the President unwittingly launched a clown show by sending the House and Senate a bundle of secret missives that soon became infamous as the "John Henry letters." As the letters showed, Henry was a British agent who had scoured New England in 1809 for Federalists willing to join a movement to dislodge that region from the United States and annex it to British Canada. For his troubles, Henry received only £200 from Canada's Governor-General, Sir James Craig, and nothing from his case runners in London. So in vengeance he turned to France, his country's enemy, enlisting the support of a French operative who used the false identity of Edouard, Comte de Crillon.*

Delighted to pit the British against the Americans, the French Minister in Washington, Louis Sérurier, helped Crillon win an audience with Secretary Monroe, who instantly saw the letters' potential to both discredit the Federalists and stimulate war fever by revealing eye-catching details of a British conspiracy to divide the American Union. With atrocious bad judgment, Monroe took every penny available from a fund for secret operations to buy the letters, sight unseen, from Henry and Crillon for the vast sum of $50,000.† After buying the letters, Monroe was disheartened to find that the names of the treasonous Federalists had been redacted, which reduced their political utility. Madison sent the cache to Congress anyway, expressing outrage that a British "secret Agent" had been "fomenting disaffection" with the eventual aim, "in concert with a British force, of destroying the Union and forming the Eastern part thereof, into a political connection with Great Britain." He did not disclose that his Secretary of State had used taxpayers' money to buy the Henry letters. The President wrote Jefferson

---

* The slimy Crillon tried to cash in himself by offering to sell the embarrassing letters to Minister Foster, who would then be free to destroy them, but Foster declined.

† More than $900,000 two centuries later.

that he hoped public outrage over the letters would make Federalist New England behave.

At first, the Henry letters evoked the indignation that Madison sought. "What national evil to be compared with a *dissolution of the federal compact?*" asked one Republican journal. "Yet the British government or at least *British agents,* have contributed and endeavored to effect this.—Does not our blood freeze at the thought!" Sérurier, delighted to see Americans so furious at the British, observed, "If this event does not produce a war, nothing will do so." Federalist leaders called the letters "an electioneering trick," and claimed that all they proved was that Henry "could not find ONE FEDERALIST" to back his conspiracy.

Then the Henry archive blew up in Madison's face. After some digging, the Federalists announced that Monroe had secretly paid a vast sum of public money to Henry—"this Spy and Traitor"—for his letters, and a king's ransom too. They further revealed that Madison had gone on to arrange Henry's appointment as a special US government messenger and put the charlatan safely beyond the reach of a congressional subpoena by smuggling him to England, at public expense, aboard the USS *Wasp.* Federalist journals had a field day. Hartford's *Connecticut Mirror* complained that the President "had no more right" to spend the people's coin with such cavalier abandon "than a burglar has to take money out of his neighbour's desk." *"What a national disgrace!"* cried Boston's *Columbian Centinel.* The *Berkshire Reporter* of Pittsfield, Massachusetts, published this rhyme (to be sung to the tune of "Yankee Doodle Dandy"):

> *We espi'ed a* Henry, *who to Washington was bound, sir,*
> *To sell our Chief a* Dreadful PLOT *for many thousand pounds,*
>   *sir. . . .*
> John Henry *was a* cunning *dog, as many do declare, sir,*
> *Of* Madison *he made a* FOOL, *which surely was not* fair, *sir!*

* * *

O N APRIL 1, MADISON asked the Senate and House for a sixty-day embargo against all foreign vessels arriving at the United States or already in port. Monroe privately explained to congressional leaders that he and the President intended the halt to be a preface to possible war, allowing time to prepare and bring American ships home, where they would not be so exposed to the Royal Navy. The world seemed to be "running mad," Dolley Madison wrote her sister Anna. "The war business goes on slowly, but I fear twill be sure." She reported that angry Federalists were refusing her invitations and would not "enter M[adison']s door."

Congress gave the President his embargo, but the British took it as merely one more of his idle threats. So blasé was Foster about this development that he wrote his superiors in London that he was more optimistic than ever about peace—and even asked them for a six-month sabbatical. At his residence, Foster continued to host hundreds of Washingtonians of both parties for games of chess and cards, orchestral performances, and levees. While raising a glass under the cheerful striped marquee in Foster's garden, some of his Federalist guests counseled him to ignore Madison's bluffs, predicting that the little man would never take the United States to war.

The President undercut his own tough public message by privately suggesting to Foster that there was still an easy way to avoid conflict: Britain did not really have to stop the harassment of American ships, as mandated by its Orders in Council, but could simply claim in public that the policy had been canceled! As Foster wrote his new Foreign Secretary, Lord Castlereagh, "The name of the Orders in Council has become more objectionable to him than the substance." The British laughed at America's military weakness, the result of a decade of Jefferson-Madison neglect—only 6,744 regulars in the Army and sixteen vessels in the Navy, not counting Jefferson's infernal gunboats. And Congress seemed, for the most part, to be keeping its checkbook closed. Against the motley American force, Great Britain commanded the world's most powerful armada—six hundred warships—and a half million well-trained regulars.

The spring elections of 1812 showed that Americans were apprehensive about war, with the surprise defeat of many Republicans suspected of undue ardor for fighting England. Congressman John Randolph of Virginia warned that his country must not "go to war without money, without men, without a Navy." Samuel Harrison, a Madison supporter in Vermont, wrote the President that "a very large majority of the people, both in the Eastern, Western, and Northern Sections of the Union" opposed a military conflict with England:

> *Peace* is the *Element* on which the Americans ought ever to abide. . . . My Dear President, to plunge into a War without adequate preparation, would be the summit of Folly. . . . I am better acquainted with the feelings of the People than many of those sycophantic, declamatory War Hawks, who, like Homer's Thersites, are full, of empty boasts, and impotent threats; yet in time of danger will be noticed, only to be laughed at. . . . Your *real friends will dissuade* you from so destructive a measure.

Nevertheless Madison appointed Jefferson's two-term War Secretary, Henry Dearborn, as Senior General of his Army, and asked him to start planning for war.* Dearborn wrote the President that their opening strategy must be "the conquest of Lower Canada":

> After Securing the Small posts, on the southern Side of the River at st Lawrence, the Town & Garrison of Montreal, will be the first important object. . . . To afford a reasonable certainty of Success to the expedition, it would, in my opinion require an Army of at least sixteen thousand Men, Rank & File, present and fit for duty. . . . When a declaration of War, can no longer be avoided, but by the Sacrifice of our national honor, and Independence, it will be of infinite importance, that it should be

---

* While Dearborn's new troops respected his valor during the Revolutionary War three decades earlier, they derided the sixty-year-old General as rusty, referring to him as "Granny."

So prosecuted, as to produce a Satisfactory peace, in the shortest time possible.

Madison decided to wait until the USS *Hornet* arrived from Europe in late May. Unless this vessel brought news that the British would cancel their Orders in Council, he would ask Congress to declare war against England. When the *Hornet* brought no such assurance, the President was angry at the world. In private, he fulminated about the need to wage a "triangular" war against both England and France, writing to Jefferson that if he seemed to go easy on the French, he would give the Federalists new political ammunition.

Knowing what it would mean to face the British Navy, Madison made one final effort to avert a full-fledged conflict. At the Executive Mansion, he claimed to Foster that, despite appearances, the French had eased their harassment on the high seas; therefore, England should really reciprocate by scrapping the Orders in Council. Rudely Foster told him that he could not accept his contention about France without proof. He explained that Castlereagh had directed him to be firm. After Foster was gone, the President damned England's "wicked obstinacy." As Madison recalled much later, Castlereagh's order showed "an utter disregard of the complaints of the United States," and "with this final notice, no choice remained but between war and degradation."

Madison's leadership in taking the nation to the brink of war had been severely disappointing. Like most of his peers at the Constitutional Convention, he had adopted the position that their new country must go to war only as an absolute last resort, when the survival of the Republic was in immediate peril.* It was difficult to argue that Britain's impressments, as frustrating as they were, or its apparent cooperation

---

* In 1795, he had written that "of all the enemies to public liberty, war is, perhaps, the most to be dreaded, because it comprises and develops the germ of every other," and warned that "in war, too, the discretionary power of the Executive is extended; its influence in dealing out offices, honors and emoluments is multiplied; and all the means of seducing the minds, are added to those of seducing the force, of the people."

with the Indians, which was actually more casual than it seemed, came anywhere close to his standard of imminent danger. If Madison was so indignant that England treated the United States without respect, he should have built up the American military, not lurch toward a war for which his country was ill prepared.

As one of the chief architects of the American system, Madison knew that the nature of the first major war to be fought under any President would do much to shape how often and how lightly the nation went to war in the future—and that engaging in this conflict would mean relaxing the established standard in Philadelphia. Unlike General Washington, Madison had never heard guns fired in battle or seen the desperately wounded. Unlike Jefferson and Adams, he had never traveled to Europe. (He once told Jefferson that "crossing the sea would be unfriendly to a singular disease of my constitution.") For Madison, so comfortable with abstraction, it was not surprising that he had studied and sometimes quoted from the German historian Baron Samuel von Pufendorf and the Dutch scholar Hugo Grotius, who both considered war an exercise that could be waged under strict ground rules.

Inexperienced in military affairs, Madison deluded himself into thinking that this war would be predictable and brief, with a few quick battles against a British force distracted by the struggle against Napoleon, after which Canada would tumble into American hands and London would plead for peace. As a political theorist, Madison knew that if his country had to go to war, such a venture had better enjoy the overwhelming support of the American people. But he realized that nearly every Federalist opposed the idea. Should there be a war, it would be, at least at the start, almost the exclusive project of his own political party.

Madison had been warned by Henry Clay that Congress would only consent to declare war if he made an unmistakable request for it. The President remained sufficiently respectful of the constitutional limits on his war powers, which he himself had helped to establish, that he was reluctant to ask the House and Senate outright to declare war against

England. Therefore, to salve his conscience, he opted to ask the members to declare that there already existed, "on the side of Great Britain, a state of war against the United States."*

* * *

ON JUNE 1, 1812, Madison gave the most important message of his presidency to his private secretary, Edward Coles (who was Dolley's cousin), for the gallop up Capitol Hill. In it, he listed England's "injuries and indignities" to the United States—the brutal impressments, interference with ships off the East Coast, blockades, British aid to hostile Indians on the western frontier, all topped off by the hated Orders in Council, which he called "a war against the lawful commerce of a friend." He told Congress that the Constitution "wisely" gave it the task of deciding "whether the United States shall continue passive under these progressive usurpations and these accumulating wrongs, or, opposing force to force in defense of their national rights, shall commit a just cause into the hands of the Almighty Disposer of Events."

Speaker Clay wrote a friend, "Let us give, in return for the insolence of British cannon, the peals of American thunder." After three days of secret debate (antiwar members tried but failed to open the proceedings), the House approved a war declaration against Britain by 79 to 49 votes, with not a single Federalist member voting yea. Roughly half of those Congressmen opting for war came from states in the region from Maryland to Georgia, whose populations were agitated less by England's specific maritime violations than its general, persistent affront to American dignity and independence. The Senate was so casual about the necessity for war that it took two weeks to pass a declaration, also after secret debate, and by an even smaller margin than that of the House—19 to 13

---

* A precedent adopted by later Presidents through Franklin Roosevelt in 1941, when he asked Congress to declare that since the Japanese attack on Pearl Harbor, "a state of war has existed between the United States and the Japanese Empire."

votes.* Celebrating at a nearby boardinghouse, Congressman John C. Calhoun of South Carolina hugged Henry Clay and joined other War Hawks to hop around a table, in an Indian war dance.

Despite the mandate for military conflict, the atmosphere in Washington was strangely devoid of urgency or tension. Monroe sportingly invited the British Minister for tea in his office, and, as Foster recalled, the two diplomats "endeavored to frighten one another for a whole Hour by descanting on the Consequences of War." Before sailing home to London, Foster paid a farewell call on Madison, who claimed that he had tried to keep the Congress from "pushing matters to extremes." Elsewhere in Washington, wealthy locals ghoulishly weighed their bids in the auction that was soon to come for the departing British Minister's household furniture and horses.

* * *

UNBEKNOWNST TO MADISON (it took several weeks for news to travel from London), at almost the exact instant that Congress had endorsed his war with England, the British Prince Regent and his Cabinet—now ruling in "mad" King George's stead—had, in fact, made the monumental decision to cancel the central reason for that conflict, the Orders in Council. Legions of British merchants and other businessmen, suffering from a severe economic depression, had demanded that the House of Commons abort the orders and thereby reopen the American market to England. But the inflexible Prime Minister, Spencer Perceval (whom Madison called "the Great Champion & Bigot" in reference to the Orders in Council), had refused.

Then, on May 11, while Perceval was striding into Commons, a malcontent named John Bellingham raised his pistol and committed what remains, to this day, history's only assassination of a British Prime Minister. Bellingham's gunfire had the consequence of removing the obstacle to rescinding the Orders in Council, which Perceval's successor,

---

* The Senate came close to limiting its authorization to reprisals against England by American vessels and privateers.

the young Earl of Liverpool, did in late June. Word of this breakthrough would not reach the United States for about six weeks.*

When some of Madison's friends learned of Perceval's murder, they implored him to pause before unleashing America's military fury, in case the new Prime Minister should cancel the Orders. Ex-Governor Henry Lee III of Virginia begged the President to "hold back yr. ships of war & privateers—give some time to hear from the enemy" because a "growing disposition" in Britain "for the repeal of the orders in council may stop war, unless it is hastened on our part." Lee went on, "Believe me my dear sir you could by no act so widely gratify the majority of yr. Country as by standing still awhile—you immortalize yr. name too by shewing yr. deep reluctance to wade in human blood."

But Madison ignored such appeals. He did not wish to give the British enemy the gift of precious time. Moreover, he had discarded his old doubts about this war and adopted with gusto the identity of a majestic Commander-in-Chief. As he planned the American invasion of Canada, Madison could not know that he was launching a conflict—which would consume many American lives—for which the principal cause of war had just vanished.

---

* On August 3, reporting the suspension of the Orders, Boston's *Independent Chronicle* quoted a British paper: "The termination of our disputes with America is now at hand; and we trust there is not a human being on either side of the Atlantic, who will not raise his hand in thankfulness to Heaven."

CHAPTER THREE

"The Most Glorious War"

SOON AFTER OBTAINING his war declaration from Congress, Madison donned a black bicorne hat, with an outsize military cockade, and the Commander-in-Chief, touring his War and Navy Departments, watched his war open with deceptive ease.

In July 1812, General William Hull—Yale graduate, Lieutenant Colonel of the Revolution, and Governor of the Michigan Territory— led about 2,500 troops from Fort Detroit across the Strait of St. Clair into Canada, where he hoped to cut off Britain's conduits to its native American allies in the Northwest Territory. "Glory! Glory!" cried the Madisonian *National Intelligencer*, "to the volunteers of Ohio, and the Tippacanoe boys who have first planted the American Standard in CANADA." Newark, New Jersey's *Sentinel of Freedom* embraced the administration's optimism: "Should the war continue, it is supposed that Upper Canada will fall an easy prey to the Americans. And very possible, the American Eagle may be flying on the walls of Quebec by the first of January next."

Establishing a foothold at Sandwich, Ontario, where he commandeered the most palatial mansion, Hull was certain that Canadians, eager for liberation from their British masters, would welcome the Americans with laurel wreaths. "INHABITANTS of Canada!!" he grandiloquently proclaimed. "I come to protect, not to injure you. . . . If the barbarous and savage policy of G. Britain be pursued, and the savages are let loose to murder our citizens, and butcher our women and children, this war will be a war of extermination. . . . *No white man found fighting by the side of an Indian will be taken prisoner.* Instant destruction will be his lot."

Hull had been told to thrust for Fort Malden, from which the British were said to have pulled the strings on their Indian marionettes, but he erred by dawdling at Sandwich for two weeks, claiming that his men needed to prepare gun carriages. The British exploited Hull's delay to capture the American fort on Mackinac Island, which helped them to control Lakes Superior, Huron, and Michigan. As Hull later complained, this "opened the northern hive of Indians" to swarm "down in every direction."

Madison wrote to Jefferson that the loss of their island fortress now made it critical for Hull "to take Malden, and awe the Savages emboldened by the British success." But with the aid of a vengeful Tecumseh and his warriors, General Isaac Brock, the British commander in Canada, secured Malden with a small, well-trained force and chased the American Army out of Canada. Retreating to Fort Detroit, in August, Hull sadly hung out a white tablecloth of defeat and gave up almost two thousand troops as prisoners. Lexington, Kentucky's *Reporter* complained that "HULL has shamefully, ingloriously and disgracefully surrendered to the British and Indians. *A Tale* remains to be told, which will make the blood of every American boil with indignation." *Poulson's American Daily Advertiser* of Philadelphia blamed the disaster "solely" on "those men who hurried the country into war, without providing the necessary means for carrying it on with spirit and energy." "The Country is disgraced," opined the *New York Herald,* adding, "The chiefs of the Government must be the most miserable wretches that ever undertook to administer the affairs of a Nation." The *Herald* explained that "Mr. Madison's War (for in two years nobody else will father it)" had sprung from "the madness of those in power."

Madison was furious when he learned of Hull's defeat from a post rider at Dumfries, Virginia, where he and Dolley were staying the night while traveling from Washington to Montpelier. Mrs. Madison exclaimed to Edward Coles that Hull had "surrender'd Detroit, *himself* & the whole Army to the British! Do you not tremble with resentment, at this treacherous act?" "Mortifying and humiliating," Monroe wrote Henry Clay. He felt that Hull's force had been seized by "a panic." Looking for a silver lining, the Secretary of State wrote Jefferson, "This most disgraceful event may produce good. It will rouse the nation. We must efface the stain before we make peace, & that may give us Canada." But Clay thought Hull "deserves to be shot," and Jefferson agreed.

Head figuratively between his hands, Madison abruptly returned to Washington, wondering how to calm what he called the "erroneous excitements" over "Hull's catastrophe." Reverend David Jones wrote the President from Ohio, "It is impossible for me to express the Indignation of the Country here. Not a few reflections are cast on you for appointing such an infamous Rascal to Command." Hull was court-martialed and sentenced to death for treason, cowardice, and neglect of duty, but the President reduced his punishment to removal from the Army. "MR. MADISON is the author of this War," lectured the *Portsmouth Oracle* of New Hampshire. "He commenced it without preparation. He conducts it feebly—Thus far, it has disgraced us." The *Rhode-Island American* asked, "What can we expect from men, whose whole conduct has been such a tissue of folly and blunders?"

By now, Americans throughout the eighteen states of the Union were learning that Britain had revoked the Orders in Council. The *Newburyport Herald* of Massachusetts said that "Poor Mr. Madison" must be "cudgeling his dull brains to find out which way to turn, since the unlucky repeal of his *principal cause of war.*" The *Boston Gazette* inveighed against Madison's "unnecessary and ruinous war."

Without even consulting the President, General Dearborn, in August, approved an armistice to let Madison shut down the war. Already reeling from Hull's insubordination, the President abruptly canceled Dearborn's action. He suspected that England might have quashed the orders as a temporary ploy to depress American enthusiasm for the war and buy time in order to strengthen its defenses in Canada. He sent a coded message to Jonathan Russell, the American chargé d'affaires in

London, that hostilities would cease only if Britain repealed the Orders in Council in both form and fact, adding that a halt to impressments must include restoring "those already impressed."

British leaders were exhilarated to learn how their cancellation of the orders was encouraging the virulent domestic opposition to Madison's war. The epicenter of resistance was New England, which, just as under Jefferson's embargo, was likely to suffer disproportionately from the war. Some were agitating for a separate peace with England. Governor Caleb Strong of Massachusetts, which boasted more than one-third of America's shipping, asked for prayers to end this conflict "against the nation from which we are descended." The President complained to Jefferson that "the Federalists in Congress are to put all the strength of their talents into a protest against the war and that the party at large are to be brought out in all their force." Thirty-four antiwar members of Congress claimed that the British had the perfect right to issue Orders in Council against US shipping and to impress US sailors; they called on Americans to abstain from Madison's military adventure.

When Madison asked New England governors to mobilize their militias for the war, Strong risked jail in defiance. Connecticut's Roger Griswold searched for more clearly legal means to say no to the conflict. A "Yankee farmer" wrote the *Connecticut Herald* that "the Farmers of New England do not feel desirous of *wasting* their blood in support of this *most mysterious* war. . . . Let us, *every man*, rally round our STRONGS and our GRISWOLDS."

* * *

MADISON REACTED TO New England's recalcitrance with "surprize" and "pain." He dreaded that some of the antiwar states might secede, which could lead to civil war. The *National Intelligencer*, which was loyal to Madison, warned, "Were New England to become a separate country, it would be after debilitating convulsions and grievous wounds, which would leave her far more exhausted and disjointed, than she was at the close of the revolutionary war."

Eager to preserve both the Union and civil liberties, however,

Madison refused to use brute force against the New England insurgents. He insisted that the best way to stop the protest movement would be military success on the battlefield. But some of Madison's followers took vengeance against the "seditious opposition" too far. Just after the war with England began, a midnight mob broke into the Baltimore head-quarters of the *Federal Republican,* whose young Federalist proprietor, Alexander Contee Hanson, had denounced the conflict as "unnecessary, inexpedient" and French-inspired.* Armed with drum and fife, axes and clubs, they damaged Hanson's printing apparatus, hurled the parts into the street, and burned the building down.

A month later, Hanson relaunched his paper from a nearby house, insisting that he would not let vandals "destroy the freedom of speech and of the press." Generals Henry "Light-Horse Harry" Lee and James Lingan, both Revolutionary War veterans, and two dozen Federalists stood guard with muskets and bayonets. A new mob, hurling cobble-stones, forced their way into the building. Lee and his comrades fired their weapons, killing two intruders and wounding ten or more. Hanson and his defenders were marched off to protective custody, some to be tried for murder. Still another horde—crying *"Tory! Tory!"*—broke into the jail to beat and club the Federalists. According to one account, "All whom address, stratagem or fortune did not favor were assassinated and thrown into a heap as dead carcasses." Lee was crippled and Lingan killed. The *National Intelligencer* called the violence "unprecedented in the annals of the Republic." Hanson's paper decamped to Georgetown, complaining that Madison's own public silence about the Baltimore riots betokened a "sudden enmity to the Liberty of the Press."

Monroe advised the President, "The punishment even of such men as the Editors of that paper must be inflicted by law, not mob movements." But some Republicans argued that with the nation enmeshed in its first major war, Madison should constrain press freedoms and perhaps even declare martial law. In Pennsylvania, the *Lancaster Journal* warned, *"The United States swarm with British adherents and emissaries,"* adding that

---

* Hanson was the editor who had almost killed the *Chesapeake*'s Captain Gordon in their 1810 duel.

the President's own "negligence" about this internal threat "is as *criminal in him* as it is *dangerous to the nation.*" But Madison, author of the Bill of Rights, was adamant about civil liberties. In 1795, he had warned, "War is the parent of armies; from these proceed debts and taxes; and armies, and debts, and taxes are the known instruments for bringing the many under the domination of the few. . . . No nation could preserve its freedom in the midst of continual warfare."

Madison had been appalled in 1798 when President Adams, anticipating a possible war against France, signed the Alien and Sedition Acts, which forced some journalists to be locked up for criticizing the government and others to be branded troublemakers who should be expelled from the country. Madison had told Jefferson that Adams was a "hotheaded Executive" to have endorsed such measures, and deemed them unconstitutional. At the time, he wrote Jefferson, "Perhaps it is a universal truth that the loss of liberty at home is to be charged to provisions against danger, real or pretended, from abroad." Now he concurred with his Virginia childhood friend John Taylor's warning that war with England "may terminate in the destruction of the last experiment in favour of free government." Knowing that he was setting down a marker for later wartime Commanders-in-Chief, Madison admirably kept his hands off the people's liberties.

* * *

A T THE START of the war, Commodores Rodgers and Decatur had authorized raids against British ships on the Atlantic. Despite the modest size of the US Navy, the Americans won a few victories. In August 1812, the *Guerriere,* sailing between Halifax and Bermuda, fired on the *Constitution,* commanded by Captain Isaac Hull (nephew of the General who lost Detroit), but to little effect, moving one American sailor to cry, "Huzzah! Her sides are made of iron!" The captain of the mortally wounded *Guerriere* presented his sword of surrender, and his ship was set aflame, exploding as it sank under the waves. "An auspicious triumph," Madison told Congress. The *Boston Gazette* conceded that the "brilliant Naval victory" of the ship now hailed as

"Old Ironsides" would "excite the liveliest emotions in every American bosom."

That October, General Dearborn authorized General Stephen Van Rensselaer of the New York militia to go on the attack in Canada, but the small, badly trained force was captured at Queenston Heights, and Van Rensselaer was sacked. As with Hull's defeat, this debacle reflected badly on Madison's skills as Commander-in-Chief, especially while the nation was deciding on the President's reelection. Gallatin confessed to Jefferson that the "misfortunes" of "our military land operations" exceeded "all anticipations." "Mr. Madison is wholly unfit for the storms of War," Henry Clay wrote to a friend. "Nature has cast him in too benevolent a mould."

Federalist papers showed the President little mercy. The *Salem Gazette* of Massachusetts complained that "the feeble and timid mind of Mr. Madison" had conceived a war "without money, without soldiers, and without generals." The *New-England Palladium* was scathing: "History can scarce afford an instance of so miserable a war conducter! . . . People have thought him a good writer—that is, of proclamations, messages to Congress and newspaper essays. . . . Dress him up in a parson's gown, and white wig, and he might look well enough for a minister of peace, but . . . it is impossible to help laughing, when we observe the pitiful attempt of Madison to play the warrior!" Maryland's *Frederick-Town Herald* lampooned Madison as Commander-in-Chief: "Let us take Canada, if it costs millions of lives and centuries of war. Let us take Canada, the expence is nothing."

Madison was opposed for reelection by New York's Lieutenant Governor, DeWitt Clinton, a dissident Democratic-Republican backed by the Federalists. When campaigning in antiwar states, Clinton opportunistically promised to end the conflict. Where the war was popular, he pledged to fight England more fiercely than Madison. The President's supporters urged the voters not to change Commanders-in-Chief in the middle of this conflict. The *Constitutionalist* of New Hampshire replied, "Shall it be said, that because we are now engaged in a war, we shall not change our rulers after we have discovered their want of talents to conduct it? . . . We doubt whether the annals of any age can furnish an example of a war commenced under more unfavorable auspices, and conducted with so much imbecility, and such a total want of foresight."

Madison defended his war leadership in his written November message to Congress. He conceded that Van Rensselaer's defeat had been "considerable," frustrating "our expectation of gaining the command of the [Great] Lakes by the invasion of Canada from Detroit." He asked Congress to improve the Navy and soldiers' pay, intoning, "Above all, we have the inestimable consolation of knowing that the war in which we are actually engaged is a war neither of ambition nor of vain glory." To have "shrunk" from this conflict would have been a concession that Americans "were not an independent people, but colonists and vassals."

The *Providence Gazette* was not impressed by the President's "lame apology for the war." The *Massachusetts Spy* warned that if Madison were reelected, "we are to expect with absolute certainty, at least four years continuance of a vindictive, ruinous, and sanguinary conflict!" Another Federalist paper argued that Madison's proposed military pay increase was "evidence of the unpopularity of the war. . . . How debasing is it, to see the Administration resorting to such mean expedients to recruit their lean and meagre regiments?" Madison defeated Clinton by 128 electoral votes to the challenger's 89, with Clinton taking nine northeastern states, which were known for reviling Madison's war. The popular vote was much closer—50.4 to 47.6 percent. Thanks largely to disgust with the war, Federalists doubled their strength on Capitol Hill.

* * *

ON THE MORNING of Madison's second inaugural, in March 1813, a Virginia farmer witnessed the President's arrival at the Capitol: "A carriage with four spanking greys drove like Jehu to the door, and out popped a little man in black, with a powdered head. This, I was told, was the Lord's anointed: he stepped four paces from the carriage, then slackened his gait and turned hesitatingly towards it again, as if he had forgot his cane. . . . Here he drew his breath twice, winked three times and went into the house, preceded by the marshal, who cleared the way for him." After taking his oath in the Senate chamber, Madison emerged outdoors to deliver his address, smugly claiming that the war against England, and his "means of conducting it" deserved "the smiles of Heaven." The *Federal Republican* claimed that when Chief Justice John Marshall heard the President's "preposterous eulogiem upon himself," his face assumed an angry glare and that when Madison "encountered his eye, a guilty suffusion spread over his cheeks."

Madison's self-satisfaction belied the fact that Gallatin had warned him that the war had so drained the US Treasury that they could not make it to the end of March. Congress had approved borrowing $16 million but Federalists were trying, with considerable success, to block the loan in an effort to bring down Madison's regime. With Gallatin postponing payments to stay afloat, the Frenchman Stephen Girard, who lived in Philadelphia, and two German-born financiers, David Parish and John Jacob Astor—the latter was the first multimillionaire of the New World—ponied up the $9 million difference, which meant, ironically, that America's sacred crusade to wrench itself from the Old World was thenceforth financed by Europeans.[*]

By that month of March, the US Army still numbered only about nineteen thousand men. Congress tried to swell the ranks by slashing the term of enlistment from five years to one, offering bounties and recruiting minors, but with only mild success. The President had John Armstrong—who had replaced the stumbling Eustis as Secretary of War—ask Congress to impose a draft, but they ran into a Federalist brick wall. "Any thing like a Pledge by Federalists to carry on this wicked war, strikes a Dagger at my heart," said that party's Gouverneur Morris of New York. "What are you to gain by giving Mr. Madison Men and Money?"

Struggling with money and manpower, Madison accepted the offer of the Russian Tsar, Alexander I, to arbitrate the Anglo-American war. At this moment, the President would have been relieved to find some

---

[*] Later in 1813, "with fear and trembling," the Republican Congress, at Madison's behest, imposed taxes on real estate, slaves, sugar, whiskey, carriages, and other items.

kind of "honorable peace." In Frenchtown, Michigan Territory, marching in the January cold, many of William Henry Harrison's soldiers had been killed by the British and native Americans. The *National Intelligencer* described the "terrors of the tomahawk and scalping-knife" and the "indiscriminate slaughter by the savages of the wilderness." The *Alexandria Gazette* noted that "many were burned alive in the houses."

In April 1813, the modest American force led by Brigadier General Zebulon Pike crossed Lake Ontario by corvette, brig, and schooner, and seized the provincial capital of York. Swarming into the little legislative assembly building, the troops rejoiced to discover, hanging above a mace, a trophy they took to be a "human scalp," but it turned out to be the parliamentary speaker's wig. The Battle of York claimed the life of General Pike, whose back was broken by a stone fragment from an exploding British powder magazine. Intoxicated by unaccustomed victory, the American soldiers plundered private houses and provincial headquarters and set them aflame, spurring angry British commanders to vow revenge.

By May, British vessels, led by the Admiral of the Fleet, Sir George Cockburn, reached the coast of Maryland. The invaders hazed US merchant ships, raped American women, threatened to provoke slave uprisings, and burned parts of Fredericktown, Havre de Grace, and other towns north of Annapolis. There were rumors that Cockburn's next stop would be Washington. The former House Speaker Jonathan Dayton, a Federalist who had been the youngest man to sign the Constitution, warned Madison of a plot "to seize your person and papers and convey you to the fleet" of Admiral Cockburn.

Dolley heard that Cockburn and his confederates were planning "to land as many chosen *Rogues* as they can about 14 miles below Alexa[ndria] in the night, who may arrive before day & set fire to the offices & Presidents House." She wrote Edward Coles, "I do not tremble at this, but feel *affronted* that the Admiral . . . should send me notis that he would make his bow at my Drawing room *soon*." Mrs. Madison explained that although she was a Quaker, "I have allways been an advocate for fighting when assailed. . . . I therefore keep the old Tunesian Sabre within my reach."

* * *

IN JUNE 1813, Madison became so sick that he almost died. Shivering in bed at the Mansion, although it was almost the zenith of summer, the President wore a nightcap and flannel gown, with Dolley hovering in despair. "A bilious fever," recorded Monroe, "of that kind called the remittent." No one could say for certain that Madison's deathly sickness, with vomiting and diarrhea (perhaps a malady of the liver or gall bladder, provoked by a parasitic infection or yellow jaundice), had been incurred by a frustrating war. But it could not be wholly coincidental that this was the instant when Madison's never-robust body broke down.

Since youth, the fussy Madison had been something of a hypochondriac.* He occasionally suffered from trembling fits that resembled epilepsy. His removal from public view now led to hateful rumors. Ex-President John Adams wrote a friend he had heard that Madison "lives by laudanum and could not hold out for four months." The *Federal Republican* claimed, "His recent sickness has made havoc of his constitution, and left him, it is confidently believed, but a few months, perhaps a few days to live." The journal went on to report that the President was "*now* utterly sinking beneath his high duties—and now bursting forth in paroxisms of rage, violence and extravagant folly, which would disgrace a spoiled child of twenty. . . . Not a few, who have recently visited him, have left his chamber under a full conviction, of the derangement of his mind."

When Madison was finally well enough for Dolley to take him to Montpelier, their departure led to comment that the presidential couple was escaping out of fear that Admiral Cockburn's legions were about to attack Washington. A Boston paper offered a soothing rebuttal: "It is not from an apprehension of the enemy, but for the *search of Health,* that Mr. Madison *deserts the Capital.*" Dolley wrote Gallatin's wife, Hannah, that no outsider could fully comprehend the gravity of the President's illness "and the despair, in which I attended his bed for nearly five

---

* His brother Reuben and sister Elizabeth had perished from illness as young children.

weeks! Even now, I watch over him as I would an infant, so precarious is his convalessence—added to this, the disappointments & vexations, heaped upon him by party spirit."

When she married James in 1794, the smiling, extroverted, Rubenesque Dolley Payne Todd had opened the door to his cage, helping the awkward groom, who was seventeen years older, connect to the social and diplomatic life of Philadelphia, which was then the national capital.* Dolley had tragically lost her first husband and younger son in a yellow fever epidemic. The following year, the never-married Congressman Madison asked for an introduction to Mrs. Todd, and within three months, they were engaged. For marrying out of her faith, the Quakers expelled her.

Called (like Martha Washington) the "Presidentess," Dolley lushly renovated the Executive Mansion and staged sumptuous receptions and banquets, even in wartime, presiding with her curlicued coiffure, ample décolletage, and fealty to the most current fashions. She chatted with Henry Clay about their mutual affinity for snuff, using her charm on friend and foe (although one rude British diplomat complained that she had "an uncultivated mind" and was "fond of gossiping"). Dolley had spittoons strategically placed about the state floor for the many tobacco-chewing guests. Discarding Jefferson's austerity—Madison's predecessor had moved about Washington on his own horse—the Presidentess had Philadelphia's finest coach maker build a quasi-royal carriage with brass-mounted harnesses that emulated the vehicles used by Washington and Adams. Fretting that James's small stature and lack of personal grandeur might tempt people to deny him proper respect, she started a tradition, which persists to this day, for an anthem to be performed when the President entered a room.†

That summer, the House and Senate, after having their sleeves

---

* Contributing to Madison's shyness with women was the fact that his first serious love, a fifteen-year-old girl named Catherine Floyd, had crushed her thirty-two-year-old suitor by dumping him for a medical student in 1783.

† At that time the anthem was "Hail, Columbia," which was later replaced by "Hail to the Chief" under President Andrew Jackson.

tugged by influential clergymen, demanded that Madison proclaim a national wartime "Day of Public Humiliation and Prayer" to "acknowledge our dependence upon Almighty God." The President had long been a champion of American religious liberty—he was the Founder who proposed that "Congress shall make no law respecting an establishment of religion." Like many of his Federalist critics, Madison was at least nominally an Episcopalian but once said that if he had to join any sect, it would be the Unitarians.

Madison did not wish to violate the separation of church and state, but he also feared that if he flatly refused the clerics' request, Congress might reduce its support for his war against England. Thus he agreed to issue a proclamation, carefully worded in order not to encourage future Presidents to recommend that Americans pray or otherwise use the excuse of a war to violate religious liberty. In it, he specifically stated that he was doing so in response to a congressional resolution, and that "on times of public calamity such as that of the war brought on the United States," it was "especially becoming" that "all who shall be piously disposed" assemble and honor "the Great Parent and Sovereign of the Universe."

Hanson's *Federal Republican* argued that even this cautious statement was too openly religious to come from a President. It published a letter from a "gentleman of Maryland," who wrote, "I wish never to see the president of the United States, *ex officio* president of God's house. . . . We have seen the evils, which have resulted from an union of church and state, when those in authority were pious."*

* * *

BY JUNE 1813, with the British tightening their blockade of the Atlantic coast, the United States suffered a defeat with painful

---

* During Madison's retirement, noting that Jefferson had never issued any such decree, he regretted his wartime proclamation to honor the "Great Parent." Returning to the vehemence of his early days as a Founder, the ex-President demanded that state and church be separated by unbreachable walls, or else "bigotry may introduce persecution; a monster, that feeding & thriving on its own venom, gradually swells to a size & strength overwhelming all laws divine & human."

historical resonance. Six years after its battering by the *Leopard,* the restored USS *Chesapeake* had ranged the Atlantic and seized five British vessels, but its new captain, James Lawrence, had felt "extreme repugnance" to be assigned to what he considered "the worst ship in our Navy," an "unlucky ship" that was shunned by the best American sailors.

Before Lawrence sailed from Boston, the captain of the HMS *Shannon,* which was lying in wait, sent him a written challenge, chivalrously offering to hold fire until the *Chesapeake* was prepared to fight, but Lawrence never received the British note. Thus when he spied the *Shannon* he ordered his crewmen to fire. After six minutes of "tremendous broadsides," many on the *Chesapeake* were killed or wounded. Lawrence took a musket ball in the viscera. While being carried below deck, mortally injured, he ensured his place in US naval history by ordering, "Don't give up the ship!" But these almost final words were in vain. After seizing the American warship, the British took it to Halifax so that they could send it back into battle against the Americans, defiantly renamed as the HMS *Chesapeake.*

Three months later, Commodore Oliver Hazard Perry, the young US naval commander on Lake Erie, stood at the helm of the newly built brig *Lawrence,* named for the *Chesapeake*'s martyr. Concentrating fire on Perry's ship, the British killed most of his crew. Amid the smoke and flame, the Commodore bravely had himself rowed to the nearby brig *Niagara,* where he took command of his remaining flotilla. Amid cannon fire so thunderous that people heard it 160 miles away, Perry's vessels pounded the British warships to the point of surrender.

Perry proclaimed, "We have met the enemy, and they are ours." Proudly he wrote Madison, "It hath pleased the Almighty to give the arms of the United States a signal victory over their enemies on this lake." The President exulted in what he called *"the brilliant atchievement of Perry,"* which had "opened a passage to the territory of the enemy."*

---

* So ravaged was Britain's Lake Erie flotilla, it was said, that "not a boat was left to carry back the melancholy tidings" to British commanders, who, on receiving the news, torched Forts Amherstburg and Detroit in order to thwart the Americans.

In October, Perry and General Harrison joined in the Battle of the Thames, leading US forces to a mammoth victory over the British and their Indian "savages." Tecumseh was killed, and the western front was secured on behalf of the American struggle for Upper Canada. The President assured Americans that these victories were "the best auguries of eventual victory." But in December, the British captured Fort Niagara, killing sixty-five Americans. One Federalist paper blamed the "horrid massacre" on the "wretched policy" of Madison's generals. Another warned that since the President was hell-bent on seizing all of Canada, "the present war will continue at least seven years."

✳ ✳ ✳

I N THE SPRING of 1814, the long conflict between Britain and France paused with Napoleon's abdication, letting England devote itself to winning the American war. The United States still lacked command of Lake Ontario, which provoked it to engage the British on the Niagara Peninsula in some of the harshest fighting of the conflict.

Madison ordered Secretary Armstrong to "be prepared for the worst the enemy may be able to effect against us," adding that if the British were looking for targets, "the Seat of Govt. can not fail to be a favorite one." Dolley Madison warned Hannah Gallatin of "the depredations of the Enemy approaching within 20 miles of the City" and that people were saying "that if Mr. Madison attempts to move from this House in case of an attack they will *stop him,* and that he shall *fall with it.* I am not the last alarmed at these things, but entirely disgusted, and determined to stay with him."

At the start of July, Armstrong assured the President that the British would attack not Washington but the more alluring military target of Baltimore. However, Madison felt that Armstrong was ignoring the psychological impact of conquering the American capital city. He demanded that the War Secretary and General William Winder draft a plan for Washington's defense, which should employ ten thousand militiamen.* But Armstrong and Winder dragged their heels. Except for asking questions from time to time, the President refused to push them, although he knew of Admiral Cockburn's warning that "Mr. Madison will have to put his armor on and fight it out."

On Thursday, August 18, Madison learned that twenty British transports and thirty other warships on the Patuxent River, thirty-five miles southeast of Washington, were disgorging perhaps six thousand well-trained, well-supplied regulars. They began slowly marching up the road to the American capital. By the following Monday morning, more anxious about the redcoats, the President decreed that the federal archives be removed from Washington for safekeeping. He sent militiamen from Maryland and Virginia to the crossroads town of Bladensburg, nine miles from the Capital.

Madison bravely rode with a gaggle of aides, his new Attorney General, Richard Rush, and Navy Secretary, William Jones, to visit the soldiers gathered to protect Washington. Spending the night at a nearby house, he sent a message to Dolley that the troops were in "high spirits" but the enemy appeared more menacing than forecast: she "should be ready at a moment's warning" to flee the Capital because British troops might soon arrive "with intention to destroy it." Returning to the Executive Mansion on Tuesday evening, August 23, Madison received Winder, who had accidentally fallen into a ditch that day and still had not made up his mind how to use the troops called up by the President. Monroe had ridden out to gauge the scene for himself. He wrote Madison with alarm, "The enemy are in full march for Washington." With Monroe's warning in his troubled mind, Madison retired with Dolley for what would prove to be the last night they would ever spend in the White House.

On Wednesday morning, so Madison later wrote, he was handed a note from Winder, requesting "the speediest counsel." The British were moving toward Bladensburg, amid rumors of pillage and rape.

---

* Winder was an obscure lawyer who had received his military post as a sop to bipartisanship: his uncle, Levin Winder, was Maryland's Federalist Governor.

Galloping through the heat and dust to the Secretary of War's quarters, the President was warned by Armstrong that their ill-trained volunteers were about to be defeated by the British regulars. Madison ordered him to go to Bladensburg and confer with Winder. Strapping on two dueling pistols, the President rode to the battleground himself, along with Rush. Madison's aides feared that the British might try to kidnap the American President.

In Bladensburg, someone noted that "the thermometer marked blood heat." When Madison arrived, he was taken to a hilltop and told by the petty Armstrong that he would collaborate with Winder only if the President forced him to. Madison bravely refused to depart, thus becoming the first sitting American President to be vulnerable to enemy fire. Through a spyglass, he watched his forces retreat, losing their final chance to block the British from invading Washington.* Sunburned from hours in the blistering heat, Madison "fell down into the road," as he later put it, by carriage toward the Capital, past terrified families escaping in the other direction. "There goes the President!" they cried.

When Madison reached his Executive Mansion, he doffed his pistols. The big house was deserted, and Dolley was already gone. Knowing that people were watching him carefully for signs of cowardice, he climbed into his coach, along with several servants, Rush, and John Mason, Commanding General of the Capital's militia. They rode to the nearest ferry landing on the Potomac, one of the rendezvous points where he had asked his wife to meet him, should the worst befall Washington. But, with darkness coming, Dolley was not there. Forlorn, Madison boarded the barge. Looking backward, as it moved onto the river, he could see the capital city drifting away from him.

✳ ✳ ✳

R EACHING THE ROCKY Virginia shore, the fugitive President mounted a horse and wandered the forest with Rush in search of

---

* Georgetown's *Federal Republican* later claimed that as soon as he heard enemy fire, the "panic struck" President had fled.

Wiley's Tavern, another place of rendezvous, located on Difficult Run, near the Great Falls, but still he could not find Dolley. By some accounts, when Madison encountered Washingtonians who had fled to Virginia, he heard himself reviled with loud, angry epithets for letting their city be burned—including demands that he be shot.* By midnight, he was still about five miles from Wiley's Tavern. The brutal experience of the day had taken its toll, and the President could ride no more. A Presbyterian minister, William Maffitt, gave him a bed for the night at the farmhouse on his estate, which was called Salona.†

The next day, Thursday, August 25, Madison searched on horseback for his wife through what was called a minor hurricane, with "heaving black clouds of rain." He returned in soaking clothes to Reverend Maffitt's home to learn that Dolley had arrived there and gone. Finally, that evening, drenched and hungry, he was gloriously reunited with his wife at Wiley's.‡ A violent wind throttled the apple trees around the inn, and flying apples struck the windowpanes.

Madison dined on cold leftovers that Dolley had saved for him and collapsed into bed. But at midnight, someone shouted that the British were coming (although there was probably no enemy soldier within twenty miles). Leaving his wife at the tavern—he warned her to wear a disguise if she emerged—Madison took off into the foul, wet night with Rush, Mason, Secretary Jones, and several dragoons, looking for Mrs. Conn's Ferry, which they hoped to take across the Potomac to Maryland, where Madison hoped to rejoin some of Winder's soldiers.

But the wild, storm-tossed river would not let him. Having been in the saddle for up to ten hours or more a day since the morning he left the

---

* Reflecting the racism of the time, Charles Ingersoll, a Republican Congressman from Pennsylvania, later recounted a rumor that Admiral Cockburn had succeeded in provoking a slave revolt, and that "thousands of infuriated negroes, drunk with liquor and mad with emancipation," were raping white women across the countryside.

† Later, during the Civil War, Salona served as a headquarters for the Union's General George McClellan.

‡ It turned out that Dolley had slept only about a mile away from Madison the previous night, at an estate called Rokeby, owned by family friends.

Executive Mansion to inspect General Winder's troops, the President of the United States—defeated first by the British, now by the elements—lay down his head and slept, with one eye open, for only a few hours, it was said, in a dilapidated "hovel," hidden by a tangle of bushes.

On Friday, August 26, the tousled Madison and his party crossed the river into Maryland, but failed to find Winder's men at Montgomery Court House.* Instead, that night, at nine o'clock, the President, along with General Mason and dozens of dragoons, limped into the Quaker settlement of Brookeville. One local warned that "people are heaping curses on the government" and "all parties unite in execrating Madison." This suggested that finding the President a resting place might not be easy. A pathfinder took Madison's party to a substantial home. As the President discreetly lurked in the dark on his horse, the guide carefully asked "if General Mason and suite" could stay the night, even if they had to sleep on the floor. "No," replied the owner, "my house is filled with families who have fled from Washington and Georgetown." Finally the frazzled Madison and his companions found hospitality with the Brookeville postmaster, Caleb Bentley, a Quaker silversmith, whose wife, Henrietta, happened to be Dolley's friend.

They sat down for supper with fellow refugees from the Capital and Brookeville townspeople. Some were Quakers who detested Madison's war, but the President received what were called the "kindest and most touching attentions." At the crowded table, he sat so close to the other diners that in the flickering candlelight, they could see the gouge on his nose caused by long-ago frostbite during winter electioneering. (Madison once quipped that it was a "scar of a wound" obtained while defending his country.) Loading his plate, the President explained that he had ridden "thirty miles since breakfast, over a dreadful road, without any dinner." As someone recalled, Madison was "quite talkative and cheerful for some minutes, but occasionally relapsed into silent gloom."

Also present was Madison's revenue commissioner, Samuel Harrison Smith, who had likewise fled the British. Tactlessly Smith mentioned that Alexander Hanson of the *Federal Republican* had inveighed against

---

* Today the town is called Rockville.

"the disgrace of the President flying around from place to place" after the British invasion, as well as Madison's failure to keep his pledge to "rouse the nation" from a government of exile in Fredericktown. Clearly annoyed, Madison changed the subject by asking what had happened to Monroe and Armstrong. Some buffoon tweaked the President's raw nerve by observing that Winder's force must have been awfully small to have been so easily "routed" at Bladensburg. Barely able to contain his fury, Madison glared at the offender. That night, Mrs. Bentley slept on her living room floor in order to vacate her bedroom for the President, and fretted that outside the house his guards were trampling her flower beds.

On Saturday morning, after a brief night of rest under the Bentleys' roof, Madison showed signs of traumatic shock and disorientation. Although he knew that the White House had been badly burned, he bizarrely hoped aloud that his valuable book collection had survived, and invited a fellow boarder to visit him at the Mansion, "seeming to forget for the moment," as one witness observed, "that his palace was burnt." Soon Monroe, armed with two pistols and a sword, arrived with good news: the windstorms had so threatened Cockburn's fleet that the British had retreated from the Capital. Ready to leave, Madison wrote his "dearest" Dolley—still at Wiley's Tavern and wearing borrowed clothes to conceal her identity from potential British kidnappers—that she should "remain in your present quarters" until they were sure that the danger to Washington had fully passed. He told her that he knew not where they would "hide our heads; but shall look for a place on my arrival."

Elsewhere in America, people were wondering who was now in charge. The Federalist *Salem Gazette* attacked the President for his absence: "Ever since the battle of Bladensburg, MADISON has been missing— he does not even know where he is himself—entirely lost and bewildered! . . . He ought to have thrown himself before his Capitol with a determination to bury himself under its ruins. . . . For misconduct like this, a Roman or a Grecian General would have suffered banishment or death." New York's *Commercial Advertiser* asked, "Why this mysterious silence at a crisis so momentous? . . . Why has not the President issued a Proclamation, acknowledging his blunders, and announcing the extent of our disasters? . . . Where—ten thousand tongues are daily asking—where are the constituted authorities of our Nation?"*

* * *

R ETURNED TO WASHINGTON on Saturday night, August 27, Madison accepted a bed from Attorney General Rush, whose townhouse stood in the Six Buildings row on Pennsylvania Avenue.† Inspecting the city the next day, the President found his Executive Mansion "in ashes, not an inch but its cracked and blackened walls remained." Surrounded by dead horses, the Capitol was in "smouldering ruins" that were "yet smoking." Because no food stores were operating, one of the two White House milk cows, which had both survived Cockburn's attack, was slaughtered to feed the President. Madison also partook of hams and casks of wine that had been saved from his kitchen.

Calling at the F Street mansion of Dolley's sister Anna and her husband, Richard Cutts, ex-Congressman from Massachusetts and now Superintendent General of Military Supplies, Madison was overjoyed to find his wife, who had returned by carriage to the cheers of a crowd. Surveying the city, she had exclaimed, "Such destruction! Such confusion!" Furious at the British, she wished she could "sink our enemy to the bottomless pit," and later recalled, "My heart mourned for my country."

The President summoned Armstrong, who had been hiding in a Maryland farmhouse, intently reading a Walter Scott romance novel. Madison told him frankly that, in the aftermath of Washington's burning, each soldier was threatening to break his sword and "tear off his

---

* Wincing at this spectacle, many investors stopped buying US bonds and pulled their silver and gold out of American banks, which almost upended the nation's financial structure.

† Cockburn's soldiers had kept their torches away from most private homes in the District. In London, Lord Liverpool, the British Prime Minister, claimed his parliament that no invading Army had ever acted "more humanely." He went on to insist that Cockburn had burned Washington in revenge for US atrocities at York—a ridiculous comparison, for York was a tiny outpost and the several buildings set afire by the Americans were small, wooden, and easily rebuilt.

epaulettes" rather than serve under Armstrong as Secretary of War.* After first insisting that he would not cave in to the "humors of a village mob," the General resigned. Adding to Armstrong's pain, Madison let the General's hated rival Monroe replace him as Acting Secretary of War while remaining Secretary of State.†

Catching his breath for the first time all week, Madison was exposed to the blast of attacks against him. The *American Watchman* told its readers, "Our country disgraced." "JAMES MADISON IS THE CAUSE OF THIS," charged the *Federal Republican*. "When will the reign of insanity terminate? When will our infatuated rulers turn from the path of folly—when will they cease to render our unhappy country to the scorn and derision of the world?" The *Delaware Gazette* reported that even "the Madisonians feel ashamed of the conduct of our rulers," noting "the torrent of curses" poured upon the President. The *Newport Mercury* demanded that Madison and his entourage be "constitutionally impeached, and driven with scorn and execration from the seats which they have dishonored and polluted." Addressing the President directly, Boston's *Palladium* asked, "Do you ever blush? If not, let the blood rise and encrimson your cheeks; it may give some relief to your agitated mind."

The *Boston Gazette* pronounced Madison "an elegant scholar" but "the most incompetent executive functionary that ever disgraced a nation." It complained that the President, "instead of abdicating his chair, as he is called upon to do by all America, excepting a few lick-pans and office-holders," was trying to "conceal from an abused people his infamous weakness in leaving the capital of the U. States without a sufficient defence against 5000 famished troops. . . . The people will be bamboozled no longer. . . . They are determined to have nothing more to do with James Madison, nor John Armstrong, nor any of the junto."

---

* On one of the burned walls of the Capitol, someone had drawn an image of the General being hanged, adding the words "Armstrong the Traitor."

† Armstrong had hoped to run against Monroe for President in 1816, but with his political career now in tatters, he retired to the Hudson Valley county of Dutchess, where he built an imposing mansion (his daughter had married a rich man) and wrote a pamphlet warning that Monroe's "lust for power is insatiable."

The *New York Evening Post* issued a biting couplet: " 'Fly, Monroe, fly! Run, Armstrong, run!!' / Were the last words of Madison."

✳ ✳ ✳

Here the dismal state of the war, and of Madison's reputation, might have calcified but for a military achievement that—to the country's good fortune and the President's—occurred in mid-September 1814, only a fortnight after his tail-between-the-legs return to Washington. Striking at the crucial port of Baltimore, fifty British warships, commanded by Admiral Cockburn and Major General Robert Ross, landed about four thousand men and, by morning, started bombarding the star-shaped Fort McHenry, but they failed and Ross was killed.

This success, just at the moment Americans had been feeling so dejected about the war, was immortalized by the Washington lawyer Francis Scott Key. Aboard a nearby British ship, Key was bargaining over US prisoners when he was inspired to record that at the fortress, "the rockets' red glare, the bombs bursting in air, gave proof through the night that our flag was still there."* Suddenly Americans no longer thought of Madison quite so much as the nincompoop who had, however briefly, lost their Capital. Now he was also the leader who had overseen the glorious Battle of Baltimore, as well as a concurrent, more strategically important victory at Lake Champlain. Even the *Federal Republican* agreed that the Baltimore victory had retrieved, "in some degree, our national character from the disgrace."

With the Capitol ruined, the House and Senate took up temporary quarters in Blodgett's Hotel, at Seventh and F Streets, Northwest. Some members tried to exploit the disaster to have the nation's Capital moved

---

* Key's poem was sung to the tune of the drinking song "To Anacreon in Heaven," an ode to free love and the grape. The Greek poet Anacreon had exalted excessive drinking, and the song's original lyrics included the lascivious refrain "May the Sons of Anacreon intwine / The Myrtle of Venus with Bacchus's Vine!" Nevertheless the Prohibition-era Congress of 1931 chose "The Star-Spangled Banner" as the nation's anthem.

back to New York or Philadelphia—or, some even suggested, Baton Rouge. Those who were disenchanted with the Compromise of 1790, which placed the Capital roughly midway between North and South, now saw their chance to undo it. A decade and a half into its life as the federal city, Washington's streets and amusements were primitive, the summer climate steamy and disease-prone. Both Madison, who, as a Congressman, had helped President Washington to fashion that deal, and Dolley, who had tried to elevate the Capital's social life, argued in response that for Americans to give up on the city named after the Father of His Country would grant a belated victory to the British torchmen.

By the time the Capital's magnolias dropped their leaves, the Madisons had moved into the three-story, red brick Octagon House, not far from the charred hulk of the presidential Mansion. Built by a well-known Federalist, Colonel John Tayloe III, known as the richest Virginia planter of his day, the Mansion had been graciously vacated by Louis Sérurier, the French Minister, whose cook had also been kind enough to shelter Mrs. Madison's bird, Uncle Willy. Trying to show the world that nothing had changed, Dolley resumed some semblance of her old entertaining. The *Washington City Gazette* sniped at her, regretting that the British flames had not "put an end to drawing-rooms and levees; the resort of the idle, and the encouragers of spies and traitors."

Madison received a visit from his Virginia friend William Wirt, who later informed his wife that the President "looks miserably shattered and woebegone. In short, he looked heart-broken. His mind is full of the New England sedition." Madison told another friend, Wilson Cary Nicholas, that the northeastern states were "the source of our greatest difficulties in carrying on the war, as it certainly is the greatest, if not the sole, inducement with the enemy to persevere in it." The people of that region, he said, were "under a delusion scarcely exceeded by that recorded in the period of witchcraft; and the leaders are becoming daily more desperate in the use they make of it. Their object is power." The President was right to worry about New England, where "blue-light" Federalists—so named for those whose blue lanterns warned British vessels at night against US blockade-runners—had long blustered about wrenching their region away from the United States and making their own separate peace with Great Britain. Now, with the British occupying a small part of Maine, the dissenters called a convention at Hartford, Connecticut, where the British flag was flown side by side with the Stars and Stripes. One Republican joked that the secessionists would vote to create "a handsome new British crown, cut at Hartford, and set in diamonds."

Madison feared that these "plotters of sedition, insurrection and ruin" would embolden the British Prince Regent to keep battling the United States under the illusion that he need only wait for New England to succeed in halting the war. The Republican pamphleteer Mathew Carey of Philadelphia demanded that Madison use military force, if necessary, against New England's "daring, powerful, unprincipled and formidable conspiracy," but the President maintained his self-restraint. As it turned out, the secret sessions at Hartford resulted only in *"talk, mere talk,"* so said one Republican. Boston's *Independent Chronicle* sneered, "The *Mountain* was in labor, and out crept a *Mouse.*" Showing relief, the *National Intelligencer* observed that the schemers had "found that it is not so easy to get up a civil war."

As 1815 began, having failed to conquer Baltimore, the British turned their fury against New Orleans, hoping to shake American dominion over the entire Louisiana Purchase. "Our anxieties cannot be expressed," Dolley Madison wrote to Hannah Gallatin on January 14. "The fate of N. Orleans will be known to day—on which so much depends." In the Battle of New Orleans, General Andrew Jackson swiftly won the most heroic ground victory of the entire war, killing 251 of the British enemy, including the commander, Sir Edward Pakenham, while losing only perhaps a dozen of his own men. "Glory be to God, that the barbarians have been defeated," said *Niles' Weekly Register,* "and that at *Orleans* the intended plunderers have found their grave!" The President and Dolley were jubilant. But not even they could know that the War of 1812 had already ended before Jackson's triumph.

★ ★ ★

THE PREVIOUS SUMMER, the British and Americans had met for peace discussions in the neutral Flemish city of Ghent. Madison had sent five envoys, including Gallatin, John Quincy Adams, and Henry Clay—the last to assure fellow War Hawks, in case of a deal, that the President had not gone soft. Before their departure, Monroe told them that a halt to the "degrading practice" of impressments was not negotiable.* In Ghent, the priggish Adams began by refusing to dine with his fellow Americans, recording, "They sit after dinner and drink bad wine and smoke cigars, which neither suits my habits nor my health, and absorbs time which I cannot spare."

When the talks began, the British haughtily insisted that the United States surrender much of Maine and most of the Northwest Territory, the latter to become an Indian "buffer state," as well as New Orleans, ceding to England the power to control the Mississippi River, the entire Louisiana Territory, and other western lands. The American team dug in for what they expected to be a long, tortuous struggle. But to their astonishment, the British proved to be open to a settlement. In London, the Duke of Wellington, standing tall after defeating Napoleon, had been asked to go to North America and take command of the British armies, but he had advised that the ex-colonists would never allow themselves to be conquered. After brisk negotiations, a peace compact was signed, over eggnog, on Christmas Eve. Henry Clay and the War Hawks had once vowed not to accept any settlement that did not include the US acquisition of Canada. But the Treaty of Ghent essentially restored the state of affairs that prevailed before the War of 1812. At Plymouth, England, an American clerk took the peace document aboard the British sloop of war *Favourite,* and braved forty-two days of winter storms to reach New York.

On Tuesday, February 14, 1815, at the Octagon House, Madison sat in his round upstairs study as he heard the tap-tap-tap of Monroe's steps across the black-and-white checkerboard marble floor below. The

---

* Aiming to put his delegates on equal footing with the British, Monroe required them to wear uniforms of special design—a blue coat with standing collar and gold-embroidered cuffs, to be worn with white knee breeches—which he pronounced "handsome . . . national and economical."

President walked down the winding staircase and saw the grinning Monroe, who was holding out several pages of parchment. Bound by a thin black ribbon and emblazoned with six red wax seals, the document was entitled "Treaty of Peace and Amity between His Britannic Majesty and the United States of America." In joy, Dolley threw open the front door of the Mansion, and soon the public floor was packed with visitors, cheek by jowl. Federalists and Republicans celebrated together, "crazy with joy," and Madison's enslaved servant Paul Jennings played "Hail, Columbia" on his violin.

When the President walked upstairs to confer with Monroe, Dolley was the focus of all eyes. According to one witness, "No one could doubt who beheld the radiance of joy, which lighted up her countenance and diffused its beam all around, that all uncertainty was at an end." "Our glorious Peace," Dolley wrote a friend the following month. "Congress adjourn'd last night, still our house is crouded with company—in truth ever since the peace my brain has been turn'd with noise & bustle."*

In Federalist Boston, while a choir sang "Te Deum," seventeen horses, celebrating "the happy return of PEACE," pulled a sled with cotton bales inscribed *"General Jackson."* Rockets were fired from the gold-domed roof of the State House. At a mass meeting, Boston Republicans apologized to President Madison for New England's misbehavior, pledging that all good citizens "will commemorate your Name in the American Annals with lasting honor & Applause." In the western Massachusetts town of Pittsfield, "Patriots of '76" mingled with soldiers of the War of 1812 "in joyous hilarity." In Hartford, den of secessionist intrigue, one journal crowed that now, with *"Peace abroad,* we could have *Union at home."* Fairfield, Connecticut, "exulted as an Ox was roasted whole, and at evening their joy was illuminated by the blaze of fifteen barrels of tar!" A witness in the nation's capital noted that "all of Washington is now jumping alive."

Many Federalist organs were appalled by the Treaty of Ghent.

---

* American sensitivities about domination by England remained so strong that when the Senate ratified the Treaty of Ghent, it appended a note that no one should presume that the US bargainers had deliberately abased themselves by signing the document underneath the Britons.

"Instead of rejoicing they ought to clothe themselves in sack-cloth and ashes at this *'disgraceful peace,'*" observed New York's *National Advocate*. Maine's *Hallowell Gazette* complained that the United States had obtained no guarantee of maritime rights or even a foot of Canadian ground: *"What has this country gained by the sacrifice of so much blood and treasure?"* The *New York Evening Post* grumbled that the war had been "adopted without cause; declared without being prepared, and carried on for more than two years amidst every disaster and disgrace." The *Salem Gazette* cited "the needless suffering that has been endured, of the widows, orphans and fatherless that will ever look back to this war with sorrow!" Hanson's *Federal Republican* battered Madison—"Is no one accountable for the blood thus wantonly spilt?"—and Rhode Island's *Newport Mercury* agreed: "The blood and misery of thousands rest upon his head."

Republicans attacked their opposition by recalling old Federalist prophecies that England would never stop fighting until Madison was ousted from the presidency. The *Rhode-Island Republican* taunted, "Yes, a Peace is made, and Madison is still in the chair of state. Miserable federalists—go hide yourselves—you are covered with shame, and disgrace has marked you forever." Vermont's *Rutland Herald* praised Madison's decision to fight: "If ever there was a necessary war, a war founded on moral principles of just resistance to oppression, it was the war declared against England. Thank GOD we did declare war; it has raised us a name and character which is not to be valued by dollars and cents. . . . 'MADISON'S WAR,' as the faction have called it, has given us a name and character as a nation, and 'MADISON'S PEACE' has secured those blessings forever."

* * *

THE WAR OF 1812 had cost the nation perhaps 2,260 combat deaths and 4,505 wounded.* Americans might well have asked why this

---

* The US population in 1810, according to the official census, was 7,239,881 (including over a million who were enslaved). The British lost an estimated 1,160 in battle.

sacrifice had been justified, since they had failed to annex Canada or compel the British to formally respect American rights on the high seas. To divert all eyes from this question, Madison's party leaders quickly moved to claim that the conflict had ended in victory. The Republican George Troup of Georgia congratulated his House peers "on the glorious termination of the most glorious war ever waged by any people." Pennsylvania's Charles Ingersoll boasted, "Not an inch *ceded* or *lost.*" Other Republican leaders romanticized the effort as "the second war for our independence."* This slogan was a gross exaggeration, almost a slur on the generation that fought the Revolution, for, unlike in that conflict, there was no imminent threat of British attack in the summer of 1812.

Republicans also tried to force respect for Madison's war by casting aspersions on its skeptics. On the floor of the Massachusetts Senate, John Holmes of Cape Cod displayed an early example of the ignoble tradition, which would later expand through American history, of charging that critics of a war were disparaging the warriors. Holmes told his Federalist colleagues, "It is an additional slander upon the brave men whom you refuse to honor or thank for glorious deeds, to say that the war is disgraceful."

As the first sitting President to take the nation into a major war, Madison had been compelled to improvise. On the surface, he had abided by the Constitution he had helped to write when he insisted that Congress be the branch of government that launched the War of 1812. But he made it very clear that he wanted a war against England, which helped to persuade an ambivalent House and Senate, thus starting the long presidential encroachment on Congress's war-making power that marked the next two centuries. And by pleading for a war in the absence of a large, immediate threat to American survival, Madison lowered the threshold so that future Presidents and Congresses could—contrary to

---

* In retirement, Madison gratefully accepted this characterization, writing Ingersoll in 1818, "If our first struggle was a war of our infancy, this last was that of our youth; and the issue of both, wisely improved, may long postpone, if not forever prevent, a necessity for exerting the strength of our manhood."

the spirit of most of the Founders—more easily enmesh the nation in sundry military conflicts for lesser purposes.

In certain ways, Americans should be grateful that Madison was their first major war President. A leader who lacked his experience in devising much of the Constitution and Bill of Rights might have crushed civil liberties, tried to shut down hostile newspapers, harassed insolent Congressmen, or used force to bring New England secessionists into his fold. He did not unduly violate the boundary between church and state to rally support for his war, and his public statements were remarkably free of hyperbole or demagoguery. His restraint established benchmarks worthy for his wartime successors.

But Madison established other, more dangerous traditions for later Presidents to follow during time of war. He had been willing to mislead Congress (for example, in vouching for the Cadore letter). He had let the American military effort unfold with too little money and too few soldiers, sailors, ships, and other resources, with almost half the Congress and almost certainly a majority of Americans opposing it. A century and a half later, the historian Samuel Eliot Morison rightly called the conflict of 1812 "the most unpopular war that this country has ever waged, not even excepting the Vietnam conflict."

At times, it seemed that Madison prosecuted his war with almost intentional incompetence, as if an amateur performance would show the purity of his intention not to seize unconstitutional power. In the same manner, he tolerated bad mistakes by his military leaders, calling them inevitable in a country "without those large standing armies which even in peace are fitted for war." At the start of the conflict, he never warned Congress or the American people of the lives, national treasure, and years it might require, or of the serious chance that the United States might lose the war, ending its democratic experiment once and for all. If later Americans loathed a lack of candor and forthrightness in their wartime Presidents, they would be justified to point an accusing finger at Madison for setting expectations too low.

* * *

EXHAUSTED BY HIS wartime presidency, Madison left office in 1817 and shunned the Capital for the rest of his life. In the spring of 1836, at Montpelier, a few months before the sixtieth anniversary of the Declaration of Independence, he was eighty-five years old and nearing death.* That May, a month before his demise, he received Charles Ingersoll, who was writing a history of the 1812 war. The visitor found that Dolley, in turban and cravat, "looks just as she did twenty years ago" and that she "seldom leaves the house, as her devotion to Mr. Madison is incessant." Ingersoll wrote that the ex-President "never was strong, and is now extremely emaciated and feeble . . . with a difficulty of breathing, which affects his speech," but noted that "his understanding is as bright as ever."

Since leaving the presidency, the laird of Montpelier had rarely expressed himself in public about the War of 1812, suggesting that he found it a painful subject. Now, as he recounted the conflict's domestic political furies for Ingersoll, he harped not on the antagonisms but the unexpected moments of comity. After the burning of Washington, he revealed, his nemesis Alexander Hanson, of the *Federal Republican,* had quietly cautioned him against assassination plots—and when the Federalist Congressman Cyrus King of Massachusetts, who hated the war, refused an invitation to his White House table, King had done so with a handwritten note of kindness and respect. As Ingersoll recorded, the ex-President complained "somewhat mysteriously" and "with emotion" that Congress had blocked certain of his intentions at the start of the War of 1812, saying, "There was something I never could understand, and will not characterize, but leave it to history to do so." (By this, Madison probably meant the refusal of his own party's leaders to give him the money, military, and other tools he deemed necessary to win the war.)

Madison had clearly changed in his later years. By Ingersoll's account, he now "showed the strongest dislike of hostilities" and warned against the American system's "perpetual liability" to enter a war. Ingersoll believed that by now, the old man's politics were "simple and lovely . . .

---

* With the sixtieth anniversary of the Declaration of Independence approaching, some of Madison's friends suggested that he take stimulants in order to emulate his mentor Jefferson's famous feat of expiring, along with John Adams, on the fiftieth. But he scoffed at the suggestion.

to avoid war at almost any price, and to preserve the Union." The ex-President did not sound like the militant Madison of 1812. It was as if he had circled back, through time, to become the shrewd political theorist he had once been, cautioning the nation against war as "the true nurse of executive aggrandizement."

* * *

A S THE WAR of 1812 receded into history, it would have been healthier had Americans viewed the episode as a cautionary tale, which should have made them suspicious of future Presidents who called them to battle. But instead, it seemed that with each retelling, the conflict became more glowing a success. In 1826, John C. Calhoun, by then John Quincy Adams's Vice President, insisted, with only some exaggeration, that "all are now united in the wisdom" of Madison's war, "and the happy results that have followed."*

The grandest national hero of the era was Andrew Jackson, whose bravery encouraged Americans to look back fondly at Madison's conflict. For a half century, January 8, the anniversary of the Battle of New Orleans, was a national holiday, the only time a single American battle has ever been thus commemorated. Many of the time considered this date to be second in importance only to the Fourth of July, boosting the War of 1812 almost to the level of the Revolution.† Madison's war gained additional popularity from romantic folk memories of Dolley saving George Washington's portrait, "Old Ironsides," and epigrams like "Don't give up the ship" and "We have met the enemy, and they are ours."

---

* One reason the Federalist Party evaporated was that it was vilified as "the opposers of the war of 1812, when our country stood most in need of the unanimity and concert of our fellow citizens." When Monroe ran for President in 1816, in the afterglow of the Ghent treaty, he won 183 electoral votes to 34 for the Federalist, Rufus King. Senator Daniel Webster was later forced to use his formidable powers of argument to explain why, as a young Federalist Congressman from New Hampshire, he had castigated the war.

† In 1832, the centennial of George Washington's birth, Rhode Island's *Providence Patriot* observed that as the nation honored "the illustrious Hero of the *first* war of independence," the current President, Andrew Jackson, had been "the illustrious Hero of the *second* war of independence."

When Americans sang of the Battle of Baltimore in "The Star-Spangled Banner," they were honoring the War of 1812. Madison's ig-nominious escape from burning Washington and Hull's surrender at Detroit shrank in the public recollection.* Another reason the shadow of the War of 1812 fell so long was that each of Madison's half-dozen suc-cessors had played a role during the conflict. Monroe was Secretary of State and War, Quincy Adams a peace commissioner, Jackson the victo-rious general, Martin Van Buren "straining every nerve" to support the war as a New York State Senator, William Henry Harrison the scourge of the Indians, and John Tyler a Virginia militia warrior.

More susceptible than most to the mystique of the War of 1812 was James Knox Polk of Tennessee, who became President in 1845. At the White House, by then long restored and repainted to conceal the black scars left by the British flame bearers, Polk and his wife, Sarah, happily welcomed back Dolley Madison, still glowing in her midseventies. After her husband's death, Dolley had left Montpelier for the Capital and a corner house on Lafayette Square, across from Stephen Decatur's.

Polk had been seventeen in 1812, but was too frail to fight—a fact that, as friends noted, seemed to make the young man all the more in-trigued by military adventure. An Andrew Jackson protégé, Polk nostal-gically recalled how Old Hickory, "pre-eminent for his patriotism and unbending will," had "concluded the war, most happily for his Country, by the brilliant Victory of New Orleans." Polk owned what he referred to in his diary as "a curiously wrought Hickory walking cane," carved with scenes of the Battle of Baltimore.† He swung that walking stick as President, while plotting how to take the nation into war against Mexico.

---

* In his history of the War of 1812, published in 1849, Ingersoll went so far as to insist that "dia-ries have been burned and narrations suppressed" in order to impede those eager to write about the burning of Washington, DC.

† Polk received this gift during his first year as President from a Baltimore admirer, John Hennick, who informed him that the cane had been "cut on the spot where the citizens of Baltimore stood, who defended that City in 1814, and near the spot where General Ross fell."

CHAPTER FOUR

"The Country Is Now Virtually Ours"

J AMES POLK'S WAR against Mexico was spurred in the spring of 1846 by the ambush, near the Rio Grande, of a slight, high-strung thirty-year-old dragoon with a drooping mustache, Captain Seth Thornton.

The previous December, when Texas, formerly Mexican, became the twenty-eighth state of the Union, Mexico angrily broke relations with the United States. Defying the Mexicans' assertion that their border with Texas was the Nueces River, not the more southerly Rio Grande, Polk ordered General Zachary Taylor's "Corps of Observation" (whose four thousand soldiers constituted almost half the entire US Army) to the Rio's dry, barren north bank. There they built a star-shaped fortress of pork barrels, mud, sand, and crisscrossed twigs, surrounded by a broad, deep ditch, and dubbed it "Fort Texas." Taylor's men blockaded the river in an effort to starve out six thousand Mexican troops on the other side. On Friday, April 24, 1846, Taylor ordered Thornton to range about twenty miles to investigate a report that two thousand Mexican troops had crossed the Rio Grande in order to attack Fort Texas.*

---

* As a brutal warning to the Yankees, the Mexicans had lately murdered one of Taylor's colonels, Trueman Cross, whose naked body was discovered four miles from the fort, "horribly mutilated" by lances. Cross's killers had made off with his pistols, watch, and horse. Vultures had bitten

A patrician soldier, born at Rumford, his family's Virginia estate, Thornton was a descendant of Pocahontas; his father, who died young, was the second cousin of George Washington. Young Seth was called "the comfort and delight of his mother, to whom he ever rendered the most dutiful love and care." After suffering an emotional breakdown at Trinity College in Hartford, he decamped to Kentucky, where he stayed with relatives for two years of recuperation, then joined the Second Dragoons, newly established by President Andrew Jackson to fight the Seminole Indians in Florida. One of Thornton's friends felt that "a braver and more warm-hearted soul never animated a human frame." Determined to prove his mettle, Seth impressed some who knew him as "too ardent and impetuous for his physical structure."*

Now, undertaking his mission for General Taylor, Thornton led a squadron of twelve officers, forty-nine privates, and a bugler for fifteen miles along the Rio Grande. After sundown, they paused for a few hours' sleep. The next morning, he took his men up into the flatlands. There his Mexican guide dug in his heels, insisting that the region was "full of Mexicans" who could kill them all. However, as Thornton's second in command, Captain William Hardee, later recalled, Seth was certain "that the Mexicans had not crossed; and if they had, that they would not fight" because such action would risk full-fledged war against the United States.

Thornton thus ordered his troops to march three miles farther, to a seemingly abandoned riverside plantation called Rancho Carricitos, which was enclosed by a tall chaparral fence. Recklessly refusing to send sentries ahead, he entered the property by sliding between two heavy bars at the gate. Misreading Thornton's hand signal to remain a safe distance behind him, his troops followed, in search of drinking water. Some took a nap while Thornton inspected one of the cottages and questioned

off most of his flesh, so he could be identified only by his teeth, a shred of scalp, and a shoulder strap from his uniform.

* In 1838, when the steamboat *Pulaski* sank off the Atlantic coast, Thornton bravely rescued fellow passengers by pulling them onto bobbing pieces of wreckage and then tied himself to a floating hen coop, using a piece of wood for a rudder and a woman's shawl he had found on the water as a sail. Fishermen found him "famished and reduced to a state of raving insanity."

what he took to be an elderly caretaker. After a loud war whoop, hundreds of Mexicans with muskets sprang into view, producing what was called a "blaze of fire."

Commanding his troops to dash past the Mexicans, Thornton shouted, *"Charge!"* Riding his longtime mount, he leapt the chaparral fence, but his horse, injured in the jump, rolled over him. Knocked unconscious, Thornton was hauled away by the Mexicans. A brevet Major, Philip Barbour, wrote in his diary, "I very much fear that he has either taken his own life or been overtaken and put to death. . . . He has often told me that he would blow his own brains out before he would surrender to the Mexicans." But Thornton was actually alive, a prisoner in a Mexican jail. When the muskets fell silent, Hardee sent the opposing General, Anastasio Torrejón, a white flag of truce. With a dozen or more Americans dead, Hardee delivered himself and forty-five other men into Mexican custody at Matamoros.[*]

Zachary Taylor had been waiting at Fort Texas for his dragoons' safe return. Told of the attack, the furious General responded that it meant all-out war against Mexico. He wrote the Army's Adjutant General, Roger Jones, "Hostilities may now be considered as commenced." One of Taylor's soldiers recorded, "We hope soon to avenge the deaths of these brave fellows, who have fallen in the glorious cause of their country. The American flag, we flatter ourselves, will, ere long, float over the city of Mexico."

By Saturday morning, May 9, President Polk had not yet received Taylor's report on the ambush, which took weeks to get to Washington. Nevertheless he had already secured the concurrence of his Cabinet, except for one member, that in case of any hostile action against Taylor's troops, the President should ask Congress to declare war against Mexico. Polk insisted that the Mexicans had already provided "ample cause of war," and that the country was "excited and impatient" for it. That evening, at six o'clock, Roger Jones arrived at the White House with Taylor's letter. Polk summoned his Cabinet, recording afterward, "It was

---

[*] Hardee found his jailers "most gracious," and was grateful that they seemed eager to show that Mexicans were not "barbarous."

so agreed that a message should be sent to Congress . . . laying all the information in my possession before them and recommending [a] vigorous & prompt measure to enable the Executive to prosecute the War."

* * *

BY CONTRAST WITH James Madison, who shared his three predecessors' lifelong obsession with England, there is little evidence that James Polk gave much of a damn about Texas or Mexico before he campaigned for President in 1844.

Born the first child of ten in 1795 in Mecklenburg County, North Carolina, to Jane Knox and Samuel Polk (the Scottish family name had been Pollok), James was eleven when his family sold its land in favor of larger, cheaper acreage in Columbia, Tennessee. The boy grew up frail.* After graduation from the University of North Carolina—at the top of his class—he read for the law, won a seat in the Tennessee legislature, and married the affluent, well-connected Sarah Childress. Their romance had been encouraged by their mutual family friend Andrew Jackson (Sarah called him "Uncle Andrew"), who had been grooming the young man whom one Polk friend called the "Possum looking fellow" for politics.

In the House of Representatives, the taciturn, shrewd, suspicious Polk served seven terms as a Jackson Democrat, the last as Speaker—his champions called him "Young Hickory." Then, at forty-three, he went back home to be elected Governor of Tennessee, dreaming of the White House. But then Polk suffered two narrow defeats for reelection by a backlands beanpole called "Lean Jimmy" Jones. Polk's political career seemed virtually over.

By 1844, his best hope appeared to scheme his way onto the Democratic ticket as Vice President.† The party's likeliest standard-bearer was

---

* At seventeen, he was diagnosed with urinary stones, which were excruciatingly removed by forceps, with only brandy as a painkiller. Polk was left almost certainly sterile and perhaps without sexual function.

† By 1844, the Jacksonian Democrats were opposed by the Whig Party.

the gray-and-red-haired ex-President Martin Van Buren, eager to avenge his 1840 defeat by William Henry Harrison, the hero of Tippecanoe, who had died after a month as President, leaving the office to John Tyler. Polk's efforts to butter up Van Buren failed when he could not deliver Tennessee's delegates to the "Little Magician."* Then, during the election year, Tyler proposed a treaty to annex what was at that time the independent Republic of Texas.

After President Monroe signed a compact conceding Spain's dominion over Texas in 1819, America's relationship with Texas had been complicated. Although Mexico's war of independence in 1821 transferred Texas to the Mexicans, US settlers like Moses Austin and his son Stephen were encouraged to develop the land. In 1836 came the struggle over the Alamo, capture of the Mexican General Santa Anna in the Battle of San Jacinto, and the founding of an independent Texas republic. Coveting protection against future attacks from Mexico, the first President of Texas, Sam Houston, favored annexation by the United States.

Acquiring Texas would fulfill Tyler's ambitions to expand American territory. (He also hoped that it might move Whig leaders, who disliked him, to let him run for a full presidential term.) He feared that if America did not act on Texas now, the British might offer it military protection and then exploit its new foothold to control the Mississippi River. Tyler's Secretary of State, John C. Calhoun, savored the prospect of admitting Texas as a slave state, which would strengthen the power of his slaveholding South. Calhoun did not recoil from the possibility that Northern outrage at such a development might compel the South to secede from the Union. "If the Union is to break there could not be a better pretext," he was assured by his fellow South Carolinian, Governor James Hammond. "With Texas, the slave states would form a territory large enough for a *first rate power . . .* that would flourish beyond any on the Globe."

---

* Polk's friends tried to explain that Tennesseans were not drawn to any candidate "who did not squirt tobacco juice," but Van Buren was not mollified.

After Tyler signed a compact to acquire Texas, Calhoun sent it to the Senate, along with what was called a "bombshell" appendix, which praised annexation as a means of preventing the abolitionist British from tampering with slavery. Disgusted by Calhoun's argument, Van Buren said he would oppose annexation unless Texas first made peace with Mexico—an unlikely event, because so many Texas citizens who wanted statehood were motivated by desire for US military protection against the Mexicans. Van Buren warned that since the Mexicans still had their eye on Texas, "annexation and war with Mexico are identical." His refusal to endorse annexation left many fellow Democrats furious. Some of Polk's cronies advised him to ditch the Little Magician and jump onto the Texas bandwagon.

For Polk, the decisive factor was Andrew Jackson, still his chief patron. By now seventy-seven and failing, Old Hickory knew that the Texas issue could be used to thwart the presidential ambitions of his political enemy Henry Clay, now a US Senator, whom Jackson rightly viewed as the Whigs' likely nominee.* Jackson believed that national expansion was essential if the nation was to become a world power. From the Hermitage, his estate outside Nashville, he explained, in writing, to his protégé Sam Houston how annexation could bring "the prosperity & permanent happiness of Texas."† Jackson also issued a public letter saying that if Texas were annexed, "our western boundary would be the Rio Grande" and "with such a barrier on our west we are invincible."

Jackson had pondered backing Van Buren, but not after his onetime Vice President's statement against Texas annexation. The General was so shocked by Van Buren's heresy that he exclaimed, "It's a forgery!" He sadly wrote his old running mate that now there was no greater chance

---

* The mythic rivalry between the Kentucky patrician and the self-styled tribune of the people had begun in 1815, when Clay resented that Jackson had won so much more acclaim for the Battle of New Orleans than Clay had attracted for his labors on the treaty ending Madison's war. It deepened after the disputed election of 1824, when, in Jackson's fiercely held view, a "corrupt bargain" was made by Clay ("the Judas of the West," said Jackson) to let John Quincy Adams become President in exchange for being named Secretary of State, and in 1832, when Jackson won reelection by trouncing Clay.

† Houston had been a Tennessee Congressman and Governor before moving to Texas.

of restoring him to the White House than reversing the current of the Mississippi. Hoping to win Jackson's support for the presidency, with the political calculus clear, Polk now decided that he felt more strongly about Texas than he had ever realized. "I have no hesitation," he announced, "in declaring that I am in favour of the immediate re-annexation of Texas." With delight, Jackson then gave his blessing to Polk, demanding that the Democrats nominate a Southwesterner who wanted Texas in the Union.

With the support of his party's god, when the Democrats convened in Baltimore's Odd Fellows Hall, Polk was nominated for President after nine ballots. "You should have heard the cheers," one of Polk's friends wrote him. Balancing the Polk ticket with the Pennsylvania Senator George Dallas, the delegates approved a platform asking for Texas annexation at the "earliest practicable" moment. To assuage the losers for the nomination, Polk pledged to assume the presidency "with the settled purpose of not being a candidate for re-election." The happy Jackson wrote to Sarah Polk, "Daughter, I will put you in the White House if it costs me my life!"

When told of Polk's nomination, the astounded Henry Clay asked if the Democrats were "serious." The Whig Senator Daniel Webster concluded that Polk had been chosen "expressly for Texas." Tongue in condescending cheek, the *New Hampshire Sentinel* told its readers, "Mr. Polk (pronounced *Poke*) was the Speaker, we believe, of the House of Representatives." The *New-York Tribune* dismissed Polk as "a third rate politician—who never devised a measure nor said a thing worth remembering." The *Milwaukee Sentinel* referred to the Democratic nominee's claque as "Polkats."

The Senate took up Tyler's annexation treaty in June 1844. Henry Clay urged fellow Whigs to oppose it, arguing that Texas was not worth the danger of "national dishonor, foreign war, and distraction and division at home." (Clay also complained that Tyler, as an accidental President, had overreached his placeholder's role.) General Jackson thundered from the Hermitage that foes of annexation "have no patriotism or love of country. . . . The people of the South and West will withdraw all confidence from them, and send them to their own native dunghills, there to rest forever." But Tyler's treaty was killed by Whigs and Northern Democrats, led by Missouri's Senator Thomas Hart Benton.[*]

Polk's enemies insisted that he wanted Texas in the Union because, as a slaveholder himself, he hoped to extend the reach of the "peculiar institution." They recalled that he had denounced abolitionists for their "fanatical wicked and dangerous agitation." A Whig paper reported that "Mr. Polk himself traffics in slaves and *burns the initials of his name into their flesh* in order to identify his 'property.'" (The *Nashville Union* lamely tried to shield Polk from such attacks by insisting that the ex-Governor "has never owned a slave who would consent to be sold or transferred to another master.") Polk champions posted a "POLK, DALLAS & TEXAS" banner next to the slave bazaar of Washington, DC, the largest in the country. Vermont's *Phoenix* warned that Polk and "the whole locofoco party are for rushing into a foul and disgraceful war with Mexico, to *rivet the chains of slavery* forever in our land! Slave-buying and slave-selling will be brisk when Texas is annexed to our Union . . . The old slave states will become large breeding fields to supply the Texan market."[†]

That fall, Polk received 170 electoral votes to Clay's 105 (but in the popular vote, only 49.5 percent to Clay's 48.1 percent). His position on Texas had helped him to sweep the Deep South, but, ironically, he owed his election to the antislavery movement: except for the presence of a third-party candidate, the abolitionist James Birney, who siphoned off Whig voters, Polk would have lost New York and hence the election. The angry *Barre Patriot* of Massachusetts brayed at Birney supporters, "YOU have elected as President of the United States, the TOOL of the Southern

---

* Some Southern Democrats demanded that their region secede from the Union unless the Senate reversed itself. Furious that Northern Senators had violated their party's platform, they started planning a raucous demonstration in Nashville, featuring Polk. Knowing that he would lose the election if he should be marginalized as a sectional candidate, however, Polk, with Jackson's help, managed to quash the spectacle.

† Polk's critics had branded him with the term "locofoco," which had once been reserved for radical Jacksonians but was now used to describe all Democrats. A Whig journal in Alabama quoted the gibe of Tennessee's ex-Congressman Balie Peyton that Polk "has never had command of any body of men, and I have never heard of his fighting but one battle, and that was with his brother at Columbia, who gave him a most unfraternal flogging."

Slavocracy, and have thereby ensured the Annexation of Texas." Ex-President John Quincy Adams disparaged Polk's election as a "victory of the slavery element." After the voting, a Vermont Whig in the Capital peered out of his window at the Polk-Dallas banner hanging near Washington's slave market and said, "That flag means *Texas*, and *Texas* means *civil war*, before we have done with it!"

* * *

IN JANUARY 1845, the Polks stayed for a night at the Hermitage. There the bedridden Jackson told them he could now depart this earth confident of "the perpetuity of our glorious Union." James and Sarah were borne by the steamboat *China*, along the Ohio River, to Wheeling, Virginia, and by carriages and a special railroad car to Washington, where they checked into S. S. Coleman's hotel on Pennsylvania Avenue.

Tyler was still President, and the churlish, grandiose Virginian wished to establish a historical niche for himself as something greater than "His Accidency." Many constitutional experts suggested that a President must annex Texas by treaty, which would require consent from two-thirds of the Senate. Instead the lame-duck President tried to skirt the problem by asking Congress for a joint resolution empowering him to annex Texas. The Democratic House passed a motion by a renegade Whig, Milton Brown of Tennessee, to admit Texas as a slave state and then haggle with Mexico over their final boundary. Had it succeeded, Brown's resolution would have allowed Texas to be sliced into five new slave states, which would increase the number of pro-slavery Senators by one-fifth. "Every Texas Planter, with fifteen slaves," warned the horrified *Milwaukee Sentinel*, "will have as much voice in Congress, as ten New York Farmers or Mechanics!"

Those who called on the President-elect at Coleman's were surprised by Polk's obsession with the issue. "He is for Texas, Texas, Texas," someone said, "& talks of but little else." Some Senators proposed a compromise bill that would have Polk choose between the House approach and a proposal by Senator Benton, which would admit one part of Texas as a state and another as a territory, leaving slavery and other disputed issues to a five-man commission. (Benton fondly recalled how President Madison had resolved the War of 1812 with such a delegation at Ghent.) In order to get the bill passed, Polk gave Benton and other undecided Senators the impression that if given such a choice, he would opt for Benton's plan. Only on the basis of this expectation did Benton and other swing Senators support the bill, which barely passed, by 27 to 25, and was greeted with serenades, bells, and cannon fire.

Congress had clearly intended to give the choice between the two approaches to Polk, with his fresh national mandate. But the outgoing Tyler was desperate in his historical vanity and he detested Polk. He therefore stuck a broomstick into the machinery by seizing the prerogative for himself and choosing the House version. During his last full day in the White House, Tyler asked Old Hickory's nephew, Andrew Jackson Donelson, the chief US diplomat in Texas, to take a written invitation to the Texas government, settled at its capital of Washington-on-the-Brazos, to join the United States immediately. "The deed is done!" exclaimed the *Farmer's Cabinet*. Flabbergasted, Senator Benton considered Tyler's caprice "prolific of evil, and pregnant with bloody fruit." Mexico responded to the departing President's action by severing diplomatic relations with the United States.

The next day, March 4, 1845, Tyler pulled up in an open barouche at Coleman's. The President-elect climbed in for the journey up to the Capitol, now grandly rebuilt, with three wooden domes, after the British inferno of 1814. They were preceded in their parade by "a little band of veteran soldiers of the Revolution, with hoary locks and steps apparently unfaltered by age." Then the rains came, so the new Chief Executive gave his inaugural oration from the Capitol's eastern steps "to a large assemblage of umbrellas," as John Quincy Adams gibed in his diary. One onlooker recorded that Polk—standing, ramrod-straight, to his full five feet, eight inches—read his speech "with the air of a man profoundly impressed by it himself." In it, he pledged to acquire Texas "by all constitutional, honorable and appropriate means." That night, the new President took Sarah—who wore a "deeply fringed" blue velvet gown and bonnet, and waved an ivory-handled fan adorned by portraits of her husband and his predecessors—to a $10-per-ticket inaugural ball at Carusi's Saloon, owned and managed by the son of the late patriarch Gaetano, who had survived the British attack on the USS *Chesapeake*.

During his years in the House, Polk had struck many colleagues as a charmless, nerveless wheeler-dealer, given to political sleight of hand. He behaved precisely in this spirit during his first days in office. He knew that Benton and several other Senators had grudgingly voted for annexation only because of what the Missourian called Polk's "full assurance" that he would adopt the Senate's conciliatory approach to Texas. But Polk now claimed that he had never made any firm commitment to Benton's plan. He wrote Donelson that he would embrace Tyler's approach in order to "most speedily and certainly" bring Texas into the Union. Polk added that if this made Texans nervous, they should rely on the "well-known justice and liberality" of the United States and its military, which would defend Texas all the way down to the Rio Grande. To this message Polk appended a threat: if the Texans tried to bargain or add even a single caveat, annexation would be "placed in jeopardy."

The furious Benton complained that the new President had "cheated" him and his peers and won their votes by "fraud." He demanded to know what secret instructions Polk had sent to Donelson. The imperious Polk refused, citing George Washington's doctrine of executive privilege, which held that a President need share with Congress only "such papers as the public good would permit."

Polk did not say so, but he had something else in mind. Sharing his hero Jackson's belief that America's path to world greatness would be expansion to the West, he hoped, by the end of his single term, to acquire Mexico's California territories. If the Mexicans would not sell him that land at a reasonable price, he might just feel compelled to seize it in the course of a war that might happen to break out between the United States and Mexico. That summer, John O'Sullivan, a Democratic editor and Polk supporter, gave the President's philosophy a name by writing that it was "our manifest destiny to overspread the continent allotted by Providence for the free development of our yearly multiplying millions."*

* * *

OFFENDED BY POLK'S take-it-or-leave-it offer, the sitting (and last) President of the Republic of Texas, Anson Jones, signaled that he might prefer instead to seek an alliance with England. Under such an arrangement, the British military would help to guard the Texas Republic against Mexico and, if necessary, the United States. British agents were reliably said to be making "magnificent offers" for such a partnership. On Polk's behalf, Donelson warned Jones that if Texans now spurned this chance to join the United States, "it may never be recovered."

Sam Houston, who was known to be the power behind Jones's throne, was furious at Polk's high-handedness. Had Texas, he asked, been offered so much as a dime for all of its land? And if Texas made a deal with the United States, what might it expect when Polk and his Democratic Congress were succeeded by politicians who were less respectful of Texas customs (in other words, slavery)? Moving into action, the ailing Andrew Jackson, only weeks from death, invited his old friend Houston to the Hermitage and persuaded him that his future lay with the United States. Afterward, in triumph, Old Hickory wrote Polk, "I knew British gold could not buy Sam Houston."

What followed was a strange escapade that brought a considerable chance of drawing the United States into war with Mexico. The case officer for this venture was the "bombastically aggressive" Robert Field Stockton, whom Polk had just styled a Commodore of the Navy.† Under

---

* While professing to be neutral about what it called the slavery "of an inferior to a superior race," O'Sullivan's article advocated the "ultimate disappearance of the negro race" from the United States.

† Stockton had championed Polk's presidential candidacy in New Jersey. Many complained of his self-avowed affinity for "creative disobedience" and found him an "egotistical braggart." Born in Princeton, New Jersey, the wealthy grandson of a Declaration of Independence signer, Stockton had served as a War of 1812 midshipman, bought land on Africa's west coast for possible

orders from Polk's Navy Secretary, the historian George Bancroft, Stockton sailed on May 12, 1845, aboard the brig *Porpoise* to the Texas port of Galveston, where he secretly met with Polk's trusted emissary and friend Charles Wickliffe, a former Kentucky Congressman and Governor. Wickliffe was quietly maneuvering to pit Texas against Mexico over the disputed territory between the Nueces and Rio Grande; he spread false information that Mexican soldiers had come north across the Rio. Under Wickliffe's plan, when hostilities began, the United States would openly join in the Texans' defense. Congress and the American people would be ignorant of the fact that the conflict would have been waged on a false pretext.

On May 22, Stockton informed Bancroft that General Sidney Sherman of the Texas militia had pledged to have his troops "clear and protect the boundary" to the south. He persuaded the Secretary to quietly provide the Texans with Navy powder and provisions, and sent an aide, Dr. John Wright, to help Sherman persuade the skeptical Anson Jones to accede to the venture. Wright frankly explained to Jones that the purpose of Stockton's exercise was to push Texas into conflict with Mexico, adding that if Texas joined the Union, the United States would bear the burden of the war. By Jones's later account, Wright assured him that President Polk was behind Stockton's gambit but wished to conceal his role.

Jones told Wright and Sherman, "So, gentlemen, the Commodore, on the part of the United States, wishes me to manufacture a war for them." They nodded. Jones explained that the Texas Congress must sanction such a venture. Hoping to scare the Americans into offering better terms, he revealed to his guests that the British had informed him that they had convinced Mexico to recognize the independence of the Texas republic. If that happened, why should Texas bother colluding with the United States at all? Therefore, Jones said, he would present his legislature with two

---

colonization by ex-slaves, made a killing with early investments in canals, and dabbled in Jacksonian politics. In February 1844, on the Potomac, he staged a demonstration of the screw-propellered USS *Princeton*, a steam-powered warship with heavy guns, for President Tyler. But a new, little-tested gun of Stockton's design—the world's longest—blew apart, killing nine people, including the Secretaries of State and Navy and, nearly, the President.

options—either US statehood or continued independence under a British military guarantee against Mexican attack. In June 1845, at Washington-on-the-Brazos, the Texas Senate and House convened (the latter in a rustic loft above a bar) and unanimously opted for US statehood. Astonished by the decision, Jones charged that Donelson and other Americans had bribed the lawmakers with money and job offers. On the Fourth of July, in Austin, a convention of Texans ratified their entrance into the United States "with becoming dignity and self-respect."*

One Northern paper exulted, "The die is cast—the long agony is over! *Texas is again ours!*" Washington, DC's *Daily Union,* which was close to Polk, predicted "that Mexico will declare war" against Texas, and if the United States did not respond, it would "sacrifice our own rights, disregard our obligations to Texas, violate our honor, and cast a stain upon the American escutcheon." Reflecting its access to the President's private thinking, the *Union* warned, "A corps of properly organized volunteers (and they might be obtained from all quarters of the Union) would invade, overrun, and occupy Mexico. They would enable us not only to take California, but to keep it." Forty thousand soldiers deployed against Mexico "would end the war in *one year.*" Referring to the mythical bloodstained garment that had killed Heracles, the *Union* concluded, "Texas has proved the Nessus shirt to the whig party. . . . If they are wise, they will not prosecute the game any further! The country is now virtually ours."

To "deter and prevent" Mexico from rash behavior, Polk ordered General Taylor to send two thousand soldiers from Fort Jesup, Louisiana, westward into Texas, referring to the force as an "Army of occupation." He warned that the country had been "so long at peace," since the War of 1812, and much of the American military had become "so fond of their ease & personal comfort" that they now required "the most rigid discipline." He told a friend that Mexico would have already attacked US territory "but for the appearance of a strong naval force in the Gulf and our Army moving in the direction of her frontier on land."

The President knew that even should the Mexicans swallow their

---

* Texas officially became a state on December 29, 1845.

outrage about statehood for Texas, they were unlikely to accept the American claim that Texas territory extended all the way south to the Rio Grande. The *National Intelligencer*, by now a Whig paper, warned that if Polk employed Taylor's troops to enforce this contention, it would constitute an invasion of Mexico—"*offensive war*, and *not* the necessary defence of Texas." "Soon our Army will be on the Rio Grande del Norte, with the flag of Freedom at their head, and an endless procession of Slaves in their rear," warned the abolitionist *New-York Tribune*. "The Army will dispossess the Mexican authorities; the chained and cuffed procession behind will subdue and cultivate the soil, dancing to the music of the overseers' whip."

* * *

IN AUGUST 1845, Polk and his Cabinet resolved that if Mexico declared war or sent even a single soldier across the Rio Grande, Taylor's force should seize Matamoros and other strategic points on the Mexican side of the river. Acting in concert, the US Navy would blockade the country's eastern Gulf coast.

With his penchant for secret agents, Polk sent an American dentist, William Parrott, to assess the mood in Mexico City. Parrott reported back that the Mexicans would not seriously try to compose their differences with the United States "until after we shall have given them a positive proof of our superiority" by going to war. Best for Mexico to be "well flogged by Uncle Sam's boys, ere we enter upon negotiation." But after he was in the capital for a while, Parrott found the Mexicans more conciliatory; he predicted that if Polk sent them an emissary, they might settle the two countries' problems with comparative ease. American diplomats agreed, noting that Mexico, despite its overheated threats, had failed to attack Texas after annexation.

That fall, testing the opportunity for negotiation, the President appointed the Spanish-speaking Congressman John Slidell of Louisiana as his special envoy, with the rank of Minister. He told his Cabinet that Slidell's "great object" would be to persuade Mexico to accept a permanent boundary along the Rio Grande and on to the Pacific, ceding to the

United States all Mexican territory above this line. Under the President's plan, the United States would absorb what would later become the states of Texas, California, Arizona, New Mexico, Utah, and Nevada, as well as portions of Oklahoma, Kansas, Colorado, and Wyoming. "For such a boundary," said Polk, "the amount of pecuniary consideration to be paid would be of small importance." He was hoping to pay $15 million but was willing to offer $40 million. He told Slidell, "I am exceedingly desirous to acquire *California*. . . . If you can acquire both *New Mexico* and *California,* for the sum authorized, the nation, I have no doubt, will approve the act."

Polk's Secretary of State, James Buchanan of Pennsylvania, informed the US consul in Mexico City, John Black, that the President's desire for peace was "so strong" that he would "waive all ceremony" and bargain. Black replied that the Mexican Foreign Minister, Manuel de la Peña y Peña, had agreed, provided that Polk's envoy had "full power" to settle their outstanding problems. Peña had also asked, as a show of goodwill, that the US Navy withdraw from Veracruz Harbor. Polk agreed.

But when Slidell reached Mexico City, Peña and his chief, the tee-tering interim President José Joaquín de Herrera, deflected him to a truculent "council of government" that was breathing down Herrera's neck. The council quickly sent Slidell packing; it complained that since Mexico did not enjoy good relations with the United States, receiving him would jeopardize its "dignity." Furious, Slidell complained to Peña that from no other "civilized nation" had there been "so many wanton attacks upon the rights of persons and property" as Mexico's against the United States. If war came, Mexico would bear "sole responsibility." Slidell wrote Polk that he felt upset by his "mortifying" failure. He advised that "a war would probably be the best mode of settling our affairs with Mexico."

The President responded to Mexico's insult by commanding General Taylor to move his restive troops from Corpus Christi—on the safe, uncontested side of the Nueces River—down to the Rio Grande. A New Hampshire paper warned, "So the President, instead of Congress, has DECLARED WAR, by invading the territory we *want very much.*"

* * *

BY EARLY 1846, although girding for war, Polk still hoped to obtain Texas, California, and other treasure lands by paying hard cash to the Mexican government, which was now headed by the anti-American General Mariano Paredes y Arrillaga. In this effort, Polk twice received a mysterious adviser to General Santa Anna, who was now exiled in Cuba. The agent, Alexander Atocha, advised the President that his chief wished to return to power in Mexico City. He claimed that Santa Anna was willing to sell the United States the Mexican lands that Polk wanted (for $30 million) and sign a peace treaty. But the General would require a quiet incentive for himself—perhaps $500,000 up front. Atocha told Polk that the only way the Mexicans would make concessions was if they were scared; he urged that the US Navy therefore be menacingly restored to Veracruz Harbor. Polk wisely concluded that Atocha could not be trusted.

The President directed Slidell to ask for an audience with the new Paredes government. He knew, and perhaps even hoped, that Slidell would be rebuffed, providing the United States with yet another grievance against Mexico. He told Slidell that if his mission failed, he would ask Congress for "the proper remedies." By this, he meant war. Alluding to this possibility, Buchanan explained to Slidell that Congress might reject an "energetic" recommendation from Polk for action against Mexico "if it could be asserted that the existing government had not refused to receive our minister." Taking Buchanan's hint, Slidell wrote to the new Mexican Foreign Minister, Joaquin Maria del Castillo y Lanzas, assuring him that the United States was "unwilling to take a course which would inevitably result in war, without making another effort to avert so great a calamity." Outraged by the reference to war, Castillo slammed the door in Slidell's face, exclaiming that Mexico had been "despoiled" by his letter. Slidell then wrote Buchanan that the only recourse now left for the United States was the musket, pistol, and bayonet: "Be assured that nothing is to be done with these people, until they shall have been chastised."

Polk learned of the new Mexican affront in April 1846. The only thing staying his hand now was his wait for Slidell's return to Washington to help draft a war message to Congress. The President asked Buchanan to compile a list of every recent Mexican offense, including physical violence against US citizens, and all outstanding US commercial claims against Mexico (perhaps a total of $5 million) to make a "succinct" case for military conflict.

Should Polk go to war with Mexico, he did not wish to have to wage a simultaneous conflict with Great Britain. After the War of 1812, the United States and England had agreed to jointly govern the Oregon Country, which roughly spanned the distance between the forty-second parallel north and the parallel fifty-four degrees forty minutes north. During the 1844 campaign, many Democrats had demanded that America take control of the entire parcel; they cried, "Fifty-four forty or Fight!" But that April, pragmatically ignoring his party's most extreme expansionists, Polk made a deal with the British to divide the land at the forty-ninth parallel north in order to clear the decks for a conflict with Mexico.

South of the Rio Grande, General Pedro de Ampudia massed six thousand Mexican troops near Matamoros and sent General Taylor an ultimatum: retreat to east of the Nueces or else his Army would settle the matter of their contested territory in battle. Taylor's response was to blockade the Rio Grande, which cut off supply lines to Mexico's troops, constituting a new provocation to war.

On Sunday, May 3, 1846, after attending church, Polk asked Senator Benton, who was Chairman of the Committee on Military Affairs, to the White House. Benton told the President that he felt "a decided aversion to war with Mexico, if it could be avoided consistently with the honor of the country." Polk replied that he "could not permit Congress to adjourn without bringing the subject before that body." On Tuesday, he warned his Cabinet of "the possibility of a collision between the American and Mexican forces." On Wednesday evening, he received a several-weeks-old report from General Taylor that, as Polk described it in his diary, "hostilities might take place soon." On Friday, Slidell, back in Washington, told the President that there remained "but one course towards Mexico." On Saturday morning, Polk asked his Cabinet whether he should ask Congress for a declaration of war on the following Tuesday. Everyone said yes, except Bancroft, who argued that it would be more effective to wait for the Mexican Army's attack against Texas, which, he insisted, was sure to come.

That evening, Polk studied the message from Roger Jones, in Texas, about the ambush of Seth Thornton and his dragoons at Rancho Carricitos. With his adrenaline flowing, he started scrawling out his request of Congress to declare war. But the next morning, after he went to church with Sarah, his mood had changed. Somberly absorbing the magnitude of his next step, the usually stoical President wrote in his diary that he was suffering from "great anxiety."

* * *

O N MONDAY, May 11, 1846, just before sending his war message to Congress, Polk asked Benton back to the White House. By now, he may have regretted double-crossing the Senator over Texas annexation the previous year, because this time Benton was not much open to persuasion. From Benton's point of view, Polk had deliberately instigated this war by acquiring Texas, "with which Mexico was at war," and then marching the US Army to the Rio Grande and "pointing cannon" at Matamoros, which had provoked Mexican troops to cross the river and attack. ("And this," Benton later wrote in his memoirs, "is what is called spilling American blood on American soil.")

Polk gave the Senator a copy of his written message to Congress, which Benton took to an adjoining room to read. He returned to tell the President that he could not support the war. Polk later told his diary, "He was willing to vote men and money for defence of our territory, but was not prepared to make aggressive war on Mexico. . . . He did not think the territory of the U.S. extended West of the Nueces River."

At noon, Polk's nephew and private secretary, Joseph Knox Walker, took his message to Capitol Hill. The President was asking Congress for consent to deploy the US militia and armed forces, summon up to fifty thousand one-year volunteers, and spend $10 million to reach "a speedy and successful termination" of the war within two years. He explained that after rejecting Slidell, who had enjoyed "full powers to adjust every existing difference," the Mexicans, "after a long-continued series of menaces, have at last invaded our territory and shed the blood of our fellow-citizens on our own soil. . . . Our forbearance has gone to such an extreme as to be mistaken in its character." In a separate preamble, which resembled Madison on England in 1812, he asked Congress to declare that "a state of war exists" with Mexico.*

As Polk's appeal was read aloud to the House of Representatives, members listened in "breathless silence." A few questioned whether all-out war already existed. The South Carolina Democrat Isaac Holmes asked, "Suppose the Mexican Congress should not recognize the conduct of their general, and condemn it, and send here a remonstrance, or rather an apology—is it war? The invasion of any set of men in any capacity is not war." Holmes went on, "I remember—there are men on this floor who remember—all know that our frigate, the *Chesapeake*, was captured in 1807 by the frigate *Leopard*. Was that absolutely war? Will any man say that it created war?"

Jacob Brinkerhoff, Democrat from Ohio, argued, "If the War of 1812 taught any lesson . . . it is the folly, the insanity of prosecuting a two-penny war. I am in favor of prosecuting this war in such a manner that our enemy shall be at once crushed—such a war as should fully, instantly, at once bring them to our feet."

The Whig Congressman Garrett Davis of Kentucky insisted, however, that the southern Texas border was the Nueces. Davis recalled that when Polk had ordered Taylor's Army to the Rio Grande, the Mexicans warned that the United States would "be deemed to be making war upon Mexico." Nevertheless Taylor had ordered a blockade of Matamoras, mounting "a battery of cannon within three hundred yards of it, bearing upon its public square, and from whence he could, in a few hours, batter it down." Davis complained that now Polk's friends in

---

* The *Baltimore Sun* obtained Polk's message over Samuel Morse's new "Magnetic Telegraph," the first time a long document had been so conveyed, showing the potential of the invention "more than volumes of argument could possibly do."

Congress were being asked to "protect" him by pointing an accusing finger at the Mexicans, "to cover his mistakes and incompetency." After only a half hour of debate, the House declared war on Mexico by 174 to 14, with the objectors calling themselves the "immortal fourteen."

In the Senate, John Clayton, a Delaware Whig, accused Polk of deliberately provoking a war: "Why was it necessary to cross the desert, and take up a position immediately in front of the friendly town of Matamoras? . . . It was as much an act of aggression on our part as is a man's pointing a pistol at another's breast. . . . Congress has not been consulted, nor either branch of it." The Senate was so divided over the issue that it adjourned that day without voting on a war declaration.

Still disposed to block Polk's war, Benton now asked the President in writing how much money and men it would take to "defend" the United States. To Benton, defense was not the same thing as the more ambitious war he suspected that Polk actually wanted to wage. In another effort to persuade, the President asked him that evening to the White House. There, with Buchanan and his Secretary of War, William Marcy, as witnesses, Polk gave Benton a solemn pledge. As he later recorded in his diary,

> I told him that . . . if the Bill which had passed the House to-day should also pass the Senate, no more men would be called out and no more money expended than would be absolutely necessary to bring the present state of hostilities to an end. I told him that if the war [should be] recognized by Congress, that with a large force on land and sea I thought it could be speedily terminated.

If not a deliberate lie, Polk's assurance was as deceptive as his slippery, false intimations to Benton a year earlier about Texas annexation. His new language implied a quick and limited war. But Benton (correctly) suspected that Polk actually envisioned military action of such scale and ferocity that Mexico would give up California and the other territory he coveted. Having been duped once by this President, Benton told him no, adding that "in the nineteenth century, war should not be declared without full discussion and much more consideration" than that day's perfunctory debate in the House of Representatives.

Polk wrote in his diary that it was "useless to debate the subject further" with Benton. He now feared that the Senate would deny him his war:

> The Whigs in the Senate will oppose it on party grounds and probably, if they can get Mr. Calhoun, Mr. Benton and two or three other Senators professing to belong to the Democratic party to join them, so as to make a majority against the Bill. . . . The professed Democratic members who by their votes aid in rejecting it will owe a heavy responsibility not only to their party but to the country. I am fully satisfied that all that can save the Bill in the Senate is the fear of the people by the few Democratic Senators who wish it defeated.

But the next day, prompted by the White House, Sam Houston, now representing Texas in the US Senate, implored his peers not to let the "imbecile" Mexicans "commit outrages upon our country."* Lewis Cass, Democrat from Michigan, told colleagues, "A Mexican Army is upon our soil. Are we to confine our efforts to repelling them?" Cass recommended marching all the way to Mexico City, after which the United States could dictate terms. In response, Willie Mangum, a North Carolina Whig, demanded "a grave inquiry" into whether Polk had provoked war. John C. Calhoun said he was willing to offer soldiers and supplies, but that Polk's "monstrous" contention, without proof, that a state of war now existed would strip Congress of its war-making power and give "that power to every officer—nay, to every subaltern commanding a corporal's guard."

Senators came close to striking down the preamble, by 20 to 25.†

---

* Houston's fellow Senator from Texas was Thomas Jefferson Rusk, who had been Secretary of War of the Republic of Texas, and whose descendant, Dean Rusk, would help President Lyndon Johnson wage war in Vietnam.

† Vice President Dallas, as presiding officer, noted that Whigs "almost got on their knees to beg to be spared from voting on the preamble."

Holmes explained that he could not endorse "so bold a falsehood." Calhoun refused to vote on the final bill, as did two other Senators. Benton was tempted to oppose Polk, but finally decided that if he, as Military Affairs Chairman, did so, it would make the President "a ruined man." The Senate finally approved Polk's war by 40 to 2.*

After the vote, a disconsolate Benton mused that had Mexico spilled no American blood, it would have been "difficult—perhaps impossible" to convince Congress to endorse a war, but that "with it, the vote was almost unanimous." Benton observed that many in both houses had given Polk his war declaration in the ignorant belief, encouraged by Polk's party whips, that the ambush of Seth Thornton and his dragoons, soon called the Thornton affair, would be the final gunfire between Americans and Mexicans, and that a peace treaty, bursting with Mexican concessions, would be signed before autumn.

When the nation learned what Congress had done, much of the opposition would come from abolitionist New England. Boston's *Emancipator* warned that the Whigs had embraced a conflict that would extend slavery in America, out of "fear of being nicknamed 'Old Federalists' if they dared refuse to vote a lie." Connecticut's *Middletown Constitution* exclaimed, "What no previous Congress has dared to do without long consideration and solemn deliberation has now been done in a few hours and without scarcely a show of debate!" The *Vermont Phoenix* charged that Polk had larded his war message with "gross and palpable *falsehoods!*" Massachusetts's *Berkshire County Whig* complained that Congress had made Polk "into a monarch." In Wisconsin, the *Milwaukee Sentinel* called the House and Senate "lickspittles and toadeaters. . . . The rashness of this said whole proceeding is as remarkable as its lawlessness." The same journal asked why Polk had "excused himself" from military service in the War of 1812.

On Tuesday evening, May 12, at 7:00 p.m., a jubilant Knox Walker

---

* When the roll call reached the Whigs John Crittenden of Kentucky and William Upham of Vermont, both Senators said, "Ay, except the preamble." The two voting nay, John Clayton of Delaware and John Davis of Massachusetts, were also Whigs. The final bill, as passed, included the assertion that "a state of war exists."

arrived at the White House, informing Uncle James that the Senate had backed him to the hilt: the war debate had been "animating and thrilling." The next day, an exhausted Polk signed the declaration of war and issued a proclamation—echoing Madison's language of June 1812—that Americans had been "forced" to take "the last resort of injured nations."

At Wednesday evening's Cabinet meeting, the President was wire-tense from nervous strain. Buchanan read aloud from a dispatch he had drafted for American Ministers in Europe. It pledged that the United States would not fight this war with the intention of acquiring California, New Mexico, or any other Mexican territory. The Secretary of State reminded his chief that no such war ambition had been mentioned in either his appeal to Congress or the war declaration he had just signed. "Astonished," as he later confided to his journal, by Buchanan's obtuse presumptuousness, Polk gruffly ordered him to take that promise out of his dispatch.

CHAPTER FIVE

"A Presidential War"

As the war began, New Yorkers marched with placards crying "MEXICO OR DEATH!!!" The *Brooklyn Eagle* proclaimed, "This outrage upon humanity—this insult to our country—must be avenged!" "We can send out 25,000 men from this city in 24 hours, the finest in the world," boasted the *New York Sun*. A rally of twenty thousand Philadelphians pledged "to sustain the country in its emergency." New Orleans was reported to be "glowing with a spirit of patriotism worthy of ancient Greece," and "all Mississippi is ready to take the field." Galveston echoed with the cry "To arms, Texans! To arms!" A few Whig papers complained about the Commander-in-Chief's inexperience. New York's *Albany Evening Journal* warned that the Army, including a lieutenant colonel "who has not had his harness off" since the War of 1812, would now be called to fight under "a man who has seen no service, endured no privation, and dared no death!"

On the second floor of the White House, the taciturn Polk was pursued in his office, down the hall from his bedroom, by pushy Congressmen and other visitors, who peddled friends, constituents, and relatives for prestigious military posts. (A newly formed regiment of mounted riflemen was a particular draw.) Forced to extend his daily office hours from morning to the late afternoon, the President was annoyed by what he called this "harassing." A Kentuckian told him that John C. Calhoun's "friends" were charging that Polk had invented this war as a ploy to run for reelection. The President replied by restating his "fixed and unalterable" intention to retire after a single term. Someone warned him that senior Army men, jealous of their own authority, were trying to sabotage his call for new generals to help command the tens of thousands of new volunteers. "These officers are all whigs & violent partisans," Polk fumed into his diary, "and not having the success of my administration at heart seem disposed to throw every obstacle in the way of my prosecuting the Mexican War successfully."

Polk was exhilarated by the victories achieved even before he had signed the formal war declaration. Just a week after learning of Seth Thornton's ambush, he was told that in the Battle of Palo Alto, General Taylor's Army had defeated a three-times-larger Mexican force, with a death toll of five hundred Mexicans and only four Americans. After that, in the Battle of Resaca de la Palma, it was said that Taylor rode majestically on his horse, exposed to Mexican bullets and cannonballs, "as unmoved and selfpossessed as if on parade." While retreating across the Rio Grande, about three hundred Mexican soldiers drowned. Taylor's Army lost thirty-four troops, Mexico over five times that number. Georgia's *Macon Telegraph* claimed that Resaca de la Palma was "like another Thermopylae." The *New York Courier* crowed, "We look in vain in modern warfare, for any such triumphs of courage and skill over numbers, in the history of civilized nations." At the Executive Mansion, Polk and his wife were presented with a spent canister and war-shredded Mexican flags by a crippled Army major just back from the Rio Grande. Leaning on his crutches, the major proudly told the President about each of his battle trophies.

As soon as Congress had declared war, Polk had started machinating to expand its goals far beyond what the two houses had explicitly authorized. According to his diary, he hoped "my friends in Congress and elsewhere would suffer me to conduct the War with Mexico as I thought proper, and not plan the campaign for me." He told his Cabinet that it would not be enough for Taylor to seize northern Mexico and hold it until peace was made. He also wanted General Winfield Scott, hero of the 1812 war, to "occupy the country on the lower Del Norte and in the interior."

But that was not all. During these first few weeks of combat, the maverick President was already planning his grab for Upper California.* He had ordered Colonel Stephen Kearny to lead his regiment and a thousand Missouri volunteers to Santa Fe, "to protect our traders," and then "proceed towards California," providing that he could get there by winter.† As Polk's journal shows, on May 26, he proposed to the Cabinet "that an expedition be immediately fitted out against Upper California," with "two or three mounted regiments to be assembled and marched from Independence in Mo. to the Sacramento before the setting in of winter." He confided to George Bancroft, now Acting Secretary of War, that "the more I reflected on the subject the more important I thought it." On May 30, the President revealed his intentions to his department secretaries, later writing in his diary,

> I stated that if the war should be protracted for any consider-
> able time, it would in my judgment be very important that the
> U.S. should hold military possession of California at the time
> peace was made, and I declared my purpose to be to acquire for
> the United States California, New Mexico, and perhaps some
> others of the Northern Provinces of Mexico whenever a peace
> was made. In Mr. Slidell's Secret instructions last autumn these
> objects were included. Now that we were at War the prospect of
> acquiring them was much better.

The Cabinet agreed, but neither Congress nor the American people were informed about this portentous expansion of the war's mission. Resolution of a border skirmish was leading to the radical expansion

---

* As opposed to Baja California, to the south. Polk's circle used the term interchangeably with the word "California."

† Santa Fe had been claimed by the old Republic of Texas but had been seized by Mexico. After Polk gave him his assignment, Kearny was promoted to Brigadier General and commander of the "Army of the West."

of the United States. Thomas Hart Benton much later recalled of Polk and his circle, "War was a necessity and an indispensability to their purpose. . . . Never were men at the head of a government less imbued with military spirit, or more addicted to intrigue."

On the final day of June, Polk and his Cabinet discussed what he called the ultimate "objects of the War." Buchanan proposed that they seek all Mexican lands north of the Rio Grande to El Paso, and above a boundary of about thirty-two degrees latitude, west to the Pacific. He argued that Americans of the North would oppose the acquisition of territory farther south out of fear that it would be carved up into new slaveholding states. In response, Secretary of the Treasury Robert Walker, a well-known champion of slavery from Mississippi, demanded more: Why not seize all Mexican land down to about twenty-six degrees latitude? He would rather "fight the whole world sooner than suffer other Powers to interfere in the matter." Praising Walker's voracious appetite, the President replied that "in any event, we must obtain Upper California and New Mexico."

* * *

POLK QUIETLY LOOKED for ways to make a deal with the Mexicans that would obviate the need for more fighting. He had Alexander Slidell Mackenzie take a new secret message to Santa Anna in Havana.* While the United States intended to fight Mexico fiercely, it said, the President would prefer a negotiated peace and would bargain "with pleasure" if Santa Anna returned to power. Mackenzie added that Polk wanted Mexico to agree to the Rio Grande as its boundary and relinquish California, all the way up to San Francisco, for which Polk was ready to pay cash. Feigning interest, Santa Anna went on to advise Mackenzie on how best to wage war against Mexico. Polk had asked his emissary to come straight back to Washington after his

---

* Mackenzie was John Slidell's brother; he had reputedly added the surname in a bid to inherit money from an uncle.

mission, but instead the excited Mackenzie took Santa Anna's military advice to General Taylor, who guffawed at the notion of collaborating with the duplicitous Mexican General.

The President had Buchanan propose to his Mexican counterpart that they jointly broker an end to "the present unhappy war," but without result. Polk asked Senator Benton to help him get $2 million from Congress—supposedly for "extraordinary expenses" but actually to buy California when the United States and Mexico finally worked out their peace settlement.* This required Polk, for the first time, to confess to the Senate—albeit in a confidential message—that he viewed the Mexican War, at least partly, as a vehicle by which to expand the United States. The Senators gave him the money, along with a resolution asking the President to "conclude a treaty of peace, limits, and boundaries" with Mexico. Polk construed the Senate vote as consent for him to bargain over Mexican real estate.†

The Whigs demanded that Polk take public responsibility for widening the war's ambition, which he did. Then a new, young abolitionist Pennsylvania Congressman from the President's own party, David Wilmot, submitted what was soon dubbed the "Wilmot Proviso." It would demand that slavery be excluded from any territory acquired from this war. In disgust, Polk replied that he found no connection between slavery and a Mexican peace, but the House passed the proviso by 83 to 64. Using a shrewd parliamentary maneuver, the abolitionist Senator John Davis of Massachusetts exploited the moment to block Polk's $2 million bequest.‡ Dejected by the rebuff, Polk told his diary

---

* Polk's requested $2 million was exactly the same contingency sum that Congress had twice given Jefferson—first for the Louisiana Purchase from France and then to buy East and West Florida from Spain.

† Thanks in part to tariff cuts Polk had pressed upon Congress, US trade was thriving and the nation's coffers were flush, which meant that he did not need to ask for new taxes to finance his war.

‡ Davis had been one of the two Senators who opposed Polk's declaration of war. Eager to scuff him up, the Democratic *New Hampshire Patriot* now reviled him as "the same individual, if we mistake not, who gave *three cheers when he received news that the British had burnt the city of Washington.*"

that had he obtained the money, "I am confident I should have made an honorable peace by which we should have acquired California, & such other territory as we desired, before the end of October." Now, if the war dragged on, "the responsibility will fall more heavily upon the head of Senator Davis than upon any other man, and he will deserve the execrations of the country."

With his grim work ethic, Polk had stayed in Washington, without serious respite, since becoming President. For most of his life, he had been vulnerable to exhaustion, intestinal problems—notably chronic diarrhea—and physical collapse. As his troops advanced into Mexico, he refused to curb his compulsive overwork, night after night, until dawn. His face looked more skeletal, his eyes more hollow, his lank hair whiter. Sarah told him, "When I think of the labor and fatigue you have to undergo, I feel sad and melancholy and conclude that success is not worth the labor." In August, trying to escape the tensions of the war, they went to visit the Navy yard at Norfolk, Virginia, passing the USS *Chesapeake*'s old dock, as well as the resting place of the now-dilapidated *Constitution*. From Hampton Roads, the Polks set off on the steamboat *Curtis Peak* for the vacation hamlet of Old Point Comfort. Both severely prone to seasickness, they staggered off the vessel beneath bursting fireworks, while a military band from Fort Monroe performed patriotic airs. The next morning, feeling shaken and fatigued, with a painful headache, Polk remained in his bed.

After returning to the White House, the President was exhilarated by momentous news from the West. Having taken Santa Fe, Stephen Kearny's force had gone on to conquer the Mexican province of New Mexico without bloodshed. And from the settlement of Los Angeles, the onetime secret envoy Robert Stockton had pronounced the United States in control of California, over which he would now preside as military governor. Polk had rightly expected Mexican domination of the territory, under the unpopular General José Antonio Castro, to collapse after a few showy displays of US force. Thus Stockton, backed by only several thousand troops, had landed at San Pedro, while his chief lieutenant, the well-known explorer John C. Frémont (who was also Senator Benton's son-in-law), brought a similar contingent to San Diego. Stockton appointed Kearny to succeed him as military governor, and the latter had Frémont, his rival, court-martialed for insubordination (which made Benton furious at Polk). Nevertheless the President exulted that both New Mexico and California had fallen to the United States.

The fighting in Mexico had reached a stalemate. Polk tried to break it with an amphibious landing at the Mexican port of Veracruz, which, he hoped, would, along with the victories by Kearny and Stockton, bring the enemy to the negotiating table. He was especially optimistic because Santa Anna had returned to Mexico, with his faithful Atocha at his side. But, showing few signs of the old amity he had once affected toward Polk, the chameleon General now demanded that Mexico retake Texas.

From the Mexican front, Zachary Taylor complained, by slow letter to Polk, that the untrained volunteers under his command had been given too little preparation to march five hundred miles through mountains to Mexico City. Instead he asked the President to let them be used to seize the country's northern provinces. Polk grudgingly consented but griped into his diary, "General Taylor, I fear, is not the man for command of the Army; he is brave but he does not seem to have resources or grasp of mind enough to conduct such a campaign." He suspected that Taylor, with his not-so-latent Whig loyalties, was "most ungrateful, for I have promoted him, as I now think, beyond his deserts, and without deference to his politics. I am now satisfied that he is a narrow-minded, bigoted partisan, without resources and wholly unqualified for the command he holds."

In the autumn of 1846, Taylor and his troops marched south toward Monterrey, which they seized after a three-day battle.* Preaching "magnanimity" and with his men exhausted, he infuriated Polk by letting General Pedro de Ampudia's seven-thousand-man Army go free under a two-month armistice.

---

* Taylor's force included the Mississippi Rifles, commanded by Colonel Jefferson Davis, who had been married to Taylor's daughter Sarah for three months before her death at age twenty-one of malaria.

* * *

WHILE CAMPAIGNING FOR the fall 1846 midterm elections, many Whigs encouraged a backlash against the war. At a campaign rally in Boston's Faneuil Hall, Senator Daniel Webster employed his vaunted oratorical skills against what he called Polk's "universally odious" conflict. Having served Harrison and Tyler as Secretary of State, Webster had his eye on the presidency for 1848. He told the crowd that "the war, in its origin, was *a Presidential war.*"* Polk had "ordered the Army south of the Nueces, to take possession of the Mexican land! That was the origin of the war." Webster insisted that *"Congress alone* has power to declare war, and yet it is obvious, under the present construction, that if the President is resolved to involve the country in a war, he may do it. . . . A clear violation of his duty. In my judgment, it is an *impeachable offense.*"

Known as the "Defender of the Constitution," Webster noted that "the great objection to this war is that it is illegal in its character." When it was won, he asked, did Polk plan to seize all of Mexico "as American territory—a territory equal to the formation of forty new states?" Then the Senator brought down the house: "It is time for us to know what are the objects and designs of our government. . . . I am for taking the Constitution as our fathers left it to us, and *standing* by it—and *dying* by it!"†

Shielding the President from Webster's attack, the *Washington Daily Union,* which enjoyed tight connections to Polk, charged that the Massachusetts Senator was merely reprising his old disloyalty during the War of 1812: "With all due pomp and preparation the Federalists have

---

* While opposing the war declaration against Mexico, Ohio Congressman Columbus Delano had also warned that if America pursued this conflict, it would be a "Presidential war—a war commenced by the President in an unconstitutional manner and by illegal means." Delano was a maternal ancestor of President Franklin Delano Roosevelt.

† Unlike Webster, some more cowardly Whigs, cognizant of how the Federalists' opposition to the 1812 war had killed their party, were muffling their antagonism toward the Mexican War. The Chicago Whig leader Justin Butterfield, who had once been a Federalist in New England, joked, "By G-d, I opposed one war, and it ruined me, and hence forth I am for *War, Pestilence and Famine.*"

at last hung out their *Great Blue Light*," with Webster "shamefully" trying to "strengthen the arms of the enemy." Adopting the same theme,
the Worcester, Massachusetts, *Palladium* blustered, "The country is at
war with Mexico, and Mr. Webster, instead of putting his herculean
shoulder to the wheel, as every true patriot does, talks of impeaching
the President!"

That fall, Polk's Democrats gained four new seats in the Senate. But
the Whigs took narrow control of the House of Representatives, gaining thirty-seven seats. Their number would now include a thirty-seven-
year-old attorney from Illinois named Abraham Lincoln. Overjoyed by
the House victory, a Whig paper welcomed "the hope of soon putting a
check on the monstrous and wicked policy of the Administration."

Unsettled by his midterm defeat, Polk knew that the new, slender
Whig majority in the House, using its subpoena powers to haze the administration, was likely to make it more difficult for him to wage his war.
But in his December annual written message to Congress, he did not
mention the election results. Defiant as ever, he boasted of the American
victories at Palo Alto, Resaca de la Palma, and Monterrey, all "won against
greatly superior numbers." He added that without bloodshed, the nation
had vanquished New Mexico and California—more territory "than that
embraced in the original thirteen States of the Union." Polk pledged that
the war would be "vigorously prosecuted" until an "honorable peace"
compelled the Mexicans to pay the United States for its war expenses and
the "large pecuniary demands" of "our much-injured citizens."

Responding to Webster and other critics, the President claimed that
the conflict "was neither desired nor provoked by the United States" and
"has not been waged with a view to conquest." Having committed this
whopper to parchment, he lambasted those who called the war "unjust
and unnecessary." Casting aspersions on their motives, he accused his
critics of using language "devised to encourage the enemy and protract
the war," lending Mexico "aid and comfort"—a phrase that was the
Constitution's definition of treason, as Polk well knew. Echoing Polk's
calumny, the *Union* argued that while some of the President's detractors might not be strictly treasonous by law (which required provable

intention to encourage the enemy), they were certainly guilty of "the open and burning shame of 'MORAL TREASON!' "*

Firing back, the Whig *New Hampshire Sentinel* complained that Polk had claimed it was "treasonable" to doubt his "infallibility . . . or the correctness of his decisions." A pseudonymous Whig columnist called "HILLSBOROUGH" wrote that by using the words "aid and comfort," the President had cast "odium upon at least one half of the people over whom he presides." He contended that the war, "its inception, in the manner it occurred, was a gross violation of the Constitution," as were "the acts of the President's agents in annexing conquered territory and compelling its inhabitants, at the point of the bayonet, to swear allegiance to the United States." Acidly the *Cleveland Herald* remarked, "Taking Mr. Polk's word for it, no nation ever went to war with a cause more just than ours."

With the war dividing the country, civility broke down in the House of Representatives. Meredith Gentry, a Tennessee Whig, insisted that Polk's assertion that the United States legally owned the Texas land between the Nueces and the Rio Grande was a "lie." The Georgia Democrat Seaborn Jones complained that Gentry's "disgust—his hatred—his violence of feeling" against Polk had driven him to use the word "lie," a term of "coarseness and vulgarity" that was "most certainly unfit to be applied to the President of the United States." Barclay Martin, a Tennessee Democrat, vilified Gentry as "an advocate of Mexico."

* * *

Like the madisons during the War of 1812, the presidential couple now found their dinner invitations spurned by members of the opposing party. Mrs. Polk bolstered her husband's spirits by observing that there was "always somebody opposed to everything."

Sarah Childress Polk was the daughter of a wealthy planter in Murfreesboro, Tennessee. After being privately tutored, she was sent to the

---

* With dark historical symmetry, the term "moral treason" had been hurled by James Madison's liege *National Intelligencer* at critics of the 1812 war.

Moravian Female Academy in North Carolina; after a year, her father died, and she returned home to inherit a fourth of his estate, which included thirty-four slaves.* According at least to legend, James Polk first glimpsed Sarah in the looking glass at a stylish Nashville reception, as the tall teenage girl bantered with her father's friend Andrew Jackson. Old Hickory encouraged the relationship by reminding Polk that "her wealthy family, education, health and appearance are all superior." But the ambitious young woman did not consent to marry James for four years, until he had been elected to the state legislature.

As her husband rose in politics, Sarah gave him constant counsel, vetted his speeches, and shared his night reading. When they were apart, she would write him ("Dear Husband") about political intrigues within their home state.† Especially with no children to play alongside the family hearth, she fretted about James's health when he campaigned, once writing him, "I never wanted to see you more in my life than now." (Alarmed that she had written him so "despondingly," he replied, "You must cheer up.") Sarah's observations were often more biting and partisan than his, moving him to caution her, "I understand you, but others might not, and a wrong impression might be made." Polk cherished her us-against-the-world feistiness. When Andrew Jackson's onetime court painter Ralph Earl rendered Sarah's portrait, James told the artist he had captured "exactly the look of mischief that few people outside of myself ever see." After the Polks entered the White House, Vice President Dallas wisecracked, "She is certainly master of herself, and I suspect of somebody else also." Dallas did not understand that nobody ruled James Polk. While traveling with the President, Buchanan buttered up Mrs. Polk by writing her, "We have gotten along as could be expected in your absence."

---

* When they entered the White House, the Polks saved money by dismissing ten servants and replacing them with slaves—some newly purchased, some imported from their family retinue in Tennessee.

† In 1840, appraising a groundswell for James to seek a Senate seat, she wrote him, "It does strike me that this is the right thing for you to do." In 1841, while he was running for reelection as Governor: "I do not think it likely that the Democrats will get out any candidates in this county." Consoling him about brickbats from a Nashville journal, she wrote, "I do not believe anything that they put in the papers will have any effect so you need not be uneasy."

When Polk's wife entertained, her religion and sense of the dignity of the Executive Mansion moved her to ban dancing, band concerts, and hard liquor, the last earning her the nickname of "Sahara Sarah." During the Mexican War, revealing her vision of her husband's place in history, she hung a heroic portrait of Hernán Cortés, the conquistador of the Aztecs, in the Blue Room. The Massachusetts Whig Charles Sumner praised Sarah's "sweetness of manner," but others found her "a little too formal and cold." Called, like Dolley Madison, "the Presidentess," she adopted Polk's toughness about political methods. During a White House dinner, when Sarah asked one ex-soldier to recount his battle experience, he was startled to hear her demand "whatever sustained the honor and advanced the interests of the country, whether regarded as democratic or not."

Polk shared his wife's strong belief in God; on most Sundays, although he preferred Methodist hymns and ritual, they attended a Presbyterian service. Because Polk's father was a skeptic, his mother's request to baptize him as a baby had been rejected by a Presbyterian minister. Under the strain of his wartime presidency, Polk felt the urge to be baptized but lacked time for what he called the "solemn preparation." His secular father had taught him respect for secular government. As President, Polk observed, "Thank God, under our Constitution there was no connection between church and state." The President refused Christian ministers who exhorted him to claim God's sanction for the Mexican War; he earnestly assured the Catholic Bishop of New York, John Hughes, that US troops would not try to transform the conquered Mexicans into Protestants.

Despite Polk's willfulness, his record on civil liberties was surprisingly good. Although he condemned opponents of his war for "moral treason" in his diary, he did not ask to lock them up, as John Adams had during his struggles with the French. Unlike Madison, Polk never asked Congress or state governors to force young Americans to fight. Nor did he make a major effort to have his government censor the dispatches sent from the Mexican front by the nation's first generation of foreign war correspondents. Polk could afford to be magnanimous: achievements on the battlefield buffered him against gripes about the war's conduct, and the tens of thousands of Americans pleading to fight in Mexico preempted the need for a military draft.

Nevertheless, the Polk-connected *Daily Union* horrifyingly proposed that every US town and village create a "war-register" of all Americans who spoke out against the Mexican conflict, listing "where an individual expresses sympathy for the enemy, or wishes the death of the President, or the downfall of the National Administration." Did this demand for a national enemies list quietly originate with Polk or one of his cronies?

* * *

A S 1847 OPENED, despite the new political strength of the antiwar Whigs, Polk aimed to escalate the war. He planned to ask the states for enough fresh volunteers to stage a great amphibious assault on Veracruz. Newly disenchanted with Taylor over the petulant General's refusal to keep him informed and fulfill his exact orders, Polk told his diary that Taylor had "acted with great weakness and folly" in Monterrey and seemed "giddy with the idea of the presidency."* He had wanted to sack Taylor as commander in Mexico, but the only obvious substitute was the sixty-year-old Winfield Scott, "Old Fuss and Feathers," who had fought in the 1812 Battle of Queenston Heights and whom Polk mistrusted. Nevertheless he summoned Scott and asked him to lead an attack on Veracruz. According to Polk's diary, the General was "so much affected that he almost shed tears."

The President asked Congress for ten new volunteer regiments, as well as $3 million in cash and $23 million in borrowing authority. The Whig Senator John Berrien of Georgia demanded a caveat: Polk could not use the money to fight Mexico unless he renounced "the acquisition, by conquest, of any portion of her territory." Berrien got nowhere, but

---

* In the spring of 1847, the *Cincinnati Morning Signal* asked Taylor if he would be "willing" to be President. The General replied, "I am not prepared to say that I shall refuse." Taylor went on to pledge that he would not become "the candidate of any party," implying that both the Whigs and the Democrats might nominate him. The *Union* later marveled that the Whigs "would force General Taylor into the presidential canvass as their candidate solely and avowedly on the ground that he has fought with success and glory in a war which they abhor!"

Polk's own Democratic Senate rejected his bid for ten regiments. The dumbfounded President asked Senators, as a matter of "patriotism," not to show Mexico "a course of indecision." John Calhoun responded by demanding "masterly inactivity": hold the territory already conquered until Mexico begged for peace. He explained that of all the reasons he opposed the Mexican War, the principal outrage was "the manner in which it was brought on," when Polk had provoked the Mexicans by sending General Taylor to the Rio Grande.*

Rising to Polk's defense, Tom Benton told the Senate that Calhoun should not blame Polk for the war. He asked whether Rome's civil war had been caused by Caesar crossing the Rubicon, or America's Revolutionary War by British soldiers at Lexington and Concord. Like those earlier struggles, "the causes of this Mexican war were long anterior to this march." Then Benton threw his punch: "The Senator from South Carolina is the author of those causes, and therefore the author of the war!" He recalled 1819, when, as Secretary of War, Calhoun had pressed President Monroe to approve the Adams-Onís Treaty, which gave Texas to Spain as the price of acquiring Florida—and 1844, when, as Secretary of State, Calhoun had urged President Tyler to annex Texas, forcing the United States to inherit Texas's war with Mexico: "And now he sets up for a man of peace, and throws all the blame of war upon Mr. Polk, to whom he bequeathed it!" Captivated by Benton, the Senate gave the President his cash and his regiments. Polk told his diary, "Good feeling prevailed."†

In February, although directed to stay at Monterrey, Taylor moved six thousand troops southwest to Saltillo, where, to his surprise, General Ampudia and twenty thousand Mexican warriors were waiting to pounce. Ordered by the Mexicans to surrender or be "cut to pieces with your troops," Taylor fought them in the Battle of Buena Vista, and managed to end the two-day struggle with only 267 Americans killed. Had

---

* Denouncing Calhoun's proposal, the *Union* asked, "Why we are at war! And what is inactivity in war . . . but delay and feebleness, and, in the long run, cruelty?"

† Appreciating Benton's performance, Calhoun later conceded that he had played his hand well.

Taylor not exceeded his orders, those men would not have lost their lives in a confrontation that brought their country little.

Having returned to power in Mexico City, Santa Anna sent his secret agent Atocha to Washington with a peace offer, which demanded that the United States cancel its naval blockade and remove its forces from Mexico. In no mood to bargain, the President vowed to his Cabinet in March that he would advance to Mexico City, and, as he told his diary, "pursue Santa Anna's Army, wherever it was, and capture or destroy it." Senator Benton advised him not to stop at Monterrey and instead conquer Mexico City: "Ours is a go-ahead people, and our only policy to obtain peace and save ourselves is to press the war boldly."

One American who had perished at Buena Vista was Henry Clay Jr., the son and spitting image of Polk's grand adversary.* In 1844, the elder Clay had warned Americans that Polk secretly longed for a war with Mexico. Now, after being told the ghastly tidings while dining at Ashland, his estate in Lexington, Kentucky, the ex-Senator agonized over his son's destruction by "this most unnecessary and horrible war." It soon emerged that while holding several Mexicans at bay so that some of his men could escape ("Leave me, take care of yourselves!"), the younger Clay was stabbed to death by Mexicans with bayonets.† His father, once a War Hawk of 1812, now wrote a friend, "I find it extremely difficult to sustain myself under this heavy calamity. . . . How often, my dear friend, are the objects most endeared to us snatched away from us!" As a gesture of reconciliation, President Polk approved the request of his old rival to send his now-fatherless grandson Henry III to West Point.

The younger Clay's death on the battlefield evoked intense condolences from the Whig press. *"Henry Clay, Jr., his son!"* exclaimed the

---

* Of the West Point–trained young Henry, the *Louisville Courier* had marveled, "He can raise in an hour as noble and brave a band as ever shouldered a musket, or thrashed an enemy!"

† General Taylor wrote Clay that he would miss young Henry's "familiar face": "He gave every assurance, that in the hour of need, I could lean with confidence upon his support. Nor was I disappointed." One of Henry's fellow warriors sent the elder Clay his son's wallet, which still held $76.50, and, as he wrote, "a lock of his hair, which was taken from his head as soon as he was brought into the Camp."

Milwaukee Sentinel. "The hope of his old age. The Astyanax of his family."* "Truly Mr. Polk and his cabinet will have an awful account to settle," said the *Albany Evening Journal.* "THEY made the war—THEY introduced into the enemy's service their best Generals, and the blood of Henry Clay is shed through his gallant son in its maintenance." In response, the *Ohio Statesman,* a Democratic journal, asked, "Why single out young Henry Clay to mourn over? Where are the hundreds of fallen men that have fallen in defence of their country? . . . Why harrow up the feelings of his friends, by . . . telling them that he was killed while engaged in an *unholy act?*"

For Polk, another killing at Buena Vista struck much closer to his heart—that of his old political comrade, Archibald Yell, who had been Arkansas's first Congressman. Having urged a Mexican war on Polk, Yell had left his Democratic seat to become a Colonel in Arkansas's Mounted Devils. Now General Taylor reported that Archy had fallen "gallantly at the head of his regiment." After Yell had charged the enemy on horseback, far ahead of his troops, sword to the skies, his horse had raced out of control and thrown him; Mexican soldiers pierced his chest and forehead with lances. Disconsolate, Polk told his diary that Yell "was a brave and good man, and among the best friends I had on earth, and had been so for 25 years." He wrote the Yell family, "None of his relatives can feel his loss more sensibly than I do." Furious about Yell's death, the President stormed into his journal about Taylor's insubordination, which—Polk was certain—had provoked a needless battle that had killed Archy. Of Taylor, Polk wrote, "The truth is that from the beginning of the War he has been constantly blundering into difficulties, but has fought out of them, but at the cost of many lives."[†]

---

* In Greek legend, Astyanax was the son of Hector, the Trojan crown prince.

† Polk felt a keen obligation to Yell's son DeWitt. Fearing death, Archy had sent the President a $400 money order, explaining that if the worst transpired, half the sum should go for his son's schooling. Polk now invited DeWitt, a student at Georgetown College (later University), to spend a few days together at the White House. He offered to appoint him to West Point, but did not dissuade DeWitt when the son recalled that his father had criticized the academy. Instead DeWitt returned to Arkansas for the study of law.

* * *

IN MARCH 1847, General Scott reported to Washington that his Army, aided by the US blockade of the east coast of Mexico, had landed "in fine style, and without direct opposition (on the beach), accident, or loss." A month later, Polk learned the "joyous news," as he told his diary, that after five days of shelling, General Juan Morales had surrendered Veracruz, which opened the way to Mexico City. "We have taken the Gibraltar of the western continent," rejoiced the President's ever-faithful *Union*.

Polk had sent a new special envoy to Mexico with sanction to negotiate a peace treaty as soon as the foes threw up their hands. The agent was Buchanan's tall, officious, Spanish-speaking chief clerk Nicholas Trist, a Virginia patrician.* Polk had characteristically cautioned Trist to act with "absolute secrecy," but Trist's mission was soon leaked to the *New York Herald*. The irate Polk fulminated into his diary about this "great outrage upon me," writing that he had not "been more vexed or excited since I have been president." Fearing that Whig critics would now try to gum up the works by sending their own emissaries to the Mexicans, he tried without success to ascertain the source of the leak, personally interrogating at least one suspect.

In early May, Trist reached Veracruz. Instead of observing the protocol of calling on Winfield Scott, he sent the General, by messenger, a sealed letter from Buchanan for transmission to the Mexican Foreign Minister, Domingo Ibarra, as well as instructions from Marcy, the Secretary of War, to Scott, saying that if Trist negotiated a truce, the General should treat it as "a directive from the President." Furious, Scott complained to Trist, in writing, that Marcy had chosen to "degrade

---

* With impeccable Democratic lineage, Trist was married to Thomas Jefferson's granddaughter and had served as Andrew Jackson's private secretary. Trist was instructed to ensure that Mexico formally ceded New Mexico and California, as well as permanent rights to cross the Isthmus of Tehuantepec between the Gulf and the Pacific. All commercial claims by American citizens against Mexico should be relinquished, and the United States should pay the Mexican government between $15 million and $30 million in cash.

me" as a mere courier when, in fact, a potential armistice was "most peculiarly a military question." He insisted on being the bargainer: "The safety of this Army demands no less." Scott flatly refused to deliver Buchanan's sealed letter, writing Marcy that he was "too much occupied with the business of the campaign."

Adding insult to injury, Trist wrote Scott that US government policy was "what any man of plain unsophisticated common sense would take for granted that it must be; and it is not what your exuberant fancy and over-cultivated imagination would make." Trist wrote his wife, back home, that the old General was the "greatest imbecile" he had ever encountered: "If I have not *demolished* him, then I give up." After reading Trist's insolent letter, Scott wrote Marcy, "I entreat to be spared the personal dishonor of being again required to obey the orders of the chief clerk of the State Department." Scott added that he was not surprised to receive such treatment, since he had heard rumors that the President wished to replace him with Tom Benton.

Shown Scott's letter to Marcy, Polk demanded that the "insubordinate" General be fired: "The golden moment to make a peace . . . may be lost because of Gen'l Scott's arrogance & inordinate vanity." Then, in another letter to Marcy, Scott threatened to quit, citing the "many cruel disappointments and mortifications I have been made to feel." Polk was so irked by Scott's letter that he threatened to have him court-martialed. The President also wished to fire the disobedient Trist, but with the war in the balance, his Cabinet persuaded him not to rock the boat.

In June, Polk escaped the pressures of war by traveling up the Eastern Seaboard to Augusta, Maine. Having been apprehensive about venturing into abolitionist New England, he was relieved to inform his diary that "my reception was everywhere respectful & cordial." He wrote Sarah, "Nothing of a party or of an unpleasant character has occurred anywhere."

Meanwhile, in Mexico, Trist and Scott had bonded over their common antipathy to Polk. Told that Trist was ill, Scott graciously sent him a jar of guava marmalade; as Trist later recalled, the General's gift ended "all constraint & embarrassment between us." They became such good friends that both men asked their superiors in Washington to destroy their sniping letters about each other. From long conversations, Trist and Scott endorsed a British diplomat's suggestion that they put some cash in Santa Anna's back pocket in hopes of ending the conflict fast. Scott even offered to provide the money from his own war chest. Trist assured the General that although their superiors had not approved such a gambit, it was their "duty to disregard" such formality, since such a deal would "entirely supersede the necessity for the occupation of the capital." Scott duly sent off a $10,000 payment as an icebreaker. But Santa Anna replied, through the British, that the Mexican congress had barred him from seeking peace.

By the late summer of 1847, US troops were fighting their way toward the ancient city of the Montezumas. With eerie symmetry, the first American soldier killed in this battle, which proved to be the last of the Mexican conflict, was Captain Seth Thornton, who had been wounded at the start of the war's opening act. Released from the Matamoros jail in a prisoner exchange, the young dragoon had been sent back to Washington for both hospital care and a court-martial, which cleared him of malfeasance. Thornton had demanded to rejoin the Army for its culminating march to Mexico City. While he was on reconnaissance, a battery of masked Mexican gunners knocked him off his horse and killed him. "Seth Thornton is cut in two by a nine-pound shot!" went the cry. According to one later account of the battle, Thornton was "known to the whole Army, and the news of his death created a greater shock than the fall of a hundred persons."

Almost five thousand Americans broke through a wall of seven thousand Mexicans at Contreras, killing about seven hundred and seizing eight hundred more, clearing an approach to the enemy's capital. After three further such assaults, Santa Anna implored his colleagues for one last-ditch effort to defeat the Americans. To buy time, he acceded to Scott's offer of a cease-fire. ("Too much blood has already been shed in this unnatural war," the General had written him.) When Polk heard about the pause, he groused that Scott should have exploited his advantage by forcing Santa Anna to accept American terms or else suffer a brutal attack on Mexico City. But as it happened, the pathologically unreliable Santa Anna soon violated the armistice.

Finally in September, Scott led his Army, through defensive troops, into Mexico City, hoisting the Stars and Stripes over the palace of government. Santa Anna escaped his capital to preserve his own skin. Wearing resplendent full uniform, Scott reviewed the American conquest from atop a handsome bay charger.

The following month, after word of Scott's triumph reached the White House, Polk demanded to hold all conquered territory until the Mexicans pleaded for peace. Then he learned that Trist had surpassed his instructions by apprising the Mexicans that the US might give up the land between the Nueces and the Rio Grande to create a neutral buffer zone. The furious Polk ordered Buchanan to pull Trist ignominiously back to Washington.*

* * *

IN LEXINGTON, KENTUCKY, on a gray, drizzly Saturday morning in November 1847, Henry Clay Sr., aged seventy years, emerged from his grief to address a public meeting about the Mexican War. Since the death of Henry Jr., Clay had had himself baptized as an Episcopalian. Rising with thousands of others who cheered when Clay arrived was Congressman Abraham Lincoln, whose wife, Mary, had grown up as a Lexington belle. Young Lincoln revered the old Whig statesman and, like Clay, hated the Mexican War.

"The day," Clay began, "is dark and gloomy, unsettled and uncertain, like the condition of our country, in regard to the unnatural war with Mexico." The ex-Senator exclaimed that the number of their countrymen slain in Mexico was now "equal to one half of the whole of the American loss during the seven years war of the Revolution!" The United States, he noted, would not be at war but for the Texas annexation (which he had warned against) and Polk's "warlike" dispatch of Taylor's force to the Rio Grande. Knowing that some might blame him, as the War Hawk of 1812, for launching a tradition of American

---

* Polk told his diary that Trist's offer had "embarrassed" him by suggesting that he was willing to surrender the original premise for which the Mexican War had been fought.

belligerence that had led to this struggle against Mexico, Clay insisted that the old conflict against Great Britain

> was a war of National defence, required for the vindication of the National rights and honor, and demanded by the indignant voice of the People. President Madison himself, I know, at first, reluctantly and with great doubt and hesitation, brought himself to the conviction that it ought to be declared. . . . How totally variant is the present war! This is no war of defence, but one unnecessary and of offensive aggression. It is Mexico that is defending her fire-sides, her castles and her altars, not we.*

With his new moral stature as a father who had lost his son in battle, Clay explained,

> A declaration of war is the highest and most awful exercise of sovereignty. The Convention which framed our federal constitution had learned from the pages of history that it had been often and greatly abused. It had seen that war had often been commenced upon the most trifling pretexts; that it had been frequently waged to establish or exclude a dynasty; to snatch a crown from the head of one potentate and place it upon the head of another . . . and, in short, that such a vast and tremendous power ought not to be confided to the perilous exercise of one single man. The Convention, therefore, resolved to guard the war-making power against those great abuses. . . . And the security against those abuses . . . was to vest the war-making power in the Congress. . . . Whenever called upon to determine upon the solemn question of peace and war, Congress must consider and deliberate and decide upon the motives, objects and causes

---

* Clay also observed, "How different also is the conduct of the whig party of the present day from that of the major part of the federal party during the war of 1812! . . . Who have rushed to the prosecution of the war with more ardor and alacrity than the Whigs? . . . Who have more occasion to mourn the loss of sons, husbands, brothers, fathers, than whig parents, whig wives and whig brothers, in this deadly and unprofitable strife?"

of the war. And, if a war be commenced without any previous declaration of its objects, as in the case of the existing war with Mexico . . . the President of the United States may direct it to the accomplishment of any objects he pleases. . . . Either Congress or the President, must have the right of determining upon the objects for which a war shall be prosecuted. . . . If the President possess it and may prosecute it for objects against the will of Congress, where is the difference between our free government and that of any other nation which may be governed by an absolute Czar, Emperor, or King?

Clay's two-and-a-half-hour oration was the most eloquent, well-argued case by a leader of the time that Polk's style of war making had trampled the intentions of the Founders. Thanks to the growing reach of the telegraph, Clay's warning could soon be peddled as a pamphlet on street corners in Boston and Philadelphia. Despite his melancholy and physical deterioration, Clay allowed himself to hope that his speech might vault him toward another presidential nomination.

The other most famous Whig to revile Polk's war was Daniel Webster, and it is poignant and ironic that the Mexican conflict killed Webster's son too. When the Senator's lovable, adventurous Edward—"Neddy," known as the "pet of the family"—had volunteered from Massachusetts, his siblings were upset by his eagerness to join the conflict their father so abhorred. Webster was especially distressed because he had long feared for the safety of his high-spirited son. Neddy once wrote home from Dartmouth College that he had been "wounded by a sword." His father had (fruitlessly) replied, "What had you to do with swords? . . . You are to have nothing to do with horses, dogs or guns." Now Webster was told by the War Department that Neddy had died of typhoid fever after braving the rains and bitter cold during the American march toward Mexico City.

"I hardly know how I shall bear up under this blow," the Senator wrote his son Fletcher. "It has almost crushed us." Webster's daughter Julia raged against Neddy's demise in this "wicked & cruel war . . .

without one friend to smooth his dying pillow. . . . *Now* I feel nothing but how my brother in the flower of his youth, was a useless sacrifice—to what?—ambition & vainglory." In the wake of his son's death, Webster demanded that fellow Senators (the *National Intelligencer* had never seen him "so deeply moved and earnest") "return our friends, and our brothers, and our children—*if they yet be living!*—from a land of slaughter."

In December 1847, Abraham Lincoln rose in the House of Representatives to question the origins of the Mexican War. Recalling the Thornton affair at Rancho Carricitos, he demanded that Polk provide the nation with "all the facts which go to establish whether the particular spot of soil on which the blood of our citizens was so shed, was, or was not." Lincoln's Whig colleague George Ashmun of Massachusetts, a Daniel Webster protégé, successfully proposed an amendment to an Army supply bill charging that the President had "unnecessarily and unconstitutionally begun" the Mexican conflict. In support, Lincoln gave a forty-five-minute speech—audacious for an obscure backbencher—building a prosecutor's argument that Polk had created a counterfeit pretext in order to fight a gratuitous war. (Unlike the abolitionist "conscience Whigs," Lincoln did not also contend that the President had fabricated the war to extend slavery.)

Deriding Polk's "naked *claim*" that the territory of Texas extended to the Rio Grande, Lincoln insisted that Polk was "deeply conscious of being in the wrong" and "feels the blood of this war, like the blood of Abel, is crying to Heaven against him." Polk had tried to "escape scrutiny" by "fixing the public gaze upon the exceeding brightness of military glory—that attractive rainbow, that rises in showers of blood—that serpent's eye, that charms to destroy." Lincoln added that Polk's mind had been "tasked beyond its power . . . running thither and hither, like some tortured creature, on a burning surface." A month later, Lincoln told the House that Polk's justifications for his war were "like the half insane mumbling of a fever dream."

After the Congressman attacked their President, some Democratic journals in Illinois derided him as "Spotty Lincoln" and "Benedict

Arnold."* But in his home state, the length and bloodiness of the Mexican conflict was exhausting the patience of even some Polk Democrats. The national press responded to Lincoln's complaints mainly by ignoring them.

* * *

WHEN THE NEW Congress convened in December 1847, Polk was anxious about coping with the new Whig majority in the House. He confided to his diary that with two-thirds of his presidency elapsed, he wished that "the remaining third was over." But in his annual message, he bragged about his war with Mexico. "History presents no parallel of so many glorious victories achieved by any nation within so short a period," he asserted. "While every patriot's heart must exult and a just national pride animate every bosom in beholding the high proofs of courage, consummate military skill, steady discipline, and humanity to the vanquished enemy exhibited by our gallant Army, the nation is called to mourn over the loss of many brave officers and soldiers, who have fallen in defense of their country's honor and interests."

Polk went on to insist that he had never aspired, "as an object of the war, to make a permanent conquest" of all Mexico, but now realized that New Mexico and California "should never be surrendered." The new territories "would soon be settled by a hardy, enterprising and intelligent portion of our population." San Francisco Bay and other harbors would permit "an extensive and profitable commerce" with China and the rest of eastern Asia. Polk argued that other Mexican lands should be held only "as a means of coercing Mexico to accede to just terms of peace." Offended by the President's belligerence, the *National Intelligencer* caviled that Polk sounded like "the bully of the bailiwick, who chewed up an ear or nose, or scooped out with thumb a prostrate adversary's eye."

---

* In the courtly Springfield tradition, Lincoln had pledged to serve only one term in Congress, to allow others to serve in the House, so whatever he, as a lame duck, said was not even big news at home.

John Calhoun was unconvinced by Polk's promise not to seize all of Mexico. He called on the Senate to make sure this would never happen, and his motive was racist. Aghast that Mexicans might be placed on an equal basis with white Americans, Calhoun claimed on the Senate floor, "We have never dreamt of incorporating into our Union any but the Caucasian race—the free white race. . . . Ours, sir, is the government of the white man." Calhoun went on to lambaste Polk's war leadership: "Has the avowed object of the war been attained? . . . Have we obtained a treaty? . . . No, sir. . . . We have for all our vast expenditure of money—for all the loss of blood, and men—we have nothing but the military glory which the campaign has furnished."

The Senate defeated Calhoun's resolution. But, with the Whigs feeling their oats, the House changed by 85 to 81 a resolution applauding General Taylor in order to complain that Polk had launched the Mexican War "unnecessarily and unconstitutionally." One member charged that in 1845, the President had sent John Slidell to Mexico "for the express purpose of 'kicking up a fight.'" The House demanded that Polk supply any documents illuminating Slidell's mission, as well as any secret maneuvering by the President to ensure Santa Anna's safe passage back to Mexico. Polk feared that releasing such papers, which recorded some of his naive attempts to influence the Mexicans, "would exhibit me in a ridiculous attitude." Buchanan warned him that if he obliged the House, no foreign official "would ever trust us again" to keep diplomatic conversations secret.

Polk thus withheld most of the archive, citing, as his "constitutional right," the doctrine of executive privilege. Outraged, John Quincy Adams, who had returned to the House after his single term as President, proclaimed, "This House ought now to assert, in the strongest manner, this right to call for information, and especially in such cases as those where questions of war and peace are depending."* Another Whig member, Ohio's Robert Schenck, asked, "Should it go abroad that all the power we have here, as the people's representatives, is to record the edicts of a master?" But Polk prevailed.

---

* Adams died two months later, after collapsing on the House floor.

* * *

IN JANUARY 1848, the President was shocked to be told by Buchanan that Trist—rather than come home, as ordered—was still in Mexico City, negotiating with the vanquished enemy. The new Mexican President, Pedro María de Anaya, had implored Trist, even though he now lacked official status, to bargain with him anyway. James Freaner of New Orleans, a journalist friend, had told the American clerk, "Make the treaty, sir! It is now in your power to do your country a greater service than any living man can render her." Straightening his spine, Trist agreed: "I *will* make the treaty."

Polk speculated that Trist had absorbed General Scott's "hatred" of him and was "lending himself to all Scott's evil purposes." The President believed that Scott, with his "vanity and tyrannical temper," was angry at him, in part because the old General had not been portrayed as "the exclusive hero of the war." He feared that Trist would "greatly embarrass the Government." Confirming Polk's suspicions, Secretary of State Buchanan received a long letter from Trist, denouncing the President's supposed intention to conquer all of Mexico; Trist added that Polk lacked "infallibility of judgment."* The President told his diary that Trist's letter was "contemptably base," as well as "arrogant, impudent" and "personally offensive," adding that he had "never in my life felt so indignant." Polk appointed General William Butler to replace Scott as commander of US soldiers in Mexico City and to seek a peace treaty with the Mexicans.

But by the time Polk's directive reached Mexico City, Trist had already concluded a treaty. To keep one step ahead of the sheriff, he had warned the Mexicans that they had to settle by the end of January.

---

* Trist also attacked General Gideon Pillow, a longtime Tennessee political ally of Polk's who had been wounded in Mexico, blaming Pillow for the fact that the President saw everything "upside down." Eager to turn Polk against Pillow, who was a rival of General Scott's, Trist claimed that Pillow was representing himself as "the *maker* of the President (by having procured his nomination at the Baltimore convention), and as the President's *other self*—a pretension which I have reason to believe but too well founded."

The formal documents were signed at the town of Guadalupe Hidalgo. They directed that the Texas boundary be the Rio Grande, and that the border between El Paso and the Pacific be settled by a joint commission. New Mexico and the part of California that was north of this boundary would be ceded to the United States for $15 million, and Mexico would be paid for its outstanding claims up to about $5 million. Trist had fulfilled almost all of his instructions, even wangling a bargain price for the territories. With his disdain for convention, he gave a signed copy of the agreement to the journalist Freaner, who took it to Washington.

On Saturday evening, February 19, Buchanan brought Trist's compact to Polk at the Executive Mansion. The President later told his diary that Trist had "acted very badly" but that the treaty "should not be rejected on account of his bad conduct." On Sunday evening, he assembled his Cabinet to secure its support for the settlement. To Polk's fury, the self-seeking Buchanan, who had once opposed his efforts for territorial expansion, now insisted that they go back to the Mexicans and demand even more land. Polk berated his Secretary of State for his "total change of opinion." But with his pledge to serve only one term, Polk was a lame duck, and Buchanan, who aspired to be President, clearly felt there was little penalty for opposing his chief now. In the presence of Polk and his stunned Cabinet colleagues, he now criticized Polk for overruling his advice against waging the battle for Mexico City, which had "spent much money and lost much blood."

Polk later told his diary, "No candidate for the presidency ought ever to remain in the Cabinet. He is an unsafe adviser." He wrote that Buchanan's motive was "to throw the whole responsibility on me of sending the Treaty to the Senate. If it was received well by the country, being a member of my administration, he would not be injured by it in his presidential aspirations, for these govern all his opinions & acts lately; but if, on the other hand, it should not be received well, he could say, 'I advised against it.'" Polk presumed that Buchanan was also incensed that Trist, a mere clerk, had stolen the honor of making peace, which the Secretary of State had planned to achieve himself.

On Monday at noon, overruling Buchanan, Polk told his Cabinet that he would send the treaty to the Senate for ratification, along with a caveat deleting a provision for Mexican land grants in the ceded territories. According to his journal, he cautioned the secretaries that if he should scrap the peace settlement, Congress would probably refuse to "grant either men or money to prosecute the war." If that occurred, "the Army now in Mexico would be constantly wasting and diminishing in numbers, and I might be at last compelled to withdraw them, and thus loose the two Provinces of New Mexico & Upper California." Polk emphasized the "immense value" of those provinces.

The petulant, disloyal Buchanan now tried to scotch the Mexican treaty by leaking a copy of it, as well as other confidential documents, to his close friend John Nugent of the *New York Herald,* who wrote under pseudonyms such as "Chee Wah-Wah." In a sensational report, now posing as "Galviensis," Nugent wrote that Polk's "infamous" treaty was full of "illegality and fraud," negotiated by a "prostrate" Mexican government through "tricks," adding that the President had enjoined his Cabinet "not to breathe a word" about it.*

When Polk read the *Herald* account, he angrily concluded that Buchanan was behind it. He told his diary that if the Secretary of State should be proven the source, he would fire him. Perhaps averring to the fact that Buchanan was widely thought in Washington to be gay, Senate investigators informed Polk that the Secretary of State was "in habits of intimacy" with Nugent, and that Senators had reported that they often had a difficult time getting in to see Buchanan "because this fellow, Nugent, was closetted with him." The President told his diary that his Secretary of State was "selfish" and "very weak," and that before now he had "overlooked" Buchanan's "weaknesses" for "the sake of the public good." Polk added that he was shocked that the Secretary would have "constant and intimate intercourse" with "so unprincipled a man" as Nugent; he feared that Buchanan "has placed himself in his power."

During a showdown between Polk and his Secretary of State, Buchanan denied leaking to Nugent and complained of a conspiracy of

---

* Chee Wah-Wah was a bastardization of the Mexican city of Chihuahua.

"certain Senators" to embarrass him. Buchanan claimed that he had be-friended Nugent only to win the *Herald*'s support for the President and the war. Tartly Polk replied that given the "infamous" Nugent's eager-ness "to calumniate and abuse me," Buchanan's friend had a singular way of "giving the support of the *Herald* to my administration."

The *Milwaukee Sentinel*, a Democratic paper, welcomed the prospect of a Mexican treaty: "GOOD NEWS! GREAT NEWS! Peace upon almost any terms will be joyfully welcomed by the American People. They have long since tired of the war." The *New-York Tribune*, published by Hor-ace Greeley, a Whig, agreed: "The country demands peace now, for it is sick to nausia of this miserable war and its more miserable authors." The *Trenton State Gazette*, a Whig journal, sputtered, "These terms of peace—so humiliating to the war-men—involving so mortifying an abandonment of all the lofty pronunciamentos with which they began and carried on the war—this mercenary buying off of a contemptible and defeated enemy—this paying them for peace, is the disgraceful con-clusion of this unnecessary war."

On February 23, Polk sent the proposed treaty, including his caveat, to the Senate. Fifteen Whigs proposed an amendment that would hand all conquered territory west of Texas back to Mexico. Dismissing the treaty, Daniel Webster sniffed, "Not worth a dollar." Stupefied by such myopia, Polk told his diary that the treaty would bring the United States "an immense empire, the value of which 20 years hence it would be dif-ficult to calculate." Eleven Senate Democrats suggested that four Mexi-can provinces be added to the land ceded to the United States under the compact. After a two-week debate, the Senate ratified Polk's treaty and caveat by 38 to 14, with the negatives precisely divided between Democrats and Whigs. The Mexican War had seen 1,733 Americans killed in combat, 11,550 others who died—mainly of disease—and 4,152 wounded. The Mexicans suffered perhaps 5,000 battle deaths.

* * *

AFTER THE MEXICANS told American diplomats, at Queré-taro, that they would accept the caveat, Polk planned to sign the finished treaty on July 4, 1848. His timing was intentional: he considered his acquisition of more than nine hundred thousand square miles of land, all the way to the Pacific, to be almost as important a gift to his country as the Declaration of Independence. Adding to the historical significance of the day, he would also cement the cornerstone of the unfinished Washington Monument.

On a brilliant summer morning, escorted by the cavalry and other troops "waving plumes, bristling arms and floating banners," the Commander-in-Chief and Sarah mounted a platform near the stump of an obelisk (the monument was not completed until 1884), accompanied by the still-vibrant, eighty-year-old Dolley Madison, revered for supporting her husband through the War of 1812. Dolley's smiling presence seemed to bless the conflict that Polk had just concluded and the annexation of land with which he had settled it.* This day's celebration was the final scene of Polk's war. "Wherever you cast your eye," reported the Polk-friendly *Union,* "you were arrested by the appearance of some distinguished man in civil or in military life; and many of the last from the late glorious battlefields in Mexico." The crowd included Congressmen Abraham Lincoln of Illinois and Andrew Johnson of Tennessee.

Donning the gloves and apron of his fellow Mason, George Washington, Polk dipped the first President's Masonic trowel into mortar and spread it around the edges of a large marble block. Inside it was a zinc-lined case containing a copy of the Constitution, a proud description of the telegraph, and a silk Lone Star banner from Texas, woven by "the ladies of Galveston" and provided by Senator Sam Houston. Rising to offer the day's main oration, the Speaker of the House, Robert Winthrop of Massachusetts, a Whig who had supported Polk's war, obliquely reminded the crowd of the dangerous issue of slavery. The vast territorial expansion, he warned, would produce "many marked and

---

* Mrs. Madison had moved into the house on Lafayette Square after her ne'er-do-well son Payne had taken financial risks and lost the family's Montpelier estate. Congress had bailed Dolley out by paying $25,000 for her husband's papers. Sarah Polk invited her for carriage rides, as well as entertainments at the Executive Mansion.

mourned centrifugal tendencies"; therefore the Washington Monument must, in the future, serve as "an emblem of perpetual Union."

An hour before midnight, in the East Room of the White House, with many witnesses, Polk signed the Treaty of Guadalupe Hidalgo. In a written message, he assured Congress that the Mexican War had endowed the United States with "a national character abroad which our country never before enjoyed." But Polk had paid his own price. The tense-lipped President had not confided to outsiders how much the years of war had damaged his health. In his diary, he repeatedly wrote of his "great labour & anxiety" and that he was "exceedingly fatigued."

∗ ∗ ∗

IN RETROSPECT, POLK deserves credit for adding almost a million square miles to the United States, making it, once and for all, a truly continental nation. But his repeated corner-cutting—and his awareness that he would have only one term as President in which to achieve his aims—kept him from making a serious, extended effort to discover whether the new lands might be obtained without a major, bloody war, which should have been his last resort.

Just a half century into the life of the American Republic, Polk had crushed the Founders' hope that their gleaming new country would not indulge in the Old World monarchs' habit of manufacturing false pretexts for wars that they sought for other, more secret reasons. Presuming that Polk was involved with the Stockton adventure of 1845, the first effort to invent a predicate for a Mexican war failed, but the second—sending General Taylor to the Rio Grande—achieved its intended goal. It allowed the President to persuade Congress and the American people to back a war that was supposed to be largely in retaliation for Seth Thornton's border skirmish but, in fact, was a device for Polk to secure Texas, New Mexico, and California. In the absence of the Thornton affair, Polk would have been forced to ask Congress for a war declaration in response to a list of Mexican provocations that it might have found far more abstract than it had found Madison's list of British offenses to be in 1812—and Polk might not have obtained his war.

Instead, riding the crest of public outrage against the attack at Rancho Carricitos, Polk deceived Congress by asking for a conflict supposedly intended to avenge the assault and compel the Mexicans to repay outstanding debts. It does not seem to have occurred to him to have candidly informed the members that one of his war aims was acquiring California and New Mexico, which might require a long and costly war—even though, in the militant atmosphere of the moment, they might not have refused him. Didn't the Americans he was sending to Mexico deserve to know what they would be dying for?

As a result of Polk's obfuscation, he later had to cope with the fury of Americans who demanded to know why the war was taking so long and why he had expanded its objectives without specific congressional authorization. In response to this public anger, members of Congress too often behaved like Polk's lapdogs—despite the opposition of Clay, Webster, and other prominent Whigs. By letting Polk get away with his obfuscations, they sent an unintended message to later Presidents that when they asked the House and Senate for war, those Commanders-in-Chief could be duplicitous too.

Polk's compulsive secrecy violated the open, democratic tradition that the Founders had tried to encourage. He loved not only secret war aims but secret agents (Slidell, Atocha, Stockton, Mackenzie, Trist) and secret documents, which he concealed by asserting executive privilege against members of Congress who were afraid to risk being called unpatriotic. When Polk lied to Congress with his ludicrous claim that he had neither "desired nor provoked" the Mexican War and waged it with no "view to conquest," his mendacity compromised his moral stature and established another bad example for later Presidents. Polk also echoed Madison's tendency to marginalize opponents of his war as unpatriotic, although the Founders had exalted the role of criticism in a democracy. Benjamin Franklin had advised his contemporaries in 1756 to "Love your Enemies, for they tell you your Faults."

Throughout his time in office, Polk showed himself virtually indifferent to the central moral issue of his time. At best, he hoped that

Congress could keep papering over the issue of slavery, writing in his diary that an open clash "would be attended with terrible consequences to the country and cannot fail to destroy the Democratic Party, if it does not ultimately destroy the country." Polk the slaveholder knew that his vast territorial expansion might make it safer for slavery to survive. His actions aggravated the national struggle over the issue, making that struggle more bitter and violent when it erupted into war twelve years after he left office.

* * *

IN NOVEMBER 1848, Zachary Taylor, running as a Whig, was elected President, over former Senator Lewis Cass of Michigan.* With few notable qualifications beyond his triumphs at Palo Alto and Monterrey, the General won because of the popularity of Polk the Democrat's war. The following March, during their carriage ride up Capitol Hill for the inaugural, Taylor still resented how Polk had sought to deny him credit for the Mexican success. He jolted his predecessor by musing aloud that perhaps he should try to block California and New Mexico from becoming states of the Union, since their physical distance from Washington might make them difficult to govern.

When Polk, spent from his years at war, walked out onto the Capitol steps, one witness could scarcely recognize "the broken down old man, with thin white hair hanging from his brow." Rather than head straight home to Nashville, the ex-President treated himself and Sarah to a nine-state victory trip, by rail, stagecoach, and steamer, absorbing the accolades of the South, source of his most loyal support. After a cold rain in Macon, Georgia, Polk, "greatly fatigued and quite unwell," displayed a "violent cold and cough." Then he and Sarah boarded the steamboat *Emperor*, bound from Mobile to New Orleans, although both cities were overcome by cholera epidemics. Polk explained in his diary that he was "too far on my journey to change my route" and did not wish to "act

---

* Taylor won 47.3 percent of the popular vote, with 42.5 for Cass, and 10.1 for ex-President Martin Van Buren, nominee of the abolitionist Free Soil Party.

rudely." Truth be told, he did not want his "triumphal march" to stop: "The cordial welcome which has been extended to me by thousands of my fellow-citizens, without distinction of political party, far exceeds anything I had anticipated."

Four fellow passengers on the steamer *Caroline E. Watkins* succumbed to cholera. Feeling severe pain in his abdomen, Polk canceled visits to Natchez and Vicksburg to avoid more exposure to disease. Near collapse, Polk staggered off the vessel at Smithland, Kentucky, and spent four days under the care of Sarah's brother-in-law, a physician. After a week with his aged mother in Columbia, Tennessee, Polk traveled with his wife to their new home, Polk Place, in Nashville. In the final entry of his diary, Polk wrote that he was "arranging my library of books."

By then, the former President was feeling so sick that a Presbyterian cleric was summoned. Trembling from severe fever and diarrhea, the sinking Polk told him, "I am about to die, and have not made preparation. I have not even been baptized. Tell me, sir, can there be any ground for a man thus situated to hope?" At the last moment, he had himself christened by a local Methodist minister. On June 15, 1849, with his mother and wife kneeling at his bedside, the ex-President spoke his last words: "I love you, Sarah, for all eternity, I love you." At his wife's behest, he was buried at Polk Place, with a copy of the Constitution at the foot of his coffin.

After Polk died, President Taylor did not trouble himself to make any public comment. "This silence speaks of Gen. Taylor's want of common courtesy—aye, his want of a *heart*," complained the *Vermont Gazette*. Some abolitionist journals lauded Polk's demise. "The memory of the wicked shall rot," said one paper in Herkimer, New York. In Boston, William Lloyd Garrison's *Liberator* recalled that Polk had "left his slaves in their chains" and committed "the horrors and atrocities of the Mexican war." One reader noted that Polk, with "criminal disregard of national law," had usurped Congress's constitutional responsibility to make war: "And did Congress impeach and try the usurper? No. The members, with a few HONORABLE exceptions, became accomplices by a vote of men and money. . . . To kill, without authority, is murder. The sentence, death." Later that year, William Jay, a New York abolitionist and son of the Founder John Jay, published a widely read pamphlet charging that the Mexican War had been a conspiracy intended to expand the slave territory of the United States: "Not only Texas, but all New Mexico, will for a long period be doomed to the ignorance, degradation, and misery, which are inseparable from human bondage."

Then came California's Gold Rush. Flakes of the precious metal had been discovered at Sutter's Mill. With tens of thousands of Americans flooding the West in quest of wealth, Polk's efforts to acquire California gained new respect. But as the 1850s unfolded, amid the growing national conflict over slavery, Polk—the last President for whom slavery was not the paramount, obsessive national issue—seemed to shrivel into a minor historical figure, more distant in time than he actually was.

Sarah Polk was outraged that Americans could forget her James so rapidly. During the Civil War, citing his commitment to the Union, she pronounced herself neutral, which later helped to protect her from recriminations when Nashville fell to the North. During her decades as a widow, when Sarah ventured out from Polk Place, she wore black. On her parlor mantelpiece, under a framed copy of her husband's inaugural address, she proudly displayed a California gold nugget. After Sarah died in 1891, she and James were buried on the Tennessee state capitol grounds, in a tomb adorned with the boast that Polk had "planted laws of the American union on the shores of the Pacific."*

* * *

WHEN ABRAHAM LINCOLN ran for President as a Republican in 1860, some Democratic journals castigated him for his opposition, while in Congress, to the way that Polk had made war. The *Constitution* of Washington, DC, accused him of having taken sides "against his own country" with an "unpatriotic and anti-American speech." The *New Hampshire Patriot* charged that Lincoln "did more to embarrass his own country and to encourage the Mexicans to a desperate and bloody resistance than he could have done by voting against

---

* Polk Place briefly served as the Tennessee Governor's Mansion before it was razed in 1900.

furnishing supplies to our troops." (Lincoln replied by noting that he had never voted against money or supplies for the soldiers fighting in Mexico.)

In delivering that scorching attack of 1848 on a sitting President, the intensely ambitious young Congressman Lincoln had acted in part out of self-interest. At the time, he conceded to William Herndon, his Springfield law partner, that he had been eager to "distinguish" himself on the national stage. But his emotions about Polk and Mexico were genuine and deep. A few weeks after his speech on the House floor, Lincoln was profoundly moved to hear another Whig Congressman denounce Polk's war as blatant aggression, devised to "force and compel" the Mexicans to sell their country. "My old, withered, dry eyes," Lincoln wrote his colleague, "are full of tears yet." (His colleague was Alexander Stephens of Georgia, who, in the early 1860s, would become Vice President of the Confederacy.) Lincoln was also disgusted by Polk's partisan "rascality," which, he believed, had driven him to distort military strategy and military appointments to benefit the Democrats. In 1848, Lincoln even deprecated the goal of territorial expansion, assuring a crowd in Worcester, Massachusetts, that it was better to keep "our fences where they are and cultivating our present possession, making it a garden, improving the morals and education of the people."

When Billy Herndon, that same year, questioned his friend about his antiwar zeal, Lincoln replied that if Americans should "allow the president to invade a neighboring nation whenever *he* shall deem it necessary to repel an invasion . . . you allow him to make war at pleasure." Evincing his close reading of constitutional law, Lincoln explained that the Philadelphia convention of 1787 had assigned the war-making power to Congress because "kings had always been involving and impoverishing their people in wars, pretending generally, if not always, that the good of the people was the object." The Founders, he wrote, had decided "that *no one man* should hold the power of bringing this oppression upon us."

CHAPTER SIX

Fort Sumter

IN NOVEMBER 1860, forced onto the knife's edge between North and South, the newly installed Union commander in Charleston, South Carolina, was enduring a dark night of the soul. A Southerner to his viscera, Major Robert Anderson had been sworn to protect the Union and federal property, including this fortress. But local citizens were changing their allegiance to Anderson's old friend, Senator Jefferson Davis of Mississippi, who would soon be president of the Confederate States of America. Anderson wrote another friend, "God grant that our blessed land may not be bathed in blood. The fanaticism, the madness and folly of man are being exerted to ruin and disgrace our people."

Fifty-five years old, with intense hazel eyes, Anderson was bookish, fragile, and sensitive. While crouching under enemy fire during the Mexican War, he scrawled to his much younger wife, Eba, "I just this moment hear a mocking-bird warbling his sweet notes." He wrote her of how much he detested "killing each other to find out who is in the right," adding, "This will, I hope, be the last war I shall take an active part in." He was also rich. Largely from his marriage to Eba, his net worth was about $300,000 (perhaps about $7 million today).* And he was highly intelligent, having graduated fifth out of thirty-seven in his West Point Class of 1825.

Anderson enjoyed family ties to many eminent Americans. His father had fought under General Washington and served as aide-de-camp to Lafayette before moving his family (Robert was the eighth of sixteen children) from Virginia to Kentucky.† Visitors to the family's Louisville plantation, called Soldiers' Retreat, included Henry Clay, James Monroe, and Andrew Jackson. At Robert's grand New York City wedding to Eba, the bride was given away by General Winfield Scott, whom Anderson had once served, calling him "my best friend." As a West Point field artillery instructor, Anderson had taught cadets who would one day fight on both sides of the Civil War (among them were Generals William Sherman, George Meade, Joseph Hooker, Jubal Early, and P. G. T. Beauregard).

But he was a casualty of the Mexican War. While fighting his way to Mexico City, he was wounded five times, once almost fatally, and had a musket ball lodged in his right shoulder. Combined with the lingering impact of dysentery and an old case of malaria (contracted when embattled in Florida's Seminole Wars), his body and emotional life were damaged. Daguerreotypes taken of him after the Mexican War show a soldier mournful, shaken, and haunted.

As a modest Southern gentleman, Anderson once said he would rather "cut my tongue out" than push himself forward for Army promotions. But by the late 1850s, he was so bored by his assignment—inspecting government ironwork—that he daydreamed about life as an Iowa farmer and almost quit the Army, writing Eba that when future history was written, "I fancy we shall not have much ink wasted on us."

---

* Her Army father, Duncan Lamont Clinch, who served for a year as a Whig Congressman, was laird of a substantial Georgia plantation. Eba was an invalid, suffering from vaguely diagnosed maladies that may have included neurasthenia. For much of their marriage, while Robert moved to various Army posts, she stayed with their five children in New York's palatial Brevoort House on Fifth Avenue.

† Anderson's relatives included Chief Justice John Marshall and the brothers William Clark, who joined Meriwether Lewis to explore the Northwest for President Jefferson, and George Rogers Clark, who conquered the Northwest Territory.

Then, in 1860, General Winfield Scott, who treated Anderson like a son, recommended him for the Sumter command. He could have no more powerful champion. In 1852, the Whigs had run Scott for President against Franklin Pierce, who defeated him. By now, the seventy-four-year-old Scott was the top professional military officer in the United States, the only soldier since George Washington to be honored with the brevet rank of Lieutenant General. Born in Virginia, Scott now argued that, like himself, Anderson hailed from a slave state and could use "his rich voice and abundant gesticulations" to persuade the Charleston locals to accept the federal presence there. And in case reconciliation proved impossible, the old General wanted his own man in the eye of the maelstrom.[*]

That November, Abraham Lincoln was elected President without a single electoral vote from a Southern or border state. General Scott had predicted to President James Buchanan that if the winner should be Lincoln, the known enemy of slavery, seven Southern states would leave the Union. When Republicans had nominated the little-known lawyer at Chicago's Wigwam the previous May, they recalled his stirring opposition to both slavery and disunion through seven Senatorial debates of 1858 against the "Little Giant," Illinois Senator Stephen A. Douglas. At the core of their new, six-year-old party were Northern abolitionists incensed by the Kansas-Nebraska Act of 1854 and the Supreme Court's *Dred Scott* decision of 1857, which held that African Americans could not be treated as citizens and Congress could not limit the spread of slavery.[†] Congressman William Boyce of Charleston bellowed that if Republicans took the White House, "the question of negro equality is settled against us, and emancipation only a question of time," allowing South Carolina "no choice but to immediately withdraw from the Union."

---

[*] Whoever commanded Sumter would have to be quick on his feet, because in those days, orders from the War Department were sent in sealed US Mail bags that took days to arrive.

[†] Citing the alleged boast of at least one Southern leader, the disgusted New York Governor William Seward warned that the *Dred Scott* ruling would let slave masters call the roll of their slaves while standing at such sacred revolutionary landmarks as Bunker Hill, Concord, and Lexington.

Now, after Lincoln's victory, secessionism was raging through the South. Before Anderson assumed command in Charleston, he called on President James Buchanan's Secretary of War, John Floyd of Virginia, who warned him that Charleston was combustible and he must do nothing to create a spark. Devoutly religious, Anderson took with utmost gravity his oath to defend the federal Union. He had not cast a ballot in the presidential contest of 1860, nor, in the style of other Army officers who wished to show their respect for civilian authority, ever in his life. (One nephew recalled that "few men ever lived who came so near to having no political opinions.") Still both Anderson and Eba had owned slaves themselves, which had been key to their joint wealth.* One of Anderson's colleagues thought he felt "hatred and contempt for the people of the North and East." Sharpening the Major's agony was his long friendship with Jefferson Davis, dating back to West Point and the Black Hawk War of 1832, when Colonel Zachary Taylor assigned both Anderson and Davis to escort Chief Black Hawk to jail after his capture.†

In seething Charleston, Anderson's new duties included the virtually unoccupied Fort Sumter, as well as Castle Pinckney and Fort Moultrie. He took up residence with the garrison that was now his at Moultrie, which was on land, looking toward Sumter, which sat on its own artificial island in Charleston Harbor. Locals were threatening to shoot from the high dunes down at the vulnerable Moultrie and the garrison stationed there, which Anderson found "so weak as to invite an attack." He warned Washington that "the storm may break upon us at any moment," and asked for more garrisons, to be stationed at Castle Pinckney and Sumter, "the key to the entrance of this harbor," both of which, if seized by a secessionist mob or militia, could be used to bombard Moultrie.

Anderson advised his superiors to hurry. South Carolina's legislature had called a special session for December, after which the Palmetto State

---

* Anderson once recorded that Eba was growing richer because of "the increase of her darkies," but by 1860 they had both sold their slaves.

† The Black Hawk War was fought against the famous Sauk chief and his native American allies over the rich lands east of the Mississippi.

would probably become the first to depart the Union. He reported that after secession, the newly independent state would most likely demand that the federal government vacate Moultrie, Pinckney, and Sumter at once, and if this were not done, it could "cause some of the doubting states to join South Carolina." Personally, Anderson regarded secession as a "sin." He told his men that the fate of their country was at stake: "If we divide our Union once, then we can divide it a thousand times."

✳ ✳ ✳

Lincoln would not be sworn in until March, so the choice of holding on or letting go of Sumter and the other federal installations in Charleston fell to President Buchanan, who, alas, was no less opportunistic than he had been while Polk's Secretary of State. Old Buck, as the sixty-nine-year-old Buchanan was now called, wished to shirk the decision and let others take the blame for whatever then transpired.

On December 3, he told Congress that federal "property" should be retained, but that the House and Senate should decide exactly how. (Ironically, if Congress approved Buchanan's proposal, one of those ruling on how the seceded states should be stopped from snatching federal military bases would be Jefferson Davis, who had not yet resigned as chairman of the Senate's Committee on Military Affairs.) Buchanan obtained what he deemed an assurance from South Carolina's Governor, William Henry Gist, that so long as there were no reinforcements, Sumter and the other two federal sites in Charleston would be left alone. Furious at Buchanan's failure to act more decisively, his Secretary of State, Lewis Cass, resigned.

Early that same month, Eba Anderson paid what she found to be a "painful" call on the President, conveying her anxieties that her husband, as an emblem of the federal government, might be attacked or killed by a Charleston mob. Buchanan quietly sent a War Department officer, Don Carlos Buell, to the city, with orders to put nothing in writing: Buell should quietly tell Anderson to do whatever was necessary to keep federal control of the forts and "defend yourself to the last extremity." Disinclined to take the blame for whatever violence occurred, Buell flouted his instructions and recorded Buchanan's message in a memorandum, which he gave to Anderson; he kindly advised the Major that he "ought to have written evidence" of direction from above. Touring the three forts, Buell concluded that while Moultrie could be easily assaulted from behind, Sumter looked almost impregnable. He offered Anderson his "personal advice" to move his garrison to Sumter.

When Buchanan saw a copy of the document that Buell had given to Anderson, he blanched at the words "to the last extremity" and forced Secretary Floyd to write the Major that if he should be "attacked by a force so superior that resistance would, in your judgment, be a useless waste of life, it will be your duty to yield to necessity, and make the best terms in your power." Anderson was told not to share Floyd's mild new directive with anyone. Disgusted by Buchanan's flip-flopping, although accustomed to it from the many times they had butted heads during the Mexican War, Winfield Scott implored the President to strengthen the federal presence at nine forts in the South, including Moultrie. In response, Buchanan foolishly assured him that no other state was likely to follow South Carolina out of the Union.

On the evening of December 20, after their state proclaimed itself an "Independent Commonwealth," delirious Charlestonians got drunk, lit bonfires, fired off rockets, and hung out a sign that said "THE WORLD WANTS IT." With eerie timing, Ralph Farnham, the last known survivor of the Revolutionary War's Battle of Bunker Hill, died a few days later in Acton, Maine, at the age of 104. Heartsick over the impending national rupture, an Indiana poet called Sarah Bolton imagined Farnham delivering a final, piteous monologue, after hearing of South Carolina's apostasy:

> Do they talk of dissolving the Union? . . .
> Well may the old man tremble, and his heart beat faint and low,
> When he thinks of the price it cost us some four score years ago! . . .
> If God has forsaken our country, the only boon I crave
> Is that he will delay its ruin till I have gone down to my grave;

For I could not breathe with traitors, nor turn my face to the sun,
Nor dwell in the land of the living, when the States are no
longer one.

With Charleston's fever soaring, Robert Anderson decided to move his garrison from the vulnerable Moultrie to Fort Sumter. Named for a revolutionary General, Thomas Sumter of South Carolina, the still-uncompleted fort was a severe brick pentagon, perched on a two-and-a-half-acre, human-made island created from 2,423,250 blocks, hewn partly by slave labor. Sumter's strongest side was the one facing the Atlantic, because its architects presumed that any hostile fire would come from the sea—certainly not from the city of Charleston!

Under a faint moon on the evening after Christmas, Anderson, holding a folded thirty-three-star flag, quietly sailed with the men of Companies E and H, as well as some wives and children, across the water to the fortress. When they arrived, the Major lit a candle and wrote Eba that he was safe. Unsettled by the change, South Carolina's bombastic new Governor, Francis Pickens, sent two aides to see Anderson, threatening violence. Anderson informed them that he had made his move to avoid a confrontation. He said, "My sympathies are entirely with the South," and that he believed that any sectional problems had been "brought on by the faithlessness of the North." But he refused the Governor's demand to return his men to Moultrie: "I cannot and will not go back." After Pickens's men departed, Anderson raised the American flag over Sumter, on a flagstaff ten stories high, dropping to his knees while "The Star-Spangled Banner" was played and his men shouted, *"Huzzah! Huzzah!"*

In Washington, when Jefferson Davis heard of what he termed the "calamity" at Sumter, he marched, angry, into Buchanan's upstairs office at the Executive Mansion and told him he was surrounded by "blood and dishonor." Dropping his tall, plumpish frame into a chair, the haggard, sleep-deprived President claimed that Major Anderson had violated his orders. After Davis was gone, Buchanan's new Secretary of State, Jeremiah Black, warned the President that he too would resign—after only twelve days in office—unless Buchanan stood up to South Carolina. Behaving, as usual, like a weather vane, Buchanan agreed to sign a defiant statement, drafted by Black, refusing South Carolina's demand to pull the federal garrison from Fort Sumter ("This I cannot do; this I will not do"). Then Palmetto State emissaries came to the White House and warned the President, "You have probably rendered civil war inevitable."

* * *

WHILE OLD BUCK was whining over his troubles, Abraham Lincoln boarded a special train at the Great Western station in Springfield, Illinois, on February 11, 1861. He had told a crowd of neighbors that he would take up a task "greater than that which has devolved upon any other man since the days of Washington," not knowing "whether ever, I may return." During his twelve-day trip, stopping at Cleveland, Buffalo, New York, Philadelphia, and dozens of other towns and cities, Lincoln generally avoided making a specific response to the secession of Southern states (seven at the start of February) and threats against Fort Sumter.

An exception was Indianapolis. Speaking from an upper floor at the Bates House to twenty thousand Hoosiers, the President-elect asked whether it would be coercion if the federal government "simply insists upon holding its own forts, or retaking those forts which belong to it." Anyone who thought that way, he said, must consider the Union to be nothing "like a regular marriage at all, but only as a sort of free-love arrangement." How could "one fiftieth or one nineteenth of a great nation, by calling themselves a state, have the right to break up and ruin that nation as a matter of original principle?" With even this lawyerly challenge, Lincoln proved to be provocative. As the *Baltimore Sun* reported, many Americans found his statement "a declaration of war against the South." In retaliation, some Southerners who had not yet resigned from Congress threatened to bring the legislature to a halt. Kentucky's *Louisville Daily Journal* warned that the incoming President was "sporting with fireballs in a powder magazine."

When Lincoln and his family reached New York City, on February 19, Mayor Fernando Wood told the President-elect, at an Astor

House reception, that New Yorkers were "deeply interested" in the secession crisis because "we fear that if the Union dies, the present superiority of New York may perish with it."* The *New York Herald* reported that the unruly crowd, with "hair disheveled, clothes awry, faces grim and sweaty and bulging eyes," surged forward to meet Lincoln. People cried, "Keep off my toes, God damn you!" and "Make room for this lady!" The *Herald* tactfully noted that "toilettes were anything but complete." When a Charleston visitor extended his hand, Mayor Wood anxiously told Lincoln he hoped a handshake would not be "beyond the pale." Lincoln chuckled, "I will shake hands with South Carolinians if they will shake hands with me!"

That evening, under guard by twenty policemen, Lincoln attended the opera.† For security's sake, he was slipped into his box, at the Academy of Music, after the overture. In the near dark, New Yorkers swiveled their heads and pointed up at what someone described as the "plain black cravat, the next shirt collar turned over the neckcloth, the incipient whiskers, and good humored face." An ovation built. Gentlemen and ladies rose ("Jump up! Jump up!") to cheer the President-elect, waving hats and handkerchiefs. Lincoln took a faint bow, then, as the acclaim grew louder, stood up, towering above the others in his box. When the orchestra played "The Star-Spangled Banner," the audience sang along and a large American flag was unfurled from the proscenium. The night's opera was a lugubrious choice for a leader taking power against the backdrop of impending national violence—Verdi's *Un ballo in maschera,* about the assassination of Sweden's King Gustav III by a conspiracy.

As the President-elect reboarded his railroad car, he was told about a plot to kill him when he changed trains in Baltimore, known as a "Mobtown" of Confederate sympathizers, thugs, and rampaging political murderers like the Blood Tubs and the Plug-Uglies. Keeping a

---

* Soft on the rebels, Wood had already proposed that New York City itself consider secession, becoming a "free city," in order to protect its commerce with the South.

† One New Yorker presumed that Lincoln had clearly never before had such an "excellent opportunity" to see such "wealth, intelligence and respectability." When a similar slighting comment was made to Mary Lincoln, she fibbed that their Springfield life had "always" included such fancy scenes.

scheduled date to raise a new, thirty-four-star flag at Philadelphia's Independence Hall, he evinced his inner worries by insisting that he "would rather be assassinated on this spot" than surrender the Union.* The next day, on the train, Lincoln's young secretary John Hay found his boss "so unwell he could hardly be persuaded to show himself." Arriving at pro-Union Pennsylvania's capital of Harrisburg, Lincoln, in his upset mood, disrupted his effort to conceal his exact intentions toward the South: he reported that a military parade he just saw had heartened him about "what may be done when war is inevitable." Later that day, someone asked him how soon he would send boys into Dixie; another called out, "We will all go, if you want us!"

Convinced that he might be risking his own murder, Lincoln agreed to skip Baltimore and enter Washington in disguise, although one adviser warned it would be "a damned piece of cowardice." Wearing a frayed coat and wool cap, the President-elect looked, so one friend thought, like "a well-to-do farmer," as he stepped off the train in the Capital, on February 23, with two bodyguards, Allan Pinkerton and Ward Hill Lamon. Unfortunately, the swaggering, hard-drinking, self-inflating Lamon, who had been one of Lincoln's temporary law partners during his circuit rides (usually armed with gun and knife, he once joked to Lincoln, "I might not be mighty in Counsel, but *might be useful in a fight*"), cabled the *Chicago Journal* about his chief's costumed arrival and his own role in the scheme.

Soon appeared an embarrassing cartoon of a timorous Lincoln, clad in military cloak and Scotch plaid beret. The *New York World* wondered why the President-elect would "blench at the first show of danger." The *Cincinnati Enquirer* called him "more than coward." Lincoln's supporter Congressman Samuel Curtis of Iowa called it "humiliating to have a President smuggled into the capital by night." "As if he were an absconding felon," observed another Lincoln man, Senator John Hale of New Hampshire. "Frightened at his own shadow," said someone else. When the President-elect's official train—bearing Mary Lincoln and her sons—finally rolled into Baltimore, his family was heckled with loud catcalls.

---

* The new flag reflected Kansas's admission to the Union in January 1861.

That same week, in Montgomery, Alabama, Jefferson Davis, having resigned from the US Senate, was installed as the provisional Confederate president. This slaveholder, champion of states' rights, and ex–Secretary of War (under Franklin Pierce) had been chosen by a congress of the by-now seven departed states (South Carolina, Mississippi, Florida, Alabama, Georgia, Louisiana, and Texas). After a gun salvo, Davis told his fellow secessionists, "If we must again baptize in blood the principles for which our fathers bled in the Revolution, we shall show that we are not degenerate sons, but will redeem the pledges they gave, preserve the sacred rights they transmitted to us, and show that Southern valor still shines as brightly as in 1776, 1812, and in every other conflict." He warned that his region would "make all who oppose us smell Southern powder and feel Southern steel."

Davis wrote Governor Pickens in Charleston, "We are probably soon to be involved in that fiercest of human strife, a civil war." He asked Pickens, in the meantime, not to demand the surrender of Major Anderson's troops at Fort Sumter: "The little garrison in its present position presses on nothing but a point of pride." Pickens replied that he hoped the federal soldiers would surrender peaceably, "but if not, blood must flow." He counseled Davis that "48 hours hot fire will do the work."

* * *

LODGED AT WILLARD'S Hotel on Pennsylvania Avenue, Lincoln received members of the "Peace Conference" chaired by former President John Tyler, now seventy. Derided as an "Old Gentleman's Convention," these were mainly retired officials from both North and South who were trying to find a compromise. They warned Lincoln that holding Fort Sumter was "but a barren honor," which would cost "thousands of lives." Lincoln retorted that "a state any day is worth more than a fort!" If Virginia would pledge to stay in the Union, "I will withdraw the troops from Fort Sumter." As Lincoln had expected, this proposal quickly vanished into the chamber's heavy cigar smoke. After the delegates left, he dismissed them as "Southern Pseudo-Unionists."

On March 4, 1861, under cloudy skies, the morose Buchanan arrived in his open barouche, at the front of Willard's, to pick up his successor. When the two men reached the Capitol, with its partially constructed new dome, John Hay studied the outgoing President, curious about "what momentous counsels were to come from that gray and weather-beaten head." He noticed that Lincoln had "that weary, introverted look of his, not answering." Buchanan was prating about the White House water supply, assuring his successor that the Mansion's right-hand well was more effective than that on the left.

The specter of Lincoln's possible assassination lingered. The *New York Times* ominously noted that some seven hundred men had arrived in Washington—"most of the worst characters of Baltimore and some places in Virginia," including "a large gang of 'Plug-Uglies,'" arousing "grave fears" about an attack "against Mr. Lincoln's person. . . . Strange to say, heavy bets are pending on the question of his safety." Five hundred special policemen, imported from other cities, joined a legion of volunteers, federal troops, and bodyguards in double strength, orchestrated by Winfield Scott to forestall any violent "surprise." Among the forty thousand spectators were people who said they had journeyed from "Varmount" or "Indianny," and "few Southerners, judging from the lack of long-haired men."

In his inaugural address, the new President acknowledged that he took office "under great and peculiar difficulty. A disruption of the Federal Union, heretofore only menaced, is now formidably attempted." He employed conciliation, constitutional argument, unvarnished threat, homely metaphor, and near-seduction to keep the South from pressing its cause to the point of civil war. He said that Southerners should not fear for "their peace and personal security," and renounced, for himself, any right or inclination to interfere with "slavery, in the States where it exists." As for the Fugitive Slave Act, "the intention of the lawgiver is the law." He pledged no bloodshed, "unless it be forced upon the national authority."

Nevertheless he insisted that "the Union of these States is perpetual" under the Constitution, and "no State upon its own mere motion can lawfully get out of the Union." (The crowd cheered almost every time Lincoln mentioned the Union.) Violent acts against the federal

government would be "insurrectionary or revolutionary." He warned
that "the power confided to me will be used to hold, occupy and possess
the property and places belonging to the Government"—an unmistakable reference to Fort Sumter. (Cries of "Thank God!" and "We'll stand
by you!")

Having drawn the line, Lincoln contended that North and South
had only one "substantial dispute": "One section of our country believes
slavery is *right* and ought to be extended, while the other believes it
is *wrong* and ought not to be extended." Physically, North and South
could not separate: "A husband and wife may be divorced . . . but the
different parts of our country cannot do this." If it tried, the South alone
would be to blame for the result: "In your hands, my dissatisfied fellow-
countrymen, and not in mine, is the momentous issue of civil war. . . .
You can have no conflict without being yourselves the aggressors."

Moving some in the crowd to tears, Lincoln closed, "We must not
be enemies. Though passion may have strained, it must not break our
bonds of affection. The mystic chords of memory, stretching from every
battlefield and patriot grave, to every living heart and hearthstone all
over this broad land, will yet swell the chorus of the Union, when again
touched, as surely they will be, by the better angels of our nature." By
the custom of the time, only then, after a booming ovation, was Lincoln
sworn in by the eighty-three-year-old Chief Justice, Roger Taney, after
which the new President bowed and kissed the Bible.

In Montgomery, successive takes of Lincoln's speech rattled out of
a telegraph machine. As Davis pursed his lips in cold anger, his provisional vice president, Alexander Stephens, cried, "The man is a fool!"*
From Washington, the two leaders received a cable sent by Senator
Louis Wigfall of Texas, exclaiming, "WAR WAR WAR." South Carolina's
Charleston Mercury rebuked Lincoln: "If ignorance could add anything
to folly, or insolence to brutality, the President of the Northern States of

---

* Stephens may have felt especially piqued because his old friend and colleague Lincoln had written him before Christmas, "Do the people of the South really entertain fears that a Republican
administration would, directly or indirectly, interfere with their slaves, or with them, about their
slaves?" He had assured the Georgian that "there is no cause for such fears."

America has, in this address, achieved it." The *Memphis Appeal* warned, "The Southern people do not fear, but despise the threats fulminated by this abolition despot." The *Richmond Dispatch:* "Every Border State ought to go out of the Union in 24 hours." The *Richmond Enquirer:* "Virginia must fight."* Still some who read Lincoln's words, such as Winfield Scott, thought the new President might be calling for a negotiated settlement between North and South.

* * *

A T THE WHITE House, on the day after his inauguration, Lincoln was handed a message from Major Anderson, who warned that his men at Fort Sumter would be out of food and supplies in just a few weeks.

Watching the rebels across the water, as his provisions disappeared, Anderson had written that he felt like "a sheep tied watching the butcher sharpening a knife to cut his throat." Eager to resupply Fort Sumter without provoking the South, General Scott ordered the charter of a private double-decked steamer, the *Star of the West,* and had it loaded with soldiers, small arms, vegetables, and newly slaughtered beef. The *Star's* captain, John McGowan, took the reinforcements to the mouth of Charleston Harbor under cover of darkness, but someone gave word of the mission to the press, and rebel artillery was waiting for him. Signal flares were sent up by a Confederate steamer called the *General Clinch* (named, improbably enough, for Eba Anderson's father). Then, after a warning volley, a nineteen-year-old cadet named Tuck Haynsworth tugged the lanyard of his cannon, launching what was called the first shot fired in anger in the momentous confrontation between North and South. The *Star* was struck by three rounds, and the unnerved McGowan hightailed his ship back to New York.

---

* The *Chicago Times,* a Democratic paper but no Southern mouthpiece, charged that Lincoln had pushed Dixie to the abyss: if the new President fulfilled his "loose, disjointed, rambling" address, "there must be civil war within thirty days, or the Southern people are a set of arrant braggarts and cowards."

In his dispatch to President Lincoln, Anderson said he now saw no serious alternative to surrendering the fort. The Major added that he had asked his officers how large a force would be required to relieve the garrison, and the estimates ranged up to twenty thousand soldiers, backed by a US Navy armada. Lincoln found Anderson's report so pessimistic that he asked the Acting Secretary of War, Joseph Holt, a Buchanan holdover, whether Anderson, in light of his Southern allegiances, could be trusted to provide an accurate portrait of the Sumter problem. Holt weakly replied that he could think of no reason to doubt Anderson.

Lincoln's query was not casual. After the assault on the *Star of the West,* Anderson's second in command, Captain Abner Doubleday, had complained about the Major's gloominess in a letter to his wife, Mary.* He also wondered why Anderson had not responded in kind when the *Star* had been fired upon. Doubleday's Republican brother, Ulysses, had sent a copy of Abner's letter to Lincoln before the latter departed Springfield, along with a scrawled warning: "Depend upon it, Maj. A's heart is not with his duty." Now the President startled Mrs. Doubleday by coming to see her in Washington. Behaving as if he were still a private attorney, he asked her to show him any other letters from Abner that might illuminate Anderson's character. General Scott later vouched for his old protégé, and Lincoln swallowed his doubts about the Major's fealty to the Union.

Affected by Anderson's grim warning, Scott told the President that he endorsed a colleague's view that there seemed "no alternative but a surrender." Lincoln asked how long Fort Sumter's provisions might last. Scott reckoned that the garrison would be starved out within seven weeks. Breaking through Confederate strength to bring reinforcements, he said, would require twenty-five thousand soldiers and a considerable fleet; their training would take six to eight months—and perhaps an act of Congress. Lincoln shared Scott's disheartening message with his new Cabinet. Attorney General Edward Bates told his diary, "I was astonished to be informed that Fort Sumter, in Charleston Harbor, *must*

---

* Wrongfully credited with the invention of baseball, Doubleday was later falsely said to have directed that the pastime's home plate be shaped like a pentagon to commemorate Fort Sumter.

be evacuated." Scott's dark prognosis quickly made its way into the newspapers and thus to the men of Fort Sumter. Disgusted by what he took to be Lincoln's duplicity, Sumter's assistant surgeon, Samuel Wylie Crawford, wrote bitterly, "All this talk of 'occupying, holding, and possessing' the forts is nonsense."

On March 15, Lincoln sent a scrawled request to his department secretaries: "Assuming it to be possible to now provision Fort-Sumpter, under all the circumstances is it wise to attempt it? Please give me your opinion, in writing, on this question." Treading carefully in handling the other politicians he had named to his Cabinet, the President clearly wanted their recommendations on paper: in case his decisions produced a fiasco in Charleston Harbor, no one could then falsely claim that Lincoln had ignored his superior advice. Most of the Cabinet warned him that any effort to bolster Sumter would probably fail, thus tarnishing the new administration. Bates advised the President that he could not see "any great national interest" in holding the fort. Pondering a solution, Lincoln wondered whether giving up Sumter might be more politically palatable if he tightened the federal grip on Fort Pickens, off the coast of Pensacola, Florida, which was also in danger.

Postmaster General Montgomery Blair, an abolitionist lawyer from Maryland, felt so alienated by Lincoln's lack of pugnacity that he was tempted to quit.* His father, Francis, who had been Andrew Jackson's right-hand man, warned the President, to his face, that relinquishing Sumter would be "virtually a surrender of the Union" and might cause the House to impeach him. (Blair informed his son, "I may have said things that were impertinent & I am sorry I ventured on the errand.") The angry Republican Senator Benjamin Wade of Ohio went to the White House and warned Lincoln, "Go on as you seem to be going— give up fortress after fortress—*and Jeff Davis will have you as prisoner of war in less than thirty days!*"

Weighing these and other demands for militance, Lincoln quietly

---

* Blair cautioned the President that General Scott's political views shaped his judgment and "whilst no one will question his patriotism, the results are the same as if he was in fact traitorous."

sent Ward Hill Lamon to gauge the scene for him in Charleston. Lamon took it upon himself to suggest to Major Anderson that his garrison would soon be evacuated; he also asked Governor Pickens if he would allow the US Navy to do the job. (Pickens counseled him to hire a civilian steamboat instead.) Even worse, after misunderstanding Anderson's private comment that he had installed some defensive booby traps around Sumter and mined its wharf, Lamon oafishly warned Pickens that the Major was planning to blow up his fort. After receiving this misinformation, General Scott rapped Anderson's knuckles, writing him, "I forbid it as your commander, it being against your duty as soldier & Christian."

Anderson's months under pressure had strained his emotions, and, with the dwindling food supply on the island, he was starving. After reading Scott's reprimand, he wrote back that he was "deeply mortified at the want of confidence in me"—especially the aspersion against his Christianity. Knowing his own limitations, Anderson confided to the General that the only thing enabling him to survive this crisis was his reliance on God: "I must say that I think the Govt. has left me too much to myself, has not given me instructions, even when I have asked for them, and that responsibilities of a higher and more delicate character have been devolved upon me than was proper."

* * *

BY LATE MARCH 1861, Lincoln had concluded that the days for Anderson's garrison to stay at Fort Sumter were numbered. If there had to be a civil war, it would be easier for the President to unite Americans of the North and get them to fight should it be clear that the Confederacy was the aggressor. The Union side would enjoy a moral and emotional advantage if this conflict began with an assault by the South, and Lincoln was not above tinkering with the lights and scenery to make sure that this military drama had maximum impact.

With this in mind, he sent a thirty-nine-year-old ex–naval officer named Gustavus Vasa Fox to do more reconnaissance for him at Fort Sumter. Fox was Montgomery Blair's brother-in-law, and he boasted to his wife, "Uncle Abe Lincoln has taken a high esteem for me." As Captain Fox strolled around the fort's parapet by moonlight, Anderson strongly warned him that any military expedition to rescue the installation would be thwarted by the superior weaponry of his onetime West Point student General Beauregard, now Jefferson Davis's Army commander in Charleston. Fox did not contest this claim because he suspected that Anderson was swayed by his "Southern sympathies." Fox urged the Major to place his men on half rations to extend the time until they were driven out by starvation.

Lincoln was worried about looking timid.* When Fox reported to him at the White House, the President asked what would be needed to resupply Fort Sumter. Fox provided a wish list, which Lincoln gave to Secretary of War Simon Cameron and Secretary of the Navy Gideon Welles, the latter wearing his customary wig, along with orders to prepare to bolster the Sumter garrison. Influenced by Fox's insinuations about Anderson's Southern loyalties, the President complained to General Scott that the Major had "played us false."†

On April 3, Anderson warned Washington that his food supply would soon be exhausted: "Our bread will last four or five days." He "urgently" hoped "that definite and full instructions will be sent to me immediately." After receiving Anderson's message, the President summoned Captain Fox and issued a formal order to aid Fort Sumter. If the rebels tried to stop the expedition, the US Navy would be authorized to shoot. Fox appealed for more preparation time, but Lincoln refused: "You will best fulfill your duty to the country by making the attempt."

---

* Adding to this concern, Lincoln had been charged with softness and bungling in March when his order to reinforce Fort Pickens was thwarted by a US Navy commander whose three sons were Confederate soldiers.

† Suspicions in Washington about Anderson's motives spilled into the *New-York Tribune*, which reported growing concern "that Major Anderson has been playing a deep game for three months, and one which has deceived his military superiors. For many weeks the steady tenor of his daily dispatches had been, 'Send no reinforcements or supplies—I need neither troops nor provisions; therefore let me alone.' Suddenly—the moment that Mr. Lincoln takes the reins of government— the tone changes, and now Anderson cries, 'Send me supplies, or I starve—send me more troops, or it will be impossible to defend the fort.' Why this sudden change?"

At Lincoln's request, Cameron wrote to Anderson that his message had brought "some anxiety to the President," who had not realized that starvation was so imminent. A relief mission would set out for Charleston immediately: "You will therefore hold out, if possible, till the arrival of the expedition." Cameron informed Anderson that the President expected him to "act as becomes a patriot and soldier, under all circumstances," but if, "in your judgment, to save yourself and your command, capitulation becomes a necessity, you are authorized to make it."

When Anderson received Cameron's dispatch, he felt as if he had been punched in the solar plexus. He took the Secretary's command to act like a "patriot and soldier" as a gratuitous aspersion on his allegiance to the Union. And Lincoln's directive that the Major make the decision to capitulate, if necessary, suggested to him that he was about to be made into the President's scapegoat for the demise of the federal presence at Fort Sumter, which, by now, Anderson deemed inevitable.* He hoped that God would provide some way to "avert the storm."

The Major wrote his friend Colonel Lorenzo Thomas, Adjutant General of the Army, an agonized letter, confiding that Cameron's message about the relief expedition "surprises me very greatly." Since the Southern side had been "erroneously informed" that there would be no such mission, for Captain Fox to stage such an attempt "would produce most disastrous results throughout our country." Anderson went on,

> Even with his boat at our walls, the loss of life (as I think I mentioned to Mr. Fox) in unloading her, will more than pay for the good to be accomplished. . . . We have not oil enough to keep a light in the lantern for one night. The boats will have to, therefore, rely at night entirely upon other marks. . . . We shall strive to do our duty, though I frankly say that my heart is not in this war, which I see is to be thus commenced.

---

* The Major noted that the Confederate batteries at Charleston were almost battle-ready. That same week, the *Richmond Dispatch* had predicted that the President of the United States would "throw the responsibility of evacuation upon Major Anderson, and make him the scape goat."

Thomas never received Anderson's letter. By now, Governor Pickens had ordered his authorities to steal mail sent from Fort Sumter. After reading the purloined message, Pickens and Beauregard discussed how to exploit it to discredit the Union cause.

Lincoln assured Pickens, by letter, that "an attempt will be made to resupply Fort-Sumter with provisions only." If the effort should not be resisted, the Union would not try to bring in new "men, arms or ammunition" without advance notice, except "in case of an attack on the fort."* Lincoln's written hope that the rebels would tolerate the mission was intended mainly for the record; he knew they were likely to retaliate. On the same day he appealed to Pickens, he wrote to six Northern governors that battle might be imminent. From three others he secured pledges to send thousands of militiamen in case civil war broke out, explaining to Pennsylvania's Governor, Andrew Curtin, "I think the necessity of being *ready* increases. Look to it."†

The President told a visitor that they would soon find out "whether the revolutionists dare to fire upon an unarmed vessel sent to the rescue of our starving soldiers." Amid the growing crisis, Lincoln kept his sense of humor, wondering whether he could dispel the crowd of government job seekers outside his office by sending them to Fort Sumter, where they could "demonstrate their patriotism."

* * *

ON WEDNESDAY, April 10, 1861, Jefferson Davis ordered General Beauregard to demand the immediate surrender of his old West Point teacher, Major Anderson, and, if Anderson refused, to decimate Fort Sumter. Afflicted by severe migraine headaches, the rebel leader argued that transforming the tension between North and South into

---

* Since Lincoln refused to acknowledge the secession of any state, he wrote to Pickens as one of the Union's governors, instead of contacting Jefferson Davis, whose Confederacy he did not recognize.

† Deciphering Lincoln's action, the *Cleveland Plain Dealer* explained that the President's decision to send the Navy to Sumter was "shrewdly inviting the secessionists to open the ball." The New York Democratic journalist John O'Sullivan, who had once coined the term "Manifest Destiny," now detected in Lincoln's directive "the cunning hand of the third rate village lawyer."

open warfare would reveal Lincoln's scheme of "coercion" and pull the eight remaining uncommitted slave states, in outrage, off the fence and into the Confederacy.

Davis had once minimized the "little garrison" at Sumter as merely "a point of pride" for the Union. His secretary of state, Robert Toombs, who had resigned his US Senate seat from Georgia, had warned him that bombarding the fort would "lose us every friend at the North. You will wantonly strike a hornet's nest which extends from mountains to ocean, and legions, now quiet, will swarm out and sting us to death." Some rebels predicted that Lincoln would land four thousand soldiers, with artillery and horses, to not only bolster the fort but teach a vicious lesson to the people of Charleston. Aided by the half of the city's population who were black, the Northern intruders, under this racist theory, would supposedly loot stores, kill gentleman planters, and rape their wives. One plantation lady asked her diary, "What if Lincoln gain the advantage— & with sword in hand . . . ravaging the land & destroying our firesides with ruthless revenge." Louis Wigfall, having now quit the US Senate, urged Davis in a cable from Charleston to "take Fort Sumter before we have to fight the fleet and the Fort."

Inside Sumter, Anderson's men, each by now down to only half a cracker and a few bites of salt pork, were almost dizzy from lack of food. The Major had tried to keep them from hearing about the relief expedition, but they quickly figured out what might be ahead guessing by the new, different chores he gave them, as well as his order to move their bedrolls to hardened gun rooms. Foreseeing casualties, Dr. Crawford, the assistant surgeon, prepared his amputation instruments.

On Thursday afternoon, April 11, by Davis's order, three of Beauregard's aides, including the resigned US Senator James Chesnut of South Carolina, sailed to Fort Sumter, lashed their rowboat to the stony wharf, and asked to be escorted to Major Anderson, who was in his guardroom. They handed him Beauregard's ultimatum, pledging transport for the commander and his men "to any post in the United States." It said, "The flag which you have upheld so long and with so much fortitude, may be saluted by you on taking it down." After consulting his officers, Anderson gave the rebels a sealed reply for Beauregard. Thanking his old student "for the fair, manly, and courteous terms proposed," it said, "I regret that my sense of honor, and of my obligations to my Government, prevent my compliance." Walking his visitors to the gate, the Major asked, "Will General Beauregard open his batteries without further notice to me?" Improvising, Chesnut said, "I think not." Making a final effort to forestall a Confederate attack, Anderson told them, "Gentlemen, if you do not batter the fort to pieces about us, we shall be starved out in a few days."*

At 1:30 the next morning, the Major was rousted from bed. Beauregard's envoys had returned with another offer: "If you will state the time at which you will evacuate Fort Sumter, and agree that in the mean time you will not use your guns against us unless ours are employed against Fort Sumter, we will abstain from opening fire upon you." But Anderson knew that Captain Fox's fleet was soon to arrive. When that happened, the rebels would blast the vessels, and he could not order his garrison to sit on its hands.

However, in his "desire to avoid the useless effusion of blood," Anderson made the rebels an offer that would cast a long shadow over his later reputation: he would evacuate the fort by noon on Monday, April 15. In the meantime, he would not fire on Beauregard's forces "unless compelled to do so by some hostile act against this fort or the flag of my Government," some other sign of bad intention, or "controlling instructions" from Washington. Anderson's detractors would later damn him for being willing to hand over his fort to the rebels. His explanation was that if Fox's relief mission did not arrive within three days, his starving men would have had to surrender anyway, and that his caveats preserved his right to retaliate for any assault on Fox's fleet.

Scoffing at Anderson's offer, Chesnut dictated an official rejection to his young scribe: "We have the honor to notify you that he will open the fire of his batteries on Fort Sumter in one hour from this time." Severely distressed, Anderson pulled out his pocket watch. It was 3:20 a.m. He had his officers awakened and told them to raise the large

---

* That night, the courtly Chesnut, who had helped to write the Confederate constitution, told his wife, Mary, that he felt deep empathy for Anderson.

thirty-three-star storm flag he had brought; it was big enough to make sure that the banner would be seen from far away, flapping in the brisk Atlantic air, when the rebels bombarded the fortress.

* * *

A T ABOUT 4:30 on Friday morning, April 12, 1861, a single mortar shell tore a thin yellow streak through the blue-black sky over Charleston Harbor, then dropped onto Fort Sumter, exploding into a fiery burst of red and orange. Anderson waited to respond, because in the darkness the gun rooms were too murky for the men to easily fire their weapons.* By 6:00 a.m., Fort Sumter had taken more than a hundred shells or cannonballs. To keep his men steady, Anderson tried to maintain the garrison's normal routine: roll call, breakfast (by now, the salt pork was rank), assembly. Then at 6:30, through gale-force winds and heavy rain, the men began returning the rebels' fire.

An hour after noon, amid the explosions, Anderson was informed by a lookout that he had spotted Captain Fox's armada in the Atlantic. When they heard this news, a few men cheered. But, in fact, only some of the vessels had arrived outside the harbor, and they waited in the rain until the fleet reached full strength. Annoyed that Fox seemed so gutless while his own men were braving death, Anderson hoped that Fox's ships were simply waiting until dark to land. Thus at seven o'clock, he ordered his men to stop firing for the night. The rebels stood down too, except for mortar blasts every fifteen minutes to keep his garrison off balance all night. There was still no sign of Fox's fleet, but to Anderson's relief, his only casualties were four men who were mildly wounded. Although pockmarked, Sumter's outer walls were still remarkably intact.

Told on Friday evening that the shelling of Fort Sumter had begun, Lincoln said he "did not expect it so soon." Later that night, when a Congressman asked how he liked the news, the President, described

---

* Edmund Ruffin, a Virginian who had joined the Palmetto Guards as a temporary volunteer, dreaded that Anderson's garrison might not retaliate, which "would have cheapened our conquest of the fort."

as "anxious but calm," replied, "I do not like it." "Civil war has at last begun," announced the *New York Herald*, predicting that Anderson's "brilliant and patriotic conduct" would "silence the attacks made at the North upon his character and patriotism." The *Hartford Courant* reported that "Major Anderson's fame is on every one's tongue about the hotels and streets." "War! War!! War!!!" shrieked the *Macon Telegraph.* "THE BALL FAIRLY OPENED!!!!"

At 7:30 a.m. on Saturday, the second day of what Union officers would call the "War of the Rebellion," rebels and Yankees, some shirtless, resumed their battle. A mortar shell broke through the roof of Sumter's officer quarters and started a fire, which roared through the fortress, sending up an ugly black cumulus. Gagging from the smoke, Anderson's men covered their mouths with wet handkerchiefs and hit the ground. Seizing the chance to crush the Union garrison, the rebels escalated their attack, throwing large numbers of cannonballs into the furnaces of Fort Moultrie, which they now held, for use in creating fires at Sumter. Anderson later said it was "painful" to find that, instead of helping to put out the flames at his fort, the rebels "rapidly increased their fire upon us from every battery, in total disregard of every feeling of humanity." With his head high, he ordered those of his soldiers who could to keep up their fight.

That afternoon, the bombardment knocked down Fort Sumter's towering flagstaff, but somehow its flag survived. Although "The Star-Spangled Banner" would not become the national anthem for seventy more years, every member of Anderson's garrison knew its words and the story of the Battle of Baltimore, during which Fort McHenry's banner, through those bursting bombs, was "still there." Fearing that a missing flag would signal surrender, the men of Sumter tied it onto a conspicuous gun carriage. Nevertheless, as soon as Wigfall saw the flag disappear from its pole, he set off—with no one's sanction but his own—with three slaves and a rebel private, in a leaky rowboat, destined for the beleaguered island fortress. From Wigfall's sword dangled a white kerchief, as an impromptu banner of truce. When he arrived, he told several Union officers, "You are on fire, and your flag is down. Let

Thomas Jefferson, who resisted taking his nation to war in 1807 over the British attack against the USS *Chesapeake*. Painted by Rembrandt Peale, 1800.

Commodore James Barron of the *Chesapeake*.

The HMS *Leopard* confronts the *Chesapeake*, June 1807.

James Madison, the first sitting President
to lead the United States into a major war.
Painted by John Vanderlyn, 1816.

Dolley Madison, who escaped the
White House in August 1814 before
British soldiers arrived with torches.
Painted by Gilbert Stuart, 1804.

BRITISH BURN THE CAPITOL · 1814

Redcoats attack Washington, DC, August
1814. Painted by Allyn Cox, 1973–1974.

The "Star-Spangled Banner," which
was "still there" after the Battle of Fort
McHenry, September 1814. Displayed at
Boston Navy Yard, 1873.

Andrew Jackson as hero of the Battle of New Orleans.
Painted by Dennis Malone Carter, 1856.

Sarah and James Polk, photographed in
Washington, DC, probably 1846.

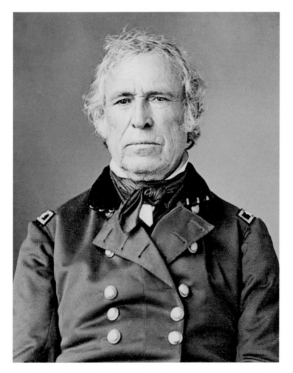

General Zachary Taylor, whose army provoked
the Mexican War at President Polk's request,
photographed probably early 1840s.

American troops entering Saltillo, Mexico, 1847–1848, in
one of the first photographs ever taken of soldiers at war.

Senator Henry Clay of Kentucky, who was defeated by
Polk for President in 1844 and hated Polk's Mexican
War but lost his own son, Henry Jr., in the conflict.
Photographed perhaps 1849.

Senator Daniel Webster of Massachusetts, who denounced
Polk's conflict as "a Presidential war," and whose son Neddy
died in the fighting. Photographed between 1845 and 1849.

General Winfield Scott leads Americans to conquer Mexico City,
September 1847. Painted by Carl Nebel and Adolphe Jean-Baptiste Bayot, 1851.

Abraham Lincoln, photographed in the spring of 1861,
as he coped with the Confederate assault on Fort Sumter.

Mary Todd Lincoln, who was shattered by the death
of their son Willie and the emotional pressures of the
Civil War, photographed about 1863.

Major Robert Anderson, haunted by his surrender of Fort Sumter, April 1861. Photographed probably that same year.

Confederate flag snapping above Fort Sumter, April 1861, after the Union Army fled.

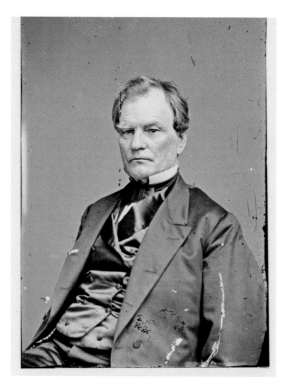

Senators Benjamin Wade and Zachariah Chandler, who complained to Lincoln's face about his mistakes and shortcomings as Commander-in-Chief. Wade photograph is 1855–1865; Chandler is 1860–1865.

Lincoln and General George McClellan meet on the
Antietam battlefield, October 1862.

African American man being lynched during July 1863
riots over race and the military draft.

Democrat Clement Vallandigham, leader of the antiwar
Copperheads, photographed between 1855 and 1865.

Lincoln's 1864 Democratic opponent, George McClellan,
photographed during the Civil War.

General Ulysses Grant, smoking a cigar outside Baptist church,
Massaponax, Virginia, May 1864.

Lincoln in February 1865, two months before his murder.

William McKinley and his ailing wife, Ida,
at the White House.

Charles Dwight Sigsbee, captain of the USS *Maine*.

The *Maine* arrives in Havana Harbor, January 1898.

Detail from 1898 poster with provocative rendering of *Maine* explosion that would move Americans to support the war against Spain.

Colonel Theodore Roosevelt and his Rough Riders, 1898.

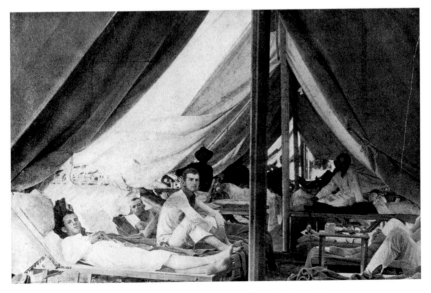

Military fever ward, Jacksonville, Florida, 1898.

McKinley witnesses signing of Spanish peace protocol,
White House, August 1898.

McKinley in Buffalo, on the day before his assassination, September 1901.

us quit." The Union men replied that, although he may not have seen it, their Stars and Stripes was, in fact, still waving.

Wigfall next called on the ravaged Anderson, saying that Beauregard wished to halt the fighting: "Upon what terms will you evacuate this fort?" Presuming that Wigfall meant a truce, not a surrender, the Major referred him to the written terms he had sent Beauregard on Wednesday. "Very well," replied the rebel. Soon Fort Sumter's Union flag was replaced by Wigfall's white kerchief. Sailing to Charleston, Wigfall, with torn shirt and muddy face, climbed out of his boat, waved his hat, and shouted, *"Sumter is ours!"* An exuberant rebel crowd hugged him and lifted his body onto its shoulders.

In the meantime, three of General Beauregard's formal emissaries arrived at Fort Sumter and offered to help douse the fire. Declining their assistance, Anderson noted that Wigfall had already negotiated a truce. Nonplussed, the envoys told him that Wigfall had not seen Beauregard for two days. Concluding that Wigfall had played him for a fool, the irate Anderson told the rebels to "return to your batteries." He had his Union flag raised again, and ordered his men to resume firing. Beauregard's envoys told Anderson that if he should be willing to write down what he considered to be his understanding with Wigfall, they would ask the General whether he could accept it. Anderson inquired how many rebels had been injured. Despite thousands of blasts exchanged, it turned out that no one had been killed on either side. "Thank God," exclaimed the Major, "there has been a higher power over us!"

Beauregard sent word that he would accept Anderson's written conditions for departing the fort, but insisted that the Union officers not salute the Union flag. Feeling at the end of his rope, the Major did not argue. At this early juncture of the struggle, Southern courtliness remained. That evening, one of Beauregard's aides told Anderson that the General had "cheerfully agreed" to let the men salute, as his own "honorable testimony to the gallantry and fortitude" of the Major, his former West Point teacher.

By Sunday afternoon, April 14, the squalls over Charleston had given way to tranquil sunshine. While children and ladies with parasols watched from sightseeing boats, Anderson's thirty-three-star Union flag at Fort Sumter was lowered, and the Major sobbed at the sight.* One of Charleston's jubilant rebels hailed their victory with a defiant song, which some called the first of the Civil War:

> Next day the fort is taken, and the stars and stripes no more
> Defiant on the ramparts wave on Carolina's shore.
> Lincoln and Scott and all the rest we boldly now defy.
> They may want to get it back, but we'd like to see them try!

Anderson was still furious at Captain Fox's failure to help them. Finally Fox made himself useful by arranging for the defeated men of Fort Sumter to sail to New York City aboard the steamer *Baltic*, with the fort's battle-ripped flag hanging from a spar, lashed to the vessel's mizzenmast. As they boarded the boat, "Yankee Doodle" was played on drum and fife. The Major wrote Governor Pickens, "If we do not meet again here, I hope we will meet again in a better world."

Reunited in Manhattan with Eba and their five children, Anderson wondered whether citizens of the North would vilify him for the Fort Sumter defeat. At a rally in Union Square on April 20, the Major stood under the Sumter flag, which was hung from the statue of George Washington on horseback. He was astounded and deeply moved when more than one hundred thousand people gave him a vast admiring roar.[†] Some called it the largest public gathering that the nation had ever seen. City authorities gave the Major a gold medal for his "brilliant defence of a national fortress from the most wanton, atrocious and treasonable assault known in the history of the world," as well as a snuffbox depicting the Goddess of Liberty crowning him with a laurel wreath. Throughout

---

* Jefferson Davis had cabled Beauregard, "If occasion offers, tender my friendly remembrance to Major Anderson." Unwilling to add to Anderson's "distress and natural mortification," the General declined to call on him.

† Anderson's flag was later displayed, as a sacred relic, at fund-raising rallies for the Union cause, where it was put up for auction and the winner was expected to give it back.

the city, Anderson's stern portrait adorned lampposts and horse-drawn wagons. The *New York Leader* asked, "When has the world witnessed a spectacle of nobler heroism?" In the euphoria, one of Anderson's officers fondly wrote him, with hyperbole, "The whole Country looks to you with a depth of affection which has not had its parallel since the days of Washington."

But not every Northerner called Anderson a hero. The *New York Courier* charged that Anderson's "defense" of Fort Sumter had been "a sham," adding that the "traitor" had deviously "arranged with Beauregard for the surrender of Sumter before it was assaulted" because his "sympathies were all with the Rebels." Boston's abolitionist *Liberator* reported that some officials in Washington "strongly suspected" the Major of "treachery," adding that the idea was "preposterous."

The week after Fort Sumter's demise, Secretary Cameron wrote Anderson to convey "the approbation of the Government of your gallant and judicious conduct." But Lincoln kept his distance from the Major. As a cagey politician, he realized that if Northerners should conclude that Anderson's Southern sympathies had kept him from zealously guarding his fort, this political backlash would damage the President who had kept him there. Lincoln was also no doubt concerned by what was called the Major's "greatly disabled" condition. One journal published a claim that at Sumter Anderson had "surrendered from sheer exhaustion."

Then came Anderson's resounding welcome in New York, which raised the question of why his Commander-in-Chief had not thanked him for his leadership in person. Lincoln now sent Anderson what he called "a purely private and social letter," saying, "I shall be much gratified to see you here at your earliest convenience, when and where I can personally testify my appreciation of your services and fidelity, and perhaps explain some things on my part which you may not have understood."

Anderson came to the Executive Mansion in May, and Lincoln wryly asked, "Major, do you ever remember meeting me before?" Anderson respectfully said he had no such recollection. "My memory is better than yours," Lincoln charmingly replied. "You mustered me into the service of the United States in 1832, at Dixon's Ferry, in the Black Hawk War!"

The Major was astonished. Basking in the credit the President now gave him for launching his public career, Anderson remained a fervent Lincoln man until the day he died. For good measure, the President also made him a Brigadier General.*

Having ensured that Anderson was on his team, Lincoln sent the veteran of Fort Sumter on the road to sign up Union volunteers.† In May 1862, the President named Anderson as Union commander of the border state of Kentucky, which was flirting with secession, and asked him to take his post "at once." But Anderson realized that his "heart was not in it." The Army retired him, explaining that since the "severe shock" of Fort Sumter, "he has not been equal to the fatigue and excitement incidental to service in the field." Lincoln was informed that Anderson felt "grieved" at his dismissal but understood why he must bow out. Using the parlance of the time, Army medics attributed his emotional breakdown to a "softening of the brain."

Confederate leaders took retribution. Anderson's Southern land and physical property, as well as the fortune that he and Eba had kept in Dixie banks, were confiscated, forcing him to support his family on his Army pension. Much later, after the Civil War, Anderson pleaded with Congress to compensate him for the Southern larceny but was rebuffed. (The *Philadelphia Inquirer* sniffed that Anderson's $4,125 annual pension was "a much larger income than hundreds of thousands of his countrymen enjoy.") To keep his family afloat, Anderson sold his book collection for a quarter of his asking price.

---

* By letter, Eba Anderson had asked Lincoln to promote her husband, saying, "He would die rather than ask for—or connive at getting—an appointment for himself." She explained "how keenly his sensitive nature would feel his Juniors in the service being placed above him" and that she "could not *bear*, Mr. President, to see him endure that trial."

† During one such meeting, Anderson described the rebels' "inhuman treatment" when they revved up the battle against the flaming Sumter. South Carolina's *Charleston Mercury* struck back at the Southern "turncoat" who had surrendered his fort: "Did anybody prevent him pulling down his dirty stripes?"

Heartbroken and bitter at what he considered his country's ingratitude, looking more wizened than his age, the Brigadier General abandoned the United States in 1869 for the less expensive South of France—his doctor hoped that the benign climate of Nice might succeed in "saving his life"— but Anderson died there in 1871, at the age of sixty-six.

Pinching pennies, Eba returned to America, surviving her husband by decades, long enough to present, at age seventy-six, pink roses to President Theodore Roosevelt's wife, Edith, at the White House on Election Night 1904. In her old age and penury, Mrs. Anderson clung to her most prized possession—Robert's ravaged flag from Fort Sumter. She urged her children to fight anyone who flung out the "slander" that their father, on that dreadful island in Charleston Harbor, had acted as a tool of the benighted Confederacy.*

* * *

FROM LINCOLN'S POLITICAL point of view, the Battle of Fort Sumter had been almost perfect, especially because it involved no loss of life. If civil war was inevitable, better for Northerners to react against this appalling scene than by some less dramatic display of federal assertion that might not have been so effective in uniting them for the struggle ahead. The alternatives might have included seaborne federal tax collectors braving Confederate fire in some Southern harbor, or terrified US postmen raising their hands in front of Southern muskets—or, far more damaging in its political optics, some Sumter-in-reverse, such as Union soldiers bombarding Fort Moultrie to get the rebels out, which might have moved Americans of the North to ask what kind of war Lincoln was asking them to fight.

Of the struggle in Charleston Harbor, the President later told his Illinois friend Orville Browning, "The plan succeeded. They attacked Sumter—it fell, and thus, did more service than it otherwise could."

---

* In 1911, on the fiftieth anniversary of Fort Sumter, an Anderson daughter, also named Eba, published a nineteen-page defense of her father's "dignified silence under ingratitude and lack of appreciation," which rejected the "dastardly" charge that he "was not a Union man."

Browning agreed: "The effect upon the public mind is better than it would have been had Anderson sustained himself in the Fort. The outrage, the very atrocity of the unprovoked assault, followed by the capture, has aroused the indignation of all patriots."

The day after Fort Sumter's demise, Lincoln's ardent friend Joseph Medill, publisher of the *Chicago Tribune,* wrote him, "There is but one opinion in Chicago. . . . *Sumter must be retaken.* . . . Crush the head of the rattle-snake. That was where the trouble was hatched. . . . The North West will back you with their last man, dollar and bushel of corn." The *Philadelphia Inquirer* rallied its readers: "It is now for the people of the United States to wipe out the insult and disgrace inflicted upon their defenders at Fort Sumter." "Civil war is a dire calamity," argued the *Vermont Phoenix,* "but it is by no manner of means so great an evil as anarchy." Horace Greeley's *New-York Tribune* predicted that "Jeff Davis & Co. will be swinging from the battlements at Washington at least by the 4th of July."

From the Confederate side, the *Lynchburg Virginian* warned of Lincoln, "Let him send his myrmidons to invade our soil, and they shall be welcomed with bloody hands to hospitable graves." The *Macon Telegraph* chortled, "Anderson's force is supposed to be dreadfully cut up. Hurrah for the Confederate States of America." In Montgomery, happy rebels serenaded Jefferson Davis and his secretary of war, LeRoy Pope Walker, who vowed "in an insolent and braggart speech" (so described by a Northern correspondent) that the Confederate flag, "which now flaunts the breeze here, will float over the old Capitol at Washington." Several days after the showdown at Fort Sumter, the prized state of Virginia— with all of its wealth and importance to American history, contributing a third of all US Presidents before 1861 (as well as some of Lincoln's ancestors)—seceded from the Union. The Old Dominion was followed within seven weeks by Arkansas, North Carolina, and Tennessee. Davis prepared to move his capital from Montgomery to Richmond.

Lincoln had no more than about a year of formal education, as a boy in Indiana, but from his long study of American history, he knew how the British invasion of Washington had demoralized the Americans of 1814. He fully expected an early Confederate lunge against Washington, which was geographically surrounded by secessionists in Virginia and Maryland (although the latter voted, at the end of April, to remain in the Union). Federal officials warned of furtive rebel sympathizers, who would spring into action from shanties and back alleys at a moment's notice, slicing telegraph cables and blasting bridges. General Scott reputedly asked the President to send Mary and their sons Willie and Tad back to Springfield, away from the peril, but Lincoln refused.

Responding to the cascade of events, the Commander-in-Chief flexed his muscles without consulting members of the House and Senate, most of whom were still back in their home states. He could have called Congress back into session, but in that era of limited telegraph and railroad lines, it might have taken so long to assemble the members that the intense Northern anger over Sumter would dissipate.* Throwing the matter to Congress would also risk the danger that the military behemoth that Lincoln was ambitious to create—and quickly—would be stalled by pettifogging debates over military logistics, presidential power, state prerogatives, and civil liberties. Preferring to operate, for at least a time, without such strangling constraints, he instead summoned Congress for an extraordinary session, which would start on the intentionally symbolic day of July 4. He hoped that this session would ratify his initial efforts to suppress the Southern assault.

At no time—not ever—would Lincoln ask the House and Senate for a declaration of war against what he called the "so-called Confederacy." That would be to accept the Southern proposition that secession by the states was legal, which would mean that the Union was fighting a foreign power. From Lincoln's perspective, since the Constitution forbade a state from departing the Union, Davis's cabal was staging an illegal insurrection against the federal government. The oath to defend the Constitution which Lincoln had sworn just five weeks ago now compelled him to crush that insurrection. For him, there was a better precedent for inaugurating this war than Madison in 1812 or Polk in 1846. It was

---

* With congressional elections pending in Kentucky and Maryland, Lincoln was also apprehensive about calling a special session of the old Congress, which could have included rabid secessionists.

the Whiskey Rebellion of 1794, when angry frontiersmen in western Pennsylvania and elsewhere had raucously flouted federal taxes on distilled spirits. Recalling that the American Revolution had begun with tea parties like this, President Washington had asserted federal authority by sending thirteen thousand militiamen, under Light-Horse Harry Lee, to stop the defiance. Starting with Parson Weems's popular, semifictional hagiography of the first President, Lincoln had studied and revered Washington since boyhood.

While Anderson's garrison was sailing out of Charleston Harbor in defeat, Lincoln had issued a formal proclamation warning that federal laws were being defied in various Southern states "by combinations too powerful to be suppressed by the ordinary course of judicial proceedings." At the time, the US Army consisted of about sixteen thousand men, most stationed west of the Mississippi River. Perhaps up to a third of their number were departing to join the Confederacy. The President asked state governors for seventy-five thousand militiamen (the number recommended by General Scott—Lincoln did not want to provoke heretofore undecided border and upper South states by seeking a larger number, which would imply that he was plotting a massive invasion of the South). He implored "all loyal citizens to favor, facilitate, and aid this effort to maintain the honor, the integrity, and the existence of our National Union, and the perpetuity of popular government; and to redress wrongs already long enough endured." Lasting for ninety days (the legal limit, under a 1795 militia law), the first mission of this force, he said, would "probably be to repossess the forts, places and property which have been seized from the Union," taking "the utmost care" to "avoid any devastation and destruction of or any interference with property, or any disturbance of peaceful citizens in part of the country."

After reading this statement, Lincoln's two-time rival Stephen Douglas told fellow Illinois Democrats that "the shortest way to peace is the most stupendous and unanimous preparation for war." In support of Lincoln's request, Governor John Andrew of Massachusetts cabled the President, "By what route shall I send?" From Boston, Oliver Ellsworth, grandson of the nation's third Chief Justice, wrote Lincoln that the patriotic fervor in his city was so great that he had been "*retarding* men from rushing into the office, eager to add their names to the rolls—men, money and all honor are devoted, the North is aroused. . . . *We know no party.* . . . The loss of Sumter was the greatest victory the people ever realized; it has done its work *effectually.*" From western New York, the ex-Congressman Elias Holmes, whom Lincoln had known while in the House, wrote him, "The hot air of Rebellion breathed thro' wet cloth at Ft. Sumter has fully cemented the people in this locality in favor of force *defensive* and *offensive.* . . . Never since the days of Adam was a change so rapid and so radical."

But the *Richmond Whig* called the request by the "dictatorial" Lincoln "a gross and flagrant usurpation." From Raleigh, North Carolina, Governor John Ellis wrote the President to protest his "wicked violation of the laws," adding, as if Lincoln needed to be warned, "You can get no troops from North Carolina." Although Kentucky had abjured joining the Confederacy, Governor Beriah Magoffin wrote to Lincoln, "Kentucky will furnish no troops for the wicked purpose of subduing her sister Southern states." Alexander Stephens bellowed that Lincoln could send seventy-five times seventy-five thousand men in his effort to intimidate the South, and even then, Lincoln would fail.

At the White House, braced for a possible Confederate effort to seize the Capital, straining to hear the first military salvos with his own ears, the anxious Lincoln waited for the promised militia. "Why don't they come?" he asked. "Why don't they come?" This President, who had been so ridiculed before Sumter's capture for his casualness and restraint, now transformed himself into the most powerful Chief Executive that Americans had ever seen—and by means that, as Lincoln later confessed, were not "strictly legal." During the eighty days he had preserved for himself with no Congress in town, he acted with self-awarded autonomy of a kind enjoyed by no previous President. Ex-Justice Benjamin Curtis, who had resigned from the Supreme Court after dissenting from the *Dred Scott* decision, charged that Lincoln was building "a military despotism."

Responding to the rebels' announced intention to take up privateering, the President proclaimed a naval blockade of rebel ports, which, in conflicts between rival nations, was traditionally an act of war. (Scott had advised him that such a blockade could bring the South to terms "with less bloodshed than by any other plan.") Due to the Southern insurrection, Lincoln explained, the federal government could not "comfortably" collect revenue from the renegade region, which obstructed the Constitution's demand for "uniform" enforcement of laws throughout the Union. Using language designed to signal European powers not to aid the Confederacy, he warned that the rebels had also issued "pretended letters of marque to authorize the bearers thereof to commit assaults on the lives, vessels, and property of good citizens of the country lawfully engaged in commerce on the high seas, and in waters of the United States." He cautioned that if the new blockade should be violated, offending vessels could be seized "as prize." The *New York Times* crowed, "The pirates of the Confederacy will be dealt with according to the universal law of the high seas."

By May, Lincoln realized that his manpower request had been too modest. With no congressional sanction of the kind required by the Constitution, he bolstered the US Army with eight new regiments (including tens of thousands of new men for the cavalry and infantry) and the US Navy with about eighteen thousand new seamen.

Lincoln explained to John Hay that the "central idea" of the gathering conflict was to prove "that popular government is not an absurdity." But in his ardor to save the endangered Union, the President encroached on civil liberties. After Fort Sumter, pro-rebel rioters in Baltimore blocked troops who were on their way to protect Washington, killing four members of the Sixth Massachusetts Regiment. The *New York Times* reported that "parties of men half frantic are roaming the streets, armed with guns, pistols and muskets" and "a general state of dread prevails." With Congress away, the angry Lincoln suspended the writ of habeas corpus for the area between Philadelphia and the Capital, allowing Americans suspected of plots against the federal government, or otherwise abetting the "so-called Confederate states," to be detained indefinitely, without indictment or hearing in court. He later noted that he had done so "very sparingly" and that the Constitution empowered him to do so.* Against the menace of Maryland, with its Plug-Uglies and rebel mobs, he declared martial law, a sanction unmentioned by the Constitution. "The excitement is fearful," the state's Governor, Thomas Hicks, had cabled him. "Send no troops here." Lincoln ignored the request.

Chief Justice Taney, acting as a circuit judge, issued a writ for the appearance in court of a member of the pro-rebel Maryland militia named John Merryman, a suspected saboteur who had been jailed for treasonous acts, including participation in the Baltimore riots. Ironically, Merryman was being held at Fort McHenry, scene of the sacred "Star-Spangled Banner." Abiding by Lincoln's suspension of habeas corpus, McHenry's commander refused. Taney demanded that the President "perform his Constitutional duty" so that the Union would still be "living under a government of laws." In June, the Chief Justice wrote *Ex parte Merryman*, which found that only Congress enjoyed the right to suspend habeas corpus. But *Merryman* was not a Supreme Court ruling. Lincoln defied the order by extending the area in which the writ was canceled, insisting that the life-or-death struggle against the South superseded normal procedure.

The Senate and House finally convened on Independence Day. With members absent from, by now, eleven Confederate states, Republicans easily controlled both houses. In a written message, by far his longest to date on the war, Lincoln defended his position on habeas corpus, asking, "Are all the laws, *but one,* to go unexecuted, and the government itself go to pieces, lest that one be violated?" He insisted that the Constitution endorsed such action "when, in cases of rebellion or invasion, the public safety may require it." More broadly, he explained that the Southern rebellion had compelled him "to call out the war power of the government and so to resist force employed for its destruction by force for its preservation." He added that his orders, "whether strictly legal or

---

* Attorney General Edward Bates advised Lincoln, "When the very existence of the Nation is assailed, by a great and dangerous insurrection, the President has the lawful discretionary power to arrest and hold in custody, persons known to have criminal intercourse with the insurgents."

not, were ventured upon under what appeared to be a popular demand and a public necessity, trusting then, as now, that Congress would readily ratify them."

Lincoln insisted that the rebel attack on Fort Sumter "was in no sense a matter of self-defense." The South had "forced upon the country" a choice between "immediate dissolution or blood," leaving him no alternative but to use federal authority to resist the Union's "destruction by force." With the "deepest regret," he asked Congress for at least four hundred thousand men and $400 million to make "this contest a short and decisive one." He insisted that his overriding desire was "to preserve the Government," and that he had "no moral right to shrink" from this duty. Since he expected the House and Senate, in time, to "readily ratify" his actions, he had taken no actions beyond his "Constitutional competency." At stake was the survival of not only the nation but "free government upon the earth."

The danger of assassination still troubled Lincoln. In his message to Congress, he said he had no right to consider the dangers to his "own life in what might follow." He knew that if the rebels should overrun the Capital, he might be shot or hanged. His sometime bodyguard Lamon promised him, in writing, that "if there is any prospect of an attack on Washington," he would hurry to his aid, but added, "I very much fear that there are eavesdroppers and traitors lurking about the White House. . . . There is too much known of what transpires between you and others on state secrets. . . . I wish you would look after it at once." However, still ashamed of what he now considered his overreaction to the pre-inaugural threats, the President remained casual about his safety.

When the Senate debated a joint congressional resolution to approve Lincoln's unilateral actions since Fort Sumter, Trusten Polk of Missouri balked. A cousin of the late President, and, like him, a Democrat, Polk denounced Lincoln's seizure of power and blamed him for maneuvering the Union into "a war, monstrous in its character," against the South. In a historical sense, the Senator was—probably unwittingly—turning the tables against Lincoln, who in 1848 had denounced President Polk from the House floor for grabbing unwarranted power and scheming the country into war. Polk now noted that the Constitution provided a means for a President to seek a declaration of war; he complained that Lincoln had "usurped the war power" when he raised armies, "suspended the writ of habeas corpus," and "blockaded ports." Polk insisted, "There is no necessity in peace or war that justifies a violation of the Constitution."

As Lincoln himself had conceded, he had reached for authority beyond that granted by the founding document. Had the House and Senate now been inclined to judge him harshly, they might have been justified to consider impeaching and removing him for abuse of power. But instead, weighing the President's ends against his means, Congress overwhelmingly approved his argument that he had had to act swiftly in order to save the endangered Union. Exceeding his request, it gave the President $500 million and half a million men to fight the South, and it backed him on habeas corpus.*

Trusten Polk's Republican colleagues responded to his rant against Lincoln by complaining that the Missouri Senator was performing the rebels' dirty work. Six months later, they had Trusten expelled from the Senate, and the cousin of the eleventh US President became a Confederate colonel.

* * *

LINCOLN WAS BESEECHED by many Americans to retaliate at once against the South. Alexander Hamilton's son James, a New York Democratic lawyer, wrote the President that "a short war is the most humane, and least expensive," so he should send ten thousand men forthwith into Virginia, "to protect and encourage the Union sentiment and there to recruit, to march to Richmond." In a public letter, the *New-York Tribune*'s Horace Greeley warned Union soldiers that they had "already been accused of cowardice for not pursuing the enemy"; therefore, "On to Richmond!"

---

* Compared with the mammoth initial force allotted to Lincoln by Congress, James Polk had had to make do with only fourteen thousand men.

General Scott warned Lincoln that the Union Army was not yet ready to fight. But the President knew that if he waited much longer, he would be jeered for being timorous. He also feared that Scott's self-restraint might encourage the rebels to make a vicious strike on Washington. Thus on July 21, Lincoln sent thirty-five thousand volunteers, as well as a number of militia and regulars, to Virginia's Bull Run Creek, near Manassas, to wage what quickly became the largest battle that had ever been fought in North America. At first, there was good news from the Union side. "Our troops engaged the enemy with a large force," reported the Associated Press. "Washington was wild with excitement and joy!" But not for long. For Lincoln, Bull Run proved to be a painful defeat, with perhaps 481 Union soldiers killed.

When it was over, the victorious Jefferson Davis strutted the battle-field, with bleeding rebels waving their caps while lying on the ground as he passed. "Washington Shrouded in Gloom!" cried Southern papers. "The Line of Retreat Strewed with the Dead and Dying!" Raising the subject of assassination, the *New Orleans Times-Picayune* warned that Lincoln, "who has inaugurated this war upon his own countrymen," should worry about "the safety of his own vile and guilty body, and well may the residents of Washington fear for the transfer of the struggle to the streets of their own city!"

Some Northern papers lacerated Lincoln for the rout at Bull Run. The *Brooklyn Daily Eagle* reported, "upon excellent authority," that General Scott had told the President "that he had acted like a coward . . . in yielding to the urgency of the public, the press, and members of Congress, and advancing upon Manassas before he was ready." The *New York Herald* claimed that the Manassas campaign had been forced on a malleable, neophyte President by its rivals, the *New-York Tribune* and *New York Times*, "as well as by the bloodthirsty Jacobins of Congress." All were "drunken madmen, with loaded pistols in their hands, who conspire to force the engineer, at the peril of instant death, to go ahead at full speed." Because of Lincoln's "terrible blunder," predicted the *Herald,* the national conflict was no longer likely to be a "short war."

After Bull Run, Lincoln signed two bills calling for a vast number of volunteers to be recruited by the states and mustered into federal service for two or three years. He had once dreamt that there might be at least a chance to cauterize the Southern insurrection fast. But now, in his humiliation, he confronted the enormity of what lay ahead, and felt deeply shaken, saying, "If to be at the head of Hell is as hard as what I have to undergo here, I could find it in my heart to pity Satan himself." After a visit with the President in August, his Illinois friend Orville Browning wrote him, "I was sorry to find you a little despondent, and not at all hopeful of your own individual future. . . . Be of good cheer. You have your future in your own hands, and the power to make your name one of the most justly revered, and illustrious in the annals of the human race."*

What was tormenting Lincoln was his new comprehension that victory over the South would require him to be the executioner of immense numbers of Americans on both sides. He lacked the ability to keep his emotional balance by transforming the images of piled-up corpses and mothers collapsing in grief into some kind of mental abstraction. Empathy was part of Lincoln's political genius. But through the coming four years of pathos, it made misery his unshakable companion. Within a year of Bull Run, out of a mixture of emotions like no President before him, Lincoln would ask an old circuit-riding friend, Congressman Daniel Voorhees of Indiana, "Doesn't it strike you as queer that I, who couldn't cut the head off of a chicken, and who was sick at the sight of blood, should be cast into the middle of a great war, with blood flowing all about me?"

---

* Browning had been appointed to the US Senate after Stephen Douglas's sudden death from typhoid fever.

CHAPTER SEVEN

"Blood Flowing All About Me"

B Y THE START of 1862, Lincoln was under siege. Many members of the House and Senate were outraged at the Union's failure to advance against the South, especially the previous October's defeat in the Battle of Ball's Bluff, Virginia. Lincoln had been disconsolate to learn that Oregon Senator Edward Baker, whom he once called "my dearest personal friend"—from their days as rivals in Springfield—had been killed at the height of the bluff.* He and Mary had named their second son Edward, who had died at almost four, to honor Baker. When Lincoln was told of the Senator's death, he was seen "heaving with emotion," and "wept like a child" at Baker's funeral, which he insisted on hosting at the White House.

The abolitionist firebrand Benjamin Wade, Republican from Ohio, considered his party's President an impressionable rube. From Washington, Wade wrote his son James, "In view of the late defeat on the Potomac, all is gloomy & despairing here." Wade and Senator Zachariah Chandler of Michigan had both been witnesses to the Confederate victory at Bull Run. Like their Radical Republican colleagues, both

---

* Baker remains the only sitting US Senator in history to die in battle.

Senators wished the President would define this conflict more openly as a struggle against the evils of slavery. They contended that addressing the full moral dimension of the war would electrify the soldiers of the Army of the Potomac, as well as the Northern Americans who backed them.*

Wade complained to Chandler that the President's unassertive position on slavery "could only come of one born of 'poor white trash' and educated in a slave State." Chandler and Wade were also furious at Lincoln for firing General John C. Frémont, alumnus of the Mexican War and now commander of the Union's western armies, for mismanagement. Frémont had issued an edict liberating the slaves in his region, which Lincoln had canceled, largely out of worry that it might compel Kentucky to secede.† Chandler warned fellow Senators that some Army officers were enemy sympathizers and were calling the conflict a "damned black Republican" war.

Trying to make up for his deficiencies, Lincoln studied books from the Library of Congress on military history and strategy. Wade, Chandler, and Senator Lyman Trumbull of Illinois went to the Executive Mansion and urged him to be more aggressive on the battlefield. Chandler told the President that reluctance to attack the rebels in Virginia would be "infinitely worse than another Bull Run." But Lincoln put off his visitors. Afterward the disgruntled Chandler wrote a political friend back home that "we can win a victory in 24 hours," but "there is no plan for a fight here."

Lincoln had not refuted the Senators' complaint that the aging Winfield Scott was inadequate to the magnitude of this struggle. In November 1861, after consulting his Cabinet, he accepted Scott's resignation ("for reasons of health") in favor of General George McClellan. He

---

* Embracing this point of view, one Pennsylvanian wrote his Congressman, Edward McPherson, that half of the Army volunteers would most likely refuse to renew their service unless the Army directly attacked "the virus of slavery . . . the root of the evil."

† Frémont had, of course, been accused of insubordination before, when, as military governor of California during the Mexican conflict, he was court-martialed, and President Polk commuted his sentence. After earning a fortune during the Gold Rush, Frémont became the first presidential nominee of the Republican Party in 1856.

warned McClellan that being General-in-Chief as well as commander of the Army of the Potomac would be strenuous, but the egotistical McClellan replied, "I can do it all."

Lincoln's choice of McClellan disturbed many Republicans. To them, McClellan, as a Democrat, was a totem of the party that for decades had abetted the South as it clung to the evil institution. McClellan wanted the struggle against the Confederacy to be limited, with prisoners of war "handled humanely and their civilians' property scrupulously protected"; he had little respect for volunteers or civilian control of the military. He considered Lincoln "an idiot," "the original gorilla," and "nothing more than a well-meaning baboon," confiding to his wife, Ellen, "I will not fight for the abolitionists." He told her he was responding to a "call on me to save the country," and that when he went among his soldiers, "I can see every eye glisten. . . . You never heard such yelling. . . . I believe they love me." "Help me dodge the nigger," McClellan wrote a friend. "I am fighting to preserve the integrity of the Union & the power of the Govt.—on no other issue." Years later, he charged that the goal of congressional Republicans "was not the restoration of the Union but the permanent ascendancy of their party."

The well-heeled McClellan lived in the house, facing Lafayette Square, where the aged Dolley Madison had resided as a widow during the Polk years. One evening, a few weeks after Ball's Bluff, Lincoln and his Secretary of State, William Seward, came to see him and were told that the General was out. They waited for an hour; when McClellan arrived, he went upstairs and let his visitors wait for another half hour before having them informed that he had gone to bed. "Better at this time not to be making points of etiquette and personal dignity," Lincoln told John Hay. "I will hold McClellan's horse if he will only bring us success."

Lincoln had seized unprecedented power to address the national emergency, and with mixed results. So when the Thirty-seventh Congress first officially convened in December 1861, some Senators tried to restore at least some of the balance. Chandler asked the Senate to launch a committee to investigate the "disasters" of Bull Run and Ball's Bluff, "with the power to send for persons and papers." Upping the ante, the

Iowa Republican James Grimes proposed a joint committee with the House which would probe a larger range of military disasters: "Let the country know what are the facts." Others insisted that this should be the exclusive province of the military, but Maine's William Fessenden noted that the Constitution gave Congress the power to declare war and provide the money to wage it with: "We must satisfy the people of this country that things go on well."

Ohio's John Sherman asked that any new panel be empowered to investigate every aspect of the conflict, and Congress agreed. By an overwhelming vote, it created the Joint Committee on the Conduct of the War, with three Senators and four members of the House, and Wade as chairman.* The *Chicago Tribune* predicted that the new panel would "rake things fore and aft in their search to place responsibility for our Army's inaction." But John Crittenden, now a member of the House, complained that Congress should not be allowed to meddle in executive matters: "Let the Army do its own business and we do ours."

Worried that the committee would seek to undermine him, Lincoln invited its members to the Executive Mansion on New Year's Eve 1861. Wade and Chandler assured him, unconvincingly, that their purpose was to help. But the Ohioan could not keep himself from rebuking the President: "You are murdering your country by inches in consequence of the inactivity of the military and the want of a distinct policy in regard to slavery." In a later meeting, several committee members asked Lincoln when General McClellan planned to act. The President shocked them by replying that he did not think he had "any right to know" because he was "not a military man" and it was his "duty to defer" to the General. Lincoln admitted to the Army's Quartermaster General, Montgomery Meigs, that "the people are impatient," and asked Meigs, "What shall I do?" He pondered making a public display of command by leading Union soldiers across a battlefield.

When Wade's committee convened, a New York militia major was asked about the sluggishness of the Army, and he replied, "It is sort

---

* Appointed by the Vice President, Hannibal Hamlin, and Speaker of the House Galusha Grow, the members included Senator Andrew Johnson of Tennessee.

of a standing joke among us that this is a very civil war." The tough, patrician, goateed General Charles Stone was interrogated about his responsibility for the Ball's Bluff debacle. "It is said of you," noted Wade, "that you take slaves and return them to secessionists." Weakly, Stone replied that he followed orders from the War Department and considered himself to abide by the Fugitive Slave Act of 1850, which was still in force. (The *Chicago Tribune* crudely claimed that Stone's "chief distinction" was "nigger catching.") Other witnesses claimed that Stone had colluded with rebel officers and deliberately jeopardized his own men. Wade and other members charged him with errors such as faulty transportation and tolerance of rebel plans to build fortifications. Some called Stone a symbol of Democratic efforts to undermine the Union cause. Forbidden to see his accusers' testimony or confronting them in formal session, he called his treatment a "humiliation."

Out for blood, Wade and Chandler wanted the new Secretary of War, Edwin Stanton, to have General Stone arrested for treason and disloyalty. Attorney General Edward Bates advised caution, warning against "a precedent for Congressional interference with the command of the Army." McClellan complained that Wade's committee wanted "a victim."* Complying with the Senators' demand, Stanton had Stone imprisoned, without charge or trial, at Fort Lafayette in New York Harbor. Senator James McDougall, a California Democrat, indignantly asked whether the American "form of government" had been transformed into a "council of seven . . . who wield absolute power and domination." Wade replied, "I am tired of hearing these arguments in favor of traitors." Lincoln accepted "general authority" for Stone's arrest, saying imperiously that the General would be charged and tried "in due season."†

---

* Of the committee's attacks, Lincoln privately said, "I do the very best I know how—the very best I can; and I mean to keep doing so until the end. . . . If the end brings me out wrong, ten angels swearing I was right would make no difference." Richard Nixon recited Lincoln's quote to defend himself during the Watergate scandal in 1974.

† After being moved to Brooklyn's Fort Hamilton, Stone asked the President, on Independence Day 1862, for resolution of his case; he was released the following month and restored to the Army. In the 1880s, he served as chief engineer for the new Statue of Liberty.

When McClellan appeared before Wade's committee, he was asked why he seemed so reluctant to assault the rebels. The General explained that new bridges across the Potomac were suited mainly for advance and that any sound commander would ensure his soldiers' means of retreat. "Before you strike at the rebels, you want to make sure of plenty of room so that you can run in case they strike back?" Chandler taunted. Wade added, "Or in case you get scared." Afterward Wade told Chandler, "I don't know much about war, but it seems to me that this is infernal, unmitigated cowardice."

* * *

IN FEBRUARY 1862, the President and Mary lost their eleven-year-old son Willie, probably to typhoid fever. The weeping President told his aide John Nicolay, "My boy is gone—he is actually gone!" The next day, Lincoln was seen as "completely prostrated with grief." At the funeral in the East Room, which was decked in black crepe, the President trembled and sobbed as he studied his son in his casket. He observed that Willie "was too good for this earth" and "It is hard, hard to have him die!" Soon an office seeker demanded to speak with him, and Lincoln exclaimed, "That crepe is hanging there for my son; his dead body at this moment is lying unburied in this house. . . . Couldn't you at least have the decency to wait until after we had buried him?"

Mary was mercurial and insecure, and her married life with Lincoln had been difficult, but she had once been a source of his self-confidence, assuring him in 1860, "You've got no equal in the United States!" But losing another son, amid the other tortures of the Civil War, flattened her. Medicated by laudanum, she was overcome by "paroxysms of convulsive weeping," it was said, and could not bring herself to attend Willie's service; she stayed in bed for weeks. The President implored his forty-three-year-old "child-wife" to "control your grief or it will drive you mad."

That same month, the Joint Committee on the Conduct of the War renewed its attack on the stalled McClellan. At the White House, Wade and Chandler threatened to open a Senate debate on the General's fitness to serve unless McClellan met the President's written demands to get moving. A week later, Wade told Lincoln that McClellan must go. The President asked him who should fill the job. "Why, anybody!" said the chairman. Lincoln replied, "Wade, *anybody* will do for you, but I must have *somebody*."

In March 1862, Lincoln removed McClellan as General-in-Chief and asked him to concentrate on the Army of the Potomac. That May, more confident of his own skills of military command, the President thrust himself into the center of battle. After a struggle over Yorktown, rebel soldiers were withdrawing to Richmond, but Norfolk was still holding out. The Commander-in-Chief took a Coast Guard revenue cutter, the *Miami,* to Ocean View, Virginia, where he took charge of planning an amphibious landing to seize the port, using a tugboat to search for landing spots. By early light, Lincoln watched Union troops hit the beach at Willoughby Spit. That evening, wearing his nightshirt, he learned that the rebels of Norfolk had surrendered, and, by at least one account, performed a dance of joy.

McClellan's Peninsula offensive against Richmond failed, and Lincoln said the defeat left him feeling "as nearly inconsolable as I could be and live." The fevered Chandler told the Senate that McClellan must "suffer the extreme penalty of law" because the nation had been "disgraced." He insisted that the General had committed treason and "deserves to be shot." McClellan assured a friend that Senator Chandler was "beneath my notice, & if the people are so foolish as to believe aught he says I am content to lose their favor & to wait for history to do me justice."

The Radical Republicans were chafing more than ever at Lincoln's avoidance of the slavery issue. In his inaugural address, he had pledged not to disturb the institution in the states where it prevailed, saying he had "no lawful right" to do so. He had later warned Congress against taking "radical and extreme measures" that might transform a war to reunite the Union "into a violent and remorseless revolutionary struggle."* In response, the President's Chicago friend Joseph Medill pleaded with him "for God's sake and your Country's sake" to recognize that this conflict was "a Slave-holders rebellion." He warned Lincoln that there would be "a feeble response" to his new request of state governors to send three hundred thousand fresh volunteers if the men were "to serve under proslavery generals to fight for 'Union and Slavery.'"

That March, Lincoln recommended to Congress a plan for the federal government to compensate any state that "may adopt gradual abolishment of slavery." Contending that emancipation was not a federal matter, he argued that slaves in every border state, as well as Washington, DC, could be liberated for roughly the cost of waging three months of the current war. His proposal fizzled when the border states refused this incentive, leaving compensated liberation to be restricted to the District of Columbia. Lincoln said he was "a little uneasy" about the "time and manner" of the District's abolition, and would have preferred that it be gradual and slow. Sounding like no abolitionist, he warned Orville Browning that "families would at once be deprived of cooks, stable boys &c and they of their protectors without any provision for them." But Frederick Douglass saluted "that first great step towards that righteousness which exalts a nation." Congressman Owen Lovejoy of Illinois exulted that Lincoln had "taken the Abolition wedge, and struck it into the log of Slavery," knowing "that the thin end of the wedge must first enter the wood."† The Washington reporter of the Democratic *Chicago Times* complained that Lincoln's government had "nigger on the brain, nigger in the bowels, nigger in the eyes."

In July, Lincoln confided to Secretaries Seward and Welles that he

---

* Lincoln was thinking, in part, of potential defections by Democratic soldiers from the US Army, as well as possible racial massacres and whatever political backlash might follow.

† The President also obtained modest funds from Congress to send freed slaves to colonies in Central America or elsewhere but failed to launch this notion beyond one experiment at Ile de Vache, in the Caribbean.

was nearing the conclusion "that we must free the slaves or be ourselves subdued" in the war, adding that "something must be done." Since the start of the struggle, Senator Charles Sumner, now a Republican, and other Radicals had insisted to Lincoln that he had the legal right to liberate slaves held by a wartime enemy. Seeking quiet in the War Department's cipher room, across the street from the Mansion, the President dipped his pen in ink and slowly scrawled out versions of a draft executive order that would grant the slaves their freedom. As Lincoln later recalled, he had decided "that we had about played our last card, and must change our tactics, or lose the game!" He later wrote that the thousands of slaves willing to enlist behind the Union were a matter "of physical force": "Throw it away, and the Union goes with it."

Meeting with his Cabinet on Tuesday, July 22, Lincoln read aloud a draft announcement that on the following New Year's Day, "as a fit and necessary military measure," he would declare that all slaves in any state "wherein the constitutional authority of the United States shall not then be practically recognized" would "thenceforward, and forever, be free."* He told the department secretaries that he was not requesting their advice, merely informing them. Postmaster General Blair warned that if the President took this step, he would lose the November midterm elections. Seward told Lincoln that the world would view his proposal as the desperate "last measure of an exhausted government, a cry for help." To avoid such embarrassment and keep from estranging the border states, the President resolved to defer his proclamation until the Union had enjoyed a major military victory.

In the meantime, on Thursday, August 14, he invited African American leaders to the Mansion—the first such social gathering in the history of the President's house—and made the case for colonization, advising them that "we have between us a broader difference than exists between almost any other two races" and "it is better for us both, therefore, to be

---

* The order would liberate slaves only in enemy areas, because while Lincoln's war power allowed him to capture the other side's resources, he could not change the law against slavery without consent from Congress.

separated."* Colonization had been proposed by Lincoln's onetime hero Henry Clay. Eager to affirm that he did not intend to change the Union's overriding aim in fighting this war, the President wrote a public letter to the *New-York Tribune*'s editor Horace Greeley, who was demanding immediate emancipation, that "if I could save the Union without freeing *any* slave I would do it, and if I could save it by freeing *all* the slaves I would do it." Lincoln's public suggestion that he was contemplating some form of emancipation stepped far beyond what earlier Presidents had done. But Senate Radicals remained dissatisfied. Charles Sumner joined with Governors of Northern states, who, after Union setbacks, were having a hard time meeting their quotas for military volunteers, to insist that Lincoln employ African Americans on the battlefield. But the President replied that this "would produce dangerous and fatal dissatisfactions" among Union soldiers: "half the Army would lay down their arms and three other States would join the rebellion."

Growing fed up with the insolent McClellan, Lincoln appointed Henry Halleck as General-in-Chief of all of his land forces, telling Halleck that he could decide whether to retain McClellan in command of the Army of the Potomac. When the Second Battle of Bull Run began, at the end of August, the President hoped for the victory that would let him unveil his preliminary Emancipation Proclamation. But the Union's warriors, under General John Pope, were turned back, leaving Lincoln badly depressed, saying that he was "wrung by the bitterest anguish" and felt almost ready to "hang" himself.

Evincing the religious subtext of some of his reactions to wartime events, he wrote to himself, "The will of God prevails. . . . In the present civil war it is quite possible that God's purpose is something different from the purpose of either party. . . . God wills this contest, and wills that it shall not end yet. . . . He could have either saved or destroyed the Union without a human contest. . . . Yet the contest proceeds." What other wartime American President besides Abraham Lincoln would

---

* Frederick Douglass complained that Lincoln's "silly and ridiculous" comments exposed "his pride of race and blood, his contempt for negroes and his canting hypocrisy," and that the President was essentially telling African Americans, "I don't like you, you must clear out of the country."

have been so skeptical about himself and his cause to concede—even in private—that Providence might not necessarily be on his side? More important, Lincoln was expressing his suspicion that by withholding victory from both sides and prolonging the war, God must wish the conflict to end not simply with the reunion of North and South but with emancipation.

* * *

B Y SEPTEMBER, AFTER the second Bull Run debacle, the despondent President opted to accommodate McClellan, wage this struggle as a defensive war, and eschew a more radical approach on slavery. Lincoln prodded a group of Christian abolitionists from Chicago to help him solve his dilemma: "What *good* would a proclamation of emancipation from me do, especially as we are now situated?" He added that with the South in full defiance, he did not wish "to issue a document that, the whole world will see, must necessarily be inoperative, like the Pope's bull against the comet!" But in the spirit of his earlier private note, he assured the Chicagoans, "It is my earnest desire to know the will of Providence in this matter. And if I can learn what it is, I will do it!" As Lincoln later recalled, he now privately concluded that "if God gave us the victory in the approaching battle," he would construe it as a divine signal to "move forward in the cause of emancipation."

Confronted that same month with the mixed results of the Battle of Antietam, Lincoln convened his Cabinet secretaries and read them his "preliminary" Emancipation Proclamation, having "fixed it up a little."* He told them he wished there were "a better time" to act and that the Union side was "in a better condition," but had concluded that "the time has come now."

Lincoln was renowned for his ability to speak to Americans in imperishable prose redolent of emotion and history, but that facility was

---

* Claiming about 4,300 deaths, the day of that confrontation has been called the bloodiest in American history, with a toll exceeding that of Pearl Harbor and the terrorist attacks of September 2001.

nowhere evident in this document. He knew that the Radicals would be attracted to the content and that hostile federal judges would seize upon any fault in his legal reasoning. He did not want to scare away others with incendiary language. Thus the language of his proclamation was dry and legalistic, with repeated references to his existing constitutional authority. It was intended to avoid alienating border states and Northern conservatives.

In it, Lincoln assured the public that the war would still be prosecuted to restore the Union. He would once again ask Congress to endorse compensated "immediate or gradual" abolition of slavery and colonization for freed slaves. But on the next New Year's Day, "all persons held as slaves within any State, or designated part of a State . . . in rebellion against the United States, shall be then, thenceforward and forever free."* Reacting to Lincoln's proclamation, Frederick Douglass later said he gave out a "shout for joy" but lamented that it lacked "one expression of sound moral feeling against slavery."

Until the Southern states were firmly reinstalled in the Union, Lincoln's document could not liberate a single slave. It solved some of his short-term political problems by affirming for fellow Republicans that he understood his role as the leader of a party founded to abolish slavery. But Lincoln knew there was a more profound reason to make it clear to the world that his struggle was not merely to save the Union but also to destroy the evil institution that had provoked this Civil War. He understood that it was an intense feeling of soaring mission that had spurred American patriots to jeopardize their lives fighting British oppressors in the Revolutionary War. He hoped his proclamation would lift the stated war aims of the Union side beyond merely the legal reunion of North and South to the more exalted aspiration that he would soon come to call a "new birth of freedom."

Predictably, New England celebrated Lincoln's surprise. Joyous

---

* In his proclamation, striving to demonstrate that he was acting within the intentions displayed by Congress, Lincoln also noted the act passed by Congress in March 1862 "to make an additional article of War," which prevented the US military from being used to return fugitive slaves—as well as its measure of July 1862 holding that all slaves held by people in rebellion against the US government that took refuge within Union lines would be deemed "captives of war" and "forever free."

citizens of Bangor, Maine, fired off a hundred guns at noon and lit bonfires at night. The *Boston Journal* predicted that Lincoln's order "may become the most important ever issued in this country since the Declaration of Independence." The *Daily Green Mountain Freeman* of Montpelier, Vermont, applauded the President for taking "the decisive step . . . on which the war is to be hereafter waged. . . . The mighty word which will make this Republic free, has at last been resorted to." The *New York Evening Post* said it "animates our soldiers with the same spirit which led our forefathers to victory under Washington."

But the Democratic *New York Evening Express* warned that Lincoln's order was designed "to degrade and destroy white labor, and to reduce the white man to the level of the negro." The *Indianapolis Star* argued that the action was unnecessary because "the freeing of the slaves of the rebels can be attained when our forces occupy rebel territory." It warned of a forecast "from high authority" that "in sixty days we should have either an ignominious peace, acknowledging the Southern Confederacy, or else a dictator." The *Signal* of Joliet, Illinois, a Democratic paper, agreed that the document revealed the President's "despotic tendency," since he "has no more right to abolish slavery than he has to abolish the institution of marriage." Kentucky's *Louisville Journal* called Lincoln's "wholly pernicious" order a "gigantic usurpation . . . aggravated by the menace of great and unmixed evil. Kentucky cannot and will not acquiesce in this measure. Never!" The *Richmond Enquirer* castigated Lincoln: "Let the civilized world fling its scorpion lash upon him!"

* * *

Lincoln did not campaign in the 1862 midterm elections. He considered it unfitting for a war President and knew that—tainted by what he privately called the "ill-success of the war"—he was too unpopular to do much good for Republicans. He was pained to learn that Democrats were exploiting his actions on habeas corpus and the Emancipation Proclamation as campaign issues. In New York, Horatio

Seymour, running for Governor, vowed to stop the President's unwarranted arrests "even if the streets be made to run red with blood." Mary Lincoln tried to help improve her husband's standing with a visit to the Brooklyn Navy Yard, arriving with Fort Sumter's General Anderson.

That fall, the President issued what amounted to a national extension of his suspension of the writ—an edict that gave military officers authority to arrest Americans deemed "guilty of any disloyal practice" or "aid and comfort to the Rebels," including efforts to block the draft or signup of volunteers. Maryland's abolitionist ex-Congressman Henry Winter Davis, seeking to reenter the House, called Lincoln's action "court martial despotism." Denouncing the Emancipation Proclamation, many Ohio Democrats demanded "the Constitution as it is, the Union as it was." To this slogan a few appended, "the Negroes where they are." William Allen, the state's former Democratic Senator, warned that liberated slaves, "with their hands reeking in the blood of murdered women and children," might "cross over into our state" and compete with white Ohioans for jobs.

Lincoln had to cope, as well, with the fact that his Treasury was in trouble. After the Bull Run defeat of 1861, many banks had declined to help the federal government. Eschewing a property tax like that of the 1812 war as an unfair gift to wealthy owners of stocks and bonds, Congress instead passed the nation's first income tax, on upper-income Americans, and established a Bureau of Internal Revenue; the President approved the measure in July 1862. With considerable success, he also encouraged Americans "of small means" to purchase war bonds.

As the fall of 1862 began, Lincoln was morose over his political prospects. However, he soon told a visitor that "there is no use in being blue" and that he felt "a good deal better" after seeing a poll showing that eight hundred out of a thousand in one regiment backed him. In the midterm elections, although Republicans gained a seat in the Senate, they lost a fifth of their seats in the House. The *New York Times* believed that the balloting revealed a "want of confidence" in the President. In Illinois, Lincoln's close friend Leonard Swett, who lost his own congressional election, wrote a friend that the Emancipation Proclamation "did great harm" when "Negroes from the south were taken into our state." Senator Trumbull found that many Republicans "believed that their sons & relations were being sacrificed to the incompetency, indisposition or treason of a great many Democratic generals." Angry about the House defeat, the Maine Congressman Frederick Pike, a Republican, wished that Lincoln "would leave off story telling long enough to look after the war."

The President privately concluded that announcing the preliminary emancipation before the midterm election had been a "great mistake." He had hoped it would bring "greater gain than loss."* A few Republican Congressmen from Pennsylvania came to the Executive Mansion and told Lincoln that some of their state's party chiefs "would be glad to hear some morning that you had been found hanging from the post of a lamp at the door of the White House." The President replied that they should not be surprised to hear someday that this had come to pass. He regained his sense of humor when asked about the victory of Horatio Seymour, the Democratic candidate for Governor of New York, explaining that he felt like the Kentucky boy "who stubbed his toe while running to see his sweetheart" and "said he was too big to cry, and far too badly hurt to laugh."†

Now Lincoln had to act on McClellan. About a month before the election, he had seen the General at his field headquarters, spoken with soldiers, and slept in a tent overnight, after which he concluded, "I am now stronger with the Army of the Potomac than McClellan." In late October, McClellan refused the President's request to go after General Robert E. Lee's forces, explaining that his horses were "absolutely broken down from fatigue." Lincoln curtly replied, "Will you pardon me for asking what the horses of your Army have done since the Battle of Antietam that fatigue anything?"

---

* In December, House Democrats proposed a resolution that Lincoln's emancipation was "a high crime against the Constitution"—not accidentally echoing the Constitution's requirement for a President's impeachment—but were rebuffed by the Republican majority.

† Adlai Stevenson, great-grandson of Lincoln's close Illinois friend Jesse Fell, quoted these words on Election Night 1952, in Springfield, while conceding to Dwight Eisenhower.

The President had decided not to remove McClellan before the elections because it might look panicky or as if he was avoiding the blame for Union military frustrations. But after the results came in, he took the action and solemnly promised Senator Chandler that the "war shall henceforth be prosecuted with tremendous energy." The following month, Lincoln told Congress, "We cannot escape history. . . . The fiery trial through which we pass will light us down in honor or dishonor to the latest generation. . . . We shall nobly save or meanly lose the last best hope of earth." When Lincoln issued his final emancipation document on New Year's Day 1863, Senator Wade said, "Now hurrah for Old Abe and the *proclamation*." Later that month, the President boasted to abolitionist leaders that he had "knocked the bottom out of slavery."

* * *

LINCOLN'S STRENGTH AMID his own trial by fire was all the more admirable in light of his lifelong struggle with depression. His childhood had been one of loss and alienation. As he later said, he was a "poor, friendless boy." His mother, Nancy, had perished when he was nine, his only brother, Thomas, at three days old, and his only sister, Sarah, who had looked after him, when he was eighteen. He felt so estranged from his gruff, willful, illiterate father, Thomas, that he never permitted Thomas or his second wife, Sarah, to meet Mary or their children. When Thomas was dying, Lincoln asked his stepbrother to "say to him that if we could meet now, it is doubtful whether it would not be more painful than pleasant," and he declined to attend his father's funeral.

Despite his natural melancholy, Lincoln did not try to wall himself off from the agonies of the national struggle. He believed it was important for him to see fallen Union soldiers being buried in the cemetery near the Soldiers' Home, the presidential summer retreat up the hill from the White House; the sight would confront him, however traumatically, with the fearsome results of the decisions he made about the war.

This President had few close friends, and amid the sadness and chaos

of these years, the instability of Mary Lincoln deepened his anxieties.*
Replying to her abiding dread that someone would murder him, he tried
to assuage her: "All imagination! Don't worry about me, Mother, as if
I were a little child." Once an overnight guest at the Mansion heard,
through a wall, the agitated First Lady telling her husband, "Need to
be taught a lesson—yes, sir! Promise me what I asked you, or I won't
leave go of them!" Lincoln replied, "Ma—come now! Be reasonable. . . .
How do you reckon I can go to a Cabinet meeting—without my *pants*!"
After the President spoke at a fair, she loudly told him, "That was the
worst speech I ever listened to. . . . I wanted the earth to sink and let me
go through!" Orville Browning later recalled that Lincoln told him more
than once "that he was constantly under great apprehension lest his wife
should do something which would bring him into disgrace."

Mary lost two Confederate half brothers to the Civil War, but
wild, unfounded rumors had it that she was a secret secessionist, even
an enemy spy. When her rebel brother-in-law, Ben Hardin Helm,
died in the Battle of Chickamauga, the President wired sanction for
Mary's sister Emilie to return to Kentucky. Asked to swear allegiance
to the United States, she refused, and Lincoln took the political risk
of harboring her at the White House. When General Daniel Sickles
complained to him about it, the President bridled and said that "my
wife and I are in the habit of choosing our own guests." Defying aspersions about her political loyalties, the First Lady raised money for military hospitals and comforted wounded Union soldiers, touching their
faces. For some of the veterans whose hands no longer functioned, she
wrote letters home. Sometimes the President came too, thanking the
patients for their courage. In one clinic, they handed out Christmas
turkeys, paid for by Lincoln with $1,000 (about $19,000 today) of his
own money.

As the war ground on, although Lincoln told friends, "I have all

---

* Lincoln had told William Herndon, his Springfield law partner, that he contracted syphilis in
the mid-1830s. Whether or not this was true, he may have suspected that he had passed the disease
to Mary, hastening her deterioration and imbuing him with a sense of guilt.

my life been a fatalist," he found some surcease in religion. As a young man, he had written an essay doubting Jesus Christ's divinity and the notion that the Bible was a reliable indicator of God's purposes, and it was burned by a friend, Samuel Hill, who feared for Lincoln's political future. Campaigning for Congress in the mid-1840s, he had to deny rumors that he was "an open scoffer at Christianity." But as President, he pronounced himself "an humble instrument in the hands of the Almighty, and of this, his almost chosen people." Late in the conflict, Joshua Speed, Lincoln's Springfield roommate, was startled to find the old skeptic absorbed in his Bible. The President admonished Speed, "Take all of this book upon reason that you can, and the balance on faith, and you will live and die a happier and better man."

* * *

IN JANUARY 1863, Clement Vallandigham, Democrat from Ohio, rose in the House of Representatives to demand that Lincoln's efforts to crush the Southern rebellion be adjudged an "utter, disastrous and most bloody failure." (One reporter noted "the unpleasantly conspicuous pieces of gold in his front teeth.") Vallandigham called for the military struggle to be shut down through arbitration by France, resulting in "informal, practical recognition" of the Confederacy, which would let North and South reunite gradually in peace.

"I did not support the war, and today I bless God that not the smell of so much as one drop of its blood is upon my garments," the Ohioan boasted.

> I have denounced, from the beginning, the usurpations and the
> infractions, one and all, of law and Constitution, by the President
> and those under him—their repeated and persistent arbitrary ar-
> rests, the suspension of *habeas corpus,* the violation of freedom
> of the mails, of the private house, of the press and of speech . . .
> which have made this country one of the worst despotisms on
> earth. . . . Has sufficient blood been shed, treasure expended,

and misery inflicted in both the North and the South? . . . Stop
fighting! Make an armistice. No formal treaty. . . . Let slavery
alone. . . . Let us choose a new President in 'sixty-four.

The *Journal* of Gallipolis, Ohio, groused that Vallandigham was
asking for "surrender to the rebels by changing the Constitution to
suit Jeff Davis." Republicans called the Ohioan and other Democrats
who shared his views "Copperheads," in honor of the lowly, poison-
ous snake that struck without warning. Lincoln knew that the Copperheads were not the only Northerners feeling disenchanted by his
war. Voluntary enlistments to fight with the Union Army seemed in
danger of drying up, so the President persuaded Congress to impose
the first wartime draft in American history. Millions of men from ages
twenty to forty-five had to register. The rich could avoid going to war
by hiring a substitute or paying a fee of $300 (about $5,600 today).
Of this loophole, Joseph Medill wrote to his *Chicago Tribune* Washington correspondent, Horace White, "Since I have lived in Illinois,
I never witnessed greater hostility to any public measure. . . . There
is no possible defense, justification or apology that can be made for
this outrage."

At Medill's behest, White shared this letter with the President, who
was well informed on the rising opposition to both his conscription program and the Emancipation Proclamation in the Midwest and western
states. Lincoln was warned of chatter that citizens in these disgruntled
regions, provoked by secret pacifist societies and rebel agents, might flee
the Union and join the Confederacy. He told Senator Sumner that he
dreaded "the fire in the rear more than our military chances." Richard
Yates, the Governor of Illinois, a Republican who was Lincoln's friend,
persuaded the President to send federal regiments to Springfield to guard
against this internal danger.

Lincoln asked General Ambrose Burnside, who now commanded the
Department of the Ohio, to make sure that the American West stayed
in the Union. Having failed in the Battle of Fredericksburg, Burnside
now acted against "treason, expressed or implied," issuing General Order

Number 38, an edict that anyone suspected of aiding the country's "enemies," which—in defiance of the First Amendment—included "declaring sympathies" for the rebels, would be arrested for treason and/or espionage. Deliberately flouting the order, Vallandigham, by now seeking the Democratic nomination for Governor of Ohio, publicly decried the "wicked, cruel and unnecessary war" being waged "for the purpose of crushing out liberty and erecting a despotism" and seeking "the freedom of the blacks and the enslavement of the whites." He urged young men to defy the draft or desert their comrades on the battlefield, and vowed to "hurl King Lincoln from his throne."

Burnside retaliated by sending soldiers to Vallandigham's home in Dayton, where they knocked down doors to subdue the Congressman in his bedroom. That night, in protest, five hundred or more of Vallandigham's angry backers stormed over to the pro-Lincoln *Dayton Daily Journal*, burned down the building, and destroyed the city's telegraph lines, with the flames consuming the neighborhood. Burnside had his quarry tried in a military court for "declaring disloyal sentiments and opinions" with the object of weakening the government's "efforts to suppress an unlawful rebellion." Vallandigham was convicted and sentenced to prison for the war's duration at Fort Warren, in the harbor of abolitionist Boston.

At a protest by three thousand people in New York's Union Square, when someone mentioned Lincoln's name, there were calls of "Hang him!" Another speaker warned that "never since this country was founded has human liberty been in such jeopardy." Someone else noted that the words Vallandigham had spoken were tamer than Lincoln's criticism, while in Congress, of President Polk and his Mexican War. Worried that Vallandigham would become a dangerous martyr, Lincoln had his sentence commuted, directing instead that he be sent through enemy lines to the South, from which it would be more difficult for him to undermine the Northern war effort. Vallandigham pronounced himself "a prisoner of war." When he reached the Confederacy, the *Macon Telegraph* noted that the visitor was "cheerful, and seems to breathe freer on escaping Lincoln's despotism." Despite his presence in the nest of the enemy, Ohio's Democratic leaders made him their choice for governor.*

Lincoln's infringements of civil liberties were being castigated within both parties. Browning, his friend, called them "illegal and arbitrary." The President defended himself by replying to a public letter from Democrats of Albany, New York, who had complained that his treatment of Vallandigham and other actions were unconstitutional. Lincoln explained that he was facing "a clear, flagrant and gigantic case of rebellion." He noted that the Constitution said that habeas corpus should not be suspended "unless when, in cases of rebellion or invasion, the public safety may require it," and this was "our present case." He was dealing with "a most efficient corps of spies, informers, suppliers and aiders and abettors" of the rebels. Vallandigham had not been arrested, he wrote, for "damaging the political prospects of the administration," but for "laboring, with some effect, to prevent the raising of troops, to encourage desertions from the Army . . . and this gave the military constitutional jurisdiction to lay hands upon him. . . . Must I shoot a simple-minded soldier boy who deserts, while I must not touch a hair of a wiley agitator who induces him to desert?"† Burnside had the *Chicago Times* shut down for attacking Lincoln's emancipation as "a criminal wrong" and the war as "national suicide," but the President ordered him to desist. In mid-June, up to one hundred thousand haters of Lincoln's war staged a mass meeting at the fairgrounds in his hometown of Springfield and cheered for Vallandigham.

Lincoln privately insisted that military victories would overcome public unhappiness with his other policies, and was dispirited when the Union's defeat at Chancellorsville in May was followed by other

* When Ohio Democrats demanded Vallandigham's return, Lincoln wrote them, "We all know that combinations, armed in some instances, to resist the arrest of deserters, began several months ago; that more recently the like has appeared in resistance to the enrolment preparatory to a draft; and that quite a number of assassinations have occurred from the same animus. These had to be met by military force, and this again has led to bloodshed and death. . . . I solemnly declare my belief that this hindrance, of the military, including maiming and murder, is due to the course in which Mr. V. has been engaged . . . in a greater degree than to any other one man."

† Lincoln's letter was widely circulated in pamphlet and other forms. The New York Republican Roscoe Conkling called it "the best campaign document we can have in this state."

setbacks. Then, on the Fourth of July, Lincoln was told of General Meade's triumph at Gettysburg, followed by news of another at Vicksburg, Mississippi, raising hopes that the Civil War might soon be over. The President grew furious when he realized that Meade had neglected a "golden opportunity" to finish off Lee's Army; he complained that the General and his men had "held the war in the hollow of their hand, and they would not close it." With moist eyes, Lincoln told his son Robert, "If I had gone up there, I could have whipped them myself." In an unsent letter, he wrote Meade that General Lee had been "within your easy grasp, and to have closed upon him would, in connection with our other late successes, have ended the war." But now "the war will be prolonged indefinitely" and "I am distressed immeasurably because of it."

The week after Gettysburg saw three days of riots in New York City against Lincoln's draft law and the unfairness of letting rich men pay for substitutes. A mob had rushed into the office where a blindfolded official was spinning a wheel and calling out conscription numbers. Draft officers were attacked with stones, clubs, and brickbats, and their records were "dragged into the street, torn into fragments and scattered everywhere with loud imprecations and savage yells," the New York Times reported. The building was set aflame. A deputy provost marshal stepped outside to assure the rioters that all draft materials had been destroyed. He was beaten to death. Some shouted that they would be willing to fight if rich men would shoulder the same musket. One protester called out, "Old Abe will pay $300 to keep quiet!" As the melee spread, the Times wrote that one of its "most cowardly features" was "the causeless and inhuman treatment of the negroes of the City." More than a dozen African Americans were maimed and killed, including one man who was hanged and his corpse then burned by a "devilish" crowd. Washington's Evening Star reported that, "thirty thousand strong," the wild mobs had the nation's largest city "in their possession and were burning and destroying on all sides." More than a hundred people died.

New York's Governor Horatio Seymour wrote Lincoln that the military draft was illegal and his state was bearing too much of the burden. The President scrawled out for Seymour a more succinct public notice that he would not stop conscription unless the Supreme Court ruled it unconstitutional, noting that the enemy "drives every able-bodied man he can reach into his ranks, very much as a butcher drives bullocks into a slaughter pen." The Union could no longer "waste time to re-experiment with the volunteer system." Lincoln wanted to justify his rich-man's loopholes as a benefit to the poor but wisely kept silent. Feeling more hopeful about the war, he assured his aide John Hay that the enemy "will break to pieces if we only stand firm now."

* * *

INFURIATED BY REPORTS of the pro-Vallandigham rally in his own beloved Springfield, Lincoln was eager to return to his hometown for the first time since leaving to become President. His old friend James Conkling was staging a "grand Mass Meeting" at the same fairgrounds, uniting "War Democrats" and Republicans in support of Lincoln, the Union, and "constitutional government." Conkling wrote the President, "We intend to make the most imposing demonstration that has ever been held in the Northwest." Conkling urged him "to abandon, for a few days, the fatigues and anxieties of official duties and indulge in some relaxation, which perhaps the state of your health may require." As an additional spur, Conkling warned that "the Presidential campaign for your successor (if any) has already commenced in Illinois."

But Lincoln feared leaving his duties in Washington. Instead he wrote out a letter for Conkling to read aloud at the rally (he asked him to do it "very slowly"). This statement was aimed at his critics in the crowd. It would warn that for the moment there was no reason to think that any compromise with the South to preserve the Union was possible:

> To be plain, you are dissatisfied with me about the negro. . . .
> You dislike the Emancipation Proclamation. . . . You say it is
> unconstitutional—I think differently. I think the constitution
> invests its Commander-in-Chief with the law of war, in time
> of war. . . . Some of the commanders of our armies in the field

who have given us our most important successes believe the emancipation policy, and the use of colored troops, constitute the heaviest blow yet dealt to the Rebellion, and that at least one of those important successes could not have been achieved when it was but for the aid of black soldiers. . . . You say you will not fight to free negroes. Some of them seem willing to fight for you; but, no matter. Fight you, then, exclusively to save the Union.

General Ulysses Grant had assured the President that the emancipation had been "the heaviest blow yet given the Confederacy" because ex-slaves "will make good soldiers and taking them from the enemy weakens him in the same proportion they strengthen us." Now, in his public letter, Lincoln explained, "I issued the proclamation on purpose to aid you in saving the Union."

When the rally was held, the crowd size roughly matched that of the earlier Copperhead event. After Lincoln's letter was heard, the *Joliet Signal* claimed that participants had been falsely told "that Abraham would honor the occasion with his distinguished presence" and that "greenbacks were distributed liberally to arouse a feeling of enthusiasm." Lincoln's letter was widely published and read out at other rallies. The *Boston Evening Transcript* lauded the President's rebuke to Vallandigham, the "worthless demagogue," and "skulking traitors who are aiming to give our soldiers a stab in the back."

Lincoln wished to issue a compact, elegant new statement of why this war had to be fought that was more than merely a rebuttal to the Democrats or Copperheads. A cemetery was to be dedicated at Gettysburg on Thursday, November 19. Lincoln accepted the invitation to offer a coda to the main address, to be delivered by Edward Everett of Massachusetts, a former Senator, Governor, and Secretary of State (under Millard Fillmore). It was announced that the First Lady would accompany the President to Gettysburg, but on Wednesday morning, just before their departure from the Executive Mansion to board a special four-car train, Tad grew ill. Panicked by the possibility of danger to still another son,

Mary demanded that her husband forgo his speech and stay home, and was outraged when he told her that he could not stay home.

On an unusually warm autumn day at Gettysburg, the President, wearing his black stovepipe hat, climbed onto a horse and joined a funerary parade to the battleground. "A great many citizens of Gettysburg are in the relic business," one witness reported, "and sold immense numbers of shot and unexploded shell, during the day, at stiff prices." The throng was jammed into a modest area, it was said, "like fishes in a barrel." Everett spoke for more than two hours, and Lincoln vigorously shook the orator's hand before the performance of a special new hymn.[*] Then he stepped forward to deliver, from notes, what would become the most famous address ever uttered by an American President in time of war or peace.

"Four score and seven years ago," he began, "our fathers brought forth on this continent, a new nation, conceived in Liberty, and dedicated to the proposition that all men are created equal." This reaffirmed Lincoln's public insistence, which had started with the emancipation, that this war be waged not only to restore the Union created by the Founders but also to advance their commitment, as stated in the Declaration of Independence, to equality. He went on, "Now we are engaged in a great civil war, testing whether that nation, or any nation so conceived and so dedicated, can long endure." To those demanding the restoration of the Union without disturbing slavery, he was saying that fulfillment of both of those missions was required to fully realize the dreams of the Founders. With the remains of rebel and Union soldiers lying all around him, the President concluded, "From these honored dead we take increased devotion to that cause for which they here gave the last full measure of devotion—that we here highly resolve that these dead shall not have died in vain—that this nation, under God, shall have a new birth of freedom—and that government of the people, by the people, for the people, shall not perish from the earth."

After speaking these few poetic words, Lincoln was done. His

---

[*] Afterward Everett wrote Lincoln, back at the White House, "I hope your anxiety for your child was relieved on your arrival."

listeners responded with a great wave of applause, not knowing whether he had more to say. But he had not been asked to provide the main oration, only a postscript. He was trying to influence not only those at Gettysburg but a national audience, and he knew that a brief statement was more likely to be widely republished and taken to heart.

Although the speech was widely admired, Democratic papers complained that Lincoln had turned his blessing of the Gettysburg "necropolis" into a partisan occasion, "coldly calculating the political advantages" of "an offensive exhibition of boorishness and vulgarity" that was "more for his benefit" than the "honor of the dead." One asked, "Is Mr. Lincoln less refined than a savage?" Some journals contended that the President's reference to the Founders' commitment to equality was "gross ignorance" or a deliberate "perversion of history." Deriding Lincoln's "silly remarks," Madison, Wisconsin's *Daily Patriot* noted that the Constitution "does not say one word about equal rights" and "expressly admits the idea of the inequality of human rights." Of the Gettysburg dead, the Lincoln-hating *Chicago Times* asked, "How dared he, then, standing on their graves, misstate the cause for which they died, and libel the statesmen who founded the government?"

✳ ✳ ✳

EARLY IN 1864, Lincoln told his Illinois friend Reverend Owen Lovejoy, "This war is eating my life out. I have a strong impression that I shall not live to see the end." Another home state friend, Leonard Swett, found him "much more eager" to be reelected than he had been to seek a first term. Despite her sorrows, Mary started entertaining again, hoping to reward important allies in an election year. Lincoln feared that if turned out of office before the war ended in victory, history would view him as a President so inept that he could not subdue the errant rebels, despite the strategic advantages enjoyed by the Northern side, with its formidable industry and four times greater population. He knew that no other Republican was as likely to win in 1864, and that a Democratic successor might well try to shut down the war without achieving either emancipation or reunion of North and South.

But Republican leaders were by no means all agreed that Lincoln should run again. Some, like his Secretary of the Treasury, Salmon Chase, hankered to replace him. In February, Chase's backers in Congress sent out broadsides that derided Lincoln's "vacillation and indecision" and called his reelection "practically impossible." Chase claimed not to have been involved, but Lincoln quickly retaliated. He called a meeting of the Republican National Committee, which consisted mainly of men to whom he had given jobs, and they endorsed the President by 80 percent. Soon thereafter, Lincoln's Maryland friend Francis Blair publicly demanded a probe of corruption in Chase's department and decried the Secretary's disloyal, ungentlemanly "intrigue" against the President who had hired him. In early March, Chase pulled out of the race. General Grant, who now commanded Lincoln's armies, loyally rebuffed those who urged him to run against his Commander-in-Chief.

Republicans went to Baltimore in early June as part of what they now called the National Union Party, in an effort to pull in pro-war Democrats. John Nicolay, who was present, noted that the delegates were seeking a Democrat to be Vice President, "provided he would add strength to the ticket." They chose Andrew Johnson, the pro-Union Democratic Military Governor of Tennessee. Lincoln had conveyed his "wish not to interfere" in the contest to be his running mate, and there was an element of fatalism in his diffidence. He had earlier joked that Vice President Hannibal Hamlin, of Maine, was his insurance against assassination by the Confederacy, because Lincoln's murder would usher in a new President who was a Radical. By allowing Johnson to take the number two role, Lincoln was discarding that insurance.

Then, in July 1864, one month short of a half century since the British had torched James Madison's White House, the rebels launched a surprise attack against the Capital. "Let us be vigilant," said Lincoln, "but keep cool." Despite his measured words, one of his generals thought the President looked "almost crushed." Secretary Stanton stationed a gunboat on the Potomac in case Lincoln, like President Madison, had to flee the federal city. The anxious Treasurer of the United States had the currency in his vaults stuffed into sacks for removal by tugboat.

Under General Jubal Early, the rebels soon reached the fortifications defending "Mr. Lincoln's City." Eager to show his bravado, Lincoln mounted a horse and rode uphill to Fort Stevens. There, standing on a parapet, he picked up a pair of field glasses and watched the advancing enemy while bullets whizzed past him—the only time in American history that a sitting President has been exposed to this degree of immediate danger. It was said that a young Union officer and future Supreme Court Justice named Oliver Wendell Holmes shouted at the tall man in stovepipe hat and frock coat, "Get down, you fool!" The President was bravely joined by Mary, who, by one account, collapsed in shock and grief when she saw a wounded surgeon and thought it was her husband.

When the battle was over, Early cried, "We haven't taken Washington, but we've scared Abe Lincoln like hell!" Lincoln was embarrassed, knowing that many Northern voters would now once again wonder whether their Commander-in-Chief knew what he was doing. Furious that the enemy had managed to escape, he complained that his generals hadn't bothered to chase the rebels because they might "actually catch some of them."

By late August, with Union forces bogged down near Petersburg and Atlanta, Lincoln had become convinced that he would lose the fall election to the expected Democratic nominee, General McClellan. Mary Lincoln was terrified of the prospect of defeat. Unbeknownst to her husband, she had run up large hidden debts for fancy clothes and other luxuries that would come due if he lost. To one visitor, the President said, "You think I don't know I am going to be beaten, *but I do*—and unless some great change takes place, *badly beaten*." Seized by a new spell of melancholy, he took out a sheet of stationery and wrote in black ink that "it seems exceedingly possible that this Administration will not be re-elected." After his defeat, "it will be my duty to so co-operate with the President elect, as to save the Union between the election and the inaugeration [*sic*]; as he will have secured his election on such ground that he cannot possibly save it afterwards." In a strange ritual, Lincoln signed and dated this political testament, sealed it in an envelope, and then asked the seven members of his Cabinet to sign it, sight unseen.

On Monday, August 29, the Democrats met in Chicago. They endorsed a platform written by none other than Vallandigham, who was there as a delegate. In the summer of 1863, the Ohioan had made his way from the South to Canada by way of Bermuda. After Ohio Democrats nominated the absentee Copperhead for governor, Lincoln privately said he could not accept that "one genuine American" could be "induced to vote for such a man as Vallandigham," but confessed that he regarded the Ohio balloting with "more anxiety" than he had felt about the election of 1860. Vallandigham lost badly to a War Democrat, John Brough. ("Glory to God in the highest," Lincoln wired Brough. "Ohio has saved the nation.") In Canada, the Copperhead met with rebel agents seeking to seize the state governments of Ohio, Illinois, Indiana, and Kentucky, then, in disguise, sneaked back to his home state. Alerted to this in June 1864, Lincoln scrawled a request to Brough to "watch Vallandigham" and consider his arrest, but did not send it.

Vallandigham's Democratic platform demanded an immediate end to what it called Lincoln's failed "experiment of war" against the South, and would not even require a Southern pledge to rejoin the Union. The presidential nomination went to General McClellan, who was joined on the ticket by Congressman George Pendleton, an Ohio Copperhead crony of Vallandigham's, to prevent the Peace Democrats from bolting the party—a choice that repelled many Union warriors. In one cartoon, a Northern soldier told McClellan, "Goodbye, 'little Mac'—if that's your company, Uncle Abe gets my vote." McClellan announced that, while willing to run, he would not accept the party's platform "for a thousand Presidencies." He added that if peace would not be contingent on the Union's restoration, he could not "look in the face of my gallant comrades of the Army and Navy" and tell them that "the sacrifice of so many of our slain and wounded brethren had been in vain."

Along with McClellan's renown came deep political liabilities. He could not escape his own responsibility for whatever frustrations voters felt about the length and ferocity of the war. Nor was he well poised to denounce Lincoln's unpopular program of military conscription. Noting that the Democrats' "principal thunder" had been directed against the President's "arbitrary arrests" and "reckless overthrow of all the safeguards against despotism which our fathers erected as the rights of the States," the *Pittsburgh Daily Commercial* recalled that McClellan had himself, in the fall of 1861, ordered the "seizure and imprisonment" of secessionist members of the Maryland legislature.

* * *

IN THE PREDAWN hours of Thursday, September 1, 1864, while Democrats were still haggling in Chicago, the skies over Atlanta were lit by soaring rockets as the Army of William Tecumseh Sherman took the city. Lincoln had endorsed Sherman's "hard war" approach, intended to make conquest so excruciating that Southerners would plead for an early peace. "So Atlanta is ours," boasted the General's cable to his superiors, "and fairly won." In Chicago, Joseph Medill, who had feared that his friend Lincoln would be defeated for reelection, now wrote, "The dark days are over. . . . Thanks be to God! The Republic is safe!"

Two weeks later, the President was told that Jubal Early's troops had been pushed out of the Shenandoah. With relief, Lincoln chuckled that it looked as if "the people wanted me to stay here a little longer." One of his Illinois loyalists wrote him, "The September victories have changed it all, and as we reason here, your reelection is certain." But Democratic journals did not relent. Ashland, Ohio's *States and Union* warned that Lincoln "will carry on the war to free the negro, and you would be taxed to pay the bill," while McClellan "is in favor of a restoration of the Union on the basis of the Constitution without any more bloodshed." Ebensburg, Pennsylvania's *Democrat and Sentinel* predicted that if Lincoln were reelected, "no man's life or liberty would be secure at any time he might give offense to some pimp or spy of the Administration, and he might be kidnapped and put into some bastille, there to rot into oblivion."

On Tuesday, November 8, 1864, at the Executive Mansion, Lincoln was pulled to a window by his son Tad to watch Union soldiers lining up to vote. Of Mary, he told aides, "She is more anxious than I." By midnight on that rainy evening, it was clear that the President had won an Electoral College landslide. He told supporters arriving to serenade him, "If I know my heart, my gratitude is free from any taint of personal triumph." Had McClellan been elected and then shut down the war, Lincoln might thereafter have been viewed as a catastrophic President who had spent untold lives to restore the old Union, then ruined the effort by transforming it into a doomed crusade against slavery.

In December, Lincoln asked Congress to pass a constitutional amendment against slavery. He contended that the recent election had shown this position to be the will of the majority: "May we not agree that the sooner, the better?" He argued that if border state members of Congress endorsed the amendment, the South "would soon see they could not expect much help from that quarter . . . and quit their war upon the Government." He assured Missouri Congressman James Rollins that "it will bring the war, I have no doubt, rapidly to a close." Favors and federal appointments were dangled to encourage support for the President's objective. Lincoln told one Congressman, whose brother had been killed in battle, that it was his "duty" to end slavery because "your brother died to save the Republic from death by the slaveholders rebellion."

The President prevailed and, although it was not legally necessary, made a point of signing this Thirteenth Amendment. He told a crowd at the White House that for the war to end, it was essential to root out "the original disturbing cause." The *Liberator* proclaimed, "Glory to God, America's Free!" In Massachusetts, Governor John Andrew asked churches to ring their bells. Referring to the horse-trading, Congressman Thaddeus Stevens of Pennsylvania later recalled that "the greatest measure of the nineteenth century was passed by corruption, aided and abetted by the purest man in America."

Lincoln acceded to Francis Blair's request to be allowed to see his old friend Jefferson Davis in Richmond about making peace. During their visit, Blair told Davis that slavery should no longer be an "obstruction" between them, since the Confederacy was in the process of freeing African Americans in order to fight in its Army. He even suggested that

Davis sign an armistice with the North and transfer his forces to Texas, where they could thwart the designs of the new French-installed Mexican Emperor Maximilian.

In February 1865, Lincoln and Secretary Seward met quietly with three Davis envoys—Alexander Stephens, Robert Hunter, and John Campbell—aboard the steamboat *River Queen* at Hampton Roads, Virginia. The President was in no mood to make serious concessions. Stephens asked him what would happen, should the war end. According to Stephens, Lincoln replied that he considered his Emancipation Proclamation to be a "war measure" that would, by then, be defunct. He had earlier told Orville Browning that he had "never" intended to make slavery's abolition a condition for stopping the war and restoring the Union. Lincoln's reply to Stephens may have sounded as if he was backing down on the issue, but, in fact, he knew that with passage of the Thirteenth Amendment, slavery was finished. He felt that such a negotiating gambit might help Davis save face while surrendering, which could prevent American blood from flowing for another year or more.*

With the war approaching an end, Lincoln struggled with the lame-duck Congress over how to reconstruct the vanquished South. Eager to coax Southern states to give up their arms, he had proposed requiring only that 10 percent or more of a state's population pledge allegiance to the Union and that it honor the emancipation. But the Radicals, led by Benjamin Wade and Henry Winter Davis, feared that such a gentle approach would empower the planter aristocrats and endanger postbellum African American rights. Seizing the initiative in July 1864, the House and Senate had passed the Wade-Davis Bill, which would require a majority of voters in each Southern state wishing to reenter the

---

* At Hampton Roads, Lincoln also revived his old notion of paying the South for emancipation. After the meeting, he drafted a request for Congress to offer $400 million, in two installments, to the rebel states if they stopped resisting federal authority by July, conditioned upon ratification of the Thirteenth Amendment. He told his Cabinet that such a deal was worth the expense since "we are now spending three millions a day" and he could not hope to end the war "in less than a hundred days." But the secretaries demanded that the war be ended "by force of arms," and Lincoln replied, "You are all against me."

Union to swear they had never backed the Confederacy. The fuming President had refused to sign it, telling Seward he wished to know "whether these men intend openly to oppose my election—the document looks that way."

After the 1864 election, Congressman James Ashley, an Ohio Republican, suggested a compromise measure that would recognize the government of Louisiana under Lincoln's 10 percent approach while demanding black voting rights and other Wade-Davis provisions. But Ashley's approach failed, leaving the President, with his imposing reelection majority and a more favorable Congress soon to convene, in command of Southern Reconstruction.* Henry Winter Davis, cosponsor of the Radicals' bill, complained, "Congress has dwindled from a power to dictate law and the policy of the government to a commission to audit accounts and appropriate moneys to enable the Executive to execute his will—and not ours." Senator Sumner, using the filibuster, managed to block recognition of Louisiana, moving Lincoln to gripe, "He hopes to succeed in beating the President so as to change this government from its original form and make it a strong centralized power."

* * *

A T THE CAPITOL, on a rainy, muddy Saturday, March 4, 1865, Lincoln was ready to take his second-term oath. First, Andrew Johnson was sworn in as Vice President on the Senate floor. Recovering from typhoid fever and his journey from Tennessee, Johnson had downed several tumblers of whiskey or brandy, and it showed. In a long rant, the class-conscious ex-tailor noted the guests "with all your fine feathers and geegaws," and thanked God for the fact that he was a "plebian." Lincoln closed his eyes with what the Senate secretary called "unutterable sorrow." Charles Sumner shielded his face with his hands. Zach Chandler later wrote his wife that Johnson had "disgraced himself & the Senate by making a drunken foolish speech. I was never so

---

* Members also recognized that the sooner Southern states were readmitted with a pledge to end slavery, the earlier the Thirteenth Amendment would be ratified.

mortified in my life, had I been able to find a hole I would have dropped through it out of sight." The President told a parade marshal, "Do not let Johnson speak outside," and later observed, "It has been a severe lesson for Andy, but I do not think he will do it again."

When Lincoln stepped outside, onto the platform before the Capitol's East Front, one spectator, John Downing Jr., thought the President "looked, with his fatherly smile and beaming spectacles, like a real paterfamilias." In his brief inaugural address, Lincoln confessed that neither North nor South had "expected for the war the magnitude or the duration which it has already attained. . . . Fondly do we hope, fervently do we pray, that this mighty scourge of war may speedily pass away." Nevertheless, he warned, God might will "that it continue until all the wealth piled by the bondsman's two hundred and fifty years of unrequited toil shall be sunk, and until every drop of blood drawn with the lash shall be paid by another drawn with the sword." Affirming his desire for a gentle peace, he closed, "With malice toward none, with charity for all, with firmness in the right, as God gives us to see the right, let us strive to finish the work we are in, to bind up the nation's wounds, to care for him who shall have borne the battle and for his widow and his orphan, to do all which may achieve and cherish a just and lasting peace among ourselves and with all nations."

The President later said he thought his speech might wear better than "anything I have produced." That night, even though it was wartime, he and Mary rode in their open barouche to the Patent Building for an inaugural ball of four thousand guests, with "a thousand jets of gas lighting up the long hall," so reported the *Philadelphia Inquirer*. At midnight the Lincolns repaired to "a gorgeously fine supper table a thousand feet long," with three bands "discoursing their sweetest airs."

Returning to the Executive Mansion, the depleted President collapsed into bed for several days. Mary told Elizabeth Keckley, her assistant and milliner, that while her husband had won a second term, "I almost wish it were otherwise. Poor Mr. Lincoln is looking so brokenhearted, so completely worn out, I fear he will not get through the next four years." She felt all the more upset because their son Robert, a new Harvard graduate, had joined the Army, and, as she told her husband, she was "frightened he may never come back to us." Trying to calm the First Lady, Lincoln had persuaded Grant, "as though I was not President, but only a friend," to include Robert at "some nominal rank" in his entourage.

In late March, the Lincolns and Tad took the *River Queen* to visit Grant's headquarters at City Point, Virginia. With Grant about to wage a final offensive, Lincoln wanted to make sure it succeeded. But the visit exacerbated Mary's insecurities. She complained after Lincoln rode by horse with Grant, General Ord, and Ord's attractive wife, Mary, while First Lady and Julia Grant followed by ambulance. She accused her husband of making eyes at Mary Ord and thereafter refused to leave her cabin.* Having watched as Mary "repeatedly attacked her husband" in front of the officers, Grant's aide Adam Badeau found it hard to watch his Commander-in-Chief "subjected to this inexpressible public mortification."

Vice President Johnson arrived uninvited and, some thought, drunk again. By Mary's account, her angry husband told her, "For God's sake, don't ask Johnson to dine with us." During formal meetings, the President reiterated the need for postwar reconciliation with the South, telling Grant, "Let them all go, officers and all. . . . I want submission, and no more bloodshed. . . . I want no one punished. Treat them liberally all round. We want those people to return to their allegiance to the Union and submit to the laws." During their visit, Grant asked the President whether he had ever doubted the "final success" of the Union, and Lincoln replied, "Never for a moment." When he learned that Union soldiers were marching into Richmond, he said, "Thank God that I have lived to see this! . . . I have been dreaming a horrid dream for four years, and now the nightmare is gone."

On the sunny spring morning of April 4, wearing his stovepipe hat, Lincoln, along with Tad and Admiral David Porter, toured vanquished Richmond, where Confederates had set fires as they ran away. Throwing

---

* Tart and sure in her opinions, she had complained to Lincoln that Grant was "a butcher" and "not fit to be at the head of an Army. . . . He loses two men to the enemy's one. . . . I could fight an Army as well myself." She rudely told Mrs. Grant, "I suppose you think you'll get to the White House yourself, don't you?"

their caps into the air, African American laborers cried, "There is the great messiah!" and dropped to kiss Lincoln's feet. "Don't kneel to me," he told them. "You must kneel to God only, and thank Him for the liberty you will hereafter enjoy." He told an assembly of black people in Capitol Square, "My poor friends, you are free—free as air. You can cast off the name of slave and trample on it." Asking to visit the "Confederate White House," which Jefferson Davis had just fled, he sat in Davis's club chair, asked for water, and inquired about the daily life of the Mansion. Then he toured the abandoned Virginia State House, its chamber strewn with Confederate currency and upended chairs and desks. Its doorknobs were embossed with the commonwealth's motto, *"Sic semper tyrannis."*

The next day, aboard his steamer, the *Malvern,* half a dozen eminent Virginians asked Lincoln to let their legislature meet and repeal secession, compelling General Lee to surrender without further bloodshed. The skeptical President preferred to leave the task to his armies. On his cruise home, when he saw Mount Vernon, he remembered his own home in Springfield: "How happy, four years hence, will I be to return there in peace and tranquillity!" Arriving back in Washington on the evening of April 9, Lincoln called on Seward, who was in bed, recovering from a carriage accident, and said, "I think we are near the end at last." He did not know that the war was truly over: Lee had surrendered to Grant that afternoon at Appomattox Court House, with the victor magnanimously allowing the rebels to keep their horses for spring plowing.

On the evening of April 11, with torches and banners, an excited, celebratory throng burst onto the North Grounds of the White House, where the President spoke from a second-story window. To make sure he expressed exactly what he meant, he stuck to his manuscript, voicing his hope for "a righteous and speedy peace." But his didactic discussion of the new government of Louisiana under Reconstruction was a disappointment to some of his listeners, who had come for a rousing victory address. Lincoln told the crowd that he hoped to confer the "elective franchise" on "the very intelligent" African Americans, "and on those who serve our cause as soldiers." One of those present, the well-known Shakespearean actor John Wilkes Booth, growled, "That means nigger citizenship. Now, by God! I'll put him through. That is the last speech he will ever make."

The President told his Cabinet the next day that he hoped there would be "no persecution, no bloody work" in the South when peace came. Two days later, he conceded to the department secretaries that he had "perhaps been too fast" in asking for an early Reconstruction. Still, he said, "we can't undertake to run state governments in all these Southern states. Their people must do that, though I reckon that, at first, some of them may do it badly." More than 618,000 Americans may have perished in the Civil War, which remains the largest US death toll for any military conflict.

* * *

LINCOLN WISHED TO make sure that Friday, April 14, 1865, would be immortalized in history. He envisaged the date as a closing bookend to the Civil War, a holiday that future Americans would celebrate. Exactly four years earlier, the Stars and Stripes at Fort Sumter had been lowered in defeat. But on this new fourteenth, under the President's orders, the very same Old Glory would be raised there once again, expunging the humiliation of 1861 and symbolizing, for all time, the victory of the Union armies and reunion of North with South. At the President's request, hoisting what someone called "the old smoke-stained, shot-pierced flag" would be the same officer who had presided over the earlier debacle— Robert Anderson, now a Major General, who had kept it in a New York City bank vault. As it happened, this day would be Good Friday.

At Charleston, South Carolina, "salvos of artillery were fired, and every vessel in the harbor put on its gayest attire," said the *New York Times*. "The national ensign floated from all the principal fortifications, with the exception of Sumter, where was shortly to take place a scene never to be forgotten." The crowd at the old, battered fort featured federal dignitaries—including, by Lincoln's special invitation, the Boston abolitionist William Lloyd Garrison, who had once scorned him as too timid about slavery—and "between 2,000 and 3,000 of the emancipated race, of all ages and sizes. Their appearance was warmly welcomed."* The journalist Theodore Tilton described Sumter's appearance that morning as "a Coliseum of ruins," standing "in its brokenness a fit monument of the broken rebellion."

After noon, on a platform adorned by flowers, myrtle, and bunting, General Anderson stepped forward, vowing "to fulfill the cherished wish of my heart through four long years of bloody war—to restore to its proper place this very flag which floated here during peace, before the first act of this cruel rebellion. I thank God I have lived to see this day." With tears in his eyes, Anderson pulled the halyard that brought the old banner to the top of its standard. According to the *New York Times,* "No sooner had it caught the breeze than there was one tumultuous shout. It was an inspiring moment, grand and sublime, never to be experienced again. Our flag was there, its crimson folds tattered but not dishonored, regenerated and baptized anew in the fires of Liberty." Reverend Theodore Cuyler, a Brooklyn abolitionist, called it "the most exciting moment in my life."

By Lincoln's order, there was a hundred-gun salute—to commemorate the one ordered by Anderson in 1861 before he gave up—and then "a national salute from every fort and rebel battery that fired on Fort Sumter." During a very long speech, Reverend Henry Ward Beecher cried, "No more war, no more accursed secession, no more slavery that spawned them both!" That night, at a jubilant Charleston Hotel banquet, Garrison toasted the President of the United States. He exulted that Abraham Lincoln's "brave heart beats for human freedom everywhere." Raising his glass to this "great" and "honest man," Anderson recalled the threats of assassination before Lincoln's first inauguration. He boasted that by now, the Commander-in-Chief was so beloved that he "could travel all over the country with millions of hands and hearts to sustain him."

✷ ✷ ✷

---

* A white Northern visitor, Edward Cary, found that in Charleston that morning, white locals showed "curiosity" more than "patriotism" but that "Negroes of every shade thronged the streets; gray haired 'uncles' and turbaned 'aunties,' grinning and giggling children, and 'picaninnies,' all manifesting joy to see us."

LINCOLN NEVER GOT to hear about the ceremony he had orchestrated. While the crowd was cheering at Fort Sumter, he and the First Lady climbed into an open carriage, bound for the Washington Navy Yard. In the Capital's spring air, Mary found her husband "almost joyous" and told him, "Dear Husband, you almost startle me by your great cheerfulness." He replied, "And well I might feel so Mary. I consider *this day*, the war has come to a close. . . . We must *both* be more cheerful in the future. Between the war and the loss of our darling Willie, we have both been very miserable."*

That evening, after an early supper, Lincoln told the Speaker of the House, Schuyler Colfax, that he wished to visit California "now that the rebellion is overthrown." Harkening back to the time of Polk and the Mexican War, and eager to pay off the country's Civil War debt, Lincoln said, "I have very large ideas of the mineral wealth of our nation. I believe it practically inexhaustible. . . . Immigration, which even the war has not stopped, will land upon our shores hundreds of thousands more per year from overcrowded Europe. I intend to point them to the gold and silver that wait for them in the West." The presidential couple had planned to go to Ford's Theatre, but Mary's head was aching. Lincoln reminded her that their attendance had been announced, adding that if he stayed at the White House, he would have to deal with "overjoyed, excited people" and "I must have a little rest."†

When the Lincolns arrived at Ford's, the audience rose to the strains of "Hail to the Chief." The President bowed, and a spectator, Daniel Beekman, observed "the most heavenly smile I ever saw on a man's face." Watching *Our American Cousin* from their box, Mary felt that her husband was distracted while laughing at the actors' jokes. Sitting near the stage, John Downing Jr., who had seen Lincoln at his second inaugural,

---

* Mary later assured a friend that "the last day he lived was the happiest of his life."

† Swelling the audience, newspapers had reported that the Lincolns would be accompanied by General Grant and his wife, Julia, but they had declined at the last moment. One theatergoer, Frederick Sawyer, later mused that had Grant attended, "he might have shared the same dreadful fate" as Lincoln. Sawyer added, "How many more martyrs to slavery!"

noted how he "rested his face in both of his hands, bending forward and seemingly buried in deep thought." Just before John Wilkes Booth entered their box, the President told Mary that when his second term in office was done, he wished to go to Jerusalem.

Booth fired his Derringer pistol, waved his dagger, and shouted, *"Sic semper tyrannis!"* He leapt to the stage, breaking his shin. (Some thought he also said, "The South is avenged!") With Lincoln unconscious, people cried, "Stand back! . . . Give him air! . . . Has anyone stimulants?" and, out of fury against the assassin, "Hang him! . . . Kill him!" Weeping intensely, Mrs. Lincoln crooned, "They've murdered Papa! They've murdered Papa!" The full reach of Booth's conspiracy was unknown, and still is. One of his fellow plotters slashed the ailing Secretary Seward at home in his bed.

Rejecting a call to take the President back to the White House, an attending surgeon, Charles Leale, warned that "he would die as soon as he would be placed in an upright position." Thus Lincoln was carried, through the hysterical mob, to a boardinghouse across the street. A military officer waved a sword: "Out of the way, you sons o' bitches!" After gauging the scene, Secretary Stanton wrote down, "It is not probable that the President will live through the night."* "Why didn't he kill me?" cried the First Lady. "Why was I not the one?" In the morning, she wailed and prostrated herself on the floor. Stanton gave an order: "Take that woman out and do not let her in again." When death came at 7:22, Mary, in another room, was told, "It is all over! The President is no more!" She asked her pastor, Phineas Gurley, *"Why did* you not *tell* me?" At the White House, the twelve-year-old Tad Lincoln later observed that perhaps his father belonged in heaven, because "he never was happy after he came here."

Andrew Johnson was sworn in as President while standing in the parlor of his two-room suite at the Kirkwood House, on Pennsylvania

---

* Among the items found in Lincoln's pockets after his murder were his wallet, which contained a five-dollar Confederate bill—probably a souvenir from his Richmond visit—as well as his ivory pocketknife, spectacles, and clippings from newspapers that had praised him. After his granddaughter donated this collection to the Library of Congress in 1937, it was withheld from public view until 1976.

Avenue. Johnson said that while he felt "incompetent" to hold the job, "the duties now are mine" and "the consequences are God's."

Shockingly some of the most prominent Radicals in Congress pronounced themselves glad that Lincoln had been replaced by Johnson, so that a more audacious President could launch the Reconstruction of the South. Henry Davis said he had not spoken with anyone in Washington "who did not consider the change a great blessing." Senator Zach Chandler opined that God had kept Lincoln "in office as long as he was useful, and then substituted a better man to finish the work." Senator Ben Wade assured the new President Johnson that "Mr. Lincoln had too much of human kindness in him to deal with these infamous traitors."

✷ ✷ ✷

T o wage the most momentous war that Americans had ever fought, Abraham Lincoln had made himself, by far, the most powerful President they had ever seen. Convinced that the entire democratic venture was in danger, he took for himself unprecedented authority, but the crucial fact is that he did so within the democratic process, and Congress and the courts, for the most part, affirmed him.* He had closely studied the Constitution and deeply respected it. When he suspended habeas corpus, he did so reluctantly—there was no sign of hunger for personal power. Throughout the war, he made clear that his expansion of presidential authority was intended merely for the duration of the conflict and should not be taken as a precedent either by himself in peacetime or by later Presidents. He expected that "the Executive power itself would be greatly diminished by the cessation of actual war."

Unlike Polk, Lincoln did not trick or lie to Congress. There is no question that he wanted the drama of Fort Sumter in 1861 to unfold in

---

* For instance, in the *Prize Cases* of 1863, by a vote of 5 to 4, with Chief Justice Taney dissenting, the Supreme Court affirmed Lincoln's order to blockade the South in the spring of 1861, while Congress was out of session, without a war declaration by Congress. The Court ruled that the Southern insurrection had provoked a conflict tantamount to war: the President had been compelled to "resist force with force" and could not wait for Congress to "baptize" the struggle "with a name."

a way that would appear most favorable to the Union cause; but, unlike Polk with Mexico, he did not deliberately provoke a counterfeit incident to launch his war. When Lincoln went to battle, he had no concealed private agenda like Polk's to grab new territory. He wished only to fulfill his oath of office by crushing the Southern insurrection and restoring the Union, confessing that if he could do so "without freeing a single slave, I would do it."

Inexperienced in military affairs, aside from his youthful stint in the Black Hawk War, Lincoln had to learn on the job. His talent in managing generals was slow to come, and he had to learn military strategy. What his leadership shows, however, is the overwhelming importance of political skill to a President's ability to wage war. Throughout the conflict, using his deep parliamentary experience, Lincoln made a supreme effort to keep in touch with Congress, consulting members when he thought they differed. The Radical Republicans often exasperated him, but he learned from them and used them to understand public opinion. Without the Radicals' influence, he would have been slower in sacking generals who did not deliver, issuing the Emancipation Proclamation, and, at the end of his life, embracing black suffrage. The same legislative skills that enabled him to build coalitions in Congress helped him to invent strategies that would ultimately knit North and South back together.

Lincoln earnestly tried to inform and educate Americans about his conduct of the war. By contrast with Polk's furtiveness, Lincoln constantly expressed himself to the public—in speeches, public letters, and meetings with visitors who would later divulge the President's utterances to reporters. His sublime abilities as thinker and writer, his legal background, his Bible reading, and his self-acquired knowledge of history let him, at almost every turn, connect his aims to Americans' shared historical memory, their understanding of the Constitution, and their sense of morality. His persuasive eloquence—which no other American President, earlier or later, surpassed—assuaged the people about setbacks on the battlefield and steeled them to support the Union cause, however long and bloody the conflict turned out to be. His decision to widen the aims of the conflict to include abolition lifted the Union struggle to a higher level of moral intensity, which, as he argued, helped to ensure victory.

By the night of his murder, Lincoln had won the Civil War, but in death, to a tragic degree, he lost the peace he had sought. The martyred President had badly erred by allowing the selection of an 1864 running mate who shared neither his talent for leadership nor his vision for the peace. Lincoln's gloomy acquaintance with the unexpected dangers of life should have made him more aware that, with death threats all around and a defeated, furious South, he might not survive a second term: therefore, it was crucial who was Vice President. But instead he had shown uncharacteristic carelessness by letting the hard-drinking, impulsive, ill-tempered Andrew Johnson be first in line to succeed him.

Some argued later that, having won the war, Lincoln was murdered at exactly the right moment to preserve his reputation, since after the war he was bound to collide with the Radical Republicans demanding a punitive Reconstruction of the South.* But that ignores Lincoln's unparalleled political acuity, which had enabled him to wage the Civil War without a direct smashup with the Radicals. After Lincoln's assassination removing the political giant from the presidential chair, the issue of Reconstruction was left to be handled by a Lilliputian, thwarting Lincoln's hope to bind the nation's wounds.

Andrew Johnson's lenience toward the South, including his opposition to granting voting rights to freed African Americans, provoked a backlash in the midterm elections of 1866, which put Congress firmly under the authority of the Radical Republicans. When Johnson was impeached in 1868, escaping conviction by a single vote, Congress dramatically moved the pendulum back from the historic power that Lincoln had acquired for the presidency. Under the sway of the Radicals, Johnson's successor, Ulysses Grant, transformed the South by force until the Democrats seized control of the House of Representatives in 1874.

---

* Alluding to the popular notion that Lincoln had secured his reputation by being assassinated at his political peak, President Kennedy told his brother Robert in October 1962, when Nikita Khrushchev acceded to his demand to remove Soviet missiles from Cuba, "This is the night I should go to the theater."

In November 1876, the Democrat Samuel Tilden, Governor of New York, defeated the Republican Rutherford Hayes, Governor of Ohio, in the popular vote. A fierce dispute over twenty electoral votes was resolved by a tacit deal in which Hayes obtained the presidency in exchange for his pledge to remove federal troops from the South. This bargain closed down Reconstruction, handed political dominance of the region to the Democrats, and postponed a chance for reconciliation of the races, and between North and South, by at least a century. In that same election, Hayes's close friend and protégé, young William McKinley, who had served under him during the Civil War as an Army Major, won his first elective job, as a Congressman from Ohio.

CHAPTER EIGHT

"Maine Blown Up"

O N HAVANA HARBOR, on Tuesday evening, February 15, 1898, aboard the battleship USS *Maine,* sailors stripped off their shirts and fanned themselves in the stagnant heat, which intensified the foul odor of the contaminated water. In his wood-paneled quarters, Captain Charles Dwight Sigsbee, the *Maine*'s commander, sat at his mahogany desk, atop an Oriental carpet; he was writing a letter to his wife, Eliza. Of modest height, the fifty-three-year-old Sigsbee wore wire spectacles and a carefully cultivated thick brush mustache.

Like his men, Sigsbee was shirtless, but out of respect to his rank, even while alone, he wore a sack coat, which had been handed to him by his cabin mess attendant, James Pinckney. Sigsbee described Pinckney as "a light-hearted colored man, who spent much of his spare time in singing, playing the banjo and dancing jigs." The captain was compulsively anxious about the social impact of his manners and clothes, as well as those of other people. Only an hour before his death in 1923, the old, ailing Sigsbee rebuked his male nurse for wearing no socks.

The constellation Orion should have been visible tonight, but when the captain looked through his porthole, he could see only a blue-black overcast sky. In the distance, across the harbor, glowed the pink, ocher, and red stucco and brick of Havana, dominated since Christopher

Columbus's arrival in 1492 by the minions of Spain. It was the second night of the city's wild, gaudy annual Carnival, and the streets were full of music and laughter. But the *Maine's* bored sailors could not join in. Sigsbee had banned them from shore leave for the duration of their stay in Havana Harbor, to prevent any jarring incident that might enrage Spanish officials and thus jeopardize the men on his ship and relations between the United States and Cuba.

The previous month, President William McKinley had ordered the *Maine* to sail from Key West to Havana, to protect "American life and property" from riots and other violence. Three years had passed since the last US ship had visited the city. Sigsbee received the order by code word ("TWO DOLLARS") from General Fitzhugh Lee, US consul general in Havana, who had fought for the Confederacy under his uncle, Robert E. Lee. As Sigsbee later recalled, he had been told to make a "friendly visit" to Cuba, so he had the *Maine* "steam in when the town was alive and on its feet," with his crewmen in Navy blue and officers in frock coats. But Sigsbee soon discovered how combustible the Cuban political climate was. When he attended a bullfight outside Havana, he was handed an angry Spanish broadside, which complained that the "Yankee pigs who meddle in our affairs" had sent the *Maine,* "a man-of-war of their rotten squadron." It proclaimed, "Spaniards! The moment of action has arrived. . . . Death to the Americans!"

Barred from enjoying Havana's Carnival, Sigsbee's sailors on this Tuesday night held their own more tepid celebration aboard the *Maine.* Along the starboard gangway, they danced to accordion music. On the after turret, a gunner's mate strummed a mandolin. Everyone was counting the days until the *Maine* could return to the United States. But many members of that crew now had less than two hours to live.

∗ ∗ ∗

BORN IN ALBANY, New York, Sigsbee was the son of Nicholas, founder of the *Freeholder,* the official journal of the state's Anti-Rent Party, which upheld the rights of struggling tenant farmers like him against the Dutch patroons who had ruled the Hudson Valley for two centuries. Eager to improve his son's social station, Nicholas sent his son to school with the well-to-do boys of the Albany Academy, which contributed to Charles's lifelong fussiness about his appearance and status. In 1859, the father used his political connections to the Democratic Congressman Erastus Corning to help Charles win appointment to the US Naval Academy.* On graduation, the young Sigsbee fought in the Civil War, serving under Admirals David Farragut and David Porter; in early 1865, he joined the retaking of Fort Fisher, North Carolina, which was considered, until World War II, the largest amphibious operation in American history.

Despite his Gilbert-and-Sullivan look and pompous demeanor, Charles Sigsbee stood out in the Navy as the inventor of an important deep-sea sounding device and other oceanographic equipment. He served, for a time, as the Navy's chief hydrographer and discovered what is now still called Sigsbee Deep, the most profound basin in the Gulf of Mexico. A talented amateur cartoonist, he drew sketches of prominent Navy men that were good enough to be published in New York's *Daily Graphic*.

Sigsbee snapped up command of the *Maine* in April 1897 in part to get away from his wife, Eliza, who stayed behind with their children in the family's brick townhouse on Riggs Place in northwest Washington.† His toxic marriage filled him with resentment and sadness. He once told his journal that Eliza was "rarely demonstrative of affection for me" and treated him like "a coal bearer or servant," despite his own "better education and immensely greater experience." Complaining of her lack of panache, he scrawled, *"My house is not managed according to my position. . . .* I requested her to put on the dinner table, habitually, four little bon bon dishes to contain certain candies . . . or salted nuts. . . . She did this twice and never since has it been done." He further carped, "I never

---

* Since Annapolis, Maryland, was dangerous terrain for federal officers after the attack on Fort Sumter in April 1861, the academy was temporarily moved to Newport, Rhode Island.

† The Sigsbees had five daughters (two of whom died young) and a son, Charles Jr.

think of taking a brother officer to a family meal, because I know that in most cases I should be mortified. My wife *never has* had even the most remote idea of tact or *finesse*. . . . Never for one single instant has she been able to realize her responsibility for me as a naval officer—a public man! This is true—quite true! Alas for it! Hell!" Much later, Sigsbee's daughter May angrily wrote him that "your only God is public opinion and your only sense of honor 'Can I get away with it' (at least in regard to your family)."

Sigsbee blamed Eliza's surliness, her experimentation with religious "mushroom cults," and her possible infidelity on her West Point father, General Henry Lockwood, whom he called "a most excellent man but very eccentric."* Sigsbee wrote in his journal that his wife had "always been a 'nagger' of the most pronounced and vulgar type: She nags as the negroes nag each other. And she is a *vindictive* nagger." He asked himself, "Should I submit to nagging, vulgarity, neglect, separation from friends, vindictiveness and pettiness and narrowness of life in every way, and abase myself and appear to like it all?" He wrote, "I wish I could try life all over again, for I believe I am at least a loyal and right thinking gentleman—at least I try to be." But, as a friend recalled, Sigsbee finally opted to "stick it out" in the marriage "and make the best of a bad bargain." While in Washington, he escaped from what he called his "cheerless existence" by seeking out other women. When he was at sea, he found that his relations with Eliza improved; he explained to chums that he kept his "equilibrium" by writing her warm letters, trying to convince himself that his wife was actually everything he had "really hoped that she would be." That is what the captain was doing on his fateful Tuesday night aboard the *Maine*.

While donning his sack coat, Sigsbee had found a ten-month-old letter from one of Eliza's friends, which had gone unanswered. On the ship's tricolor stationery, he started writing Eliza ("My darling Wife")

---

* Early in their marriage, Sigsbee had found a letter suggesting that Eliza had been sexually involved with another man just before her wedding; he hid the letter for use as ammunition against her, should he later seek a divorce.

to apologize, and heard the *Maine*'s Marine bugler, "Fifer" Newton, the popular third baseman for the ship's baseball team, play "Taps." Sigsbee put down his fountain pen to listen. Then, at 9:40, just as he slipped his completed letter ("Lovingly, C.D.S.") into an envelope, he heard the horrific boom.

Sigsbee found it "a bursting, rending and crashing sound or roar of tremendous volume . . . followed by a succession of heavy, ominous metallic sounds, probably caused by the overturning of the central superstructure and by falling debris." After that came "intense blackness and smoke." As he later recalled, "For a moment, the instinct of self-preservation took charge of me, but this was immediately dominated by the habit of command." He later wrote Eliza, "When the shock occurred I knew what was the matter and that the vessel was lost. I immediately pulled myself together and thereafter felt no excitement whatever and was much better prepared, than commonly, to do the proper thing calmly. My mind was very active but I was not emotional. I knew that I could not permit myself to *feel* sentimentally."

Rejecting his impulse to crawl through an air vent, Sigsbee took "the more dignified way of making an exit through the passageway leading forward through the superstructure." In the darkness, an orderly, Private William Anthony, bumped into him hard. Rather than run for his life, Anthony saluted, formally apprised the captain that the *Maine* had been "blown up" and was "sinking," and made himself useful.* When Sigsbee's eyes began to function, he saw "white forms on the water" and heard cries for help, but when he commanded the lowering of the boats, he discovered that only three of fifteen vessels had survived the explosion. From atop the poop deck, Cadet Wat Cluverius heard terrible sounds from below, as, in Sigsbee's words, "the poor wretches, pinned down and drowning, mangled and torn, screamed in agony."

---

* Anthony soon became well known when Sigsbee publicly praised his "heroism," saying that "at great personal risk," the orderly "hung near me with unflagging zeal and watchfulness." In November 1899, however, unable to find a permanent job, Anthony committed suicide by drinking liquid cocaine in New York's Central Park. His burial costs were paid by the *Philadelphia Times* and the Democrats of New York's Tammany Hall machine. The US Navy later named destroyers in Anthony's honor during both world wars.

The *Maine* was sinking fast. Sigsbee cried, "Get into the boats, gentlemen!" Two of his officers presented their hands to help the captain move from the flaming wreck into a lifeboat, but Sigsbee insisted on being the final man to depart his ship. His deck officer, Lieutenant John Blandin, thought his commander seemed "as cool as if at a ball." Before Sigsbee stepped into his gig, he was presented with his pug dog Peggy, who had survived the blast and fire. As the oarsmen rowed away, the captain called out, "Are there any left alive? If so, for God's sake, speak!" From the doomed battleship, there was only silence. Some of the *Maine*'s survivors had been rescued by the Spanish cruiser *Alfonso XII*.

Climbing aboard the merchant steamer *City of Washington*, Sigsbee was told that only 84 or 85 Americans had withstood the *Maine* disaster, leaving 265 missing or killed.* (The dead included Sigsbee's cabin aide Pinckney and Newton, his bugler.) "A wholesale murder of sleeping men!" exclaimed Lieutenant Richard Wainwright, Sigsbee's executive officer.† In the *City of Washington*'s dining saloon, Sigsbee looked after some wounded men lying on mattresses. Then he stepped onto the deck to watch a few last sputtering explosions aboard the dying *Maine* before it slipped beneath the waves.

Seeking refuge in the captain's cabin of the steamer, Sigsbee penciled a cable to Secretary of the Navy John Long in Washington, which, as he well knew, would soon be published around the world. "Maine blown up in Havana Harbor at nine forty to-night and destroyed," it began. "Many wounded and doubtless more killed or drowned." Whatever Sigsbee's motives in writing it, one sentence in his message stands out: "Public opinion should be suspended until further report."

Even amid the trauma and confusion of this terrible night, Sigsbee clearly understood that he, almost single-handedly, had the power to stampede Americans into a war against Spain. A more grandiloquent or

---

* The final death toll was established as 266, with 94 survivors.

† In the stream of American history, Wainwright's uncle George Dallas had been Polk's Vice President during the Mexican War. Another relative, Jonathan Wainwright, fifteen years old in 1898, would become the Allied commander who surrendered the Philippines in 1942, during World War II.

impulsive commander, or one who sought such a conflict, might have—even in the absence of unambiguous evidence—accused Spain, which would have ignited a fever for immediate retaliation that would have been very difficult for Congress or President McKinley to stop. Sigsbee's restraint gave his political superiors in Washington the chance, should they wish to use it, to restrain Americans from insisting on war against Spain until there was a serious investigation of why the *Maine* had been sunk. This reflected Sigsbee's underlying respect for the constitutional notion that such ultimate decisions of war and peace should be made by civilian, elected authorities, not the military.

That having been said, Sigsbee was also well aware that if it should appear that the *Maine* had been destroyed because of any negligence by him, he would become a national pariah. He later confessed that when the *Maine* exploded, "to tell the truth, my first thought was—what will the newspapers say at home?" The day after the catastrophe, Sigsbee sent a cable to Eliza in Washington that is astonishing in its solipsism:

MAINE BLOWN UP LAST NIGHT. TOTALLY WRECKED. ALL OFFICERS SAVED BUT JENKINS AND MERRITT WHO WERE PROBABLY KILLED.* ABOUT 250 KILLED. I AM UNINJURED BUT HAVE LOST ABSOLUTELY EVERYTHING BUT THE SACK COAT TROUSERS AND SHIRT. WILL BORROW MONEY OF GENERAL LEE. ESTIMATE MY PECUNIARY LOSS FIFTEEN HUNDRED DOLLARS.

＊ ＊ ＊

ABOUT THREE O'CLOCK on Wednesday morning, February 16, William McKinley was asleep in his second-floor White House bedroom, which he shared with his beloved invalid wife, Ida. A winter wind rattled the windowpanes. A watchman rapped loudly on the heavy wooden door to wake up the President, who donned a dressing gown and rushed to his office down the hall, where he spoke on the telephone

---

* The bodies of Lieutenant Friend W. Jenkins and Assistant Engineer Darwin R. Merritt were indeed found later.

with Secretary Long and looked at cables, including Sigsbee's, describing the attack in Havana Harbor. "The *Maine* blown up!" McKinley exclaimed. "The *Maine* blown up!" He told a naval aide that, beyond the tragic loss of life, the political timing of this disaster was terrible; he asked how it could have transpired.

McKinley often thought about his four years in the Civil War. Having enlisted as an eighteen-year-old in the Twenty-Third Ohio Volunteer Infantry Regiment, he considered the Union effort "the most sacred cause in history."* Referring to his final wartime rank, Ida still called him "the Major." During the war, he had told his diary that if he were killed, he would "fall in a good cause and hope to fall in the arms of my blessed redeemer." As a Methodist, he found group prayer with fellow warriors "precious to my soul—in fact, I felt more of the love of God in my heart at these meetings than I felt for some time before." Raised by abolitionist parents, William espoused African American suffrage and praised the service of black US soldiers.

In August 1862, McKinley and his comrades went to the Executive Mansion "to see Uncle Abraham." As one recalled, President Lincoln "made us quite a speech." The following month, as a commissary sergeant during the fighting at Antietam, McKinley bravely risked enemy fire to bring food and coffee to his comrades. When the battle was done, Lincoln came to review the soldiers and, as McKinley noted, "his indescribably sad, thoughtful, far-seeing expression pierced every man's soul." After the war, McKinley sought an Army career until his father told him he had "never thought that soldiers amounted to much in times of peace," so William became a lawyer.

During McKinley's fourteen years in Congress and four years as Governor of Ohio, he had paid little attention to the large, sprawling island that was ninety miles south of Florida. In 1878, Cuban insurgents were defeated after a decade of war trying to throw off their Spanish

---

* Suffering from depression, McKinley had earlier dropped out of Allegheny College in Pennsylvania, worried, as he later said, "that my whole life was to be spoiled by my unfortunate nervousness." Unable to afford more college, he taught school and debated in his spare time. One topic was whether the federal government should evacuate Fort Sumter.

overlords. When a Cuban Army of about 30,000 soldiers renewed this effort in February 1895, Spain sent an imposing 220,285 men across the Atlantic to retain control of its colony, which was later called the largest force to cross the Atlantic before World War II. Since they could not match the Spanish in numbers, the Cuban insurgents waged guerrilla war against railroads, marketplaces, and agriculture.* General Valeriano "Butcher" Weyler of Spain responded by forcing about one-third of all Cubans, with only one week's notice, into camps, surrounded by barbed-wire fences and watchtowers. The inmates suffered from primitive shelter, inadequate food, and rampant disease. It was estimated that a quarter of the Cuban population died there.

Newspapers across the United States, especially those owned by William Randolph Hearst and Joseph Pulitzer, published harrowing accounts of the Spanish atrocities in Cuba. The natural American affinity for freedom fighters induced anger at Spain and growing sympathy for the Cuban rebels. Businessmen who backed McKinley for President in 1896 implored him to do something to stop the uncertainty about Cuba, where there was about $50 million (about $1.5 billion today) of American investment.

In March 1897, on the night before McKinley's inauguration, the departing President, Grover Cleveland, warned him that within the next two years, he would inevitably be hauled into war with Spain. McKinley did not wish to end the nation's long peace since Appomattox. Trying to fix the Cuba problem, he offered to buy the island, but the Spanish turned him down flat. McKinley sent a personal envoy, his friend William Calhoun of Illinois, to Weyler's Cuba. Calhoun reported back that the island was "wrapped in the stillness of death and the silence of desolation." In the countryside, "every house had been burned, banana trees cut down, cane fields swept with fire." Calhoun wrote that the "destitution and suffering" caused his heart to "bleed for the poor creatures."

---

* A similar approach was employed by Fidel Castro's guerrillas to depose President Fulgencio Batista in the late 1950s, and by CIA-backed forces trying, without success, to oust Castro in the early 1960s.

The devout McKinley was shaken by Calhoun's account of what he considered to be Spain's un-Christian behavior in Cuba. As a result, he gave a tenth of his presidential salary that year to the Cuban relief effort of the Red Cross, and demanded that the Spanish government abide by "the military codes of civilization." Spain replied by reminding the President of the Union Army's excesses during the Civil War. Frustrated, McKinley privately said that if he could not succeed in getting Spain to relax its brutalities, he wanted at least "to show that we had spared no effort to avert trouble."

In September 1897, through his Minister in Madrid, Stewart Woodford, McKinley warned the Spanish that the United States could no longer ignore the "injury and suffering" in Cuba. If Spain refused to seek "a settlement honorable to herself and just to her Cuban colony and mankind," he would have to make "an early decision as to the course of action which the time and the transcendent emergency may demand." A month earlier, the Spanish Prime Minister, Antonio Cánovas del Castillo, had been murdered while relaxing at a Basque spa. McKinley was cheered when Cánovas's more liberal successor, Práxedes Mateo Sagasta, fired General Weyler and offered Cubans a form of home rule under Spanish military dominion. That December, in his annual message, McKinley told Congress that the "near future" would show whether Spain really intended to seek "a righteous peace" in Cuba. If not, he ominously warned, the United States might take "further and other action." Backing the President's veiled threat of war, Secretary Long publicly ordered his European Squadron to keep sailors at their posts, extending their tours of duty.

In January 1898 came evidence that the Spanish were playing a double game. From Havana, Fitzhugh Lee reported that after Spain had unveiled its plan for limited home rule, "mobs, led by Spanish officers, attacked today the offices of the four newspapers here advocating autonomy." Democrats in Congress, as well as Catholic and Protestant groups, demanded that McKinley take a more truculent approach. Determined to show the Spanish that he meant business and to protect American citizens in Cuba, McKinley chose to send the *Maine* to Havana; it arrived on January 25.

To make sure that the battleship's visit did not push the Spanish toward an unnecessary war, the President had his birdlike, red-mustachioed Assistant Secretary of State, William Day, an ex–Ohio judge who had long served as his close political adviser, remind the hard-line Spanish Minister in Washington, Enrique Dupuy de Lôme, that their two countries were "at peace." Dupuy was informed that, despite the pressure from Congress, McKinley was willing to give Spain's new reforms in Cuba time to succeed. During a diplomatic banquet at the White House, over cigars and brandy, the President, dressed in white tie, greeted Dupuy, in gold-braided uniform with decorations, and assured him, "You have no occasion to be other than satisfied and confident."

Then Hearst's *New York Journal,* eager to provoke a conflict with Cuba, published an intercepted private letter that Dupuy had written to a friend two months earlier. In it, Dupuy belittled the "weak" McKinley as "catering to the rabble . . . a low politician who tries to leave a door open behind himself while keeping on good terms with the jingoes of his party." Dupuy explained that the Spanish reforms in Cuba were merely an insincere feint intended to stall for time with the Americans.

The yellow press hyperbolically called the Spaniard's letter the "Worst Insult to the United States in Its History." Dupuy responded by falsely claiming that the letter was fake. Judge Day (as he was widely called) brought some of Dupuy's other letters to the White House; he and McKinley concluded that the handwriting was identical to that of the facsimiles published in the newspapers. During a "frigid" conversation at the Spanish legation, Day compelled Dupuy to confess that the offending letter was indeed his, and ordered him to leave the United States. Washington's *Evening Times* predicted that the Dupuy affair would now usher in "the crisis in Cuban affairs which has been expected for some time," warning that the situation was "very grave." Five days later came the destruction of the USS *Maine.*

✳ ✳ ✳

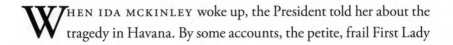

WHEN IDA MCKINLEY woke up, the President told her about the tragedy in Havana. By some accounts, the petite, frail First Lady responded with "hysteria," and her husband had to calm her down. This would not have been unusual. Ida suffered from nervous and spinal disorders, migraines, fevers, severe anxieties, depression, vertigo, phlebitis, a partially paralyzed leg (she moved by cane or wheelchair), fainting spells, and sudden, alarming seizures, which were secretly diagnosed as epilepsy. Ida once said, "My husband's arm has so taken the place of my foot that I have never been deprived of any enjoyment in life because of my lameness." McKinley and his handlers worked hard to make sure that Ida's name was not published in the same sentence as the word "epilepsy," which, in those days, was often linked to insanity. They feared that Americans would feel unsettled if they believed that the wife on whom the President so lovingly doted was on the verge of becoming deranged.

McKinley's initial instinct in dealing with the *Maine* crisis was to throw on the brakes. He knew there would be shrill demands for immediate war against Spain from yellow journalists, provocateurs on Capitol Hill, and American groups who loved the Cuban insurgents. They would insist—despite the absence, so far, of reliable evidence—that the *Maine* had been sunk by a deliberate Spanish attack. McKinley felt that his first job was to let a Navy court of inquiry find out who or what had actually caused the *Maine* disaster.

The President privately warned his younger friend Senator Charles Fairbanks, Republican from Indiana, that many Americans would be "so influenced by the horror of the tragedy" that they would clamor for war. However, McKinley insisted, "I don't propose to be swept off my feet by the catastrophe. My duty is plain. We must learn the truth and endeavor, if possible, to fix the responsibility. The country can afford to withhold its judgment and not strike an avenging blow until the truth is known." He would ensure that his country "will not be plunged into war until it is ready for it." The President told his Army physician, Leonard Wood, "I shall never get into a war until I am sure that God and man approve. I have been through one war. I have seen the dead piled up, and I do not want to see another."

But in public, throughout the week after the *Maine* sank, McKinley said nothing. He was no doubt anxious that any comments from him, beyond expressions of grieving solicitude for the families of the martyred sailors, might be exploited to create a national frenzy for war. On February 22, when he spoke at the University of Pennsylvania in honor of Washington's birthday, the audience expected enlightenment about the *Maine* and the possibility of armed conflict. Instead he offered a long, anodyne paean to General Washington ("his noble unselfishness, his heroic purposes, the power of his magnificent personality") and did not mention the *Maine* tragedy.* The *Washington Sentinel,* a Democratic weekly, complained that McKinley had uttered "not a sentence, not a word, not a syllable, not a hint of the great, all-shadowing national sorrow. So far as history records, there is nowhere a parallel for this amazing silence."

While McKinley maintained his sphinxlike self-restraint, the yellow press served up often-fabricated stories intended to prove that Spain was behind the *Maine*'s sinking. "MAINE IS A GREAT THING," the warmongering Hearst cabled his London bureau. "AROUSE EVERYBODY. STIR UP MADRID." Two days after the calamity, his *New York Journal* featured a front-page drawing of a Spanish torpedo lurking under the vessel ("The Warship Maine Was Split in Two by an Enemy's Secret Infernal Machine"). One day later, it proclaimed, "The Whole Country Thrills with War Fever." Three days after that: "Havana Populace Insults the Memory of the Maine Victims." None of the tabloids ever managed to explain why, if Spain had indeed engineered the destruction of the *Maine,* its government never took public credit for the act.†

The influence of such high-decibel journalism was later exaggerated. Most American newspapers treated the *Maine* disaster with more equanimity, and so, at first, did the American people. The *Springfield Republican* of Massachusetts marveled three days after the *Maine* was sunk

---

* The closest McKinley came to the subject on everyone's mind was to note, with approval, Washington's admonition to "observe good faith and justice" toward "all nations," and "cultivate peace and harmony with all."

† General Weyler publicly insisted that American "indolence" had caused the *Maine* to sink by accident. An official Spanish study, quickly issued in hopes of slowing the Americans' rush to war, concluded that the *Maine* had suffered from a spontaneous coal bunker explosion next to the place on the ship where munitions were stored.

that "there have been no mass meetings in any American community to emit cries of rage. Not a stone has been thrown, nor an effigy burned." It averred that "the great majority of American newspapers do not share with Mr. Hearst the infamy of his patriotism for dollars." The *Baltimore Sun* noticed on Capitol Hill "a general avoidance of radical utterances, as if everyone was drawing a long, long breath before deciding whether anything is to be done." The *Philadelphia Inquirer* called it "a condition of painful suspense." Senator Henry Cabot Lodge, Republican from Massachusetts, told reporters that the predicament over Cuba was "too serious to talk about at present." His colleague Shelby Cullom, Republican from Illinois, chimed in, "I am too mad to talk about it."

But within a week, Congress erupted over the issue of who should investigate the *Maine.* From the Senate floor, Republican William Mason of Illinois said McKinley was wrong to give the task to Navy leaders, who suffered from an insuperable conflict of interest, since they would be "trying their own case." Instead "let this disaster to our Navy and to our country be thoroughly investigated by Congress." Mason complained that Navy investigators were being too leisurely—they would not reach Havana until the following week: "*Manana! Manana!* Tomorrow, always tomorrow!" He warned that in the meantime, someone in Havana Harbor might use dynamite to destroy "the evidences of the catastrophe," obscuring the causes of the *Maine* disaster forever.

Angry at Mason, Republican Senator Edward Wolcott of Colorado went on the attack, saying he didn't know "what slums" his Illinois colleague may have "dragged" to find some lack of trust in the Navy. But every "patriotic citizen" knew that "the officers of our Navy are honorable, courageous, upright men—and, above all, they tell the truth." Referring to Sigsbee, Wolcott added that "the awful disaster that overtook his ship will count for nothing by comparison with the degrading insinuations made here." Cabot Lodge insisted that the *Maine*'s commander had shown "a coolness and a nerve which are an honor to the American name. Does anyone suppose that Captain Sigsbee, capable of such splendid conduct, is going to lie about his ship?"

As it turned out, just as Mason had warned, the five-man court of inquiry was indeed badly compromised. Its appointed chief, Rear Admiral

William Sampson, had been Sigsbee's teacher at the Naval Academy. Sampson knew that his chances for future promotion would depend on whether his superiors were happy with his panel's procedures and verdict.* Sampson knew that key Navy officials were hoping that his board would avoid any conclusion that the *Maine* had been sunk by accident, which would suggest that the Navy had been incompetent. Assistant Secretary of the Navy Theodore Roosevelt was pumping for war with Spain. Sampson had a clear motivation to please TR, who admired him and had taken a conspicuous interest in his career. And although the Sampson board had been assigned to deal merely with the specific issue of whether the *Maine* had been lost due to Navy negligence, the public would inevitably presume that the panel had chosen between placing the blame on an accident or on the Spanish.

Ten days after the *Maine* sank, McKinley convened his Cabinet upstairs at the White House, at the same heavy table Lincoln had used throughout the Civil War. Amid the winter chill, the Secretaries of both State and War were sick at home. McKinley asked those present to reserve judgment about why the ship sank until the Navy's court of inquiry issued its report. Afterward one Cabinet secretary insisted that the President "will not be jingoed into war." Tamping down public complaints that he was too much inclined to be lenient toward Spain, McKinley let it be known that he was trying to ascertain, as the *New York Times* reported, whether public opinion "would be with him" should he "employ vigorous measures in Cuba." But he was also quoted as saying in private, "You may rest assured there will not be war with my consent, except for a cause which will satisfy good men here, the nations of Europe and Almighty God."

Almost certainly speaking on McKinley's behalf, his close friend and political patron Senator Mark Hanna of Ohio told reporters, "As long as the President and the Secretary of the Navy and all the rest of the Cabinet keep cool and quiet, there is no need for the rest of us to get

---

* And, in fact, after delivering its conclusions, Sampson was promoted to command the North Atlantic Squadron throughout the Spanish-American War.

alarmed. No, I honestly do not see any reason for the excitement that is being created. There will be no war."

* * *

SINCE THE TRAGEDY, Sigsbee had remained in Havana Harbor, sleeping aboard the US dispatch boat *Fern,* supervising attempts to retrieve the corpses of his crew from the twisted, partially submerged wreck of the *Maine.* Back home, he had become a national celebrity and was widely praised for his aplomb on the fatal night. Hearst's *New York Journal* said it was "reassuring to contemplate" the captain's "cool, courageous and confident figure." "The reporters bothered me so much that I thought it prudent to leave the city," Sigsbee's Chicago brother Luther ("Lufe") wrote him. "There is much excitement. For yourself there is but one opinion, of *praise*." A few American women asked the captain, by letter, to father their children.

Predictably, Sigsbee loved his new fame. From the *Fern,* he proudly wrote Eliza that, according to one Congressman, when President McKinley had learned that the captain had been the last to depart the *Maine,* "tears came into his eyes." Sigsbee told her, "I am amazed at the general opinion of my career. As you know, I have always felt rather stiff as to the requirements of official duty . . . and it seems to have worked out in my favor." Referring to his initial request that public opinion be suspended about the cause of the explosion, he went on, "I knew that my first telegram would help the government to control the situation. . . . The public praise of my course seems strange to me because it assumes that I must have been obliged to curb the violence of my feelings in order to write my telegram." He marveled, "It seems that I am lauded from the pulpit for being a man of peace. A great thing that for a warrior."

Sigsbee reported to his wife, "One body was recovered yesterday; no one today. . . . I feel very much relieved to have all the wounded away from Havana. Now if I can only clear the wreck of the dead! . . . All the men sleeping over the zone of explosion must have been blown to atoms. One of the men sent to Key West today told me that he knew nothing about any explosion or injury until he found himself aboard the Spanish Man-of-War, *Alfonso XII,* and remembered nothing. This shows that most of those who died had 'painless' deaths." Noting a request by Spanish officials to investigate the battered *Maine* themselves, he wrote her, "My pennant still flies and the colors fly at half mast day and night. He who disturbs the Maine and her dead attacks the flag."

Being Sigsbee, he also wondered whether the federal government would pony up the cash to replace the clothing he had lost on the fatal night. He wrote Eliza, "I understand that in similar cases the Treasury allows one dozen shirts. I never had less than two dozen at sea in my life. Suppose a chap leaves port suddenly with a big lot of clothes ready for the week or ten days and arrives in a stupid port about Friday? What then? . . . I could not possibly replenish my naval wardrobe within two years without help."

In Havana Harbor, on Monday, February 21, Sigsbee became the first witness before Sampson's court of inquiry, testifying in secret at a round wooden table in the plush parlor of the lighthouse tender *Mangrove.* He was nervous about the court's conclusions. "I hope that something will be done to express continued confidence in me unmistakably," he wrote Eliza. "I don't want to appear as having merited any lack of confidence."*

Sigsbee knew that his testimony would likely have more influence over the investigation's outcome than anyone else's. If the *Maine* should issue a verdict adverse to Sigsbee and his crew, his career might be ruined. (As a Naval Academy cadet, Sigsbee had been required to study the history of the US Navy, including how an official investigation had destroyed Commander James Barron's career by blaming him for the attack on the *Chesapeake* in 1807.) But if the court found that the Spanish had sunk the *Maine,* the United States might be thrust into a major war of retaliation. Before the court of inquiry, Sigsbee never flatly insisted that the Spanish had deliberately caused the disaster. Instead he claimed,

---

* Sigsbee, who was carefully following press reportage about the *Maine,* could not have failed to note, for instance, that even while lavishly praising him, Senator Wolcott had warned that the court of inquiry's verdict could mean that Sigsbee's Navy career would be "ended forever."

sentence by sentence, that his command and crew discipline aboard the *Maine* had been letter-perfect. He also painted a stark portrait of the hostility that Spanish officials in Havana felt toward the Americans, and dropped clues about how Spain might have conspired against his ship.

Sigsbee testified that when the *Maine* arrived, the Spanish had assigned it to "the least-used buoy in the harbor." He said he had "rarely known merchant vessels to be anchored there," observing that Spain's *Alfonso XII* was anchored about 250 yards away, too close for comfort. Sigsbee recalled how on the *Maine*'s first Sunday in Havana, a ferryboat crowded with Spaniards—both civilian and military, returning from a bullfight—had issued "yells, whistles and apparently derisive calls." Then, after he held a private onshore meeting with Spanish officials, someone had provocatively leaked to two Havana journals that Sigsbee was pushing for Cuban autonomy from Spain. Remaining within the bounds of his job and expertise, he told the court of inquiry, "I have no means of knowing whether my apparent interference in the political concerns of the island had any relation to the destruction of the *Maine*."

Defending his own conduct aboard ship and that of his crew, Sigsbee insisted there had never been a sign "that any coal had been too long in any bunker," adding that "the fire alarms" were "sensitive." Inflammables had been "stowed in chests aft, according to regulations." Ship discipline was "excellent." As for the ship's magazines, "I do not think there was any laxity in this direction." He said he had taken greater than "ordinary precautions" for his ship's protection. He had ordered his master-at-arms to scrutinize all packages brought on board, since they might include dynamite.

Back in Washington, unaccustomed to the spotlight, Mrs. Sigsbee raised eyebrows by telling a *New York Herald* correspondent she had been "delighted to learn" that her husband's dog Peggy had survived the *Maine* explosion: "The children have been grieving and wondering if the dear little dog has been killed." In early March, Eliza and their daughter May attended a "Grand Concert" at the Capital's National Theatre, along with Washington officialdom, to benefit the relatives of perished *Maine* crew members. Enjoying her own sudden prominence,

Eliza reported to Charles by letter that "the house was packed with a large & fashionable audience. . . . The President & Mrs. McKinley were in a box, also Secretary Long." Daughters of naval officers sold programs and little American flags to those assembled. "May was one of these," Eliza wrote. "After people knew who she was, she sold a great many. There were many people who would not buy flags of anyone but *waited* for *Miss Sigsbee*."

McKinley was preparing his next steps. Hoping to intimidate Spain to relax its grip on Cuba or, if that failed, bolster the United States for a possible war, he asked Congress for a $50 million blank check for national defense. The House and Senate galleries were packed for the two-day debate over this "patriotic action." The President got his money, with no dissenting votes. The *Washington Evening Star* observed, "The great moves toward war are going on without check." Noting how rapidly the Spanish were building up their Navy, McKinley and Secretary Long told the Cabinet that the US would acquire new torpedo boats and warships. From Madrid, General Woodford advised him, by cable, to set an April 15 deadline for Spain to satisfy all American demands on Cuba: "They should see that the United States mean business, and mean it *now*." Through all of these maneuvers, McKinley told friends, "I pray God that we may be able to keep the peace."

In Havana Harbor, members of Sampson's jury examined the carcass of the *Maine*. Returning to the *Mangrove,* they questioned other survivors, eyewitnesses to the explosion, and divers who had swum around the wreckage. Throughout their deliberations, however, with Sampson as chair and Sigsbee as chief witness, there was never significant doubt that the panel's verdict would clear Sigsbee and his men of blame for the disaster, leaving Spain as the likely culprit.

At the Executive Mansion, after sundown on Thursday, March 24, McKinley was handed a copy of Sampson's brief, still-secret report. It insisted that crew discipline aboard the *Maine* had been "excellent" and that the ship's loss "was not in any respect due to fault or negligence." With no equivocation, it concluded that the *Maine* "was destroyed by the explosion of a submarine mine, which caused the partial explosion of two or more of her forward magazines." It noted that after the incident, the ship's hull "bent" inward, which suggested an external explosion. Ignoring the fact that within the three previous years thirteen other American vessels had suffered fires connected to spontaneous combustion in their coal bunkers, the panel noted that the *Maine* had never encountered such a problem. Its report conceded that the panel had not been able to find "evidence fixing the responsibility for the destruction of the *Maine* upon any person or persons." But Sampson and his colleagues knew that all Americans would understand that the only country with a strong motive to destroy the *Maine* deliberately, and the means to do so by submarine mine in Havana Harbor, was Spain.

In retrospect, Sampson's verdict was almost certainly in error. Two later studies of the *Maine* explosion, both performed by the Navy, concluded that the cause was probably not a Spanish mine. In 1911, after the Army Corps of Engineers pulled the wreckage out of Havana Harbor, a new naval court of inquiry argued that the *Maine*'s explosion could be explained by "the action of gases of low explosives, such as the black and brown powders with which the forward magazines were stored." In 1974, a study led by Admiral Hyman Rickover, father of the nuclear Navy, suggested that the *Maine* exploded and sank because its coal bunker blew up, igniting its magazines. A 1998 study, commissioned by the National Geographic Society, using a computer model, concluded that if a mine sank the *Maine,* it would have had to be "perfectly placed," which would have been "a matter of luck," and that "a coal fire could have been the first step in the *Maine*'s destruction."

As time went on, the sinking of the *Maine* became shorthand for a disaster that would quickly unite Americans in support for a retaliatory military attack on another country, just as the Thornton affair had generated immediate passion for James Polk to start a war against Mexico. During the Cuban Missile Crisis in 1962, President John Kennedy and his brother Robert, his Attorney General, considered scenarios that might win public support for the US military to bomb and invade Fidel Castro's Cuba, after which it could destroy nuclear-capable missiles that had been secretly slipped onto the island by the Soviet leader Nikita Khrushchev. As the President's hidden tape machine recorded their voices, Robert told his brother that perhaps they should find "some ship" and "you know, sink the *Maine* again or something."*

* * *

AFTER HOLING UP at the White House with advisers to study the Sampson findings, McKinley made a final, ill-fated effort to avert a collision with Spain. At his request, General Woodford privately told the Spanish that if Spain would promise the Cubans "full self-government," then, during a six-month armistice, the President would use his "friendly offices" to broker a deal between Spain and the Cuban insurgents. On Monday, March 28, he sent the Sampson report to Capitol Hill, along with a polite cover note asking that Spain act with a "sense of justice" and "honor" compelled by its "friendly relations" with the United States. Listening in the Senate galleries as McKinley's message was read aloud were Eliza Sigsbee and the President's younger brother, Abner.†

The *Philadelphia Inquirer* reported that McKinley's message "fell like a wet blanket on Congress." Salem, Oregon's *Capital Journal* demanded that McKinley "do something radical" to "purge himself from suspicion" and "give the lie to all the stories regarding his supineness." Montana's *Anaconda Standard* wrote that "a Court of Inquiry will have to investigate the President's sanity." William Mason told other Senators that the *Maine*'s "widows and orphans cry out to us. . . . If we believe that murdering our men, sinking our ship, and lowering our flag is not cause for war, say so." Mason demanded, "Awake to glorious war against a nation that burns homes and murders women and children!"

---

* In the spring of 1962, Kennedy's Joint Chiefs of Staff had secretly pondered ways to generate antagonism toward the Castro regime. One was to engineer the sinking of an American ship in Guantánamo Bay, for which the blame would be falsely placed on Castro. A staff document advised that the ruse be patterned on "the *Maine* incident."

† Standing in the long tradition of presidential siblings who cut corners, Abner McKinley was "frequently mentioned in connection with the sale of vessels to the government at very high rates," recalled the *New York Times* on his death in 1904. "Very large contracts for supplies were awarded to firms of which the president's brother was the representative."

While contemplating probable conflict with Spain, McKinley, on Saturday night, April 2, met the *Maine*'s captain for the first time, at a lavish reception in Sigsbee's honor, hosted by the National Geographic Society at the Capital's most luxurious hotel, the Arlington, just above Lafayette Square. Alexander Graham Bell, the society's president, joined Sigsbee, who was just back from Havana, in a receiving line to greet a thousand luminaries, including "nearly every public man in Washington."

Secretary Long told the now-famous captain, "I don't think you and I need any introduction." One military officer tastelessly gibed, "This is nearly as bad as being blown up, Sigsbee, isn't it?" The guest of honor replied, "It is very good, all this. I never thought people felt so about me." Among the throng, so it was reported, were "little boys whose parents had brought them to see the famous sailor and man, who gazed at him with awe." Sigsbee shook so many hands that sweat poured from his brow. Eliza Sigsbee, wearing a velvet gown and holding a bouquet of roses, joked to her husband, "Can I be permitted to shake hands with you?" Two of their daughters laughingly told him, "Charmed to meet you!" As the US Marine Band played "Hail to the Chief," McKinley arrived, and the ballroom cheered. Rather than go to the head of the line, the President modestly waited his turn to see the *Maine*'s commander. Clutching Sigsbee's hand, he gravely said, "Captain, it gives me great pleasure to have the honor of meeting you."

For Sigsbee, the Arlington fete was the fulfillment of his lifelong fantasies of personal glory. He would not have been irrational to take the celebration as evidence that he had been cleared at the highest levels of any suspicions about the *Maine*'s demise. It might have seemed to augur for Sigsbee a lasting, honored place in American history and a major assignment in the war against Spain that was about to commence.

But, in fact, any such dreams were already behind him. McKinley and Long were content to honor Sigsbee because it was in their momentary interest to affirm that the *Maine* had not been sunk because of Navy negligence. Soon, however, they would demonstrate how little they really thought of him. While others in the Navy were being granted prestigious assignments for the coming conflict with Spain, Sigsbee was merely offered command of the USS *St. Paul*, a transatlantic passenger steamship that was being converted into an auxiliary cruiser. The *Baltimore Sun* called the assignment "A SET-BACK FOR SIGSBEE."

Flabbergasted and deflated, the captain implored his new friends in the press to demand that the Navy treat him with greater respect. Pleading on Sigsbee's behalf, one wire service argued, "In any other country, he would have been raised several degrees in rank and loaded with decorations. . . . Having been in command of a battleship, he cannot be expected to take anything of lower grade unless the Department proposes to humiliate him for the loss of his vessel."

* * *

ON MONDAY, APRIL 11, exhausted from two months of agonizing over Cuba, McKinley sent a seven-thousand-word war message to Congress. "In the name of humanity," he requested approval to "use the military and naval forces of the United States" to end the hostilities between Spain and Cuba, and establish a new Cuban regime to oversee "the functions of a separate nation." The Cubans required protection from "the misery that afflicts the island." American involvement was "specifically our duty, for it is right at our door," and "a constant menace to our peace." If this effort succeeded, "then our aspirations as a Christian, peace-loving people will be realized."

Surprising some in the House and Senate, McKinley did not base his request for war primarily on the sinking of the *Maine*. Still uncertain about whether Spain was truly behind the attack, he acknowledged that, according to the naval court of inquiry, the ship had been vanquished by a "submarine mine," noting that responsibility for that mine "remains to be fixed." Nevertheless, he wrote, "the destruction of the *Maine*, by whatever exterior cause, is a patent and impressive proof of a state of things in Cuba that is intolerable."

Expecting to hear from a lion, some thought McKinley sounded like a mouse. "An outrage," complained the Democratic Congressman John Lentz of Ohio. "A stench in the nostrils of every decent American."

House Minority Leader Joseph Bailey, Democrat from Texas, called McKinley's message "the weakest and most inconclusive sent out by any President." Ohio's Republican Senator Joseph Foraker said he had "no patience with the message." The *Omaha World-Herald* asked why McKinley was "utterly incapable" of confronting "the assassins of 266 American sailors."

The House approved the President's request by 325 to 19. But the Senate attached conditions that McKinley recognize the Cuban insurgents as the island's "lawful government" and renounce any American effort to seize permanent control of the island. The President replied that such caveats would "usurp" his prerogatives; they were withdrawn. When he signed the final resolution, Spain broke diplomatic relations with the United States. McKinley established a naval blockade of Cuba's northern coast and its southern port of Cienfuegos. In response, the Spanish declared war.

With events having spun beyond his control, on Monday, April 25, McKinley sadly asked Congress, in writing, to declare that a state of war existed with the far-off Spanish kingdom. Newspapers published a purple rhyme of vengeance:

> *Remember the* Maine *when great guns roar,*
> *When cannon belch on the hostile shore.*
> *Remember the dead in a sunken ship,*
> *And pass the cry from lip to lip.*
> *Forget the shriek of shot and shell;*
> *Forget for the hour that war is hell.*
> *For over there, beneath the Bay,*
> *Two hundred sailors lie to-day.*

With fighting language like this ringing in their ears, Americans were once again off to war—this time impelled, more than anything else, by their fierce desire for retribution for a Spanish assault against the *Maine,* which, as we now have substantial reason to believe, had most likely never occurred.

CHAPTER NINE

"We Must Keep What We Want"

IN WASHINGTON ON Sunday morning, May 1, 1898, wearing his signature carnation boutonniere, McKinley took Secretary Long to All Souls Church, on Fourteenth Street, where they heard its young Unitarian minister, Bradford Leavitt, tell his flock, "The national conscience has been wrought up to a high pitch over the condition of affairs in Cuba. You and I know that there are some things far worse than war."

Of the Spanish-American conflict, the President later recalled, "The storm broke so suddenly that it was here almost before we realized it." The nation's standing Army had been allowed to dwindle since the Civil War, leaving only about 19,000 troops available. Thus McKinley called for 125,000 new volunteers, and then for 75,000 more. With a US naval blockade around Cuba, he and Long had directed Commodore George Dewey to move his forces from Hong Kong to the Philippine port city of Manila, where Dewey was told to strike Spain's Asiatic squadron. "Capture vessels or destroy," said the dispatch to Dewey. "Use utmost endeavor." McKinley later called that order "the greatest single act of my life."

On Sunday night, at the White House, before he and Ida were to host a Cabinet dinner, the President came down the stairs, reporting, "There has been a big fight in the Bay of Manila. We've had a cable from Dewey. The Spanish fleet has been annihilated. Seven men injured—poor boys!" After dessert, while the young soprano Geraldine Farrar performed in the Blue Room, McKinley vanished upstairs to his new War Room, there to read cables from the battlefront.* The next morning, the President enjoyed a cigar—he smoked ten to twenty per day—and, with delight, read out wire service accounts of Dewey's success to his aides. Within a week, Commodore Dewey cabled Washington that he controlled Manila Bay "completely" and could take the city "at any time." McKinley told Long to inform the press of this achievement, but Theodore Roosevelt had already stolen his superiors' thunder by doing so. As in Lincoln's time, excited crowds gathered outside the Executive Mansion to cheer the Commander-in-Chief.

McKinley wrote Congress about Manila that "the magnitude of this victory can hardly be measured by the ordinary standards of naval warfare. . . . The great heart of our nation throbs, not with boasting or with greed of conquest, but with deep gratitude that the triumph has come in a just cause." Despite the President's disavowal of conquest, many Americans, spurred on by some of the more fevered newspapers, were developing an interest in a possible American empire extending far across the Pacific, enabling the United States to gain new markets and convert "heathens" to Christianity. The religious Ida was dreamily inspired by this potential for evangelism. McKinley may not have sought this conflict, but his ambitions for glory from the conflict with Spain were expanding by the day. A war launched mainly—whether the President admitted it or not—in retaliation for the sunken *Maine* was growing into a much larger crusade. McKinley scrawled in a private memo, "While we are conducting war and until its conclusion we must keep all we get; when the war is over we must keep what we want."

Anxious that Germany or Japan might try to seize the Philippines,

---

* The Signal Corps had provided a telephone switchboard connecting McKinley with his eight Cabinet departments and the House and Senate. Newly installed telegraph lines let him communicate with General William Shafter, commander of the Fifth Army Corps in Cuba, with only twenty minutes' delay.

he decided that at least part of the archipelago should be subdued and acquired for the United States—although not as a state of the Union. On similar terms, he was also eager to annex Guam and the Hawaiian Islands. Although the Hawaiians had been more than helpful to American military vessels, McKinley demanded the acquisition of Hawaii as a strategic necessity of the war, and pushed it through the opposition of House Speaker Thomas Reed, who, although a Republican, was skeptical of the entire Spanish conflict and the President's burgeoning imperialism. Only in early summer did the Senate consent—after a thwarted filibuster and widespread anxieties that if defied McKinley might annex Hawaii by executive order anyway. Sounding almost like James Polk during the Mexican War, the President told his personal secretary, George Cortelyou, "We need Hawaii just as much and a good deal more than we did California. It is manifest destiny."

After reporting the invigorating news of Dewey's triumphs at Manila, American papers cried, "On to Havana!" Unlike with the Philippines, Guam, and Hawaii, McKinley avowed no ambition to annex Cuba, only to liberate it from its cruel Spanish rulers. After voting to declare this war, Congress had gone on to pass an amendment, sponsored by the Republican Senator Henry Teller of Colorado, stipulating that any American military action in Cuba must culminate in handing "control of the island to its people."

By now, Admiral Sampson had taken up his command of the North Atlantic Squadron, having pocketed the promotion he sought by ensuring that the *Maine* court of inquiry produced the verdict that most of his superiors wanted. Sampson wished to bomb Cuba, but his Navy chiefs, averse to placing armor-clad ships in danger, preferred blockading Havana and other major ports.* Secretary Long demanded an early assault on Cuba, but his Army counterpart, Russell Alger, warned that, although

---

* This foreshadowed the secret White House debate over Cuba during the Missile Crisis of 1962, when the Joint Chiefs of Staff demanded that the island be bombed, followed by an invasion, and President Kennedy overruled them by insisting that their first step instead be a naval blockade (which he euphemistically called a "quarantine").

many excited young Americans were signing up as volunteers, only about twenty-eight thousand fighters would be available. Major General Nelson Miles warned against attempting an invasion with such a small force: if it lasted into the rainy Cuban summer, many of the warriors would die of yellow fever.

Behind his veneer of eternal self-confidence, McKinley was learning how to manage a military conflict. He agreed with Miles that sending soldiers into Cuba during the rainy season would menace their health. He would have preferred to start by attacking Spanish-held Puerto Rico, which presented no similar problem. Dewey's victory in Manila, however, had led the President to hope that the Spanish might collapse on Cuba as quickly as they had in the Philippines. Nor did McKinley wish to disappoint those Americans eager for their armed forces to march into the Cuban jungles now. During the second week of May, the President told Miles to assault Havana with a seventy-thousand-man Army, but the General had to gently inform him that they lacked enough ammunition for such a force to wage a single battle. Sheepishly, McKinley had to suspend his order.

The President also had to contend with embarrassing insubordination. In mid-May, Sampson ordered Admiral Winfield Scott Schley to move his Flying Squadron to Cienfuegos in quest of Spanish ships, but had to revise his directive after being told that the Spaniards were in fact off Santiago, on the opposite Cuban coast.* In a message to Secretary Long, which Long considered "one of the most infelicitous in history," Schley flouted the order, dubiously claiming that his squadron had to retreat to Key West to pick up more coal. When McKinley heard about Schley's defiance, he was shocked and furious. Secretary Long later recalled that the President considered this the darkest day of the entire war. At McKinley's request, Schley was ordered to Santiago, but for a brief time, he refused, risking court-martial. McKinley was grateful that Schley's flippancy did not become public until the war was over.

---

* Schley was so named because his uncle Henry had served under General Scott during the War of 1812.

Sailing to Cuba to take personal command, Sampson informed Washington in early June, "Bombarded forts at Santiago today." He added that "if ten thousand men were here, city and fleet would be ours within forty-eight hours. Every consideration demands immediate movement." Frustrated by Sampson's delays and alibis, McKinley read his dispatch and ordered that any available Americans be sent to Cuba immediately. Two days later, soldiers marched onto ships at Port Tampa, Florida, but after false reports of danger from nearby Spanish cruisers, they were stalled for a week. Then about seventeen thousand Americans headed, aboard coastal steamers, for Santiago, and were soon called the biggest army of invaders that had ever left American shores.

They included Lieutenant Colonel Theodore Roosevelt and his Rough Riders, the volunteer cavalry of cowboys, ranchers, miners, and other adventurers that Roosevelt had quit his number two job at the Navy to raise. Waiting impatiently in San Antonio, Roosevelt had fired off telegrams to Washington, pleading to join the invaders in Tampa. At wits' end, he finally telephoned the First Lady, whom he had charmed, and persuaded her to intervene. Afterward Roosevelt wrote the President, "Pray present my warm regards to Mrs. McKinley, and tell her that she will never have cause to fear being ashamed of the First Volunteer Cavalry, which is, in a peculiar fashion, her regiment."

Calculating that his chances of being killed were about one in three, TR wrote his wife, Edith, that if he did not return from Cuba, she must give his pistol and sword to their sons Theodore and Kermit. She wrote him that when she read this request to their boys, they "put their heads in my lap and sobbed bitterly." On July 1, astride a horse called Texas, leading his men up Kettle Hill, Roosevelt fired a pistol reclaimed from the wreckage of the sunken *Maine*.

* * *

AS MIDNIGHT APPROACHED on Saturday, July 2, McKinley was upstairs at the White House, anxiously perched near his telegraph machine, waiting for word from the battlefront in Santiago. Around

Sunday noon, he received a wire from a despondent General Shafter that he could not succeed in Santiago with his current modest force and was contemplating retreat to a position five miles away. Deflated, the President repaired with his advisers to the Cabinet Room. He knew that withdrawal would be a humiliation, showing haste, unpreparedness, and incompetence. He opted to let Shafter decide what to do, asking Alger to offer reinforcements to encourage the General to stay where he was. A new cable reported to Washington that the Spanish squadron on Santiago Bay had been eliminated.

Before dawn on Independence Day, Shafter wired, "I shall hold my present position." Admiral Sampson sent a dispatch to Washington two hours later that was intended to echo General Sherman's message of 1864 offering President Lincoln the capture of Savannah as a Christmas gift. Sampson cabled that "the fleet under my command offers the nation a Fourth of July present," the "whole" of the Spanish fleet.* Sampson's message was published, and McKinley publicly replied, "You have the gratitude and congratulations of the whole American people." Before long, however, newspapers made Sampson the butt of jokes by reporting that Admiral Schley, whom Sampson had failed to mention, deserved far more of the credit for this accomplishment—and that Sampson had not even been closely involved with the steps that led to victory. Schley graciously told the press that their triumph was big enough for everyone. But the angry Sampson tried to damage his rival's reputation by leaking details of Schley's earlier failures to pursue the Spanish squadron.

Before midnight on July 6, McKinley asked Americans, with "yet fresh remembrance of the unprecedented success" in the bays of Manila and Santiago, to pray that "our gallant sons may be shielded from harm alike on the battlefield and in the clash of fleets, and be spared the scourge of suffering and disease while they are striving to uphold their

---

* Sampson reported, "At 2, the last ship, the *Cristobal Colon,* had run ashore 75 miles west of Santiago and hauled down her colors. The *Infanta Maria Teresa, Oquendo* and *Viscaya* were forced ashore, burned and blown up within 20 miles of Santiago."

country's honor." But Spain refused to give up Santiago, and the Americans had to fight. Shafter had advised letting the Spanish preserve their dignity by withdrawing with their forces undisturbed, but McKinley, unwilling to give up his moment of victory, demanded that the General press for unconditional surrender. He approved a cable to Shafter, which said, "What you went to Santiago for was the Spanish Army. If you allow it to evacuate with its arms you must meet it somewhere else. This is not war." The Navy was ordered to shell the city.

General Miles warned Washington that if the engagement was not shut down now, the Americans on Cuba would be subjected to serious risk of mortal disease. Hastily convening his Cabinet, McKinley told the secretaries that Spain must not be let off so easily. Others in the room agreed that the Spanish were "tricking" the American generals. McKinley had Miles informed that if he considered victory within his grasp, he should either demand total submission from the Spanish or else attack. On July 15, Shafter reported to Washington that the Spanish had surrendered not only Santiago but the whole eastern part of Cuba.

The suspicious McKinley worried that Shafter would waffle while bargaining with Spain over terms. At his direction, Alger wired the General, "It is not possible that you are entertaining the proposition of permitting the Spaniards to carry away their arms." The Army's Adjutant General, Henry Corbin, told Shafter that the Spaniards must be shown that "the way to surrender is to surrender." Shafter warned that the Spanish were pleading to take their weapons back to their homeland, and that, if denied, "we may have to fight them yet." The President was informed of the enemy's surrender, and he asked that the occupation be "as free from severity as possible." Later in July, a volunteer force led by General Miles moved to seize most of Puerto Rico.

Shafter's Army superiors ordered him to remove his soldiers in Cuba, who were already short of food, to the mountains, beyond the region of the island that was most vulnerable to yellow fever. Shafter suggested that he bring his troops back to the United States, but neither ships nor receiving facilities were ready. Told again to move his men to higher ground, Shafter dragged his heels, claiming that the situation was "somewhat improving." Outraged by Shafter's lassitude, a group of his commanders wrote him, "This Army must be moved at once or it will perish. Persons responsible for preventing such a move will be responsible for the unnecessary loss of many thousands of lives." Protecting himself, Shafter now warned Washington that a yellow fever epidemic might be imminent: if his force in Cuba, "an Army of convalescents," was not quickly transferred to the United States, there would be "very few to move." By early August, the General's letter made it into American newspapers, along with a cri de coeur from Theodore Roosevelt, who wrote that his cavalrymen were "so weakened and shattered as to be ripe for dying like rotten sheep."*

When McKinley read both letters in the papers, he was furious. They showed him, for the first time, the scale of the peril to his troops. He also feared that the letters would undermine his position when he haggled with Spain over peace terms, by showing the enemy that his occupation force in Cuba was so enfeebled that it must be abruptly withdrawn. Alger suggested to the President that they divert public attention from the problem by moving a large number of the soldiers to Puerto Rico, to back up General Miles, but McKinley rebuked him, asking what Americans would think if they discovered that their government had acted "unnecessarily and at great expense."

* * *

THOSE AROUND THE President noted that months of leading his country in wartime had left him with signs of "severe physical and mental strain." Short on sleep, McKinley confided to friends, "The days merge into each other." He took solace from his Methodism. As a young man, he had told his pastor, Aaron Morton, "Religion seems to me to be the best thing in all the world," and had himself baptized in a stream. Both Morton and McKinley's mother, Nancy, had predicted that William might become a minister. As President, he read the Bible to Ida at

---

* The McKinleys had two nephews who had enlisted to fight in Cuba. When Ida learned of the island's yellow fever scourge, she lobbied to have them both transferred to Puerto Rico, where they were assigned to General Miles.

night, and insisted that Christianity was "the mightiest factor in the world's civilization."

Throughout the war, McKinley spent considerable energy caring for his ailing, doll-like wife. His physician, Dr. Presley Rixey, recalled that Ida's "whole life, without children, was tied up in her husband, and in his absence, she was never really happy." Rixey noted that the President "reduced his absence from her side to a minimum," and thus took no more outdoor exercise than "a short walk or ride beside his wife, usually in a closed carriage." He prompted McKinley to drive himself "in an open trap with a good pair of horses, his wife beside him," but the First Lady soon halted their outings. "Then," said Rixey, "I tried short horse-back rides," but "this took him too much from her presence."

McKinley would tell friends, "Oh, if you could have seen what a beauty Ida was as a girl!" The daughter of James Saxton, a prosperous burgher of Canton, Ohio, she had rolled bandages for Union soldiers during the Civil War before marrying the Major. After the birth of their first daughter, Katie, followed a second, whom they called Little Ida. Then the younger child died of cholera at the age of four months. McKinley's brother Abner recalled that after the baby's death, Ida "would sit for hours in a darkened room, holding Katie in her lap, weeping in silence." When Abner asked Katie to join him for a walk, she replied, "No, I mustn't go out of the yard, or God'll punish Mamma some more." Then at the age of three, Katie also died, and Mrs. McKinley said she felt deserted by God. A family friend recalled that "Ida would have died years ago, but William would just not let her go."

Ida had long expected her husband to become President, but on the night of his election in 1896, she was filled with dread. Citing the murders of Lincoln and James Garfield, she was said to have told him, "Oh, Major, they will kill you! They will kill you!" The President acted as her buffer against the world, explaining that he "never went into her presence without a smile on my face" because "there was my wife's life at stake." During setbacks in the war, he tried to keep the bad news from Ida. Before playing cards with friends, he whispered instructions: "Mrs. McKinley always wins." Almost daily he consulted various doctors about her emotional and physical maladies and strove to conceal her propensity for seizures from outsiders. Once when Ida started to tremble during dinner at a friend's home, the President leapt up and draped a large napkin across her face.

* * *

NEAR THE END of July, the French Ambassador, Jules Cambon, came to the White House with a peace feeler from Spain. Knowing that McKinley was religious, the envoy told him that he hoped that the President would "be humanely Christian and generous." Judge Day, by now Secretary of State, warned that the United States would not make a limited deal on Cuba; any talks must address how to end hostilities "in all the points where they now exist." After consulting his Cabinet, McKinley drafted a possible settlement, which codified his intent, under the Teller Amendment, to give Cuba to its people and help the island form an independent, constitutional government. Spain would cede Puerto Rico and other islands to the United States, as well as Manila.

Worried about "questions of race, climate, etc.," in the Philippine Islands, McKinley had been skeptical "about our keeping the whole group." Now he weighed how much of the archipelago should become American territory. The Filipino revolutionary Emilio Aguinaldo and his forces had been struggling against Spanish dominion for two years. When Aguinaldo formed an authoritarian government-in-waiting in the spring of 1898, McKinley had ordered Dewey to avoid making pledges to him that would "incur our liability to maintain their cause in the future." Day warned the President that absorbing the entire Philippines, with its millions of unlearned people, would be a tall order for America, which believed in the consent of the governed.

Raising the matter with his Cabinet, McKinley pretended to be undecided, but Cortelyou saw his chief's "guiding hand" in the discussion. Joking about his Secretary of State's limited conception of America's role on the islands, McKinley joked to the Cabinet, "Judge Day only wants a hitching-post." He told his more acquisitive Secretary of Agriculture,

James Wilson, "You Scotch favor keeping everything, including the Sabbath!" When Day privately chided the President for ignoring his request for an American naval base in the Philippines, McKinley confessed, "I was afraid it would be carried."

The President summoned Cambon and gave him his own peace proposal. After reading it, the Frenchman said, "They are very hard terms." McKinley replied that if Spain had sued for peace just after Dewey's triumph in Manila Bay, he might have been more generous. But now, if the Spanish stalled, he might further tighten his demands. He refused Spain's request to provide compensation for any past American injuries to Spaniards and their property in Cuba or Puerto Rico. After their talk, Cambon persuaded the Spanish government that if it refused McKinley's demands, Spain would "have nothing more to expect from a conqueror resolved to procure all the profit possible from the advantages he has obtained."

On Friday afternoon, August 12, through heavy rain, Cambon returned to the White House to sign a peace protocol on Spain's behalf in advance of a final treaty. Averse to theater, McKinley barred the press from the Cabinet Room. The French envoy and Day sat down at the table once used by General Grant, while the President, glowering with his thick eyebrows, stood above them, wearing a black Prince Albert coat, pale waistcoat, and black bow tie.* After the little ceremony, Day murmured to Cortelyou, "Let's see what we get by this."

On a very hot day at the start of September, McKinley arrived, by open carriage, at Camp Wikoff, on Montauk Point, near the tip of Long Island. Named for the first American officer felled in the Cuba campaign, the camp had been hastily built to care for the sick, wounded, and dying, and to guard the public against soldiers suffering from yellow and scarlet fever, typhoid, malaria, dysentery, and other maladies. Theodore Roosevelt stayed there briefly, along with various Rough

---

* In 1899, Théobald Chartran rendered a large, excellent painting of McKinley's treaty signing. President George W. Bush hung it in that same room, which he and other modern Presidents used as a private office, and sat in front of it, using Grant's old table as a desk, while conducting wars in Afghanistan and Iraq.

Riders. The camp was overcrowded, with about eighteen thousand inhabitants. One chaplain complained of "typhoid fever patients rolling in filth and without attention of any kind" and "only one nurse to every thirty-five sick men." McKinley hoped his visit would help to counteract complaints about the camp's mismanagement, bad conditions, and inefficiency. To preserve her own health, Ida stayed behind, shopping in New York City.

Wearing a light straw boater with formal attire, the perspiring McKinley looked out at the acres of crisp, pointed tents above the blue Atlantic. Thankful to Wikoff's gray-bearded commander, General Joseph Wheeler, for bettering conditions before his arrival, the President chirped, "This is beautiful" and "I never saw a handsomer camp." He was driven to the tent of General Shafter, who had returned ill from Cuba. Shaking hands, he told the red-faced, feverish Shafter, "Don't get up, General. You are entitled to rest. How are you?" "A little achy" came the reply. Touring some of the hospital tents, McKinley said, "How sorry I am to see these brave fellows in such a condition." One nurse confronted him: "There are men lying out in the grass in the regimental camps, dying." After speaking with one soldier whose life was ebbing away, the normally stolid President was on the verge of tears.

McKinley's voice broke with emotion as he addressed about five thousand of the soldiers in the heat: "You have come home after two months of severe campaigning, which has embraced assault and siege and battle. . . . The names of brave officers and men who fell in battle and those who have died from exposure and sickness will live in immortal story." For two minutes, the crowd shouted, "Hurrah! Hurrah!" and some of the men wept. "Three cheers for the President!" shouted General Wheeler. The armed yacht *Aileen* fired off twenty-one guns.

* * *

IN LATE SEPTEMBER, McKinley established a peace commission to bargain with the Spaniards in Paris. It would be chaired by Judge Day, who had resigned as Secretary of State, after only five months, to accept the job. To ease Senate ratification of a treaty, the President also appointed the Chairman of the Senate Foreign Relations Committee, Cushman Davis of Minnesota, and William Frye of Maine, the Senate's President Pro Tempore, despite Frye's plea that he would prefer "to fish and hunt." For bipartisanship, he secured the Delaware Senator George Gray, a Democrat.* Anxious that his Republicans might lose control of the Senate in November, he asked the envoys to try to conclude a treaty in time for current Senators to ratify it before the current Congress adjourned in March.

During the second week of October, McKinley boarded a train for what amounted to a victory tour, with fifty-seven formal appearances in six states. As President, he had never traveled west of Chicago. Unlike Lincoln during his war, McKinley had done very little to inform Americans about what he was doing and why. Now he had the opportunity to explain the Spanish conflict to the public and confide his aims for the future. It was a month before the 1898 midterm elections, and he knew that speaking in public about the nation's military triumph was likely to boost Republican chances. Since Andrew Johnson, no President had gone out to campaign for his party in midterm, and in 1896, McKinley had famously pressed his cause from his own front porch in Canton, Ohio—partly to avoid unfavorable comparisons with the brilliant oratory of his opponent, William Jennings Bryan. But he feared that a dramatic midterm loss of congressional seats would undermine him as he tried to arrange the peace. To avoid the crass appearance of a President campaigning so soon after the guns had fallen silent, he told Republican leaders that while he was "entirely willing" to discuss "current events," he would not allow himself to make "political speeches."

Disembarking from his train in Cedar Rapids, Iowa, McKinley told the crowd, "This war, that was so speedily closed through the valor and intrepidity of our soldiers, will bring to us, I trust, blessings that are now beyond calculation. It will bring also burdens, but the American people never shirk a responsibility and never unload a burden that

---

* McKinley had asked Chief Justice Melville Fuller and Associate Justice Edward White, both appointed by Democrats, to join the commission but both declined.

carries forward civilization. We accepted war for humanity." At a "Peace Jubilee" in Bryan's bailiwick of Omaha, the President recalled, "It has been said by someone that the normal condition of nations is war. That is not true of the United States. . . . Ours has never been a military government." Exuberantly he boasted about his war: "What a wonderful experience it has been from the standpoint of patriotism and achievement! . . . Matchless in its results! Unequaled in its completeness and the quick succession with which victory followed victory! Attained earlier than it was believed to be possible!"

In Hastings, Iowa, McKinley insisted, "We have pretty much everything in this country to make it happy. We have good money, we have ample revenues, we have unquestioned national credit. But what we want is new markets, and as trade follows the flag, it looks very much as if we are going to have new markets." Moving on to the Iowa town of Glenwood, he asserted, "There was no malice in our conflict," noting that the first ship to enter Santiago's harbor after the Spanish surrender bore the Red Cross, with "provisions and medicines" for suffering Cubans: "And so all through the war, we have mingled with our heroics our splendid and glorious humanity."

At the Illinois State House in Springfield, where Abraham Lincoln had been a lawmaker, McKinley, the son of abolitionists, recalled how the "Martyr President" had "liberated a race—a race which he said ought to be free because there might come a time when these black men could help keep the jewel of liberty within the family of freedom. . . . These brave black men ascended the hill of San Juan in Cuba." In Chicago, from his box at the elegantly ornamented Auditorium Theatre, McKinley bowed as Booker T. Washington, from the stage, thanked "our wise, patient and brave Chief Executive for the generous manner in which my race has been recognized during this conflict."

Two nights later, in the same hall, McKinley confessed that before the Spanish conflict he had not fully foreseen its ultimate result:

> The war with Spain was undertaken not that the United States should increase its territory but that oppression at our very

doors should be stopped. . . . Looking backward, we can see how the hand of destiny builded for us and assigned us tasks whose full meaning was not apprehended even by the wisest statesmen of their times. Our colonial ancestors did not enter upon their war originally for independence. Abraham Lincoln did not set out to free the slaves but to save the Union. The war with Spain was not of our seeking, and some of its consequences may not be to our liking. . . . Territorial expansion is not alone and always necessary to national advancement. There must be a constant movement toward a higher and nobler civilization.

After the President spoke, a ceremonial toast was offered to the Navy. And who should deliver the response but Captain Sigsbee, late of the USS *Maine*? The *Chicago Tribune* later reported that the renowned Sigsbee had arrived in "gorgeous attire. Nothing handsomer than the gold epaulets and gold lace of a naval officer of high rank." Sigsbee told the audience, "I am glad that the issue of the *Maine* was not used as a cause of war," adding that it was "absolutely untrue" that "any fleet or squadron of the United States has gone into this war flying the official signal 'Remember the *Maine!*'* I, as the captain of the *Maine*, glory in it." To thunderous applause, the captain went on, "I trust that we will all remember the *Maine*, but in the right sense and the right way—never for revenge. A nation may go to war to punish, but never for revenge. Not this nation!" Despite the applause, much of the audience may have been dumbfounded to hear Sigsbee claim that their country had not gone to war against Spain in retaliation for the *Maine*.

Traveling eastward, the President stopped at Columbus, where he had reigned as Governor of Ohio. Of the war, he bragged, "No desire for new territory, no motive of aggrandizement but that we might stop the oppression of a neighboring people whose groans we could almost

---

* By "cause of war," Sigsbee meant McKinley's war message and the congressional war declaration. That summer, he had told the *New York Times*, "How could it be possible for me to think of revenge? I have never had the least idea who blew up my ship."

hear. . . . My countrymen, the past is secure. We know the extent of our country now." In Logansport, Indiana: "The flag never seemed so dear to us as it does now, and it never floated over so many places." (A member of the crowd shouted, "It will stay there!") In Tipton, Indiana, the President made a different claim: "We have had such a revival of patriotism in this country as we have never had since the earliest days of our history. . . . That is what the war has done for the people of the United States." In Philadelphia, as a million people watched and cheered, the smiling McKinley led a military parade, riding behind four white horses, with the crowds cheering nonstop and the President mouthing his thanks. Then, with Ida present but deliberately obscured from the raucous crowd, McKinley reviewed the troops for three hours, standing under a large, newly designed presidential flag of fire-engine red.

The *New York Times* complained that McKinley had been discussing the war during his tour "with the recklessness and the cheerfulness of a child. . . . Because we have beaten a bankrupt and retrograde nation of 17 millions, his position is, therefore, that we can beat anybody." Citing the President's boast of raising two hundred thousand volunteers within sixty days, the *Times* noted that these men had been badly led, equipped, fed, clothed, and disciplined: they were "not an Army but a mob, and they would have been an easy prey to a quarter of their number of real soldiers." A New York City Democrat, running for Congress, tried to take McKinley down an additional peg. Captain William Astor Chanler, a rich patrician who had fought at San Juan Hill, claimed to a crowd that the President's brother Abner had corruptly "made a pot of money" from the Spanish war as "counsel for the firm that supplied clothing to the Army." (Chanler ultimately won his election.)

That fall, McKinley's Ohio patron Senator Mark Hanna had exhorted Republican candidates to "make their appeal on the issue of the war." Theodore Roosevelt exploited his Cuba heroism to run for Governor of the Empire State. Employing a Rough Riders bugler to announce his appearance at campaign stops, TR asked voters, "Is New York going to prove false to the Administration, false to the flag, false to what it did last summer, false to what the Navy and Army won for the country? . . . If New York State goes wrong at the next election, you will have given a blow to the interests of the United States heavier than any Spain was able to strike." The *New York Times* carped that Roosevelt's "ardent jingoism" was "arrogance and audacity" and "partisan clap-trap of the rankest sort," based on the assumption that the victory over Spain "was exclusively an achievement of the Republican party."

In November, riding in the railroad car *Cleopatra,* McKinley and Ida returned home to Canton, where the President voted, along with perhaps a dozen old friends, at an old carpenter shop, placing his black silk hat on the shelf of the voting booth. Returning to the White House on Election Day, he stayed up until midnight, reading bulletins. With sixteen million people voting, his party had gained 6 seats in the Senate, commanding a 44 to 34 majority, while losing 21 seats in the House, which left it in control by 189 to 161. Roosevelt had narrowly won his governorship. Looking ahead to the President's reelection was his new Secretary of State, the same John Hay who had once been Lincoln's aide. Hay assured McKinley, "You have pulled us through with your own strength. This makes the work for 1900 simple and easy."

* * *

AT THE FRENCH Foreign Ministry on the Quai d'Orsay, under crystal chandeliers, amid garish green and red upholstery, the chief Spanish negotiator, Eugenio Montero Ríos, told the Americans that "you are the victors and we are the vanquished," and that "magnanimity becomes the victor."

McKinley had asked his commissioners for "no joint occupation with the insurgents" in the Philippines. Beyond that, he pondered what to do with the islands. Before Thanksgiving, in his White House office, he told a group of fellow Methodists that after returning from his railroad speaking tour, "I walked the floor of the White House night after night, until midnight, and I am not ashamed to tell you, gentlemen, that I went down on my knees and prayed Almighty God for light and guidance more than one night. And one night, late, it came to me this way—I don't know how it was, but it came."*

From his epiphany, the President concluded that returning the archipelago to Spain "would be cowardly and dishonorable." Letting it fall to Germany or France "would be bad business and discreditable." Filipinos were "unfit for self-government, and they would soon have anarchy and misrule over there worse than Spain's was." Therefore "there was nothing left for us to do but to take them all, and to educate the Filipinos, and uplift and civilize and Christianize them, and, by God's grace, do the very best we could by them, as our fellow men for whom Christ also died." Ida enthused to her husband about "converting" the Philippines' Igorot tribe.† McKinley asked aides to add the Philippines to the map of the United States on his wall, vowing, "There they will stay while I am President."

On McKinley's behalf, Secretary Hay cabled the commissioners in Paris, "Grave as are the responsibilities and unforeseen as are the difficulties which are before us, the President can see but one plain path of duty—the acceptance of the archipelago." Hay wrote that Americans were insisting that "the people of the Philippines, whatever else is done, must be liberated from Spanish domination." Senator Frye recommended closing the deal with the Spanish by offering them $10 million or $20 million in cash. Hay replied with "cheerful concurrence," reporting that McKinley found this "a reasonable sum" that fell "under established precedents." After holding out for more than a month, the Spanish agreed to give the Philippines, Guam, and Puerto Rico to the United States, and Cuba to its own people. On Saturday night, December 10, the final parchment was signed, with ribbons and seals attached,

---

* Always eager to emulate the sixteenth President, McKinley may have been recalling a Lincoln story he had told in 1892 in Youngstown, Ohio, when he quoted the Civil War leader saying that before Gettysburg, he had "knelt on my knees" and "prayed to God as I had never prayed to Him before."

† Colonel Benjamin Montgomery, the White House telegraph chief, felt that the First Lady's "incessant talk on the conversion of the islanders influenced the President to retain the Philippines."

before a hearty fire. Then the doors of the chamber were flung open, and the Spaniards told reporters, *"C'est fini."* By then, perhaps less than 400 Americans and 800 Spaniards had died in battle, thousands more from disease.

The following week, the President resumed his victory trip, riding his train to Georgia, Alabama, and South Carolina. In Dixie, McKinley contended that the Spanish conflict had helped to bridge the old cleavage between North and South, so that "sectional lines no longer mar the map of the United States." He told the Georgia legislature that since "every soldier's grave made during our unfortunate Civil War is a tribute to American valor," the time had come for the federal government to "share with you in the care of the graves of Confederate soldiers." Surprised to hear such a conciliatory offer from the man who led the party of Lincoln and Radical Reconstruction, those in the chamber cheered.

The *Atlanta Constitution* praised McKinley's statement and proclaimed, "We Are Now One Nation in Heart." The *New York Times* reported that since Appomattox, "nothing has more deeply stirred a Southern audience." One Georgia woman said, "We are all McKinleyites now." More churlishly, the *Chattanooga News* insisted that Southerners would continue to feel affronted so long "as the Republican politicians of the North insist on placing Negroes in office."*

* * *

O N JANUARY 4, 1899, McKinley sent the Paris treaty to the Senate, where Henry Cabot Lodge was one of its champions. Lodge warned, "The repudiation of the President in such a matter as this is, to my mind, the humiliation of the United States in the eyes of civilized mankind and brands us as a people incapable of great affairs or of taking rank where we belong, as one of the greatest of the great world powers." Lodge dropped this point of view exactly twenty years

---

* Later, in Macon, a Confederate veteran gave McKinley a rebel badge with his picture on it and asked him to put it on. "I do not know that it will be proper," said the President. "But you must," said the veteran, and McKinley complied.

later, while dealing with Woodrow Wilson's League of Nations compact. To McKinley's good fortune, William Jennings Bryan endorsed the treaty, refusing pleas to lead the opposition. Bryan said he preferred "to ratify the treaty and end the war, release the volunteers [and] remove the excuse for war expenditures." The great isolationist thought it "safer to trust the American people to give independence to the Filipinos than to trust the accomplishment of that purpose to diplomacy with an unfriendly nation."

But the effort to capture two-thirds of ninety Senators proved to be difficult. George Hoar, Republican from Massachusetts, warned that the treaty would "make us a vulgar, commonplace empire, controlling subject races and vassal states, in which one class must forever rule and other classes must forever obey."

Two days before the roll call, McKinley learned that warfare had broken out in the Philippines between the Americans and the insurgents. At the White House, leaning back in his chair, he said, "How foolish these people are. This means the ratification of the treaty. The people will understand now. The people will insist upon its ratification." But he remained two votes short. His floor managers converted one holdout Senator by offering political favors. The President turned around the defiant racist Samuel McEnery of Louisiana, who worried about all of those brown people in the Philippines, by agreeing to endorse the latter's resolution that the United States should not annex the archipelago. (McKinley anticipated that McEnery's edict would be defeated by the House, and he was right.) Thus the Senate ratified the Treaty of Paris by 57 to 27 votes.

The following week, McKinley traveled to Boston, where he inspected the city's gleaming new subway and made his first major statement on what the United States would now do in the Philippines. At the vast dinner of the Home Market Club in Mechanics' Hall, he exulted in a loud ovation. Behind him, illuminated by electric lights, were large portraits of George Washington, Lincoln, and himself, looming above the word "LIBERATOR." With two thousand diners and four thousand other guests present, the North Adams Transcript contended that "more people were fed than at any previous banquet in the country's history."

McKinley told the crowd that, "like Cuba and Puerto Rico," the Philippines was "a trust we have not sought" but "from which we will not flinch." After liberating the Philippines, he asked, "could we have left them in a state of anarchy and justified ourselves in our own consciences or before the tribunal of mankind?" He went on,

> Until Congress shall direct otherwise, it will be the duty of the Executive to possess and hold the Philippines, giving to the people thereof peace and order and beneficent government. . . . No imperial designs lurk in the American mind. . . . Our priceless principles undergo no change under a tropical sun. . . . I cannot bound my vision by the blood-stained trenches around Manila, where every red drop, whether from the veins of an American soldier or a misguided Filipino, is anguish to my heart.

Instead he looked forward to "a people redeemed from savage indolence and habits," whose grandchildren "shall for ages hence bless the American republic" because it "set them in the pathway of the world's best civilization."

As "The Star-Spangled Banner" was played, one diner, F. E. Taft, a fifty-year-old manufacturer from Newburyport, fell dead of a heart attack; his body was quietly removed from the hall. Then a fifty-three-man choir sang "Ode to President McKinley," specially composed for the occasion: "All hail to our great Chief Magistrate, / Appointed in God's wide plan. . . . A wider scope for the whole world's hope, / And a happier age for Man."

* * *

WHILE ISSUING ORDERS about the Philippines, McKinley told intimates he felt "strange" about wielding presidential power so far from the American mainland. He had ordered that US military government be "extended with all possible dispatch to the whole of the ceded territory." The American arrivals should "proclaim in the most public manner that we come not as invaders or conquerors but as friends—to protect the natives in their homes, in their employments and in their personal and religious rights."

From Manila, General Francis Greene warned that most Filipinos wanted "a Philippine republic under American protection," similar to what was being envisaged for Cuba—and that the insurgents were not willing to go quietly. Told that Aguinaldo wished to establish "a dictatorship of the familiar South American type," the President decried the "sinister ambitions" of what he called the Filipino "insurrection." Leading the charge against it would be General Arthur MacArthur, a Civil War veteran, whose ambitious nineteen-year-old son Douglas was a West Point cadet that fall. As the struggle escalated, some Americans charged that US forces were committing atrocities in the Philippines that rivaled those of Butcher Weyler in Cuba. By the start of 1900, MacArthur's soldiers had subdued enough of the archipelago that the President asked William Howard Taft, then a federal appeals court judge in Cincinnati, to "go there and establish civil government." Taft noted that the rising American casualties were causing the President "great grief."

By the summer of 1900, McKinley felt so robust about expanding the powers of his office that he sent five thousand US soldiers to China without consulting Congress, in the name of guarding American civilians. When they arrived, they joined other forces against the Boxer Rebellion, provoking the Chinese to declare war against the United States. The President did not ask Congress to back him, but American courts ruled that a state of war prevailed nevertheless.*

McKinley's new muscularity outraged members of the Anti-Imperialist League, created after the start of the Spanish-American War to uphold the principles of nonintervention and consent of the governed appearing in the Declaration of Independence, President Washington's Farewell Address, and Lincoln's Gettysburg Address. Its leaders included Mark Twain, the philanthropist Andrew Carnegie, and Samuel Gompers of the American Federation of Labor. Many of its members complained that the idealistic

---

* Cabinet members explained on background that McKinley had not called the Senate and House back into session to bless his actions because he feared they would exploit such an opportunity to pass other bills "that will hurt the President in the campaign."

volunteers who had signed up to fight in Cuba were now being compelled to wage McKinley's more ignoble war against Filipino insurgents.

During a League rally at New York's Cooper Union in May, ex-Senator Carl Schurz of Missouri, a Union General during the Civil War and McKinley's onetime friend, exclaimed that during the conflict with Spain, the United States had let the Filipinos "believe that in fighting on the same side with us, they were fighting for their own independence." Then "we deliberately turned our loudly-vaunted war of liberation and humanity into a shameless war of conquest. . . . We killed many, many thousands of them, and still go on killing them at the rate of 1,000 to 1,500 a month." Schurz called on Americans to show "that the Republic of Washington and Lincoln still lives."

In June, at Philadelphia, the Republicans nominated McKinley for reelection. Anxious about potential dangers to her husband's life, Ida had hoped to take him home after one term to Canton. She had long had premonitions that the Major would be killed in office, and told friends, "I dread all his speeches." Cortelyou noted that one afternoon, after returning late from an event, the President found her weeping in fear that "something might have happened to him." Despite Ida's anxiety, McKinley was eager for a second term that would crown his success in transforming the United States into an undeniable world power. With the death of Vice President Garret Hobart, the President's new running mate would be Governor Theodore Roosevelt. TR's maverick activism unsettled mossbacks like Mark Hanna, but McKinley knew that his heroism in Cuba would serve as a vote-getting advertisement for his war.

After a brief springtime boomlet for Dewey, by then appointed to the highest rank as Admiral of the Navy, the Democrats, at Kansas City, once again chose William Jennings Bryan. In Indianapolis, accepting the nomination outdoors in the stifling heat, Bryan devoted his whole speech to what he called McKinley's imperialism:

> Those who would have this nation enter upon a career of empire must consider not only the effect of imperialism on the Filipi-nos. . . . We cannot repudiate the principle of self-government in

the Philippines without weakening that principle here. . . . The spirit which will justify the forcible annexation of the Philippine Islands will justify the seizure of other islands and the domination of other people—and with wars of conquest, we can expect a certain, if not rapid growth of our military establishment. . . . A large standing Army . . . is ever a menace to a republican form of government. . . . In what respect does the position of the Republican party differ from the position taken by the English government in 1776?

Defending his criticism of a President during wartime, Bryan later recalled that Congressman Abraham Lincoln had upbraided Polk during the Mexican War.

That November, McKinley defeated Bryan with 51.6 to 45.5 percent of the popular vote, and 292 to 155 electoral votes. At a Union League banquet in Philadelphia, the reelected President proclaimed that his "unquestioned endorsement" showed "the obligations of a righteous war and treaty of peace unrepudiated. . . . We have reached that period in our history when there is no closed door to America. The nations of the earth recognize this, and accord to the United States, as her right, the position of one of the great powers of the world." He told the diners, "Be not disturbed. . . . There is no fear for the Republic."

* * *

MCKINLEY USED THE Spanish-American War to launch the United States as a global power, extending its territory in the Pacific and western Atlantic and the reach of its troops to China. But one test of a President's accomplishment is how much it grew out of that leader's aforethought and long-standing philosophy, and by that measure, McKinley's achievement shrinks.

During his first year in office, he had told Carl Schurz, "You may be sure that there will be no jingo nonsense under my administration. You need not borrow any trouble on that account." Before the spring of 1898, McKinley was more passionate about tariffs than military and foreign policy, and his steps toward world influence for his country were largely reactions to the events of the war. Had the *Maine* not happened to suffer a boiler accident, as it probably did, McKinley might not have been quite so motivated to extend American might and territory beyond the nation's continental limits.

This President showed appealing indignation after learning the full extent of Spanish brutality in Cuba, but it is unlikely that, without provocation, either McKinley or Congress would have pushed the matter to the point of war in the Caribbean and Pacific in order to stop it. He deserves to be honored for his restraint after the sinking of the *Maine*. A more vainglorious or war-happy President might have linked arms with Hearst, Pulitzer, and the most militant members of Congress to rush the American people headlong into conflict. But McKinley's restraint resembled less that of Thomas Jefferson, who had the political skill to keep his country out of war after the *Chesapeake* was attacked in 1807, than that of Madison, who lacked such a talent for command in 1812. As much as McKinley might have liked to slow the stampede toward war, he was not up to the task. And although, unlike Polk, McKinley did not manufacture the immediate predicate for this conflict, the fact remains that the Spanish-American War was heavily promoted to Americans as retaliation for a supposed attack that was probably false.

Once the conflict began, despite his inexperience as Commander-in-Chief, McKinley managed to overcome the limits of his tiny standing Army to help his country secure a quick victory. He did not exploit the crisis to grab unwarranted power for himself. But he was guilty of what became known in later times as "mission creep." For McKinley, a war that was accelerated by the desire to punish the Spanish for the *Maine* disaster, drive them out of Cuba, and grant the Cubans their independence became—without his consulting the Congress or the American people—a struggle for an American empire, including new aims such as Christianizing the Filipinos.

Unlike with Polk's territorial expansion during the Mexican War, however, McKinley's mission creep was not the result of a concealed agenda that the President suddenly sprang on the country. It grew from his spontaneous reactions to the unfolding of his war and the demands from Congress and the public to push American power beyond the limits of the mainland. It is a sign of McKinley's candor that he readily admitted to the public, after it was over, that he had been improvising. When he spoke in Boston in early 1899, he asked, "What nation was ever able to write an accurate program of the war upon which it was entering, much less decree in advance the scope of its results?" and said, "No accurate map of nations engaged in war can be traced until the war is over."

In his decision to seize the Philippines, McKinley underestimated the risk that it would take years and thousands of lives to quash the local insurgency, and that this effort would cast the United States before much of the world as an oppressor. By the time he ran for reelection, he had hastily transformed himself into an apostle of empire with the zealotry of a convert, but he showed little understanding of how the nation's new imperial role might ultimately compromise its image before the world—and its original revolutionary conception of itself.

Professor Woodrow Wilson of Princeton wrote in 1900 that the Spanish-American War and its "most striking and momentous consequence . . . the administration of distant dependencies" had helped to make McKinley's presidency more powerful than any since the early nineteenth century, except for Lincoln's. "When foreign affairs play a prominent part in the politics and policy of a nation," Wilson explained, "its Executive must, of necessity be its guide: must utter every initial judgment, take every first step of action, supply the information upon which it is to act, suggest and in large measure control its conduct. . . . Upon his choice, his character, his experience hang some of the most weighty issues of the future." With more prescience than he knew, Wilson forecast that "interesting things" might emerge from this "singular change."

＊ ＊ ＊

CELEBRATING THE DAWN of a new century, on Thursday, September 5, 1901, McKinley and his wife arrived at the Pan-American Exposition in Buffalo, New York. With whitened hair, great dark wells around his eyes, and a massive gut, the President had aged rapidly during his war years. Now, in what proved to be the last speech of his life, he marveled at the advance of new technology: "The telegraph keeps us advised of what is occurring everywhere, and the press foreshadows, with more or less accuracy, the plans and purposes of the nations. . . . The quick gathering and transmission of news, like rapid transit, are of recent origin, and are only made possible by the genius of the inventor and the courage of the government." He recounted that at the close of the War of 1812, it took nineteen days for federal officials to inform General Jackson in New Orleans that the conflict was over:

> How different now! . . . We knew almost instantly of the first shots fired at Santiago, and the subsequent surrender of the Spanish forces was known at Washington within less than an hour of its consummation. . . . God and Man have linked the nations together. No nation can longer be indifferent to any other. And as we are brought more and more in touch with each other, the less occasion is there for misunderstandings.

That night, as if looking into the future, the President and Ida watched as the buildings of the fair, some with domes, were illuminated, glowing into the sky. Then there were brilliantly colored fireworks, which depicted American ships from the Spanish-American War and the profile of McKinley.

The next afternoon, at four o'clock, the President rode in his open carriage to the fair's Temple of Music. While an organist played selections from Bach, a receiving line formed so that McKinley, in his frock coat, could shake hands with members of the public, including a young anarchist called Leon Czolgosz, whose right hand was swathed in what seemed like a cloth bandage. It concealed a revolver. As the President reached out, gunfire knocked him back on his heels. He asked, "Have I been shot?" Watching his assailant be pummeled, McKinley ordered, "Don't let them hurt him!" With a bloodstain widening on his white vest, he advised Cortelyou, "Be careful—tell Mrs. McKinley gently."

Taken back to the house where they had been staying, he asked, "Poor, brave little woman, what will she do?"

At first, after surgery, the doctors allowed themselves to hope that the President would survive the attack. Having rushed to Buffalo, Vice President Roosevelt told reporters, "God wouldn't let such a noble man die by an assassin's bullet!" But within the week, McKinley's heart began to falter, and he murmured to Ida, "God's will, not ours, be done." As the President sank into a coma, Dr. Rixey told the First Lady that her husband was entering "that sleep which knows no awakening."

After midnight, on Saturday, the fourteenth, McKinley died. Reproaching himself, his doctor recalled how he had failed to get the President to take more exercise and fresh air, and cited McKinley's anxieties over Ida, who was "constantly on his mind." Rixey attested that had the President been more vital, he might have survived the assassin's bullet, but "his enfeebled constitution could not stand the shock, and gangrene around the wounds caused death."*

Summoned from a hiking trip, TR took the presidential oath in Buffalo, vowing to uphold the policies of his martyred predecessor. Within a day, however, he was telling reporters that he would behave "as if I and not McKinley" had been elected President in 1900. The war in the Philippines ended nine months later, with more than 4,200 American combat deaths, and a Filipino combat death toll of more than 20,000. The US Congress provided for a Philippines legislature, and gave it the protection of the American Bill of Rights. Back in Canton, Ida McKinley recalled to friends that "the Major had planned a trip to the Orient." She said that if she had enjoyed any physical strength, she "would go and teach the babies of the Philippines."

Before the United States pulled its troops from their island, it

---

* A week after McKinley was interred at Canton, Abraham Lincoln was reburied in a new concrete vault at his Springfield tomb. (In 1876, the remains had nearly been stolen for ransom.) When the coffin was opened to be sure it was Lincoln, witnesses noted that the Great Emancipator's melancholy face was "chalky white." With the passage of time, Lincoln's eyebrows had vanished and his black suit was flecked with shreds of red cloth—almost certainly the remnants of an American flag.

compelled the Cubans to change their constitution to include the language of an amendment sponsored by the Republican Senator from Connecticut, Orville Platt. It forbade Cuba to conclude any treaty with a foreign power that might impair its independence, gave the United States the right to intervene there, if necessary, and provided for US naval installations on the island, including one at Guantánamo Bay.

In their new Hawaiian territory, the Americans transformed the Iolani Palace of the deposed final queen, Liliuokalani, into a capitol building. They also set about building a home for US warships on a great lagoon that, according to Hawaiian legend, had hosted an ancient shark goddess. The new base was called Pearl Harbor.

CHAPTER TEN

"The World Is on Fire"

O N WEDNESDAY MORNING, January 17, 1917, mired in the third year of its Great War against Germany and the other Central Powers, Great Britain was almost desperate for the United States to come to its aid.* In London's Whitehall neighborhood, Rear Admiral William Reginald Hall, the director of British naval intelligence, looked out his office window at the falling snow, while rolled-up messages shot from pneumatic tubes into wire baskets. In came one of Hall's best code-breakers, Nigel de Grey, perspiring with excitement. De Grey asked the Admiral, "Do you want to bring America into the war? . . . I've got something here which—well, it's a rather astonishing message which might do the trick, *if* we could use it."

De Grey produced his handwritten version of a partially decoded German telegram: "It isn't very clear, I'm afraid, but I'm sure I've got most of the important points right." The cable, from the German Foreign Secretary, Arthur Zimmermann, told his Ambassador to the United States and Mexico, Johann von Bernstorff, that two weeks hence, Germany would start "unrestricted submarine warfare" on the Atlantic. When

---

* At the time, the Central Powers included Germany, Austria-Hungary, the Ottoman Empire, and Bulgaria.

the U-boats were unleashed, the government of the Kaiser, Wilhelm II, would try "to keep America neutral" but "war with the U.S.A." would be likely. In the dispatch, Bernstorff told Zimmermann to prepare for such a conflict by asking their Minister in Mexico, Heinrich von Eckardt, to lay the groundwork for a German-Mexican military alliance against the United States.

Now the audacious Hall ordered de Grey to ignore standing rules that such an acquisition be shared with the Admiralty and Foreign Office. Knowing that the cryptographer was "absolutely trustworthy," Hall told him, "Nothing is to be put on the files. This may be a very big thing—possibly the biggest thing of the war. For the present, not a soul outside this room is to be told anything at all." The Admiral was delighted by the possibility that he might now go down in world history as the man who helped his country win the Great War by spurring the United States to join Britain in the struggle. He locked de Grey's notes into his desk, and, as he later recalled, "sat down by myself to evolve a plan of campaign."

Hall was a charming, hot-tempered maverick, who blinked his intense, clear blue eyes so rapidly that his colleagues called him "Blinker." His false teeth made clicking noises when he spoke. A Manchester *Guardian* editor once called him "half Machiavelli and half schoolboy." But an American diplomat who worked with the Admiral in London found him "the coldest-blooded proposition that ever was—he'd cut out a man's heart and hand it back to him." Blinker Hall's interrogations of German prisoners of war were said to be "as ruthless as anything the Old Bailey had ever seen."

Hall was born in 1870 to a father who had been England's first naval intelligence chief but died at fifty-two; the son said it was always "my ambition to sit in his seat." Blinker started in the Navy at fourteen and became captain of the battle cruiser *Queen Mary* in 1913, but his weak lungs aborted his career at sea. Winston Churchill, the First Lord of the Admiralty, gave him command of naval intelligence at the start of war against Germany. Citing his "energy and dash," Churchill found Hall's capacity for hard work "almost frightening." For his team, reaching outside the Navy, Blinker recruited brilliant scholars such as John Beazley, an Oxford archaeologist, Alfred Dillwyn "Dilly" Knox, a Cambridge papyrologist, who decrypted German cables while soaking in his office bathtub, and de Grey, an actor, painter, and book editor, who was called the "Dormouse" because of his modest height and mien.

Blinker asked his codebreakers to find a complete, authentic version of the Zimmermann telegram. When and if it was provided to the Americans, he did not want it dismissed as a British fabrication. He kept the cable's distribution severely limited, out of concern that the Kaiser's regime would discover that the British had broken their codes, and hence change them. The telegram had been sent on an American transatlantic circuit; if the Yanks discovered that London had been illicitly reading their messages, there could be an anti-British tempest in the US Congress making it more difficult for President Woodrow Wilson to take his country into the war. Thus Hall asked his men to find a version of Zimmermann's message sent by some other channel, which he could show to Washington without making it obvious how aggressively England was spying on the Americans.

On January 31, just as the Zimmermann cable had forecast, Germany announced its renewal of unrestricted submarine warfare. With excessive optimism, Blinker Hall anticipated that Wilson would respond by asking the House and Senate for a declaration of war, obviating the need to release the telegram. Two days later, Hall heard from Captain Guy Gaunt, the British naval attaché in New York City, who had been running various covert schemes to nudge the Americans into the war. Gaunt reported he had just been told by Wilson's confidential adviser, Colonel Edward House, that the President would soon break diplomatic relations with Germany and expel Ambassador Bernstorff.* Gaunt was so delighted that he cabled Hall, "I'll probably get soused." Hall asked him to "try and get copies of all telegrams" sent recently between Bernstorff and Eckardt.

---

* The courtesy title used by House, a wealthy Houstonian, had been granted by the Texas Governor Jim Hogg.

To prod the Americans toward action, Hall called on their Ambassador to the Court of St. James's, Walter Hines Page, who was ostentatiously pro-British. Blinker had long cultivated Page, handing him intelligence secrets like bonbons.* Now he briefed the envoy on Gaunt's warning about the impending German-American fracture. Knowing what it could mean, Page gave Hall a whiskey and soda to celebrate.

After guarding the Zimmermann telegram for weeks, Hall finally shared its main points with his counterpart at the Foreign Office, Charles Hardinge; he suggested that the Foreign Secretary, Arthur Balfour, provide a copy to Wilson's government. But Hardinge feared that the Americans would conclude that Britain had been running a *chambre noire* spy operation against them, and might be offended by such a blatant effort to push them into the war.

Then, on February 19, Gaunt sent Hall a coded near-duplicate of the Zimmermann telegram, which Bernstorff had sent to Eckardt. The document had been obtained from the Mexican telegraph office, which meant it could be given to the Americans without tipping them off that the British were intercepting their cable traffic. This version contained alarming new details. While warning that the United States would enter the war, Zimmermann was asking Eckardt to "most secretly" persuade the Mexican President, Venustiano Carranza Garza, that "the ruthless employment of our submarines" could force England to beg for peace in a few months. Germany and Mexico should "make war together" and then "make peace together." Berlin would grant the Mexicans "generous financial support and an understanding on our part that Mexico is to reconquer the lost territory in Texas, New Mexico and Arizona." Zimmermann was offering Mexico the chance to take back some of the territory won by James

---

* In 1918, after his country entered the European conflict, Page wrote Wilson, "Hall is one genius that the war has developed. . . . I shall never meet another man like him. . . . For Hall can look through you and see the very muscular movements of your immortal soul while he is talking to you. Such eyes as the man has! My Lord!"

Polk's armies in the Mexican War. Bernstorff also suggested trying to dislodge Japan from the Allied cause to fight alongside Germany and Mexico.

Hall now asked his US intelligence liaison, Edward Bell, to come to his office. Without seeking Balfour's permission in advance, Blinker took it upon himself to show the cable to Bell, who read it, aghast, exclaiming, "Mexico to reconquer the lost territory! . . . Why not Illinois and New York?" Hall said His Majesty's government had not yet decided whether to formally offer the telegram to President Wilson. Hall asked Bell to "beg" Ambassador Page "to make no use of the information until Mr. Balfour has made a decision." Bell pledged to "sit tight" for "as long as you say." Having already shared the secret with Bell, Blinker belatedly asked the Foreign Office for sanction to give "the substance" of Zimmermann's cable to Bell, who "would see that it reached the President." Balfour directed that Hall "clinch this problem," since "he knows the ropes better than anyone." Hall gave the Zimmermann telegram to Page, who read it and then pounded his fist on his desk in both indignation and triumph.

On Friday afternoon, February 23, at the Foreign Office, Balfour formally handed Page an English version of the cable, explaining that it had been "bought in Mexico" and urging that it be published. Knowing that the telegram could have the ultimate impact of allowing England to win the Great War, Balfour later called it "as dramatic a moment as I remember in all my life." Moved to tears, Page cabled Washington that he would soon "send a telegram of great importance to the President and Secretary of State": Zimmermann's telegram had "so greatly exercised the British Government that they have lost no time in communicating it to me." Now Washington could decide how to gird against "the threatened invasion of our territory." The self-dramatizing Hall cabled Gaunt in New York, "Alone I did it."

At the White House, before dinner on Sunday, February 25, President Wilson was presented with the Zimmermann evidence by Acting Secretary of State Frank Polk, who, by unlikely coincidence, was the son of a cousin of the President who had gone to war against Mexico.* For three years, Wilson had asked Americans to be "impartial in thought, as well as action" about the European war. Now, as Winston Churchill later wrote, the fate of the conflict would depend on Wilson's "mind and spirit," which gave the American President "a part in the fate of nations incomparably more direct and personal than any other man."

✳ ✳ ✳

BORN IN VIRGINIA'S Shenandoah Valley in 1856, Thomas Woodrow Wilson grew up amid the Civil War. "I know what war is, for I have seen its wreckage and terrible ruin," he later said, as President. He was old enough to remember hearing about the election of Abraham Lincoln. (By then, the family had moved to Augusta, Georgia.)

His father, Joseph Ruggles Wilson, a Presbyterian minister, was an undaunted champion of slavery. Three months before Fort Sumter, Joseph preached that "the Bible brings human slavery under divine authority," and that the institution, "by saving a lower race from the destruction of heathenism, has, under divine management, contributed to refine, exalt and enrich its superior race!"† When war came, Reverend Wilson served as a Confederate chaplain and lent his church to serve as a hospital for rebel soldiers; his churchyard housed Union prisoners of war. After Appomattox, eight-year-old Tommy watched the captured Jefferson Davis brought through town on his way to federal prison.

When Wilson arrived at the College of New Jersey (later called Princeton) at eighteen—by then calling himself Woodrow—a friend found him "very full of the South and quite secessionist" and "quite

---

* Polk was on duty because Secretary of State Robert Lansing was spending the weekend at the Greenbrier resort in West Virginia.

† The elder Wilson later proudly had this sermon published, writing that he hoped it would provide "a service to my slaveholding brethren throughout the state"; he added that it was "high time" to "meet the infidel fanaticism of our infatuated enemies."

bitter about it." But, as befit a nimble, ambitious young man, he later tried to minimize the impact of the losing side on his upbringing. In a shorthand note scrawled during his early twenties, Wilson insisted, "To *me* the Civil War and its terrible scenes are but a memory of a short day." As a law student at the University of Virginia, Wilson wrote in the university magazine that "*because* I love the South, I rejoice in the failure of the Confederacy." When he took a wife, his choice was Ellen Louise Axson, of Rome, Georgia, daughter of another Presbyterian minister.

By the time of America's next war, against Spain, Wilson was a Princeton political scientist whose family by then included three daughters. Watching as William McKinley tried to handle the Cuba problem without military action, Wilson derided the President's "leaderless government," where "no man stands at the helm to steer."* Once the Spanish War erupted, Wilson was caught up in the country's fighting spirit. As his brother-in-law, Stockton Axson, recalled, "he was belligerent—regretted he was not free to enlist in the armed forces and fight—read each day's news with the eagerness of a boy." Wilson's Princeton colleague Bliss Perry thought he "romanticized the Army and Navy too much." Unlike more anti-imperialist Democrats, Wilson approved of McKinley's seizure of the Philippines, Hawaii, and Guam.

No other future President had so closely studied the nation's most significant wars. Wilson's five-volume *History of the American People* (1902) revealed his attitudes toward earlier war Presidents. Describing Thomas Jefferson's response to the *Leopard*'s attack on the *Chesapeake* in 1807, Wilson criticized the President's restraint: although Jefferson "saw the face of war" in the British assault, he was "unalterably opposed to war" and "would not propose any means of redress." Wilson lambasted Jefferson's embargo against Britain "as a substitute for war in bringing foreign nations to terms of reason," but lauded the fact that, while

---

* In *Congressional Government* (1885), Wilson had decried the failure of post–Civil War Presidents to stand up to a provincial, sluggish Congress.

confronting Congress, Jefferson "had his way to the utmost." Scathingly Wilson wrote that before the War of 1812, James Madison was "not strong enough" and "saw no way of retreat not too humiliating to be borne," and so caved in to the "foolhardy and reckless" War Hawks. Still the author conceded that by halting impressment on the high seas, Madison's "clumsy, foolhardy, haphazard war" against Great Britain was "sufficient guarantee that another for a like purpose would never be necessary."*

Wilson punctured James Polk's official version of how the nation came to fight Mexico, writing that Polk "ordered" General Taylor to advance to the Rio Grande so that his soldiers could provoke the Mexicans to attack. Wilson lamented Polk's power grab from Congress, which he "had not consulted" before bringing "this momentous matter to a head. . . . War indeed existed, but by whose act Congress was no longer at liberty to inquire." There remained "nothing for it but to vote supplies and an Army." Wilson wrote that Polk had "broadened the scope and meaning of the war beyond all expectation" by seizing "not merely the disputed territory which Texas claimed, but also the whole country of the Pacific slope beyond, from Oregon to the Gila River, to which the United States could have no conceivable right except that of conquest."

Describing Southerners' determination to preserve slavery, Wilson as historian sounded like an apologist: "black people had multiplied among them" and "hired labor had been, once for all, driven out." He wrote that "the care of the slaves, their maintenance like a huge family of shiftless children, remained a duty and a burden which the master could not escape, good season or bad, profit or no profit." He claimed that "where the master was himself at hand, there was almost always moderation, a firm but not unkindly discipline, a real care shown for their comfort and welfare." Wilson insisted that by departing the Union, rebel leaders were trying to provoke "a constitutional crisis, but not a civil war," hoping to bargain for "better terms" from the federal government, but that

---

* Wilson considered it "a tragical but natural accident that the war should be against England, not against France."

"when the sound of the guns at Sumter was heard, it became at once another matter." Like other Southerners, the author castigated Lincoln's seizure of presidential power, writing that the Civil War President "acted oftentimes with the authority almost of a dictator" and that "many plain people everywhere" feared that he was "permanently weakening the foundations of individual liberty."

Addressing the Spanish-American War only three years after it was done, Wilson wrote that after the *Maine* was sunk, "sensational newspapers exaggerated every phase of the disturbing incidents of the time, to make news and increase their sales. . . . Politicians were quick to say and do what they hoped would enhance their credit." Although he respected William McKinley's civility, Wilson complained that this war President lacked the "mastery" to restrain congressional impulses for "radical action," and too heavily inhaled "the subtle airs of opinion abroad out-of-doors." To Wilson, the Spanish conflict was "a war of impulse" but nevertheless a historic watershed, in which Americans had "given themselves a colonial empire, and taken their place of power in the field of international politics."

In 1902, Wilson became president of Princeton, and nine years later, reform Governor of New Jersey. Nominated by the Democrats for President in July 1912, he warned a friend, with impressive self-knowledge, that in the public mind, he was "a vague, conjectural personality, made up more of opinions and academic prepossessions than of human traits and corpuscles." That November, he won 42 percent of the popular vote, defeating ex-President Theodore Roosevelt and the sitting Chief Executive, William Howard Taft. Elected as a progressive reformer, with no military or international experience, Wilson told a Princeton colleague it would be "an irony of fate" if his administration "had to deal chiefly with foreign problems."

* * *

WILSON HAD SCARCELY mentioned foreign policy during his campaign (nor had Taft or, with one exception, Roosevelt). His first inaugural address included not a single sentence on world affairs.

Then, in the dramatic summer of 1914, a Bosnian Serb started a chain reaction by killing the Austrian Archduke, Franz Ferdinand. That August, Germany declared war against Russia and France. German troops invaded Belgium, whose neutrality had been guaranteed by Great Britain and others, thus moving the British to make war against the Germans. Austria-Hungary declared war on Serbia and Russia. France and Britain retaliated with a war declaration. Britain, Russia, and France, soon widely referred to as the Allies, each pledged by treaty to reach no separate peace with its enemies.

When the news of Europe's impending smashup reached Wilson during the first week of August, he was kneeling over Ellen's deathbed, upstairs at the White House. By the light of dawn, she expired from Bright's Disease. The tearful President walked to the window and asked, "Oh, my God, what am I to do?" The next day, he wrote, "God has stricken me almost beyond what I can bear." He told his doctor, Cary Grayson, that he sometimes felt "that the presidency has had to be paid for with Ellen's life." Colonel House recorded after seeing Wilson in New York that his distraught friend had confided that "he could not help wishing when we were out tonight that someone would kill him."

After watching Ellen's burial, the President told her brother Stockton, "I am afraid something will happen on the high seas that will make it impossible for us to keep out of the war." Wilson felt a "compulsion of necessity and duty" to have the United States mediate among the European combatants. Determined to prevent a spiraling of outrage in the tabloids and the streets, like that after the destruction of the *Maine,* which might draw the nation into the conflict, the President personally implored reporters "not to give currency to any unverified rumor, to anything that would tend to create or add to excitement."* He ordered all US military officers—even retired ones—to abstain from public comment on the European situation. He read aloud to Colonel House

---

* Wilson was so apprehensive about providing any hint of allegiance to one European alliance or the other that he canceled a speech planned for the centennial of America's victory of September 1814, at Baltimore's Fort McHenry.

a passage from his *History of the American People* about how Madison had been swept, against his will, into war. "Madison and I are the only two Princeton men that have become President," he said. "The circumstances of the War of 1812 and now run parallel."

The President reembraced American neutrality, warning Congress that "it will be easy to excite passion and difficult to allay it." Even though Americans came "chiefly from the nations now at war," they must not be "divided in camps of hostile opinion, hot against each other." Instead the nation should assume "the fine poise of undisturbed judgment."* Backed by his Secretary of State, the devoutly isolationist William Jennings Bryan, Wilson told the House and Senate in his annual message of December 1914 that "we have nothing to do" with Europe's war, whose "causes can not touch us."† The following April, the President said, "Our whole duty—for the present, at any rate—is summed up in this motto: 'America First.'"‡

Then on May 7, 1915, off the Irish coast, a German submarine sank the British transatlantic ship *Lusitania,* the fastest and most luxurious ocean liner in the world. Of the 1,198 passengers killed, 128 were Americans. Shocked by the attack, Wilson strode out of the White House into the rain, through Lafayette Square and up Sixteenth Street, "to get my mind in hand." Knowing from the *Maine* how the sinking of one ship could move Americans to cry war, he refused to "indulge my own passionate feelings" against the perpetrators in public.

By now, the President had taken up with Edith Bolling Galt, the widow of a Washington jeweler. He had just asked Edith to marry him.

---

* One New Yorker took President Wilson's plea so literally that she wrote the *New York Times,* "with regret," that people were showing "partisanship" while watching movies about war in the theaters. She recommended that such films be "preceded by an announcement that no demonstration be made during their projection."

† Wilson had restored the old presidential practice, suspended by Jefferson, of speaking to Congress in person, well aware that the scene would enhance a Chief Executive's power.

‡ Ironically Wilson had provided a name for the national movement, founded in the late 1930s, which opposed intervention against Adolf Hitler's Germany trampling on many of Wilson's beliefs, while Americans struggled over whether to enter the conflict ultimately known as World War II. Donald Trump adopted the term during his 2016 presidential campaign and used it in his inaugural address.

"You can't love me, for you really don't know me, and it is less than a year since your wife died," she replied, while adding, "I thrill to my very finger tips" at the proposal. Wilson wrote her to lament "my pitiful inability to satisfy and win you, and to show you the true heart of my need." On the night he was told of the *Lusitania*'s destruction, he wrote Edith, "My happiness absolutely depends upon your giving me your entire love." Soon he informed her that "a new certitude and confidence has come to me."

Speaking to an audience of newly naturalized citizens in Philadelphia three days after the *Lusitania*, he refused to mention the disaster. To tamp down public indignation, he asserted that there was "such a thing as a man being too proud to fight," as well as "a nation being so right that it does not need to convince others by force that it is right." Almost immediately he regretted those comments as "foolish." With disgust, Theodore Roosevelt warned that Wilson's approach would not let the United States "retain or regain the position won for it under Washington." Wilson demanded that Germany apologize and offer reparations for America's losses on the *Lusitania,* and was turned down. He wanted to send Germany a tough reply, but Secretary Bryan, dreading war, advised him instead to fix the problem by preventing Americans from boarding belligerent ships.

Wilson was afraid of a public showdown with Bryan, especially one year before he had to seek reelection. The three-time Democratic presidential nominee represented the isolationist vote that was a crucial element of the Democratic coalition. But Bryan quit, complaining to Wilson that "Colonel House has been Secretary of State, not I, and I have never had your full confidence." Eager to keep his country out of Europe's struggle, Bryan told his wife, Mary, that Wilson "does not seem to realize that a great part of America lies on the other side of the Allegheny Mountains." Of Bryan, Wilson told Edith, "No stranger man ever lived, and his naivete takes my breath away."

In August 1915, a German torpedo sank the British White Star Line's *Arabic;* the forty-four passengers killed included two Americans. Some of Wilson's advisers told him that sending another diplomatic note would look timid. Instead the President authorized a leak

to Washington reporters that he was contemplating severance of diplomatic relations with Germany. This helped to elicit a public pledge
from the Kaiser's government not to sink more passenger ships without
warning, but the statement included no apology or compensation for
either the *Lusitania* or the *Arabic*. That fall, Wilson persuaded Congress to augment the nation's defense with fifty destroyers, ten battleships, and a hundred submarines, as well as a one-third increase in the
US Army.

A week before Christmas, the President married Edith Galt. Taking
her into his professional life, he encouraged her to read the contents of
"the Drawer" in his office desk, where urgent documents were left for
him, and asked her advice on state affairs. She helped him by coding
and deciphering correspondence with his envoys in Europe.

At the start of 1916, Wilson told his private secretary, Joseph Tumulty, "If my reelection as President depends upon my getting into
war, I don't want to be President. . . . I have made up my mind that
I am more interested in the opinion that the country will have of me
ten years from now." He understood that America "wants action" but
would not "be rushed into war, no matter if every last Congressman
and Senator stands up on his hind legs and proclaims me a coward."
But Wilson scheduled a speaking tour on "preparedness" to demonstrate his mettle. In Des Moines, making up for his remark about
being "too proud to fight," he promised never to ask Americans to "pay
the price of self-respect" for peace. In St. Louis, he warned against
the perils posed by "one reckless commander of a submarine." In
Pittsburgh, he cautioned that "the world is on fire, and there is tinder everywhere," and, in Cleveland, that there were "things I cannot
control—the actions of others."

In March 1916, a reckless German commander sank the French passenger ferry *Sussex* on the English Channel; the eighty casualties included four injured Americans. Wilson told Congress that unless the
Kaiser's government "immediately" vowed to stop its "relentless and indiscriminate" submarine attacks against passenger and cargo vessels, he
would break relations with Berlin. The Germans replied by demanding
that the United States press the British to relax their maritime blockade,

but they pledged to abide by existing international rules against attacking ships without warning.

Wilson was vastly relieved. If the Germans kept their commitment, he could campaign for reelection without fearing, every hour, that another submarine incident might force him to make crucial decisions about war amid a domestic political circus. He knew that Germany probably believed it was in its self-interest to aid Wilson's cause, since many Republicans were more truculent than the President about entering the war on Britain's side. In their party's platform, they charged that with his "shifty expedients" and "phrase-making" Wilson had "destroyed our influence abroad and humiliated us in our own eyes."

The President's handlers devised a new campaign slogan—"He Kept Us Out of War." They claimed they were thinking of Wilson's policy toward Mexico, but the candidate worried that this tagline seemed to promise Americans a blissful state of peace that he might not be able to keep. Yet he did not prevent the motto from serving as the overwhelming public rationale for his reelection. Wilson knew that campaigning as a peace seeker would help to secure the Bryan vote for himself, all the more important since warlike Americans might gravitate to the Republican nominee, the former New York Governor and Supreme Court Justice Charles Evans Hughes. The President also knew that emphasizing peace could appeal to women, who at the time were legally empowered to vote for President in twelve states.

Lacking the advantage of the brutal Republican cleavage between William Howard Taft and Theodore Roosevelt that had enabled him to become President, Wilson understood that if he prevailed in 1916, the result would likely be very close. Accepting the Democratic nomination that September in Sea Girt, New Jersey, Wilson embraced his peace theme, insisting that America would best "serve mankind" by "reserving our strength and our resources for the anxious and difficult days of restoration" that would follow the European war. He later charged that Republicans "do not want a peace obtained as gentlemen obtain it, but only as braggarts obtain it."

Campaigning that fall, Hughes tried to focus on domestic issues, such as the Wilson reforms that the Republicans called anti-business. But he also complained that the President "backs and backs, and talks and talks, and never stands." Theodore Roosevelt had written a friend that Wilson was "as insincere and cold-blooded an opportunist as we have ever had in the Presidency," and that Wilson resembled "an apothecary's clerk." Now Roosevelt told crowds that "He Kept Us Out of War" was "the phrase of a coward" and that Wilson's view of neutrality was "Pontius Pilate–like." Noting that a German U-53 submarine had been sighted off America's East Coast, TR warned that "the war has been carried to our very shores" and "we face it without policy, plan, purpose or preparation." The *Tucson Citizen* sardonically agreed: "He kept us out of war—while hundreds of our men, women and children were drowned while traveling, as was their undoubted right, upon unarmed ships." The *Chicago Tribune* snickered, "When the sword is at our throat, he will write a little note." Republican newspaper ads said it would be honorable to *"keep out of* war but not to spinelessly *creep into* war," and that "A Nation Which Does Not Protect Its Own Citizens Has Already Begun to Die."

That November, Wilson barely edged out Hughes, with 277 to 254 electoral votes, and 49.2 to 46.1 percent of the popular vote. The President would have been defeated but for the 3,806-vote lead he won in California. A third of the California electorate was estimated to be women, and, as the *Philadelphia Inquirer* reported, "the greatest proportion of women for Wilson in any state seems to have been California." If those female voters were attracted by Wilson's peace strategy, then "He Kept Us Out of War" may have saved him from defeat. He carried ten of the twelve states in which women could vote for President. But his share of the electoral vote was smaller than what he had amassed the first time, which had been true of only one earlier President— his fellow Princetonian, James Madison. Of Wilson's narrow victory, the *Kansas City Star* said, "It was as if the American people had boxed his ears soundly and sent him back with the admonition to mend his ways."

* * *

AFTER THE ELECTION, Wilson aspired to mediate the conflict between "German militarism" and "British navalism," as he wrote to himself. He believed that "decisive victories" were seldom conclusive, and therefore a leader should try to eliminate war as "a means of attaining national ambition." With this in mind, he drafted a new diplomatic note attesting that since the European belligerents all insisted that they were fighting for survival and security from aggression, the United States was "ready to join a league of nations that will pledge itself to their accomplishment," starting with a conference, supervised by neutral countries, to hash out their differences.

Colonel House warned the President that his evenhanded language would drive the British and their allies *"frantic with rage."* Secretary of State Robert Lansing, who had succeeded Bryan, advised Wilson that if the United States entered the struggle, *"we must* go in on the side of the Allies, for we are a democracy." Lansing asked what would happen if Germany agreed to Wilson's conference and the British stayed home. Dismissing such worries, the President told House, "The time is at hand for *something!"*

That same week, Wilson issued his note on naval combat in the Atlantic. Theodore Roosevelt called it "profoundly immoral and misleading." Lansing cabled his diplomats in belligerent countries that "we are drawing nearer the verge of war ourselves," and that Wilson's note raised "the possibility of our being forced into the war." Furious at this indiscretion, Wilson almost fired him. He would not have disagreed with Colonel House's view that the best Secretary of State was someone who had "not too many ideas of his own," but he knew that losing two of them in sixteen months might convince the public that his government was in chaos. Thus he let Lansing stay, but only after offering a public apology.

On Monday afternoon, January 22, 1917, with little advance notice, Wilson went to the Senate chamber and urged "a peace without victory" in Europe—an "organized peace," guaranteed by the United States— because "only a peace between equals can last." He explained, "I am speaking for the silent mass of mankind everywhere who have as yet had no place or opportunity to speak their real hearts out concerning the death and ruin they see to have come already upon the persons and the homes they hold most dear." The Illinois Senator Lawrence Sherman, an isolationist Republican, scoffed that Wilson's appeal would "make Don Quixote wish he had not died so soon." Theodore Roosevelt charged that Wilson's "spiritual forebears" were the Tories of 1776 and the Copperheads of 1864: they too had "demanded peace without victory." The President confessed to his New York financial backer Cleveland Dodge that after the frustration of his plea to the Senate, he was feeling "a little low."

Wilson did not know that in early January 1917, the Kaiser had secretly approved "full employment" of German submarines against "all sea traffic" in the neighborhood of the European war zone. Wilhelm told his Army and Navy chiefs that the action would probably provoke the United States to enter the war on Britain's side, but he hoped that the brutal show of force would resolve the long stalemate in Germany's favor. It was a week after the Kaiser made this move that Zimmermann sent his telegram, which revealed that Germany would start expanded submarine warfare at the start of February, and proposed a military alliance with Mexico.

* * *

A T THE END of January, Wilson learned the staggering news about the German U-boats.* Lansing told him that the United States must now immediately break diplomatic relations with Berlin: "The time for patience has passed." The President responded that he was "not sure." If he refused to sever relations, he was "willing to bear all the criticism and abuse which would surely follow." Wilson told Colonel House that it would be "a crime" if the United States entered the war in a way that made it "impossible to save Europe afterward." The President wanted to eliminate, if possible, Europe's balance-of-power

---

* Under the new policy, any ship sailing within a zone that encompassed Britain, France, Italy, and part of the Mediterranean would be vulnerable, although, it was said, a few well-identified US ships might be allowed to sail in the area over one specific route.

struggles and end the old tradition of its authoritarian leaders dragging their peoples into war without soliciting their views in advance. Wilson insisted that he was still determined to avoid taking his country into the conflict, if humanly possible. House found the President "sad and depressed."

On February 2, in an effort to nudge his Cabinet in the direction of peace, Wilson crudely based his appeal on race. He warned the secretaries that if the United States joined the war, the "white races" would suffer "a depletion of manpower," and asked, "Would the yellow races take advantage of it and attempt to subjugate the white races?" This argument went nowhere. Most of his Cabinet urged him to break relations with Berlin. Bewildered, the President confessed to the secretaries that by now, he could not "fully trust anybody's judgment"—not even his own.

The next day, looking stunned, Wilson told a Joint Session of Congress that the Germans had left him "no alternative" but to break with their government. He added that he could not imagine that Germany would follow through on its threat, which would include dispatching submarines against American ships: "Only actual overt acts on their part can make me believe it even now." After the speech, Roosevelt wrote his friend Senator Henry Cabot Lodge that Wilson was "yellow all through in the presence of danger." In the weeks to come, German U-boats sank one merchant ship after another, including American vessels. Wilson reluctantly acceded to his Cabinet's demand that US ships be fortified with armaments and protective convoys.

Then, on Saturday evening, the twenty-fourth, Frank Polk brought the Zimmermann telegram to the White House. Polk found that after reading it, Wilson was angry and "much disturbed." Lansing later told the President that Zimmermann had exploited the Americans' transatlantic circuit to send his proposal, making them the "innocent agents" of his planned conspiracy against them. *Good Lord!* exclaimed Wilson. *Good Lord!* Colonel House urged him to publish the Zimmermann cable immediately and make "a profound impression" on Congress and the nation.

But still Wilson held back. He was anxious that, on the heels of the diplomatic collision with Germany and the arming of US vessels, revelation of Zimmermann's message might send Americans into the war hysteria he had taken such care to prevent. But there was a more profound reason for caution. When Zimmermann had tempted Mexico with an alliance, he was not speaking idly. For years, the United States and its southern neighbor had been on the verge of war.

In 1913, when the authoritarian General Victoriano Huerta seized power, Wilson had refused diplomatic relations with the new "government of butchers." The following April, after the Mexicans arrested several US sailors who had strayed into a prohibited area of Tampico, Wilson sent the US Navy to Veracruz, launching a series of events that led to Huerta's resignation in favor of President Carranza, whom the United States then recognized. Eager to provoke the mighty northern neighbor into war against Carranza's government, his rival Pancho Villa, in March 1916, conceived a border raid into New Mexico, in which several Americans were killed. Wilson was in no mood to show weakness, especially in an election year. In quest of Pancho Villa, he sent fourteen thousand soldiers, under General John Pershing, across the Mexican border, which was legally an act of war. It revealed Wilson's willingness to employ military force to pursue what he considered to be democratic ideals.*

The President knew that unless he handled Zimmermann's message carefully, he could provoke a war with the Mexicans, who might now have the Germans on their side. Anxious that the Germans might also be trying to subvert the wobbly government of Cuba, he sent a US Army division to that island. Without divulging the Zimmermann secret, he told his Cabinet that "so many things are happening" that he could not afford to let Cuba be subject to German "plots."

Wilson was painfully aware that suppressing Zimmermann's telegram could be fruitless because the British, eager to push the United

---

* During the 1916 campaign, some Republican orators had cited Wilson's Mexican intervention to charge that he was a hypocrite in claiming that he had kept America out of war.

States into the war, might release it themselves. Despite the President's Scots-Irish ancestry, his love of England's scenery and architecture, and his reverence for its parliamentary system, his Anglophilia had strict limits.* In the summer of 1916, he had been disgusted to learn that the British government had been intercepting Americans' mail and drawn up a "blacklist" of US companies trading with Germany. He complained to Colonel House, "This blacklist business is the last straw."† He could easily imagine British agents slipping the Zimmermann telegram to the newspapers, which would not only demand that Wilson respond by waging war against Germany but also vilify him—who so priggishly preached about government openness—for trying to conceal the secret from the American people.

Before reading the Zimmermann cable, the President had hoped that he could somehow broker the differences between Britain and Germany, and keep his country out of the conflict. But with the Kaiser's regime vowing to destroy American ships on the Atlantic and courting Mexico to fight the United States together, the scales had finally fallen from Wilson's eyes. That week he bluntly told a group of Quaker and other antiwar visitors, "If you knew what I know at this present moment . . . you would not ask me to attempt further peaceful dealings with the Germans." On February 26, the President went before another Joint Session of Congress but did not reveal the Zimmermann telegram. He told the members that despite his defensive actions to "defend our commerce and the lives of our people," he was "not now proposing or contemplating war or any steps that need lead to it." He insisted that "war can come only by the willful acts and aggressions of others."

---

* As a youth, Tommy Wilson had read voraciously about Prime Minister William Gladstone, and kept above his desk a portrait of the Liberal leader, whom he called "the greatest statesman that ever lived," telling his mother, "I intend to be a statesman too."

† In September 1916, Wilson had told Page in Washington that he had privately started out the war feeling "as heartily in sympathy" with England "as any man," but Britain had "gone on doing anything she wished," sometimes trampling American rights. As the startled Page later recorded, his old friend also "spoke of England's having the earth, of Germany's wanting it," explaining that the war sprang from "many causes," not all of which cast Britain in a noble light.

Knowing how the assault on the *Chesapeake,* the Thornton affair, and the sinking of the *Maine* had shocked the American people to ask for war, Wilson now decided to let the Zimmermann telegram do its work. On Wednesday evening, February 28, after a quiet presidential go-ahead, Lansing asked Edwin Milton Hood, of the Associated Press, to his home, where he gave him a copy of the secret German cable. "U.S. BARES WAR PLOT," blared the next morning's *Chicago Tribune.* "CAPITAL STIRRED BY GERMAN INTRIGUE TO EMBROIL UNITED STATES IN HUGE WAR," said the *Daily Record* of Hickory, North Carolina. The *Washington Herald* added, "JAPAN ALSO CHARGED WITH PLAYING PART IN MONSTER INTRIGUE." The *New York Herald* warned that "the United States stands on the brink of war." "At last the nation has no excuse for failing to understand the gravity of the international crisis," said the *Kansas City Star.* The *Daily Traveler* of Arkansas City, Kansas, announced it would no longer "string along with President Wilson in his policy of peace without victory" and that "Germany is in need of the worst licking she ever got or ever will get."

Responding to the new, more militant atmosphere, the lame-duck House of Representatives rushed to enact Wilson's bill to arm US ships against the Germans by 403 to 14. But there was trouble in the Senate. Robert La Follette, the emotional isolationist from Wisconsin, planned a filibuster. Told that his father had brought a loaded pistol onto the Senate floor, La Follette's son Robert Jr. counseled him, by note, "Do not try to fight Senate physically. I am almost sick with worry."

On Sunday, March 4, at noon, the old Congress adjourned without a Senate vote. Wilson had come to the Capitol to be sworn in for his second term in a private ceremony: in deference to the day of rest, his formal inaugural would be the next day. When he found out that his bill had been stalled in the Senate, the fuming President denounced the "little group of willful men" who had rendered the government "helpless and contemptible." He asserted that he could go ahead and arm American ships without congressional consent. On Monday, standing before the Capitol, he proclaimed into a cold wind, "We are provincials no longer. The tragic events of the thirty months of vital turmoil through which we have just passed have made us citizens of the world. There can be no turning back."

His efforts to stay out of war in tatters, Wilson collapsed into his White House bed, suffering from a severe cold and sore throat. For nine days, he saw almost no outsiders, and one may suspect that his problems were emotional as well as physical. From his sickroom, true to his word, he issued an executive order to fortify US merchant ships with Navy guns and sailors. While this was being fulfilled, German U-boats sank four American vessels within a week. In a state of near-denial, Wilson assured Lansing that these attacks did not necessarily require the United States to go to war. When the President did not act, an impatient British diplomat in Washington expostulated that Wilson was "the most agile pussy-footer ever made."

Recovering from his illness, on Tuesday, March 20, the President convened the Cabinet, whose members were, by now, unanimous for entering the European conflict. Lansing told them that the time was ripe because Russia was shedding its monarchy, which would allow the United States to frame the European war in terms of self-governed nations against autocracies. Postmaster General Albert Burleson reported that Americans were insisting on war. Stiffening, with his jaw visibly clenched, Wilson replied, "I want to do right, whether popular or not." That evening, he tried to divert himself by watching vaudeville at Keith's Theatre, on Fifteenth Street, near the White House.

Within the next week, Wilson finally came to understand that his notion of "armed neutrality" would be futile. He told a Washington friend, Matthew Hale, a shipping executive, that "apparently, to make even the measures of defense legitimate, we must obtain the status of belligerents." Over dinner at the White House, he confessed to Colonel House that he did not feel suited to be a warrior President. House indeed found Wilson was "too intellectual, too cultivated not to see the incongruity and absurdity of war." House believed that, by contrast to Wilson, a wartime President should be of "coarser fiber and one less of a philosopher than he."

Wilson retained the devout Christianity of his youth, telling a lawyers' group of the "perfectability of human life." He had defied those asking for war "in the name of God and humanity," observing privately that "war isn't delivered in the name of God." But now, resigned to the inevitable, he typed out a speech to Congress, with two fingers, on his curved Hammond Multiplex typewriter. "I never knew him to be more peevish," recorded the White House Chief Usher, Ike Hoover. "He's out of sorts, doesn't feel well, and has a headache."

＊ ＊ ＊

O N MONDAY, April 2, 1917, at 8:30 p.m., members of the new House and Senate cheered and waved little American flags as the President walked into the chamber. A glowering Senator La Follette chewed gum, lowered his chin to his chest, and kept his arms crossed in defiance.

In his address, Wilson was frank about his own change of heart. During the previous two months, while Germany had sunk vessels "without warning and without thought of help or mercy for those on board," he had been "for a little while unable to believe" that a government would show such "reckless lack of compassion or of principle." But the new German submarine attacks were clearly "warfare against mankind." More armed neutrality would be "ineffectual" and "practically certain to draw us into the war."

"With a profound sense of the solemn and even tragical character of the step I am taking," he asked Congress to recognize that Germany was waging war against the American people. The misbehavior of the Kaiser's Germany, he said, reminded him of "the old, unhappy days, when peoples were nowhere consulted by their rulers, and wars were provoked and waged in the interest of dynasties, or of little groups of ambitious men who were accustomed to use their fellow men as pawns and tools." Referring to the Zimmermann telegram, he warned that Germany "means to stir up enemies against us at our very doors," but he asked Americans to "put excited feeling away," including that of "revenge."*

---

* An obvious reference to the *Maine*.

Their motive must be instead "the vindication of right." He insisted that "the world must be made safe for democracy."

On that historic night, the President rode upstairs in the White House elevator with his young cousin Fitzwilliam Woodrow, who was a decade out of Princeton, and told him, "Fitz, thank God for Abraham Lincoln." Recalling Lincoln's slowness in building his Civil War effort, Wilson vowed, "I won't make the mistakes that he did."

CHAPTER ELEVEN

"Salvation of Mankind"

O N WEDNESDAY, April 4, 1917, the Senate was first to debate Wilson's war declaration. Henry Cabot Lodge of Massachusetts, ranking Republican on the Foreign Relations Committee, warned that "national cowardice" would be worse than joining the struggle "against barbarism." Lodge went on, "This is not, and cannot be, a party war. . . . We must fight for all we are worth. . . . The most merciful war is that which is vigorously waged and which comes quickly to an end." Warren G. Harding, a backbench Ohio Republican, averred that entering the conflict would "at least put a soul into our American life." The Democrat Claude Swanson of Virginia cautioned that unless the United States upheld its rights, "Old Glory will be sunk to new depths of shame and humiliation."

But James Vardaman, a Mississippi Democrat, replied, "Each Senator should remember that he may, by his vote, be signing the death warrant of hundreds of thousands." He insisted that if Americans were to make the decision themselves, they would, "in thunderous tones, direct the President to find some other way than war." Nebraska's isolationist George Norris, a Republican, claimed that behind the "war fever" were "munitions makers, stockbrokers and bond dealers." He cautioned, "We are about to do the bidding of wealth's terrible mandate and make millions of our countrymen suffer, and untold generations bear burdens and shed their lifeblood, all because we want to preserve our commercial right to deliver munitions to the belligerents. I feel we are about to put the dollar sign on the American flag."

Leaping to his feet, the Missouri Democrat James A. Reed bellowed that Norris's insinuation "grazes the very edge of treason." The galleries erupted in applause. Vice President Thomas Marshall threatened expulsion unless the spectators grew quiet. Reed charged that Senator Norris had not only insulted the President but given "aid and comfort" to the enemy. Norris replied that his "war crazy" colleagues had lost their reason.* "All except him!" burst out John Sharp Williams, Democrat from Mississippi, evoking a laugh from fellow Senators.

Gesturing wildly, Robert La Follette, almost shouting, complained that "poor" Americans, lacking an "organized mouthpiece," would now be "called to rot in the trenches." John Williams objected, calling La Follette's utterance "pro-German and pretty nearly pro-Goth and pro-vandal," as well as "anti-American, anti-President and anti-Congress." Furious at the insult, La Follette stormed out of the chamber. Williams went on to say he could imagine the "groans" of parents and children sent to "watery graves" by German U-boats: "I am getting tired of this talk that this is a Wall Street war. That's a lie! Wall Street did not sink the *Lusitania*, the *Arabic*, the *Sussex* and these other ships." At 11:11 p.m., after thirteen hours of debate, the Senate passed Wilson's war resolution in its exact original form by 82 to 6.†

The House took up the matter on Thursday. "Cotton Tom" Heflin and John Burnett, both of Alabama, neared a fistfight when the antiwar Burnett challenged Heflin to resign and enlist. Heflin said, "My nephew will go into this war," and Burnett replied, "It's easy enough to fight through somebody else." The House sergeant at arms had to separate them with his mace. By evening, couples in white tie and fancy dresses had entered

---

* Norris declined to cite the Senate prohibition against accusing a colleague of unworthy motives.

† All six dissenters were included in the "little group of willful men" that Wilson had earlier denounced. The eight Senators absent made it known that they backed the President.

the galleries, eager to watch history unfold. The United Press reported that women with "shoulders flashing from décolleté gowns leaned nervously far over the edge, listening to every word being said from the floor beneath." When the first roll call on the war began, well after midnight, there was a collective gasp in the chamber when Wilson's House Majority Leader, Claude Kitchin of North Carolina, a Bryanite isolationist, voted no. One of his friends said, "Kitchin is sweating blood."

All day long, Jeannette Rankin, Republican from Montana, who in 1916 had become the first woman elected to Congress, avoided the House floor, torn by conflicting emotions. A pacifist, she had been warned that opposing the war might jeopardize the chances for women's suffrage. She arrived in the chamber to hear her name called for the second time. Taking a breath, she tremulously announced, "I want to stand by my country, but I cannot vote for war." "Vote! Vote!" members shouted. Puzzled by Rankin's comment, the House clerk asked, "Do you intend to vote no?" She nodded, collapsed into her chair, covered her eyes, thrust back her head, and let out an audible sob.

Outside the Capitol building swirled a nor'easter. The rains pounded the stained-glass skylights above the House chamber. By 3:13 a.m., the House had endorsed the President's bid for war by 373 to 50.[*] It was Good Friday.

At noon, a nervous, distracted Wilson lunched with Edith and his cousin, Helen Woodrow Bones, at the White House. Informed that the official parchment had arrived from Capitol Hill, he refused advice to sign it in his formal West Wing office.[†] He was in no mood for ceremony or gloating, and wished it known that he had ratified the resolution as soon as possible. He led the ladies into the tiny chamber of the tailcoat-clad Chief Usher, Ike Hoover, just inside the Mansion's north

---

[*] Sensitive to symbolism, Wilson had asked that the Senate and House enact a joint resolution, which—even though Congress had the constitutional power to declare war on its own—would legally require the President's signature, suggesting also that America's involvement in the world war would be a collaboration between both branches of government.

[†] In 1902, Theodore Roosevelt had moved the presidential offices from the second floor of the White House to a new West Wing.

door, without official guests or photographers. "Stand by me, Edith," said the President, before accepting from his wife a gilded fountain pen as he sat down at Hoover's desk. At 1:18, with the muscles bulging in his lantern jaw, Wilson scrawled, "Approved."

Lieutenant Commander Byron McCandless rushed out of the West Wing and waved his arms, sending the word "WAR" by semaphore to an Annapolis classmate of equal rank, Royal Ingersoll, who was waiting across the street at the gray Second Empire building that housed the State, War, and Navy Departments.* Wireless radio operators then flashed the alert to American vessels around the globe. From his grand office in the same building, Assistant Secretary of the Navy Franklin Roosevelt, thirty-five years old, who had been one of the loudest champions in the government for entering the European conflict, was already planning how to collaborate with his British and French counterparts as they fought shoulder to shoulder.

* * *

WILSON BEGAN HIS war short of full national unity. The *Chieftain* of Pueblo, Colorado, excoriated him for his "counterfeit and lying campaign slogan" of "He Kept Us Out of War." It went on, "The pacifists who supported Mr. Wilson last fall must now admit either that he did not deserve the credit they gave him for keeping us out of war, or else that he has betrayed the confidence they placed in him."

With the United States officially embattled, Wilson wrote an old friend, Harry Fine, "My days are so full now as to come near to driving me to distraction." His son-in-law Francis Sayre wrote him, "It seems hard to think that we can do nothing to lighten the wearying load which you have to bear. But all the country now is beginning to understand as never before your ideal of America."

On his Hammond machine, the President typed out a written appeal to his countrymen. "There is not a single selfish element, so far as I can

---

* Today it is called the Eisenhower Executive Office Building.

see, in the cause we are fighting for," he said. "We are fighting for what I believe and wish to be the rights of mankind and for the future peace and security of the world." American miners, farmers, railway workers, manufacturers, and others would determine "the fate of the war." They must build "ships by the hundreds" and "help clothe and equip" soldiers of the United States and its new partners, providing "mules, horses, cattle for labor and for military service—everything with which the people of England and France and Italy and Russia have usually supplied themselves but cannot now afford the men, the materials or the machinery to make." Wilson closed with a martial burst: "We must all speak, act and serve together!"

Wilson's first job was to build an adequate fighting force. At the start of the war, the US Army numbered little more than a hundred thousand soldiers. Wilson had hoped to rely on volunteers to fulfill America's new obligations in the Great War but was quickly brought to reality when, after war was declared by Congress, only about seventy-three thousand young men signed up for the conflict. For the first time since Lincoln in the Civil War, the President asked the House and Senate to endorse military conscription. Every male American from twenty-one to thirty-one would have to register, creating a draft pool of more than ten million, engaging virtually every family in the war effort, as Wilson said, "with thoughtful devotion to the common purpose of us all."

The week after the war declaration, Theodore Roosevelt arrived at the White House, proposing to raise and command a volunteer infantry division to fight in France, including all four of his sons. Sitting in the Green Room, he told Wilson, "I could arouse the belief that America was coming." Trying to charm his host, TR predicted that if the President could "translate" his war message into fact, it would rank "with the great state papers of Washington and Lincoln." He managed to soften the wary Wilson, who later told Joe Tumulty that Roosevelt was "a great big boy," with "a sweetness about him that is very compelling."

But Wilson wanted to win this war with the "scientific definiteness and precision" of conscript soldiers, not some "Charge of the Light Brigade." In this, he was backed by the top ranks of his War Department, both civil and military. He knew that if the irrepressible Theodore got his foot in the door, it would be hard to keep him from trying to meddle with war strategy and tactics. TR might try to run for President again, and Wilson, who had not ruled out seeking a third term, did not wish to give a possible future opponent such a golden chance to expand his credentials. Thus he had his Secretary of War, Newton Baker, decline Roosevelt's offer by letter.* Theodore's beloved niece, Eleanor Roosevelt, later observed that Wilson's rejection of her uncle was "a bitter blow from which he never quite recovered."

When the President sent his draft bill to Congress, TR's close friend Henry Cabot Lodge proposed an amendment to allow volunteers like the ex–Rough Rider. Senator Hiram Johnson of California, who had been Roosevelt's 1912 running mate, argued that Theodore had "the tenacity and the pluck to win." "Roosevelt has no respect for authority, constitutional or otherwise," responded Senator William Stone, Democrat of Missouri. "True, he headed a regiment in the Spanish war," but, "as everyone knows," he "led them into a hole, and they would have been decimated and cut to pieces but for a Negro regiment."† Wilson contrived to have Lodge's amendment quashed.

La Follette claimed that the President was "trying to force the draft system on the country as a permanent institution after the close of the war." Even the Democratic House Speaker, Champ Clark of Missouri, warned that "conscription will never pass," and accused Wilson's War Department of trying to "bulldoze the people into passing this bill." Nevertheless, in May 1917, the draft bill cleared the Senate by 81 to 8 and the House by 397 to 24.‡ Launching the national summons, Secretary Baker pulled the first capsule containing a draft number out of a

---

* Wilson also rejected TR's suggestion that the President appoint a nonpartisan, coalition war Cabinet, "calling the best men of the nation."

† A reference to the African American "Buffalo Soldiers," who fought alongside the Rough Riders.

‡ The Selective Service Act of 1917 would specifically differentiate itself from the conscription of Lincoln's time by forbidding registrants to hire substitutes. In January 1918, the Supreme Court unanimously rebuffed a challenge to the draft, which had charged that it violated the Thirteenth Amendment's ban against involuntary servitude. The Court ruled that conscription was part of Congress's power under the Constitution to make war.

large glass bowl, and nearly three million draftees ultimately fought in the war. Against the objections of Senator Vardaman and other notorious Southern racists, Wilson's draft Army included African Americans, but the white supremacist President, despite his high-flown rhetoric about elevating humankind, kept them restricted to segregated units. Wilson believed that separating the races within the government was "in the interest of the colored people" because it avoided "friction."

Wilson's scholarship had foreshadowed that he would try to maximize his power, within democratic limits, during wartime. In *Congressional Government*, he had lambasted House and Senate committee chairmen who obstructed the aims of war Presidents who enjoyed broader vision. Addressing the vital problem of food production and distribution, the President told Congress, "It is absolutely necessary that unquestionable powers shall be placed in my hands." When Wilson named a mining mogul, Herbert Hoover, as what was called a "food czar," the Republican Senator John Weeks of Massachusetts complained about making "a food dictator" out of a "man who had emerged from obscurity only a short time ago." Lodge contended that Wilson was demanding "powers to interfere with every form of human activity, to be placed in the hands of men of whom the country knows absolutely nothing." The Republican Senator Albert Fall of New Mexico charged that the administration wanted "to hug everything to itself," with the Senate as "rubberstamp."

Wilson was irritated when he heard that some Senators were proposing an amendment to sharpen their oversight of wartime spending. In a letter to Senator Robert Owen, Democrat from Oklahoma, he cited the Civil War's Joint Committee on the Conduct of the War, which had "distressed Mr. Lincoln so constantly," adding that he hoped "with all my heart" that this constraint would not be imposed: "It would be impossible for me to conduct the war with success if I am to be placed under daily espionage." Wilson wrote Senator Thomas Martin, Democrat from Virginia, that his "burden of responsibility is already all but too great to carry," and he was "very anxious that my friends in the Senate should understand how serious this is."

Responding in part to Wilson's pleas, Congress passed measures granting him wide influence over the wartime domestic economy. The *Washington Times* warned that the new strictures would make Wilson the "virtual dictator of the United States," with "dominion over practically every inhabitant and every industry." With a verbal shrug, Warren Harding said, "He is already, by the inevitable force of events, our partial dictator. Why not make him complete and supreme dictator?" The Ohio Senator noted that as the Civil War progressed, Congress had "all but abdicated" in favor of Lincoln: "The same thing must occur in this war, and the sooner it comes, the better for all of us."

While debating how to finance his war, Wilson listened to congressional Democrats, who angrily recalled how "millionaires" had been spared during the Spanish-American conflict. He accepted the need for large-scale borrowing, even though it would embolden the Wall Street financiers who had opposed his domestic reforms. But he insisted on hikes in the permanent income tax, authorized in 1913 by the Sixteenth Amendment, as well as new corporate and estate taxes and a surtax that would target the richest Americans.

This President showed that his intellectual affection for civil liberties had strict wartime boundaries. Under a new loyalty test, an executive branch employee could be fired if there was reason to suspect that he or she was "inimical to the public welfare" because of "conduct, sympathies or utterances."* Wilson also demanded from Congress an espionage bill that would outlaw "insubordination, disloyalty, mutiny, refusal of duty" in the military, as well as efforts to block enlistment. This measure would give him extraordinary control over published materials and free speech. Many cautioned that it could be used to punish critics of Wilson's conduct of the war. The *Hartford Evening Post* predicted that Americans would not "tolerate a gag" that would help the administration "cover up errors." The *New Orleans Item* warned, "The light of liberty will be smothered under the bushel of oppression."

But Congress gave the President most of what he wanted. The new

---

* In the fashion of Lincoln, Wilson pledged that the order would be "withdrawn when the emergency is passed." In *Schenck v. United States* (1919), the Supreme Court unanimously ruled that his Espionage Act did not violate the constitutional guarantee of free speech.

act authorized prosecution of citizens who championed "treason, insurrection or forcible resistance" to American laws. The following year, Congress overwhelmingly passed a Sedition Act, which specifically prohibited "disloyal, profane, scurrilous or abusive language" about the US government, the armed forces, or the flag, or which caused American institutions to be viewed with contempt.* Wilson's Department of Justice exploited the two acts to convict nearly a thousand people. In 1919, the Harvard legal scholar Zechariah Chafee Jr. wrote that "never in the history of our country, since the Alien and Sedition Laws of 1798, has the meaning of free speech been the subject of such sharp controversy as today."

Attorney General Thomas Gregory used the new laws to pursue the antiwar union Industrial Workers of the World, the "Wobblies," and their president, William "Big Bill" Haywood. Postmaster General Albert Burleson fought some magazines that questioned the conduct of the war by revoking their privilege of low second-class postal rates. Wilson refused to overrule him, using the dodge that "the line is manifestly hard to draw." When the Socialist Party leader Eugene V. Debs gave a speech in Canton, Ohio, William McKinley's hometown, about the war as an outgrowth of capitalism, he told the crowd he must be "exceedingly careful" because "certain limitations" had been placed on free speech. "I would rather a thousand times be a free soul in jail," he proclaimed, "than to be a sycophant and coward in the streets." Despite Debs's caution, he was prosecuted and slapped with a ten-year prison sentence.

* * *

BY THE SUMMER of 1917, the weary President was trying to pace himself. He played golf, rode horseback with his wife, and took

---

* The act was supposed to prevail only "when the United States is in war," but was repealed in December 1920. The Trading with the Enemy Act of 1917 forbade the publication "in any foreign language" of any comment about the war's conduct unless an English version had been cleared in advance by the US Post Office.

her out to Keith's to see vaudeville. He played a record on their Gramophone machine and showed her "how to do a jig step." In the White House basement, he tried, with less success, to teach her to ride a bicycle. From a weekend cruise on Chesapeake Bay aboard the presidential yacht in July, he wrote his daughter Jessie,

Edith and I are on the *Mayflower* to-day to get away from the madness (it is scarcely less) of Washington for a day or two. Not to stop work (that cannot stop nowadays) . . . but to escape people and their intolerable excitements and demands. . . . We try to take things light-heartedly and with cool minds, but it is not always possible, and I fear that I notice little signs of its Telling on Edith. As for myself, I am surprisingly well, by all tests that the doctor can apply, though *very* tired all the time.

Just after Labor Day, wearing a white straw boater and white ducks and carrying a flag, Wilson marched up Pennsylvania Avenue in an "honor parade" with newly inducted soldiers. He joked to his Secretary of the Navy, Josephus Daniels, "I understood they wished good-looking men, and so I agreed."

While an academic, Wilson had written at length about a President's need to educate the people, especially during war. But now, to a surprising degree, he gave the task of explaining the "real facts" of the conflict to a new Committee on Public Information, chaired by an ex–muckraking reporter and early Wilson backer, George Creel, which published patriotic pamphlets and encouraged production of anti-German films like *The Kaiser, the Beast of Berlin*. Creel aspired to generate a "passionate belief in the justice of America's cause" that would "weld the people of the United States into one white hot mass instinct with fraternity, devotion, courage and deathless determination."

For most of 1917, Wilson made little extended public comment about the war. Just when Americans needed their President to guide them into a conflict so distant from their country, which many still did not understand, Wilson allowed his singular public voice to fall nearly silent, satisfied that his actions would speak louder than rhetoric. Many people presumed that this ex-professor loved making speeches. But, in fact, as Wilson confided to Colonel House that year, he became anxious when he had to face an audience; while walking across a crowded stage, he "always" feared that he would collapse before reaching the podium. Encouraged to repeat one oration in a studio for a sound recording, Wilson declined, explaining that he had never "succeeded in getting the 'emotional power' into my voice when speaking into a phonograph," and "as a matter of fact, I sound like a machine."

Wilson's rare public remarks about the war during that first year of American engagement offered glimpses into his thinking. On Flag Day, he told a crowd at the Washington Monument that if the Allies prevailed, "the world may unite for peace, and Germany may be of the union." In August, he warned a labor committee of his new Council of National Defense, "We have not yet felt the terrible pressure of suffering and pain of war, and we are going presently to feel it." In November, he told the American Federation of Labor in Buffalo, "You can explain most wars very simply, but the explanation of this is not so simple." Attacking the "fatuous" assertion that peace could be achieved without waging war, he revealed his pique at the antiwar opposition: "What I am opposed to is not the feeling of the pacifists, but their stupidity. My heart is with them, but my mind has a contempt for them. I want peace, but I know how to get it, and they do not."

Wilson's late wife's sister Madge Axson Elliott recalled that on New Year's Eve 1917 at the White House, "the news from France had been bad, and Woodrow's eyes were grave." She felt that with so many Americans dying, "he was taking the war hard." In the wake of its revolution, Soviet Russia had established an armistice with the Central Powers and was seeking peace at Brest-Litovsk. As the *New York Times* had reported that morning, "The German line, although repeatedly and severely dented, has not been broken." In the presence of his family, Wilson read aloud from Wordsworth: "Another year! Another deadly blow. . . . And we are left, or shall be left, alone / The last that dare to struggle with the Foe."

The President decided it was time "to formulate the war aims of the United States," as Colonel House told his diary. "I never knew a man who did things so casually." Wilson's goal was worthy but the nation had already been at war for eight months. House solicited ideas from "the Inquiry," a rump advisory group he had created, which included his brother-in-law, Sidney Mezes, a philosopher, the *New Republic*'s Walter Lippmann, and experts on Europe. At the White House, on Saturday morning, January 5, 1918, as the Colonel recalled, he and the President started "remaking the map of the world." Having jotted shorthand notes on a memo from the Inquiry, Wilson typed out fourteen ideas and asked House to help rank them, finishing after midnight. The next day, the President typed an address for Congress, hoping that it would be one of his greatest public utterances.

On Tuesday morning, the eighth, before going to the Capitol, Wilson felt so excited that Colonel House and Edith sent him to the golf course to calm himself. He told the Joint Session that "the moral climax of this, the culminating and final war for human liberty, has come." Listing what he called his "Fourteen Points," he explained that "we entered this war because violations of right had occurred which touched us to the quick and made the life of our own people impossible."* Now the country demanded that the world "be made safe for every peace-loving nation, which, like our own, wishes to live its own life, determine its own institutions, be assured of justice and fair dealing by the other peoples of the world, as against force and selfish aggression."

Speaker Clark called Wilson's Fourteen Points speech "the most luminous the President has ever delivered, clear as crystal, and the man who cannot understand it must be exceedingly dense." But it did not silence complaints about his handling of the war. Senator George Chamberlain, Democrat from Oregon, Chairman of the Military Affairs Committee, proposed a bill for a "War Super-Cabinet," composed of three private citizens, who would help to manage the conflict, independent of Wilson's department secretaries. Chamberlain said that "the

---

* Beyond specific proposals for ending the war, Wilson's Fourteen Points included "open covenants of peace, openly arrived at . . . absolute freedom of navigation . . . removal, so far as possible, of all economic barriers . . . national armaments . . . reduced to the lowest point consistent with domestic safety . . . free, open-minded and absolutely impartial adjustment of all colonial claims," as well as insistence that "a general association of nations must be formed under specific covenants for the purpose of affording mutual guarantees of political independence and territorial integrity."

military establishment of America has fallen down" because of "inefficiency in every bureau."

Wilson decried Chamberlain's charge as "an astonishing and absolutely unjustifiable distortion of the truth." The Associated Press forecast that the confrontation between the two branches of government would be "a historical struggle." In a three-hour reply to the President on the Senate floor, with the galleries packed, Chamberlain asserted that he had "nothing but the kindliest feeling" toward the President, but "no man can keep me from telling the truth. I have no fear of God, man or the Devil." Objecting to Wilson's aspersions on his integrity, after all of his support for the war, he asked, *"Et tu, Brute?"* Citing American delays, Chamberlain went on, "In God's name, are we going to get over to France? . . . You Senators know that there are men along the Atlantic Seaboard that ought to have gone to France six weeks or two months ago. . . . If America is going to play any part in this war, she will have to get at it pretty soon."

Delighted to inflict some damage on the President who had elbowed him out of the war, Theodore Roosevelt publicly took Chamberlain's side. Speaking at the National Press Club, he noted that Wilson himself had written, in *Congressional Government,* that Congress must scrutinize the Executive. "In the first six months after this war opened," said TR, "the Navy Department showed very poor work, owing to indecision and delay."* As the Senate debate went on, Democrat Gilbert Hitchcock of Nebraska claimed that the President "does not know the real situation," adding that the Navy's laggard shipbuilding was "worse than a farce" and "nothing short of a crime."

Rising to Wilson's defense, Senator Williams of Mississippi warned that Chamberlain's "stupid bill" would "put the President in a hole." Recalling the Committee on the Conduct of the War, he said that "of all the asses that ever existed, the worst was the typical council of asses that came very near ruining Lincoln and Grant in the Civil War." Turning to Hitchcock, Williams asked, "What do you know about running this

---

* Theodore knew of the Navy's problems in detail because he was in close touch with his fifth cousin and nephew-in-law Franklin, who privately shared his frustrations over Wilson's shortcomings.

war? . . . Let the President alone!" At Wilson's request, Lee Overman of North Carolina proposed that Senators reaffirm the President's power to "coordinate and consolidate" all war functions. Appalled, Hitchcock exclaimed, "We might as well abdicate!" But the Senate gave its vote of confidence to Wilson.

There was no serious chance that the Democrats who controlled that chamber would have forced a war council on their President, and even if they somehow did, he would have vetoed the measure. The *New York Times* rightly argued that "there would have been no clash" if Wilson "had taken the leaders of Congress into his confidence, either publicly or privately." The President was not showing the nimbleness that had enabled him to push a controversial and historic domestic reform program through Congress during his first term. Madge Elliott, who revered her brother-in-law, later wrote that he was "too thin-skinned to get out and wrestle with the 'tough guys.' He hated chicanery and scheming, and perhaps he allowed the other conferees to see his scorn of their methods."

✳ ✳ ✳

WILSON MAY HAVE kept an iron grip on the domestic side of his war, but for a leader so eager to be in control, he granted extraordinary autonomy to the commander of the American Expeditionary Force, General John Pershing. The two men met only once during the entire conflict, a week after Congress's war declaration. The President delighted Pershing by asking him, when he started fighting alongside the other Allies, to keep regarding US soldiers as a self-standing force, "the identity of which must be preserved."

By the summer of 1918, Wilson had in mind a postwar "peace league" that could undergird a lasting world order. On Thursday, July 4, he sailed on the *Mayflower* to Mount Vernon, where he told ten thousand guests, wilting under the heat, that after this war, such an institution would "check every invasion of right" and sanction any "international readjustment that cannot be amicably agreed upon. . . . What we seek is the reign of law, based upon the consent of the governed and sustained by the organized opinion of mankind."

Although there were few actual sinkings that summer, German subs were attacking merchant ships and other vessels near New Jersey and Delaware, as well as a tugboat and four barges off Cape Cod; the last was viewed, with fright, by people on the beach. The President reassured his anxious daughter Jessie, who was vacationing on nearby Nantucket, that the Germans posed no "real danger" to her island: "If the stupid submarine commanders should seek to create terror anywhere, it would be on some crowded coast like that of New Jersey." He explained that he himself, however, could not visit Nantucket because "the naval people think it might be taking unnecessary risks for me to cross the open waters opening from Long Island Sound, if I did so in the slow and easily recognizable *Mayflower*."

More than a million American soldiers were marching into France, there to bolster the Allies in the final offensive of the Great War, which included battles at Saint-Mihiel and the Argonne. After Saint-Mihiel, Wilson cabled "warmest congratulations" to General Pershing: "The boys have done what we expected of them, and done it the way we most admire." Theodore Roosevelt's youngest boy, Quentin, having joined the war effort, along with his three brothers, was killed while flying over France. At his Long Island home of Sagamore Hill, suppressing his despair, TR told reporters, "Quentin's mother and I are very glad that he got to the front and had a chance to render some service to his country, and to show the stuff there was in him before his fate befell him." Wilson cabled his old rival to praise Quentin's "fine gallantry": "I am deeply grieved that his service should have come to this tragic end."

With the war moving toward culmination, the President feared that a Democratic loss in the November midterm elections would damage his world standing. He told the banker Thomas Lamont that "the peoples of our allies would never understand" and "would say I had been repudiated," damaging his ability to win "the sort of peace that I have set my heart upon." Wilson had an unappealing tendency to combine high-flown rhetoric with tough partisan politics, blinded by his conviction that, unlike his opposition, he acted out of disinterested motives that were above reproach. Thus, two weeks before the 1918 election, he issued a statement imploring Americans to vote Democratic "not for my own sake or for the sake of a political party, but for the sake of the nation itself." This was "imperatively necessary," he wrote, because "at almost every turn," Republicans in Congress had tried to take "the conduct of the war out of my hands."*

Theodore Roosevelt's emotions were roiling after Quentin's death, and now he lashed Wilson without mercy. At the end of October, thundering for two hours at a standing-room-only night rally at Carnegie Hall, TR charged that the President "does not ask for loyalty to the nation," only "support of himself." Wilson's pronouncement, he said, revealed "a greedy unscrupulousness as to methods, and a complete subordination of national interest to partisan warfare never before known in our history during a great war." He was "glad that Mr. Wilson has now cast off the mask." Roosevelt carped that the President was claiming "that Republicans are not good enough to serve the Republic in Congress at this time, but they are good enough to die for the Republic in the Army and Navy!" Alluding to Quentin's loss, TR said, "We have sent our sons and our brothers to spill their blood like water overseas under the flag," only to be told that this sacrifice did "not entitle us to any word in saying how the war is to be waged!" He insisted that "the world would be better off now, by hundreds of thousands of lives, if Mr. Wilson had been willing to supplement his own self-sufficient ignorance by the counsel of those who would gladly have counseled him wisely, but who would not creep into his presence as slaves." From the crowd came cries of "Hit him hard, Teddy!" and "Three cheers for a fighting man!" Roosevelt shouted back, "Don't cheer for me—I'd have been in the fight, if I'd have been allowed!"

Shared fury at the sitting President moved Roosevelt to bury the hatchet with his onetime protégé, William Howard Taft. They issued a

---

* Worried about the impact of this statement, Edith had beseeched Wilson to kill it, but he told her that he had promised fellow Democrats that "I would do it." The acting Democratic National Chairman, Homer Cummings, had persuaded the President to delete another passage, which would have mentioned Lincoln's request in 1864 not to change horses in midstream as an "honourable precedent for what I am doing."

joint public statement that if voters elected a Republican Congress, then Wilson, instead of relying on his "academic theories" in making the peace, would be compelled to face "a courageous, coordinate branch of the government to moderate his uncontrolled will." Speaking in Manchester, New Hampshire, Taft insisted that before Wilson, "never, in peace or war, have we had a more partisan administration," and now the President was asking Americans for "unlimited control over the settlement of a peace that will affect them for a century." The Republican National Chairman, Congressman Will Hays of Indiana, complained that Wilson was an "autocrat" who "wants only rubber stamps," and that he was scheming to end the war prematurely in order to help Democrats at the polls.

On Monday, November 4, the day before the election, the State Department let it be known that the Allies had agreed on surrender terms to be leveled against Germany. "The end of the world war is in sight," said the *New York Times,* reporting a "conviction in Washington" that the Germans were "ready to accede." It added that Wilson was being given "unstinted credit" for playing "a wonderfully skilled diplomatic hand in his dealings with the Central Powers." But the prospect of peace was too little and late.

Had the President managed to lock down a German surrender, he might have saved the Democrats. Instead voters gave the Republicans control of the Senate, by 49 to 47 seats, and the House, by 240 to 192. Domestic questions, including widespread unease about the war's social and economic dislocations, had a large influence on the Democratic loss; this was aggravated by Wilson's misguided preelection statement, which moved some voters to punish him for arrogance. The President claimed to his daughter Jessie that he was "not at all dismayed or disheartened" by the electoral rebuff, because he would "see to it" that Republicans were "put in a position to realize their full responsibility." Undermining his own President with an official of another nation, Theodore Roosevelt wrote the British Foreign Secretary, Lord Balfour, that "in any free country, except the United States," the rejection "would have meant Mr. Wilson's retirement from office and return to private life."

Wilson's midterm defeat would badly undermine him as he tried to secure a postwar world order. The new Chairman of the Foreign Relations Committee, which would rule on any peace treaty, would now be Senator Lodge, who, like his close friend TR, detested this President. Even before the war, Lodge had written Theodore, "I never expected to hate anyone in politics with the hatred I feel toward Wilson."

* * *

O N SUNDAY, NOVEMBER 10, Kaiser Wilhelm II was dethroned, and he fled to Holland for his life. Britain's King George V, who was his cousin, told his diary that Wilhelm was "the greatest criminal known for having plunged the world into this ghastly war," having "utterly ruined his country and himself."

Keeping vigil at the White House, the President and First Lady learned by telephone, at three o'clock that morning, that the Germans had signed an armistice. As Edith later recalled, "We stood mute—unable to grasp the significance of the words." From Paris, Colonel House, who had bargained for the armistice as Wilson's envoy, wired the President, "Autocracy is dead. Long live democracy and its immortal leader. In this great hour my heart goes out to you in pride, admiration and love."

At 1:00 p.m., wearing a cutaway and gray trousers, Wilson faced a Joint Session of Congress, where he read out Germany's surrender terms. He told the members that "this tragical war, whose consuming flames swept from one nation to another until all the world was on fire, is at an end," and "it was the privilege of our own people to enter it at its most critical juncture." He added that the war's object, "upon which all free men had set their hearts," had been achieved "with a sweeping completeness which even now we do not realize," and Germany's "illicit ambitions engulfed in black disaster." This time, Senator La Follette clapped. Theodore Roosevelt and Senator Lodge complained that Wilson should have held out for unconditional German surrender.

Driven down Capitol Hill, Wilson was cheered by joyous crowds on the streets. Eleanor Roosevelt recorded that Washington "went completely mad" as "bells rang, whistles blew, and people went up and down the streets throwing confetti." Including those who had perished in theaters of conflict from influenza and other diseases, the nation's nineteen-month intervention in the world war had levied a military death toll of more than 116,000 Americans, out of a total perhaps exceeding 8 million.

There were rumors that Wilson planned to sail for France and horse-trade at the peace conference himself. No previous President had left the Americas during his term of office. The *Boston Herald* called this tradition "unwritten law." Senator Key Pittman, Democrat from Nevada, told reporters that Wilson should go to Paris "because there is no man who is qualified to represent him." The *Knickerbocker Press* of Albany, New York, was disturbed by the "evident desire of the President's adulators to make this war his personal property." The *Free Press* of Burlington, Vermont, said that Wilson's presence in Paris would "not be seemly," especially if the talks degenerated into "bitter controversies." The *Chattanooga Times* called on Wilson to stay home, "where he could keep his own hand on the pulse of his own people" and "translate their wishes" into action by wireless and cable to his bargainers in Paris.

Lawrence Sherman threatened to push a Senate resolution saying that if Wilson dared to leave the country, his job would be pronounced vacant and Vice President Thomas Marshall sworn in as the new President (even though no one had done this to Theodore Roosevelt when he spent seventeen days, in 1906, sailing to Panama and Puerto Rico). Secretary Lansing counseled Wilson that attending the conference personally "would be a mistake": the President could "practically dictate the terms of peace" if he stayed more aloof. But as Lansing recalled, his chief replied with "that harsh, obstinate expression which indicates resentment at unacceptable advice." Unlike all previous American war Presidents, Wilson wanted to represent himself while shaping the peace.

Confronted by a new Republican Congress, Wilson had been urged to augment his peace delegation with members of the opposing party and of the Senate, two-thirds of which would have to approve any treaty.* McKinley had done that in 1898. But for Wilson, appointing

---

* Josephus Daniels had proposed his old comrade William Jennings Bryan, saying it was "the crowning ambition of his life," but Wilson felt that "Mr. Bryan is soft-hearted and the world just now is very hard-hearted."

the hostile Lodge was out of the question. As for other Republicans of stature, the President was still fuming at Taft for his campaign attacks and felt there was "no room big enough" for him to coexist with Charles Evans Hughes. Instead, as his token Republican, Wilson pulled out of oblivion Henry White, an ex-diplomat who confessed after his appointment that he had "never been more surprised in my life." The others in his delegation would be Lansing, House, and General Tasker Bliss, the Army's ex–Chief of Staff. Lodge dismissed them as "mouthpieces of the President."

On Monday, December 2, before sailing for Europe, Wilson gave his annual address to Congress and rhapsodized about the war: "Our men went in force into the line of battle just at the critical moment. . . . Thenceforth it was back, back, back for their enemies, always back, never again forward! . . . And throughout it all, how fine the spirit of the nation was. What unity of purpose, what untiring zeal!" Secretary of the Navy Daniels told his diary that congressional "Republicans had said they would give him an ice bath, and they were sullen and quiet."

Wednesday morning, in Hoboken, New Jersey, saw Wilson, Edith, and their party, guarded by a thousand soldiers, board the USS *George Washington,* a renamed former German passenger ship that had been seized for use as an American troop transport. The troublemaking *New York Sun* asked who was "legally the Republic's President," now that Wilson was "sailing away on a mission unknown to our Constitution and laws." Aboard ship, Dr. Grayson told his diary that with "every whistle valve in New York City sounding . . . the din was terrific." The President was looking forward to this cruise as his "first real rest" since taking office almost six years earlier. Since winter was fast approaching and Wilson grew seasick in choppy waters, the vessel's captain took a ten-day southern route, by way of Portugal's Azores.

Strolling after dark on the *Washington*'s deck, Wilson confided to George Creel that he had few illusions about the peace conference to come: "These ancient wrongs, these present unhappinesses, are not to be remedied in a day or with a wave of the hand. What I seem to see—with all my heart, I hope that I am wrong—is a tragedy of disappointment." He told another member of his party, "It frightens me when I think of what the people of the civilized world are expecting." When his ship arrived at Brest, on December 13, the smiling Wilson walked down the gangplank, bowing and waving his tall silk hat as the masses roared. The city's mayor called out, "Long live the champion and apostle of international justice!"

In Paris, the President and the well-tailored Edith, wearing a black hat with gray feathers, rode up the Champs-Élysées while crowds threw bouquets and cheered, "Wilson! Wilson! Wilson!" and *Vive l'Amérique!* The First Lady wrote her family, "So many emotions crowded into a small space of time that my mind is tired. . . . Here the *world* seemed to be waiting to welcome and acclaim my wonderful husband." This was heady wine for a President who had barely managed to get reelected and whose party had just been rudely overturned in Congress. In private, Colonel House found Wilson "visibly nervous"; he observed that the President was "acting a new role and on a new stage and he was not sure of himself."

Wilson met with Prime Minister Georges Clemenceau and, on Joe Tumulty's advice, went, along with his wife, to greet injured American and French soldiers in the hospital. Disgusted by the notion of exploiting the visit for political gain, he declined to pose for pictures. "It was an awful trial to see some of the badly wounded," Edith wrote home afterward. "They are all so grateful & appreciative & it breaks your heart that personally you can do so little for them." The President and First Lady shared Christmas with General Pershing at his command post outside Paris.

Arriving in London the next day, the Wilsons were feted by King George and Queen Mary at Buckingham Palace. Sensitive to the charge back home that the United States had been dragooned into the war to save Britain's skin, the President offended the King by asking him to stop calling his countrymen "brothers" or "cousins" or "Anglo-Saxons"; the last term, he said, could "no longer be applied" to the American people. He added that in the future, the only thing that would unite America and Great Britain would be "community of ideals and of interests." After Wilson departed, the King told an aide, "I could not bear him. An entirely cold academical professor—an odious man." The President also conferred with the British Prime Minister, David Lloyd George, who told colleagues that Wilson had "insisted definitely on his point of view."

At the start of January 1919, the American couple went to the Vatican, where the Wilsons were blessed by Pope Benedict XV. Moving on to Turin, Italy, the President was informed that Theodore Roosevelt had died; he cabled TR's widow that the news "has shocked me very much."

* * *

THE GREAT PARIS conclave formally opened on Saturday, January 18, at the Quai d'Orsay, the same place where William McKinley's peace commissioners had ended the Spanish-American War. Diplomats from dozens of countries gathered under the leadership of the "Big Four," which included Italy's Prime Minister, Vittorio Orlando, as well as Wilson, Clemenceau, and Lloyd George. The British contingent in Paris did not include Blinker Hall. Knighted for his handling of the Zimmermann telegram, the Admiral had hoped to join his country's delegation as an adviser but was elbowed out by the first Sea Lord, Sir Rosslyn Wemyss.*

Clemenceau had tearfully insisted that the peace talks be held in his capital; he specifically wanted them to open on the same day the Kaiser's father, Wilhelm I, had been crowned in 1871, at the start of the Second Reich. Uncaptivated by Wilson's idealism, the seventy-seven-year-old Frenchman privately lectured him, "We have become what we are because we have been shaped by the rough hand of the world in which we have to live, and we have survived only because we are a tough bunch." Clemenceau was not feeling charitable toward the vanquished. By the end of the war, fully a fourth of his country's men between the ages of eighteen and thirty had been killed. He later told an American reporter, "My life hatred has been for Germany because of what she has done to France." It was claimed that Clemenceau asked to be buried standing

---

* Hall quit the Navy and got elected to Parliament as a Conservative. Shortly before his death in 1943 at Claridge's Hotel in London, the mortally ill Sir Reginald showed he had not lost his sense of humor: when someone came to fix the plumbing in his suite, he said, "If you're the undertaker, my man, you're too early."

up, facing Germany, so that he could keep eternal watch against the menacing foe.

When Wilson had arrived in Paris, Clemenceau's government demanded that he visit their country's ravaged battlefields, but the President dismissed the idea as an effort to manipulate his emotions in order to persuade him to accept French arguments about the peace. Wilson irritably told his aides that even if France had been turned into "a shell hole, it would not change the final settlement." During a token visit to Reims, he infuriated the French by claiming that the renowned local cathedral had survived the German onslaught more intact than they had suggested.

Wilson wished to take a large step toward a League of Nations before he had to return to the United States, at least briefly, for the opening of the newly elected Congress. Clemenceau insisted that any League be able to enforce its collective decisions, if necessary, with its own Army. Like Lloyd George, Wilson took the Frenchman's proposal as a ploy to transform the League into an armed, anti-German coalition.* He explained that his Congress would never allow an international body to decide when the United States would go to war; it would be "unconstitutional and also impossible." The Associated Press reported that the talks were being hampered by "distrust and bitterness." Wilson complained to Dr. Grayson that the French "talk and talk and talk," repeating points "that have already been thoroughly thrashed out." The British diplomat Lord Robert Cecil warned the French that if they did not play ball, they might have to face an Anglo-American military alliance.

By the time of Wilson's departure in mid-February, the Big Four had agreed on a "Draft Covenant" for a League, with no dedicated military force and a requirement that most of the enforcement actions of its executive council be unanimous.† As the President and Edith boarded the

---

* In London, Winston Churchill scoffed that no League could "substitute for the British fleet."

† The President also prevailed in demanding that the covenant respect the Monroe Doctrine, which warned European powers against trying to subvert the independent nations of North and South America. He knew that this provision would please Senators who would have to ratify his treaty.

George Washington, Wilson said he felt like the man who fell out of a twelfth-story window and shouted while passing the fifth story, "I'm all right so far!" Aboard the vessel were the Assistant Secretary of the Navy and his wife, Eleanor, whom Edith found "very delightful companions." Franklin Roosevelt had been in Europe to manage the closing of US Navy operations. Over a shipboard luncheon, Wilson warned the Roosevelts and other guests that if Americans did not back his League of Nations, it "would break the heart of the world." So dangerous were the crashing winter seas that they swept a lieutenant and a quartermaster away from one of the ship's escorting destroyers. For safety, Roosevelt ordered the vessels to disperse.

After their rough crossing, the Wilsons and their traveling party were forced by a New York dock strike to come ashore, on February 24, in Boston. There the President rode past cheering multitudes to speak in Mechanics' Hall before a flag-waving crowd of eight thousand people, which included both Roosevelts. This was the same auditorium where William McKinley had been feted as a "liberator" in 1899. Wilson was welcomed by the Bay State's Republican Governor, Calvin Coolidge, who called the reception "more marked" than any accorded to George Washington, and "more united" than any for Abraham Lincoln. Clenching his right fist, Wilson told the throng, "I have fighting blood in me." Senator Lodge took the President's defiant appearance in his own bailiwick as a deliberate shot across his bow, privately calling it "a piece of small cunning in which he is fond of indulging."

When Wilson and the First Lady rode their special train home to the Capital, they stopped in Providence. From the rear platform, the President told the crowd that what had pleased him most of all in Paris was that European peoples had come to trust the United States; he added that rejecting the League would "disappoint" them. But while Wilson was away, the isolationist Senator William Borah, Republican from Idaho, had announced that he would oppose a League even "if the Saviour of mankind should revisit the earth," asking for one.

In his absence, the President had been so determined to keep the reins in his hands that he had refused to let his Cabinet secretaries and friends start trying to educate Congress and the American people about the need for a League. In his 1908 book *Constitutional Government in the United States,* Wilson had argued that presidential control of foreign relations must be "very absolute," adding that when a Chief Executive bargained with a foreign power over a treaty, "he need disclose no step of negotiation until it is complete."

At Colonel House's suggestion, Wilson asked the Senate and House Foreign Affairs Committees to dine at the White House and hear about his experience in Paris—a device intended to honor the tradition by which Presidents did not formally testify before Congress. Lodge was seated next to the First Lady, who tactlessly boasted to him about the President's "magnificent reception" in his home city of Boston. Senator Frank Brandegee, Republican from Connecticut, groused that no liquor was offered. The punctilious Lodge felt that Mrs. Wilson's fingernails were unclean. After dessert, the President took the diners to the East Room, where he unveiled his plans for the League. In a bad humor, Lodge later complained to Henry White that Wilson's understanding of the situation was superficial and "we learned nothing." The President told Colonel House that "your dinner was a failure as far as getting together was concerned."

March 3 was the final evening of the expiring Congress. On the Senate floor, Lodge revealed the names of thirty-seven Republican Senators in that body who would oppose a League "in the form now proposed by the peace conference." Two other Republicans sided with them, as did one Democrat, Missouri's James Reed, which brought the total to forty, suggesting that Wilson could not command the two-thirds of the Senate required to ratify a treaty. Lodge was clearly trying to tie Wilson's hands before he returned to France.

Hoping to strengthen his political position before his voyage to Paris, Wilson appeared onstage at New York's Metropolitan Opera House with ex-President Taft—so recently his critic, but a tenacious supporter of a world peace organization—who now praised the League as a safeguard against "world suicide." Wilson denounced the "selfishness" of the League's opponents, and warned that it would be impossible to separate its covenant from the rest of a peace treaty "without destroying the whole vital structure." Edith later wrote, "My husband never failed to get his audience, and on this night, they really seemed to go wild."

In mid-March, the President and First Lady reached Paris. Wilson had asked House to press the Allies to accept his qualms about dividing Germany and saddling the country with heavy reparations, which, he feared, "would simply give a cause for hatred and a determination for a renewal of the war." Now he was shocked when the Colonel told him that he had failed. Edith, who disliked House, noted that as her husband heard the bad news, he "seemed to have aged ten years."

As the talks wore on, Wilson's press aide Ray Stannard Baker thought the President appeared "grayer & grimmer all the time." Exploding at French intransigence, Wilson told Lloyd George that he would "never sign a French peace" and would go home before doing so. The President collapsed into bed, suffering from high fever, headaches, diarrhea, and possible bronchitis. Clemenceau inquired of Lloyd George whether they could "bribe" Wilson's doctor to have him stay there. Grayson later speculated that the President may have suffered one or more small strokes, but in public, at the time, said that it was merely influenza. Wilson remained so angry at the French that he asked his doctor to have the *George Washington* stand by for his possible imminent departure. Disgusted by Wilson's tactics, Clemenceau relented, sputtering later that the President had behaved like a petulant cook "who keeps her trunk ready in the hallway."

By May 1919, after transforming much of the world's map, the Big Four confronted Germany with its terms for peace. Privately Wilson told aides that these demands were so strict that "if I were a German," he might refuse to sign, "but I have striven my level best to make them fair." One of the President's young advisers, William Bullitt, complained that the terms were much harsher than what Wilson had promised. He feared that such demands would subject "the suffering peoples of the world to new oppressions, subjections and dismemberments," ensuring "a new century of war." Bullitt persuaded about a dozen of his junior colleagues to join him and quit in protest. Even Lansing felt that the peace was "immeasurably harsh and humiliating."

The final treaty was signed on June 28 in the Hall of Mirrors of Louis XIV's Versailles Palace. It was five years to the day after Franz

Ferdinand had been murdered in Sarajevo, unleashing the events culminating in world war. Boisterous spectators almost knocked Wilson over
into a palace fountain. After the ceremony, he told Lansing, "I did not
know I was excited until I found my hand trembling when I wrote my
name." The President asserted, in a written statement, that the Versailles
treaty was "severe only because great wrongs done by Germany are to be
righted and repaired."

* * *

HAD WILSON REMAINED at the White House and let the peace
be shaped in Paris by a diplomatic team that justified his confidence, he could have spent the previous six months campaigning among
Senators and the American people for his cherished League of Nations.
Instead, while Wilson was almost four thousand miles away, he had left
the arena largely to his adversaries.

Sailing back on the *George Washington* in July, he was forced to catch
up. In his stateroom, he worked on an address to the Senate, churlishly
telling Dr. Grayson that he had "very little respect for the audience."
Still, knowing the high stakes that might rest on what he said on the
Senate floor, Wilson, for perhaps the first time in his presidency, re-
hearsed for this speech. In New York City, standing up in his open car,
the smiling President was lauded by almost a half million people in a
ticker-tape parade. When his train reached Union Station in Washington, a hundred thousand cheered him after midnight.

Speaking to the Senate the next morning, Wilson sounded more
erratic and halting than the President of old.* He explained that the
nation had entered the war "not because our material interests were directly threatened" but because it saw "right everywhere put in jeopardy."
The "indispensable" new League of Nations would help to maintain the
"new order" emerging from the war. Wilson noted that after ending its
isolation with the Spanish-American War, the United States had reached
its "majority" as a world power: "The only question is whether we can

---

* Dr. Grayson informed the press a week later that his patient had been afflicted by "dysentery."

refuse the moral leadership that is offered us, whether we shall accept or reject the confidence of the world. . . . The stage is set, the destiny disclosed. . . . We cannot turn back. . . . It was of this that we dreamed at our birth." The Democrat Henry Ashurst of Arizona complained that Senators had "wanted red meat" but the President "fed them cold turnips." Warren Harding, who opposed the League, pronounced Wilson's address "utterly lacking in ringing Americanism." Wilson wrote Colonel House that month, while lobbying Senators, that he was "very tired" because it seemed that "there never were so many problems per diem."

Lodge opened hearings on the League treaty in early August. Lansing asked the President to try to woo the nine Senate Republicans thought to have "mild" reservations. But as he wrote in his diary, he found that Wilson "would have none of it, and his face took on that stubborn and pugnacious expression." The President groused to his son-in-law William Gibbs McAdoo, who had been his Treasury Secretary, that as soon as he made one concession, the reservationists would demand more. But as a gesture of comity, he agreed to take questions, on the record, from the Senate Foreign Relations Committee. To soften this new departure from precedent, he staged this encounter at the White House.* The *New York Times* reported that Senators had "no disposition to nag Mr. Wilson or to do anything that would infringe upon the dignity of his high office."

On Tuesday, August 19, at 10:00 a.m., Wilson sat down at the corner of a table in the East Room with Chairman Lodge and eighteen of his nineteen committee members. Lodge's chief objection to the League was Article Ten, which called on member states to help protect the "territorial integrity" of any member against "external aggression," which the Chairman regarded as a threat to the sovereign right of the US government to decide when and where to deploy its own military force. As the President was questioned, a team of six Senate stenographers produced transcripts, which were rushed to news reporters waiting in the Mansion's basement. Borah asked Wilson whether a country that wished to withdraw from the League would be the "sole judge" of whether it

---

* Although willing to relax the separation of powers doctrine, Wilson rejected the Senators' appeal for secret documents related to the Paris talks, citing executive privilege.

had fulfilled its obligations under the treaty. The President replied, "The only restraining influence would be the public opinion of the world." But Harding, noting that the covenant specified that signers must fulfill their obligations before departing the League, asked, "Rather a far-fetched provision, is it not?" Irritably, Wilson replied, "That phraseology is your difficulty, not my idea."

Porter McCumber, a Republican from North Dakota, asked whether the treaty could compel the United States, against its will, to go to war. Wilson said "there might be a very strong moral obligation" but "we would have complete freedom of choice." The Indiana Republican Harry New asked how the presence of a League of Nations might have altered the outcome of the War of 1812 or the Spanish-American War. Wilson wryly said that while he "tried to be a historical student," he could not "form a judgment."

Around one thirty, Wilson asked, with Virginia courtesy, "Will you gentlemen not come into lunch with me? It will be very delightful." Over cold ham from his birth state, he shared anecdotes about his visits to London and Paris, then assured Lodge that he would be "very glad" to "resume the morning conference." Lodge told him there was nothing more to ask. Later he complained that Wilson had shown "ignorance and disingenuousness in his slippery evasions." Hiram Johnson told his son that the President's face had looked "hard, and cold, and cruel," with his "ponderous lower jaw" resembling that of "a vicious horse." But Johnson had to concede that in his presentation, Wilson had maintained the upper hand.

The next day, on the Senate floor, Wilson's friend Key Pittman proposed four "interpretative reservations," which, he said, had been endorsed by the President and would not require renegotiation of the Versailles treaty. But Lodge demanded a "much more drastic" revision of the treaty's provisions on the League. Believing that he and Pittman had gone hat in hand to meet Lodge more than halfway, the furious Wilson concluded that if opposing Senators would not listen to reason, he would have to take his case to the people.* He told Edith, "I promised our soldiers, when I

---

* Wilson may have recalled how McKinley had made a similar tour to extol his own Treaty of Paris.

asked them to take up arms, that it was a war to end wars. . . . If I do not do all in my power to put the treaty in effect, I will be a slacker and never able to look those boys in the eye."

After the strain of Paris and the domestic political warfare over the League, both the First Lady and Dr. Grayson were anxious about Wilson's health. Americans did not know it, but their President had long been struggling against cardiovascular disease. During their last weeks in Europe, Ray Stannard Baker had noticed that the Commander-in-Chief had developed a facial tic and could not remember some of his own conversations.

* * *

AT UNION STATION in Washington, shortly before dusk on Wednesday, September 3, 1919, the President, sporting his straw boater, a blue blazer, white trousers, and white shoes, and Edith boarded their special seven-car train for a four-week westward journey. Planned by Joe Tumulty, it was scheduled to include thirty major speeches, as well as more informal talks from the rear platform. Wilson planned to visit every state beyond the Mississippi but four.

Josephus Daniels had warned the President that such a trip might damage his health, but Wilson insisted that it would be "a relief" because he was "spoiling to tell the people all about the treaty." This was just before widespread use of the loudspeaker, so for Wilson to shout so many orations would be especially exhausting. In October, he planned to repeat this performance in New England, facing down Lodge in his own lair. Sensing the drama ahead, twenty-one reporters signed up for Wilson's western trip—more than for any previous such tour. Unfortunately for Wilson, the time of Presidents speaking on radio had not yet arrived; despite Wilson's misgivings about the sound of his own voice, such broadcasts would have increased the impact of his speeches.

In the maiden speech of his journey, Wilson told the crowd he had longed for "the pleasure of leaving Washington" and "of feeling the inspiration that I would get from you. . . . The real voices of the great people of America sometimes sound faint and distant in that strange city" (Columbus, Ohio). Referring to the Treaty of Versailles, he proclaimed, "I came back from Paris, bringing one of the greatest documents of human history. . . . In spirit and essence, it is an American document" (Kansas City, Missouri). He confessed, "My pulses quicken at the thought of it" (Omaha, Nebraska). He predicted that the treaty would increase "the probability of peace" by "about ninety-nine percent" (St. Paul, Minnesota).

Insisting that "the League of Nations has gone to the heart of this people," he noted that "thousands of our gallant youth lie buried in France, and buried for what? For the redemption of America? America was not directly attacked. For the salvation of America? America was not immediately in danger. No, for the salvation of mankind." He confided that "one of the hardest things for me to do during this war" had been "merely to try to direct things and not take a gun and go myself" (Billings, Montana). "Everywhere in Europe there is that poison of disorder and distrust, and shall we take away from this unsteady world the only thing that reassures it?" he asked (Coeur d'Alene, Idaho).

Wilson asserted that the United States was "the only national idealistic force in the world, and idealism is going to save the world. . . . Narrow selfishness will tie things up into ugly knots that you cannot get open, except with a sword." He recalled "those voiceless graves, those weeping women" who had lost family members in the Great War (Helena, Montana). Citing the Senate skeptics about the treaty, he asked, "Have these gentlemen no hearts? Do they forget the sons that are dead in France?" (Los Angeles). Wilson reported that "everywhere we go, the train, when it stops, is surrounded with little children. And I look at them almost with tears in my eyes, because I feel my mission is to save them. These glad youngsters with flags in their hands—I pray God that they may never have to carry that flag upon the battlefield" (Tacoma, Washington).

The President reported, "I have had women who had lost their dearest in the war come up to me, with tears upon their cheeks, and say, 'God bless you!' Why did they bless me? I advised the Congress to go into the war and to send their sons to their death. . . . There can be only one explanation. They are proud of the cause in which their sons died, and, my friends, since we all have to die, the way those fellows died is the best way, after all" (San Diego).* He claimed it was better to "die upon the field of freedom" than "quietly in your bed, never having done anything worth anything," and asked, "Do you think anybody outside the family is going to be interested in any souvenir of you after you are dead?" By contrast, anyone would "touch with reverence any sword or musket or rapid-fire gun or cannon that was fired for liberty upon the fields of France" (Reno, Nevada).

One of Wilson's addresses was clairvoyant. At the Palace Hotel in San Francisco, he told the audience, about his League of Nations, "I have it in my heart that if we do not do this great thing now, every woman ought to weep because of the child in her arms. If she has a boy at her breast, she may be sure that when he comes to manhood, this terrible task will have to be done once more." Without his treaty, "I can predict with absolute certainty that within another generation, there will be another world war." Wilson made this forecast exactly two decades, to the month, before the outbreak of a second world war.

Three weeks into his speaking tour, nearing the end of his rope, the weary President defended his treaty by descending into nativist demagoguery. Ridiculously, he claimed that aside from his Senate opposition the "only popular forces" organized against it were "hyphenated Americans."† Questioning the patriotism of citizens who were not of Anglo-Saxon origin, he asked, "Shall we, by the vote of the United

---

* After Wilson spoke in San Diego, the *New York Times* reported that he had enjoyed the novel experience of hearing his voice amplified for the audience by an electrical device.

† As early as his 1915 annual message to Congress, Wilson had warned against American citizens "born under other flags . . . who have poured forth the poison of disloyalty into the very arteries of our national life. . . . Such creatures of passion, disloyalty and anarchy must be crushed out." The President was especially angry at the many Americans of German and Irish origin who had called for American neutrality. His hostility echoed that of TR, who had told the Knights of Columbus at Carnegie Hall in 1915 that "a hyphenated American is not an American at all," and "the one absolutely certain way of bringing this nation to ruin" was "to permit it to become a tangle of squabbling nationalities."

States Senate, do for Germany what she could not do with her arms?" (Salt Lake City). ——

On Thursday afternoon, September 25, Wilson appeared at City Hall Auditorium in Pueblo, Colorado, where the local paper had complained the previous year that the President had betrayed the implied promise of his "counterfeit and lying" slogan of 1916 to keep the nation out of battle. Now the President used his Pueblo visit to rant bitterly against "hyphenated" citizens: "I cannot say too often—any man who carries a hyphen about with him carries a dagger that he is ready to plunge into the vitals of this Republic whenever he gets ready. If I can catch any man with a hyphen in this great contest, I will know that I have got an enemy of the Republic." Although Wilson had not often spoken such ugly words in public as President, it is painful for his memory that he did so during this speech, which turned out to be his final public address as President.

Two days earlier, Wilson had been told that, after the Foreign Relations Committee had referred the treaty to the Senate with forty-five amendments, Lodge had cobbled together a coalition that would block Senate consent to his treaty unless it was extensively changed. Now, in Pueblo, Wilson explained to the crowd that the "heart of the whole matter" of the League was Article Ten, which, he insisted, merely gave the League's council the power to "advise" member nations "what steps, if any, are necessary to carry out" its goals. No one should "fear" that Congress would be forced to "do something that it did not want to do." If the League succeeded, it would lead all peoples "out into pastures of quietness and peace such as the world never dreamed of before." As Woodrow finished his speech, Edith was in tears.

Before this journey, Wilson had rarely spoken in public with such intensity and passion, and the cost was severe. Having taken the country into the war and fashioned a peace, he had now made forty addresses over eight thousand miles, trying to rescue the League from rejection. During this tour, he had suffered from stomach illness, choking fits, and pounding headaches, exacerbated by the heat and, later, high altitudes. Before he spoke in Pueblo, Edith and Dr. Grayson had made him pledge to keep it to twenty minutes. "This will have to be a short speech," Wilson had joked with reporters. "Aren't you fellows getting pretty sick of this?" But the President could not restrain himself; he spoke for more than an hour.

About twenty miles after his train departed Pueblo, Grayson persuaded the depleted Wilson to make a stop and take Edith for a three-mile walk in the fresh mountain air. Back on the train, bound eastward that night for Wichita, the President, after writhing with pain in his bed, went to Edith's compartment and told her that his headache had become "unbearable." She summoned Grayson, who noted that Wilson's facial muscles were twitching and he was about to vomit.

Edith later recalled that night as "the longest and the most heart-breaking of my life." Grayson warned the President it would be "suicidal" if he did not halt his tour, but Wilson complained that foes would call him a "quitter." Waking after a brief, fitful sleep, the President, with tears welling in his eyes, told Tumulty he had never felt more exhausted: "I just feel as if I am going to pieces!" At first, he demanded to complete his tour, explaining that otherwise the treaty would be sunk. But after Edith's persuasion, he allowed his last five stops (Wichita, Oklahoma City, Little Rock, Memphis, and Louisville) to be canceled, and the train rushed back to Washington.

Once Woodrow was back in their upstairs White House quarters, the First Lady noted that he "wandered like a ghost." Then, after less than a week, he suffered a massive stroke, which paralyzed his left side. Grayson claimed to reporters that Wilson was merely suffering from "nervous exhaustion."

* * *

WERE WILSON IN greater command of his faculties, and in closer touch with reality, he might have looked for some kind of compromise with Chairman Lodge and the reservationists, but not now. Signaled by the White House, Democratic Senators loyally promised not to bargain over the treaty until the President was ready to guide them. Thus, in the meantime, Republicans with mild objections to the League were more susceptible to Lodge's influence.

Edith and Grayson made certain that the public did not know the full extent of the President's disability. Running interference between her husband and the outside world, she was later hyperbolically called "the first woman President." In early November, when the senior Democrat on Lodge's committee, Senator Hitchcock, was admitted to Wilson's White House bedroom, he was shocked to find the President, lying on his Lincoln-era bed, "an emaciated old man with a thin white beard." Hoarsely Wilson asked how many Senators would vote unqualifiedly for the treaty. "Not over forty-five," Hitchcock guessed. The President replied, "It is possible." When the Senator returned later that month, Wilson told him that although "a sick man, lying in this bed," he intended to visit the home states of his Senate foes, there to denounce them, "if I have breath enough in my body." Angrily he hissed, "I will get their political scalps!"

In their initial vote, on November 19, Senators refused to give the treaty its necessary two-thirds vote, endorsing it without reservations by only 53 to 38. The opposition included five Democrats. Urged to make concessions, the President told Hitchcock, "Let Lodge compromise!" Encouraged by Tumulty and Edith, Wilson briefly dabbled with making a challenge to the treaty's foes: they should quit their Senate seats and seek reelection; if a majority of them succeeded, he would resign the presidency and get out of their way. Explaining her husband's refusal to bargain, Edith told Ray Stannard Baker that Woodrow "still has in mind the reception he got in the West, and he believes the people are with him." At one point, she asked Wilson, for her sake, to "accept these reservations" and "get this awful thing settled." But he replied, "Little girl, don't you desert me; that I cannot stand." He assured her that it was "better a thousand times to go down fighting than to dip your colors to dishonorable compromise."

At the start of 1920, the depressed Wilson suffered what Grayson called "a sharp attack of the 'flu.'" The President told his doctor, "It would probably have been better if I had died last fall," and spoke of being rolled onto the Senate floor in his wheelchair to resign. In February, Wilson was incensed to learn that Lansing had sympathized with a public statement by a British special envoy, Lord Grey, that the Allies should revise the League treaty to soften the US Senate's opposition. By letter, the President asked his Secretary of State whether this was true, and whether he had also convened the Cabinet without asking his permission, which Lansing had done. The Secretary believed that Wilson's complaint "sounded like a spoiled child crying out in rage," revealing "a species of mania." Wilson told Tumulty it was "time to spike disloyalty," and fired Lansing. As his new Secretary of State, the President chose the far more malleable Bainbridge Colby, a minor New York lawyer who had twice run for the Senate as nominee of TR's Progressive Party.

Tumulty warned Wilson that Democratic support for his treaty in the Senate was "rapidly disintegrating" and that the only way to win consent might be to accept Lodge's reservations. But the President issued a public letter to Hitchcock that any revision "strikes at the very heart" of the treaty; should he accept, "I could not look the soldiers of our gallant armies in the face again." Senator Brandegee marveled that Wilson had "strangled his own child."

On March 19, the Senate considered a version of the treaty including reservations, all but one issued by Lodge. Forty-nine Senators endorsed the diluted version; thirty-nine refused. American participation in Wilson's cherished League of Nations had been effectively killed. Warren Harding blamed the defeat on Wilson's own "towering ambition." "If I were not a Christian, I think I should go mad," the President told Grayson, "but my faith in God holds me to the belief that He is in some way working out His own plan through human perversity and mistakes."

That June, the Republicans in Chicago's "smoke-filled rooms" chose Harding for President and Calvin Coolidge as his running mate. Accepting the prize, the Ohio Senator denounced Wilson's treaty as a "supreme blunder," which the President had "intolerantly urged and demanded." He pledged that no League, no "world super-government," would be permitted to "summon the sons of this Republic to war." Wilson remembered Harding's stumbling performance as part of the Foreign Relations Committee in the East Room: of all those present, only Harding "asked such unintelligent questions." Unwilling to believe that the Ohioan could be elected President, Wilson consoled himself with his private conviction that "Harding is nothing."

At the end of June, the Democrats met in San Francisco. Astonishingly, the stricken Wilson still clung to his secret ambition to win an unprecedented third term. After the delegates deadlocked, the President asked Colby, by telephone, to propose his name. But Tumulty and other old Wilson loyalists warned Edith that such a hopeless flier "would mar his place in history." Instead Governor James Cox of Ohio was chosen on the forty-fourth ballot. Cox's running mate was Franklin Roosevelt. Feeling ostracized by his own party, Wilson felt "deeply resentful" of young Roosevelt, who had accepted the Democratic platform, which refused to endorse the League unconditionally.

On a Sunday afternoon in July, Wilson greeted his party's two nominees while sitting in his wheelchair on the White House South Portico; his paralyzed left shoulder and arm were covered by a shawl. As Roosevelt for the first time realized the magnitude of the President's incapacity, Edith was moved by the obvious "shock and sympathy" on his face. With tears in his eyes, Cox assured Wilson that he and Roosevelt were "a million percent with you and your administration—and that means the League of Nations." Saying he was "very grateful," their host told them, "That battle can still be won."

That fall, the President told intimates that Harding, campaigning as the anti-Wilson and pledging to restore "normalcy," would be "deluged" because Americans always responded to a "moral occasion." But Harding won by a landslide.* Republicans took the House by 303 to 131 seats and the Senate by 70 to 26. Lodge crowed, "We have torn up Wilsonism by the roots." Wilson assured his late wife's brother Stockton

---

* After laboring for more than a year to present an image of steadiness at the White House, Edith took Harding's promise of "normalcy" as a rank insult.

Axson, "I have not lost faith in the American people. They have merely been temporarily deceived."

Although still in prison, the Socialist nominee, Eugene V. Debs, had won 3.4 percent of the popular vote against Harding and Cox. Prominent Americans, including some of Wilson's Cabinet, backed clemency for Debs, but the President refused. "They will say I am cold-blooded and indifferent, but it will make no impression on me," he told Tumulty. "This man was a traitor to his country and he will never be pardoned during my administration." Wilson added, "While the flower of American youth was pouring out its blood to vindicate the cause of civilization, this man Debs stood behind the lines, sniping, attacking and denouncing them."*

Despite the huge Republican majority, Wilson continued to hope that the Senate would reverse its "gross and criminal blunder" of rejecting his League. In the East Room of the silent White House, he and Edith reached back to a more joyous time by watching newsreels of their triumphant arrival in France, which, by now, must have seemed decades ago. Wilson had the moving picture screened at least seven times.

After Harding's inauguration, the Wilsons moved to a newly built mansion on S Street in Washington. During his retirement, when the Senate wished the ex-President a happy birthday, by voice vote, he acidly joked to Grayson he would have preferred that "three Senators get together and have it passed with sincerity." With no logic, he dreamt of running for President again.

In the autumn before his death, in February 1924, he told his daughter Margaret that it was "best, after all," that the nation had not entered the League after his return from Paris. She asked, "Why, Father darling?" The timing might have made it "only a personal victory," he explained. "Now when the American people join the League, it will be because they are convinced it is the only right time for them to do it." With a faint smile, Wilson told Margaret, "Perhaps God knew better than I did, after all!"

* * *

---

* President Harding commuted Debs's sentence in December 1921.

FOR HIS LEADERSHIP while waging his world war and seeking a durable peace, Wilson deserves credit for his intelligence, eloquence, use of American history, and genuine idealism about spreading what has been called the "contagion of liberty" around the globe. He kept his country out of Europe for as long as he could. Then he managed to persuade Congress to grant him a war declaration, even though, as he later confessed, America was "not directly attacked" or "militarily in danger." He built a formidable governmental machinery, and raised armies and an arsenal that helped the Allies to win the war. With acute vision, he understood from the start what an organization like the League of Nations could do to forestall future wars.

What is striking, however, is the derangement between Wilson's modest domestic political standing and the radical aims for which he was asking the acquiescence of Congress and the American people. He had been reelected by one of the smallest presidential margins in American history, and on the bogus hint, which not even he really believed, that he could continue to keep Americans "out of war." At the start of 1917, his party base included a large, isolationist element that still revered William Jennings Bryan. The President had few close friends in Congress, even among Democrats, and made little effort to make new ones. So often chilly in public, this Calvinist ex-professor was devoid of the kind of charisma that had enabled Theodore Roosevelt to entice voters and members of Congress to support some of his more unconventional goals. The Kansas editor William Allen White complained that Wilson's handshake felt like "a ten-cent pickled mackerel in brown paper."

For all his high-flown scholarly rhetoric about liberal democracy, the moment Wilson became a war President, he grabbed for authority with some of the passion of an autocrat, claiming that "unquestionable powers" were "absolutely necessary," and stepped on civil liberties. As a scholar, he had overestimated the ability of a President to change public opinion. In 1907, he had written that the Chief Executive possessed "the only national voice in affairs. Let him once win the admiration and confidence of the country, and no other single force can withstand him, no combination of forces will easily over-power him. . . . If he rightly interpret the national thought and boldly insist upon it, he is irresistible."*

But even this overblown theory required a President to make a vigor-ous effort to educate the public. Throughout America's war effort and its immediate aftermath, however, Wilson's public voice was far too often silent, Fourteen Points or not. He who had studied Lincoln should have remembered how the sixteenth President had continually spoken out or issued written statements about the Civil War in an effort to shape how Northerners viewed the conflict. Wilson was also unable to keep himself from saying things that were likely to be misinterpreted and which dam-aged his cause, such as the nation being "too proud to fight" and seeking "peace without victory."

Wilson's wartime leadership revealed the same disdain for Congress he had shown in *Congressional Government*. He often felt affronted when members of the House and Senate offered advice or otherwise chal-lenged him. Leading a wartime nation nourished his sanctimoniousness and extreme predilection for boldness, which, at times, blinded him to the stark limits of his political power. To Wilson, his own motives were almost always above suspicion, and almost never those of his critics. He had appointed few aides or Cabinet members with the intellect, ability, or stature to stand up to him. His wife, Edith, although a reliable source of loving support, did not have the ability or inclination to restrain some of his most self-damaging impulses.

After the victory of November 1918, Wilson overplayed his hand. Given his country's horrifying death toll of perhaps 116,000 soldiers—during those nineteen months, Americans had died in Europe at an even faster rate than during the Civil War—it would have behooved the President to adopt a public stance of respectful, self-effacing gratitude, instead of parading around Paris, with his top hat and toothy smile, suggesting to some countrymen back home that he thought he had won the war almost single-handedly. He refused to put a single Republican of stature on his peace delegation in Paris.

---

* These words can be read with bitter irony if one knows what happened to Wilson after Versailles.

Wilson asked his foes in the newly Republican House and Senate and among the American people for something far beyond his originally stated war aim of helping the Allies defeat the Central Powers. He wanted them to ignore Thomas Jefferson's warning against "entangling alliances" and join a mysterious new world organization that—so many suspected, and Wilson never persuaded them otherwise—might encroach on their future right to decide for themselves when and how America should go to war. Wilson refused to roll up his sleeves, acknowledge the magnitude of such a political departure, and bargain with Congress as a constitutional equal, or to make his case to the American people until his western tour of autumn 1919, by which time it was too late. No wonder that this President—with his theories about peace and war that seemed alien and abstract to many Americans—suffered such a resounding national backlash with the Harding landslide.

By the 1920s, many Americans were trying to rid their minds of Woodrow Wilson and his League of Nations. While they honored the World War's veterans, many were resolved that no future President should take them into a similar adventure. After Harding died in 1923, the new President, Calvin Coolidge, assured Congress that there was "no reason" to limit America's "freedom and independence" by joining Wilson's League, adding that "the incident, so far as we are concerned, is closed." The next year, Coolidge kept his job in another Republican landslide.*

Joining sixty-one other countries, in 1928, President Coolidge signed the Kellogg-Briand Pact, which renounced war as a means of resolving international disputes.† Sponsored by the Americans and French, the measure had sped through the US Senate with only a single dissenting vote. Speaking at the Civil War battleground of Gettysburg, Coolidge asked Americans to "bend our every effort to prevent any recurrence

---

* In the 1924 election, the isolationist Robert La Follette took 17 percent of the popular vote, as well as his home state of Wisconsin.

† The treaty was named for Coolidge's Secretary of State, Frank B. Kellogg, and the French Foreign Minister Aristide Briand.

of war." He noted that by then the size of the American military was "exceedingly moderate," adding, "No other nation has anything which we would think of taking by force." In Wausau, Wisconsin, Coolidge told a veterans audience that had there been a Kellogg-Briand treaty in 1914, it might have "delivered the world from all the misery which was inflicted by the Great War."

CHAPTER TWELVE

"How Could This Thing Happen?"

O N SUNDAY MORNING, December 7, 1941, at about seven o'clock, Admiral Husband Kimmel, Commander-in-Chief of the US Fleet, woke up at home in Makalapa Heights, above Pearl Harbor. He was planning to play golf with Lieutenant General Walter Short, who was in charge of defending military installations on the Hawaiian Islands.

Unshaven, still in pajamas, the blue-eyed, graying blond, wide-shouldered Kimmel answered the telephone. His duty officer, Commander Vincent Murphy, told him of a report that the US destroyer *Ward* had sunk a hostile submarine a mile from the entrance to the Pearl Harbor base. Kimmel was so accustomed to hearing similar reports, which were later proven false, that he did not warn the Army. As the Admiral donned his white uniform, Murphy called him back to warn that the *Ward* had just halted a sampan. Then a yeoman shouted, "There's a message from the signal tower that the Japanese are attacking Pearl Harbor, and this is no drill!"

Rapidly buttoning his tunic, Kimmel rushed onto the lawn of his neighbor, Captain John Earle, which overlooked Pearl Harbor's "Battleship Row." Kimmel and Earle's wife froze when they saw Japanese warplanes flying in figure eights to bomb the American vessels. The planes were so close that the Rising Sun could be seen on the wings. His face stony white, Kimmel knew "something terrible was going on" because "this was not a casual raid by just a few stray planes. The sky was full of the enemy." With horror, he watched the battleship *Arizona* "lift out of the water, then sink back down—way down."

Kimmel had his driver speed him to his office. From there at 8:12, he sent an alert to the Chief of Naval Operations, Admiral Harold "Betty" Stark: "Hostilities with Japan commenced with air raid on Pearl Harbor." While looking out of a window at the chaos and destruction, Kimmel was struck near the heart by a spent machine-gun bullet, but so lightly that the round bounced off his chest and fell to his feet. Already suspecting that he would be one of those blamed for the Japanese attack, he said, "Too bad it didn't kill me." According to one witness, Kimmel then reached up with both hands for his four-star shoulder boards and tore them off.

Especially compared with the ignominious way it would end, Kimmel's career had started with promise. Born in 1882, in the Kentucky tobacco town of Henderson, he graduated in the top quarter of his class at the US Naval Academy.[*] In 1914, during the occupation of Veracruz ordered by President Wilson, he was wounded in the arm and both legs. The following year, during a trip to San Diego, the Assistant Secretary of the Navy, Franklin Roosevelt, his elder by one month, took him on as a temporary aide. Kimmel later recalled that Roosevelt and his wife were "very charming," but he grew "tired of holding Mrs. Roosevelt's coat." In November 1918, in Scotland, as executive officer of the dreadnought USS *Arkansas,* Kimmel watched the final surrender of the German fleet.[†]

In January 1941, after Kimmel had served as the Navy's budget officer and commander of three light cruiser divisions in Hawaii, President

---

[*] Kimmel's father, Manning, was a West Point graduate who fought as a federal officer at Bull Run, then, out of fierce Southern allegiance, joined the Confederacy, which gave him the rank of Brigadier General. After Appomattox, having heard rumors that West Point graduates who became rebels would be hanged for treason, Manning hid out in Mexico, then settled in Henderson, where he prospered in the retail coal business.

[†] For Kimmel, this proved to be a bookend to December 1941, when he witnessed the assault that brought America into its next world war.

Franklin Roosevelt chose him as Commander-in-Chief of the US Fleet, which included ships in both the Atlantic and Pacific. Kimmel wrote Admiral Stark that he was "perfectly stunned," having not expected that job "in my wildest dreams." He later told his niece that he was "awfully scared" by his new responsibility. The reason for the vacancy was that the previous October, Kimmel's predecessor, Admiral James Richardson, had protested Roosevelt's decision to move the Pacific Fleet from San Diego and Long Beach to Pearl Harbor. The President insisted that the new location would provide deterrence against Japanese militarists. But Richardson warned him, to his face, at the White House, that putting these ships in the middle of the Pacific would make them more vulnerable to attack. Stung by Richardson's effrontery, Roosevelt removed him.

The President's choice of the more amenable Kimmel, whom his colleagues called "Kim," was a bad mistake, putting a solid but prosaic and unimaginative officer into what would turn out to be one of the world's most important commands. Communications between Washington and Honolulu, almost five thousand miles apart, were primitive, so much would hinge upon Kimmel's ability to think on his feet. But this Admiral was, by nature, far too content to wait for orders from the War Department.

At 1:40 p.m. that day in Washington, DC, which was five hours ahead, Roosevelt was lunching with his close aide Harry Hopkins in his private oval study, upstairs at the White House. Secretary of the Navy Frank Knox called to report that Pearl Harbor was under aerial attack. This was the first time since the War of 1812 that another country had successfully launched a major military assault on the territory of the United States. The President knew instantly that the United States would now have to enter a world war of unimaginable magnitude. He ordered Knox, "Find out, for God's sake, why the ships were tied up in rows!"

✳ ✳ ✳

Roosevelt's white house study, like other rooms at the Mansion and the family's spacious Victorian home at Hyde Park, was adorned by framed naval and war scenes. As an adolescent, Franklin had begun to amass what the *New York Times* in 1961 called "the world's largest known collection of American naval prints and paintings." The President owned the earliest surviving portrait of John Paul Jones, whose biography he had once attempted to write, and what were called the only sketches made during combat in the Mexican War (by a gunner on the US sloop of war *Cyane*). Roosevelt loved to collect ship models, as well as books, pamphlets, and documents related to his country's naval history.

The President's maternal ancestors, the Delanos, had made money on clipper ships plying the China trade, including opium, but his forebears had not fought in the War of 1812, the Mexican conflict, or the Civil War. His father, James, although thirty-two when the struggle between North and South began, did not join the Union Army; he hired a substitute. Young Franklin's fascination with war was stimulated by his fifth cousin Theodore. As a student at Groton, captivated by news accounts about the Rough Riders in Cuba, Franklin imitated TR by wearing a stylish gold pince-nez and exclaiming "Bully!"* When Theodore and the Rough Riders paraded through New York City, Franklin cheered along with the crowd. He later claimed that had he not been confined in the Groton infirmary with scarlet fever, he would have volunteered to fight the Spanish in Cuba himself.

On St. Patrick's Day 1905, in Manhattan, the twenty-three-year-old Franklin married Theodore's favorite niece, Eleanor. By then, his cousin was President, and, in the absence of her late alcoholic father, Elliott, TR gave away the bride. Before long, Franklin was telling other clerks in his New York City law firm that, although he was a Democrat, he would follow his cousin's political path, from the New York legislature to the White House. His son Franklin Jr. told me in 1978, "My father spent his whole adult life competing with TR."

As a New York state senator in 1912, the Democratic Roosevelt campaigned for Woodrow Wilson. TR was running for President that year

---

* Some Harvard classmates later ribbed Roosevelt for his fixation on his cousin by calling him "Kermit," after Theodore's second son.

on the Bull Moose ticket but, with his respect for ambition, bore Franklin no ill will. When Wilson won, Franklin successfully lobbied for Theodore's old job at the Navy, explaining that "all my life I have loved ships" and that, as a boy, he had wished to attend Annapolis. Franklin knew that being Assistant Secretary of the Navy would lend him a military patina that, as TR had shown, could enhance his political future.

At the Navy, Roosevelt's genial, long-suffering chief, Josephus Daniels, knew that his hyperactive, sometimes insubordinate young deputy, on whom he doted, yearned to be President. Franklin quickly became the champion of a much larger US Navy, while Daniels gravitated toward the pacifism of his hero William Jennings Bryan. At the end of July 1914, when war was nearing in Europe, Roosevelt rushed back from his family summer respite on the Canadian island of Campobello. He wrote Eleanor that "a complete smashup is inevitable" and that his chief "totally fails to grasp the situation." He added, "These are history-making days. It will be the greatest war in the world's history."

The Assistant Secretary was alarmed that "nobody seemed the least bit excited about the European crisis—Mr. Daniels feeling chiefly very sad that his faith in human nature and civilization and similar idealistic nonsense was receiving such a rude shock." He complained to Eleanor that Daniels and Bryan had "as much conception of what a general European war means" as their little son Elliott had "of higher mathematics." When war enveloped Europe, he boasted to his wife, "I am *running* the real work, although Josephus is here! He is bewildered by it all, very sweet but very sad." Repeatedly Roosevelt told his superior, "We've got to get into this war," to which Daniels would reply, "I hope not."

By the start of 1917, the Assistant Secretary could see that the United States was on the verge of entering the European conflict, and he hoped for a major role. On New Year's Day, he reached into his personal cache of historical artifacts and chose one as a gift for President Wilson. It was a memorandum scrawled by James Madison's Secretary of State, James Monroe, at the time of the War of 1812, warning that "a submission too long protracted, would have no other effect than to encourage and accumulate aggressions, until they become altogether intolerable." Eager to curry favor with the historian-President and to signal his eagerness for bold action, Roosevelt wrote Wilson that Monroe's argument was "interestingly parallel to the events of the day."

During the first week of March, Roosevelt went to the White House and asked the President for permission to "bring the Fleet back from Guantanamo" to be "cleaned and fitted out" for action. Wilson refused, explaining that he had "tried every diplomatic means to keep out of the war" and would do nothing now that might constitute "an unfriendly act against the Central Powers." He told Roosevelt that he wanted "the definitive historian," writing in the future, to conclude "that war has been forced upon us deliberately by Germany."

When Wilson finally went to Congress in April 1917 to seek a declaration of war, Franklin and Eleanor were in the chamber. She recorded that while listening "breathlessly" to the President, she felt "half-dazed by the sense of impending change." Uncle Theodore, recalling his own experience of 1898, told Franklin, "You must resign. You must get into uniform at once!" As Daniels later recalled, Franklin "thought actual fighting in the war was the necessary step toward reaching the White House." But Wilson told Daniels to keep the young man in place, adding that "neither you nor I nor Franklin Roosevelt has the right to select the place of service" already "assigned" by the nation.

During wartime, Roosevelt advocated a plan to build a "fence" of antisubmarine mines to close off the North Sea, which Wilson called "shutting up the hornets in their nest." Using twenty-two million pounds of explosives, the fence, when built, extended across the English Channel and between Scotland and Norway; it destroyed half a dozen or more German U-boats and helped to crack the morale of the German Navy. In the summer of 1918, Roosevelt insisted on touring the French battlefront himself and risked bombardment by enemy artillery in the English Channel.* His esteemed war record, combined with his famous surname,

---

* On the way to France, at a London dinner, he met Winston Churchill, Britain's Minister of Munitions. Roosevelt did not like him; he recalled Churchill having "acted like a stinker" and "lording it all over us." Churchill later could not remember having encountered Roosevelt at all.

youth, and political strength in what was still the nation's most popu-
lous state, led to his nomination for Vice President in 1920.

The following year, at Campobello, Roosevelt was struck by polio.
As he tried to recover the use of his legs and, with his faithful aide Louis
Howe, planned his return to national politics, he benefited from his
association with the heroic sailors who had risked their lives during the
World War. But he did not advertise how, behind the scenes, he had
been one of the chief and earliest officials pushing Wilson to enter the
conflict, which so many Americans now considered a ghastly, hubristic
mistake. A month after Roosevelt was elected Governor of New York in
1928, when he spoke at a banquet for the Woodrow Wilson Foundation, of which he was an officer, he carefully praised only aspects of the
late President's war leadership that most people deemed above reproach,
such as Wilson's probity and his refusal to send young Americans to
Europe until they had been properly trained.

When Roosevelt ran for President in 1932, with the nation stilled
by the Great Depression, Americans were not—luckily for him—very
interested in his role in Wilson's crusade. Disguising his internationalist
tendencies, Roosevelt stressed his efforts while in Albany for economic
reform and relief and defeated President Herbert Hoover in a landslide.
His experience under Wilson had shown him how a President could use
a national emergency to enhance his authority. Thus in his inaugural
address, although the crisis he faced was domestic, the new President
reached at once for the metaphor of military conflict, asking for "broad
Executive power to wage a war" against the Depression, "as great as
the power that would be given to me if we were in fact invaded by a
foreign foe."

* * *

DURING HIS FIRST term, as the New Deal President tried to rescue
the American economy, relieve widespread suffering, and reform
the broken financial system, the public made it clear that it was more
isolationist than ever. In 1934, responding to charges that the Mor-
gans, du Ponts, and other "merchants of death," concerned with "iron,

blood and profits," had schemed to force the United States into the Great War, the Senate formed a special committee to investigate the munitions industry, chaired by the isolationist Republican Gerald Nye of North Dakota.* In March 1935, Roosevelt met with Nye's panel at the White House, claiming that he had "come around entirely" to respect William Jennings Bryan's views on American neutrality. That August, recognizing the nation's antiwar fervor, he signed a bill demanding an arms embargo against all belligerents in case of overseas conflict, no matter who appeared to be the aggressor.

In 1936, the President sought a second term against the Kansas Governor Alfred Landon, who urged crowds to "mind our own business." Roosevelt was loath to get on the wrong side of the vast isolationist vote, which included so much of his own party. That spring, he and Eleanor had given their annual White House garden reception for disabled veterans. Some of the guests were pushed through the receiving line in wheelchairs, while, as usual, the standing President, using his hidden leg braces, his cane, and the arm of a military aide, pretended that he was not still similarly afflicted.

When Adolf Hitler's forces remilitarized the Rhineland, Roosevelt felt unable to act dramatically. Speaking that summer to a national radio audience from the encampment at Chautauqua, New York, he pledged to "shun political commitments which might entangle us in foreign wars" and to "avoid connection with the political activities of the League of Nations." Almost echoing the "merchants of death" narrative, he warned that "production for a war market may give immense fortunes to a few men" but "for the nation as a whole, it produces disaster . . . I wish I could keep war from all nations, but that is beyond my power. I can at least make certain that no act of the United States helps to produce or to promote war."

In the most attention-grabbing part of his speech, Roosevelt suggested

---

* The Democratic majority aborted the hearings in early 1936 after Nye claimed that President Wilson had deliberately withheld important facts from Congress as it debated entering the World War. Pounding his knuckles until they showed blood, a furious Senator Carter Glass of Virginia, who had been Wilson's Treasury Secretary, accused Nye of "dirtdaubing the sepulcher" of his sainted leader.

that his personal experience during the Great War had made him an enemy of military confrontation. "I have seen war," he declaimed, with rising emotion. "I have seen blood running from the wounded . . . men coughing out their gassed lungs . . . the dead in the mud. . . . Two hundred limping, exhausted men come out of line. . . . I have seen children starving. I have seen the agony of mothers and wives. *I—hate—WAR!*" Roosevelt did not mention that he had viewed such horrors merely as a civilian official sightseer, touring the French battlefront. Unfamiliar with his personal history, many listeners no doubt presumed from hearing these words that their President must have fought in Europe, like so many of them and their family members. That November, he was reelected in a landslide.

In the summer of 1937, Japan invaded China. Speaking that October at a bridge dedication in Chicago, the capital of Midwestern isolationism, Roosevelt warned that "innocent nations are being cruelly sacrificed to a greed for power and supremacy which is devoid of all sense of justice and humane considerations." If such behavior spread throughout the world, "let no one imagine that America will escape." He suggested a possible international "quarantine" of peace-loving nations to oppose the "contagion."

The *Washington Post* praised Roosevelt's "assurance that the United States has not forgotten all moral standards in its ostrich hunt for security." The *Baltimore Sun* agreed the President's plea was "not to be shirked merely because it is hard." But the isolationist *Boston Herald* warned Roosevelt that he sounded too much like Wilson: "For the sake of several millions of American mothers, confine your crusading to the continental limits of America!" "Don't Get Excited," implored the *Nevada State Journal.* Chilled by the failure of many congressional Democrats to endorse his appeal, Roosevelt confided to his aide and speechwriter Samuel Rosenman, "It's a terrible thing to look over your shoulder when you are trying to lead—and to find no one there."

That December, Japanese bombers sank the clearly marked American gunboat *Panay,* peaceably anchored on the Yangtze River in Nanking, China, where it was protecting local American interests. Roosevelt let it be known that he was "deeply shocked." His Secretary of State, Cordell Hull, obtained from Japan an official apology, full restitution, and a pledge against similar assaults. But the attack reminded many isolationists of how the destruction of the *Maine* and other vessels had moved Americans to fight in 1898 and 1917. Worried that Roosevelt or a successor might exploit future such disasters, they searched for new means to bar Presidents from dragging the nation into war.

Democratic Congressman Louis Ludlow of Indiana had proposed a constitutional amendment demanding that unless US territory had been invaded and Americans injured, any future effort to take the country to war would require a national referendum. Ludlow complained to a radio audience, "You can cast your ballot for a constable or a dogcatcher, but you have absolutely nothing to say about a declaration of war." In October 1937, the Gallup Poll found that 73 percent of Americans favored his proposal. Roosevelt's allies had kept Ludlow's bill from reaching a floor vote, but within a day of the *Panay* assault, a majority petition dislodged the bill from the House Judiciary Committee. The President warned Speaker William Bankhead that "such an amendment would cripple any President in his conduct of foreign relations." So strong was isolationism in the House, however, that an effort to allow a floor vote was only narrowly defeated. Republicans sided with Ludlow by 64 to 21.

In March 1938, Nazi Germany annexed Austria, despite a formal protest lodged by the British Prime Minister, Neville Chamberlain, who wished to appease Hitler to maintain tranquillity in Europe. Privately Roosevelt compared Chamberlain to a "chief of police" who "makes a deal with the leading gangsters." That September, in Munich, Chamberlain and Hitler signed the infamous compact that took the Sudetenland, home of three million ethnic Germans, away from Czechoslovakia and gave it to Germany in exchange for what Chamberlain called "peace in our time." Roosevelt told intimates that the British leader and his colleagues resembled "Judas Iscariot," but did not say so in public. The Gallup Poll found that Americans approved of Chamberlain's leadership by 57 to 43 percent.

In Germany, that November, came *Kristallnacht,* with synagogues and Jewish homes set aflame. Eleanor wrote her friend Lorena Hickok that the attack on German Jews "makes me sick." The President sought to expand the US Army Air Corps to include at least twenty thousand warplanes; he privately said that if the United States had already possessed such air power, "Hitler would not have dared to take the stand he did." He sent warplanes to France and England for their potential defense, which did not violate existing neutrality laws since those states were still at peace with the Germans. Meeting at the White House with the Senate Military Affairs Committee, Roosevelt recalled that when Hitler took power, Germany was "a complete and utter failure, a nation that owed everybody." He asked, "Would any of you have said that in six years, Germany would dominate Europe, completely and absolutely?" He warned that if the British and French collapsed, the rest of Europe would fall to Hitler, and so would Africa and Latin America.

Violating a promise he made at Munich, Hitler seized the rest of Czechoslovakia in March 1939. Roosevelt asked the House and Senate to repeal existing neutrality constraints in order to aid England and France in event of war, but the Senate refused to weigh the matter until the following year. "Well, Captain, we may as well face the facts," his grizzled Vice President, John Nance Garner of Texas, advised him. "You haven't got the votes, and that's all there is to it." That July, Roosevelt asked his Attorney General, Frank Murphy, how far he could go in "ignoring" the Neutrality Act, "even though I did sign it."

In August 1939, Nazi Germany forged a nonaggression pact with Joseph Stalin's Soviet Union. At that moment, the Führer was demanding the semiautonomous German "free city" of Danzig, which enjoyed a customs union with Poland and a transportation route across the Polish access corridor along the Vistula River, all guaranteed by the Treaty of Versailles. On Friday, September 1, after Hitler's demand was rejected, a Blitzkrieg of German divisions pierced the Polish frontier, which Britain was pledged to defend. At the White House, Roosevelt was awakened at 2:50 a.m. for a telephoned report from his Ambassador in Paris, William

Bullitt.* "Well, Bill, it's come at last," replied the President. "God help us all."

The usually buoyant Roosevelt was visibly shaken by the coming of war. Meeting with his Cabinet that Friday afternoon, he confided aloud that Bullitt's call had made him feel suddenly propelled, through time, back to the Great War:

> I was almost startled by a strange feeling of familiarity, a feeling that I had been through it all before. . . . During the long years of the World War, the telephone at my bedside with a direct wire to the Navy Department had, time and again, brought me other tragic messages in the night. The same rush messages were sent around, the same lights snapped on in the nerve centers of government. I had *in fact* been through it all before. It was *not* strange to me, but more like picking up again an interrupted routine. Unless some miracle beyond our present grasp changes the hearts of men, the days ahead will be crowded days—crowded with the same problems, the same anxieties that filled to the brim those September days of 1914. For history does, in fact, repeat.

Lest some department secretary leak that the Chief was now scheming to take the nation into Europe's new conflict, Roosevelt quickly added, "The parallel of then and now is striking, but it must go no farther. . . . True patriotism, in this hour of crisis, includes the determination that no warlike events shall be permitted to disturb the peaceful and orderly pursuits of the American people."

Two days later, on Sunday, Great Britain and France declared war against Germany. Roosevelt received a call from his despairing Ambassador in London, Joseph Kennedy, a Chamberlain friend and disciple, who told the President, "It's the end of the world . . . the end of everything." That night, in a fireside chat, Roosevelt (no doubt recalling

---

* In the Paris of 1919, Bullitt had been the Wilson adviser who inspired a mass resignation of his colleagues over the severity of the German settlement, warning that it might lead to another war.

Wilson's demand of 1914 that Americans be "impartial in thought, as well as action") told radio listeners, "This nation will remain a neutral nation, but I cannot ask that every American remain neutral in thought as well." Still he soon asked the leaders of Congress to call their members back from summer recess to repeal the Neutrality Acts.

Outraged by the growing possibility of American involvement in Europe, Charles Lindbergh, an American hero since making the first transatlantic solo aerial crossing, gave his first formal speech since the kidnapping and murder of his infant son in 1932. By radio, Lindbergh warned that the new conflict was "not a question of banding together to defend the white race from invasion" but "simply one of those age-old struggles within our own family of nations, a quarrel rising from the errors of the last war." Lindbergh predicted that if the United States got in, "we are likely to lose a million men—possibly several million, the best of American youth."

Roosevelt argued before a special Joint Session of Congress that revising the neutrality statutes would help the United States to remain a peaceful "citadel" in the Western world in which "civilization may be kept alive." He pledged to be "guided by one single hard-headed thought—keeping America out of war." After the President spoke, Gallup found that 60 percent of Americans wanted the Neutrality Acts repealed. In this, Roosevelt was aided by the hasty collapse of Poland, which was then divided between the Soviet Union and Germany. But he privately felt he was "almost literally walking on eggs." He persuaded Congress to cancel the arms embargo; still US bank loans to belligerents were barred in favor of "cash and carry." The House and Senate also forbade deliveries by US vessels on the Atlantic, whose sinking might thrust the country into Europe's war.

Before Christmas 1939, back on home leave, Ambassador Kennedy asked the President whether he planned to run for a third term. "Joe, I can't," Roosevelt replied. "I can't take it. What I need is a year's rest. You do too. You may think you're resting at times, but the subconscious idea of war and its problems—bombings and all that—is going on in your brain all the time. I just won't go for a third term unless we are in war." Knowing that Kennedy, who fiercely opposed American involvement, was listening for signs that his chief might be secretly plotting to take the nation into battle, the President caught himself: "Even then, I'll never send an Army over. We'll help them, but with supplies."

In the spring of 1940, Hitler's armies seized Norway and Denmark. By June, the Germans had conquered France, and Italy had declared war against the British and French. Before speaking at the University of Virginia's commencement, Roosevelt learned that the Italian dictator, Benito Mussolini, had deployed his forces against France. Outraged, he told the audience that "the hand that held the dagger has struck it into the back of its neighbor." Warning that the United States could not survive as "a lone island in a world dominated by the philosophy of force," he vowed to "extend to the opponents of force the material resources of this nation." The new British Prime Minister, Winston Churchill, who had replaced the discredited Chamberlain, wrote Roosevelt that he felt "fortified by the grand scope of your declaration."

* * *

NOW THE PRESIDENT faced a thicket of political challenges. He wished to persuade Congress and the American people to back his efforts to strengthen American defense and aid England, as well as the forcible draft of young men for the armed forces, unprecedented in peacetime, which would incite many people to say that he was pushing the nation into the war. Unless he helped the British people to stave off Germany, they might conclude that resistance was futile and demand Churchill's replacement by another leader who would make the best deal possible with Hitler.

At the end of June, Roosevelt was startled when the Republicans at Philadelphia nominated a dark horse, Wendell Willkie. A New York utilities executive and registered Democrat until 1939, Willkie had been promoted by northeastern internationalists who wished to aid England. Eleanor wrote her friend Lorena Hickok that she had a "hunch" that Willkie would defeat her husband. Responding to the challenge, the President broadened his Cabinet in early July by appointing two Republicans—Frank

Knox as Secretary of the Navy and Henry Stimson as Secretary of War.

To prevent the emergence of a serious opponent for his party's nomination, Roosevelt had encouraged almost every major Democrat to run, and hence split the field. It did not require much vanity for him to conclude that no one else could match his leadership skills in handling the European crisis. In July, when his convention met in Chicago, he was privately willing to become the nation's first third-term President.* He knew that the best way to do this was to feign unwillingness or indifference about staying in office and be "drafted" by the delegates.

The convention chairman, Senator Alben Barkley of Kentucky, conveyed a message from Roosevelt, at the White House, that he lacked "any desire or purpose to continue in the office of President" and that delegates were "free to vote for any candidate." This provoked a well-orchestrated demonstration, with organ music and a marching band, in which Chicago's superintendent of sewers, Thomas Garry, from beneath the hall, roared over loudspeakers, "Everybody wants Roosevelt!" and "The world needs Roosevelt!" The President was anointed on the first ballot. Roosevelt enjoyed such mastery of the convention that when delegates rebelled against his choice for Vice President—Secretary of Agriculture Henry Wallace, a Republican until 1936—he prevailed by threatening to decline the presidential nomination. Ensuring his command of foreign policy, he penciled in a crucial change to the Democratic platform, which pledged that the country "will not participate in foreign wars," adding "except in case of attack."

Two weeks after his renomination, Roosevelt called for a peacetime military draft. The isolationist Senator Burton Wheeler, Democrat from

---

* Which would allow him to best Cousin Theodore, who had failed to win what would have amounted to a third term in 1912. As early as 1935, FDR took pleasure in concluding that he had surpassed his presidential relative, writing to a friend that while Theodore could do "superficial" things like stir people's "enthusiasm," he never aroused their "truly profound moral and social convictions." And indeed, in 1938, when the Gallup Poll asked Americans which of the two Roosevelts would be regarded by history as the greater President, Franklin won by 58 to 42 percent.

Montana, warned that if Congress passed such a bill, it would "slit the throat of the last great democracy still living" and "accord to Hitler his greatest and cheapest victory." But the Army Chief of Staff, General George Marshall, insisted that there was "no conceivable way" to ensure national defense without conscription. Stimson agreed. Against the backdrop of the French defeat and Britain's valiant efforts to survive, one poll found that public support for a draft had risen from about half of the country in June to 86 percent by the end of August. Willkie helped the cause by proclaiming that conscription was "the only democratic way in which to assure the trained and competent manpower we need." Congress easily passed Roosevelt's Selective Service Act in September.

That same month, the President announced that he planned to trade fifty American destroyers, left over from the Great War, in exchange for ninety-nine-year leases to British naval installations in the Atlantic and Caribbean. Churchill had privately asked him in June for the vessels "as a matter of life and death," warning, "We will carry out the struggle whatever the odds but it may be beyond our resources unless we receive reinforcement." Roosevelt took the precaution of securing from his Attorney General, Robert Jackson, a written opinion affirming his authority to trade the ships by executive agreement. Senator Nye warned that a destroyer trade would thrust the nation into "a war of European power politics" and "seriously weaken our own defenses."

Roosevelt told Congress that his transaction would be "the most important action in the reinforcement of our national defense" since the Louisiana Purchase: "Then as now, considerations of safety from overseas attack were fundamental." Flailing, Willkie blustered that the deal was "the most arbitrary and dictatorial action" any American President had ever taken. The Gallup Poll found that the "Destroyer Deal" helped Roosevelt improve his position against Willkie from a near-tie in late August to a ten-point lead by mid-September.

Unhappy about his loss of political strength, Willkie needed an issue. In mid-September, Gallup reported that 52 percent of Americans said the nation's most important goal should be to help England win, "even at the risk of getting into the war," but 48 percent said it should be "to keep out of war ourselves." By October, the Germans were subjecting London to the Blitz, but it no longer seemed likely that Hitler would soon conquer England. The lessening of the crisis caused many voters to conclude that Roosevelt's reelection was now less essential.* Desperate to catch up with the President, Willkie transformed his campaign image into that of the man who would keep Americans out of war. He knew this would require him to hide his actual intentions, and to scare the public with lurid half-truths about what Roosevelt would do. But if that was the price of winning the presidency, he was willing to pay it.

"Who really thinks that the President is sincerely trying to keep us out of war?" Willkie demanded of crowds. Charging that Roosevelt had made secret plans to enter Europe's conflict if reelected, he insisted that the President unveil any "international understandings to put America into the war that we citizens do not know about." In Boston, where so many voters of Irish and Italian descent opposed engagement in Europe, Willkie promised that if he became President, "our boys shall stay out of European wars." In Baltimore, he warned that on the basis of Roosevelt's "past performances with pledges," if the President won a third term, "you may expect war by April 1941." Other Republicans warned of a "secret Roosevelt pact" with England that would drag American sons into battle.

The President told his Interior Secretary, Harold Ickes, that Willkie's allegations had made him "fighting mad." He knew that a major reason why Americans suspected that he would take them into war in Europe, if reelected, was that Woodrow Wilson had done exactly that after campaigning on the tricky implicit promise of his 1916 slogan "He Kept Us Out of War." At first, Roosevelt carefully resisted the temptation to pledge more than he knew he could deliver. Two weeks before the election, joining the campaign trail in Philadelphia, he offered Americans his "most solemn assurance" that "there is no secret treaty, no

---

* In August, asked whom they would prefer for President if England were defeated before the election and America might have to fight Germany, voters had said Roosevelt by 58 percent.

secret obligation" with any other government "to involve this nation in any war."

But on Halloween Eve, with Willkie said to be "within striking distance of victory," the President went one step further. At the Boston Garden, he told the throng, "I have said this before, but I shall say it again and again and again: Your boys are not going to be sent into any foreign wars!" While riding by train to Boston, Sam Rosenman, his speechwriter, had asked his chief why he did not plan to add his standard phrase "except in case of attack." "It's not necessary," replied the President. "If we're attacked, it's no longer a foreign war."

Listening to Roosevelt's speech on the radio, Willkie exclaimed, "That hypocritical son of a bitch! This is going to beat me!" Roosevelt's artful language provoked later charges that he had tricked Americans into battle. In 1944, the Republican Congresswoman Clare Boothe Luce of Connecticut charged at her party's convention that the President had "lied us into a war because he did not have the political courage to lead us into it."*

* * *

ROOSEVELT DEFEATED WILLKIE by 54.7 to 44.8 percent of the popular vote, with 449 electoral votes to his opponent's 82. Emerging from the big house in Hyde Park, under the glare of artificial lights, he told his supporters, "I don't need to tell you that we face difficult days in this country."

That same week, the *Boston Globe* published quotations from an interview with Joseph Kennedy, on home leave, who had told a reporter that "democracy is all finished in England" and there was "no sense" in getting into the war: "We'd just be holding the bag." More damaging, the envoy had predicted that democracy might also be done in the

---

* After Roosevelt's Boston speech, the *Bakersfield Californian* published a letter from one alert reader, warning that the President, "adept at evasion," had used "weasel words," and that if he won a third term, "American conscripts may then find themselves fighting anywhere from Egypt to Bessarabia."

United States because the loss of trade with Europe might "change our form of government." If America joined the war, "a bureaucracy would take over right off. Everything we hold dear would be gone. They told me that after 1918, we got it all back again, but this is different."* Roosevelt was in no position to let stand Kennedy's insistence that beleaguered Britain was a lost cause, or that the US government was headed for autocracy. After calling him to Hyde Park for a dressing-down, he told Eleanor, in fury, "I never want to see that son of a bitch again as long as I live."†

By December 1940, it was clear that both the Blitz and Hitler's invasion blueprint for England, Operation Sea Lion, were failures. But the British had lost more than five hundred merchant ships and were almost bankrupt. Churchill wrote Roosevelt that soon "we shall no longer be able to pay cash for shipping and other supplies." The President devised a way to satisfy Churchill's wish list by letting the British compensate the United States or return the borrowed goods when that was possible, which he called "Lend-Lease." With his talent for homespun imagery, Roosevelt told reporters that if his neighbor's house caught fire, he would not say, "My garden hose cost me fifteen dollars; you have to pay me fifteen dollars for it." Instead he would simply "want my garden hose back after the fire is over."‡

In a fireside chat two nights before the end of 1940, Roosevelt used

---

* Kennedy later contended that the *Globe*'s reporter, Louis Lyons, was supposed to keep at least part of their interview off the record, but Lyons's editors stood by him. After his grim visit to Hyde Park, Kennedy told ex-President Hoover that he had warned Roosevelt, "Whatever aid you extend to Britain you must regard as a bet on a losing horse," and that if America entered the war, it would become "a National Socialist state," with "no return to democratic forms."

† When Kennedy announced his resignation a week later, he insisted that he had been intending to quit and would now take up "the greatest cause in the world today"—helping the President to keep out of war. That summer, at twenty-three, Kennedy's second son, Jack, had published his rewritten Harvard senior thesis under the title of *Why England Slept;* it argued that by making the deal at Munich, the British had bought necessary time to prepare for war.

‡ During the two months after Roosevelt's reelection, the Gallup Poll asked Americans how they would vote if there should be a national referendum on intervention. Eighty-eight percent said they would vote to "stay out" of the war, with only 12 percent opting to "go in." But they agreed that America's "future safety depends on England winning this war," by 68 to 26 percent. And, by 59 to 41 percent, they expected that "the United States will go into the war in Europe sometime before it is over."

alarmist language he would never have dared employ during the campaign: "Never before, since Jamestown and Plymouth Rock, has our American civilization been in such danger as now. . . . The Nazi masters of Germany have made it clear that they intend not only to dominate all life and thought in their own country, but also to enslave the whole of Europe, and then to use the resources of Europe to dominate the rest of the world." He cautioned against "American appeasers" seeking a bargain with Hitler to keep out of the war: "Nonsense! Is it a negotiated peace if a gang of outlaws surrounds your community and, on threat of extermination, makes you pay tribute to save your own skins?" Instead, referring to Lend-Lease and his defense production program, he demanded, "We must be the great arsenal of democracy."

On Monday, January 6, 1941, Roosevelt delivered his annual message to Congress, which was now popularly called the State of the Union. Offering a history lesson, he recalled that before the Great War, Americans had never suffered a "serious" external threat to "our national safety or our continued independence." The War of 1812 had been waged "to vindicate our right to peaceful trade." Even in 1914, the European conflict seemed to raise "only a small threat of danger to our own American future." But then Americans realized "what the downfall of democratic nations might mean to our own democracies." More daring now, he insisted, "We need not overemphasize imperfections in the Peace of Versailles." When the current war ended, he proposed, the United States should seek a world founded upon "Four Freedoms"—of "speech and expression," permitting "every person to worship God in his own way," "freedom from want," and "freedom from fear."

That same week, Roosevelt submitted his Lend-Lease bill, grandiloquently called H.R. 1776. Gallup found that Americans supported it by 54 to 22 percent. Nevertheless Senator Wheeler warned that the plan would "plow under every fourth American boy." Arthur Vandenberg, the Republican Senator from Michigan, carped that it would let the President "make war on any country he chooses, any time he pleases." On the same day in February that Lend-Lease passed the House (by 260 to 165), Willkie testified for the measure before the Senate. The "merchants of death" theorist Gerald Nye reminded him of his campaign prediction that Roosevelt would have the country at war by April 1941: "Do you still agree that might be the case?" "It might be," replied Willkie. "It was a bit of campaign oratory." The Senate passed Lend-Lease in March by 60 to 31, after which Congress voted $7 billion in immediate war aid to England, a figure larger than most of the entire federal budgets of the 1930s.

Under the fragment of the Neutrality Act still in force, Great Britain would have to transport the shipments from America, and Hitler's U-boats were destroying British ships on the Atlantic. By executive order, Roosevelt expanded the area to be patrolled by US ships all the way to a longitude line, twenty-five degrees west, that ran between Africa and Latin America. He announced that the American patrols would alert the British if they spied hostile ships, but that the United States would not supply the British vessels with convoys, which were foreclosed by the Lend-Lease Act.* After conferring with the exiled leaders of Denmark, which had been overwhelmed by Germany, the President also sent American troops to occupy Greenland.

Roosevelt's decision to extend the US security zone so far across the Atlantic dramatically increased the chance that German submarines would attack American ships. As the old Navy man knew from the Spanish-American conflict and the Great War, a submarine attack on a US vessel could provoke previously skeptical Americans to clamor for war. Those who now cite Pearl Harbor in support of the argument that the President was deliberately creating the conditions for an attack by a hostile nation that would galvanize Americans to enter the conflict against Hitler may be looking in the wrong place.† In May, he told his Cabinet that he was "not willing to fire the first shot." Secretary Stimson wrote in his diary that Roosevelt "shows evidence of waiting for the

---

* Roosevelt was staying within the bounds of public opinion. In March 1941, Gallup asked Americans, "Do you think the United States should send part of our warships, manned by American sailors, to Europe, to help the British?" By 67 to 27 percent, respondents said no. In April, they opposed US convoys by 50 to 41 percent, but replied, by 71 to 21 percent, that it would be all right to use them if it was "certain" that Britain would be vanquished without them.

† It is notable that when Roosevelt amended the prohibition against war in his 1940 party platform to say "except in case of attack," he did not specify that the assault must be on US territory.

accidental shot of some irresponsible captain on either side to be the occasion of his going to war."

In June, when Germany invaded the Soviet Union, Roosevelt told reporters, "Of course, we are going to give all the aid that we possibly can to Russia." The following month, he ordered 4,400 Marines to replace British soldiers in Iceland. The Navy's Admiral Stark considered this directive "practically an act of war." In August, Roosevelt met with Churchill aboard the HMS *Prince of Wales* and the USS *Augusta,* off Newfoundland. The Prime Minister beseeched him to ask Congress to enter the war against Germany: he would rather have this, with "no supplies for six months, than double the supplies and no declaration."

Roosevelt declined, but he offered to provide British escorts with US armed vessels as far east as Iceland. He also joined Churchill to issue a public document on Anglo-American goals and principles, which was called the Atlantic Charter. The Prime Minister privately found it "astonishing" that the United States, "still technically neutral," would "join with a belligerent Power in making such a declaration." Returning to London, Churchill informed his war Cabinet that Roosevelt had confided to him that he would become "more and more provocative" and "if the Germans did not like it, they could attack the American forces." In September, near Iceland, a German sub fired torpedoes at the US destroyer *Greer.* Even though they missed, the President announced that should there be another such incident, American commanders would "shoot on sight."

At that moment, Roosevelt was considering whether to confer with the Japanese Prime Minister, Prince Fumimaro Konoye, in Alaska, for an effort to make peace in the Pacific. While the President and the American people were primarily absorbed by the crisis in Europe, his nation had been edging toward confrontation with Japan.

* * *

DURING HIS FIRST term, Roosevelt had embraced the doctrine created by Henry Stimson, while he was Hoover's Secretary of

State, that the United States would oppose any change to the territory of China or Japan that came by force. Abiding by the nation's isolationist mood, however, the President did little in 1937 when Japan attacked China. In July 1940, when the militant Tokyo regime threatened Dutch, French, and British colonial possessions in Southeast Asia, Roosevelt imposed an embargo against Japan, forbidding many exports of oil, gasoline, steel, and iron—a significant action, since at the time, Japan relied on the United States for 80 percent of its petroleum. That fall, Japan made an alliance with Hitler and Mussolini.

In early 1941, worried about the burden of a potential two-front war, the President authorized Secretary of State Hull to explore a détente with the Japanese envoy in Washington, Admiral Kichisaburō Nomura. Benefiting from information gained from deciphering Japan's diplomatic code, Roosevelt privately observed that inside the Tokyo government "the Japs are having a real drag-down and knock-out fight . . . trying to decide which way to jump." He added, "It is terribly important for the control of the Atlantic for us to keep peace in the Pacific. I simply have not got enough Navy to go round."

Then the President presided over a tragicomedy of errors. In July, although opting against a full gasoline and oil embargo, he increased the pressure on Japan by freezing its financial holdings in the United States. This would require the Japanese government to appeal for a new export license (which Roosevelt privately said he was "inclined to grant") each time it wanted resources from America. Such export licenses were officially the responsibility of Assistant Secretary of State Dean Acheson, who was disgruntled that the President had not imposed a complete ban on oil exports to Japan.* Acheson doubted that such a move would risk moving Tokyo toward war because any "rational" Japanese would know that an attack on the United States would bring "disaster for his country."

While Roosevelt was away seeing Churchill in Newfoundland,

---

* Acheson did not enjoy working under Roosevelt, later writing in his memoirs that he did not find it "gratifying to receive the easy greeting which milord might give a promising stable boy and tug one's forelock in return."

the insubordinate Acheson decided to impose his own, self-authorized ban on Japanese export licenses, which amounted to an oil embargo against Tokyo. By the time Roosevelt discovered Acheson's caprice in September, he feared that publicly reversing it would allow critics to charge him with appeasing Japan.* The result was precisely what the President had not wanted—an effective halt to trade between Japan and America. Roosevelt's Ambassador in Tokyo, Joseph Grew, who had been his Groton classmate, warned that the impending "vicious circle of reprisals and counter reprisals" would bring "eventual war" with Japan.

With Japan's oil supplies declining rapidly and its government wary of the American naval buildup in the Pacific, Prime Minister Konoye pressed for a summit with Roosevelt, saying, "Time is of the essence." But Stimson and other hawks, who were concerned about the prospect of the President improvising in private, pressed him to refuse. That October, Konoye was ousted in favor of the more militant Hideki Tōjō. The following month, Roosevelt asked Secretary Hull to make sure that his Washington talks with Nomura did not "deteriorate" and "precipitate a crisis." The Japanese, however, rejected American offers of a six-month standstill. During the final week of November, the disheartened President warned his military advisers and Hull that the United States was "likely" to be assaulted soon. As Stimson told his diary, Roosevelt noted that "the Japanese are notorious for attacking without warning," and the question was "how to maneuver them into firing the first shot without too much danger to ourselves."

On Thursday, November 27, 1941, General George Marshall wired Walter Short in Honolulu that "negotiations with Japanese appear to be terminated" and "hostile action possible at any moment." If hostilities were unavoidable, "the United States desires that Japan commit the first overt act." In the meantime, the General should "undertake such reconnaissance and other measures as you deem necessary," but not "alarm

---

* One poll in September 1941 found that Americans, by 67 percent, believed it was wiser to risk war than let Japan grow more powerful.

the civilian population." Admiral Stark's message to both Short and Kimmel was more blunt: "This dispatch is to be considered a war warning. . . . An aggressive move by Japan is expected in the next few days." Stark speculated that Japan might wage "an amphibious expedition against either the Philippines, Thai or Kra Peninsula or possibly toward Borneo."* He ordered Kimmel to execute "an appropriate defensive deployment" and "appropriate measures against sabotage."

General Short was not alarmed by the words "war warning." To him, they suggested only "that Japan was going to attack someplace." His milquetoast reply to Marshall should have alerted his superior that Short did not comprehend that Pearl Harbor was now in danger of a serious attack, but Marshall made no effort to set him straight. (The upright Marshall, willing to take blame where he deserved it, later acknowledged, "That was my opportunity to intervene, and I did not do it.") Thus Short merely moved the forces in Hawaii from their existing Number 2 alert (against an attack from the skies) to a Number 1 (defense against local sabotage).

The General was not privy to the valuable intelligence that flowed from US intercepts—through the highly secret operation called MAGIC—of coded Japanese cable traffic called PURPLE, which included messages between the foreign ministry in Tokyo and the consulate in Honolulu. This source offered clues that the Japanese were planning a spectacular surprise attack against US forces in Hawaii. The highest officials in Washington feared that sharing this intelligence with local commanders might jeopardize MAGIC by tipping off Tokyo that the United States had broken its code, after which it would be changed.

Kimmel and Short saw the rumors in the Honolulu papers. On November 30, the *Honolulu Advertiser* warned, "Japanese May Strike Over Weekend." But the two commanders kept presuming that whatever Tokyo tried would be relatively modest. When someone proposed sending Army planes to strengthen the defense of Wake and Midway

---

* Thailand's Kra Peninsula was considered a potential staging point for a Japanese invasion of Malaya.

Islands, Short's air chief, Colonel James Mollison, said, "Our mission is to protect Oahu, and shipping out these Army planes will lessen our capability to do so." Kimmel asked, "Why are you so worried about this? Do you think we are in danger of attack?" Mollison replied, "The Japanese have such a capability." Kimmel scoffed: "Capability, yes, but possibility?" He asked his war plans aide Captain Charles McMorris, "What do you think about the prospects of a Japanese air attack?" McMorris assured him, "None, absolutely none."

Convinced that the greatest plausible danger to Pearl Harbor was probably a surprise attack by Japanese subs against his ships, Kimmel did not send Navy planes off on long-range missions to watch the skies for Japanese bombers. Instead he stepped up efforts to make sure that in case the Japanese landed a major blow on the Philippines or someplace else, the US sailors and ships of Pearl Harbor would be well poised to retaliate. Short's response was, in retrospect, even worse: he ordered the Army's planes at Pearl Harbor to be massed together. This might have made them easier to protect from lurking local saboteurs; but if there should be an aerial attack, the force would be easily and quickly destroyed.

On Wednesday, December 3, Admiral Stark wired Kimmel from Washington that Tokyo's foreign ministry had sent "urgent instructions" to key diplomatic posts "to destroy most of their codes and ciphers at once and to burn all other important and secret documents." This was a clear signal that the Japanese were on the verge of war. But Kimmel did not bother to share Stark's warning with his Army counterpart, and Pearl Harbor was left grievously unprepared.

* * *

O N THE DISMAL night of Sunday, December 7, after hearing the Pearl Harbor news, Americans stood vigil in front of the White House. The American death toll would be 2,403, with about half that many wounded. More Americans would die at the hands of the Japanese attack than had perished in the entire War of 1812. After receiving the first report from Hawaii, the President had worked upstairs on his stamp collection, grimly telling his eldest son, James, "I'm trying to keep everything calm and quiet as I can." That evening, in a radio speech already scheduled, Eleanor Roosevelt confessed, "You cannot escape a clutch of fear at your heart." Roosevelt's Secret Service agent Mike Reilly noted that evening that the President's "chin stuck out about two feet in front of his knees, and he was the maddest Dutchman I, or anybody, ever saw."

In his upstairs oval study, at eight thirty, the President told his department secretaries that this was "the most serious Cabinet meeting since the spring of 1861," when Lincoln had discussed his response to the Confederate attack on Fort Sumter. With horror, Henry Stimson noted that "all the planes were in one place" at Pearl Harbor. Attorney General Francis Biddle thought Roosevelt looked "deeply shaken, graver than I had ever seen him." Secretary of Labor Frances Perkins felt that "a great change" had come over the Commander-in-Chief. Before Pearl Harbor, he had been "tense, worried" and "carrying an awful burden of decision." But now "his terrible moral problem had been resolved."

Roosevelt's closest friend in the Cabinet was his Hudson Valley neighbor, Henry Morgenthau Jr., Secretary of the Treasury. When Morgenthau went home, he told his wife, Elinor, that when Americans acquired "full knowledge" of what had occurred at Pearl Harbor, "it is going to be the most terrific shock this country has ever had." Morgenthau was outraged: "We have always been led to believe that the Navy was our first line of defense and Hawaii was impregnable. . . . The whole fleet was in this little Pearl Harbor base. The whole fleet was there! . . . They will never be able to explain it."

After his Cabinet departed, Roosevelt welcomed leaders of the House and Senate to the same room. Amid his beloved naval prints and artifacts of earlier American wars, he told his guests,

> A great fleet of Japanese bombers bombed our ships in Pearl Harbor, and bombed all of our airfields. . . . This afternoon, Guam

was being bombed by two squadrons of Japanese planes. . . . Wake Island was also attacked. . . . We believe that Manila was attacked. . . . I do not know what is happening at the present time, whether a night attack is on or not. It isn't quite dark yet in Hawaii. . . . Of course, it is a terrible disappointment to be President in time of war. . . . We have reason to believe that the Germans have told the Japanese that if Japan declares war, they will too.

Despite this awful moment of national emergency, the Chairman of the Senate Foreign Relations Committee, Tom Connally, frankly told Roosevelt that he "could not understand why we were taken off our guard" at Pearl Harbor. Connally kept asking, "Mr. President, how could this thing happen?"

* * *

ROOSEVELT KNEW THAT his war leadership would be damaged from the start if Americans condemned him for the Pearl Harbor disaster—for letting so many ships be lined up like sitting ducks or, far worse, for having deliberately encouraged an assault that would move heretofore reluctant Americans to demand involvement in war. Thus he quickly acted to make sure that serious blame was placed not on himself, Stimson, Marshall, or Knox, who would now have to lead the American fight, but on the commanders in Honolulu. Ten days after the attack, Kimmel and Short were abruptly stripped of their posts. From Missouri, an ex-judge wrote Kimmel, "You would do America a favor if you would shoot yourself." Both officers received death threats.

To establish who in the American government should be censured for Pearl Harbor, the President appointed a commission. He hoped that this would ward off calls from Republicans for a freewheeling congressional investigation. Supposedly Roosevelt's panel was independent, but, in fact, there was no possibility that he would grant it much leeway to implicate him in the Pearl Harbor disaster. If its report should indict him for mistakes or machinations that had thrust the United States into war, he and his entourage would be the target of vast public fury. Thus it was in his interest to make sure that the focus was on Short and Kimmel.

To chair the commission, Roosevelt selected the Supreme Court Justice Owen Roberts—an excellent choice for a President who wished to make sure it did not get out of control. Roberts's exalted position would bring prestige to its verdict and, as a Herbert Hoover appointee, he could not be impugned as a partisan trying to give Roosevelt political cover. Roberts was known to be unassertive, which made him subject to the President's importuning—especially at the start of a war that, at this moment, the United States was losing. The Justice was also discreet, as was later demonstrated when, after leaving the court in 1945, he destroyed his official papers.

Roberts did not insist that Roosevelt, as a potential key figure in his inquiry, be kept at arm's length. He met privately with the President at the White House on December 16, the day the commission was announced, and at least twice more, during its seven weeks of deliberation, when they could not have avoided discussing what its report would say. In mid-January 1942, Roosevelt's longtime friend Justice Felix Frankfurter, who had been a fount of confidential, shrewd advice on politics and personnel throughout the New Deal, suggested in a letter ("Dear Frank") about his colleague Roberts, "that you get him alone, and not with the other members of his Board, to tell you of things that have no proper place in their report." Frankfurter assured him that Roberts "is not only—thank God!—very modest. He is also truly shy."

In late January, the Roberts Commission issued its report, which spared Roosevelt and assigned primary blame for the Hawaii catastrophe to "dereliction of duty" by Kimmel and Short—who had refused to "confer and cooperate," and whose "errors of judgment were the effective causes" of the attack—while conceding that the two officers had not been adequately informed by Washington of the imminence of war. Stimson told his diary that if Short and Kimmel were allowed simply to retire, "it might give the impression that we were trying to let off these people without punishment because we felt guilty ourselves." He noted Roosevelt's desire to "wait about a week," and then accept the two men's retirements with a pointed warning that they might yet be court-martialed, which could not be done now "without the disclosure of military secrets." Demoted to Major General, Short resigned from the Army and took a minor role as traffic chief at a Ford Motor war plant in Dallas; he died of heart disease in 1949. Reduced to two stars, Admiral Kimmel quit the Navy to work for a Marine engineering firm in New York, living, it was said, in "suspended disgrace."

After the Roberts Commission verdict was issued, Kimmel wrote Admiral Stark, who was once his close friend, that he wished he had been "smarter than I was" about what might happen at Pearl Harbor. He did not "wish to embarrass the government." But he warned that "my crucifixion before the public has about reached the limit." Noting that "irresponsible people all over the country" were "threatening to kill me," Kimmel asked Stark to have the War Department "do nothing further to inflame the public against me. . . . You must appreciate that the beating I have taken leaves very little that can be added to my burden." In his letter, Kimmel also made a veiled threat that if pushed too far, he might one day implicate his superiors in the Pearl Harbor imbroglio: "I have kept my mouth shut and propose to do so as long as it is humanly possible."

In 1944, Kimmel's thirty-one-year-old son Manning, a Navy submarine officer in the Pacific, died in action. Furious at Roosevelt, the ex-Admiral cried, "That son-of-a-bitch killed my son!" That same year, the grieving father learned new facts about how the President's high command had broken the Japanese code to obtain tantalizing clues that the Japanese might attack Pearl Harbor. Kimmel complained that "they never sent me a damn thing that told the true story." His son Edward later recalled that his father now "changed from a very dejected, downtrodden man into a fighting tiger." At the end of 1944, Stark wrote Kimmel of his "satisfaction" that the ex-Admiral would not be court-martialed. In draft replies, which he did not send, Kimmel roared back, "You betrayed the officers and the men of the Fleet by not giving them a fighting chance for their lives" and "you betrayed me by not giving me information you knew I was entitled to." Kimmel wrote that Stark should "never communicate with me again" so that "my memory may not be refreshed of one so despicable as you." He added, "May God forgive you for what you have done to me, for I never will."

Kimmel fought in vain to regain his old military rank, and for exoneration. His son Thomas observed, "You couldn't talk to him for fifteen minutes without getting back to Pearl Harbor." In 1949, the ex-Admiral started to write a Pearl Harbor memoir, but, as he wrote a friend, the process made him "so emotionally upset I had to stop." The next year, he suffered a massive heart attack. In *Admiral Kimmel's Story*, finally published in 1955, the author wrote, "I cannot excuse those in authority in Washington for what they did. . . . They must answer on the Day of Judgment like any other criminal." In 1966, Kimmel told a reporter, "My principal occupation—what's kept me alive—is to expose the entire Pearl Harbor affair." Hard of hearing, he went on to loudly claim that Roosevelt, Marshall, and their circle had "deliberately betrayed" the men in Hawaii, and "made me the scapegoat. They wanted to get the United States into the war. F.D.R. was the architect of the whole business." Kimmel said, "It's obvious he wanted the Japanese to attack." In defiance of fact, he contended that "all incriminating documents have been destroyed," adding that he didn't know "whether the whole story will ever get out."

After Kimmel died in 1968, he was interred at the Naval Academy in Annapolis, under a gravestone defiantly emblazoned with four stars. Knowing that Marshall had been buried at Arlington National Cemetery, and that Stark (who died in 1972) would be too, the bitter old man had written his son Thomas, "I don't care where I am buried so long as it is not in Arlington."*

* * *

---

* After Kimmel's death, his descendants took up his cause. Thomas Kimmel complained in 1982, "The Navy's behavior has been outrageous" and "You talk about the scandal of Watergate—this scandal is worse and should be told." In 2003, Kimmel's grandson, also named Thomas, appeared at a conference in Washington, DC, cosponsored by the Holocaust denier Willis Carto. Joining speakers on "the power of the Zionist lobby" and "the censored history of the Luftwaffe," the young Kimmel showed slides as he argued for his grandfather's innocence.

O N MONDAY MORNING, December 8, 1941, Roosevelt awoke at seven thirty. Henry Morgenthau had ordered the Secret Service to double its guard around the President.* He warned that "somebody could put twenty men in a five-ton truck, crash in there and take over the White House." But when he asked for permission to surround the Executive Mansion with tanks, Roosevelt would accept only Army machine gunners. At midday, the President was driven to Capitol Hill.

When Roosevelt had first dictated his address asking Congress for a war declaration against Japan, he had called December 7 "a date which will live in world history."† Then, shrewdly, he had deleted the final two words of this phrase in favor of the more pungent and memorable "infamy"—a noun that Theodore Roosevelt had employed in no less than five of his messages to Congress. Now, in the same House chamber where he and Eleanor had watched Wilson deliver his war address in 1917, Roosevelt asked the Joint Session to "declare that since the unprovoked and dastardly attack by Japan . . . a state of war has existed between the United States and the Japanese Empire." In his second-to-last sentence, suggested by Harry Hopkins, he vowed, "We will gain the inevitable triumph, so help us God." The First Lady had thoughtfully invited Edith Wilson to sit next to her in the President's box; the scene filled Eleanor with "a curious sense of repetition."

Wilson's war appeal had provoked four days of congressional debate. This time, there was almost none. The Japanese bombers at Pearl Harbor had united most of the country. On the Senate floor, Arthur Vandenberg said, "To the enemy we answer—you have unsheathed the sword and, by it, you shall die." Acting within thirty-three minutes, the Senate approved Roosevelt's request by 82 to 0. In the House, the Republican Minority Leader, Joseph Martin of Massachusetts, asked for there to be not "a single dissenting vote." His colleagues endorsed a war declaration

---

* Until the Department of Homeland Security was founded in 2002, the Secret Service was part of the Treasury.

† Roosevelt had wisely refused the advice of Secretary Hull to deliver a long speech that recounted his diplomacy with Japan before Pearl Harbor.

by 388 to 1. The lone dissenter was the pacifist Montana Republican Jeannette Rankin, who had also voted against the declaration requested by Wilson. "As a woman," she now felt able to explain, "I can't go to war." Vilified for her choice, Rankin was forced to hide in a telephone booth from an angry, shouting, shoving throng before police rushed her out of the Capitol.

Returning to the Oval Office, with Senate and House leaders standing above his shoulders, Roosevelt signed the document of war at 4:10 p.m. He wired Churchill, "Today all of us are in the same boat with you and the people of the Empire and it is a ship which will not and cannot be sunk." Three days later, Germany and Italy declared war against the United States, and, at Roosevelt's request, Congress responded in kind. With a minor exception the following year, Pearl Harbor would prove to be the last time in American history that a President ever asked Congress for a declaration of war.*

---

* In 1942, Roosevelt asked to expand the American war effort to include Bulgaria, Hungary, and Romania.

CHAPTER THIRTEEN

"The Survival War"

Now, as the nation embarked on its most perilous war, Franklin Roosevelt was resolved, unlike Wilson in 1917, to constantly explain the issues at stake, his strategy, and how the conflict was unfolding. Although Pearl Harbor had united most of the country behind the war, the enemy was on the offensive in the Pacific. For the first time since the War of 1812, the United States was facing an extended period of defeat by a foreign military force. Roosevelt was worried about the damage of those setbacks to national morale. During this war, unlike every previous President waging a major conflict, he could rely on radio to broadcast his statements to a vast audience.

Americans were lucky to have a Commander-in-Chief who was not a neophyte. As Assistant Secretary of the Navy, Roosevelt had scrutinized both Wilson's accomplishments and his blunders. He had heard the private running commentary of Cousin Theodore, who had filled his ears about what Wilson was doing wrong. TR had harped on Wilson's wartime failure to reach out to Congress, especially to the opposing party.

On Tuesday, January 6, 1942, the coldest day thus far that winter, amid a vicious wind, the somber President arrived at the Capitol to deliver his State of the Union message. Normally Roosevelt wore a gray frock coat for this occasion; this time he was dressed in black. At

12:32 p.m., on the arm of his aide General Edwin "Pa" Watson, he slowly entered the House chamber, using his steel-braced legs, as members leapt to their feet for a full minute of applause.

Speaking more slowly than usual, Roosevelt told Congress that "Japan's scheme of conquest goes back half a century." That plan was to subjugate "all the peoples in the Far East" and dominate the Pacific by controlling "the western coasts of North, Central and South America." But Japan's dreams, he said, were modest compared with "the gargantuan aspirations of Hitler and his Nazis" to dominate "the whole earth." The Nazis sought a new, worldwide "pagan religion," under which "the Holy Bible and the Cross of Mercy would be displaced by *Mein Kampf* and the swastika and the naked sword." Now "Hitler and his Italian and Japanese chessmen" would face "superior forces" that would "strike at the common enemy."* He noted that twenty-six nations stood against the Axis Powers. To a resounding ovation, he vowed, "The militarists of Berlin and Tokyo started this war, but the massed, angered forces of common humanity will *finish* it."

"Every available plant and tool" must be converted to war production. The nation required 60,000 new planes and 45,000 new tanks in the next year, as well as 125,000 planes and 75,000 tanks the year after that. The same was true of ships, antiaircraft guns, and other "implements of war." Attracting the loudest response, Roosevelt said he hoped his statistics "will give the Japanese and the Nazis a little idea of just what they accomplished in the attack at Pearl Harbor." Building this arsenal would require spending more than half the nation's income, as well as higher taxes and "cutting luxuries and other non-essentials." Leveling with Americans, the President went on, "We have already tasted defeat. We may suffer further setbacks. We must face the fact of a hard war, a long war, a bloody war, a costly war." The alternative was "a world of tyranny and cruelty and serfdom."

Afterward Speaker of the House Sam Rayburn proclaimed, "Of all his great speeches, this is the greatest." Wendell Willkie called the

---

* Roosevelt's reference to the "chessmen" brought a first, modest burst of laughter from the audience.

address "magnificent," but warned that the proposed plan could not be achieved by Roosevelt's "present organization and administrative methods." That same week, Americans told Gallup that they approved of the President's job performance by 84 to 9 percent.

In late February, before Roosevelt gave a fireside chat on radio, his press secretary, Stephen Early, asked Americans to consult globes or world maps while the President described the course of the war. Maps were published in newspapers, and stores sold out of their globes. The President told his listeners, "Your government has unmistakable confidence in your ability to hear the worst, without flinching or losing heart." He pledged to keep "nothing from you, except information that will help the enemy in his attempt to destroy us"—and asked Americans to "pay little attention to the rumor-mongers and the poison peddlers in our midst." The struggle they were entering was "different from all other wars of the past." Victory would require "warfare in terms of every continent, every island, every sea, every air lane in the world."

That spring, Roosevelt tried to devise a name for the new conflict. He feared that calling it the "Second World War" might link the struggle too closely to Wilson's venture, from which so many Americans still cringed. Thus, while speaking at the Pan American Union, he proposed "the Survival War": "That is what it comes pretty close to being—the survival of our civilization."*

* * *

DURING THE EARLY months of this war, Roosevelt committed a tragic offense against civil liberties—the forced removal of Japanese Americans. At that time, to be sure, no one knew where Japan might strike next. During a western trip the week after Pearl Harbor, Eleanor wrote Lorena Hickok that "we had an anxious trip out, fearing the West Coast was being bombed." Within two days of the assault on

---

* Gallup found that only 7 percent of Americans favored "the Survival War." Forty percent proposed either the "War of Freedom" or the "War of World Freedom." Others liked the "War of Liberty," the "Anti-Dictator War," or the "War for Humanity."

Hawaii, the Federal Bureau of Investigation (FBI), consulting its "Suspect Enemy Alien" lists, arrested more than 1,200 Japanese-born US residents, most on the West Coast and in Hawaii, as well as 620 Germans and 98 Italians who were not citizens. But unlike American residents born in Germany and Italy, many of Japanese ancestry suffered from a special problem: the race-conscious Immigration Act of 1924 would not allow them to become US citizens. And unlike the huge populations of German and Italian heritage, little more than a hundred thousand people came from Japan—and they were easily isolated; except for a few thousand, all resided west of the Rocky Mountains.

Before Christmas 1941, although the news was censored, the oil tanker *Montebello* had been sunk by a Japanese submarine off the California coast, and so had two freighters. Amid widespread anxiety that Japan would invade the West Coast, California's Attorney General, Earl Warren, warned that "the Japanese situation" in his state "may well be the Achilles' Heel of the entire civil defense effort," threatening "a repetition of Pearl Harbor." After dining with Warren in California, the influential columnist Walter Lippmann, who had advised Wilson during the 1919 Paris conference, warned of a "Fifth Column on the West Coast." The conservative columnist Westbrook Pegler called for US citizens of Japanese descent to be placed "under armed guard," and "to hell with habeas corpus until the danger is over." Fletcher Bowron, the Los Angeles Mayor, fired city workers of Japanese origin, claiming that "Lincoln, the mild-mannered man whose memory we regard with almost saint-like reverence, would make short work of rounding up the Japanese."

"We have to be tough," insisted the *San Francisco Chronicle*, "even if civil rights do take a beating for a time." Congressman John Rankin of Mississippi said, "This is a race war," demanding to "get rid of every Japanese, whether in Hawaii or the Mainland. . . . Damn them!" In San Francisco, Lieutenant General John DeWitt, commander of the Fourth Army, reported by telephone to Assistant Secretary of War John McCloy, "Out here, a Jap is a Jap to these people now." McCloy replied that if the "safety of the country" was in question, "why, the Constitution is just a scrap of paper to me."

J. Edgar Hoover, Director of the FBI, argued that the West Coast had "no Japanese problem" and warned Attorney General Biddle against "public hysteria."* Hoover wrote Biddle that demands for mass removal of citizens of Japanese heritage were "based primarily upon public and political pressure, rather than on factual data." Secretary Stimson complained into his diary that Hoover did not understand the "great potential danger" of the Japanese because he could not gain access to their "secret thoughts." Biddle, known as a friend of civil liberties, declined to say that removing US citizens from their homes would be unconstitutional.† He was only five months in office and bashful about standing up to the military. But he told the President that there was "no reason for mass evacuation." He also warned that some Americans on the West Coast would welcome the removal of Japanese citizens "from good farm land and the elimination of their competition." Eleanor Roosevelt implored her husband to forestall the removals so insistently that he asked her to stop raising the subject.

Stimson appealed for a meeting with Roosevelt on what he called the "West Coast matter," but was told that the President had larger problems to deal with. Instead, on February 11, the two men spoke by telephone. As Stimson recorded, he "fortunately" found Roosevelt "very vigorous" about the issue, and the President "told me to go ahead on the line that I thought the best." The next day, Biddle told Stimson he had "no doubt" that mass removal would be legal "if deemed essential from a military point of view." At Stimson's behest, McCloy wrote to DeWitt, "We have carte blanche to do what we want to, as far as the President is concerned. . . . He states there will probably be some repercussions, but it has got to be dictated by military necessity, but as he puts it, 'Be as reasonable as you can.' "

---

* One motive for Hoover's uncharacteristically large-minded counsel may have been that he would have more opportunities to expand the FBI's investigative reach if the Japanese Americans remained in their homes than if confined by barbed wire.

† Biddle's chief lawyers at Justice, Edward Ennis and James Rowe, told him that mass removal would be unconstitutional. Rowe asked Roosevelt's secretary, Grace Tully, to warn the chief that California officials would probably ask for "one of the great mass exoduses of history." But other legal advisers, including Benjamin Cohen, Oscar Cox, and Joseph Rauh, told Biddle that in time of war, the paramount issue must be national security.

On February 19, with the Attorney General at his side, Roosevelt signed Executive Order 9066. Drafted by Stimson and McCloy, using legalistic language, it authorized Stimson "to prescribe military areas" and decide "which any or all persons may be excluded" from them. The word "Japanese" was nowhere mentioned.

Eleanor Roosevelt was shocked by her husband's decision. Just before Pearl Harbor, she had assured Americans by radio that "no law-abiding aliens of any nationality would be discriminated against by the government." When the President opted to exile the Japanese Americans, she was caught by surprise and appalled. Her biographer Blanche Wiesen Cook wrote that the internment decision "marked a turning point in their relationship," after which the First Lady staked out more "emotional distance" from her husband. In public, however, she loyally explained that the Japanese Americans were being removed "both for their own safety and for the safety of the country."

Forced to defend the order, Biddle assured the press that habeas corpus would not be suspended in the affected regions, nor would there be martial law. Asked to suggest a precedent, the Attorney General lamely recalled that during World War I, President Wilson had directed that "nobody could move in the air without a permit." But Biddle conceded that never before had the United States created a plan that might lead to this kind of mass evacuation. He claimed, "The move has been taken largely for the protection of the Japanese themselves." The *Baltimore Sun* wrote that there must be "advance safeguards" against the "treachery" of some Japanese Americans, who "may use the privileges of citizenship against the Republic."

The following month, Japanese American citizens and aliens, told to take "only what you can carry," started being moved by train and bus to makeshift assembly centers. That June, America won the Battle of Midway, reducing the chance that Japanese ships could attack the West Coast in large numbers. Although the chief rationale for the internment was fading, more than a hundred thousand evacuees were taken to barracks in ten newly built camps in California, Arizona, Wyoming, Utah, Idaho, Colorado, and Arkansas, with eight-person families confined to single rooms. Don Elberson, a conscientious objector assigned to meet some of the internees' trains, recalled, "It was too terrible to witness the pain in people's faces, too shameful for them to be seen in this degrading situation."*

After retiring as Chief Justice of the United States, Earl Warren was asked, in 1971, by an oral history interviewer about the evacuation, and he wept in mortification.† It was not until the 1980s that the US government confessed that the program had been an abomination, mocking its wartime contention that it was on the correct moral side of a war against racism and disrespect for personal liberties. Claiming that he had been "just a leg man" for Stimson, who had died in 1950, McCloy, at age eighty-six, testified before a congressional commission on the subject that the internment had been "reasonably undertaken and thoughtfully and humanely conducted." When he added that the war had "caused disruption in all our lives," the audience guffawed and booed—as they should have.

In 1988, President Ronald Reagan signed a bill that provided a formal apology and payments of $20,000 to survivors of the camps. The pugnacious, unrepentant McCloy told a friend that the hearings had been "a disgrace" and derided the idea of restitution. "Money, money, money!" McCloy exclaimed. "Why don't they dun the Japanese government? We didn't attack Pearl Harbor—they did!"

* * *

---

* When the Supreme Court ruled on curfews affecting Japanese Americans, in *Hirabayashi v. United States* (1942), Justice William O. Douglas wrote, "We cannot override the military judgment which lay behind these orders." Although concurring, Justice Frank Murphy noted that the majority opinion was "the first time that we have sustained a substantial restriction of the personal liberty of citizens of the United States based on the accident of race or ancestry," which "goes to the very brink of constitutional power." In *Korematsu v. United States* (1944), Hugo Black wrote that "compulsory exclusion" was "inconsistent with our basic governmental institutions," but since "our shores are threatened by hostile forces, the power to protect must be commensurate with the threatened danger." In a scorching dissent, Murphy replied that the exclusion "falls into the ugly abyss of racism." But the Court, in *Ex parte Endo* (1944), finally scotched the internment program for those deemed "loyal" to the United States, with Douglas writing that "he who is loyal is by definition not a spy or saboteur."

† Some later attributed the intensity of Chief Justice Warren's support for *Brown v. Board of Education,* the Supreme Court's 1954 decision desegregating the public schools, in part to penance for his complicity in the removal of the Japanese during wartime.

E LEANOR ROOSEVELT WAS deeply unsettled by the possibility that
at least one of their four sons would be killed in the war. Franklin Jr. and John had joined the Navy, Elliott a bomber squadron, and
Jimmy was a Marine. She wrote in her newspaper column, "My Day,"
that the exact whereabouts of three of her boys were "wrapped in mystery." On his Oval Office desk, the President kept little hand-colored
photographs, in a single frame, of their sons in uniform.

By the spring of 1942, some Americans were complaining about
Roosevelt's policy of "Atlantic First," which he had reaffirmed during
Winston Churchill's Christmas visit to the White House. Roosevelt told
General Marshall that crushing Japan would not vanquish Germany,
but "defeat of Germany means the defeat of Japan, probably without
firing a shot or losing a life." The President's critics argued that even
though American intervention had been provoked by an attack in the
Pacific, he was so absorbed by the British and Soviet plight that he was
neglecting US forces waging the Battle of Bataan, under General Douglas MacArthur. "Send Ships to Aid MacArthur Now" demanded the
New York Journal American, a Hearst tabloid, calling the Pacific commander "the greatest fighting general America has produced since the
Civil War."* But when the Gallup Poll asked who was the chief enemy
in this war, Americans said Germany over Japan by 50 to 25 percent.

Congresswoman Mary Norton, a Democrat from New Jersey, advised the President to make more frequent use of radio to defend himself. Roosevelt replied,

> From now on, for the duration of the war, there are going to be
> periods of hysteria, misinformation, volcanic eruptions, etc., and
> if I start the practice of going on the air to answer each one, the
> value of my going on the air will soon disappear. . . . For the sake
> of not becoming a platitude to the public, I ought not to appear
> oftener than once every five or six weeks. I am inclined to think

---

* This controversy was reflected in Paramount's motion picture *Holiday Inn*, starring Bing Crosby
and Fred Astaire, which premiered that summer. In a patriotic World War II musical tableau celebrating Independence Day, MacArthur was given equal prominence with Roosevelt.

that in England Churchill, for a while, talked too much and I don't want to do that.

Roosevelt had many allies on Capitol Hill, some of long standing, and he kept in close, jocular contact with them. For instance, Senator Carter Glass of Virginia complained to him, by letter, of a federal effort to acquire twenty-five acres next to Arlington National Cemetery, which would deprive its home county of tax income. With dark humor, Roosevelt replied that government purchase of the land "will bring a lot more people into Arlington County at once," although if "it is used as a cemetery, the later occupants will contribute only headstones!"

The President knew how to fend off congressional challenges. Three weeks after Pearl Harbor, Senator Arthur Vandenberg, Republican from Michigan, a prewar isolationist, had proposed a freewheeling House and Senate Committee on the Conduct of the War, resembling that of Civil War times, which had so nettled Lincoln. Roosevelt did not publicly denounce the premise of such a panel, as Wilson had. Instead he slathered on the syrup, writing Vandenberg that he would be "delighted" to cooperate, noting that "since war came to us," Congress had "given great comfort to all who believe in our political system." But out of public view, the President maneuvered to ensure that there would be no broad-gauged watchdog committee.*

Roosevelt's friend Justice Frankfurter counseled him to create an apparatus to ensure "centralized execution of the President's will." Emulating Wilson, the President established a War Production Board, chaired by the ex–Sears Roebuck chief Donald Nelson. Alf Landon complained that the President was leading the country to "totalitarian collectivism," treating the war "as just another political, alphabetical project." But Herbert Hoover, even though he had been Roosevelt's harsh political

---

* In January 1943, when Republicans revived this proposal, the historian T. Harry Williams wrote a letter to the *New York Times* warning that the committee of Lincoln's era had turned out to be "the most powerful body ever created by Congress in our wartime history" and "its interference with the military machine had highly unfortunate results."

foe since their showdown in 1932, told a New York audience that "to win total war" the Chief Executive must be granted some "dictatorial" powers, although he warned that the likely result would be "just plain Fascist economics."

After more than a decade of the Great Depression, Roosevelt now had to deal with inflation, brought on by a surging war economy. He warned Congress that "our standard of living will have to come down" and contended that no American should enjoy an after-tax income of $25,000 per year. The white-shoe Republican *New York Herald Tribune* called this argument "a blatant piece of demagoguery."* The President believed that when financing his war, Wilson had accepted too much borrowing, which had fueled inflation. This time, Roosevelt sought higher taxes—including an excess-profits tax that would "prevent defense profiteering" and large new taxes for the wealthy—as well as wage and price controls. But throughout the summer of 1942, the Democratic House and Senate resisted the President's demand.

On Labor Day Monday, September 7, Roosevelt wrote to Congress that if it did not act before October, he would move on his own, motivated by "an inescapable responsibility" to ensure "that the war effort is no longer imperiled by threat of economic chaos," which "makes the use of executive power far more essential than in any previous war." In Lincoln's spirit, he added, "When the war is won, the powers under which I act automatically revert to the people, to whom they belong."†

That evening at Hyde Park, he explained his ultimatum during a fireside chat, delivered from his pale green office in his new fieldstone library, built on the family estate. Sitting underneath a naval painting and next to a portrait of his mother, Roosevelt told radio listeners, "Wars are not won by people who are concerned primarily with their own comfort . . . and their own pocketbooks. . . . We need not leave it to historians of the future to answer the question whether we are

---

* The figure mentioned was equal to about $375,000 seventy-five years later.

† The historian Arthur Schlesinger Jr. much later called Roosevelt's demand the "most notorious claim to unilateral authority" of his presidency.

tough enough to meet this unprecedented challenge. . . . The answer is yes."* The Wisconsin Senator Robert La Follette Jr., son of Wilson's old foe, carped that Roosevelt had "placed a pistol at the head of Congress." Senator Robert Taft of Ohio called the President's defiant talk "so revolutionary and so dangerous that I cannot permit it to go unchallenged." But, unwilling to be viewed as an impediment to the war effort, the Democratic House and Senate gave Roosevelt most of what he wanted, including a peak wartime income tax rate of 88 percent.[†]

That fall, under supervision by the President and Colonel Leslie Groves of the Army Corps of Engineers, the Philadelphia contractor John McShain was constructing a vast new home for the Department of War, which, when completed, would be the world's largest office building. Moving from what had been called the State, War, and Navy Building, immediately west of the White House, Stimson and his top echelon had camped out in the Munitions Building, a temporary structure built during the Great War, next to what was now the Lincoln Memorial's reflecting pool.[‡] This and sister office buildings, jammed onto the site, had been built under Assistant Secretary of the Navy Franklin Roosevelt, who, at first, had recommended a hideous wood design so that officials would demand their swift demolition after the Great War.[§]

When a new War Department headquarters was built on C Street in Foggy Bottom, it was immediately found to be too small for that

---

* For wartime security reasons, the President's location was not announced, allowing many listeners to presume incorrectly that he was speaking from the White House.

† The President wrote Eleanor that the new tax law would so reduce the income from his presidential salary that they should try to reduce the White House food bill: "Next year the taxes on $75,000 will leave me only about $30,000 net and SOMETHING HAS TO BE DONE!" He suggested smaller portions at meals: "I know of no instance where anybody has taken a second help—except occasionally when I do—and it would be much better if I did not take a second help anyway."

‡ Built in the 1870s and 1880s, the old State-War-Navy edifice was renamed for Dwight Eisenhower in 1999 to honor his years working there while in the Army. As President, however, Ike had considered the building an eyesore and sought to demolish it.

§ Roosevelt's tactic failed. Ultimately the "tempos" lingered until President Richard Nixon ordered the final ones razed in the early 1970s.

epoch of rearmament and impending world war. Thus the President had approved hasty construction of the immense Pentagon, across the Potomac River, its shape resembling US forts of old, such as McHenry and Sumter. Built on a sixteen-month rush schedule, the poured-concrete structure was intended to use a minimum of steel; in order to save the material for national defense, ramps were substituted for steel elevators. When Roosevelt toured the building in May 1942, he asked why there were so many washrooms and was told that Virginia law required segregated facilities. The new Pentagon was a symbol of the fact that when this war was done, the United States would have to maintain a large defense establishment.* With the early American aversion to a large standing Army dispelled, such a development would strengthen the presidency of the future.

Roosevelt had also authorized Colonel Groves and the Army Corps to proceed with the secret Manhattan Project, which was rushing to perfect an atomic weapon. If this effort succeeded, outpacing a rival secret enterprise by the Germans, it could ensure an Allied victory and establish the United States as the postwar world's overwhelming military power. An atomic bomb, with its potential to kill millions of human beings, would endow future Presidents of the United States with extraordinary new authority.

✳ ✳ ✳

NOVEMBER 1942 WOULD bring the first national wartime midterm election since World War I. Pollsters found many voters angry about rationing, shortages, government bureaucracy, what seemed like Allied foot-dragging in striking back at the Nazis, and naval setbacks in the Pacific. The *New Republic* claimed that November's balloting would be the most crucial since the Civil War. Roosevelt told reporters

---

* As late as January 1945, Roosevelt recorded his quaint private hope that after the war, the Pentagon would become a military archive and the War Department could return to smaller digs in Foggy Bottom, "if we get a decent peace."

that such a judgment was "perfectly silly" because this time, unlike 1864, both political parties shared a passion to fight the war through to the end.

After an air raid against the US Navy base at Alaska's Dutch Harbor in June, a Japanese flotilla had established itself in the Aleutian Islands. Aroused by frenzied newspaper coverage about this invasion of US territory, some Americans feared that from its new foothold the enemy could bomb the West Coast. Senator A. B. "Happy" Chandler, Democrat from Kentucky, called the occupation "a direct threat" to Americans: "Whatever it takes, we must get those fellows out of there."

Having vetoed an effort to retake Europe that year—the Allied armies were unready for that—Roosevelt and Churchill had secretly agreed to launch Anglo-American troops into battle against the Axis in North Africa, under Operation Torch. When General Marshall briefed the President on its progress, Roosevelt pretended to pray, joking, "Please make it before Election Day." (When Marshall later told the President that they needed more time, he found that Roosevelt "never said a word" of objection and "was very courageous.")

The President remembered the backlash against Wilson's public appeal to endorse his war leadership in 1918 by voting Democratic. Instead, with Eleanor present for the early part of the railroad journey, that fall he took a two-week, 8,754-mile "nonpolitical" inspection tour of military installations, war factories, and naval hospitals. Wartime security compelled the entire trip to be kept secret until Roosevelt was safely back at the White House. The President asked the train's engineer to keep down the speed, knowing that his paralyzed legs and unpadded rear end could not protect him from jolts.

Roosevelt stopped first at a Chrysler tank factory in Detroit, rolling into the plant in his beloved open-topped Lincoln parade car, called the "Sunshine Special," with bulletproof windows that were rolled up to shield him from the side. Henry Ford showed him B-24 bombers being assembled by workers at Ford Motor Company at Willow Run, Michigan, including "midgets," as they were called at the time, hired to work

German submarine attacks British cargo ship *Maplewood*, April 1917.

Woodrow Wilson asks Congress for war, April 1917.

Assistant Secretary of the Navy Franklin Roosevelt [second from right]
and other Wilson officials strive for fighting condition, August 1917.

Blindfolded, Wilson chooses capsule in draft lottery, September 1918.

Before Paris peace conference, Wilson calls on
King George V, December 1918.

With wounded Americans, Woodrow and Edith, aboard ship,
returning from Europe to America July 1919.

Wilson and his wife in St. Louis, September 1919, during his
doomed crusade for the League of Nations.

Senator Henry Cabot Lodge, foe of the League, chairing the Foreign
Relations Committee, with Warren Harding at left, 1919.

Pearl Harbor's Battleship Row under attack, Sunday, December 7, 1941.

Admiral Husband Kimmel, whom Franklin Roosevelt was eager to blame for the disaster at Pearl Harbor, shown in January 1941.

Looking every inch the war President, FDR during wartime inspection tour, 1942.

Eleanor Roosevelt visits Gila River internment camp, Arizona,
April 1943.

Roosevelt, Winston Churchill, and Joseph Stalin celebrate
Churchill's birthday in Tehran, November 1943.

Braving Nazi fire to land on the French coast, D-Day, June 6, 1944.

Roosevelt asks Congress to endorse a postwar United Nations,
March 1945, six weeks before his death.

North Koreans invade the South, 1950.

Reeling from the Korean surprise, Harry Truman walks near the
White House with Attorney General J. Howard McGrath and
Defense Secretary Louis Johnson, June 27, 1950.

Truman meets General Douglas MacArthur for the only
time of their lives, Wake Island, October 1950.

Soldiers view headlines reporting that Truman is pondering
atomic bomb for Korea, November 1950.

MacArthur to Congress, April 1951: "Why surrender military advantages to an enemy on the field?"

California Senator Richard Nixon brandishes telegrams demanding Truman's impeachment for firing MacArthur, April 1951.

Beleaguered by Korean War, Truman, with wife, Bess, announces that he will not seek reelection, March 1952.

Lyndon Johnson signing the Gulf of Tonkin Resolution,
August 1964.

Secretary of Defense Robert McNamara, August 1964, who
deceived Congress about the Tonkin attack.

Johnson and Lady Bird visit sailors injured in Vietnam,
Bethesda Naval Hospital, Maryland, October 1965.

Ambush of US cavalry battalion, Ia Drang Valley, Vietnam,
November 1965.

Johnson and Senator Robert Kennedy at a midterm
campaign stop, Long Island, as their conflict over
Vietnam grows, October 1966.

Johnson greets armed forces, Cam Ranh Bay, South Vietnam,
October 1966.

LBJ had himself driven across the Potomac to witness the march
on the Pentagon, October 1967.

Conflagration in the streets of Chicago,
Democratic National Convention, August 1968.

Johnson and his family watch Chicago convention on television
from his bedroom at the LBJ Ranch.

Still furious about Nixon's secret machinations against his Vietnam
peace efforts, Johnson faces the President-elect in the White
House elevator, December 1968.

World Trade Center, New York City, September 11, 2001.

George W. Bush, that evening, in the White House bunker,
with Chief of Staff Andrew Card, Vice President Dick Cheney,
and National Security Adviser Condoleezza Rice.

US Marines pull down statue of Saddam Hussein,
Baghdad, April 2003.

in difficult-to-reach spots on the planes.* Outside Chicago, the President was driven through the rain around the Great Lakes Naval Training Station and Camp Robert Smalls, established the previous spring by the segregated US Navy to train African American seamen for the first time.† There he stopped to listen to recruits sing a spiritual called "Travelin'." In a dispatch embargoed until Roosevelt's return, Merriman Smith of the United Press reported that the Commander-in-Chief had watched as "several hundred negro commando sailors ran their obstacle course, screaming like demons let loose."

In Milwaukee, one plant worker shouted, "God Almighty, it's the President!" At the shipyard in Bremerton, Washington, Roosevelt joked about the secrecy, saying, "You haven't seen me!" and "I am not really here." He later recalled that throughout his tour, he was happy to find that women were not merely doing "sewing-machine-type" work but operating heavy machinery. Other stops included Portland, San Francisco, San Diego, El Paso, San Antonio, New Orleans, and Fort Jackson, South Carolina. Stopping at Uvalde, in arid south Texas, Roosevelt welcomed his ex–Vice President, John Nance Garner, into his railroad car. Despite the rift that had moved Roosevelt to bounce "Cactus Jack" from his 1940 ticket, the Texan tousled the President's hair and both men grinned for photographers. Roosevelt told Garner he had heard that thanks to war production, everyone in Texas was "making a lot of money." After their brief visit, before driving away in his tiny car, Garner said, "God bless you, Boss."

While riding the rails, the President read W. L. White's new bestseller *They Were Expendable,* about four US Navy officers in the Battle of the Philippines. Among his party were two adoring guests—his

---

* That evening, Eleanor teased him about his "affectionate manner" toward the reactionary Ford, patting his knee. Franklin replied that it must have worked, because Ford had concurred with everything he said.

† In 1862, during the Civil War, Robert Smalls had supervised the seizure of a Confederate transport and delivered it to the Union's naval blockade, thereby liberating himself and his seamen, as well as their families, from slavery. His achievement helped to inspire President Lincoln to admit African Americans to the Union's armed forces. During Reconstruction, Smalls was elected a Republican Congressman from South Carolina. His great-grandson was trained for World War II at the camp bearing his name.

purple-haired cousin Laura "Polly" Delano and his Hudson Valley friend and distant relative, Margaret "Daisy" Suckley, who was working as an archivist in his library. Daisy was moved into Eleanor's stateroom after the First Lady's departure. She told her diary, "We all get along peacefully, & of course we all just think of him, to make it nice for him." Without mentioning Eleanor, Suckley boasted that the President had told her and Polly that he had never taken a more "restful & satis-factory" trip, which she took as "a great compliment to us for not having controversial talk."

Once the Commander-in-Chief was back at the White House, his "secret" tour was heavily publicized. Republican Congressman Charles Halleck of Indiana complained that the President's "alleged inspection trips" always seemed to precede elections. In a fireside chat about the journey, Roosevelt told Americans that "when we drove unannounced down the middle aisle of a great plant," workers were "arguing as to whether that fellow in the straw hat was really the President," and the first to look up from their work "were the men, not the women."

On Election Day, Republicans almost took over the House of Representatives, reducing the Democratic margin to an advantage of 222 to 209. They also won 9 seats in the Senate, where the Democrats retained a majority of 57 to 38 seats. Now there would be fewer Democrats in Congress than at any time since Roosevelt had become President. The young Congressman Lyndon Johnson of Texas observed, with chagrin, "All the boys who went down were Roosevelt men."

Some blamed the Democrats' loss on low turnout and the absence of younger voters, many of whom were away at war or hard at work on assembly lines. The *Chattanooga Times* explained that voters "exacted re-venge in the farm states" for Roosevelt's anti-inflation bill. The *Journal* of Portland, Oregon, felt that Democrats had suffered from "the cumula-tive annoyances that the restraints of war impose upon a people." Joseph Kennedy, smarting after the President had rebuffed his efforts to gain a prominent role helping to run the war, wrote his friend the British pub-lisher Lord Beaverbrook that "dissatisfaction is rife and lack of confidence in the leaders and in Congress is definitely high," adding that "short of a miracle, the New Deal is finished." Asked by White House reporters

whether his "very close majority" in the Senate would now make a difference, Roosevelt responded, "Why should it? I assume that the Congress of
the United States is in favor of winning this war, just as the President is."*

The following Sunday, at Shangri-La, the rustic presidential retreat
in Maryland, Roosevelt watched films of his western inspection tour
and a new British picture, *Next of Kin,* about the dangers of spilling
official wartime secrets. Referring to Operation Torch, Daisy Suckley,
who was present, told her diary, "For weeks, the P. has had something
exciting up his sleeve." That Sunday began the invasion of North Africa.
After the Allies' quick victory, the President assured the New York Herald Tribune Forum, "I have made a constant effort as Commander-in-
Chief to keep politics out of the fighting of this war."

* * *

A T THE WHITE House, in the earliest hours of New Year's Day
1943, after a champagne dinner, Roosevelt, in his wheelchair, led
Eleanor, the exiled Norwegian Princess Martha and Prince Olav and
other guests to the Mansion's theater, where they viewed the new film
Casablanca, starring Humphrey Bogart and Ingrid Bergman. The President had not chosen the picture randomly; that month, he was secretly
destined, flying for the first time of any President in office, for the ancient Moroccan port city, where he would meet with Churchill. Stalin
had declined to join them.

Only on Sunday, January 24, the final day of their conversations, did
most of the world learn that the two Allied leaders were in Casablanca.
In the sunlit garden of his borrowed Art Deco villa, with Churchill at
his side, Roosevelt told reporters they had discussed "the whole global
picture—it isn't just one front, just one ocean, or one continent." He
went on, "We have all had it in our hearts and heads before, but I don't
think that it has ever been put down on paper by the Prime Minister and

---

* Referring to rumors that he might autocratically cancel the 1942 election, Roosevelt also noted,
with sarcasm, that when he had gone to vote in Hyde Park, "I was perfectly delighted to find that
the polling place was open."

myself, and that is the determination that peace can come to the world only by the total elimination of German and Japanese war power." The President noted that in his own country's Civil War, "we had a General called U.S. Grant" or "Unconditional Surrender Grant."* Now the only "reasonable assurance of future world peace" would be "unconditional surrender by Germany, Italy and Japan." "Hear, hear!" replied Churchill. "I agree with everything that the President has said."

Roosevelt may have attributed his insistence on unconditional surrender to Ulysses Grant, but he was probably more influenced by 1918, when Wilson had refused advice to keep fighting until Germany was absolutely defeated, and Cousin Theodore had complained about Wilson's choice to end the war in compromise.† But since Pearl Harbor, the President had avoided public mention of Wilson, knowing how many Americans still disparaged his old chief as the champion of an unnecessary war.

With Britain now so painfully dependent on American goodwill, Churchill was scarcely in a position to refuse Roosevelt's demand for unconditional surrender. The President had sprung the notion on him during their final luncheon, insisting that it would show militance to the Germans and reassure Stalin that the British and Americans would not try to make a separate peace with Hitler. "Perfect!" Churchill had replied, adding that he could "just see" how the Nazis would "squeal." Roosevelt had told him, "Uncle Joe might have made it up himself." Privately, however, Churchill knew that nothing would placate Stalin until the British and Americans agreed to send fifty divisions across the English Channel. He feared that unconditional surrender would steel the German people—having been told by their leaders that, if victorious, the Allies would enslave and destroy them—to fight to the bitter end, and that prolonging the conflict would hamper Germany's ability to act as a bulwark against Soviet power in postwar Europe.

---

* In 1862, at the end of the Battle of Fort Donelson, Grant had said, "No terms except unconditional and immediate surrender can be accepted," earning him that nickname from the newspapers and President Lincoln. Later in the conflict, however, Grant did not insist on unconditional surrender, notably at Appomattox.

† TR complained to others that Wilson had "turned his usual somersault."

That same month, in Washington, with Roosevelt's approval, Secretary Stimson announced that it was "the inherent right of every faithful citizen, regardless of ancestry, to bear arms in the Nation's battle." After Pearl Harbor, more than two thousand men of Japanese origin had been thrown out of the US Army, but now the War Department established two segregated combat units, composed of the sons of Japanese American immigrants, including volunteers from the camps. One was the 442nd Regimental Combat Team, which would become one of the most honored military units in American history.

In April 1943, wearing a starry blouse, beret, and broad smile, Eleanor Roosevelt arrived at the Japanese internment camp in the Arizona desert at Gila River. Feeling remorse over Executive Order 9066, she had been asking to visit one of the camps, but Franklin had refused until it was politically useful. By now, not only the racist John Rankin but other members of Congress were claiming that the camps were too luxurious, and that the government was "coddling the Japs"; some wished to transfer oversight of the facilities from the War Relocation Authority to the less benign mercies of the US military.* Thus when Franklin and Eleanor went to the southern Arizona border to meet the Mexican President, he asked her to tour Gila River, south of Phoenix, which was considered the most benign of the ten internment camps. Its guard tower and barbed-wire fence had been taken down after authorities concluded that no one was plotting to escape. The inmates raised chickens, hogs, and cattle, and grew cotton, corn, celery, and beets, feeding not only their own camp but some of the others. However, Gila River's population of fourteen thousand had been forced into barracks built for two-thirds that number.

During her six-hour surprise visit, warned in advance that the food was less wholesome than advertised, Mrs. Roosevelt asked for a glass of milk, took a sip, and said, "It's sour." Addressing the inmates, she expressed regret for their incarceration but also criticized the fact

---

* Interior's Harold Ickes warned the President that, after accepting their exile with "philosophical understanding," the Japanese Americans were growing bitter at their treatment. He felt that the government had taken the "unnecessary" step of creating "a hostile group right in our own territory."

that they had clustered before the war in Japanese neighborhoods, which had kept them from assimilating into American society; she hoped that once released, they would scatter throughout the country. After leaving Gila River, Eleanor told the *Los Angeles Times* that the facility was "certainly not luxurious" and "I wouldn't like to live that way." She added that "the sooner we get the young Japanese out of the camps, the better," because "otherwise we will create another Indian problem." Her public assurance that no one was being pampered helped the President quash a Senate proposal to hand the camps to the military. She lobbied in vain for the inmates to be set free.

Throughout the war, Eleanor reminded her husband that personal liberties must not be crushed in pursuit of the security of the nation. Unlike Wilson, this President did not ask Congress for new restrictions on the free press or public speech. Such sanctions were less tempting than in 1917 because this time, the country was far more united behind this war effort. But Roosevelt was more than willing to push the envelope in other ways. In 1940, although the Supreme Court had declared warrantless wiretapping illegal, he secretly gave J. Edgar Hoover wholesale authority to "secure information by listening devices," assuring his then–Attorney General, Robert Jackson, that the Court would not want to abet the nation's "enemies."

Roosevelt's son Elliott wrote much later that his father "may have been the originator of the concept of employing the IRS as a weapon of political retribution," and that FDR was "fascinated" by "other men's tax returns."* In 1936, with extremist political groups seeking to benefit from the continuing Great Depression, the President had asked Edgar Hoover to acquire information about "subversive activities in the United States, particularly Fascism and Communism." He also persuaded the

---

* During the Vietnam War, in 1970, President Richard Nixon approved the secret Huston Plan, to employ illegal wiretaps, mail openings, and other domestic surveillance that would combat domestic "radicals." (The plan was single-handedly blocked by J. Edgar Hoover, who was still at the FBI.) In his memoirs, Nixon justified his action by comparing himself to Lincoln when he suspended habeas corpus and Roosevelt when he incarcerated Japanese Americans, arguing that they three were all wartime Presidents trying to protect "innocent citizens." In the 2000s, while waging a struggle against terrorism, President George W. Bush's Justice Department cited Roosevelt's warrantless wiretaps as a precedent for its own.

FBI Director to investigate his political foes, including Wendell Willkie, who, during the 1940 campaign, was pursuing an affair with Irita Van Doren, the book editor of the *New York Herald Tribune*.

When eight German saboteurs, two of whom were naturalized American citizens, were arrested in the United States in June 1942, the furious President acted to forestall further infiltration and widespread terrorism in his own country. Roosevelt insisted that the two US citizens were "just as guilty as it is possible to be" of high treason. Flouting due process, he claimed that "the death penalty is almost obligatory," explaining privately that the only issue would be whether the men died by hanging or firing squad. He issued an executive order to try the suspects by military commission and told Biddle, "I won't give them up" and "I won't hand them over to any United States Marshal armed with a writ of habeas corpus, understand?" The Attorney General later argued that whatever their aims, the suspects had not yet committed any crime: "If a man buys a pistol, intending murder, that is not an attempt at murder." Nevertheless only six weeks after they were arrested, six of the men were electrocuted (they included one of the American citizens) and the other two, who had surrendered to the FBI, sentenced to prison.*

On race, the President's needle remained virtually stuck. Knowing the importance of the white South to a Democratic President and the power of white Southerners in the House and Senate, he had even once withheld his public endorsement from an anti-lynching bill. When the military draft began, A. Philip Randolph, chief of the Brotherhood of Sleeping Car Porters, came to the Oval Office and asked Roosevelt to desegregate the armed forces.† The President claimed that integration had already begun, although he knew that this was scarcely true. The expanding industry of war also remained largely divided by race. The head

---

* The Supreme Court quickly upheld both the military commission and its verdicts in *Ex parte Quirin,* but offered no written ruling until the saboteurs had been executed. The George W. Bush administration cited *Quirin* as precedent for using military commissions to deal with accused terrorists jailed at the Guantanamo Bay Naval Base in Cuba.

† Randolph noted that the new draft law forbade "discrimination against any person on account of race or color."

of North American Aviation openly vowed that "no matter what their qualifications," African Americans "will only be used as janitors."

In the spring of 1941, Randolph planned a march on Washington to demand equal opportunities. Roosevelt was privately "much upset" by such a prospect; he feared alienating Southern Democrats on Capitol Hill and claimed that a march would "stir up race hatred and slow up progress." At his behest, Eleanor wrote Randolph that a march would "set back the progress that is being made." In the Oval Office, Randolph asked for an executive order on fair employment, and Roosevelt said, "Phil, you know I can't do that." But when Randolph stood firm, the President issued a directive that there would be "no discrimination" in "defense industries or government," which also established a Fair Employment Practices Committee. (However, he refused Randolph's request for a signing ceremony.)

Eleanor saw to it that a segregated public housing project in Detroit, planned largely for war production workers, was opened to African Americans. But when the first black families moved in, there were angry white protesters and flaming crosses. A year later, a race riot in the same city killed thirty-four people, and was put down only when Roosevelt sent in federal troops. By memo, the First Lady warned her husband of "a growing feeling amongst the colored people" that "they should be allowed to participate in any training that is going on, in the aviation, Army Navy, and have opportunities for service." If he did not act, "it is going to be very bad politically, besides being intrinsically wrong." In April 1943, a first unit of African American pilots, called the Tuskegee Airmen, went to North Africa. Haters called them "Eleanor's niggers."

The Roosevelts personally experienced the impact of the stronger domestic surveillance that the President had approved. In league with J. Edgar Hoover, who detested Eleanor's politics, the Army's Counter Intelligence Corps (G-2) warned the President against a "gigantic conspiracy" involving her young friend Joseph Lash, a former socialist and pacifist of Russian Jewish heritage, who was engaged to marry a wealthy, divorced, German-born woman, Trude Pratt. Told that G-2 had eavesdropped on both her and Lash, who was being trained in Illinois as an Army weather forecaster, a furious First Lady admonished General

Marshall to respect her privacy. The spies mistakenly concluded from their surveillance that she and Lash had been "intimate."* An unverifiable FBI memorandum of the time claimed that when confronted by evidence of a romance, the President and his wife had "a terrific fight," and Roosevelt ordered the chief of the Army Air Corps to "have Lash outside the United States and on his way to a combat post within ten hours." Supposedly the President also demanded that "anybody who knew anything about this case" be "sent to the South Pacific for action against the Japs until they were killed."†

In August 1943, paying for her own travel and wearing a Red Cross uniform, Eleanor flew to the South Pacific, Australia, and New Zealand, to see the troops and the war work being performed by women. Before departure, she gave her engagement ring and other jewelry to her assistant, Malvina Thompson, explaining who should receive each item if she should not return alive. At a reception for troops in Auckland, she charmingly said she was "too old" to dance, since she only knew the waltz and Virginia reel. She wrote Lorena Hickok that "the people here are kind and they like FDR," but "these boys break your heart" because "they're so young and so tired." She found the men "grimmer" than during World War I: "There is no feeling of adventure or thrill."

She was eager to see Joe Lash, who was now at Guadalcanal, scene of the Allies' first major Pacific triumph over the Japanese. Admiral William "Bull" Halsey, fearing that such a "junket" would consume scarce resources, had warned that it would be too dangerous but finally relented. When the First Lady was taken to Sergeant Lash, Halsey said, "So this is the young man." After escorting her to see "gruesomely wounded" soldiers in military hospitals, the Admiral marveled at "their expressions as

---

* They had mistaken hotel surveillance tapes of Lash and his fiancée for an encounter between the young Sergeant and Mrs. Roosevelt.

† In April 1945, Secretary Stimson wrote Roosevelt that Lash "should not be commissioned or assigned to sensitive duties" because he had not given up his political contacts or activities while in the Army. Contradicting his alleged hostility toward Lash, the President wrote Eleanor, six days before his death, that "probably the same crowd" (most likely he meant the FBI and G-2) was "trying to 'get' Joe." He assured her that he was wiring Stimson "to do nothing further about withholding his commission until I get back."

she leaned over them," asking what they needed and whether she could call their mothers; he felt "ashamed of my original surliness."

The First Lady had been right to fear for her life, for Guadalcanal was struck by Japanese bombers immediately before and after her visit. Returning to the White House, she proudly wrote her daughter, Anna, that "Pa asked me more questions than I expected & actually came over to lunch with me . . . & spent two hours!" She told Franklin that having seen how soldiers had been "broken mentally and emotionally made me lie awake nights," and beseeched him to ask Congress for a GI bill like those she had heard about in New Zealand and Australia, ensuring them postwar jobs and education.

As Eleanor assimilated the "horror" that she had seen in the South Pacific, she sank into a depression, which deepened when her husband did not invite her to accompany him to his upcoming first summit meeting with both Churchill and Stalin. That fall, she poignantly wrote her friend Esther Lape that while there was "little or no surface friction" in her marriage to Franklin, they had "no fundamental love to draw on, just respect and affection." She vowed, "I'll be a fairly good handmaiden and with all the others to help I think FDR's sense of a place in history will keep him on a forward going path."

* * *

ROOSEVELT HOPED THAT World War II would end with creation of a durable international peace organization. While campaigning for President in 1932, he had publicly dismissed Wilson's old dream, saying the nation should take "no part" in the League of Nations. Soon after taking office, Roosevelt had suggested that the United States join the World Court, which was linked to the League. But the President was forced to change his mind after Democratic Senators opposed it, writing to his cousin Theodore's Secretary of State and War, Elihu Root, "Today, quite frankly, the wind blows against us."

By 1943, with the tide of war shifting in the Allies' favor, he did not want to repeat Wilson's mistake of waiting until the conflict was over to persuade Americans to back a postwar peace body. On New Year's

Day, Roosevelt told reporters, "It isn't an awful lot of use if there is going to be another world war in ten years, or fifteen years or twenty years." In his State of the Union that same month, he told Congress it would be "sacrilegious if this nation and the world did not attain some real, lasting good out of all these efforts and sufferings and bloodshed and death." That spring, he told the *Saturday Evening Post* that instead of another League of Nations, the postwar calm should be maintained by America, Great Britain, the Soviet Union, and China, which, by then, he was calling the "Four Policemen."

Senator Robert Taft, whose father had joined Wilson to extol the League of Nations, denounced Roosevelt's proposal as "an international W.P.A." that would restrict American "freedom of action."* Taft insisted that World War II be not construed as "any crusade for democracy, or for the Four Freedoms, or for the preservation of the British Empire."

Roosevelt knew from Wilson's ordeal that it would be easier to get Congress to support a peace organization if it was prompted to take the lead in asking him for one. In September 1943, blessed by the White House, the Arkansas Congressman J. William Fulbright, a young, first-term ex–Rhodes Scholar, asked for "appropriate international machinery" to preserve postwar tranquillity, and prevailed by 360 to 29. Even the President's isolationist foe Hamilton Fish, who represented Hyde Park, grudgingly voted yes, saying that no one wished to "vote against the Ten Commandments." The President told reporters "it would be a very fine thing" if the Senate told Americans "after this war, in order to avoid future wars in the world, that this country will cooperate with other nations." By 85 to 5, Senators endorsed a "general international organization." Although these resolutions had been drafted in vague language to ensure maximum support, they provoked a modest backlash. Congressman Clare Hoffman, Republican from Michigan, warned that by joining such a body, Americans would "repeal the Declaration of Independence."

Haunted by the memory of Paris in 1919, with Wilson acting as a

---

* The Works Progress Administration, a cornerstone of Roosevelt's early New Deal, which fought unemployment by offering millions of public works jobs, was a conservative bugaboo.

broker among dozens of unruly delegations, trying to fashion a post-war arrangement, Roosevelt was resolved to avoid the errors that had allowed or provoked Germany to rearm itself and draw the world into another, more destructive world war. In October 1943, he told Secretary Hull that postwar Germany should be sliced into three or more states, with "military activities" and "armament industries" forbidden. He wanted Germans to repay the countries victimized by Hitler; this time, the reparations should be "not money, but equipment and manpower."

That November, Roosevelt, Churchill, and Stalin were to meet in Tehran. Reminding the President by cable that his country still bore the overwhelming burden of fighting the European war, Stalin had insisted that he could not leave his post to travel any farther than Iran. During Roosevelt's voyage on the USS *Iowa,* a torpedo almost struck his battle-ship. Boldly the President told his valet, Arthur Prettyman, "Take me over to the starboard rail. I want to watch the torpedo!" When the Big Three convened in private, Churchill observed that they represented the "greatest concentration of power" the world had ever witnessed. Roosevelt puckishly replied that as the "youngest of the three present," he hoped that he and his "elders" would "work in close cooperation for the prosecution of the war" and "for generations to come." He forecast an Anglo-American invasion of Fortress Europe in the spring of 1944, di-verting at least thirty or forty Nazi divisions from their struggle against the Soviet Union. During dinner, he became ill. With his face turning green and sweat pouring from his chin, he was quickly wheeled out of the chamber.

The next morning, well enough to return, the President related his postwar vision of Four Policemen at the top of a postwar peace appa-ratus. Stalin made it brutally clear that he sought a weak postwar Ger-many. That evening, he complained that Churchill was too lax about the danger: "At least fifty thousand—and perhaps a hundred thousand—of the German command staff must be physically liquidated." Raising a glass, he said, "I drink to our unity in killing them as quickly as we cap-ture them!" Disgusted, Churchill replied, "I will not be a party to any butchery in cold blood." Trying to lighten the atmosphere with humor,

Roosevelt proposed a compromise—"say, forty-nine thousand, five hundred." But Churchill had seen the glimmerings of a postwar Anglo-American confrontation with the Soviet Union. Severely depressed, he told his doctor, Lord Moran, that night, "I want to sleep for billions of years."

* * *

ROOSEVELT RETURNED TO the White House suffering from what was diagnosed as a bad bronchial infection. In January 1944, his doctors forbade him to deliver his State of the Union in person. Instead he summarized it from the Executive Mansion in a fireside chat, describing his plan to ask Congress for a "second Bill of Rights," providing postwar Americans with economic security. Seeking new war revenues, Roosevelt asked for a $10 billion tax increase, but his Senate Majority Leader, Alben Barkley of Kentucky, later proposed only a quarter of that amount. He vetoed Barkley's bill—the first time a President had rejected such a revenue measure—publicly complaining that "not even a dictionary or thesaurus" could make its language clear, and that it was "relief not for the needy but the greedy."

Furious, Barkley complained that Roosevelt had made "a calculated and deliberate assault upon the legislative integrity of every member of Congress," and asked his colleagues to override the President, if they had "any self-respect left." Roosevelt told Margaret Suckley that "Alben must be suffering from shell shock." After quitting his leadership post, Barkley was reelected to it; then Congress overrode Roosevelt's veto. The President wrote Congressman Pat Drewry, Democrat from Virginia, that he was "doing everything in my power" to reestablish harmony with the House and Senate, "except among a very small number of people who would rather nail my hide to the barn door than win the war." Dreaming of his birthplace and of Warm Springs, where he had vacationed since his early recuperation from polio, he insisted, "I would give a great deal personally to return to Hyde Park and Georgia just as soon as the Lord will let me."

In March 1944, the President cabled Churchill, "I am very angry with myself," explaining that his "grippe" had "hung on and on, leaving me with an intermittent temperature." He was planning "a complete rest of about two or three weeks in a suitable climate." He had considered Guantánamo Bay, but concluded that "Cuba is absolutely lousy with anarchists, murderers, et cetera, and a lot of prevaricators." Instead he took a long, secret respite at Hobcaw Barony, the large South Carolina estate of the financier Bernard Baruch, who had counseled Wilson in Paris.

Roosevelt's grandson Curtis much later recalled that the ailing President asked Eleanor "to spend more time with him and not to travel so much," but she "would not alter her schedule." She had discovered his liaison with her social secretary, Lucy Mercer, in 1918, and agreed to remain in the marriage only after he vowed to give up his romance—but the First Lady maintained a distance. By 1936, she was writing Lorena Hickok, "I realize more and more that FDR is a great man," and that he was "nice to me but as a person I'm a stranger and I don't want to be anything else." Eleanor later observed that Franklin "might have been happier with a wife who was completely uncritical," and "that I was never able to be."

Lucy had married Winthrop Rutherfurd, who was rich and twenty-nine years her senior, but Roosevelt had kept in sporadic, secret contact with her. Disoriented by her husband's death in March 1944, Mrs. Rutherfurd saw the President at Hobcaw, Hyde Park, and the White House, when the First Lady was absent, and they motored together through Rock Creek Park. After meeting Lucy, Daisy Suckley wrote in her journal that with their "unselfish devotion," they both "feel the same about F.D.R.," and that Lucy "does worry, terribly, about him, & has felt for years that he has been terribly lonely."

Unbeknownst to the American people, Roosevelt was suffering from progressive, debilitating cardiovascular disease.[*] His father had died of circulatory problems at the age of seventy-two, and whatever

---

[*] Some later speculated that he also suffered from one or more forms of cancer that may have spread to his brain. Most of his medical records disappeared after his death.

genetic propensity Franklin had for cardiac illness was exacerbated by his daily life of restricted movement, chain-smoking, and inconceivable stress. He wrote Suckley from Hobcaw that after a rest, his heart was "definitely better" but "does queer things still." He told her, "I am really feeling 'no good'—don't want to do anything & want to sleep all the time." She later recorded that the President had discovered that his doctors "were not telling *him* the *whole* truth & that he was evidently more sick than they said!" He agreed to curtail his smoking and follow a low-calorie, low-fat diet. But those close to him anxiously noted how Franklin would bring conversations to an abrupt stop, with staring eyes and mouth hanging open. His old esprit was fading and he was more easily annoyed. As 1944 progressed, he lost about forty pounds. Eleanor wrote Joe Lash that "suddenly F is more dependent."

With public opinion flowing toward his cherished postwar peace organization, the President now openly praised Woodrow Wilson, telling reporters in the Oval Office in May that the League of Nations had "very, very great purpose," but "got dreadfully involved in American politics." He reminded them that Wilson's conflict "was going to be a war to end wars, and it was to be done through this altruistic unity of all the nations." Since then, "we have gone through some pretty rough times together" and "some of us—I don't think I include myself in this—are a little more cynical than we were then."

Roosevelt had hoped to join Churchill in England for the D-Day invasion. But at the start of June, he stayed in the United States as men and landing craft were quietly loaded into ships along the British coast. The President knew that even if Operation Overlord succeeded, tens of thousands of soldiers were likely to perish in the first landings in France—and that if the invasion failed, even though the Red Army was on the march, the defeat might make an Allied victory in this conflict much more difficult. He awaited the supreme moment at Kenwood, the estate of his aide Pa Watson, near Jefferson's Monticello. There he wrote a D-Day prayer, aided by his daughter Anna's husband, John Boettiger, a former *Chicago Tribune* reporter, as well as his own reading of the Book of Common Prayer. With his Episcopal aversion to wearing religion on his sleeve, he liked to say he was "a Christian and a Democrat—that's all." But Eleanor observed that Franklin's religion "had something to do with his confidence in himself," and that "in great crises, he was guided by a strength and wisdom higher than his own."

On Monday, June 5, the President returned to the White House. That night, he kept in close touch with Pentagon intelligence, and early the next morning was told that the great crusade was on. Visiting his bedroom at nine o'clock, Suckley found that "he had the radio on & all the night dispatches." By noon, Roosevelt knew for certain that the news was good. Squeezing almost two hundred reporters into the Oval Office, with his Scottie, Fala, nearby, he told them that even though the invaders were taking hold in France, "overconfidence destroys the war effort" because "you don't just land on a beach" and "walk through to Berlin." Cabling Churchill about "today's stupendous events," he wrote, "How I wish I could be with you to see our war machine in operation."

Roosevelt's staff gave the text of his prayer to afternoon papers, enabling Americans to recite it along with him when he read it on radio that evening. "Our sons," he began, "pride of our nation, this day have set upon a mighty endeavor, a struggle to preserve our Republic, our religion, and our civilization, and to set free a suffering humanity. . . . Lead us to the saving of our country and, with our sister nations, into a world unity that will spell a sure peace—a peace invulnerable to the schemings of unworthy men."

As Allied forces moved into Hitler's Fortress Europe, Roosevelt and his circle were confronted with new evidence of the Holocaust. In early 1942, he had been given information that Adolf Hitler was quietly fulfilling his threat to "annihilate the Jewish race." Rabbi Stephen Wise asked the President that December 1942 to inform the world about "the most overwhelming disaster of Jewish history" and "try to stop it." Although he was willing to warn the world about the impending catastrophe and insisted that there be war crimes commissions when the conflict was over, Roosevelt told Wise that punishment for such crimes would probably have to await the end of the fighting, so his own solution was to "win the war." The problem with this approach was that by the time of an Allied victory, much of world Jewry might have been annihilated.

By June 1944, the Germans had removed more than half of Hungary's 750,000 Jews, and some Jewish leaders were asking the Allies to bomb railways from Hungary to the Auschwitz death camp in Poland. In response, Churchill told his Foreign Secretary, Anthony Eden, that the murder of the Jews was "probably the greatest and most horrible crime ever committed in the whole history of the world," and ordered him to get "everything" he could out of the British Air Force. But the Prime Minister was told that American bombers were better positioned to do the job.

At the Pentagon, Stimson consulted John McCloy, who later insisted, for decades, that he had "never talked" with Roosevelt about the option of bombing the railroad lines or death camps. But in 1986, McCloy changed his story during a taped conversation with Henry Morgenthau's son, Henry III, who was researching a family history. The ninety-one-year-old McCloy insisted that he had indeed raised the idea with the President, and that Roosevelt became "irate" and "made it very clear" that bombing Auschwitz "wouldn't have done any good." By McCloy's new account, Roosevelt "took it out of my hands" and warned that "if it's successful, it'll be more provocative" and "we'll be accused of participating in this horrible business," as well as "bombing innocent people." McCloy went on, "I didn't want to bomb Auschwitz," adding that "it seemed to be a bunch of fanatic Jews who seemed to think that if you didn't bomb, it was an indication of lack of venom against Hitler."

If McCloy's memory was reliable, then, just as with the Japanese internment, Roosevelt had used the discreet younger man to discuss a decision for which he knew he might be criticized by history, and which might conceivably have become an issue in the 1944 campaign. This approach to the possible bombing of the camps would allow the President to explain, if it became necessary, that the issue had been resolved at a lower level by the military. In retrospect, the President should have considered the bombing proposal more seriously. Approving it might have required him to slightly revise his insistence that the Allies' sole aim should be winning the war, as he did on at least a few other occasions. But such a decision might have saved lives and shown future generations that, like Churchill, he understood the importance of the Holocaust as a crime unparalleled in world history.*

∗ ∗ ∗

ROOSEVELT'S HEALTH CONTINUED to flag. Early that summer, Dr. Frank Lahey, founder of Boston's Lahey Clinic, along with several other physicians, was quietly asked to see the President and examine his medical file. Afterward Lahey told Roosevelt's official physician, Admiral Ross McIntire, that since his trip overseas, Roosevelt had been "if not in heart failure, at least on the verge of it," which was "the result of high blood pressure he has had now for a long time." Lahey warned McIntire that if Roosevelt were elected to a fourth term, "he would again have heart failure and be unable to complete it."

But there is little evidence that Roosevelt ever seriously considered renouncing a fourth term. Even with his health problems, he—justifiably—considered himself indispensable to the winning of this war. No other Democrat enjoyed anything close to his world prestige, experience, or popularity with the voters. Had he bowed out, the White House might well have passed to a Republican in 1944. During a brief home leave, his son Franklin told him that everyone in the armed forces would think the President a "quitter" if he retired.

Roosevelt expected that if he ran, it would be a close race. He had asked Americans for the most extreme sacrifices, and knew that they might yearn, as in 1920, for normalcy. As Suckley recorded, Franklin remembered Wilson telling him that the public was "willing to be 'liberal' about a third of the time, gets tired of new things and reverts to conservatism the other two thirds of the time." Recent military successes in Europe and the Pacific might cause some voters to conclude that the war was virtually won, and that they therefore could afford to take a chance

---

* I have written at length about Roosevelt's approach to the Holocaust, as well as his preparations for postwar Germany, in *The Conquerors: Roosevelt, Truman and the Destruction of Hitler's Germany, 1941–1945* (New York: Simon & Schuster, 2002).

with the untested Republican nominee, New York Governor Thomas Dewey. With his booming voice, Dewey told convention delegates that Roosevelt's government had "grown old in office" and "become tired and quarrelsome." One Gallup survey suggested that if the end of the war was in "clear sight," the Governor would have a good chance to win. The President considered Dewey an icy, pompous know-it-all, but was relieved that he had endorsed some kind of postwar world organization.* That June, Roosevelt had signed the GI Bill that Eleanor had requested; it gave returning soldiers education, mortgages, and business loans.

Roosevelt told family members that, if reelected, he might resign once Germany and Japan surrendered; he would return to Hyde Park, where he had built a one-story woodland house, which he called Top Cottage, and be a "country gentleman," restoring his health and writing his memoirs. He pondered serving as the first Secretary-General of the postwar peace assembly. Churchill had suggested that the new institution, like the old, be called the League of Nations. The President replied, however, that there was "too much prejudice" in the United States to revive that name. Thus the two men agreed to call it the "United Nations." Roosevelt believed that locating the new organization in the United States would make it more difficult for Congress to refuse American membership. He spoke of placing the UN in Hyde Park and building a new airstrip there so that world leaders could fly in and out of his hometown.

These ruminations depended upon who would be his next Vice President and, if he renounced his job after the war was won, his successor. He considered the incumbent, Henry Wallace, too soft and idealistic to cope with the postwar world. Asking to renominate Wallace, a former Republican, would antagonize the party bosses. Roosevelt was looking hard at the youthful Justice Bill Douglas, a maverick ex–New

---

* Had Robert Taft once again sought his party's nomination (instead, since his seat was up that year, the Ohio Senator had focused on reelection) and succeeded, this might have been the campaign's chief issue, forcing Roosevelt to make compromises that could have restricted him when he ultimately tried to forge the peace.

Dealer and outdoorsman, who echoed his liberalism and could balance his age.

At a White House meeting, the Democratic National Chairman, Robert Hannegan, eager for a less audacious selection, proposed instead his fellow Missourian Harry Truman. "I hardly know Truman," said Roosevelt. Preferring a younger running mate, he asked how old the Senator was. After consulting the *Congressional Directory,* and finding that the Missourian was sixty, another Truman backer who was present hoped that the President would not ask again. Roosevelt observed that Douglas would have more "public appeal," but that Truman "would make you boys happy, and you are the ones I am counting on to win this election." He scrawled on paper that "either" Douglas or Truman "would bring real strength to the ticket."* Afterward Hannegan asked Roosevelt's secretary, Grace Tully, to have the note typed, claiming that the President actually preferred Truman's name to come first. Tully forged her boss's initials on the document, and Hannegan showed it around, claiming that Truman was really Roosevelt's choice.

The President appreciated Truman's restraint as chairman of the Senate special committee that had probed his defense programs. He knew that the Missourian could help him in the isolationist Midwest and, as a popular member of the Senate's "inner club," in ratifying postwar treaties. He sprang the trap door under Wallace by sending him on a trip to China, which distanced him from his supporters, and generated further confusion by beckoning others into the race for number two. Publicly Roosevelt claimed that he would vote for Wallace, were he a delegate, while privately warning the Vice President, on his return from China, that there would be catcalls and humiliation should his name be presented to the delegates.

During convention week in Chicago, when told of Roosevelt's interest in him, Truman at first stalled, anxious that such new national

---

* Roosevelt's language echoed that of Lincoln's aide John Nicolay about Lincoln's choice for Vice President in 1864: Nicolay's quote appeared in Carl Sandburg's volumes on Lincoln's war years, which FDR had read.

prominence might provoke the press to investigate the long-ago suicide of his wife, Bess's father, as well as her presence on his Senate payroll. Then, from the Blackstone Hotel, Hannegan placed a call, in Truman's presence, to the President, who warned that if the Missouri Senator "wants to break up the Democratic party in the middle of a war, that's his responsibility." After Roosevelt rang off, Truman exclaimed, "Oh, shit!"

The President accepted his fourth-term nomination by radio from his railroad car near the San Diego Naval Base (which, for security reasons, the press agreed to call "a Pacific Coast base"). He argued that Americans must now decide whether to give "this worldwide job to inexperienced or immature hands" or "to those who saw the danger from abroad, who met it head-on and who have now seized the offensive and carried the war to its present stages of success."

Aboard the heavy cruiser *Baltimore,* Roosevelt sailed for Hawaii, where he would view the sunken wreckage at Pearl Harbor and confer with his Pacific commander, Douglas MacArthur, who had toyed with running against him that year. When his ship reached Honolulu, the President asked, "Where is MacArthur?" The General roared up late, with screaming sirens and motorcycles, in a fire-engine-red convertible that, as it happened, had been borrowed from a local bordello. Long familiar with MacArthur's act, Roosevelt took him down a peg by asking, "What are you doing with that leather jacket on? It's damn hot today." The General explained that he had flown from "pretty cold" weather in Australia. During their private meetings, by MacArthur's account, the President confided to him, "If the war with Germany ends before the election, I will not be reelected."*

Returning to Washington, sitting under the Andrew Jackson magnolia behind the White House, the President lunched on sandwiches and vanilla ice cream with Harry Truman, both in shirtsleeves. Roosevelt's

---

* After Hawaii, eager to keep MacArthur friendly, Roosevelt charmingly wrote him that he wished they could "swap places," adding that "you would make more a go as President than I would as general in the retaking of the Philippines."

grandson Curtis, who joined them for part of the meal, felt that the President was "looking for character traits—hoping to confirm that Truman was the kind of person who might continue his liberal policies." Roosevelt told Truman that he hoped to be succeeded by someone who was "a little right of center" because after a time of activism, "you have to digest it." Shocked by how much Roosevelt had aged since he had seen him a year earlier, Truman later told a friend, "It doesn't seem to be a mental lapse, but physically he's just going to pieces." Told that soon he would be living in the White House, Harry replied, "I'm afraid I am, and it scares the hell out of me."

In September, while meeting with Churchill at Quebec City, the President ordered an after-dinner screening of Twentieth Century Fox's new film *Wilson*, starring Alexander Knox; he hoped that the picture would encourage moviegoers to embrace his imagined postwar peace organization. While watching his old chief, on the screen, collapse from a stroke while fighting for his League of Nations, Roosevelt swore, "By God, that's not going to happen to me!" When the film was over, his doctor discovered that the President's blood pressure had shot up dangerously.

Back in Washington, Roosevelt was alarmed to learn that Dewey was planning to exploit secret information to claim that the President had deliberately encouraged the Pearl Harbor attack to get into the war. Roosevelt's new Secretary of the Navy, James Forrestal, advised him that some Army officer had told Dewey's aides that before the assault, Roosevelt and his chiefs had been privy to decoded Japanese cable traffic showing that Tokyo was targeting the Hawaiian base.

General Marshall cautioned that if the Republican nominee used the information, the result would be "loaded with dynamite." Without telling Roosevelt, he sent the Pentagon's chief of cryptography, Colonel Carter Clarke, to see Dewey, who was campaigning in Oklahoma. Clarke bore a letter from Marshall, which he was supposed to read to the Governor, but only if Dewey pledged in advance that he would not share its contents with others. Disinclined to silence himself, Dewey refused to offer such "blind commitments." He asked Clarke, on his honor, to confirm that Marshall had not sent him at the President's behest. Clarke did so, but Dewey insisted that "Franklin Roosevelt is behind the whole thing." He complained that Washington had intercepted "certain Jap codes before Pearl Harbor" and "two of them are still in current use." Dewey blustered that Roosevelt "knew what was happening before Pearl Harbor, and instead of being reelected, he ought to be impeached."

Disturbed by Clarke's failure, Marshall sent him to see Dewey again, this time in Albany, with a new written warning that if the Governor divulged the Pearl Harbor secrets he knew, it would help "the enemy, German or Jap," and damage "the interests of our armed forces." In the note, Marshall conceded that for years the US government had decoded Japanese diplomatic messages, which had revealed "their moves in the Pacific" but "unfortunately made no reference whatever to intentions towards Hawaii," except for a dispatch that "did not reach our hands" until after Pearl Harbor had been bombed. Marshall went on to confide that the Pentagon was still acquiring crucial information about both German and Japanese intentions from channels still using the same code, which would stop if Dewey revealed the codebreaking to the public.

After Clarke departed, Dewey, white-faced in anger, told his campaign manager, Herbert Brownell, and other close aides that Roosevelt was a "traitor." Dewey said he would "be damned if I believe the Japs are still using those codes," and claimed that "at least twelve Senators" knew about the information that Marshall was imploring him to withhold. Brownell warned Dewey that if he seemed to be publicizing Pearl Harbor secrets, Roosevelt could charge, in response, that his opponent had handed "information to the enemy." Dewey felt deeply frustrated to be forced to let the potent issue slip through his fingers. When the President later heard, from his aide Harry Hopkins, about Marshall's quiet intervention in the campaign, he observed that Dewey "must be pretty desperate if he is even thinking of using material like this, which would be bound to react against him."

With the prospect of a campaign uproar over Pearl Harbor dispelled, Roosevelt moved to silence talk about his health. He told his Cabinet that there was "this constant rumor that I'll not live if I am elected," adding that "you all know that's not so," but "apparently Papa has to tell them." In a public display of stamina, on Saturday, October 21, wearing his Navy cape and lucky campaign fedora, he was driven in his open car, under a cold rain, for fifty-one miles, through all five boroughs of New York City. Eleanor later recalled that she was "really worried about him that day, but instead of being completely exhausted he was exhilarated." That evening, at the Waldorf Astoria, he spoke at a dinner of the Foreign Policy Association, over national radio, warning that "if the Republicans were to win control of the Congress, inveterate isolationists would occupy positions of commanding influence and power." He boasted that he lacked the support of the "isolationist press," naming such publishers as William Randolph Hearst and the *Chicago Tribune*'s Robert McCormick.* At that moment, MacArthur had just made his triumphal return to the Philippines.

On Tuesday, November 7, the President defeated Dewey by a popular majority of almost 8 percent, with an electoral landslide of 432 to 99 votes. Democrats lost one Senate seat, but gained twenty in the House.

✳ ✳ ✳

R OOSEVELT WAS SWORN in as President for the fourth time in January 1945, on the South Portico of the White House. Since Americans were dying abroad, he had asked for a more modest setting than the Capitol; he did not wish to bear the physical toll of a long ceremony. Asked if there would be a military parade, he replied that the soldiers were off fighting: "Who is there here to parade?" One of the guests was Edith Wilson, now seventy-two, who was shocked to note that Roosevelt looked "exactly as my husband did when he went into his decline."

Delivering history's second-briefest inaugural address, the President used language that sounded like that of Edith's husband, during his western trip of 1919.† Roosevelt proclaimed that this world war had taught Americans that "our well-being is dependent on the well-being of other nations far away." They must live "not as ostriches, nor as dogs in

---

* McCormick responded that "isolationist" was "the word that a man controlled by foreign influences uses for patriot."

† The shortest inaugural utterance had been delivered by George Washington in 1793.

the manger," but as "citizens of the world, members of the human community." He went on, "We have learned the simple truth, as Emerson said, that 'the only way to have a friend is to be one.'" After the ceremony, Eleanor wrote Joe Lash that she felt "so very depressed" because "the next years seem impossible to live through."

Two days later, Roosevelt secretly traveled by train to Newport News and departed, on the USS *Quincy*, to meet Stalin and Churchill at the Crimean resort town of Yalta, there to conceive the postwar world. Eleanor was hurt to be left home from a summit once again, this time passed over in favor of their daughter, Anna. When the Big Three met, Stalin tried to maximize Soviet influence in the new United Nations by demanding seats for all sixteen Soviet republics in its future General Assembly. Roosevelt countered by requesting similar treatment for all forty-eight American states. Stalin finally settled for three delegates, including the Ukraine and Byelorussia. Sailing home, the President worried about persuading the Senate, which he privately described as "a bunch of incompetent obstructionists," to empower the UN to request American troops to enforce its resolutions without the case-by-case assent of Congress.

Aboard the *Quincy*, a reporter asked Roosevelt whether the Yalta agreements would provide peace for the next generation. The President replied, "I can answer that question if you can tell me who your descendants will be in the year 2057." He predicted that "the United Nations will evolve into the best method ever devised for stopping war":

> Obviously we could have come to terms with Hitler, and we could have accepted a minor role in his totalitarian world. . . . We could have compromised with Japan, and bargained for a place in the Japanese-dominated Asia. . . . And we rejected that! . . . The United Nations must have the power to act quickly and decisively to keep the peace by force, if necessary. A policeman would not be a very effective policeman if, when he saw a felon break into a house, he had to go to the town hall and call a town meeting to issue a warrant before the felon could be arrested.

Back from Yalta, the exhausted President made his final appearance before Congress on March 1. No longer concealing his disability, he sat down at a table in front of the podium in the House chamber, explaining that "it makes it a lot easier for me not to have to carry about ten pounds of steel around on the bottom of my legs." At the end of the month, seeking rejuvenation, he traveled to his Little White House in Warm Springs, joined by Polly Delano and Daisy Suckley. The First Lady wrote her aunt, Maude Gray, "I say a prayer daily that he may be able to carry on till we have peace & our feet are set in the right direction." On April 8, she wrote to Franklin, "You sounded cheerful for the first time last night & I hope you'll weigh 170 pounds when you return."

Before going to bed at the Little White House, the President on several nights engaged in a small pantomime that showed the maternal place of Suckley and Delano in his life. As Daisy wrote in her diary,

> I get the gruel & Polly and I take it to him. I sit on the edge of the bed & he "puts on an act": he is too weak to raise his head, his hands are weak, he must be fed! So I proceed to feed him with a tea spoon & he loves it! Just to be able to run from his world problems & behave like a complete nut for a few moments, with an appreciative audience laughing with him & at him, both!*

On the last evening of Roosevelt's life, Henry Morgenthau came to dinner at the cottage. By now, there was an additional houseguest, Lucy Rutherfurd. When the Treasury Secretary arrived, he was "terribly shocked" to find that his old friend "had aged terrifically and looked very haggard," and "was constantly confusing names." Roosevelt related that two weeks hence, he would take his train to San Francisco for the opening session of the United Nations: "I will appear on the stage in my

---

* Fearing that this and similar recollections might someday embarrass the President, Suckley later drew a line through these passages in her journal.

wheelchair. . . . They will applaud me. . . . And I will be back in Hyde Park on May first."

The next morning, Thursday, April 12, the President posed for an oil portrait in the company of Delano, Suckley, and Rutherfurd.* Daisy noted that Franklin "looked smiling & happy & ready for anything." He told the ladies that the war in Europe could end "at any time" and tossed his draft card into the wastebasket. Suckley sat on the sofa, crocheting, while Delano left to pour water into a bowl of roses in her bedroom. Suddenly the President's head pitched forward, and Daisy asked, "Have you dropped your cigarette?" With clenched brow, trying to smile, he replied, "I have a terrific pain in the back of my head."

The two women tipped his chair backward, and someone called for a doctor. As Roosevelt was carried to his narrow bed, he murmured to Polly his last known words: "Be careful!" Rutherfurd held camphor to his nostrils; then, hoping to escape attention, she climbed into a car and sped away. At 3:35 p.m., the President died from a cerebral hemorrhage. That evening, when the First Lady arrived, she was stunned when Polly told her that Lucy, whom Franklin had pledged never to see again, had been present at the death scene. After midnight, the undertakers pulled a sheet away to find that someone had tied a strip of gauze under Roosevelt's chin and around his head, to keep his lower jaw from dropping open.

In May 1945, after Hitler's suicide and the Allied conquest of Berlin, the Germans surrendered unconditionally. That August, President Harry Truman ordered American bombers to drop atomic weapons on Hiroshima and Nagasaki, and Japan begged for peace. At the end of World War II, American military deaths were established at 405,399, out of an estimated global military death count of about 25 million. In December, the Senate voted, 65 to 7, for full participation in the United

---

* Suckley told her diary, "Lucy is such a lovely person, but she seems so very immature—like a character out of a book. She has led such a protected life with her husband, who was much older than herself, always living on a high scale, that she knows little about life. . . . F says she has *so many* problems & difficulties that she brings to him."

Nations, as did the House, by 344 to 15.* Henry Cabot Lodge Jr., grandson of the enemy of Wilson's League, and who had resigned from the Senate to fight Hitler in Europe, said he backed the United Nations "in every possible way."†

* * *

BY THE TWENTY-FIRST century, some Americans would think of the wartime Roosevelt primarily in terms of the mistakes that led to the Pearl Harbor disaster, the removal of Japanese Americans and other infringements of civil liberties, the failure to significantly improve the lot of African Americans and do more to thwart the Holocaust. Although more than some of such criticism is justified, the thirty-second President deserves the verdict of the *New York Times,* rendered the morning after his death, that "men will thank God on their knees a hundred years from now that Franklin D. Roosevelt was in the White House." It is difficult to imagine any other American leader of that generation guiding, with such success, a resistant nation toward intervention and ultimate victory in this most momentous of history's wars, as well as taking Americans into a postwar assembly that would strive to enforce the peace.

This feat would have been more difficult for Roosevelt to accomplish without his experience watching Wilson's achievements and failures at

---

* Congress recommended that the United States host the United Nations. To honor Roosevelt's dream, site searchers inspected the Chi-Wan-Da Summer Camp for Boys, ten miles from Hyde Park, but John D. Rockefeller Jr. made an irresistible offer of a parcel at Turtle Bay, on the east side of Manhattan. Before the Senate vote authorizing American entry into the United Nations, Burton Wheeler of Montana had demanded an amendment to make Presidents ask for congressional permission before providing armed forces to the United Nations, but the measure was voted down, 65 to 9. Robert Taft proposed that any effort by a President to use the armed forces without congressional assent be automatically canceled after three months, but his idea was killed by voice vote. The *Chicago Tribune* warned that with its action on the United Nations, the legislative branch "surrenders the constitutional power of Congress to declare war."

† Senator Vandenberg, the old isolationist, argued that such "unlimited Presidential use of force" had been employed "without challenge for 150 years." The retired Chief Justice Charles Evans Hughes, appointed by Hoover, agreed, noting that "our Presidents have used our armed forces repeatedly without authorization by Congress."

close hand, which showed him how to build a domestic wartime leviathan, as well as how not to deal with Congress in seeking a postwar peace organization; in public, he referred to the "tragic mistakes" and "ill-fated experiments of former years." While waging World War II, Roosevelt appeared so self-assured that it seemed he had been through it all before and, in a sense, he had.

If Roosevelt had not persuaded the nation to rearm before Pearl Harbor, the Allies might conceivably have lost the war. After the Japanese assault, his conspicuous personal self-confidence, through the public hysteria and beyond, was a powerful weapon of war. A President more psychologically insecure would not have been so able to reassure his country that the Allies would fight through "to absolute victory."* Unlike Wilson's public silence through so much of his war, Roosevelt gave repeated press conferences and speeches and spoke on radio, informing Americans about the current state of battle, both good and alarming. By contrast with what had seemed like Wilson's kingly remove, he relentlessly cajoled members of Congress to accede to his plans for war and peace. Emulating Lincoln, as the conflict ground on, Roosevelt lifted his war aims to a higher moral plane, eloquently citing his Four Freedoms and postwar "economic Bill of Rights."

Roosevelt's commanding performance throughout World War II rescued his reputation and pushed it to near the top of the presidential ladder. Had there been no war, and had he retired in 1941, he would have been known as a President who employed government activism to save his country from the worst of the Great Depression but who, despite his landslide reelection, was blocked by Congress during his second term and never managed to fix the economic crisis. As late as 1938, US unemployment was 19 percent, and the country was suffering from recession. It was Roosevelt's rearmament program that managed to stimulate the economy and put the jobless to work. Without it, that two-term President might today be widely viewed as a failure, with the term "Rooseveltian leadership" a synonym for ineffectuality. The war

---

* Just as in 1933, he had told the nation that it had "nothing to fear but fear itself"—even though, at a time of economic cataclysm, Americans actually had much to fear.

ultimately did so much to elevate Roosevelt's standing that it increased the temptation for later Presidents to escalate their reputations by seeking foreign conflict.[*]

The result of America's triumph in the Survival War, and Roosevelt's role in it, was a quantum increase in presidential power. As the custodian of nuclear weapons, a President now had the almost instant power, with little time to consult Congress or the public, to take the nation to war and cause untold numbers of deaths. With the advent of the Cold War against the Soviet Union, the apparatus of national security built to fight the Axis was preserved and expanded into a permanent war machine. For the next three decades, the United States was the world's preeminent superpower, and many Americans felt they could do anything. The experience of the late 1930s and early 1940s suggested to much of the country that the isolationist Congress had been wrong, and Roosevelt right, and that Presidents should be granted dominance on matters of war.

Roosevelt's vision of a postwar United Nations presented a means of dealing with future world conflicts that might spiral into another world war. But when Congress authorized American membership in the United Nations, it never quite resolved the problem that had vexed the opponents of Wilson's League of Nations—that obligations to such an organization, augmented by an elaborate network of international treaties, might draw an overstretched United States into peripheral wars against adversaries who did not directly or immediately threaten American security. With Congress eager to pass the buck on questions of war, Americans, as never before, were willing to entrust such decisions primarily to their Presidents—as history was about to witness in Korea and Vietnam.

---

[*] Ironically it was Theodore Roosevelt—with whom FDR felt so competitive and whom he had clearly surpassed by dint of his leadership in World War II—who regretted that, as President, he had never been presented with a crisis dramatic enough to fully demonstrate his leadership potential.

CHAPTER FOURTEEN

"I Am Going to Let Them Have It"

O N WEDNESDAY AFTERNOON, July 5, 1950, in a graveyard near the South Korean capital of Seoul, under a pounding rain, Private Kenneth Shadrick, eighteen, of Skin Fork, West Virginia, ducked into a foxhole. It was eleven days after the People's Army of North Korea had invaded the South. Under a UN Security Council resolution that he had engineered, President Harry Truman had rushed in US armed forces from Japan, which had been occupied by Americans since World War II, and where Douglas MacArthur was still military governor.

The quiet, blond, blue-eyed, child-faced Shadrick was a coal miner's son, the third of ten children. His father, Theodore, later recalled that Kenny "never caused us a mite of worry": "All that boy liked was to sit hunched up there with a book and a piece of cold bread." An A student, the son favored books about cowboys, as well as the lurid pulp science fiction magazine *Fantastic Novels*. Tightly wound, he played high school football until the day someone stole his uniform from his locker and he told his mother, Lucille, "I'll never go another day of school." Eager to "see some of the world," Kenny obtained written permission from his parents to join the Army. Leaving his Appalachian hollow, he went through basic training at Fort Knox, Kentucky, and shipped out to Japan. At first, he was exhilarated by the novelties. But by the spring of 1950, he was writing Lucille, "Mom, this place is getting me down."

This Wednesday was the first day of American ground engagement with the North Koreans. Twenty-two miles south of Seoul, Shadrick and others on his bazooka team fired at advancing enemy tanks. From his mudhole, he shouted, "One, two, three!" so that an Army photographer could capture the flame from one of his buddies' rocket launcher. Raising his head above ground level to see whether they had made a direct hit, Shadrick was struck by machine-gun fire. Dropping forward, he cried, "Oh, my arm!" As a lieutenant grabbed his wrist to feel his pulse, Kenny died of a wound near his heart. "They've got Shadrick, right in the chest!" a fellow soldier exclaimed. "He's dead, I guess."

Kenny's remains were taken to a nearby hut, where an Army medic observed, "What a place to die." Marguerite Higgins of the *New York Herald Tribune,* who had covered the Allied conquest of Berlin, thought the young man's lifeless face looked surprised. She much later wrote, "The prospect of death had probably seemed as unreal to Private Shadrick as the entire war still seemed to me."* The young man was awarded a posthumous Purple Heart.†

Kenny's family learned the news over breakfast from a neighbor who had heard it from the radio. His father told a reporter that all he knew about Korea was that it was where his son had been killed. Asked about Kenny's mission, Theodore could only reply that he "was fighting against some kind of government." Fury and shock over Kenny's sudden death made his brother Leroy, twenty-five, wish to fight in Korea himself. At 101 pounds, Leroy was too light to enlist, so he gorged himself for a week to become a soldier. Obsessed with what the North Koreans

---

* Higgins had just arrived in South Korea from Tokyo. General Walton Walker had tried to bar her and other women from the country, claiming that the Army did not have the resources to accommodate them, but MacArthur wired the *Herald Tribune* that the "ban on women correspondents has been lifted" because Higgins was "held in highest professional esteem by everyone."

† Although Shadrick was soon widely called the first American to perish in the Korean War, he was probably preceded there in death by other Americans who remained unidentified. Nevertheless Shadrick's gravestone, in the American Legion Cemetery of Beckley, West Virginia, says, "First U.S. Soldier Killed in Korea."

"did to my brother," he vowed to kill ten of the enemy "for every year he spent on earth."

Leroy later recalled that once he got to Korea, his mind "blanked out" and he heard his dead little brother's "voice." Discharged by the Army, he was treated in more than one mental institution and went to prison for income tax fraud. After his release in 1956, he tried to hold up a bank in North Carolina, seeking $5,000 to pay for travel to Independence, Missouri, so that he could assassinate former President Truman, whom he held "directly responsible" for his brother's death. Leroy had planned to murder Truman on the anniversary of Kenny's demise—the day, he later explained, when all of his own "troubles began."

In those days, retired Presidents did not enjoy Secret Service protection—they had none until after John Kennedy's assassination—but this did not bother Harry Truman. Before leaving the presidency in 1953, Truman had vowed, "If any nut tries to shoot me, I'll take the pistol away from him, ram it down his throat and pull the trigger."

✳ ✳ ✳

Truman had first been told of the North Korean assault on Saturday night, June 24, 1950, at the family's white clapboard Victorian house in Independence, Missouri. Planning a tranquil weekend with Bess and their daughter, Margaret, who had gone home for their annual summer respite, he had written a friend, the diplomat Stanley Woodward, that he expected to "order a new roof on the farmhouse and tell some politicians to go to hell. A grand visit—I hope?"

It was eighty-nine degrees that Saturday when the black car pulled up at the Truman home from the Kansas City airport, and the grinning President stepped out, swinging a cane. Someone in the crowd shouted, referring to the fraternal order, "Harry, we missed you at the meeting of the Eagles!" Truman explained that a President "just can't be everywhere he would like to go." After dinner, the family sat on the screened-in porch with Truman's haughty mother-in-law, Madge Wallace, who had always disdained him and still did. By 9:30, Harry retreated to his small, high-ceilinged library on the side of the house.

Secretary of State Dean Acheson called to say, "Mr. President, I have very serious news. The North Koreans have invaded South Korea." Margaret later wrote that as soon as her father heard the report, he "feared this was the opening round in World War III." Loath to scare Americans and much of the world with a sudden flight back to Washington, Truman opted to spend the night in Independence, waiting to obtain intelligence on the magnitude of the invasion.

Sunday morning journals were alive with the news ("SOUTH KOREA INVADED BY REDS," said the *Arizona Republic*). A White House press aide claimed that the President was "concerned but not alarmed" about Korea. Feigning calm, Truman made a preannounced visit to his younger brother Vivian's farm at Grandview, Missouri, where he viewed a new horse and an electric milking contraption. Back to his own house by noon, he took another call from Acheson, who reported that the North Korean action was clearly no rogue caprice but a full-scale offensive. By Truman's later recollection, he replied, "Dean, we've got to stop the sons of bitches, no matter what."

He hurried upstairs to his bedroom, where he packed his bags and donned a double-breasted suit and bow tie; he departed his hometown so abruptly that two aides were left behind. At the airport, when he climbed the stairs to his silvery presidential DC-6, the *Independence,* Margaret and Bess stayed behind on the tarmac, looking distraught. His daughter recorded in her diary that "everything is extremely tense" because "Communist Korea is marching in on Southern Korea and we are going to fight."

While flying to Washington, Truman looked out the window and recalled how Hitler had been allowed to occupy the Rhineland and Japan and march into Manchuria unchallenged in the 1930s. He mused that "the strong had attacked the weak," and that "each time that the democracies failed to act, it had encouraged the aggressors to keep going ahead." He also remembered how the League of Nations in 1936 had failed to stop Mussolini from seizing Ethiopia. He believed that if the Free World did not resist the North Koreans now, affirming the principles of the United Nations, then "no small nation would have the courage to resist threats and aggression by stronger Communist neighbors," ushering in "a third world war."

Early in the evening, the *Independence* landed at the Capital's National Airport. As Truman stepped out of the plane, spectators applauded. Greeted by Acheson and Secretary of Defense Louis Johnson, the President, clutching his Panama hat, paused for photographers, then told them, "That's all. We've got a job to do."* Riding in his car with the other two men and Under Secretary of State James Webb across the Potomac and into the city, Truman inveighed against the North Koreans: "By God, I am going to let them have it!" From the jump seat, Johnson swiveled around and vigorously shook the President's hand.

* * *

BORN IN 1884 to struggling Missouri farmers, Truman never forgot the hardships of his own family—slaveholders on both sides—in the Civil War. As a child, he was told by his mother, Martha, of how, early in the conflict, Union soldiers had forced her own mother, Louisa Young, to make them biscuits and then slaughtered the family's livestock, set the barns aflame, and "stole everything loose that they could carry." The Northern marauders nearly hanged Martha's brother Harrison while trying to force him to admit that their father, Solomon Young, was a Confederate soldier, asking where he was "hiding." Martha Truman so detested the Union victors that she felt Abraham Lincoln deserved assassination. Before she visited the White House, she told her son Vivian, "You tell Harry if he tries to put me in Lincoln's bed, I'll sleep on the floor!"

Hearing his relatives speak of the Civil War quickened young Harry's interest in history. Nearsighted, he was kept by his hardscrabble parents out of contact sports because if he broke his eyeglasses, they could not easily afford a replacement. Truman would later say that as a result he

---

* To better coordinate the armed services, the War Department had been replaced in 1947 by the Department of Defense.

read every book in the Independence public library. His favorite, however, was a set of gilt-edged volumes, published in 1895, that Martha
had bought from a traveling salesman, called *Great Men and Famous
Women*—on the presumption that females could never be great, only
famous—which offered brief profiles, by sundry authors, of over two
hundred eminent figures from Nebuchadnezzar to Sarah Bernhardt.
Truman particularly admired the generals—Hannibal, Andrew Jackson, and Martha's hero Robert E. Lee. For him, reading history was not
"romantic adventure" but "solid instruction and wise teaching which I
somehow felt I wanted and needed."

From his later vantage point of the White House, Truman believed
that if a President knew the history of his predecessors, it would be "easier
for him to go through a similar experience," and that it was "ignorance
that causes most mistakes." He insisted that "not all readers become leaders, but all leaders must be readers"—and that "the only thing new in
the world is the history you don't know." As was true of Wilson, Truman's reading helped him to form very specific views of earlier wartime
Presidents. He dismissed James Madison as a Commander-in-Chief who
"found it difficult to make decisions . . . a weak sister. . . . I don't think we
want to blame his intellectualism for the fact that he wasn't a very good
President. It was just that when it came time for him to act like an executive, he was like a great many other people. . . . They have difficulty doing
it." Truman deemed the War of 1812 "a disaster for us from the start."*

He admired James Polk's strenuous, undaunted use of presidential
power throughout the Mexican War, including his quarrels with Congress.† With Polk in mind, Truman felt that "every strong President
always has trouble with the Congress, whether there's a war on or not.

---

* Truman recalled being told a War of 1812 tale by Franklin Roosevelt, who had claimed that
after the British commander Sir Edward Pakenham was killed during the Battle of New Orleans,
his remains were "pickled" in a barrel of alcohol, which was then roped to the mast of a US ship
for transfer to Great Britain. As Truman recalled the story, when the sailors discovered what was
inside the cask, "they took a gimlet and bored a hole in it and got the alcohol out and drank it, so
Pakenham was not in any condition to be buried when he got back to England." (History tells us
that Pakenham's corpse was indeed preserved in a cask of rum, but there is little evidence that the
ship's crew drank its liquid contents.)

† Truman was John Tyler's great-great-nephew. Harry insisted that his relatives "had mean

But whenever the President knows what he's doing, and knows it's right, he can always convince the Congress [and] tell them what the situation is and why certain things have to be done. You never have any trouble with them after that." Truman honored Lincoln because he "saved the Union, and that's the important thing." He identified with Lincoln's modest origins and admired how he pushed the Constitution to its limits to wage the Civil War, knowing both "its intentions and the powers that aren't put down in writing," which were "there to be used by a President in emergencies." Truman said that Lincoln aimed to "stretch" the Constitution, but "never actually cracked it."

After high school, too poor to afford college, Truman "thirsted," so he later said, for appointment to West Point, but was disqualified by his myopia. In 1905, he enlisted in the National Guard ("they needed recruits") and, while working his family farm, stayed in for six years. In June 1917, two months after President Wilson took the nation into the Great War, Truman reentered the Guard, later writing that, as a "true patriot," he was "stirred heart and soul" by Wilson's wartime messages. He later described Wilson's Fourteen Points as "one of the greatest and most eloquent documents in the history of the country." His adulation of Wilson may have seemed to clash with his antipathy toward Ivy League intellectuals. But underneath Truman's brisk, practical facade was an idealistic core that responded to Wilson's romantic vision of a world grounded on international law. From high school, Harry had, in his own hand, copied and recopied rhyming couplets from "Locksley Hall," Tennyson's long dramatic monologue of 1835, and kept the scraps of paper in his wallet for most of his life:

> *Till the war-drum throbb'd no longer, and the battle flags were*
> *furl'd*
> *In the Parliament of Man, the Federation of the World.*
> *There the common sense of most shall hold a fretful realm in awe*
> *And the kindly earth shall slumber, lapt in universal law.*

---

dispositions" as a result of being related to Tyler, for whom he felt "grudging respect" as "a stubborn son of a bitch."

Fighting in France meant leaving his beloved Bess Wallace back in Independence. As Truman wrote in 1931, by heeding Wilson's call, "I felt that I was a Galahad after the Grail, and I'll never forget how my love cried on my shoulder when I told her I was going. That was worth a life time on this earth." Before his training at Camp Doniphan, Oklahoma, he declined to marry Bess, writing her, "I don't think it would be right for me to ask you to tie yourself to a prospective cripple." He pledged to be "just as loyal to you as if you were my wife." He would not "extract any promises" from her not to "go out with any other guy," but "I'll be as jealous as the mischief although not begrudging you the good time." Referring to the Kaiser, he wrote Bess, "I do want to be in on the death of this 'Scourge of God.' Just think of what he'd do to our great country and our beautiful women if he only could."

In March 1918, Truman and his comrades boarded the USS *George Washington,* the same ship that later took Woodrow Wilson to France. "There we were watching New York's skyline diminish," Truman later recalled, "and wondering if we'd be heroes or corpses." That July, serving with the 129th Field Artillery, he took command of Battery D, the first serious leadership assignment of his life. "Captain Harry" wrote Bess that before facing the enemy, in Alsace, amid the "great hubbub and excite-ment," he was struck by "a real creepy feeling." He confessed to her the fear beneath his bravado: "The men think I am not much afraid of shells, but they don't know I was too scared to run and that is pretty scared."

Truman's battery suffered only a single fatality. After the armistice that November, he noted that the front had grown "so quiet it made your head ache." With the war done, he complained to a cousin that Wilson's arrival in France to shape the peace had postponed his own return to Missouri; thus he was "very anxious that Woodie cease his gallivantin' around."

After the Great War, Truman married Bess and opened a haberdash-ery store in Kansas City with his Battery D chum Eddie Jacobson, which in time collapsed. Elected county judge in 1922, and to the US Senate in 1934, as a Roosevelt man, he felt deeply wounded and resentful when, during the 1940 campaign, the President encouraged Truman's primary opponent, Governor Lloyd Stark. Knowing his American history, Truman remembered how the Committee on the Conduct of the War had browbeaten Lincoln. In early 1941, he won the Senate's consent to establish a far more modest version of the panel, with himself as chairman, to monitor Roosevelt's rearmament program. Drawn to the subject by his indignation when small businesses were squeezed out of the action, the Missouri Senator was not unaware that his new role would establish him as a major Washington figure.

Unlike Lincoln's scourges Chandler and Wade, Truman made it clear that he had no interest in advising the President on which generals to promote, noting that his committee "does not go on fishing expeditions." Nevertheless Roosevelt tried to clip the new panel's wings by deploying Senate allies to keep its funding small ("the magnificent sum of $15,000," carped Truman). After Pearl Harbor, Truman tried to join the Army, at age fifty-seven, but was told by General Marshall, "We don't need old stiffs like you—this will be a young man's war." The Senator sent a message to Roosevelt, asking how his committee could help. When the President did not respond, Truman complained to Bess, "He's so damn afraid that he won't have all the power and glory that he won't let his friends help as it should be done." Throughout the war, Truman managed to scrutinize national defense with sufficient aplomb as to make him a serious option in 1944 when Roosevelt looked for a new Vice President. Then, in April 1945, as Truman exclaimed, "the moon, the stars and all the planets" fell upon him.

* * *

AFTER THE ALLIES defeated Japan, which had occupied Korea, the United States and Soviet Union divided the Korean peninsula at the thirty-eighth parallel. This dividing line, so far north, was proposed by a young State Department official, Dean Rusk of Georgia, who had been a Colonel in the war's China-Burma-India theater. Rusk was eager to include the Korean capital of Seoul in the region for which US forces would be responsible, even though it would be more difficult to defend. By 1948, the Soviet and American zones had evolved into national entities of their own, with the Communist North under Kim Il-sung and the South's Republic of Korea under President Syngman Rhee. US and Soviet troops withdrew from the peninsula.

The authoritarian Kim Il-sung was eager to invade the South, but when he went to Moscow in March 1949 to press his case, Stalin, recoiling from the danger of a shooting war with the United States, would not grant his consent. But the Soviet leader took notice when President Truman declined to employ the US military in an effort to keep China from falling to Mao Zedong's Communists. Stalin was also told by some Soviet intelligence officials that Truman did not consider it crucial enough to defend South Korea by military force.

Against this backdrop, in January 1950, Truman's Secretary of State, Dean Acheson, appeared before the National Press Club in Washington. Acheson, who had given the United States that shove toward war against Japan in 1941, without sanction from President Roosevelt, now accidentally signaled Kim Il-sung that America might not respond with military action should his armies invade the South. In his speech, Acheson described the American "defense perimeter" in East Asia but did not include Taiwan or South Korea, which, he said, would be protected by the United Nations. The Cold War scholar John Lewis Gaddis has written that Acheson's speech "significantly reshaped Stalin's thinking on the risks of war with the United States in east Asia."

After Acheson's address, Kim Il-sung secretly told Moscow that it was time to "liberate" South Korea. General Terentii Shtykov, the Soviet envoy to North Korea, wrote the Kremlin that Kim would not launch an attack on his own "because he is a Communist, a disciplined person, and for him, the order of Comrade Stalin is law," but reported that Kim believed that if he acted, South Korea would have "little hope of American assistance." That April, during another visit to Moscow, Kim reputedly assured Stalin that "the Americans would never participate in the war," and that if such a conflict began, it would last only a few days because South Koreans would welcome his Army as liberators. Stalin warned Kim not to "expect great assistance" from the Kremlin, which had "more important challenges to meet ". . . If you should get kicked in the teeth, I shall not lift a finger. You have to ask Mao for all the help." The result, as Gaddis later wrote, was "the first overt military assault across an internationally recognized boundary since the end of World War II."*

✳ ✳ ✳

O N SUNDAY EVENING, June 25, Truman arrived at Blair House, the presidential guest quarters across Pennsylvania Avenue from the White House, where the First Family was residing during the three-year reconstruction of the crumbling Executive Mansion. First he went upstairs to telephone Bess that he had landed safely. Walking down the staircase, he vowed, almost to himself, "We can't let the U.N. down! We can't let the U.N. down!" Then he joined a dozen guests for cocktails in the garden, including his Secretaries of State and Defense, his Chairman of the Joint Chiefs, General Omar Bradley, and other military and diplomatic officials. Dining at 7:45, with the French doors flung open to admit the soft evening breeze (the President later wrote Bess that the downstairs rooms were "very hot"), Truman did not get down to business until the meal—fried chicken, asparagus, biscuits, shoestring potatoes, and vanilla ice cream with chocolate topping—was over and the servers were out of earshot.

That afternoon, in a special Sunday session, ten members of the UN Security Council—still housed in temporary quarters at Lake Success, New York—had upon American request convened around a horseshoe-shaped table to discuss the North Korean invasion. In protest of the council's failure to unseat a delegate from Chiang Kai-shek's Nationalist Chinese regime after Mao's revolution, the Soviet envoy was absent

---

* Gaddis rightly argues that Kim might have been better advised to challenge South Korea with guerrillas, as Ho Chi Minh later did in South Vietnam, because "only a full-fledged surprise attack, like the one at Pearl Harbor, could have convinced Truman and his advisers to reverse their carefully considered decision to disengage from the Asian mainland."

and hence unable to veto a US-proposed resolution to condemn the "unprovoked attack" on South Korea and demand an immediate halt to "hostilities" and removal of Kim Il-sung's troops.*

As Truman later recalled, all of his Blair House guests were agreed on "whatever had to be done to meet this aggression." General Bradley noted "intense moral outrage." Acheson observed "great confusion about the crisis." The chiefs of the Air Force and Navy, General Hoyt Vandenberg and Admiral Forrest Sherman, argued that aiding their South Korean counterparts might be sufficient. The Army Chief of Staff, General J. Lawton Collins, warned that the South Korean Army might be "really broken," which would require the insertion of US ground troops. Dean Rusk, now Assistant Secretary of State for Asia, warned that if the Communists took all of Korea, it would be "a dagger pointed at the heart of Japan." All were grimly aware that the Soviet Union was now, as it had been for a year, an atomic power. Bradley insisted that the Soviets were "obviously testing us" in Korea: "Russia is not yet ready for war" and "the line ought to be drawn now." (This was in spite of his urging the previous year that American troops be withdrawn from Korea because the country had so little strategic importance and would be so difficult to defend.) Bradley said, "We should act under the guise of aid to the United Nations."

Truman agreed, "most emphatically," that the line must be drawn. Predicting that North Korea would not "pay any attention to the United Nations," he warned that the United States would have to use force if its order was to be obeyed. The Russians were "trying to get Korea by default, gambling that we would be afraid of starting a third world war and would offer no resistance." The US was "still holding the stronger hand," but how much stronger was "hard to tell." Vandenberg warned that "a considerable number of Russian jets are based on Shanghai." The President asked him whether "we could knock out their bases in the Far East." Vandenberg replied that "this might take some time," but "it could be done if we used A-Bombs." Truman asked for a contingency plan to "wipe out all Soviet air bases in the Far East."

---

* Neutral Yugoslavia abstained.

James Webb began to describe what South Korea's defense would require in terms of American domestic politics. "We're not going to talk about politics!" Truman exclaimed. "I'll handle the political affairs!" He directed that MacArthur send weapons to South Korea and that the Seventh Fleet keep Mao's China from attacking Chiang's outpost on Formosa. Before the dinner ended, the President asked his guests not to speak to the press, even on background: it was "absolutely vital that there should be no leak." Around eleven, the officials slipped out of Blair House through the back door.

Staying behind, Acheson showed the President a cable from John Foster Dulles, the New York Republican lawyer-diplomat who would have been Secretary of State had Truman been defeated by Thomas Dewey in 1948.* Dulles, now a part-time adviser to the State Department, had just arrived in Tokyo from Korea. In his dispatch, he warned that if South Korea could not repulse the Northern attack, "US force should be used even though this risks Russian counter moves. To sit by while Korea is overrun by unprovoked armed attack would start a disastrous chain of events leading most probably to world war." Dulles's recommendation meant that internationalist Republicans would probably back Truman if he acted forcefully in Korea. It also may have been a veiled warning that if the President did not so respond, those same Republicans might denounce him for cowardice.

At the core of Harry Truman's reputation was decisiveness. Fully in character, he had quickly drawn a conclusion as to what the North Korean attack meant, and how America should retaliate. However—as we can now understand from Soviet evidence released in the 1990s, after the Cold War ended—his interpretation of the invasion was not accurate. Its chief architect had not actually been Stalin but Kim Il-sung. To be sure, Stalin had secretly offered Kim a green light—if the plan worked, it would be a low-cost way to steal South Korea from the Western orbit—but the Soviet leader had made it plain that if Kim needed additional ground forces, he would have to get them not from the Soviet Union but from Mao.

---

* And who was appointed to that job by President Dwight Eisenhower in 1953.

On Monday, June 26, Truman was reminded of his decision to bolster Turkey and Greece against Soviet subversion in 1947, under his newly invented "Truman Doctrine." The outwardly unflappable President now confided in a letter to Bess, "Haven't been so upset since Greece and Turkey fell into our lap. Let's hope for the best." He fully shared Acheson's view that this crisis could be "a turning-point in world history," telling his young aide George Elsey, "Korea is the Greece of the Far East. If we just stand by, they'll move into Iran and take over the whole Middle East. There's no telling what they'll do if we don't put up a fight now."[*]

That morning, Acheson called Wisconsin's Alexander Wiley, ranking Republican on the Senate Foreign Relations Committee, assuring him that the South Koreans were "in good fighting shape." He hoped that "within a very short time" he or the President could "consult" with Wiley's panel. Wiley asked if the Soviets were involved in the North Korean attack. Acheson said there was "no evidence" of this, despite "the strong suspicion that it had been stimulated by the Russians." Calling the West Virginia Democrat John Kee, Chairman of the House Foreign Affairs Committee, Acheson warned that Korea was "a delicate situation, at the present, and at this opening moment, it really [has] to be in the hands of the President." Kee called him back that afternoon to ask for a briefing. Acheson said it would be "pretty difficult to do that now," because there were new reports from Korea that things were "not going so well": American supplies "might not be able to get in."

Shaken and weeping, the South Korean Ambassador, Chang Myon, arrived at the West Wing, which was untouched by the Mansion's construction work, and pleaded with Truman for "all possible aid" to his country's forces, which were "deficient in artillery, tanks and aircraft." The President replied that help was on the way, but South Koreans "must continue to fight effectively." He noted that the battle was only

---

[*] Elsey had served as a wartime naval officer in Franklin Roosevelt's Map Room. Comparing the two Presidents he served, Elsey reminisced in 2013, at age ninety-five, that "Roosevelt was up in the clouds, looking down on us. Truman was right down on the ground with us."

forty-eight hours old, and that freedom fighters in other countries had "defended their liberties, under much more discouraging situations, through to ultimate victory."

Senator Styles Bridges, Republican from New Hampshire, was one of the foremost leaders of the powerful China Lobby, which demanded to know only a year before, "Who lost China?" and backed Chiang Kai-shek's return to the Chinese mainland, there to supposedly overthrow Mao. Now Bridges was asking, "Will we continue appeasement?" The California Republican William Knowland warned that if South Korea were allowed to "succumb," there would be "little chance of stopping Communism anywhere on the continent of Asia." Tom Connally of Texas, the Democratic Chairman of the Senate Foreign Relations Committee, assured his colleagues that "the President of the United States is not going to sell out the interests of the United States or its people. He is not going to tremble like a psychopath before the Russian power." The post–World War II isolationist Robert Taft told reporters that while North Korea's attack might jeopardize US prestige, it was hardly cause for the nation to enter another war: "In Korea, as a result of the fool policy of Yalta, the Communists have control of half the country. We assigned them half the country. Let them set up an Army and get ready."

That evening, Truman dined at Blair House by himself, then gathered another war council at nine o'clock. MacArthur was reporting from Tokyo that "a complete collapse is imminent" in South Korea. General Collins told Truman that the South Korean chief of staff had "no fight left in him." Acheson insisted that it was "important for us to do something" in Korea, "even if the effort [is] not successful." General Vandenberg reported that the "first Yak plane"—meaning the Soviet-built Yakovlev Yak-9 fighter, flown by North Korea—had been "shot down." Truman said he hoped it was "not the last."

Everyone present knew that throughout World War II, Roosevelt had avoided sending US ground forces to the Asian mainland. Bradley now told Truman that they should study the potential dangers for at least a few days before he made a choice so fateful. For the moment, the President thus chose to aid the South Koreans with Navy and Air

Force but not ground troops. Nor would American sailors or airmen be allowed to operate above the thirty-eighth parallel—at least, "not yet." Dean Rusk suggested that if the Soviets were to make another move against the West, "Formosa would be the next likely spot." The President said he wouldn't give Chiang Kai-shek and his forces "a nickel" for any purpose whatever, noting that "all the money we [have] given them is now invested in United States real estate." Truman went on, "I don't want to go to war," explaining, "Everything I have done in the past five years has been to try to avoid making a decision such as I had to make tonight." He asked Bradley whether he should mobilize the National Guard to fight in Korea, noting that the Guard had "some pretty good air." If so, he would go to Congress to ask for funds. General Collins told the President, "If we [are] going to commit ground forces in Korea, we must mobilize."

After the meeting, the President told Acheson and his Assistant Secretary of State for United Nations affairs, John Hickerson, "Now let's all have a drink. It's been a hard day." Over a glass of bourbon, Truman told them, "I have hoped and prayed that I would never have to make a decision like the one I have just made today. But I saw nothing else that was possible for me to do. . . . Now, with this drink, that's out of my mind." He explained,

> I did this for the United Nations. I believed in the League of Nations. It failed. Lots of people thought that it failed because we weren't in it to back it up. Okay now, we started the United Nations. It was our idea, and in this first big test, we just couldn't let them down. If a collective system, under the UN, can work, it must be made to work. And now is the time to call their bluff.

On Tuesday morning at eleven thirty, having summoned leaders of Congress to the Cabinet Room, Truman read aloud a statement he was about to issue saying that the North Korean attack "makes it plain beyond all doubt that communism has passed beyond the use of subversion to conquer independent nations, and will now use armed invasion and war." Providing "assistance" to help the UN fulfill its resolution, he would send "United States air and sea forces to give the Korean government troops cover and support."

Maryland's Millard Tydings informed the President that the Senate Armed Services Committee, of which he was chairman, had that morning endorsed extending the military draft.* Some of the Republicans present were startled that Truman had moved so far toward war without making any serious effort to consult Congress in advance. New Jersey's Charles Eaton, ranking Republican on the House Foreign Affairs Committee, asked him if the United States was "now committed to defend South Korea from invasion." Truman crisply replied that his "statement made this clear." Another New Jersey Republican, Senator H. Alexander Smith, wished to know whether he intended to ask Congress to pass a resolution endorsing American military action in the Korean struggle. Cagily Truman replied that he would "take it under advisement."

That afternoon, in the Oval Office, Acheson urged the President not to ask for a congressional endorsement for his action in Korea: events were moving too quickly. Were he still a Senator, Truman might have objected had a President grabbed such unilateral authority for himself, but he now complied with his Secretary of State. Congress and the country were already consumed by arguments over the loss of China and suspected Soviet spies, such as Alger Hiss, who had been convicted of perjury in January 1950, after dramatic hearings that starred the young Congressman Richard Nixon of California. The President had no stomach to drag the issue of war in Korea into this morass, and he knew that time was of the essence. That evening, after American lobbying, the UN Security Council specifically asked its members to respond to North Korea's aggression with military force.

✳ ✳ ✳

---

* In 1948, with the start of the Cold War, Congress had launched the second peacetime draft in American history.

ROBERT TAFT WAS furious at Truman's effort to steamroll Congress. On Wednesday, June 28, he took the Senate floor to denounce the President's "bungling and inconsistent foreign policy," culminating with the North Korean attack. He complained that the President had not consulted, only informed, congressional leaders about his response. While conceding that America's obligations as a UN member had changed "traditional considerations," Taft proclaimed, "I do not think it justifies the President's present action without approval of Congress . . . If it is what it seems to me, it is a complete usurpation by the President of authority to use the armed forces of this country. . . . If the President can intervene in Korea without Congressional approval, he can go to war in Malaya or Indonesia or Iran or South America."

Taft also complained that in his January National Press Club speech, Acheson had "encouraged" the North Koreans to presume that the United States would not defend the South. He called for the Secretary of State's resignation, to the applause of Acheson's chief Senate enemies, William Jenner of Indiana and Joseph McCarthy of Wisconsin. (In February, the latter had given his notorious speech in Wheeling, West Virginia, charging that the State Department was riddled with secret Communists.) "We are now actually engaged in a de facto war with the North Korean Communists," Taft warned. "That in itself is serious, but nothing compared to the possibility that it might lead to war with Soviet Russia." Thus he pledged to support a congressional resolution supporting the President's decision and any Americans fighting in Korea.

Defending Truman, the Senate Majority Leader, Scott Lucas of Illinois, replied that when Taft blamed "everything in Korea" on the President, "the only thing such action does is to help Mr. Stalin." That same day, the President wrote Senator Joseph O'Mahoney, a Wyoming Democrat, that by using the Navy and Air Force to aid South Korea, "we will either get results or we will have to go all-out to maintain our position." He told his National Security Council (NSC) that he was doing his best "to avoid any feeling of panic, and to keep people from being scared," but did not intend to "back out" of the fight with North Korea, "unless there should develop a military situation which we had to meet elsewhere." Truman also pondered a cabled warning from his Ambassador in Seoul, John Muccio, that the "situation had deteriorated so rapidly" that if the President had not opted to aid the South Koreans, it was "doubtful any organized Korean resistance would have continued through [the] night."

On Thursday, June 29, at 4:00 p.m., Truman met the press in the Indian Treaty Room of the Executive Office Building. No longer the intimate, casual session around the Oval Office desk that it was under Franklin Roosevelt, the presidential press conference was now larger and more formal, although reporters still had to secure the President's permission to quote him. Truman was told, "Everybody is asking in this country—are we or are we not at war?" He replied, "We are not at war." Asked if reporters could publish that reply, he consented. Another question: "Are we going to use ground troops in Korea?" "No comment on that," responded the President. Someone asked about "any possibility of having to use the atomic bomb." Ominously Truman replied, "No comment."

Asked to "elaborate" on his decision to aid the South Koreans, Truman replied, for quotation, that their country had been "set up with the United Nations' help" and "was unlawfully attacked by a bunch of bandits." UN members were "going to the relief of the Korean republic to suppress a bandit raid." Asked about Taft's demand for Acheson to resign, Truman replied that the Senator's "political statement, at this time, is entirely uncalled for." Someone asked, "Would it be correct, against your explanation, to call this a police action?" Truman said, for quotation, "Yes, that is exactly what it amounts to." Final question: "Mr. President, your 'no comment' on the atomic bomb might be subject to misinterpretation. Has there been any change—" Truman interrupted by saying, "No comment will be made on any matter of strategy." Headlines after the press conferences touted the President's impromptu endorsement of the term "police action."

At a 5:00 p.m. NSC meeting in the Cabinet Room, Louis Johnson read out a new directive that the Joint Chiefs of Staff wished to cable to MacArthur in Tokyo. Expanding the General's mission, it would authorize MacArthur to send ground soldiers to the Korean port city of Pusan, there to protect American supply and communication lines. Truman replied, "I do not want any implication in the letter that we are going to war with Russia at this time. . . . We must be damn careful. . . . We want to take any steps we have to push the North Koreans behind the line, but I don't want to get us overcommitted to a whole lot of other things that could mean war." He simply wished to "destroy air bases, gasoline supplies, ammunition dumps and places like that," north of the thirty-eighth parallel, and "keep the North Koreans from killing the people we are trying to save." Fatefully the President told the Joint Chiefs they could give MacArthur "all the authority he needs to do that, but he is not to go north of the 38th parallel."

Acheson backed Truman's decision to send US ground troops to Korea: "It would be a great disaster if we were to lose now, and it [is] essential to give the commander-on-the-spot whatever he needs to stop a disaster." He insisted that US soldiers "be given the right to fight Soviet forces," if they were encountered: they must "have the right to defend themselves." According to the official record, "everybody agreed." The Secretary of State said he was "convinced that the Russians do not intend to enter directly into the Korean dispute." Consulted about offers of naval support and airplanes from US allies, Truman ordered, "Take everything—we may need them." He complained that, just as in World War II, it was "hard to get information out of MacArthur," and directed Louis Johnson to ask the General for daily reports on the fighting in Korea. He had "no quarrel with anybody" and didn't intend to have one. He just wanted to know what the facts were, and "I don't want any leaks."

The President had never met the legendary MacArthur, but he did not trust him. As early as 1945, Truman had complained to his diary about "Mr. Prima Donna, Brass Hat, Five Star MacArthur. . . . Don't see how a country can produce such men as Robert E. Lee, John J. Pershing, Eisenhower and Bradley, and at the same time produce Custers, Pattons and MacArthurs." Nor was Truman charmed when MacArthur, as a sitting General, flirted with running against him for President in 1948. The White House press aide Eben Ayers recorded Truman's belief that MacArthur was "a supreme egoist, who regards himself as something of a god." After John Foster Dulles called on Truman that week, the President confided to Ayers that the Republican diplomat had told him that "when word came to Tokyo of the outbreak in Korea, MacArthur knew nothing of it" and the General's staff was "afraid" to tell him; thus Dulles had done so himself. Truman told Ayers that Dulles was proposing that MacArthur be "hauled back to the United States," but he had reminded the visitor that MacArthur was popular among Republicans. The President had told Dulles that he "could not recall MacArthur without causing a tremendous reaction in this country, where he has been built up to a heroic stature."

At Truman's direction, the Joint Chiefs cabled the General with permission to use ground forces in Korea. At the President's direction, they carefully warned MacArthur that their message

> does not constitute a decision to engage in war with the Soviet Union if Soviet forces intervene in Korea. The decision regarding Korea, however, was taken in full realization of the risks involved. If Soviet forces actively oppose our operations in Korea, your forces should defend themselves, should take no action to aggravate the situation, and you should report the situation to Washington.

After inspecting the South Korean battlefront, MacArthur warned the Joint Chiefs on Friday, June 30, "The Korean Army and coastal forces are in confusion, have not seriously fought and lack leadership. . . . They are incapable of gaining the initiative over such a force as that embodied in the North Korean Army." The General's diplomatic adviser in Tokyo, William Sebald, cabled Acheson that Muccio was reporting from Seoul a "desperate and rapidly deteriorating situation. . . . He had spent most of night and practically all day with top Koreans . . . and feels he can hold them in line a little longer. Danger, however, is that they might soon panic. He strongly urged all-out effort before situation out of hand."

At 3:40 a.m. Washington time, General Collins and others spoke by telephone with MacArthur, who complained that the Joint Chiefs' cable of the previous evening did not give him "sufficient latitude." MacArthur warned, "Time is of the essence, and a clear-cut decision is imperative." After the conversation, Collins alerted the Secretary of the Army, Frank Pace, who called the President at Blair House at five o'clock. Truman had been awake for a half hour, and had just shaved. Told by Pace that MacArthur wanted two divisions of ground troops for Korea, he immediately said yes, later scrawling in his diary that the force was "to be used at Mac's discretion." Collins telephoned MacArthur that he could start by moving one regimental combat team into the Korean forward combat area: "You will be advised later as to further buildup." He added, "We all have full confidence in you and your command."

Truman asked Pace and Johnson to consider accepting two divisions offered by Chiang Kai-shek, noting that Nationalist China was a permanent member of the UN Security Council. He wrote in his journal,

> Since Britain, Australia, Canada and the Netherlands have come in with ships and planes we probably should use the Chinese ground forces. What will that do to Mao Tze Tung we don't know. Must be careful not to cause a general Asiatic war. Russia is figuring on an attack in the Black Sea and toward the Persian Gulf. Both prizes Moscow has wanted since Ivan the Terrible who is now their hero with Stalin & Lenin.

At an eleven o'clock meeting with department secretaries and congressional leaders in the Cabinet Room, Truman announced that he would issue a brief new public statement that "General MacArthur has been authorized to use certain supporting ground units" in Korea and was acting "under the auspices of the United Nations." Tom Connally praised the President for allowing US forces to range north of the thirty-eighth parallel "when necessary." General Bradley explained, "Sometimes the most effective way to hit your enemy is to go after his bases." Senator John Gurney of South Dakota said he hoped Truman understood that now that they were in this war, there could be no backing down. The President replied, "I certainly do."

Senator Wiley asked if Truman thought the Chinese Communists would now aid the North Koreans. The President said he had "no intelligence on that subject yet," but there were "a lot of rumors flying around" that Mao's Army would fight. Congressman John Vorys, Republican from Ohio, urged Truman to "get some Asiatic peoples in the fighting to help us, not just other white people," so that "it wouldn't look so much like 'white man's imperialism.'" The President warned that "if we got some Asiatics—like Chiang's men on Formosa, for example—we would have to be awfully careful of the Chinese Communists."

Then the Senate Minority Leader, Kenneth Wherry of Nebraska, who had opposed US involvement in the United Nations, rose from the Cabinet table, as if giving a speech, and asked if Truman had planned to inform Congress before taking the major step of sending ground troops into Korea. The President replied that he had already dispatched the force, but if there was a "real emergency," he would "advise" the House and Senate. Wherry replied that Congress "ought to be consulted" before such momentous actions. Truman insisted that the "weekend crisis" in Korea had been "an emergency. There was no time for lots of talk. . . . I just had to act as Commander-in-Chief, and I did. I told MacArthur to go to the relief of the Koreans and carry out the instructions of the United Nations Security Council."

Wherry stood firm: "I understand the action all right, but I do feel the Congress ought to be consulted before any large-scale actions are taken again." Truman responded that if he took any further such moves, he would "tell Congress about it," but made no pledge to ask for consent from the House or Senate in advance. Vice President Alben Barkley began to discuss a British offer of naval aid in Korea, but Wherry rose again to say he would "like the floor." Again he told the President that he "ought to consult Congress before taking drastic steps" in Korea. Truman replied that as soon as he had "definite information that required action by the Congress," he would "inform" its members: "If there is any necessity for Congressional action, I will come to you. But I hope we can get those bandits in Korea suppressed without that."

Changing the subject, Senator Tydings urged the President to seek troops from other countries, if only "just a company or two." Rising for a third time, Wherry broke in to say he had been studying Truman's new statement: "The President should not take such steps without Congressional approval." Breaking the tension in the room, Congressman Dewey Short, Republican from Missouri, rose to announce that he was "expressing the opinion of practically everyone in the Congress" by thanking Truman "for the quality of his leadership." The President closed with a warning: "This is all very delicate. I don't want it stated anyplace that I am telling MacArthur what to do. He is not an American general now. He is acting for the United Nations. It would spoil everything if we said he was just doing what we tell him to do."

After the meeting, still seething over his confrontation with Wherry, Truman received Joseph Kennedy, who was still one of the nation's best-known isolationists, and whose son Jack was now a backbencher in the House. Kennedy had asked to see the President about relations with the Vatican, and was surprised that, despite the Korean crisis, Truman was keeping the appointment.* As Kennedy later wrote in his diary, the President "looked rather cross." Showing his guest to a chair next to his desk, Truman reported that he had just met with members of Congress, including "some real stinkers," but all had backed him on Korea. Referring to the North Koreans and their Soviet patrons, he said he was not going to let "those sons of bitches" push him around. He doubted that the Russians had a geopolitical motive to plunge directly into the Korean struggle: "They are much more interested in the Black Sea and the oil peninsulas and Yugoslavia." As Kennedy later recorded, Truman realized "that these are horrible times and that the decisions he is making are going to affect all civilization."

Kennedy, who was close to Robert Taft, warned the President that his position on Korea reminded him of the moment Neville Chamberlain had guaranteed the security of Poland, making a European war almost inevitable. No doubt recalling how Kennedy had endorsed Chamberlain's mollification of Hitler, Truman shot back that "Chamberlain

---

* In the mid-1930s, when Kennedy was the first Chairman of Franklin Roosevelt's Securities and Exchange Commission, the new Senator Truman had been a party guest at his large rented mansion, Marwood, in suburban Maryland. In October 1944, two months after losing his namesake eldest son over the English Channel, an angry, grieving Kennedy had asked Truman, "Harry, what the hell are you doing campaigning for that crippled son of a bitch that killed my son Joe?"

quit at Munich," and that in this Korean crisis, he was "not going to appease." He added that "if the French and British had stood up to Hitler, the Germans would have retreated." Kennedy told him that Americans were "worried that we would be bombed and could not be protected." The President replied, "They are right. They can't be protected, and neither can the Russians. . . . We could drop bombs on Leningrad tonight."

* * *

THE START OF the Korean confrontation was by no means Truman's finest hour. He and Acheson had blundered into this war, which neither man wanted or expected, by leading the Soviets and North Koreans to believe that if the South were invaded, the United States might refuse to defend it. Once the war began, contrary to his reputation for plainspokenness, the President failed to level with Americans about how costly the Korean conflict might ultimately be. He had refused to ask Congress in advance to approve his use of military force in Korea, noting that instead he had asked the UN Security Council for "authority" to do so. But the United Nations Participation Act of 1945, which dictated the terms under which the United States would join the new world body, required that a President ask permission from Congress before providing armed forces to the United Nations.* Nevertheless, in the summer of 1950, a Senate and House that were both dominated by Truman's own party, operating in a mood of alarm, made no serious effort to hold the President to the letter of this law on Korea.

In July, Truman's aide George Elsey reminded his chief that drafts of a resolution by Congress approving the President's response to Korea had been "kicking around the White House." But, with his expansive view of presidential authority, Truman told Elsey, "I certainly never would have asked for anything. It was none of Congress's business. If

---

* Testifying in 1945, as Under Secretary of State, Acheson had assured the House Foreign Affairs Committee that only after obtaining congressional approval would a President be authorized to furnish a "contingent of troops to the Security Council."

Congress wanted to do it on its own initiative, that would have been all right with me, but I just did what was in my power, and there was no need for any Congressional resolution."

Thus Truman became the first President to engage the country in a major foreign conflict—this one potentially risking war with China—without bothering to ask Congress for a war declaration. The Democratic majority in the House and Senate could easily have obtained a declaration for him. But instead Truman had expediently cut the legislative branch out of the action at the start, unwilling to ask it even for a simple resolution endorsing his decision to use force against North Korea. As a result, Truman had undermined his ability to wage the Korean War and established a dangerous example for future American Presidents.

CHAPTER FIFTEEN

"I Don't Ask Their Permission"

O N MONDAY, July 3, 1950, during a meeting at Blair House, Acheson tried to persuade Truman to address a Joint Session of Congress, asking for its endorsement of the US military action in Korea. He said he had drafted a joint resolution and "tried to avoid anything which would give rise to debate." It would have Congress commend "the action by the United States," not "by the President," and it would not mention other danger spots in Asia, such as Formosa or Indochina. Truman agreed that he must be "very careful" not to appear as if he was "trying to get around Congress and use extra-Constitutional powers."

But Scott Lucas, his Senate leader, asked why any resolution was necessary, since the Korean fighting was "now going along well" and the President had "very properly done what he had to without consulting the Congress." Lucas warned Truman that he would be "practically asking for a declaration of war." "Exactly the point," replied Truman, who explained, with contrived reasoning, that by sending troops to Korea, he had been acting not as President but "as Commander-in-Chief of our forces in the Far East." Moreover, he noted, the Senate and House were now out of session; why court trouble by calling them back to Washington?

Acheson later told his aides that Truman believed that if he asked

Congress to approve what he had done, it "weakens the power of the Presidency" and "we have to be able to respond quickly in circumstances that are typical of this era." Truman told Dean Rusk that he liked James Polk "because Polk regularly told Congress to go to hell on foreign policy matters."

On Sunday, July 9, MacArthur cabled, "The situation in Korea is critical." Despite US efforts to build sufficient force to "hold the enemy," American military opposition to North Korean mechanized units and armor had been "ineffective" against "overwhelming odds of more than ten to one." The General reported that the enemy force "more and more assumes the aspect of a combination of Soviet leadership and technical guidance with Chinese Communist ground elements." Three days later, Truman wrote Bess, "It looks bad in the Far East. We can't get there in force for 3 weeks and by then it may be too late. Or there'll be an explosion someplace else." Referring to his nuclear option, he went on, "Hope we can contain it and not have to order our terrible weapon turned loose." He recounted to her that under the strain of war, "I lost my temper yesterday and gave old Sen. Wiley a tongue lashing at a conference I was having with eight Senators."

For weeks after sending US armed forces into Korea, Truman gave no extended explanation of his action to the American people. He was worried about spreading a "war psychosis." This was a mistake. By entering a war to save a regime most Americans knew nothing about, in a theater from which he had previously withdrawn US troops, he had left much of the public puzzled, asking why, only five years after winning a global war, the American goliath was bogged down in a struggle against North Koreans. Korea had shown the vulnerability in America's post–World War II position as the world's overwhelming superpower: vast global commitments could oblige the nation to engage in all sorts of local wars, like Korea's, in which American military dominance did not necessarily provide an advantage.

With a lot to explain, Truman opted to present his own televised version of a fireside chat. On Wednesday evening, July 19, from behind a lectern in the White House movie theater, he told Americans, echoing Roosevelt's language after Pearl Harbor, that the "sneak attack" on

South Korea "came without provocation and without warning." The assault had shown, "beyond all doubt, that the international Communist movement is willing to use armed invasion to conquer independent nations." He warned that "there may be similar acts of aggression in other parts of the world. . . . We know that the cost of freedom is high. But we are determined to preserve our freedom, no matter what the cost. . . . The free nations have learned the fateful lesson of the 1930s. . . . Appeasement leads only to further aggression and ultimately to war."[*] Cautioning that "it will take a hard, tough fight to halt the invasion, and to drive the Communists back," Truman read aloud from an optimistic report he had lately received from MacArthur.[†]

It is a good thing that Truman's reputation for straight talk did not depend on this speech. He gave no hint of the considerable chance that North Korea had taken the offensive because he and Acheson had signaled to Stalin and Kim Il-sung that the United States would not defend the South in a crunch. He claimed instead that the Korean assault was the inevitable, well-planned vanguard of a systematic effort by monolithic Communism to invade free nations.

Truman's early conduct of his war did not escape criticism from his own party. Lyndon Johnson, the fast-rising Senator from Texas, complained that the conflict was being fought "piecemeal," without full mobilization of American manpower and industry: US troops were being sent to Korea "with one arm tied behind their backs." Texas Congressman Lloyd Bentsen demanded that Truman insist that North Korea withdraw from the South within one week, or else the North would be "subject to atomic attack."

---

[*] In October 1962, President Kennedy borrowed some of this language when he addressed the nation during the Cuban Missile Crisis, saying, "The cost of freedom is always high, but Americans have always paid it," and "The 1930s taught us a clear lesson: aggressive conduct, if allowed to go unchecked and unchallenged, eventually leads to war."

[†] MacArthur had written, "Our hold upon the southern part of Korea represents a secure base. Our casualties, despite overwhelming odds, have been relatively light. Our strength will continually increase while that of the enemy will relatively decrease. His supply line is insecure. He has had his great chance and failed to exploit it. We are now in Korea in force, and, with God's help, we are there to stay until the constitutional authority of the Republic of Korea is fully restored."

In August, MacArthur showed disturbing signs of insubordination. After the President and Acheson rejected his appeals for a formal military partnership with Chiang Kai-shek, the General publicly wrote the Veterans of Foreign Wars to denounce unnamed exponents of "appeasement and defeatism in the Pacific," who were arguing "that if we defend Formosa, we alienate continental Asia." Acheson advised Truman that MacArthur's message raised "the issue as to who is the President of the United States." Truman ordered the General to retract his pronouncement, and MacArthur complied.

By the start of September, with US troops and matériel flowing into Korea, UN forces had built a "defensive perimeter" around Pusan. Touting this achievement in another TV address, Truman told Americans, "For weeks, the enemy has been hammering—now at one spot, now at another. . . . He has been beaten back each time with heavy loss. . . . We believe the invasion has reached its peak. The task remaining is to crush it."

MacArthur, with his long experience planning amphibious invasions and liberating the Philippines in World War II, wished to stage a dangerous, spectacular landing on the Korean peninsula, at Inchon. Although well aware of the risk, Truman told him to proceed. Thunder began at dawn, on Friday, September 15, as US forces hurried ashore. Within two weeks, they had broken the North Korean grip on Seoul and retaken the Southern capital.

Before the Inchon invasion, the President had approved military operations north of the thirty-eighth parallel, but only if the Soviets and China stayed out of the war. Now MacArthur exhorted him for permission to push northward. Truman knew that the Security Council resolution, in which he placed such heavy stock, had not authorized UN forces to conquer and occupy the North; however, noting that the Soviet delegate had returned to the Security Council, he refused advice to go back to the UN for consent to expand the mission in Korea. Feeling pressure from MacArthur and emboldened by the Inchon victory, Truman asked his new Secretary of Defense, George Marshall, brought out of retirement to wage this war, to wire MacArthur that he should "feel unhampered tactically and strategically to proceed north of the 38th Parallel."* This would mean pushing for a reunited Korea under the aegis of the United States and its allies.

On Wednesday, October 11, Truman boarded the *Independence,* which flew 315 miles per hour, for a 6,700-mile trip to see MacArthur on Wake Island, almost two-thirds of the way across the Pacific. The President was not averse to basking in the General's Inchon success and wished to size him up. He had acerbically written to a cousin that he had to "talk to God's righthand man." Truman's aide Charles Murphy privately considered the session a "public relations stunt." His more rough-edged appointments secretary, Matthew Connelly, groused, "When does the king go to the prince? I think this operation stinks!"

During a stop at California's Fairfield-Suisun Air Force Base, the President and his political supporter Harpo Marx cheered up hospitalized young soldiers who had been wounded in Korea. Stopping in Honolulu, Truman toured Pearl Harbor and pensively studied the wreckage of the USS *Arizona,* where the remains of over a thousand Americans still lay below. The President gave his staff what Dean Rusk called "outrageous" Hawaiian shirts, with instructions to wear them. They dined together at the Pearl Harbor Officers' Club, where, according to the official log, they were served by "Japanese ladies, attired in Japanese kimonos and obis."

The President landed on the tiny coral atoll of Wake at about 6:30 a.m. on Sunday, October 15. As sunlight came, MacArthur, in an open khaki shirt, extended his hand before cameramen and what Truman later called the "usual picture orgy." Alert to signs that the military icon might treat him with condescension or disrespect, the President was offended to see MacArthur's "shirt unbuttoned," as he later scrawled, and that the General was "wearing a greasy ham and eggs cap that evidently had been in use for twenty years." The two men climbed into the backseat of the island's only private car, a black Chevrolet ("an old two

---

* When Truman had fired the severely inadequate Louis Johnson in September, he told him, apologetically, "I feel as if I had just whipped my daughter Margaret." Johnson wept and begged Truman to let him keep his job.

door sedan," the President later grumbled). Soon, recalling MacArthur's defiance of August, Truman bluntly told him, "You're working for me. . . . I make the political decisions. . . . If you make one more move, I'm going to get you out of there."

Sitting down at a table inside a Quonset hut, the General produced his trademark corncob pipe: "Mr. President, do you mind if I smoke?" "Go right ahead," said Truman cordially. "I don't smoke, but for years people have been blowing smoke in my face." According to the President's later handwritten account, MacArthur claimed that he had "no political ambitions" and that victory in Korea was near. The official record says the General assured him that "Orientals prefer to die, rather than to lose face," and that he hoped "to withdraw the Eighth Army to Japan by Christmas." Truman asked about the possibility of Soviet or Chinese intervention in the war. "Very little," said MacArthur, adding that if China acted, "there would be the greatest slaughter." He gratefully told the President that "no commander in the history of war has ever had more complete and adequate support from all agencies in Washington than I have."

The talks were so amicable that a little after nine o'clock, Dean Rusk asked Truman in writing whether he wished to keep going. "Hell, no!" the President wrote back. "I want to get out of here before we get into trouble."* After the meeting, General Robert Landry, Truman's Air Force aide, found his chief "happy and jolly," feeling "very pleased" and "very much taken" with MacArthur. Much relieved, Truman played poker with his staff all the way back to Hawaii. Landing in San Francisco, he

---

* MacArthur also described for Truman the "puzzling" French struggle in Indochina: "The French have 150,000 of their best troops there. . . . Their forces are twice what we had in the perimeter, and they are opposed by half of what the North Koreans had. . . . If the French won't fight, we are up against it, because the defense of Europe hinges on them. They have the flower of the French Army in Indochina, and they are not fighting. If this is so, no matter what supplies we pour in, they may be of no use." Truman replied, "I cannot understand it either." Admiral Arthur Radford piped up that the difficulty was that "the French seem to have no popular backing from the local Indochinese." Radford warned that "the rest of Southeast Asia—Burma, Siam—is wide open if the Chinese Communists pursue a policy of aggression." Truman said, "This is the most discouraging thing we face."

told Americans by radio that on the basis of MacArthur's assurances, he felt "confident" that UN forces "will soon restore peace to the whole of Korea."

Four days later, MacArthur's Tokyo headquarters boasted that the "disorganized and retreating North Korean Army" was suffering from "a twenty-four-hour-round-the-clock pounding" by the US Air Force, and that UN troops had "smashed," from three sides, into the enemy capital of Pyongyang. The General assured reporters that the Korean War was very "definitely coming to an end." As MacArthur's forces pressed northward to the Yalu River, which separated North Korea from China, Truman spoke at the UN General Assembly in New York: "Now that the fighting in Korea is nearly ended," North and South must be reconstructed as "a free, united and self-supporting nation." At a stadium in Seoul, President Rhee staged a "victory meeting" of sixty thousand happy South Koreans.

In late October, MacArthur's staff in Tokyo discounted reports that Chinese Communist troops had crossed the border into North Korea.* But on Halloween Eve, spokesmen for the US Tenth Corps revealed that its troops had been confronted by a Chinese regiment north of Hungnam. On November 1, Acheson told reporters that he was "deeply concerned." Two days later, the United Press reported that "thirteen Chinese and North Korean divisions—up to 130,000 men—smashed at the crumbling United Nations line in northwest Korea," destroying "all hope of an early end to the Korean War." From Tokyo, Hanson Baldwin wrote in the *New York Times* that with China fielding "at least six divisions," the conflict had, as "so long anticipated and feared," become "a war against the Chinese Communists."†

---

* General Omar Bradley explained to congressional leaders, a month later, that Chinese troops had eluded aerial reconnaissance because they "come across the Yalu River at night in small numbers, and they march down through Korea in short columns, also at night."

† According to archives opened after the end of the Cold War, Stalin had secretly asked Mao, at the beginning of October, to intervene in Korea with great force, as did Kim Il-sung. Disposed to agree, Mao sent his Prime Minister, Zhou Enlai, to Moscow, where the Soviet leader pledged to help with equipment.

In November 1950, Americans were to vote in midterm elections. Even before the Chinese action, Republicans had run hard against what some now called "Truman's War." Their advertisements and placards went further: "Communists in High Places + Bungling Leadership = War in Korea." Campaigning in Wisconsin, Senator Joseph McCarthy bellowed, "The Korean deathtrap, we can lay to the doors of the Kremlin and those who sabotaged rearming, including Acheson and the President." In Illinois, Everett Dirksen, who was opposing Scott Lucas, told a crowd, "All the piety of the administration will not put any life into the bodies of the young men coming back in wooden boxes." Kenneth Wherry claimed that Acheson was spattered with "the blood of our boys." Robert Taft warned that the Korea debacle might now require "the drafting of every American boy of nineteen" and "taxes higher than we have ever levied on our people before"—all because Truman had "lost the peace after the American people won the war."

Bitterly the President wrote Senator Clinton Anderson of New Mexico that by displaying American discord, "the antics of McCarthy, Taft and Wherry have had as much as any other thing to do with bringing on the Communist attack" in Korea. In California, the Republican candidate for the US Senate was the thirty-seven-year-old Congressman from Whittier, Richard Nixon, who had gained national fame from his pursuit of the Roosevelt-Truman diplomat Alger Hiss as a secret agent of the Soviet Union. Nixon charged that his opponent, Helen Gahagan Douglas, had aligned herself with the "clique" in the State Department who had embraced the "appeasement policy" that had brought the Korean War. Nixon complained that Mrs. Douglas "flatly refuses to answer the direct question as to whether she supports the government of Red China," adding, "Doesn't she care whether American lives are being snuffed out by a ruthless aggressor?"

Three nights before the voting, Truman gave a national radio speech from the Kiel Auditorium in St. Louis. He did not refer directly to the Chinese intervention but charged that Republicans had "dragged our foreign policy into politics," and warned that "a vote for isolationism in this election would be a vote for national suicide." In the Republican reply, Harold Stassen, the former Governor of Minnesota, blamed China's new insolence on the President's "five years of coddling Chinese Communists, five years of undermining General MacArthur."* The Republican National Chairman, Guy Gabrielson, claimed that Truman officials were making an "obvious attempt" to keep voters from learning "that Chinese Communist divisions are pouring into North Korea, inflicting heavy casualties on our troops."

Truman's aide George Elsey much later recalled that only once did he ever see the President really drunk—after the election of 1950. Bess had found Harry so stressed by the war that she had made him sequester himself aboard the presidential yacht *Williamsburg* on Chesapeake Bay, where he read the grim election results and consoled himself with bourbon. While Democrats retained control of Congress, they lost five seats in the Senate and twenty-eight seats in the House.

The President told a friend, one of the "saddest things" was that voters seemed to have been affected by McCarthyism. Now that brickbats hurled at his war had worked politically for Republicans, Truman knew that it would be more difficult to maintain support for the conflict among the voters and Congress. Disgruntled over his election losses and anxious about the expansion of the war, he told his staff that "the campaign of vilification and character assassination which has been going on in this country" was "the best asset of the Soviet Union."

* * *

IN THOSE BYGONE days when American Presidents were not expected to comment instantly on important news, Truman did not publicly express himself about the Chinese intervention in Korea until November 16, at a routine press conference. Even then, all he did was

---

* Truman had mostly stayed out of the campaign, writing to an Indiana Congressman that "people do not like to be told by the Chief Executive how they should vote," especially in wartime. He noted how the voters had "demonstrated that to Woodrow Wilson in 1918."

praise a draft resolution by the UN Security Council that Chinese forces should depart Korea "immediately." But at least one poll found that Americans believed, by more than half, that with the Chinese action, World War III had begun.

That month, at Truman's behest, the Joint Chiefs asked MacArthur not to exacerbate the problem by crossing the Yalu River. The General accused them of "appeasement." Still eager to bring Americans "home for Christmas," he launched a new offensive, which was followed by a Chinese counterstrike, compelling him to undertake what, to this day, is still called the "longest retreat in American military history." MacArthur now warned the Pentagon that they were facing "an entirely new war." Champing at the bit, he advised the Joint Chiefs that it would be "utterly impossible" to stop short of the Yalu after seizing "terrain south of the river," as they had suggested: "The entry of Chinese Communists into the Korean conflict was a risk we knowingly took at the time we committed our forces."

Truman was reluctant to let MacArthur "lose face before the enemy." But Acheson warned the President that they were suddenly "much closer to the danger of general war" with China and the Soviet Union. Thus America must figure out how to "avoid getting sewed up in Korea" and "get out with honor. . . . We can't defeat the Chinese in Korea—they can put in more than we can." Trying to put the best face on MacArthur's failure, General Marshall argued that the offensive had been "necessary in order to find out what the Communists were up to. Now we know." Around this time, Truman told his doctor, Wallace Graham, about MacArthur, "You know, that son-of-a-bitch would get us involved in a war with China."

During a press conference at the end of November, Truman was asked whether he was contemplating use of the atomic bomb. He replied that while he did not want to see the bomb employed, "there has always been active consideration of its use," and "the military commander in the field will have charge of the use of the weapons, as he always has." The White House had to rush out a clarification, conceding that "by law, only the President can authorize the use of the atom bomb," adding that, if approved, the field commander would have charge of its "tactical delivery." Truman's aides referred reporters to the President's statement at his press conference that "it is a terrible weapon, and it should not be used on innocent men, women and children who have nothing whatever to do with this military aggression." Truman's military counselors were privately advising him that America's few ultimate weapons should not be squandered in Korea or anywhere else—only, if the worst happened, against the Soviet Union.

In a meeting the first week of December, Truman asked what price the Chinese Communists might demand for a Korean peace settlement. Acheson warned that Mao would, at least, insist that "we go south of the 38th Parallel." Marshall found it "most unlikely" that China "would ask for this little." Acheson warned, "The next thing they might ask is that we get out of Korea," followed by "an effort to get us out of Japan." Marshall felt they faced a "great dilemma of determining how we could save our troops and protect our national honor at the same time." Truman wrote in a note to himself that this meeting had been "the most solemn one I've had since the Atomic Bomb conference in Berlin" with Stalin in July 1945: "It looks very bad."

Unnerved by Truman's impulsive comments about the atomic bomb, the British Prime Minister, Clement Attlee, flew urgently to Washington to assure himself that this President was not rushing into atomic war against China. At the White House, Truman assured Attlee that the Chinese Communists were "satellites of Russia" and "the only way to meet Communism is to eliminate it—after Korea, it would be Indochina, then Hong Kong, then Malaya." He confessed that the military line in Korea was "too long to be held with the forces at our disposal. However, we cannot voluntarily back out of Korea." If that happened, "the South Koreans would all be murdered." Declining to admit that UN forces were "licked," he would rather "fight it to a finish." He reminded Attlee that in World War II, "after Dunkirk, the British didn't surrender." After the Prime Minister departed, Truman wrote in his diary, "I've worked for peace for five years and six months and it looks like World War III is here."

Members of Congress complained about the President's caution. Lyndon Johnson carped that for six "costly" months, the United States had "thrown up a chicken wire" in Korea, "instead of a wall of armed might." He decried the "circle of confusion" in the Pentagon and State Department: "The American people are tired and fed up with double-talk."* Angry, Truman told his diary that there were "liars, trimmers and pussyfooters on both sides of the aisle." He decided to emulate Roosevelt before entering World War II by proclaiming a state of "national emergency." During an advance congressional briefing, Robert Taft tried to smoke Truman out on exactly what new authority he intended to seek, but the President merely replied, "Time is of the essence."

On Friday evening, December 15, from his Oval Office desk, Truman frankly told the nation that "aggression has won a military advantage in Korea. We should not try to hide or explain away that fact." He promised that "whatever temporary setbacks there may be, the right will prevail in the end." To meet the emergency, he would increase the number of Americans on active duty to almost 3.5 million and expand war production. He cautioned that Americans would suffer from more inflation, which had soared since the war's start, and from shortages of civilian goods, unless there were new wage and price controls, and that "many others of you will have to work longer hours in factories or mines or mills." He warned that "all of us will have to pay more taxes and do without things we like," but "the future of civilization depends on what we do now."†

Taft complained that Truman's request would lead to "dictatorship and totalitarian government." Wherry threatened a Senate resolution withholding ground forces from NATO. Senator William Jenner insisted that if Congress had a "shred of courage and patriotism left," it would demand "either a declaration of war or the bringing back of American GIs to home shores." The President fueled the fire by telling reporters, about Congress, "I don't ask their permission—I just consult them." Appalled by Truman's comment, Taft proclaimed that the President was courting a "Constitutional crisis."

---

* Margaret Truman recalled much later that her father "never quite trusted" Johnson.

† Congress granted most of Truman's tax request, raising the highest personal income tax rate to 91 percent and the highest corporate rate to 70 percent.

Truman knew that asking Americans for more sacrifices would make him less popular. By January 1951, his Gallup Poll approval rating had dropped from 43 percent in September to 36 percent. By 49 to 28 percent, Americans felt that Truman's government had "made a mistake in deciding to defend South Korea." Sixty-six percent wished to "pull our troops out of Korea as fast as possible." The survey found that if Truman ran for reelection in 1952, as was widely expected, General Dwight Eisenhower, hero of D-Day, would defeat him by 59 to 28 percent, and that even Robert Taft—often called too extreme to be a plausible candidate—would prevail by 44 to 41 percent.* By February, Truman's disapproval rating had shot up to 57 percent. This was an astounding figure for those times, when Americans were inclined to support their Presidents, especially in wartime.

During the months after the national emergency was declared, George Elsey noted that Truman seemed "hunkered down and worked harder than ever at his desk." To make the President more visible, Elsey proposed an FDR-style inspection tour of defense plants, which Truman dismissed as "gimmickry," or a TV question-and-answer show with a friendly Senator, allowing the President to explain why Americans were fighting in Korea. Truman called this idea "a publicity stunt." To help break the deadlock in Korea, Congressman Albert Gore, Democrat from Tennessee, wrote the President to suggest creating an "atomic death belt" along the thirty-eighth parallel, which, if crossed, "would mean certain death or slow deformity."

* * *

THE FRUSTRATED MACARTHUR kept pressing Truman to wage their war more aggressively. In March, he told a reporter that with the same force strength required to defend a truce line near the thirty-eighth parallel, UN soldiers could march to the Yalu and seize all of Korea. Told that the President was exploring the possibility of

---

* Even though the Twenty-Second Amendment, ratified in February 1951, confined a Chief Executive to two terms, this stricture did not apply to the sitting President.

peace negotiations, MacArthur publicly argued that instead they should expand the war into China, which made Truman furious. Then, on April 5, House Minority Leader Joe Martin of Massachusetts read aloud on the House floor a letter he had received from MacArthur demanding that the Nationalist Chinese on Formosa be enlisted to create "a second Asiatic front" against the adversary, and saying, "There is no substitute for victory."

"The last straw," Truman told his diary. "Rank insubordination." He recalled how Lincoln had ousted McClellan (although the latter's approach was the opposite of MacArthur's—Lincoln had found his General too lethargic). As Truman much later recalled, he told Omar Bradley, "That son of a bitch isn't going to resign on me—*I want him fired!*" When word of the President's intention leaked, Bradley warned Truman that the *Chicago Tribune* had obtained the story. Instead of taking the time to send an emissary to speak with MacArthur, the President advised him of his fate in writing.

MacArthur's dismissal caused a national earthquake. The *Daily Oklahoman* called it "a crime carried out in the dead of night." Joe McCarthy claimed that "the son of a bitch" had fired the great General after imbibing "bourbon and Benedictine." The *Chicago Tribune* demanded that Truman be expelled from the presidency because he was "unfit, morally and mentally, for his high office." Joe Martin mulled over Truman's possible impeachment. Senator Jenner called MacArthur's firing proof that the United States was now "in the hands of a secret inner coterie which is directed by agents of the Soviet Union." Many Republicans demanded that MacArthur run against Truman in 1952.

"Quite an explosion," the President wrote in his diary. "Was expected but I had to act." He told aides that MacArthur was "a worse double-crosser" than General McClellan, who had worked with the Senate minority in 1862 "to undercut the administration when there was a war on." Truman wrote his adviser David Noyes that MacArthur's dismissal would "undoubtedly cause a great furor, but under the circumstances, I could do nothing else and still be President of the United States. Even the Chiefs of Staff came to the conclusion that civilian control of the military was at stake and I didn't let it stay at stake very long."

Addressing the nation from the Oval Office, Truman contended that "the cause of world peace is much more important than any individual." But Gallup found that Americans objected to MacArthur's sacking by 69 to 29 percent. Letters to the White House opposed the decision by twenty to one. Truman told his press aide Roger Tubby, "Go put them in [the fireplace] and set a match to them." He wrote a New Hampshire friend that MacArthur "seems to have lost all sense of proportion," adding, "It is too bad but I have always said Heroes know when to quit."

MacArthur created his own melodrama, emerging from his plane, which he had named the *Bataan,* at night under spotlights in San Francisco, his first trip to the mainland United States in fourteen years. The next day, before a hundred thousand people, he proclaimed, "The only politics I have is contained in a single phrase known well by all of you— God Bless America!" When MacArthur landed in Washington, Truman showed how little he thought of him by sending as his personal greeter General Harry Vaughan, a World War I Army pal who served as the President's military aide but was better known as his poker friend and "court jester."*

Before a joint meeting of Congress, employing his dramatic talents to the full, MacArthur recounted, "Why, my soldiers asked of me, surrender military advantage to an enemy in the field? I could not answer." Recalling the admonition of a ballad that "old soldiers never die—they just fade away," he said he would "now close my military career—and just fade away. . . . Goodbye." Congressman Dewey Short of Missouri intoned, "We heard God speak here today—God in the flesh." One wag claimed that on the Republican side of the House chamber, in response to the General's tear-jerking speech, there was not a dry eye, and on the side of the anxious Democrats, not a dry seat. Truman privately called himself disgusted by the sight of "damn fool Congressmen crying like a bunch of women" after hearing "nothing but a bunch of bullshit." In New York, through confetti and ticker tape, more than seven million

---

* Vaughan later gained notoriety as an influence peddler who took freezers from businessman who wanted government favors, and for accepting a medal from the fascist Argentine government.

spectators watched MacArthur ride in a hero's parade. During a speaking tour of state legislatures, he denounced Truman's "appeasement on the battlefield."

By the end of May, the forces led by MacArthur's successor, General Matthew Ridgway, had pushed the North Koreans above the thirty-eighth parallel. At Washington's Statler Hotel that month, Truman, in black tie, spoke at an Armed Forces Day banquet, which was broadcast by radio to the nation and the troops in Korea. He asked Americans to "quit your bickering here at home. . . . Did it ever occur to you that if this necessity with which we are faced is not met, that the casualties in Korea will be one small drop in the bucket from one of those horrible bombs of which we talk so much?"

Despite his doughty public persona, Truman suffered from sending so many young Americans off to die in a far-off place their families scarcely knew. Having fought in France, he could not easily distance himself from the images of hurt and death. He was aided by the unstinting adoration of his wife and daughter and, although he rarely spoke of it in public, his strong faith in God and constant reading of the Bible. He lampooned other politicians who wore their religion on their sleeves and said he liked being a Baptist because it gave a common man like him the most direct route to the Almighty. He could recite from the Scriptures and believed that global problems could be solved "if only men would follow the Beatitudes."

At sixty-seven, the President was compulsive in his efforts to remain physically able to respond to the day-and-night demands of the war. He took regular fast walks, with his Secret Service detail, near the Washington Monument, surprising the tourists. He swam almost nightly, sometimes with Dr. Graham, a D-Day veteran and son of an old Missouri friend, in the indoor White House pool installed by Franklin Roosevelt.* Graham would tell him, "You're not going to be a prize fighter. . . . Just keep in good physical condition—I will see to that." Next to the pool, the President performed calisthenics and used wall pulleys and a rowing

---

* Which President Richard Nixon ordered to be covered in 1970 to create the current White House press briefing room.

machine, after which he had a rubdown and zipped himself into a steam box, with his square, perspiring head poking out of the top, talking to Dr. Graham about the problems of the war.

Truman had been subject to severe headaches, sleeplessness, and nausea during times of stress when he was a county judge and a Senator. Margaret recalled his tendency to "ignore his illnesses." But suppressing anxiety took its toll on this emotional man who did not like to reveal his inner life. Several times while in the Senate, Truman had himself quietly hospitalized at an Army-Navy institution in Hot Springs, Arkansas, for work-related pressures. Now Graham and the First Lady urged him to unwind, whenever he could, on the *Williamsburg* and at his "Little White House" on the naval base at Key West.

The public did not know that Truman suffered from a kind of congestive heart failure called cardiac asthma. When the new President took office in 1945, a Senate physician had told Dr. Graham that he didn't envy him because Truman's pulmonary obstruction was so grave that he might not live out his term.* Truman responded to Graham's warnings in 1947 with his usual stoicism. "Doc tell's [*sic*] me I have Cardiac Asthma!" he wrote in his diary. "Aint that hell. Well it makes no diff, will go on as before. I've sworn him to secrecy! So What!" As Graham later recalled, Truman would get "really clutched up" at night, with severe coughing, rales, edema, and "bubbling in the lungs," for which the doctor gave him diuretics. At Blair House, Graham would sit by the President's bedside until the attack had subsided and Truman was ready, with the sun glinting through the blinds, to face the latest news from Korea.

* * *

IN JUNE 1951, Joe McCarthy upped his attack. In a long speech on the Senate floor, he accused Acheson and Marshall of "a great conspiracy" to hand the United States to Communism, with Truman as

---

* Although Truman's ancestors on both sides were noted for their longevity, and Truman himself ultimately survived to the age of eighty-eight.

their "front" and "captive"—"not master in his own house." The demagogue charged that Marshall was "steeped in falsehood," a "mysterious, powerful" figure who had sided with the Soviets in decisions that
"lost the peace," part of "a conspiracy of infamy so black that when it
is finally exposed, its principals shall be forever deserving of the male-
dictions of all honest men."

While dedicating a new military facility in Tullahoma, Tennessee,
Truman denounced McCarthy and his henchmen:

> They are trying to set the people against the government by
> spreading fear and slander and outright lies. . . . They have tried
> to besmirch the loyalty of General Marshall, who directed our
> strategy in winning the greatest war in history. They have delib-
> erately tried to destroy Dean Acheson, one of the greatest Secre-
> taries of State in the history of this country. . . . It's playing right
> into the hands of the Russians. . . . They want us to play Russian
> roulette with the foreign policy of the United States—with all
> the chambers of the pistols loaded.

In June the Soviets proposed a Korean cease-fire and withdrawal of
both sides to the thirty-eighth parallel. They had dropped their earlier
demands that all foreign troops depart Korea and that Formosa's seat
on the UN Security Council be given to Mao's China. In response,
Joe McCarthy forecast the "planned betrayal of 1951," which would
constitute the "death warrant of every American boy who has died in
Korea." Gallup found that Americans would favor a Korean truce at
the thirty-eighth parallel by 51 to 37 percent. Truman told aides he
was "not too optimistic" but asked Ridgway to pursue the possibility.
China consented and the talks began in July at the North Korean town
of Kaesong, near the thirty-eighth parallel.

The President wrote Bess that Korea was likely to be followed by another local war: "We are not sure where the next outbreak will come. It
can be Indo-China, Burma, Iraq, West Germany or Napal [*sic*]—and it
will be one of them, I'm sure." The Korea talks, which were later shifted
to a tent in Panmunjom, were stalemated when the North demanded that

roughly 132,000 North Korean prisoners of war be returned to its untender mercies. Truman vowed, "We will not buy an armistice by turning over human beings for slaughter or slavery." He grimaced over his inability to break the deadlock. Scrawling into his diary in January 1952, he fantasized about confronting the Soviet Union and China directly:

> Dealing with Communist Governments is like an honest man trying to deal with a numbers racket king or the head of a dope ring. . . . It now looks as if all that the Chinese wanted when they asked for a cease fire was a chance to import war materials and resupply their front lines. It seems to me that the proper approach now, would be an ultimatum with a ten day expiration limit, informing Moscow that we intend to blockade the China coast from the Korean border to Indo-China, and that we intend to destroy every military base in Manchuria, including submarine bases . . . and if there is further interference we shall eliminate any port or cities necessary to accomplish our peaceful purpose. That this situation can be avoided by the withdrawal of all Chinese troops from Korea and the stoppage of all supplies of war materials by Russia to Communist China. . . . We of the free world have suffered long enough. . . . This means all out war. . . . This is the final chance for the Soviet Government to decide whether it desires to survive or not.

Truman had been tempted to pursue another term in office as a means of vindicating himself over Korea, but Bess told him she thought he couldn't survive another four years as President. During a Key West vacation in November 1951, he called his closest aides to the poker table on his porch and told them, in strict confidence, that he would not run for reelection. To prove that he was not pulling out to avoid a defeat at the polls over Korea, he showed them an April 1950 entry from his diary, in which he had vowed not to run again, writing, "There is a lure in power. It can get into a man's blood just as gambling and lust for money has been known to do."

To succeed him, Truman wanted his close friend Chief Justice

Fred Vinson, an ex-Congressman from Kentucky who had served as his Secretary of the Treasury. He once told Bess that Vinson "believes in me, trusts me and supports me." In the more casual tradition of those days, Truman often talked politics with the Chief Justice, including cases that the Supreme Court was about to consider. Vinson was a member of the President's poker group on the *Williamsburg,* and the First Lady and Margaret called him "Poppa Vin." The Chief Justice, however, refused his friend's offer; he felt that the Court should not be used as a stepping-stone to the presidency, and his wife was worried about his health.*

Truman then turned to Adlai Stevenson, the Governor of Illinois, whom he scarcely knew. He respected Stevenson's probity, eloquence, and decency, and remembered from his childhood when Adlai's namesake grandfather was Grover Cleveland's Vice President. One evening in January 1952, Truman ushered the Governor into his study at Blair House, where they sat before a fire. He told Stevenson that he had been reading the Bible, and had done so all of his life. Startled by the President's offer to support him, Stevenson explained that he had committed himself to run for reelection in Illinois; he felt that Truman must have thought him "a complete idiot." He privately told James Reston of the *New York Times* that should Eisenhower be the Republican nominee, he did not deem it "my duty to save Western civilization" from the World War II hero. Truman invited Stevenson for another talk, but the Governor again demurred.

In March, the President was defeated in the New Hampshire Democratic primary by the calculatedly homespun Tennessee Senator Estes Kefauver, a Yale Law graduate who campaigned in a coonskin cap.† Truman disdained Kefauver as "intellectually dishonest" and "ignorant" of American history. His dander up, he now considered entering the race. Although against the idea, Bess and Margaret told him he was the only Democrat who could win the presidency in 1952. He asked his diary, "What the hell am I to do?" To discuss another campaign, he gathered his loyalists,

---

* The overweight, chain-smoking Vinson died of a massive heart attack the following year.

† Having waited to announce his plans for 1952, Truman had allowed his name to stay on the ballot.

including Vinson, but they politely urged him to retire for his health. Truman's aide Charlie Murphy privately felt that "the administration was going to seed" and the country "needed new blood." Eager to avoid the appearance that his unpopularity over Korea had driven him out of the race, Truman told the press that the war would "have no bearing whatever on what I may decide to do."

On Saturday night, March 29, 1952, during a black-tie Jefferson-Jackson banquet of Democrats at the DC Armory, Truman defended his conduct of the war. He noted that "some Republicans seem to think it would be popular to pull out of Korea" and that others wished to "expand the fighting" and "start dropping atomic bombs." If that happened, "and God forbid that it comes," such "loud talkers would be the first people to run for the bomb shelters." At the end of his speech, he surprised the audience: "I have served my country long, and, I think, efficiently and honestly. I shall not accept a renomination." Truman had sprung his news so abruptly that some listeners clapped without realizing what they were doing. Stevenson, who was present, noticed that some of his fellow Democrats were applauding Truman's withdrawal "with really macabre enthusiasm."*

* * *

TEN DAYS LATER, the lame-duck Truman staged a breathtaking assertion of presidential power, issuing an executive order for the federal government to seize American steel companies. Management and labor had been unable to reach a new contract, and the steelworkers union was threatening a strike. Truman was advised that a work stoppage could block the steel supply for weapons going to Korea. He believed that a President "has very great inherent powers to meet great national emergencies" and that it was his duty "under the Constitution to act to preserve the safety of the nation."

---

* The historian Arthur Schlesinger Jr., another guest, told his journal, "I found myself shouting 'No' with vigor; then I wondered why the hell I was shouting 'No,' since this is what I had been hoping would happen for months."

On Tuesday night, April 8, Truman went on television to charge that industry leaders were "recklessly forcing a shutdown of the steel mills." He "would not be living up to my oath of office" if he did not provide US soldiers in Korea with munitions required for their survival, so "at midnight, the government will take over the steel plants." Truman later told Roger Tubby, "My heart was in it—Jesus!" As Tubby noted in his diary, the President was clearly "played out." Truman himself confessed that he was "terribly tired." After he gave the speech, his press secretary, Joseph Short, feared that his chief would collapse.

The President was widely excoriated for the steel seizure. New York's *Daily News* claimed, "Hitler and Mussolini would have loved this." Lyndon Johnson publicly warned that Truman's decision "smacks of the practices that lead toward a dictatorship." Other members of Congress filed fourteen separate bills of impeachment against Truman. Robert Taft, campaigning for President in the Massachusetts Republican primary, agreed that the House had a "valid case" for forcing Truman into a Senate trial: "He might just as well go a step farther and draft the steelworkers into the Army without the consent of Congress." Republican Congressman George Bender of Ohio warned that the President might go on to seize the nation's broadcast and newspaper companies.

Defending himself, Truman told reporters that the steel strike posed "as great an emergency as we have ever faced. I tried to meet it. I have been abused roundly for it. I am not the first President that has been abused under the same circumstances, so I know how to take it." He recounted that earlier Presidents "have had to make decisions in emergencies," and "it made the Republic better." With his Louisiana Purchase, Jefferson had "paid $15 million for the greatest addition to this country that has ever been made" and "they tried to impeach him for that." Truman went on to praise Tyler's annexation of Texas and Polk's aggressiveness against Mexico, as well as the bold actions by Lincoln and Franklin Roosevelt in wartime.

Hidden from the public for decades was that in planning his steel seizure, Truman had grossly violated the constitutional separation of powers. Before taking this audacious action, he had secretly confided his plan to Vinson, asking the Chief Justice whether the Supreme Court would uphold it. Vinson had told him not to worry, and the President had gone ahead.

The steel companies responded to the seizure by suing the federal government, and US District Court Judge David Pine issued an injunction. On June 2, the Supreme Court found Truman's action unconstitutional by 6 to 3. For the majority, Justice Robert Jackson wrote that no doctrine could be "more sinister and alarming" than the notion that some future President might be encouraged to send US armed forces into "some foreign venture" in order to expand his personal power over domestic affairs. Shocked by the Court's ruling, Truman privately called it "crazy." In a letter he did not send, he angrily wrote Justice William O. Douglas, "I don't see how a Court made up of so-called 'Liberals' could do what that court did to me. I am going to find out just why before I quit this office."

On Monday, July 7, the Republican convention opened in Chicago. The keynote speaker was MacArthur, who, wearing a double-breasted suit, looked his full seventy-two years. He charged that Truman had lacked "the courage to fight to a military decision" in Korea, although "victory was then readily within our grasp." MacArthur privately hoped that he might be anointed as the presidential nominee after a deadlock between the two front-runners, Eisenhower and Taft. But by then the air had gone out of his national balloon. Truman chortled in a letter to Bess that MacArthur "was a complete flop as a keynoter." After an intense struggle, Ike took the nomination and chose Richard Nixon as his running mate.

As the President watched the Republicans on television, with their anti-Truman harangues, Dr. Graham noted that his chief was showing breathing trouble, abdominal pain, and "general malaise." The following Sunday at noon, Truman convened his political advisers, including Vice President Barkley. As he later wrote in his diary, "We agreed that we would support Barkley for the nomination since Stevenson could not make up his mind." Everyone present knew that the garrulous, ailing, seventy-four-year-old "Veep" was unlikely to defeat Eisenhower.

Truman now realized that he would probably be succeeded in office by a Republican who might try to overturn much of what he had achieved. After his guests departed, the President tottered and almost fell to the floor. Dr. Graham found that his patient was beet-faced, "extremely nervous and had a shaking chill," with "hot and fairly moist" skin and a fever of almost 104 degrees. Truman told his doctor that he wished to return to his desk, but Bess took command by telephone from Independence and had him removed to Walter Reed Army Hospital. There he slept almost uninterrupted for forty-eight hours, not far from wounded soldiers back from Korea.

The Democrats met in Chicago a week later. Stevenson called the President at the White House to ask whether it would "embarrass" him should he let his name be placed in contention. Although irritated by the Governor's dawdling, Truman promised support. Stevenson won the prize and chose Senator John Sparkman of Alabama for his ticket. On the final night of the convention, the President told the delegates, "We have met aggression in Korea, and we have stopped it there." He promised to "take my coat off and do everything I can" to help Stevenson win. When the nominee spoke, however, he did not even mention the stalemated Korean War. Distancing himself from Truman, he located his headquarters not in Washington but Springfield, writing a friend, "The line to emphasize is that I am *not* Truman's candidate." Arthur Schlesinger Jr., who took leave from Harvard that fall to write speeches for Stevenson, thought the nominee regarded Truman "as a kind of Old Man of the Sea, clinging to his shoulders."

Eisenhower ran against "Communism, corruption and Korea," as well as what he called "the mess in Washington."* Asked by the *Oregon Journal* whether he could clean up that "mess," Stevenson cited his record in Illinois. The President was furious over Stevenson's tacit admission that Truman had created a "mess," as well as Sparkman's comment that Truman had "mishandled" the steelworkers' strike. The President told Tubby that "they are running against me, not against Ike," and "can't win that way."

Stevenson's patrician background and Princeton education triggered Truman's class consciousness. In a letter he failed to send, the President

---

* Referring to the scandals attached to Truman's Bureau of Internal Revenue and charges of influence peddling in his entourage.

wrote Stevenson that he seemed to be "embarrassed by" and "above associating with the lowly President of the United States," adding, "I can't stand snub after snub by you." In another unsent letter to Stevenson, Truman objected to the candidate's public claim that he was indebted to no one for his nomination: "That makes nice reading in the sabotage press, but gets you no votes because it isn't true. . . . I'm telling you to take your crackpots, your high socialites with their noses in the air, run your campaign, and win if you can." Nevertheless Truman barnstormed for Stevenson by train, telling crowds, "Never let anyone tell you that the Korean episode has been a useless one. . . . For there we have stopped the Communists. We have upset their timetable, and we have pushed them back and we have surely saved the world from total war."

Eisenhower postponed making a major speech on the war until the last fortnight of the race. At Detroit's Masonic Temple, in a national TV broadcast, he called Korea "the burial ground for twenty thousand American dead" and "a damning measure of the quality of leadership we have been given." He derided Truman for having encouraged the war by pulling American forces from Korea and allowing Acheson to rule it outside the nation's defense perimeter. In the most remembered line of his campaign, Eisenhower pledged, "I shall go to Korea." Then, "unfettered by past decisions and inherited mistakes," he could "review every factor—military, political and psychological—to be mobilized in speeding a just peace." Fighting back, Truman released a statement recalling that Eisenhower had endorsed his earlier Korean withdrawal of the late 1940s. Privately he complained that if Ike knew how to end the war immediately, he should save American lives by sharing his secret blueprint with the President right now.

Eisenhower's promise that, unlike the Democrats, he could break the Korean deadlock ensured his landslide victory over Stevenson, by 55 to 44 percent. Congratulating the General by telegram, Truman told him that "if you still desire to go to Korea," he would lend him the *Independence*. Offended by what he saw as Truman's insinuation that his Korea pledge had been a campaign ploy that might now be dropped, Eisenhower refused the offer and, in late November, boarded an Air Force Constellation to fly from Long Island to Seoul. "I sincerely wish he didn't have to make the trip," Truman wrote in his diary. "It is an awful risk. May God protect him." Touring the Korean battlefront, wearing a fur-lined parka and cap, Eisenhower debriefed soldiers and concluded that letting the Korean stalemate continue would be "intolerable."*

In a December press conference, Truman deepened his feud with Eisenhower when asked about a report that he had privately been urged to bolster Stevenson during the campaign by announcing that he would visit Korea. Confirming the story, the President tartly said he had decided that flying to Korea "would be just a piece of demagoguery, and that is what it turned out to be." Asked if he meant Eisenhower's tour, Truman said, "Yes, the announcement of that trip was a piece of demagoguery, and then, of course, he had to take it after he made the statement." Roger Tubby whispered caution into his ear. Truman told the reporters, "Well, Roger suggested that maybe some good might come out of the trip. If it does, I will be the happiest man in the world."

Five days before leaving office in January 1953, Truman delivered a televised "farewell address" from the Oval Office. He called waging war in Korea "the most important" decision of his presidency. Recalling his own service in World War I, he said he knew "what a soldier goes through" and the "anguish" of military families. Now Americans were "living in the eighth year of the atomic age," and "a third world war might dig the grave not only of our Communist opponents but also of our own society." He professed "not a doubt in the world" that free countries would prevail. Prophetically, he forecast, "As the Soviet hopes for easy expansion are blocked, then there will have to come a time of change in the Soviet world. Nobody can say for sure when that is going to be, or exactly how it will come about—whether by revolution, or trouble in the satellite states, or by a change inside the Kremlin." Truman reminded Americans that "starting an atomic war is totally unthinkable for rational men."

---

* After his trip, the President-elect agreed to meet with MacArthur, who had announced that he had a peace plan. The grateful MacArthur complained to him that it was "the first time that the slightest official interest in my counsel" had been shown since his own return from Korea. Ike heard him out but felt that MacArthur had nothing new to offer.

On Inauguration Day, when the Eisenhowers' limousine rolled up at the North Portico, the Trumans were waiting inside to host them for coffee. However, still stewing over what he considered to be the President's aspersions, the General and his wife, Mamie, declined to come into the White House. During their frigid ride up Capitol Hill, by Truman's account, Eisenhower grumpily asked who had tried to "embarrass" him by calling his son John back from combat in Korea to attend the inauguration.* Truman, who had done so out of graciousness, told Ike that it had been his decision.

As President, Eisenhower sought to break the deadlock in the Panmunjom talks by sending secret messages to the Chinese—through at least three different diplomatic channels, including Prime Minister Jawaharlal Nehru of India—that if the Korean war did not end soon, the United States might turn to the ultimate weapon.† But at least as important was Stalin's death in March. The old tyrant had been secretly advising Mao Zedong to drag out the Korean War and thus damage the "military prestige" of the United States and Great Britain. "Americans don't know how to fight," Stalin had told Zhou Enlai in 1952. "They are pinning their hopes on the atom power and air power. But one cannot win a war with that." Two weeks after Stalin's death, his heirs secretly advised both Mao and Kim Il-sung that "the deepest interests of our peoples" compelled the "soonest possible conclusion of the war."

By June 1953, China relaxed its position on POWs, which opened the way to a settlement. The two sides agreed to a heavily armed truce, with the peninsula divided at the thirty-eighth parallel, amid a formal state of war that remains to this day. Eisenhower was convinced that his secret nuclear threat had made the difference. He later called the Korean armistice his "proudest achievement" as President. Learning of the truce in Independence, Truman told reporters that he was "certainly glad."

---

* In 1952, some feared that Chinese and North Korean patrols might try to kidnap John and exploit him for blackmail. Eisenhower had told his son that if he were captured, he would "have to drop out of the Presidential race." But John bravely promised his father that he would never let himself be taken alive. As he later recalled, he intended, if accosted by enemy soldiers, to commit suicide with his own pistol, "taking—I hoped—some of them with me."

† It was widely known that the United States kept atomic warheads on Okinawa.

Still nursing his grievances against Eisenhower, however, he acerbically added, "I sincerely hope—and I want to underline that word hope—that it means peace."

* * *

A T HIS BEST, Truman had supervised the final American efforts of World War II, approving the use of atomic weapons to close down the Japanese conflict, and resisted Soviet power in Europe. But he and Acheson erred by sending Moscow and Beijing unintended signals that the United States might not protect South Korea, which helped to provoke a war that ultimately killed at least 33,686 Americans and more than 1.2 million people on all sides.

It does not speak well for Truman—who liked to boast about his forthrightness and his eagerness to accept personal responsibility for his mistakes—that in *Years of Trial and Hope,* his second volume of memoirs (1956), he shifted the blame to others and claimed that the Korean conflict had been inevitable.* Refusing to concede that he or Acheson had done anything that might have enticed the North Koreans to invade, he claimed to have been confronted almost spontaneously by "the ominous threat of a third world war," adding that his decision to intervene in Korea had been the "toughest" of his presidency.

Having closely studied the Constitution, Truman had strongly defended congressional prerogatives while a Senator. But when the Korean fighting began, he refused to ask Congress for a war declaration, privately arguing that doing so would enmesh him in damaging controversy on Capitol Hill, and noting that, by using force to defend the South, he had the right to act as a member of the United Nations. Truman's refusal—and the willingness of Congress and the courts to put up with it—established a dangerous excuse for every later President

---

* In his memoirs, *Present at the Creation,* Acheson dismissed the charge that his National Press Club speech deserved blame for the North Korean invasion, noting that when he discussed the defense perimeter, "Australia and New Zealand were not included either."

to avoid asking the House and Senate for war declarations. It also gave some of Truman's congressional foes an opening to call his action in Korea illegitimate and unworthy of support.

Having failed to deter the North Korean invasion, the first major such event after World War II, Truman would have had a difficult time convincing the world that the postwar international order meant very much unless he responded, as he did, with force. For the early period of the Korean War, he subcontracted too much of his decision making to the legendary MacArthur. However, by firing the insubordinate commander, he gave future Presidents a substantial gift by reestablishing civilian control of the military. With political courage, for he knew it would jeopardize his popularity, Truman put the nation on a war footing, asking Americans to make sacrifices that would hasten rearmament and support the troops in battle. Korea was the first American war of the nuclear age, and Truman successfully kept it from escalating. When it became clear to him that the conflict was destined to end, at best, in deadlock unless he used nuclear weapons, Truman had the good judgment to cut his losses.

But this President could never quite explain to Americans exactly why they were at war in Korea, nor did he try hard enough. This left some to suspect that the only reason the nation could have gotten stuck in a losing war in Korea was that the federal government was honeycombed with Soviet secret agents. It was not by coincidence that Joe McCarthy made such headway just as Americans were hearing about setbacks in Korea. When US soldiers were mired during that first winter of this war, citizens back home turned against it—and the President responsible for it—with astounding speed, especially at a time when so many Americans were naturally disposed to believe in their President.

Although 1.5 million American men were drafted to possibly fight and die in this increasingly unpopular war, there were no large-scale protests, including on campuses. With Korea, Truman started an American tradition under which a circumscribed group of Americans gave their lives for a purpose that was never well explained, while the rest of the citizenry went on almost as normal. It was fortunate for Truman that he served at a time of a largely quiescent public who had intense trust in American institutions.

How to account for the fact that Truman's war leadership—from his failure to ask Congress for a war declaration through his attempted steel seizure—showed such impatience with the checks and balances imposed on the Executive by the Constitution? At least superficially, this was surprising from a leader who loved the Founders, had taken two years of night law school in Kansas City, and been a member of the Senate's "inner club." But Truman's personal experience of the wartime presidency had consisted of watching Wilson and Franklin Roosevelt wage two global conflicts and then closing down World War II, all of which encouraged him to act imperiously. It seems never to have registered with Truman that Korea was a very different kind of war from anything Americans had fought before, which should have compelled him to regard it with far more personal modesty and respect for constitutional constraints.

Almost instantly after the armistice was signed in 1953, the Korean War moved away from the center of the nation's consciousness. Even though Americans had all been affected in some way by the conflict, they seemed eager to forget that their country had not prevailed.* Eisenhower, who wished to heal the country and ensure peace and prosperity, had little incentive to relitigate the issue of Truman's failures in Korea.† He wished to turn the page from a time when so many members of his party had been enchanted by the poison of Joe McCarthy and the isolationism of Robert Taft, who died in 1953. Democrats too wished to

---

* This proved to be good fortune for Truman, whose reputation enjoyed a resurgence after his death in 1972, as many Americans, including scholars, came to view him as a near-great President. Had there been a stronger memory at the time of his mistakes and overassertions of presidential power while waging war in Korea, Truman's historical ascent might not have been so pronounced.

† The 1956 Republican platform recalled that when Eisenhower took office, "the Korean War, with its tragic toll of more than an eighth of a million American casualties, seemed destined to go on indefinitely," but the President did not mention the subject in his acceptance speech. Opening his fall campaign, he briefly recalled the "endless" loss of life in the war and boasted, "Today, Korea means peace with honor." Presidents Johnson and Nixon both later used that same term to describe their goal in Vietnam.

escape the partisan bitterness of the Korean period, as well as Truman's unpopularity. By the early 1960s, majorities in both parties were content to let the Asian conflict remain a "forgotten war."* Unwilling to take to heart the mistakes that Truman and other politicians had made over Korea, the American people and those who guided them were thus all the more doomed to rush into the darkness of Vietnam.

---

* A rare exception was during the second Kennedy-Nixon televised debate in 1960, when the Republican noted that during "a very famous speech at the Press Club" in 1950, Acheson had suggested "that South Korea was beyond the defense zone of the United States." Nixon added that such "woolly thinking" had "led to disaster for America in Korea."

CHAPTER SIXTEEN

"We Got Slapped"

O N SUNDAY AFTERNOON, August 2, 1964, Captain George Morrison, commander of a carrier division on the Gulf of Tonkin, off North Vietnam, was at the helm of his flagship, a US aircraft carrier called the *Bon Homme Richard*. Morrison was informed that one of his vessels, the destroyer *Maddox*, had been assaulted by North Vietnamese motor torpedo boats while collecting signals intelligence, and had fired back. As a young Navy ensign at Pearl Harbor, he had witnessed the Japanese attack that brought the United States into World War II. Now the Georgia-born captain was at the center of another moment in history that would draw his country into war.

Morrison's long assignments at sea, during the Korean War and later, had been hard on his family—especially his son Jimmy, who was now a film student at the University of California, Los Angeles. When the *Bon Homme Richard* stopped in San Diego in January 1964, Jimmy's mother, Clara, implored him not to arrive "looking like a beatnik." The son got a trim, but the captain ordered the vessel's barber to give him a crew cut like his own. From aboard ship, at his father's demand, Jimmy fired an M16 at human effigies hurled into the ocean. A year later, he broke the news to the captain that he was "going on the road with a rock band." George replied, "That's ridiculous! You're not a singer—you can't sing!" and "Get yourself a *job!*"

Jim Morrison gained world fame as lead singer for the Doors and falsely told reporters that both of his parents were dead. Like a fast-increasing share of his generation, he hated the war in Vietnam, to which his father was devoted, and as the conflict spiraled, one song, which the Doors recorded in January 1968, captured Jim's anger. It was called "The Unknown Soldier." After the sound of troops marching could be heard an officer's shout ("Pre-*sent*—Arms!"), a drumroll and rifle fire, and Morrison's mournful voice:

> *Breakfast where the news is read . . .*
> *Bullet strikes the helmet's head.*
> *And—it's all over!*

In August 1964, with only 15,500 US advisers in South Vietnam, the full blast of antiwar rage was in the future, as the report of an attack on the *Maddox* sped from the Tonkin Gulf to the Pentagon.

✳ ✳ ✳

O N THAT SUNDAY in Washington, President Lyndon Johnson took his breakfast upstairs in the White House at nine o'clock. Two hours later, wearing a narrow tie and his World War II Silver Star in his suit lapel, he was summoned to the Oval Office for an urgent meeting with a half-dozen officials, including his Secretary of State, Dean Rusk, alumnus of Truman's war in Korea. "Where are my Bundys?" Johnson genially asked, referring to his National Security Adviser, McGeorge Bundy, and Bundy's brother William, Assistant Secretary of State for Asia. Johnson joked, "They're up there at that female island of theirs, Martha's Vineyard."* Then he asked, "What's the big emergency?"

Rusk described what he was already calling the "unprovoked" attack

---

* Actually only Bill Bundy was staying on the Massachusetts island. Mac was taking a brief August family respite at his home north of Boston.

in the Tonkin Gulf. Told of the fragmentary evidence that North Vietnamese patrol boats had assaulted the *Maddox,* the President asked, "We weren't up to any *mischief* out here, were we?"

What Johnson meant was the secret OPLAN 34A program, which he had approved as a new President, after John Kennedy's assassination—covert US attacks against North Vietnamese targets. In March, he had asked Mac Bundy to "keep them off base" and "upset them a little bit, without getting another Korean operation started." Someone now conceded to the President that there might indeed have been such a raid a few nights before the *Maddox* was struck.

For Johnson, the moment was politically sensitive. The previous month, the Republicans had chosen Senator Barry Goldwater of Arizona to oppose him that fall. Accepting his party's nomination at San Francisco's Cow Palace, Goldwater had complained that "failures infest the jungles of Vietnam": "Yesterday it was Korea. Tonight it is Vietnam. . . . Don't try to sweep this under the rug. We are at war in Vietnam. And yet the President, who is the Commander-in-Chief of our armed forces, refuses to say whether or not the objective over there is victory."

This morning, Johnson did not seem anxious that the *Maddox* incident would amount to much. Presuming that the North Vietnamese were simply responding to a covert US raid, he told his advisers that it reminded him of being in a movie theater: "You're sitting next to a pretty girl, and you have your hand on her ankle, and nothing happens. And you move it up to her knee and nothing happens. You move it up further, and you're thinking about moving a bit more, and all of a sudden, you get slapped. I think we got slapped."

Thomas Hughes, the State Department's intelligence chief, scrawled Rusk a note, asking whether "now that we know what happens in the movies in Texas" he still intended to call the *Maddox* attack "unprovoked." Rusk put the question to Deputy Secretary of Defense Cyrus Vance, who said that "of course" it was unprovoked, because the *Maddox* had been sailing in international waters.

"Well, it seems a bit murky, and we won't have any retaliation," said the President. "But we will warn them against doing anything further." He would issue a public statement the next day vowing to send another destroyer to the Tonkin Gulf, along with combat air patrol, explaining that in the future, "any force which attacks them in international waters" would be attacked with the goal of "destroying" it. Now, dispensing with the *Maddox,* he abruptly changed the subject and asked this gathering of national security experts, at some length, about a pending postal pay bill.* Scratching his head, Johnson's new Chairman of the Joint Chiefs of Staff, General Earle Wheeler, asked a colleague while leaving the meeting, "Is it always like this?"

At 9:46 on Monday morning, Johnson addressed the *Maddox* incident during a telephone conversation with his old Texas friend Robert Anderson, who had been Eisenhower's Secretary of the Treasury.† He said, "There have been some covert operations in that area that we have been carrying on—blowing up some bridges and things of that kind . . . so I imagine they wanted to put a stop to it." After the North Vietnamese had fired, the Navy had responded "immediately with five-inch guns from the destroyer, and with planes overhead." Johnson added, "What happened was we've been playing around up there, and they came out, gave us a warning, and we knocked hell out of 'em."‡

Anderson warned, "You're going to be running against a man who's a wild man on this subject." He urged the President to declare that "when they shoot at us from the back, we're not soft," and "we're going to protect ourselves, we'll protect our boys." Referring to his public statement, Johnson asked, "Didn't it leave that impression?" Anderson replied, "I haven't heard any adverse criticism from anybody." But he cautioned

---

* Johnson may have changed topics to shut off demands for a harsher response to the report of a *Maddox* assault—a tactic he had learned from President Roosevelt. Once when LBJ went to the Oval Office to ask for a political favor, Roosevelt had stopped him short by asking, "Lyndon, did you ever see a Russian woman naked?" As Johnson later recalled, "I found myself in the West Lobby without ever having made my proposition."

† In 1943, Anderson had been one of the partners who had sold Johnson's wife, Lady Bird, an Austin radio station, KTBC, which became the basis of their fortune. Ike admired Anderson so much that he had tried to get him to run for President in 1960. Deeming Goldwater too conservative, Anderson was helping to orchestrate business and financial leaders for the 1964 Johnson campaign.

‡ It was ultimately found that in the exchange of fire, three North Vietnamese aboard the torpedo boats were killed. The *Maddox* had survived with but a single machine-gun hole.

that Goldwater would exploit the Vietnam issue: "I just know that this fellow's going to play all of the angles."

* * *

JOHNSON WAS BORN in the Texas Hill Country in 1908. He and his siblings were taught by their deeply literate mother, Rebekah, about the importance of books. Soon after becoming President, he reminisced to Isabelle Shelton, a social reporter for the *Washington Star,* about how Rebekah "just had the bed full of them" and "read out loud to us all of the time" from Browning, Tennyson, and biographies of Texas Governors Jim Hogg and Jim Ferguson, as well as Andrew Jackson and Abraham Lincoln. Johnson recalled that "the first President I really loved" was Jackson, because he "didn't let 'em tread on him," and then Woodrow Wilson: "Everything he wrote or said, I memorized nearly."

Johnson's keen boyhood interest in history did not survive into adulthood. Despite his faith in the value of education, he was too much in a professional hurry to teach himself much history he did not personally experience. As a rising politician with a flypaper memory, he felt that he learned more from his encounters with a wide range of people. The result was startling gaps in his knowledge of the American past. For instance, during a telephone conversation in 1964 with a political friend, he could say, "Remember this—Lincoln went back to Springfield, Missouri, after he was President." That same year, Hugh Sidey of *Time* magazine tried to find out whether Johnson actually consumed the large number of books alleged by his staff. When Sidey asked them for examples, aide after aide mentioned the same book—Barbara Ward's *The Rich Nations and the Poor Nations.*

Johnson loved the romance of Texas folklore. During his Hill Country youth, there were still a few surviving Mexican War veterans who told of the Alamo and the later battlefield gallantry that had expanded the nation's continental reach. Johnson's great-grandfather, Reverend George Washington Baines, was a lifelong friend of Sam Houston, after whom Lyndon's father was named. When Martin Luther King Jr. came to the White House, the President showed him a framed letter from Houston to his ancestor, praising Baines for helping to wrest Texas away from Mexico.* In 1964, Johnson reminded a Nashville audience that while Davy Crockett may have been "born on a mountaintop" (in the words of the ballad from the 1950s Walt Disney TV series), he "won his final glory" by dying at the Alamo.

Out of respect for the Texas military tradition, when young Johnson was elected to the House of Representatives as a Roosevelt acolyte in 1937, he asked the President to help get him onto the House Naval Affairs Committee. Roosevelt personally clinched the deal.† In the late 1930s, Johnson backed his President's efforts to nudge the country toward intervention. But, as he much later recalled, he "loved peace so much" that he signed a discharge petition to let the House debate and vote on the Ludlow Amendment, execrated by Roosevelt, which would have required a national referendum before the country could go to war. Defending his youthful mistake, Johnson later said, "Of course, that was the day before the nuclear bomb, but it was crazy even then because I had no information to vote on it."

In June 1940, Johnson enlisted in the naval reserve. When he announced for the Senate in a special election the following year, he pledged, "If the day ever comes when my vote must be cast to send your boy to the trenches, that day Lyndon Johnson will leave his Senate seat to go with him."‡ He would "never vote for war and then hide behind a Senate seat where bullets cannot reach me." Johnson was defeated by

---

* One of the public school textbooks assigned to the teenage Lyndon addressed the Mexican-American War by saying, "Though the President cannot declare war, he can bring about a situation which may make war unavoidable, as was the case when Polk sent an Army into disputed territory where our soldiers were fired upon." The volume also noted that during the Civil War, "Lincoln became almost a dictator" and "took every means which seemed necessary to win," and that "the war powers of President Wilson were very great."

† Roosevelt's Interior Secretary, Harold Ickes, noted in his diary that FDR found the young Texas Congressman "the kind of uninhibited young pro he would have liked to have been," perhaps if he had gone to a college less elite than Harvard. Ickes recorded Roosevelt's comment that in the generation to come, "the balance of power would shift south and west, and this boy could well be the first Southern President."

‡ His opponent was the Texas radio star W. Lee O'Daniel, known as " 'Pass the Biscuits' Pappy."

only 1,311 votes; the President told him, half-joking, that in the future he had better learn to "sit" on ballot boxes to prevent fraud after the votes were cast. After Pearl Harbor, Johnson, still a Congressman, told reporters that he hankered for "active duty with the Fleet" upon the attack by what he called "the Sabbath Day assassins."

Roosevelt had Johnson dispatched as a Navy observer to study the beleaguered Allied effort in the combat zone of Australia.* The Congressman left the management of his House office to Lady Bird. In June 1942, after a briefing by General MacArthur in Melbourne, Lieutenant Commander Johnson and two other observers, who were vetting air and ground forces, were flown to Garbutt Field, the launching base for aerial attacks against the Japanese in New Guinea. Johnson was to fly on a B-26 Marauder, called the *Wabash Cannonball,* but his place was taken at the last moment by Lieutenant Colonel Francis Stevens, one of his fellow observers, so he walked across the airstrip and asked the commander of another B-26, the *Heckling Hare,* if he could fly with his crew. The *Hare's* tail gunner, Corporal Harry Baren, warned Johnson that it would be "rough," and that he might "get shot up."

By Johnson's later account, an hour after takeoff, Japanese Zero fighter planes swarmed all around the *Hare,* which was struck by bullets and cannon shells, damaging the generator that drove the plane's right engine. Describing the barrage, the *Hare's* radioman-gunner, Lillis Walker, later said, "You're looking right into the face of death when *that* happens." According to Walker, the Congressman was "calm, and watching everything." When the *Hare* set down, Johnson smiled and told the crew, "It's been very interesting." Soon he was told that the *Wabash Cannonball,* under attack, had crashed into the ocean, with no survivors.

Upon Johnson's return to Melbourne, MacArthur presented him with a Silver Star, the Army's third-highest medal, but gave nothing to the actual *Heckling Hare* crewmen, who were risking their lives all

---

* The young White House aide Jonathan Daniels, son of Roosevelt's World War I superior, wrote in his diary that Johnson "wants for the sake of political future to get into danger zone though realizes talents best suited for handling speakers and public relations."

the time. One of Johnson's biographers, Robert Caro, called the award "one of the most undeserved Silver Stars in history," noting that "if you accept everything that he said, he was still in action for no more than thirteen minutes, and only as an observer." Another, Robert Dallek, concluded that Johnson had made a "deal" by which MacArthur would give him the medal if Johnson pledged to push the President to expand resources for his South Pacific theater.

In July 1942, Johnson returned to Washington when Roosevelt ordered that all members of Congress then serving in the armed forces either resign or return.[*] Back in harness, Johnson was at first modest about the episode that had brought him the Silver Star, telling his friend Marshall McNeil, a Texas journalist, "Well, I'll never wear the thing." He even wrote a letter, ultimately unsent, saying that "in good conscience" he could not accept a citation for "the little part I played for such a short time." But before long, he was insisting that his record aboard the *Heckling Hare* deserved an even more glorious reward than a Silver Star. As President, Johnson did not mind preening about his wartime bravery. In December 1963, while referring to political courage, he told House Speaker John McCormack, "I didn't want to go to the Pacific in '41 after Pearl Harbor, but I did. And I didn't want to let those Japs shoot at me in a Zero, but I did."

In November 1948, Johnson was elected to the US Senate by the eighty-seven-vote margin that earned him the derisive nickname "Landslide Lyndon." Two years later, after the Korean War began, outraged by Robert Taft's complaint that Truman had "usurped" congressional power, Johnson sent the President a note expressing his "admiration of your courageous response," adding, "For the decisions you must face alone, you have my most sincere prayers and my total confidence." Later Truman would tell Johnson, with some exaggeration, "I remember—you were the first Senator to support me."

Johnson recalled how Truman had been chair of the Senate committee investigating the defense effort in World War II. Warning that

---

[*] Half of the eight members of Congress then on active duty thereupon resigned in order to keep fighting in the war.

if Republicans retook Congress that November, scrutiny of Truman's war might fall dangerously to the panel chaired by Joe McCarthy, he persuaded his mentor, Richard Russell of Georgia, Chairman of Senate Armed Services, known as "Mr. Defense," to give him control of a new subcommittee on war expenditures, which elevated his stature. After Republicans took control in 1952, Russell helped him to become Minority Leader of the Senate and then Majority Leader after the Democratic comeback two years later.

In that capacity, Johnson collaborated with President Eisenhower and another mentor, Speaker Sam Rayburn of Texas, on what they called a bipartisan foreign policy. The trio banded together against the vestigial isolationist bloc, mostly Republicans, who were touting a possible constitutional amendment proposed by Senator John Bricker, Republican from Ohio, that would severely limit a President's power to make executive agreements with other countries. Eisenhower made Johnson feel like a copilot, a charmed experience that may later have given him illusions, as President, about how much congressional cooperation he could expect on national security.

During Johnson's miserable years as John Kennedy's Vice President, he did not feel like a copilot of anything. Well acquainted, from the Senate, with Johnson's talent for agglomerating power, JFK kept him on a short leash. Johnson later claimed that Kennedy had told "the Catholics"— meaning the President's coreligionists John McCormack and Senate Majority Leader Mike Mansfield—"to pay no attention to me." Before Kennedy's inauguration, Johnson had asked Senate Democrats to let him keep presiding over their caucus. They rebuffed him, citing the constitutional separation of powers, and Kennedy observed that "the steam really went out of Lyndon." When Kennedy called on Johnson for comment during councils on foreign policy, the Vice President would sometimes lower his large head and sadly reply that he was insufficiently informed to offer an opinion.

Throughout the Cuban Missile Crisis of October 1962, Johnson was a member of President Kennedy's impromptu advisory panel called ExComm. Attorney General Robert Kennedy observed that when his brother refused the Joint Chiefs' demand that the missile sites be bombed, followed by an invasion of the island, Johnson was "shaking his head, mad," although "he never made clear what he would do" instead. After Nikita Khrushchev agreed to pull the missiles out, however, Johnson grudgingly conceded to a friend that the President had played "a damn good hand of poker—I'll say that for him."

In November 1963, three weeks before Kennedy's assassination, the increasingly detested and authoritarian President of South Vietnam, Ngo Dinh Diem, and his powerful brother were killed after a coup that Kennedy had approved. During a Saigon goodwill visit, Johnson had hailed Diem in 1961 as "the George Washington of Southeast Asia." He thought it was a mistake for Kennedy to have expected Diem to reform his political system and "make Vietnam into an America overnight." After Johnson became President, he privately said that Diem's ouster and killing had been "a tragic mistake—it was awful and we've lost everything." Robert Kennedy was infuriated to learn that Johnson was privately saying that his brother's assassination may have been "divine retribution" for his role in the coup that led to Diem's murder.

✳ ✳ ✳

ON SATURDAY, December 7, 1963, upon Jacqueline Kennedy's departure, Johnson moved his family into the White House—with Lady Bird holding a large framed photograph of Speaker Rayburn and teenage daughters Lynda and Lucy (she later changed her name to Luci) handling the family beagles, Him and Her.

That same day, the President telephoned Richard Russell. On becoming President, Johnson had told the Georgia Senator, "I haven't got any Daddy, and you're going to be it." Now in command of the White House indoor pool, he asked his friend, "You don't feel like coming down here and going swimming? . . . This is good, warm water." Suffering from emphysema, Russell declined, explaining, "I've got this short-winded business. I can't breathe."

Johnson brought up Vietnam. Russell advised him, "We should get out, but I don't know any way to get out." He reminded Johnson of their meeting with President Eisenhower in April 1954, when the French colonialists were collapsing at Dien Bien Phu. Ike had asked for discretionary authority to use US air and sea power against Communist aggression in Southeast Asia. But Johnson and Russell had balked, advising Eisenhower that America should not act there alone. As the Georgian now reminded the new President, "I tried my best to keep them from going into Laos and Vietnam. . . . Said we'd never get out—be in there fifty years from now."

In January 1964, General Duong Van "Big" Minh, who had succeeded Diem as leader of South Vietnam, was deposed in Saigon by a junta commanded by the thirty-six-year-old General Nguyen Khanh. Under Secretary of State George Ball told Johnson that Khanh's ascent was "probably a good thing." Soon Johnson called Khanh "the toughest one they got" and asked his Joint Chiefs to proclaim that he was "our boy." Khanh demanded that Americans save South Vietnam by attacking the North. US officials asked him to wait until his government was better established. Khanh warned that by then it would be too late.

Rusk reminded Johnson that the Manila Pact, signed by the Southeast Asia Treaty Organization (SEATO) in 1954, committed the United States to South Vietnam's defense. The Joint Chiefs advised him in March that "preventing the loss of South Vietnam" was of "overriding importance" to the United States. The CIA warned him in May that if the "tide of deterioration" were not halted by the end of 1964, "the anti-Communist position in South Vietnam is likely to become untenable." Secretary of Defense Robert McNamara told Johnson's National Security Council that same month, "The situation is still going to hell. . . . Nothing we are now doing will win. . . . The question is whether we should hit North Vietnam now, or whether we can wait." Rusk, McNamara, and Mac Bundy all beseeched Johnson to "make a Presidential decision that the U.S. will use selected and carefully graduated military force against North Vietnam."

Seeking advice, on Wednesday morning, May 27, Johnson called Senator Russell, who told him,

It's the damn worst mess I ever saw. . . . And I don't see how
we're ever going to get out of it without fighting a major war

with the Chinese and all of them, down there in those rice pad-
dies and jungles. . . . It appears that our position is deteriorating. And it looks like the more that we try to do for them, the
less that they're willing to do for themselves. . . . It's just one of
those places where you can't win. . . . It frightens me. . . . It'd be
a Korea on a much bigger scale and a worse scale. . . . The French
report that they lost 250,000 men and spent a couple billion of
their money, and two billion of ours, down there, and just got the
hell whipped out of them. . . . We're just in the quicksands—up
to our very necks.

Russell recommended that the President engineer a fresh coup, this
time against Khanh: "Get some fellow in there that said he wished to
hell we *would* get out. That would give us a good excuse for getting out."
Johnson asked Russell how important South Vietnam was to American
security. The Senator replied that with America's fast-growing arsenal of
nuclear-tipped intercontinental missiles, Vietnam "isn't important to us
a damn bit," except "from a psychological standpoint."

Johnson reported to Russell that his chief advisers were telling him
"that we haven't got much choice, that we are treaty-bound . . . that this
will be a domino that will kick off a whole list of others, that we've just
got to prepare for the worst." He said that they sounded "kinda like
MacArthur in Korea—they don't believe that the Chinese Communists
will come into this thing, but they don't know and nobody can really be
sure." Then, showing his ambivalence, Johnson asked, "They'd impeach
a President, though, that would run out, wouldn't they?" Russell warned
that if Johnson sent combat troops to Vietnam, "it'll be the most expensive venture this country ever went into."

The President cited the "little old sergeant" who laid out his clothes
in the mornings: "Every time I think about making this decision, I
think about sending that father of those six kids in there. And what
the hell are we going to get out of his doing it? It just makes the chills
run up my back." Russell agreed: "It does me." Johnson said, "I haven't
the nerve to do it, but I don't see any other way out of it." Russell:
"It doesn't make much sense to do it. It's one of those things—heads

I win, tails you lose." The President closed, "I love you, and I'll be calling you."

Then Johnson telephoned Mac Bundy, confiding, "The more that I stayed awake last night, thinking of this thing . . . it looks to me like we're getting into another Korea. . . . I believe that the Chinese Communists are coming into it. I don't think that we can fight them ten thousand miles away from home. . . . I don't think it's worth fighting for, and I don't think that we can get out." Plaintively he asked, "What the hell is Vietnam worth to me? . . . What is it worth to this country? No, we've got a treaty, but, hell, everybody else's got a treaty out there, and they're not doing anything about it. Of course, if you start running from the Communists, they may just chase you right into your own kitchen." Bundy replied, "That's the trouble." Johnson cited a poll showing that 65 percent of Americans "don't know anything" about Vietnam, and "of those that do, the majority think we're mishandling it.* But they don't know what to do." He warned, "It's damned easy to get in a war, but it's gonna be awfully hard to ever extricate yourself if you get in."

With Johnson eager to be elected President in his own right, Vietnam was gaining more prominence in the campaign. That month, Barry Goldwater blamed the Vietnam stalemate on Johnson and McNamara, "those twin commanders of chaos." He claimed that low-yield nuclear weapons could be used to defoliate the South Vietnamese border, depriving Viet Cong rebels of cover, explaining that "a defensive war is never won." Everett Dirksen and Charles Halleck, Republican leaders of the Senate and House, soon warned that Vietnam would be an issue because "President Johnson's indecision has made it one." Denouncing Johnson's "contradictions, confusion and vacillation," Halleck charged that the President was "avoiding a decision" until after the election, "while we go on dribbling away both American lives and American prestige in a no-win war."

---

* A Gallup Poll released that day found that 63 percent of Americans had given little or no attention to developments in Vietnam, and that of those who had, 42 percent said the United States was "doing well as can be expected" and 46 percent said "badly."

On Wednesday evening, June 10, Johnson's close boyhood friend and Hill Country business partner A. W. Moursund admonished him: "Goddamn, there's not anything that'll destroy you as quick as pulling out, pulling up stakes and running." The President replied, "But I don't want to kill these folks." Moursund, a World War II Army Air Corps veteran, said, "I don't give a damn. I didn't want to kill 'em in Korea." Moursund told him to "stand up for America," warning, "They'll forgive you for anything except being weak."

The next day at noon, nervous about Moursund's advice, Johnson called Russell, sounding notably more hawkish about Vietnam: "I don't believe the American people ever want me to run [away]. If I lose it, I think that they'll say *I've* lost, I've pulled in. At the same time, I don't want to commit us to a war. And I'm in a hell of a shape." With astonishing foresight, Russell warned, "It would take half a million men. They'd be bogged down in there for ten years." Johnson said, "We never did clear Korea up yet." Russell replied, "Except for seventy thousand of 'em buried over there."* The Georgian went on, "I don't know what the hell to do. I didn't ever want to get messed up down there. . . . But as a practical matter, we're in there, and I don't know how the hell you can tell the American people you're coming out. . . . They'll think that you've just been whipped, you've been ruined, you're scared. It would be disastrous." Johnson replied, "I think that I've got to say that 'I didn't get you in here, but we're in here by treaty, and our national honor's at stake.'"

After dinner at the White House on Monday, June 15, the President took his friends Clark Clifford, once Truman's White House counsel, and the belligerent *Washington Post* columnist Joseph Alsop aside to discuss Vietnam. Alsop warned the President that he was in danger of presiding "over the first real defeat of the United States in history." Lady Bird later told her diary that this conversation did nothing "to solve Lyndon's dilemma—or to smooth his path for the days ahead." The next morning, Johnson told McNamara, "I was with some folks last night, and they think we're about to lose the greatest race that the United States

---

* Russell was referring to the total number of Americans and South Koreans killed in that war.

has ever lost, and it would be the first time that we've ever turned a-tail and then shoved out of a place and come home—and said we'd [have] given up the Pacific. Now I don't think it's that bad, but a lot of people do, and I think we're gonna have to make a decision pretty promptly." McNamara replied, "I just don't believe we can be pushed out of there, Mr. President. We just can't allow it to be done." He added that "you wouldn't want to go down in history" that way. (Russell had earlier warned the President that the Secretary of Defense was "opinionated as hell, and he's made up his mind on this.")

Johnson was trying to hold the line on Vietnam until November 1964, postponing his toughest choices until he did not have to operate within the unpredictable madhouse atmosphere of a campaign. By now, he had discarded Russell's advice to engineer Khanh's downfall and install a South Vietnamese leader who would demand an American withdrawal. (The Senator had bluntly told him to "get the same crowd that got rid of old Diem to get rid of these people.") The President now believed that "the greatest danger we face there now is losing Khanh and being asked to get out." He warned Speaker McCormack that if Khanh "falls over, as he may any day, and we have another coup, we're through in Asia."

Johnson thought negotiation would be fruitless. "Conferences ain't gonna do a damn bit of good," he told Russell. "We tell 'em every week, we tell Khrushchev, we send China and Hanoi and all of 'em word that we'll get out of there and stay out of there if they'll just quit raiding their neighbors. And they just say, 'Screw you!'" At the end of June, speaking in Minneapolis, the President assured Americans that he would use force "when necessary" and "risk war" to protect South Vietnam.

White House aides had been working, since May, to draft a congressional resolution endorsing "all measures, including the commitment of force," to defend the existing regimes in Laos and South Vietnam. Johnson told them that Truman had erred in failing to ask Congress for approval to wage his war in Korea. His aide Jack Valenti later observed that had some President tried to do so when Johnson was Senate leader, Johnson would have "torn his balls off." Only if Congress was in on the takeoff would it take responsibility for any "crash landing" in Vietnam.

Johnson reminded Robert Kennedy, who was still his Attorney General, that in the Korean War "we had the United Nations behind us, but we had a very divided country and a lot of hell, and we, finally, really lost—the Democrats did." He knew that House and Senate hearings on his Vietnam policy could be ferocious and damaging, especially during a presidential campaign. He told Kennedy that he would "shudder" if members debated a resolution on Vietnam "for a long period of time." They would "just talk and develop a big divide here at home." Kennedy agreed: "They'll start asking somebody to spell out what exactly is going to happen, and if we drop bombs there, then they retaliate and we eventually bomb Hanoi." Johnson said, "That's all true, and you can't go into the details of your plans. But if you take the other route, then they ask you by what authority, what executive order, do you declare war."

The Attorney General was hoping that Johnson would choose him to run for Vice President in 1964, so he was in no mood to quarrel. He advised the President that a congressional resolution was probably "not necessary constitutionally," but that in its absence, should Johnson wish to use major force in Vietnam, he had better brief House and Senate leaders beforehand. Johnson agreed: "And, I think, probably talk to the country about why we are there."

McNamara advised him, that June, not to ask for any resolution, unless he planned to send combat forces to Vietnam within the next two or three months. "If we're going to go strictly up the escalating chain, we're going to have to educate the people, Mr. President," he said. "We haven't done so yet." Mac Bundy counseled that in the meantime, public support for military action would be strengthened by "a substantial increase of national attention and international tension."

* * *

ON MONDAY, August 3, 1964, at 10:20 a.m., the day after the North Vietnamese attack on the *Maddox,* Johnson asked Rusk and McNamara to meet privately with Senate and House leaders, and "tell 'em what happened" in the Tonkin Gulf: "They're gonna start an investigation if you don't. . . . It would be better to do it up on the

Hill. . . . I'd tell 'em awfully quiet though, so they won't go in and be making a bunch of speeches."

The Secretary of Defense urged that the leaders be told about the secret OPLAN 34A, since there was "no question" that it "had bearing" on the attack. He reminded the President that on Friday night, "we had four PT-boats from Vietnam, manned by Vietnamese or other nationals, attack two islands," and that the adversary had "undoubtedly" connected the assault with the presence of the *Maddox.* Johnson consented. He asked McNamara to "leave an impression on background" that "we're gonna be firm as hell." He reported that "the people that are calling me up" were saying "that the Navy responded wonderfully, and that's good. But they want to be damned sure I don't pull 'em out and run. . . . That's what all the country wants because Goldwater is raising so much hell about how he's gonna blow 'em off the moon."

McNamara told the President he would inform the members that should there be another incident like the *Maddox,* Johnson would be "fully prepared" to respond by striking the North Vietnamese mainland: "As a matter of fact, in ten minutes, I am going over, with the Chiefs, the final work on this. We have pictures, analyses, numbers of sorties, bomb loadings—everything prepared for all target systems of North Vietnam." The President warned him to be careful: "If you go put this in the paper, and your enemy reads about it, then he thinks we're already taking off and obviously you've got us in a war."

That evening, Senator George Smathers, Democrat from Florida, told the President that McNamara's meeting had gone well: even Senator Wayne Morse, the maverick Democrat from Oregon, "was nice, didn't ask too many of his usually obnoxious questions."* Johnson asked how members had reacted to his public statement that the Navy should "destroy" any future attacker: "They like my orders to 'em?" Smathers

---

* Senator Morse, then a Republican, had served on Johnson's subcommittee investigating Korean War expenditures. Finding him a contentious, annoying publicity seeker, Johnson had kept him out of his hair by assigning him to focus on the defense of Alaska and the Pacific Northwest, an issue that would help the Oregonian in his 1950 reelection battle. It was Johnson who persuaded Morse in 1955 to become a Democrat.

confessed that some of those present had asked why he had not already issued such a command before the *Maddox* incident. Annoyed, the President replied, "You can't give 'em orders to chase hell out of and destroy a boat that they don't know they've even seen."

Johnson was furious to learn that after McNamara's briefing, his Senate Whip, Hubert Humphrey of Minnesota, when asked by the press why the North Vietnamese had attacked an innocent destroyer, explained that the United States had been conducting covert operations in the area. The President told their mutual friend, the Washington lawyer James Rowe, "That is exactly what we *have* been doing" and Hubert had "blabbed everything." Humphrey's gaffe was badly timed, because he was desperate to be Johnson's running mate. The President sputtered, "The damned fool . . . just ought to keep his goddamned big mouth shut on foreign affairs, at least until the election is over. . . . He's hurting his government, and he's hurting *us*! . . . He just yak-yak-yak, just dancing around with the bald head. . . . That can ruin a man mighty quick."

$$* * *$$

O N TUESDAY, AT 9:12 a.m., in the White House Family Dining Room, Johnson was hosting Democratic leaders of Congress at their weekly breakfast when he was ushered away for an urgent call from McNamara. The Secretary told him the *Maddox* was reporting that, according to radar and communications intercepts, nearby North Vietnamese ships and aircraft were poised to wage another attack. Complying with the President's standing orders, fighter planes had been launched from the USS *Ticonderoga*.

After saying good-bye to the leaders, Johnson went to the Oval Office and resumed his conversation with McNamara at 9:43. The Defense Secretary reported that Admiral Ulysses S. Grant Sharp Jr., US commander for the Pacific, had suggested by cable that the track of the *Maddox,* now eleven miles away from the North Vietnamese coast, be shifted three miles closer, to show that the vessel would not accept a twelve-mile limit. McNamara said that he and Rusk disagreed with

Sharp: "This ship that's allegedly to be attacked tonight—we don't like to see a change in operation plan of that kind at this time. Certainly no military purpose is served by it." Johnson agreed.

The Defense Secretary reported that Sharp had also proposed that should there be another attack, the US commander be authorized to pursue the offender and destroy his base. McNamara warned, "If we give such authority, you have, in a sense, lost control of the degree of our response to the North Vietnamese. . . . I personally would recommend to you, after a second attack on our ships, that we do retaliate against the coast of North Vietnam some way or other—and we'll be prepared."

Johnson told him that while eating breakfast, it had occurred to him that "the weakness of our position is that we respond only to an action," while the North Vietnamese felt free to "shoot at us." He told McNamara to pull out his target list, and if the North should attack again, "just hit about three of them damn quick and go after them." The Secretary pledged that he and Mac Bundy would "be prepared" to recommend "a retaliation move against North Vietnam, in the event this attack takes place within the next six to nine hours." Worried about press leaks that might force his hand, Johnson ordered, "Let's just try to keep it to the two of us."

At 10:53, McNamara called Johnson again: "We had just had a report from the commander of that task force out there that they have sighted two unidentified vessels and three unidentified prop aircraft." The *Ticonderoga* had reacted by launching two F-8 fighters, two A-4D jet attack aircraft, and four A-1H propeller-driven planes to examine the situation and protect the destroyers *Maddox* and *Turner Joy*. McNamara went on,

> The report is that they have observed—and we don't know by
> what means. . . . I suspect this is radar—two unidentified vessels
> and three unidentified prop aircraft in the vicinity of the destroy-
> ers. . . . We have ample forces to respond not only to these attacks
> on the destroyers but also to retaliate, should you wish to do so,
> against targets on the land. . . . Seventy percent of the petroleum
> supply in North Vietnam, we believe, is concentrated in three

dumps. And we can bomb or strafe those dumps and destroy
their petroleum system. . . . In addition, there are certain prestige
targets. . . . For example, there is one bridge that is the key bridge
on the rail line south out of Hanoi, and we could destroy that.

At 11:06, the Defense Secretary called back with a fateful message:
"Mr. President, we just had word by telephone from Admiral Sharp
that the destroyer is under torpedo attack." Johnson asked where the
torpedoes were coming from. "We don't know," replied McNamara.
"Presumably from these unidentified craft that I mentioned to you a
moment ago." The President asked, "What are these planes of ours doing
around while they're being attacked?" McNamara said, "Presumably the
planes are attacking the ships."

During a previously scheduled National Security Council meeting at
noon, Secretary of the Treasury Douglas Dillon, a Republican who had
been Eisenhower's number two man at State, warned, "There is a limit
on the number of times we can be attacked by the North Vietnamese
without hitting their naval bases." Adamant about leaks, Johnson made
his actual decisions afterward, over lunch in the Executive Mansion,
with Rusk, McNamara, Mac Bundy, Vance, and CIA Director John
McCone. Citing the conflicting signals from the Tonkin Gulf, he directed McNamara to ascertain that there had actually been a second
attack. He hoped that the report from Sharp would remain secret unless
or until it was confirmed. Then he would want a "firm, swift retaliatory
strike" against North Vietnamese military bases and an oil depot at
Vinh. After lunch, the President, who had suffered an almost-fatal heart
attack in 1955, withdrew for a nap in his four-poster bed.

Returning to the Pentagon, McNamara asked the Joint Chiefs, at
4:47 p.m., to "marshal the evidence to overcome lack of a clear and convincing showing that an attack on the destroyers had, in fact, occurred."
But while the Chiefs tried to gauge whether the report of a second attack was genuine, someone leaked the news to wire services that House
and Senate leaders had been summoned to the White House, where the
President would "brief the lawmakers on the latest PT-boat attack."

Disconcerted, McNamara called Johnson, who was in the Oval

Office, at 5:09: "Mr. President, the story has broken on the AP and the UP." Johnson walked over to the wire service machines that stood to the left of his three large black-and-white television sets (each tuned to NBC, CBS, or ABC). By contrast with his French counterpart, Charles de Gaulle, who did not permit even a telephone in his formal work chamber, Johnson had asked for this bulky equipment, which was housed in specially constructed cabinets. Now, looking down at the story that had just rattled out of the wire service "ticker," he told McNamara, "Yeah, I see it."

"Anyway, it's broken," said the Defense Secretary. He wished to issue a statement that "during the night . . . the two destroyers were attacked by the patrol boats. The attack was driven off. No casualties or damage to the destroyers. We believe several of the patrol boats were sunk. Details won't be available until daylight." Johnson said, "That's okay. I'd just go on and put that out." McNamara said he had talked to Dillon, who "fully agrees" with the President's desire to strike North Vietnam that evening. As for the Attorney General, McNamara said, "I couldn't get ahold of Bobby. He's nowhere that he can be found."

Johnson took a call at six o'clock from Senator Olin Johnston, Democrat from South Carolina, who had fought in World War I France. The latter informed the President that he had just told reporters, "I'm for keeping us out of war, and I'm voting for Lyndon Johnson." The President frankly replied, "Well, I don't know whether I can do that. I'm going to do my best, Olin."

As Johnson and his advisers knew, evidence of a second assault on the Gulf of Tonkin was still far from conclusive. But at the Cabinet table, starting at 6:16, McNamara informed the President and National Security Council without ambiguity that North Vietnamese PT boats had "continued their attacks" on the *Maddox* and *Turner Joy.* Rusk replied, "This unprovoked attack on the high seas is an act of war, for all practical purposes."

At 6:45, the President faced the congressional leadership of both parties at that same table. Now he spoke as if the evidence about a second incident were irrefutable: "After we were attacked yesterday and today, and nine torpedoes were shot at our destroyers, forty miles on the high seas, we had to answer that attack. . . . We can tuck our tails and run, but if we do, these countries will feel all they have to do to scare us is to shoot the American flag."

He disclosed that he would send the leaders a draft resolution of "Congressional concurrence" with his plan of action, warning that "it would be very damaging to ask for it and not get it." He explained that his draft would be based on earlier congressional endorsements for President Eisenhower's military actions in the region of Formosa and the Middle East. For Vietnam, "I don't think any resolution is necessary, but I think it is a lot better to have it, in light of what we did in Korea."* To put each guest firmly on the record, he "went around the table," as his aide Walter Jenkins recorded, and each "made an expression of support, one way or another." After the meeting, the President told his congressional liaison, Lawrence O'Brien, whom he had inherited from Kennedy, that he would be "bombing the hell out of the Vietnamese tonight."

With her finely tuned awareness of her husband's moods and needs, Lady Bird called him at 8:35 from the Mansion. Picking up the receiver, he said, "Darling, did you want me?" She replied, "Yes, beloved. . . . I just wanted to see you whenever you're all alone, merely to tell you I loved you. That's all." He asked whether there was "any other news." She told him, "Nothing in comparison to yours, darling." He promised, "I'll come over just as soon as we get through."

Johnson planned to announce his air strikes against North Vietnam on television after 10:00 p.m., Washington time, once the US bombers would have been launched from their aircraft carrier, so that the adversary would have no advance warning. At 9:15, he asked McNamara, "When they leave the carrier at ten, how long does it take them to get over the target?" McNamara replied that the last plane should reach its target about midnight. Johnson asked, "Do we want to give them two

---

* Meaning President Truman's refusal to ask Congress for any resolution of support for his decision to go to war.

hours' notice? Better check that, Bob. . . . I'd sure as hell hate to have some mother say, 'You announced it and got my boy killed.'"*

At 10:06, the President called Goldwater, who had been cruising on the yacht *Sundance* near the Balboa Bay Club in Newport Beach, California: "Barry, I'm going to make a statement in a little bit, and I wanted to talk to you before I did." Johnson read his statement aloud, and the Senator admitted, "I don't know what else you could do." Johnson added, "Just very confidentially, we're going to take all the boats out that we can and all the bases from which they come." Goldwater pledged, "Like always, Americans will stick together." The President said, "Thank you, Barry. Bye, fella."

After a brief dinner in the Mansion with Lady Bird, Valenti, and Mac Bundy, Johnson went to the Fish Room in the West Wing, where, at 11:36, he gave a six-minute speech. Wearing his Silver Star from the *Heckling Hare,* a morose-looking President announced that Sunday's "initial attack" against the *Maddox* had been "repeated today by a number of hostile vessels, attacking two U.S. destroyers with torpedoes." Thus "aggression by terror against the peaceful villagers of South Vietnam has now been joined by open aggression on the high seas" against the United States. "Repeated acts of violence" had compelled a "limited and fitting" reply from US armed forces. "That reply is being given as I speak to you tonight," including air action "against gunboats and certain supporting facilities in North Vietnam." Johnson vowed to "seek no wider war."

On Wednesday morning, August 5, the President formally sent up to Capitol Hill his draft congressional endorsement of "all necessary measures" in Southeast Asia. Johnson told McNamara, "We may have to escalate. I'm not going to do it without Congressional authority." Mac Bundy later said, "In my time with Lyndon Johnson, I do not remember a large decision more quickly reached." Following Truman's example on Korea, Johnson also ordered that the Gulf of Tonkin issue be referred

---

* When precisely this criticism was later issued on the House floor by Republican Edgar Foreman of Texas, Johnson complained to Speaker McCormack about "this little shitass Foreman," and called the charge "just a pure lie and smokescreen."

to the UN Security Council. But unlike Truman, this President did not have the luck of finding the Soviet delegate absent and unable to cast a veto.

Just before noon, in a speech at Syracuse University, Johnson claimed that there had been two sets of "deliberate" North Vietnamese attacks and that both were "unprovoked." (The latter was the same adjective used by Presidents Polk, McKinley, Roosevelt, and Truman to describe the offenses that pushed them toward war.) In retrospect, it seems surprising that the self-protective Johnson would have knowingly allowed himself to make two such public assertions that could later be proven false. He knew there was some chance that the August 4 assault had not occurred at all—and that, even if it had, neither this nor the previous attack by the North, in light of the OPLAN 34A raids, could be honestly construed as unprovoked. But he was eager to inoculate himself against Goldwater's charges of cowardice on Vietnam.

Should some journalist or disgruntled official release evidence demonstrating that what happened on the Tonkin Gulf was not what the President had claimed, Johnson knew he could always insist that he had been misinformed by his advisers. Long afterward, Mac Bundy said that Johnson believed that establishing the facts about the episode was McNamara's job, not the President's, and that the Defense Secretary had assured him he could "count on" the fact of a second attack. Bundy cavalierly added that, despite the lingering confusion about whether or not the North Vietnamese had actually fired on the second occasion, this was "all, in a sense, show business anyway" because the real question was "whether you wanted to stay and fight in Vietnam."

By now, Johnson had clearly decided that both Rusk and McNamara, although Kennedy holdovers, met his high standards of loyalty, which he once described as being eager to "kiss my ass in Macy's window at high noon and say it smells like roses." He felt that if he ever needed McNamara or Rusk to protect him, each would be willing to take the blame and depart quietly. Johnson had watched how faithfully the Secretary of State had served Kennedy, despite the constant needling of his brother Robert. The President joked with Rusk about which of them had more humble and rustic origins, and knew how grateful the

Secretary of State was to be treated now with respect. In McNamara, Johnson saw a man of steel-elbowed ambition almost equal to his own, who knew it was in his interest, at least for now, to jump through flaming hoops to please the chief. That summer, Johnson had enchanted McNamara, an ex–Ford Motor president who had no previous political experience, by letting it be known that he was considering him for Vice President.*

* * *

D URING AN OPEN hearing on Thursday morning, August 6, McNamara badly stretched the truth while testifying to the Senate Armed Services and Foreign Relations Committees. He claimed that what happened to the *Maddox,* while performing "a routine mission," was not connected to the patrol boat raids of the end of July. A skeptical Wayne Morse replied, "I think we are kidding the world if you try to give the impression that when the South Vietnamese naval boats bombarded two islands a short distance off the coast of North Vietnam, we were not implicated."

This was not the first time that a Cabinet member deceived Congress and justified it to himself on grounds of national security. In 1960, for instance, Secretary of State Christian Herter had falsely told a Senate committee that the issue of U-2 spy flights over the Soviet Union, which constituted an act of war, had "never come up to" President Eisenhower. McNamara himself had lied to the House Armed Services Committee in 1963, when he claimed, during secret testimony about the Cuban Missile Crisis, that there was "absolutely no connection" between the Soviet Union's decision to take its missiles out of Cuba and what he

---

* Aside from his wish to attract Republicans in 1964, Johnson could not have been serious about McNamara as his running mate. This President, so seasoned in politics, and who took such care with personal relationships, knew how abrasive others found his Defense Secretary. Speaker McCormack had called the President in April 1964 to warn him that, after having "the most uncomfortable experience I've ever had in my life" with McNamara, he never wanted to meet with him again. Johnson would also have been unlikely to spend his political capital to persuade Democrats to nominate a registered Republican, even though he claimed that McNamara, by writing checks for the other party, had merely been "trying to satisfy" his then boss, Henry Ford II.

called "not the removal but the modernization" of NATO missiles in Turkey and Italy.

After Thursday morning's Tonkin Gulf hearing was over, McNamara told Johnson that he had had "a hell of a time with Morse" but "I think I finally shut him up." He reported that the members had shown "just near-unanimous support for not only everything you've done" but "for everything you may do in the future, and generally a blank-check authorization for further action."

That afternoon, the House passed what was now widely called the Gulf of Tonkin Resolution, by 414 to 0.* The Senate endorsed the bill by 88 to 2. It was opposed by Democrats Morse and Ernest Gruening, the latter of Alaska, who decried the document as merely a "predated declaration of war power" that properly belonged not to the President but to Congress. Morse deprecated the Tonkin Gulf incident as "another sinking of the *Maine*"—a "deliberate" pretext "to justify making war against North Vietnam." Gruening said he would not send "our boys into combat in a war in which we have no business, which is not our war, into which we have been misguidedly drawn, which is steadily being escalated in private." Told about the dissenters, the President, who had wanted a unanimous endorsement, complained that Morse was "undependable and erratic," and that Gruening was "worse than Morse. He's just no good—I've spent millions on him up in Alaska."[†]

The Tonkin Resolution achieved a short-term political purpose. In late August, at the Democratic convention in Atlantic City, the keynote speaker, Senator John Pastore of Rhode Island, reminded the delegates that "only three weeks ago, in the Gulf of Tonkin . . . Hanoi and Peking felt the sting of President Johnson's determination." After Congress

---

* The Harlem Democrat Adam Clayton Powell, who had supported his friend Johnson over John Kennedy in 1960, voted "present," explaining that he was a minister and a pacifist. The isolationist Republican Congressman Eugene Siler of Kentucky, a Robert Taft admirer who hated foreign aid and American alliances and wanted US troops removed from Vietnam, opposed the Tonkin Resolution but absented himself that day from the House floor. He insisted that Presidents obtained such votes of support "to seal the lips of Congress against future criticism."

† Johnson meant that Gruening should have been grateful for the federal money he had directed toward Alaska, including rescue funds after a major earthquake in March 1964.

passed the resolution, Goldwater toned down his complaints about the issue, and for the remainder of the 1964 campaign, Johnson saw fit to mention the word "Vietnam" in public only half a dozen times.

∗ ∗ ∗

WITHOUT A TONKIN Gulf–style minidrama, Johnson's resolution would never have passed the House or Senate so resoundingly. During debate, members would have demanded that Johnson and McNamara reveal exactly what they planned to do in Vietnam. Instead, with almost no serious examination, in the wake of a counterfeit "unprovoked attack" against the United States, Congress hastily passed the President's own document intact. Both Johnson and his successor, Richard Nixon, used the Gulf of Tonkin Resolution as their warrant to prosecute a doomed war in Southeast Asia that—just as Russell had privately warned the President—would consume the next decade.

Johnson proudly kept a copy of the resolution in his wallet throughout his presidency. While defending his military struggle in Vietnam, he would yank out the slip of paper and wave it at interlocutors. In February 1965, when Congress considered his first major escalation in Vietnam, the President told Rusk, "I would keep those 502 Congressmen right chained to me all the time with that resolution." McNamara was summoned to testify, and Johnson told him,

> Bob, I think if you do run into any questions, you ought to say when we went into Korea, there was some question about the Congress not expressing themselves. . . . And for that reason, last summer . . . we asked the Congress for a resolution. . . . I read it last night again. . . . We all said, "We are not trying to seek any wider war, but here is what the Congress says." Now anytime anybody asks me . . . I would say, "Now the Commander-in-Chief has certain inherent powers . . . but it so happens, in this instance, that Congress has expressed theirself very definitely. And so here's what it has said—period."

During a private conversation that spring with George Mahon of Texas, the House Appropriations Chairman, Johnson contended that he had leveled with Congress by asking for the resolution:

> I've got a vote of confidence—502 to 2. . . . I thought . . . this would be a masterstroke with the Congress to show them I was frank and candid, and when I needed something, I would put it right in their belly . . . and if they gave it to me, why, they'd say, "We can trust the guy. Although he's got authority, he didn't write his check. He let us in on it." . . . If I hadn't been there thirty years on the Hill, I would have just signed the document that came to me transferring funds. . . . So I laid my cards on the table.

In 1969, back on the LBJ Ranch, ex-President Johnson defended his decision to ask the House and Senate for the Tonkin document. During an interview with Walter Cronkite of CBS, he explained, with intense emotion, "Congress gave us this authority to do whatever may be necessary. That's pretty *far-reaching*! That's 'the sky's the *limit*'!" When Cronkite asked why he had not asked the Senate and House for a full declaration of war, Johnson said, "I didn't know what treaty *China* might have with North Vietnam, or *Russia* might have with North Vietnam. The Communists *have* these agreements among themselves. And if we declared war against North Vietnam, that might automatically declare war against China and bring them in, triggering the thing—or the Soviet Union."* That same year, discussing his early decisions on Vietnam, he told two members of his postpresidential staff, "If you let a bully come in and chase you out of your front yard, tomorrow he'll be on your porch, and the next day, he'll rape your wife in your own bed."

In later decades, when Americans were more jaundiced against their

---

* After the program was aired, realizing that such claims were unlikely to impress viewers, Johnson told aides, "I did lousy."

leaders, many came to view the Gulf of Tonkin incident as a pretext deliberately produced by a President thirsting for war, in a dishonorable tradition extending from Polk's provocative behavior in Mexico to whatever legerdemain some people thought Franklin Roosevelt might have been up to at Pearl Harbor. It was fortunate for Johnson that Americans of his own time did not learn that soon after Congress passed the Tonkin Resolution, he was secretly informed that, thanks to further investigation by the Pentagon and US intelligence, there was probably never any August 4 attack by the North Vietnamese. When he was told of this new finding, Johnson responded that he had already felt skeptical about that second assault. He said, also in private, to George Ball, "Hell, those dumb, stupid sailors were just shooting at flying fish!"*

After receiving the later evidence that the second enemy attack might have been a chimera, the President refused to take the political risk of informing Congress and the public that his information had been faulty. Certainly he did not dream of asking the House or Senate to revise or retract the resolution that was based on that attack. In September 1964, Johnson privately showed his tough-minded attitude about the supposed second assault when McNamara telephoned him to report a possible new incident in the Gulf of Tonkin. The President replied,

> Now, Bob, I have found, over the years, that we see and we hear and we imagine a lot of things in the form of attacks and shots. . . . I don't want them just being some change-o'-life woman running up and saying that, by God, she was being raped just because a man walks in the room! . . . A man gets enough braid on him, and he walks in a room, and he just immediately concludes that he's being attacked. . . . And then, in a day or two more, we're sure it didn't happen at all.

---

* Interviewed for Errol Morris's 2003 film *The Fog of War,* McNamara admitted that evidence of an August 4 attack had later turned out to be "just confusion" and "didn't happen."

Johnson went on to remind the Defense Secretary that on Tuesday morning, August 4, McNamara had called him from the Pentagon and said, "Damn, they are launching an attack on us," and then, "when we got through with all the firing, we concluded maybe that they hadn't fired at all!"

The Chairman of the Senate Foreign Relations Committee, J. William Fulbright, grew suspicious about the Gulf of Tonkin incident earlier than most of his colleagues. In January 1968, with more than a half million Americans fighting in Vietnam and Johnson's war by then a catastrophe, Fulbright ordered a secret study by his committee of whether the Tonkin episode had been a charade engineered by the President to push an unwitting country into conflict. Recalling that Johnson had framed the Tonkin Resolution as a means of keeping out of war, not getting in, Fulbright now angrily said that if Americans had been told otherwise, they would have been "shocked." About Johnson, who had once been his friend, Fulbright now complained, "I was taken in."

Fulbright and his Foreign Relations colleagues considered the secret study, and their discussion of it, sufficiently explosive that the transcripts of them were withheld from public view until the year 2010. The Committee's longtime Chief of Staff, Carl Marcy, who had served under both parties, informed the Senators that in August 1964, although he may not have "deliberately lied," McNamara had "misled the Committee in stating that the Navy was unaware of attacks of the South Vietnamese on North Vietnam." Frank Church, Democrat from Idaho, recalled that Johnson and McNamara had presented the August 4 incident "as though the attack did, in fact, occur without any question." Albert Gore chimed in, "And 'deliberate' and 'unprovoked.'"

"We were just plain lied to—just in so many words," said Fulbright. "I don't think they told us the truth." The Arkansan expressed his fear that the United States had lost "a form of democracy." He explained, "It is a very serious matter—how a country of this importance in the world can make a decision of this kind to go to war." The New Jersey Republican Clifford Case charged that Johnson, "a very political animal," had conducted "a campaign of suppression" to conceal the true facts of the Tonkin incident. John Sherman Cooper, Republican from Kentucky, told the other Senators that if they decided that "the country and the Congress were the subject of a giant hoax" about the Tonkin Gulf, they might have to demand that the House of Representatives impeach Lyndon Johnson.

"I Do Not Have a Parachute"

I N HIS INAUGURAL address, on Wednesday, January 20, 1965, Johnson spoke not a word about Vietnam. He had defeated Goldwater in what was the largest presidential landslide in modern history. Benefiting from his coattails, more Democrats dominated the Senate (62 to 38) and House (295 to 140) than under any President since Franklin Roosevelt. In his speech, opposite to Kennedy's in 1961, he spoke exclusively of domestic affairs, for he planned to make fundamental changes in American life—with his War on Poverty, voting guarantees for all Americans, Medicare, aid to education, and other initiatives—that would install the architect of the Great Society in the record books.

Three days after being sworn in, at 2:26 on Saturday morning, Johnson was hurried by ambulance from the White House to Bethesda Naval Hospital. Lady Bird, who had been resting up from the inauguration at Camp David, feared that he had suffered another heart attack. As she later told her diary, when she arrived at the hospital, she "just patted him and sat down and held his hand. It could have been a frightening day. It was a day I had expected and thought about." Without telling him, she bought a black dress, in case she needed one for her husband's funeral.

When Johnson returned to the White House after three days at Bethesda, Lady Bird told her journal that Lyndon was feeling "washed out" and "depressed." He called Nicholas Katzenbach to ask what the Constitution said about presidential disability.* Eight days after his collapse, the First Lady recorded that "Lyndon spent most of the day in bed," and "for a man of his temperament, it means you have time to worry." She told her diary, "It's sort of a slough of despond. . . . The obstacles indeed are no shadows. They are real substance—Vietnam, the biggest." His malaise reminded her of William Butler Yeats's poem "The Valley of the Black Pig" (1896), which portrayed a desolate man facing an apocalyptic war:

> The dews drop slowly and dreams gather: unknown spears
> Suddenly hurtle before my dream-awakened eyes,
> And then the clash of fallen horsemen and the cries
> Of unknown perishing armies beat about my ears.

Soon the First Lady's fears came to pass. On Saturday, February 6, the Viet Cong attacked a US Army barracks in Pleiku, killing eight Americans. That evening, Johnson called Speaker McCormack, Senate Majority Leader Mike Mansfield, McNamara, and other advisers to the Cabinet Room, and told them he would order retaliatory air strikes against three North Vietnamese targets. He explained he had "kept the shotgun over the mantel and the bullets in the basement for a long time now," but now they had to act because "cowardice has gotten us into more wars than response has." Citing history, he contended that the United States could have avoided both world wars "if we had been courageous in the early stages." As Lady Bird recorded on Sunday, the seventh, Lyndon took repeated calls from the Situation Room: "The ring of the phone, the quick reach for it, and tense, quiet talk. . . . We'll probably have to learn to live in the middle of it—for not hours or days, but years."

Then, on Wednesday morning, the tenth, Mac Bundy called the President to report that the Viet Cong had attacked a US aircraft

---

* Robert Kennedy had resigned the previous August to run successfully for the US Senate from New York, leaving Katzenbach, his deputy, in charge.

maintenance barracks in Qhy Nhon, probably using a "sabotage bomb." Twenty-three Americans were killed, the most of any single incident yet in Vietnam. Bundy told Johnson that he was reluctant to "get in a position that only white men get avenged," but "McNamara and I feel very strongly about it." He noted that the North had recently attacked train facilities; therefore the United States and South Vietnam could together retaliate against a northern railroad, "an extremely easy target." Afterward he said, "within the next two or three nights," the President should go on television and, "coolly and directly," offer "a full-dress account of this affair." Johnson replied that he would not be "getting inflammatory or bombastic, but let's proceed." He asked that General William Westmoreland, the US commander in Vietnam, be told to notify captains on aircraft carriers: "Let's just get them to loading their stuff, and let's pick the targets." Eager to bring in Congress, Johnson called McCormack and said, "We've got to meet right quick on targets."

The President knew the gravity of the step he was taking. He loped across the street to see his new Vice President, Hubert Humphrey, who now occupied the chamber in the Executive Office Building that Johnson had once used. "I'm not temperamentally equipped to be Commander-in-Chief," he told Humphrey. "I'm too sentimental to give the orders." That evening, after briefing congressional leaders on his planned air strikes against North Vietnam, he repeated those same words to Lady Bird, who told her diary, "Somehow I could not wish him *not* to hurt when he gives the orders."

On Friday, Johnson's directive was executed. Seeking reassurance and hoping to thwart Republican opposition, Johnson called former President Eisenhower at his winter home in Palm Desert, California: "I don't want to put it up like we are in deep trouble, because I don't think it's reached that point," but "you could be more comforting to me now than anybody I know." He asked, "Why don't you come stay all night with me? I'll put you in Lincoln's bed." The General chuckled: "Lincoln's bed?" Johnson offered to send a presidential JetStar, but cautioned that he did not want the public to think "that we've got an emergency or something."

During his White House visit, Eisenhower advised Johnson that if it took eight American divisions, in a "campaign of pressure," to protect South Vietnam from a Communist takeover, "so be it." He recalled that "we had a long time in Korea." Should China or the Soviets threaten to intervene, "we should pass the word back to them to take care, lest dire results occur to them." With this, Ike was suggesting a reprise of the hints of nuclear attack that he had quietly dropped in his effort to obtain a Korean armistice. He told Johnson that the "greatest danger" now would be if China concluded "that we will go just so far and no further" in pursuing the Vietnam War. At Johnson's request, the General described how he had conveyed his nuclear threat to the Chinese in 1953 through "three channels." Johnson asked how he might convey a similar warning to the Chinese. Eisenhower suggested using the Pakistani President, Mohammed Ayub Khan, "a very fine man," whom he knew from his own time in office.

Recalling Korea, Johnson asked Eisenhower what to do if Chinese forces crossed the border into Vietnam, requiring "eight or ten U.S. divisions" in response. Eisenhower advised him, should that happen, to "hit them at once with air" and "use any weapons required"—including tactical nuclear weapons. He complained that during the Korean War, the Chinese believed that Truman had made "a gentleman's agreement" not to cross the Yalu or use nuclear arms. By contrast, in Vietnam, "we should let it be known that we are not bound by such restrictions." He warned Johnson that the United States must "never allow itself to get overdeployed." Instead he should "hit the head of the snake."*

With Korea on his mind, Johnson also called Truman in Independence: "I'm having hell!" Paternally the eighty-year-old ex-President asked him, "What's the trouble?" Johnson replied, "A little bit with Indochina. I'm doing the best I can. My problem is kind of like what you had in Korea." Eager to charm, he told Truman that he had just looked at the letter he had sent him in June 1950, which said that "what you've done is wonderful" and "I'm behind you in whatever you do." He

---

* Eisenhower was driven to the White House by his onetime aide Bryce Harlow, who recalled that before such visits, "the General would bitch and moan and groan that 'Johnson is using me,'" but that Ike "loved it—at least initially."

reminded the ex-President, "That was before old Bob Taft got up on the floor and started raising hell about you ought to have had a resolution." Truman laughed. Johnson told him, "I think when they go in and kill your boys, you've got to hit back. And I'm not trying to spread the war, and I'm not trying—" Truman broke in, "You bet you have! You bust them in the nose every time you get a chance, and they understand that language better than any other kind." Johnson said, "I need your counsel, and I love you." Truman replied, "Well, that's mutual."

Objecting to the President's air strikes, Democratic Senators George McGovern of South Dakota and Frank Church publicly asked him to negotiate. Furious, Johnson told Mac Bundy that "neither one of them really fought in many wars" or were "really outstanding experts in this field."* He said the two Senators "ought to be told" what "hurts us most is not the hitting our compound" but "these Goddamned speeches that the Communists blow up, that show that we are about to pull out." He asked Bundy to remind the dovish, skeptical Mike Mansfield that his President was "the poor bastard that stays awake every night" and "sends these men to die." Of Mansfield, Johnson later moaned, "Why do I have to have a saint for Majority Leader? Why can't I have a politician?"

McGovern went to see Johnson, who warned him that the North Vietnamese leader Ho Chi Minh was a tool of the Chinese. The Senator, who had taught history at Dakota Wesleyan, rejoined that the Chinese had been struggling against the Vietnamese for a thousand years. By McGovern's later account, the President told him, "Goddamn it, George, you and Fulbright and all you history teachers down there—I haven't got time to fuck around with history. I've got boys on the line out there."

Johnson told his old friend Everett Dirksen, the Senate Republican leader, that the North Vietnamese "can't come bomb us, kill our people and expect us to go in a cave." To his delight, Dirksen replied that his only mistake had been not to have attacked the North hard enough. Invoking the appeasement of prewar Nazi Germany, as well as the domino

---

* Johnson's once-fabled knowledge of senatorial biographies was slipping. During World War II, McGovern had flown three dozen dangerous combat missions in Europe.

theory, the President replied, "We know, from Munich on, that when you give, the dictators feed on raw meat. If they take South Vietnam, they take Indonesia, they take Burma, they come right on back to the Philippines." Johnson was outraged to find that his own Vice President wished to get out of Vietnam. Humphrey wrote him that "involvement in a full scale war" would not "make sense to the majority of the American people." He conceded that it was "always hard to cut losses," but for the newly elected President, "1965 is the year of minimum political risk." As Humphrey later recalled, his letter made Johnson so angry that he threw him into political "limbo."

Johnson was trying to expand his struggle against the North by stealth. When the US embassy in Saigon confirmed, in late February, that the United States had used B-57 and F-100 jet bombers for the first time against the Viet Cong, Johnson complained to Rusk that this news looked "desperate and dramatic" and that "all of TV" was heralding "an entirely new policy."

That month, the President had quietly approved McNamara's proposed Operation Rolling Thunder, a gradual, sustained bombing campaign intended to ratchet up pressure against the North. But privately, as he started escalating the war, Johnson was gloomily unable to convince himself that it would ultimately lead to victory. In a telephone call to the Secretary of Defense, on Friday morning, February 26, he spoke these bone-chilling words: "Now we're off to bombing these people. We're over that hurdle. I don't think anything is going to be as bad as losing, and I don't see any way of winning." To this day, it is difficult to understand how this bighearted man could have brought himself to send young Americans to risk their lives in a conflict for which, even at the start, he privately seemed to have so little hope. No earlier Chief Executive, not even Madison, had pushed Americans into a major war with such initial pessimism.

✳ ✳ ✳

FLOUTING THE PRECEDENTS for transparency set by some earlier war Presidents, on Monday, March 1, Johnson told McNamara to unleash Rolling Thunder without public announcement.* But that same day, the *New York Times* reported that the "highest" US officials in Saigon were confiding that Johnson had "decided to open a continuing, limited air war." McNamara told the President, "I don't know how in the world that came out." Furious at the leak, Johnson snapped, "Am I wrong in saying that this appears to be almost traitorous? . . . Somebody ought to be removed, Bob." He added that it was "not good to say that we've got a plan to bomb this specific area before we're *bombing* it. Because, *Christ,* I guess every anti-aircraft and everything they can get is alerted."

The next day, Rolling Thunder began, with more than a hundred US aircraft—more planes than had ever been used in a single day against the North—striking a munitions depot and Navy base. During the following three years, Rolling Thunder would unload more bombs on the North than struck all of Europe during World War II. As if to make up for the private helplessness he seemed to feel about the general contours of the war, Johnson made sure that he scrutinized the aerial forays, boasting, "They can't hit an outhouse without my permission!"

Poignantly, the President stayed up late into the night hoping for assurance that his "boys" had returned safely, saying later, "I want to be called every time somebody dies." After the first mission, a Situation Room duty officer called him very early on Tuesday, March 2, to report that two planes were probably missing. Johnson asked, "What's it look like—our two pilots lost?" He was told that rescue efforts were "underway," and, later, that while six US aircraft had been shot down, five of the pilots had survived. Lady Bird told her diary that her husband "can't separate himself from it. Actually I don't want him to, no matter how painful."

By Friday, Johnson was pondering Westmoreland's request for Marines to protect US fliers and air bases in South Vietnam, which Rusk, McNamara, and the Joint Chiefs had approved. The President told Mac Bundy, "Now, the Marines! I haven't made that decision. I'm

---

* One reason was that Johnson was still smarting from public criticism for having announced the bombing of North Vietnam in August 1964 long before all of the fliers had returned.

still worried about it." Bundy told him, "Thirty-five hundred—two battalions. How far do you want us to go?" Johnson suggested that McNamara consult the Armed Services committees in Congress. Bundy replied, "He didn't want to give them that much leeway. . . . He didn't want to get you a lot of advice *not* to do it." Johnson darkly predicted, "They're going to say not to do it later."

The next day, the President told Senator Russell, "I guess we've got no choice, but it scares the death out of me. I think everybody's going to think, 'We're landing the Marines—we're off to battle.' " He predicted that the North would "get them in a fight, just sure as hell. They're not going to run. Then you're tied down." Russell replied, "We've gone so damn far, Mr. President, it scares the life out of me, but I don't know how to back up now." "That is exactly right," said Johnson. "We're getting in worse." Morosely the President confided, "The great trouble I'm under—a man can fight if he can see daylight down the road somewhere. But there ain't no daylight in Vietnam." "There's no end to the road," replied Russell. "There's just nothing." Johnson agreed: "The more bombs you drop, the more nations you scare, the more people you make mad, the more embassies you get—" Russell said, "It's the worst mess I ever saw in my life." Johnson exclaimed, "If they'd say I 'inherited,' I'll be lucky. But they'll all say I *created* it!"[*]

Two hours later, the President told McNamara that "if there's no alternative," he could send the Marines to protect the US airmen: "My answer is yes, but my judgment is no." Straining for optimism, Johnson estimated the Marines' chances of "fighting with the Viet Cong and really starting a land war" as "maybe sixty-forty against." Perhaps they "might prevent it." But the "psychological impact" would be bad, with every American mother saying, "Uh-oh, this is it!" Johnson asked the Defense Secretary whether they could buffer the political shock by using some euphemism for Marines, such as "Military Police." McNamara replied, "No, sir, we can't really say that. They're quite different from

---

[*] Appealing to the Georgian's racism, the President also said, "You're paying a mighty big price on an Anglo-Saxon white man to make his boy go and fight in Vietnam. But none of the others can because . . . they don't have the exact IQ."

the MPs, and all the press knows it." He pledged to "minimize the announcement," but warned that it would provoke "a lot of headlines." Johnson replied, "You're telling *me*!"

On Sunday evening, in private with Lady Bird, he was disconsolate about his oncoming war: "I can't get out, and I can't finish it with what I have got. And I don't know what the hell to do!"

✳ ✳ ✳

IN APRIL 1965, hoping to avert further dramatic escalation, the President publicly offered Ho Chi Minh a billion dollars to develop the Mekong River Delta, so long as Ho would guarantee the freedom of the South. But the money was refused. McNamara and Westmoreland that month persuaded Johnson to approve nine new battalions for Vietnam, which would increase US forces there to eighty-two thousand.

The President asked Congress for $700 million "to meet mounting military requirements in Vietnam," pointedly adding that his request was not "routine." He warned that every legislator who endorsed it was "also voting to persist in our effort to halt Communist aggression in South Vietnam." He knew that this would be an easy sell, explaining to Humphrey that if the House and Senate refused him, he could tell them in public, "You're not giving a man ammunition he needs for his gun. . . . You got him standing out nekkid and letting people shoot at him." He told George Mahon of House Appropriations that he was "being frank and candid and open with them." He asked Senator John Stennis of Mississippi to show Hanoi "that we got the money and that the Congress is behind us."

The House and Senate backed the President, almost unanimously, but the newly elected Robert Kennedy told colleagues, on the Senate floor, that his yes vote should not be taken as a "blank check" for any "wider war." Escalation, he warned, could bring "hundreds of thousands of American troops" to Vietnam and "might easily lead to nuclear warfare." Johnson complained to McNamara, who had maintained his friendship with the New York Senator, that Kennedy was making "little snide remarks" in the Senate cloakroom that the President had "manipulated" the Congress on Vietnam: "You've just got to sit down and talk to Bobby."*

After still another military coup, the Saigon junta was replaced in early June by a new Prime Minister, Air Force General Nguyen Cao Ky—who wore a zippered flight suit with pearl-handled revolvers and later said his country needed "four or five Hitlers"—as well as a new head of state, General Nguyen Van Thieu. Bill Bundy called the duo "absolutely the bottom of the barrel." McNamara warned Johnson that they faced "a very dangerous situation." General Maxwell Taylor, the new US envoy in Saigon, reported that if there should be a new Viet Cong offensive, exploiting the monsoon season, which could make it harder to defend ground troops from the air, "it will probably be necessary to commit U.S. ground forces in action."

Some of the Joint Chiefs of Staff now advised Johnson to bomb Hanoi. The President told congressional friends that he had "stalled them off" by warning that this might force China to enter the war. He warned Senator Vance Hartke, Democrat from Indiana, "If you'd see what some of the Joint Chiefs are recommending here to me, you'd drop the phone and go see your grandchild." Johnson later reported to Russell that some of the military leaders were "awfully irresponsible. They'll just scare you. They're ready to put a million men in right quick." Senator Russell Long, Democrat from Louisiana, told Johnson, "We may have to face up to the $64,000-question and bomb China." Finding the President "very pessimistic about Vietnam," Mansfield implored him not to bomb the North's capital city.

On Monday, June 7, Westmoreland wired McNamara from Saigon that he urgently needed 41,000 more combat forces, and 52,000 later on, which would mean 175,000 troops in Vietnam. He argued that the United States must abandon its "defensive posture" and "take the war to the enemy," in which case "even greater forces" may be required. McNamara told colleagues, "We're in a hell of a mess." Long afterward,

* In January 1965, Johnson had told McNamara that the "Kennedy crowd" was warning that the President was plotting to withdraw from Vietnam and blame the existing military involvement on John Kennedy's "immaturity and poor judgment," saying that it had "brought havoc to the country."

he called Westmoreland's "bombshell" the most disturbing cable he ever received as Secretary of Defense, explaining, "We could no longer postpone a choice about what path to take."

Calling the President, McNamara now said, "Unless we're really willing to go to a full potential land war, we've got to slow down here and try to halt, at some point, the ground troop commitment."* The President refused, noting that the North was "putting their stack in, and moving new chips into the pot." The choice, he said, was either "tuck tail and run" or respond to those who were telling the United States, "The Indians are coming!" McNamara reported that Robert Kennedy was asking Johnson to explain to the American people, on television, "how far we're going to go." The President said, "I can't do that, can I?" McNamara replied, "No, no, you can't." Johnson asked him,

> Do you know how far we're going to go? Or do the Joint Chiefs know? What human being knows? I would imagine if they wiped out a thousand boys tomorrow, we might go a hell of a lot further than we'd do if they just wiped out four. . . . We're trying to be prudent. . . . Now, not a damn human thinks that fifty thousand or a hundred thousand or a hundred and fifty thousand are going to end that war. And we're not getting out.

To gauge the attitude of the doves, the President called Mansfield, confiding that his "military people" were warning that "our 75,000 men are going to be in great danger unless they have 75,000 more." But then "they'll have to have another hundred and fifty. And then they'll have to have *another* hundred and fifty." The Majority Leader said, "We've got too many in there now. . . . Where do you stop?" Johnson replied, "You don't. . . . To me, it's shaping up like this, Mike—you either get out or you get in." "But Hanoi and Haiphong are spit clean, and have been for months," said Mansfield. "You bomb them, you get nothing. You just build up more hatred."

---

* McNamara later informed Johnson that Rusk "doesn't want to give up South Vietnam under any circumstances—even if it means going to general war."

Johnson replied, "I think that's true," adding that the United States had done "nearly everything that you can do, except make it a complete white man's war." Mansfield, who had once taught Asian history, cautioned, "If you do that, then you might as well say goodbye to all of Asia, and to most of the world." The President later told Eisenhower that, according to his intelligence, many Chinese, Soviet, and North Vietnamese officials had concluded that "we almost got a Civil War Congress again, with all of them telling every day what ought to be done," and, although it wasn't true, that "a good many of them are sympathetic with the Communists."

Even at this early stage of the war, Johnson knew the enemy was not likely to give up. Westmoreland cabled that "short of decision to introduce nuclear weapons against sources and channels of enemy power, I see no likelihood of achieving a quick, favorable end to the war." Johnson reminded Eisenhower that "Ho Chi Minh said he'd fight on for twenty years, if he needed to." He predicted to Senator Birch Bayh, Democrat from Indiana, that ultimately the Viet Cong would "last longer than we do" because their soldier was willing to hide out in a "rut" for two days "without water, food or anything, and never moves, waiting to ambush somebody. Now, an American—he stays there about twenty minutes and, God damn, he's got to get him a cigarette!"

That month, the President told McNamara, "I'm very depressed about it. Because I see no program from either Defense or State that gives me much hope of doing anything, except just praying and gasping to hold on during monsoon and hope they'll quit. I don't believe they're *ever* going to quit. . . . And I don't see . . . that we have any . . . plan for a victory—militarily or diplomatically."

In late June, seeking comfort, Johnson called Harry Truman in Independence and said, "I thought I might invite myself out to see you," adding that he could stay in a "tourist court" near the Kansas City airport. He would be on his way to make a speech in San Francisco on the twentieth anniversary of the United Nations. He told Truman, "I remember how much you did for 'em, and how you saved 'em in Korea." Johnson turned the telephone over to a visitor, Justice Arthur Goldberg, who joked with Truman, "Do you feel peppy enough to seize the steel industry again, if they act up against the President here?"

With cold candor, Johnson told McNamara, at the start of July, "We know ourselves, in our own conscience, that when we asked for this [Gulf of Tonkin] resolution, we had no intention of committing this many ground troops. We're doing so now, and we know it's going to be bad. And the question is, do we just want to do it out on a limb by ourselves?" He warned that if they did not consult Congress before a major escalation, "you'd have a long debate about not having asked them." That same week, he confided to Lady Bird, "Vietnam is getting worse every day. I have the choice to go in with great casualty lists or to get out with disgrace. It's like being in an airplane and I have to choose between crashing the plane or jumping out. I do not have a parachute." She told her diary, "When he is pierced, I bleed. It's a bad time all around."

* * *

ON THURSDAY, July 22, 1965, Johnson made his decision. At 5:30 a.m., agitated in his bed, he turned, woke up Lady Bird, and told her, in torment, "I don't want to get into a war and I don't see any way out of it. I've got to call up 600,000 boys, make them leave their homes and their families." She told her journal, "Feeling like the boy that leaves the burning deck, I went to my own room to try to get another hour or two of sleep—fitful and unsatisfactory."

That afternoon, the President asked the Joint Chiefs whether, if he approved Westmoreland's requests, "we are in a new war" and "this is going off the diving board." McNamara replied that they had been relying on the South Vietnamese to "carry the brunt," but "now we would be responsible" for the war's outcome. Johnson asked, "Do all of you think the Congress and the people will go along with 600,000 people and billions of dollars ten thousand miles away?" Stanley Resor, Secretary of the Army, insisted that most Americans supported the obligation in Vietnam. Johnson replied, "But if you make a commitment to jump off a building, and you find out how high it is, you may want to withdraw the commitment."

The President was counseled by some to declare a state of national emergency, as he himself had urged on Truman during Korea, asking Americans for higher taxes and other forms of sacrifice. But, recalling how Truman's proclamation had damaged his popularity, Johnson refused, especially while he was still imploring Congress to enact the cornerstones of his Great Society. Instead he would announce his escalation in a "low-key manner." With biting humor, he explained, "If you have a mother-in-law with only one eye, and she has it in the center of her forehead, you don't keep her in the living room."

Johnson told Senator Russell that Westmoreland, "an old South Carolina boy," had "been out there messing with them long enough, and he's getting fed up with it." Russell warned, "You shouldn't send many more than a hundred thousand over there." The Senator noted that the South Vietnamese leader, General Ky, "that little old mustachioed fellow," had proposed "that *we* ought to fight the war and *his* troops ought to pacify the villages in the rear. God, that scared the hell out of me! If they're going to fight that kind of war, I'm in favor of getting out of there." Russell recalled that, by contrast, in the early 1950s, the South Koreans had "fought every inch of the way."

Referring to Arthur Goldberg, whom he had just persuaded to quit the Supreme Court in order to help him "end" the Vietnam War as Ambassador to the United Nations, Johnson told Russell that he was going to "do everything I can with this Jew" to "find a way to get out without saying so." He added that he didn't plan to "dramatize" his escalation. Russell agreed: "If that's the way you're going to play it, I'd play it down." Russell advised him to call up the reserves, but the President disagreed, saying that it would be "too dramatic" and "puts me out there further than I want to get, right at this moment."

Briefing congressional leaders, Johnson confessed, "We all know that it is a bad situation, and we wish we were ten years back—or even ten months back." Henry Cabot Lodge, who had been envoy to Saigon and was about to resume that post, claimed that pulling out of Vietnam would be "worse than a victory for the Kaiser or Hitler in the two world wars." Everett Dirksen pledged that, as leader of the opposition, he would not behave "like the Committee on the Conduct of the War" that had dogged Lincoln. Speaker McCormack assured the President that they were "united" behind him, along with "all true Americans."

Johnson rejected suggestions to announce his big decision before a Joint Session of Congress or in an Oval Office TV address. Instead, at 12:30 p.m. on Wednesday, July 28, he read out a brief statement on Vietnam during a regular East Room press conference, along with announcements that he was naming NBC's John Chancellor to lead the Voice of America and his old friend Abe Fortas to replace Goldberg on the Supreme Court.*

Sitting in the front row, Lady Bird dabbed her eyes with a handkerchief as her husband acknowledged, speaking very slowly, that people were asking why "young Americans" must "toil and suffer and sometimes die in such a remote and distant place." Vietnam, he said, was "a different kind of war." If the United States were driven out, then no nation would again have the "same confidence" in "American protection." Surrender would not bring peace, "as we learned from Hitler at Munich." Citing Westmoreland's request, he announced that he would "raise our fighting strength from 75,000 to 125,000 men, almost immediately. Additional forces will be needed later, and they will be sent, as requested."

Revealing his ambivalence, Johnson confessed, "I do not find it easy to send the flower of our youth, our finest young men, into battle. . . . This is the most agonizing and the most painful duty of your President." But unless the nation stood up against "men who hate and destroy," then "all of our dreams for freedom—all, *all* will be swept away on the flood of conquest. So, too, this shall not happen. We shall stand in Vietnam." A reporter asked how long the war would take. Johnson replied

---

* Johnson may very well have wanted Fortas to do for him on the Court what Fred Vinson had done for Truman, giving him quiet advance warning about opinions to come and advising him how to structure his Great Society and war policies in order to avoid having them ruled unconstitutional. Fortas wound up quietly helping the President write speeches and choose Vietnam bombing targets—breaches of the separation of powers that, when revealed to the Senate, helped to scuttle his 1968 nomination by Johnson to be Chief Justice.

that there would be "no quick solution," adding that after Pearl Harbor, no one "really knew" whether World War II would take "two years or four years or six years." Asked when he might ask Congress for a war declaration, the President replied, "That would depend on the circumstances." During a speech the following week, he gave no hint of his private doubts about the war, and told the crowd, "America wins the wars that she undertakes. Make no mistake about it!"

In early September, at the LBJ Ranch, Johnson suffered a gall bladder attack. "No one ever knows till they get it behind them," the President explained to Robert Kennedy during a telephone call. "They think it might rupture if I don't get it taken care of." Throughout his adult life, Johnson had broken down at times of emotional distress. Late in his first House campaign, in a 1937 special election, he had suffered from severe stomach pains but refused to be hospitalized until doctors warned that his appendix was about to rupture. Campaigning for the Senate in May 1948, suffering from kidney stones, he was secretly flown to the Mayo Clinic in Minnesota, after which, as Lady Bird recalled, "He was depressed, and it was bad."

This time, his recovery from surgery was so slow and painful that he asked Fortas what the procedure would be if he quit the presidency, and had the new Justice draft a resignation letter for him.* Johnson spent most of the last three months of 1965 on his ranch. He told aides that he had decided to stop drinking so that, night or day, his mind would be clear should he have to issue a sudden order affecting "my boys" in Vietnam.

* * *

A FTER THE PRESIDENT'S July escalation announcement, Eisenhower advised him, through his onetime White House staff secretary, General Andrew Goodpaster, that he should have avoided "using

---

* After his operation, Johnson unveiled his stitched abdominal scar for reporters, which inspired a David Levine cartoon in *The New York Review of Books* depicting the scar in the shape of Vietnam.

specific numbers" because it told the enemy "that we are limited in our determination." Instead Johnson should have said, "We will do whatever is needed." Ike said this was no time for "piddling" steps; instead they should "swamp" North Vietnam now. But Johnson was committed to McNamara's strategy of gradual escalation.

In November 1965, the Joint Chiefs came to the West Wing, asking the President for 113,000 more troops, a naval blockade of the North, isolation of its vital port of Haiphong, and a B-52 bombing assault against Hanoi. According to a briefer for the Marines, Charles Cooper, who was present, Johnson exploded, denouncing the Chiefs as "shitheads," "dumb shits," and "pompous assholes," making free use of the "F-word." He warned that he wouldn't let "military idiots" talk him into World War III and finally ordered them to "get the hell out" of the room. Afterward Johnson's Chief of Naval Operations, Admiral David McDonald, told Cooper, "This has got to be the worst experience I could ever imagine."

By December, the President was angry again at Humphrey, who had indiscreetly told reporters what kind of concessions by the enemy might move the President to relax the war. Johnson fulminated to Mac Bundy, "I've cautioned that boy seven times, and this morning, every paper is full of all the trades he's going to propose. . . . He's a fool." Remembering what had befallen his old chief Truman in Korea, Clark Clifford asked Johnson "where the hell we are going" in Vietnam, complaining that "further and further into this war," there seemed "no prospect of a return." The President confided to McNamara, "I've had little real sympathy with Fulbright, but I don't see any light down that barrel. We're getting deeper and deeper in. I bogged my car down."

In January 1966, Johnson planned to ask Congress for about $12 billion to support the Vietnam fighting. Complaining to Larry O'Brien, now Postmaster General, he observed that, compared with his own days as a strict Majority Leader, Senators were "running wild." Mike Mansfield "sits back like a pious priest, by God." When Fulbright roared, Mansfield would "crawl under the bed." Of his soldiers in Vietnam, Johnson blustered, "I'm not going to withdraw 'em! They can undercut 'em all they want to. They can raise hell. . . . They don't need to appropriate. We can just leave 'em there hungry, and take up voluntary contributions."

Trying to contain Johnson's war, Wayne Morse asked the Senate to rescind the Gulf of Tonkin Resolution. Fulbright warned Rusk that "before we can approve these large sums," it must be understood that neither that resolution, nor the SEATO treaty often cited by the administration, provided sufficient "legal basis" for the fighting. Fulbright publicly apologized for not having been "foresighted and wise" in pushing the Tonkin document through the Senate. Johnson complained to O'Brien that Fulbright had tried to "destroy" every President he had ever served with: "He's interested only in the *New York Times.*" Using his gift for mimickry, he imitated the Arkansan harassing Rusk during a hearing: "Well, you don't want to be re-*sponnnnn*-sive." He told Humphrey he had heard that the Arkansan was "going through a menopause" or was "off his rocker" because his wife had been ailing. Johnson insisted, "It's easier to satisfy Ho Chi Minh than it is Fulbright."

Robert Kennedy was growing more alarmed about the war. In a Senate floor speech, he warned that "if we regard bombing as the answer to Vietnam, we are heading straight for disaster." By telephone, Senator Russell warned Johnson against "getting into a debate with that little piss-ant." The President told Rusk that Kennedy's speech was "tragic" and "so presumptuous." The Secretary of State replied, "I think it has greatly weakened our position with Hanoi, and prolongs the war, actually." His anxieties aroused, Johnson warned, "It means a majority in the Senate against us, Dean." He feared that "the Bayhs and the Tydingses, and the two Kennedys and the Muskies—the general Catholic operation there—when the chips are down, they will pick up enough Cases and perhaps a Javits."* Johnson refused suggestions to ask for a new congressional expression of support for the war.

Drawing on information provided by Katzenbach, whom he had by now appointed as Attorney General, he asked Rusk to remind Congress

---

* Referring to Democrats Birch Bayh (Indiana), Joseph Tydings (Maryland), Edward and Robert Kennedy, and Edmund Muskie (Maine), as well as liberal Republicans Clifford Case (New Jersey) and Jacob Javits (New York).

that throughout American history, "there are 160 times the President has gone in without a declaration of war to protect the interests of the United States. The President has this constitutional power." Rusk replied, "The figure I have is 125, Mr. President." "I don't care," said Johnson. "Just assert that he has it. . . . We have an obligation, and the President wouldn't be worthy of his salt if he didn't do it, or else why have a treaty?" He had asked for the Tonkin Resolution, he said, because he knew that members of Congress would "run when the going gets tough" and wanted them "tied, bound and delivered beforehand." He recalled warning Congress in 1964 that he would not "pee a drop" unless they gave him a resolution to act in Vietnam. Now, "if they want to surrender to the Communists, then repeal it."* Even if the members did so, he would "go on fighting" in Vietnam because as Commander-in-Chief, he had "that power anyway."

Unburdening himself, Johnson confided to Rusk that, "with the Kennedy infiltration all over the place," he was "afraid" that members would say "that we ought to sit down with the Viet Cong," and that Bobby's statement may have been "paving the way." He lamented that Americans did not seem to comprehend why they had to fight in Vietnam: "When you just say it once on television . . . that doesn't get through to them. You've got to repeat, like Hitler did—twenty times—and then maybe they do." He recalled that a few days before, McNamara had estimated that "we only have one chance out of three of winning" the war: "It just shocked me and, furthermore, it shocked everybody at the table." With cattiness, Rusk said of the ex–Ford Motor chief, "Quite frankly, Mr. President, he hasn't had too much experience in dealing with crises."

Johnson told Mansfield that diluting the Tonkin Resolution would mean "I'm in a hell of a shape as Commander-in-Chief. . . . If we leave me in doubt . . . hell, I'd rather turn the authority over to Fulbright." He told Senator Eugene McCarthy of Minnesota, who was bridling against the war, "I can't get out. I just can't be the architect of surrender. . . . They don't have the pressure that would bring them to the

---

* He could casually issue such a challenge, knowing that at this moment members were unlikely to rescind the resolution because this would seem to undermine the American warriors in Vietnam.

table, as of yet. We don't know if they ever will. I'm willing to do damn near anything." Others proposed that Johnson defy custom and testify, in some fashion, before Congress, but the President asked Russell Long to call this idea out of bounds: "Just say, 'Since George Washington came down there and got in a goddamn row, ain't no President been back since. . . . This is a lot of crap about Johnson—he's refusing to testify!' "

Ever more worried about Robert Kennedy, the President warned Henry Luce, the militant *Time-Life-Fortune* founder, that "Bobby is sniping from the sidelines. . . . Now what he is doing is playing a little politics '68."[*] Johnson went on to complain that some antiwar Senators were attempting to load the Tonkin Resolution with "namby-pamby" conditions: "I think it's very bad to have a committee fighting a war—a Civil War committee." Johnson wondered aloud what to do if Westmoreland asked him for fifty thousand more soldiers by September and by then, "a majority of the United States Senate is against escalation." He asked Luce, "What does a man do that doesn't want to be a dictator, that just wants to do what's right?"

The President suspected that secret Chinese and Soviet agents were lurking behind some of the Senators and newspeople turning against his war. In April 1965, sixteen thousand protesters, sponsored by Women Strike for Peace, Students for a Democratic Society, and other groups, had marched against the war to the Washington Monument. Johnson told Senator Gale McGee, Democrat from Wyoming, that J. Edgar Hoover had brought him the files at night and was "very upset about it." The Communist agents were "going into the colleges and the faculties and the student bodies" and "urging that we have a cease-fire or stop our bombing," hoping to "bring pressure on us here to throw in the towel." The President assured McGee, "Hoover's got most of these groups infiltrated."

Johnson claimed to Katzenbach that he was "a red-hot, one-million-

* Luce's wife, Clare, was reputed to be intimate with Johnson while they were House colleagues during World War II.

two percent civil liberties man" and "I'm against wiretapping, period." In practice, he directed that such surveillance be "brought to an irreducible minimum," but not in cases of national security, which he defined in his own way, deciding that his political foes were among grave threats to the Republic. In March 1966, he asked his FBI liaison, Cartha "Deke" DeLoach, to have Hoover tighten the Bureau's watch on Eastern Bloc "contacts with opinion-molders," especially in Congress. He said it "scares hell out of me" to learn that "Chinese Communists give $3,000 to somebody" who was talking to Senator Morse, after which Morse would speak out against the war. He noted that Fulbright had once dined with the Soviet Ambassador, Anatoly Dobrynin, until after midnight, "and the next day, he's examining Rusk. That scares me." After consulting Hoover, who hated Martin Luther King Jr., Johnson told Mac Bundy that the civil rights leader was "not a Communist" but was "controlled completely by them." He pushed the CIA to go beyond its charter, which excluded "internal security," to investigate foreign manipulation of racial disturbances and antiwar organizations, and did the same with Army intelligence. As Johnson's CIA Director, Richard Helms, told me in 1989, the President pressed him "almost daily" for evidence that "foreign Communists" were secretly in charge of the campus protests, but Helms kept coming up dry.

In the Oval Office, Johnson warned six state governors about Communist subversion in America: "Don't kid yourself a moment. It is in the highest counsels of government, in our society. [Joseph] McCarthy's methods were wrong, but the threat is greater now than in his day." With Johnson's approval, his close aide Marvin Watson, a steely Texan and ex-Marine, asked DeLoach to "put a surveillance" on a *Chicago Daily News* reporter, Peter Lisagor, to "find out what he is doing and where he is getting his information." DeLoach refused, telling Watson that to monitor Lisagor, who had not been accused of any crime, "would bring considerable discredit not only on the FBI, but the President himself." Lady Bird reminded her husband that the files that so absorbed him "have a lot of unevaluated information in them, accusations and gossip which haven't been proven."

By the spring of 1966, the campuses were erupting in protest. Johnson asked his advisers "why Americans who dissent can't do their dissenting in private," claiming that "you have to go back to the Civil War to find this public dissent." In May, at a large Democratic banquet in Chicago hosted by his friend Mayor Richard Daley, Johnson openly questioned the patriotism of those who opposed his war: "There will be some Nervous Nellies, and some who will become frustrated and bothered and break ranks under the strain—and some will turn on their leaders, and on their country, and on our own fighting men." His false public optimism about ultimate victory in Vietnam caused critics like Walter Lippmann to charge him with "a deliberate policy of artificial manipulation of official news." Americans derided Johnson's "Credibility Gap."

The Joint Chiefs proposed expanding the bombing of the North to include petroleum, oil, and lubricants facilities and transport lines. "What might I be asked next?" Johnson replied. "Destroy industry, disregard human life? Suppose I say no—what else would you recommend?" General Wheeler replied, "Mining Haiphong." The Chiefs assured him that their suggested new attacks would not draw Moscow and Beijing into the war. Johnson shot back, "Are you more sure than MacArthur was?" Wheeler insisted, "This is different," noting that in Korea, "we had ground forces moving to the Yalu." Johnson asked, "Any warnings you want to give me before I go to commune with myself and my God?" Hearing none, the President soon approved the Chiefs' request. That fall, Johnson told Eisenhower, "I'm trying to win it just as fast as I can, in every way that I know how." Ike replied that this war was "the most nasty and unpredictable thing that we've ever been in."

During a Pacific tour, in late October, Johnson made a surprise trip to South Vietnam. For reasons of security, he spent only two and a half hours there, but moved closer to actual battle than any President since Lincoln at Fort Stevens in 1864. At the US base of Cam Ranh Bay, standing tall in an open jeep, clutching its safety railing, he wore a tan-colored ranch suit and brown tie, riding with Westmoreland past a crowd of soldiers. "Some seemed to think he should be treated like a general," said one reporter, "until he extended his hand" and "they rushed forward, almost like any street-corner crowd back home." Doffing his jacket, in his short-sleeved shirt, Johnson told individual troops, "Y'all come back safe and sound now!" and "Chin up, chest out—we're gonna get out of this yet." In the officers' mess, he told a lieutenant, "Quite a number of women you got there—you're a lucky man." He dined on ham, roast pork, and mashed potatoes in the mess hall, pinned medals on troops, and consoled the wounded, lying in Quonset huts.

Thieu, Ky, and Westmoreland sat by the President as he addressed an honor guard from a platform on an aluminum runway. His face glowing with sweat, Johnson told them, "There are some who may disagree with what we are doing here, but that is not the way most of us feel and act when freedom and the nation's security are in danger." Almost choking up, he said, "I could not begin to thank every man in Vietnam for what he is doing." He pledged, "We shall never let you down," and that "one day, the whole world will acknowledge that what you have done here was worth the price." Before leaving Vietnam, he called out, using the language of the American frontier, "Be sure to come home with that coonskin on the wall!"

In that fall's midterms, Richard Nixon campaigned far and wide for his party, criticizing Johnson's mettle on Vietnam. (Nixon traveled on a borrowed Learjet, previously used by the villain in the title role of the 1964 James Bond film *Goldfinger* and flown by the character Pussy Galore.) At a press conference four days before the election, Johnson scorned the former Vice President as a "chronic campaigner." Nixon responded, in a paid broadcast, by asking whether "every public figure" who questioned Johnson's handling of Vietnam would "become the victim of a Presidential attack to silence his dissent." Johnson called Fulbright and asked him, despite their differences, to "take on Brother Nixon" for his waffling on Vietnam: "One day, he wants to escalate the war, and the next day, he wants to deescalate it. . . . Sounds like he wants to permanently occupy the country and keep the boys there, ad infinitum. . . . Just ridicule him a little."

Voters dissatisfied with Johnson's advances on civil rights and other domestic affairs, as well as the stalemate in Vietnam, helped Republicans to gain forty-seven seats in the House and three Senate seats.* Democrats retained control of both houses, but Nixon rightly called it "the sharpest rebuff of a President in a generation." In the aircraft hangar of his ranch, Johnson insisted to reporters that "when the pendulum swings one way, as it did in 1964, pretty strongly, it has a tendency to swing back."

✻ ✻ ✻

IN FEBRUARY 1967, Johnson brooded over how to renew the conscription law, which would expire that year. Early in the Vietnam escalation, he had abruptly canceled President Kennedy's insistence that married men—especially those with children—be called up last. Johnson was worried that too much of the war was being fought by African Americans, Latinos, and other minorities, thanks largely to exemptions and 4,100 mostly white draft boards. He wished to go down in history as the liberator of black Americans, not their executioner. He named a commission on the draft, which proposed an end to deferments for college and graduate students (save those in medical and dental schools), increased diversity in the Selective Service System, a lottery, and a new policy for nineteen-year-olds to be summoned first. The President knew that canceling deferments would stimulate new campus protests against his war. Congress indeed extended the draft, but defied his wish to end college deferments and choose draftees more randomly, as in days of old, by lottery.

That February, *Newsweek* and the *New York Times* reported that during a trip to Paris, Robert Kennedy had received a "peace feeler" from Hanoi, suggesting that the enemy might negotiate if Johnson stopped the bombing. Sure that Kennedy himself had leaked the news, the President was furious. As Kennedy later told his staff, during a visit to the Oval Office, Johnson "started right in by getting mad at me for leaking

---

* A September Gallup Poll had asked Americans about Johnson's handling of the Vietnam War; the result was a statistical tie of 43 to 40 percent disapproval. Asked if the country had "made a mistake sending troops to fight" there, respondents said no by 49 to 35 percent.

the story." Kennedy had denied it and said he was unsure there had been a peace feeler but that the leak had probably come from "your State Department." Johnson shouted, "It's not *my* State Department. It's *your* Goddamn State Department!"* By Kennedy's account, the President had told him that within six months, the war would end with a military victory, and "I'll destroy you and every one of your dove friends."

Kennedy urged him to "say that you'll stop the bombing if they'll come to the negotiating table." Johnson replied, "There isn't a chance in hell that I will do that." He shouted at the Senator, "You have blood on your hands!" Katzenbach, who was present, later recalled that he had "never seen" the President like this—"irrational" and "almost totally out of control." Furious, Kennedy rose to his feet and told Johnson, "I don't have to take that from you. I'm leaving!"

In March, from the Senate floor, Kennedy asked the President to stop bombing the North and say he was "ready to negotiate within the week." This provoked more anger from Johnson, as did Martin Luther King Jr.'s announcement that he now opposed the war. That same month, Fulbright and other doves argued that by raising the troop level in Vietnam to 414,000, which exceeded the peak US commitment of the Korean War, Johnson had overstretched his constitutional powers by waging a major conflict without asking Congress for a war declaration. To the White House argument that Presidents had often gone to battle on the basis of various forms of approval from Congress beneath the level of a declaration, the doves rejoined that, with the exception of Korea, these conflicts had been of far more modest scale than the Vietnam War.

On the President's behalf, Richard Russell replied that the Tonkin Resolution was "almost a declaration of limited war," and that if Johnson wished to, he could legally send a *million* troops to Vietnam. Rebuking the antiwar Senators' wish to cap off American involvement at five hundred thousand troops unless war was declared, the Senate passed

---

* Meaning that many at State were holdovers from President Kennedy's time. Johnson later complained to his National Security aide Walt Rostow of Robert's "bellyaching": "I didn't select these folks that he was whoring around with."

a resolution of support, by 72 to 19, for efforts by the President and "other men of goodwill" to limit the escalation of the war and negotiate a peace. But the President refused, unless Hanoi stopped its infiltration of the South. To show his own efforts for peace, the White House released some of his theretofore-secret requests of Ho Chi Minh to bargain, which moved Russell to tell Johnson that Ho "just spit in your face."

Johnson was certain that Kennedy, who now surpassed him in head-to-head polls, was maneuvering to challenge him as an antiwar candidate in 1968. "I think he'd be President tomorrow, if he could do it," Johnson told Larry O'Brien in March. "Let's assume that he will try to defeat me for President. I don't honestly believe if he did that, he could possibly win. I just believe that my state and twenty others would be in revolt. It would be a hell of a lot worse than Teddy Roosevelt and Taft.* . . . I don't see that he wants us to have a bad record and to be defeated in '68, because they'd take all this power that he could get in '72." Johnson noted that he had never publicly blamed the war on his predecessor: "I've tried my best to play fair with Jack Kennedy. . . . I think on Vietnam that he was right where I am, and I'm carrying out his policy." O'Brien reported that Robert had assured him that "he wanted no goddamned involvement with any peacenik in the country that was trying to use him in any primary."†

In October, the President complained to Dirksen that Senate foes of the war "are being used" and "it's hurting our country . . . very, very bad. If we're going to ask these five hundred thousand men to stay out there, we can't have every Senator being a general. . . . It would just be suicide if we stopped the bombing, as these idiots are talking about. When you say 'stop the bombing,' you say 'kill more Americans'—that's

---

* Meaning the ex-President's losing challenge to his successor, William Howard Taft, for the 1912 Republican nomination.

† O'Brien told Johnson that as a durable Kennedy operative, "I've known this kid since 1951." He said he had warned Robert that instead of becoming President, he was in danger of going "down the Goddamn drain" and "you'll wind up the leader of the New Left . . . a road that I'd never think *you'd* travel." During their early acquaintance, Robert was working in the Senate for Joe McCarthy.

all it means." He added that Westmoreland had cabled him that the enemy had lately concentrated more firepower on Americans than "in any equivalent period in the history of warfare—much more than was ever poured on Berlin or Tokyo" in World War II, and that the only means of protecting Vietnam's demilitarized zone (DMZ) against enemy infiltration was to bomb the North's gun positions. He agonized over the danger that if America dropped a bomb in the wrong place, "we may wake up in World War III." When his daughter Lynda once returned after a date, her father told her, "Our planes are going into Hanoi and Haiphong tonight. . . . Some old Texas boy will be in the lead bomber and drop one right down a Russian smokestack. And we know what happened to the battleship *Maine,* the *Lusitania.* . . . So it's time to do some heavy thinking and deep praying."

From the start, Johnson had tried to conceal the full, monumental expense of his war from the public and refused calls to cover it with increased taxes because he thought they would dampen support for the conflict and move people to demand cuts in his beloved Great Society programs. Recalling how war had killed the domestic reforms of Roosevelt and Truman, he rudely badgered the Federal Reserve Chairman, William McChesney Martin, to keep interest rates low so that he could have both "guns and butter." The President finally agreed with Congress on a "temporary surcharge" of 10 percent on personal and corporate income taxes, as well as some spending cuts, but inflation soared.*

In September 1967, in the Texas city where he had married Lady Bird, Johnson unveiled what he called his "San Antonio formula" for peace: he would stop all bombing "when this will lead promptly to productive discussions," but only if the enemy "would not take advantage" of the bombing halt. That October, he asked McNamara, "How are we ever going to win?" Concluding that his chief was really asking how they could squeeze out a victory in Vietnam before he had to face the voters in November 1968, the Defense Secretary replied, "I have no idea how we can win it in the next twelve months." To others, the President

---

* The surcharge had the effect of creating a federal budget surplus for the only time between 1960 and 1998.

complained, "It looks as if all the news is bad" and "the people just do not understand the war."

Distraught over the conflict, Johnson surprised some who knew him by turning to religion. Born into the Disciples of Christ, he had once been called "a Protestant with a capital P," praying with Billy Graham in his White House bedroom. But Johnson now quietly sought comfort from Catholicism. His daughter Luci, who had converted at eighteen, brought her father to St. Dominic Church in Southwest Washington; she called its Dominican friars "my little monks." After kneeling for twenty minutes, her father would grouse about the absence of knee pads.

Lady Bird much later told me, in 1998, "During that time, I wouldn't have been a bit surprised if Lyndon had decided to become a Catholic." Recalling her own traumas, she went on to relate having traveled by railroad between New York and Washington, and realizing, with a physical shudder, that the boxes visible through the windows of a nearby train were actually the coffins of fallen soldiers back from Vietnam. Mrs. Johnson recounted to me that their first year or two in the White House had been "wine and roses," but "after that, it was *pure hell.*" She saw firsthand how difficult it was for war to be waged without national unity: "God prevent, but if ever again we're in a war, may it begin with something like Pearl Harbor or the Alamo, or else we'll go through that same eroding effect that took place in the Vietnam War." When she mused on wars of the past, she remembered how, during a Washington luncheon of 1951, the elderly Edith Bolling Wilson, still "handsome, full-bosomed, feminine," had told her about crossing the Atlantic with Woodrow, at the end of World War I, for the Paris peace conference.

On Saturday, October 21, 1967, the National Mobilization Committee to End the War in Vietnam—described by the *New York Times* as "a coalition of roughly 150 organizations ranging from church groups to the Peking-oriented Progressive Labor Party"—led a protest march from the Lincoln Memorial, across the Potomac, to the Pentagon, which some vowed to "shut down." The *Times* reported that organizers were predicting "the biggest antiwar rally in the history of the nation." Exceeding expectations, the march attracted about a hundred thousand people. Hauling an LBJ effigy, one marcher hoisted a placard: "THE DEATH

OF KING LYNDON." Another sign asked, "WHERE IS OSWALD WHEN WE NEED HIM?"* There were concurrent demonstrations against the war in Western Europe, Japan, and Australia.

At the White House, the President assured aides who were worried about his physical safety, "They are not going to run me out of town!" He was furious to hear that some demonstrators were leaving their draft cards at the Justice Department or burning them.† He predicted to his domestic policy aide Joseph Califano that "Communist elements" would exploit the protest to create "big trouble in the Negro ghetto," and ordered the White House, Capitol, and Pentagon to be guarded by Army soldiers—some incognito, in civilian clothes. The day after the march began, he secretly had himself driven with his wife and daughter Lynda to the Lincoln Memorial and then had his driver cross the Potomac and circle the Pentagon. As Marvin Watson later recalled, Johnson "was curious about what the 'hippies' looked like, their dress, age, and the flags, bedrolls, blankets, flight bags and flowers they carried." The President was later scandalized to read an intelligence report that some protesters had urinated in unison and had sex on the Pentagon grounds, and that some female peaceniks had tried to unzip soldiers' trousers, asking, "Wouldn't you rather fuck than fight?" He asked Califano to pass this information to Joseph Alsop.

Shaken by the size and impact of the Pentagon march, Johnson sought consolation by calling Eisenhower:

> We've just had hell, and these college students—I've had J. Edgar Hoover in after them—Ho Chi Minh sent a bunch of them over a wire in April. He got this fellow Dillinger—and he's properly named too . . . and Stokely Carmichael, and he asked them to

---

* Referring to President Kennedy's alleged assassin, Lee Harvey Oswald.

† Johnson was not mollified when informed that some of the "draft cards" were forgeries or duplicates. Responding to the President's anger, General Lewis Hershey, Director of the Selective Service since 1941, proposed the "immediate induction" of anyone who mishandled or forged a draft card or obstructed the draft process. Although tempted to approve, Johnson instead asked his new Attorney General Ramsey Clark, who had replaced Katzenbach, to order every US Attorney to ensure "that the right of free expression and dissent be in no way infringed."

come over there.* . . . They sat down and planned these demonstrations in Rome and in Bonn and in London and in the United States, all on the same day. . . . We arrested six hundred of them. . . . We found most of them, really, were mentally diseased. Hoover has taken 256 that turned in, supposedly, their draft card, and about fifty of them were college professors who had been examined for the draft by the Army and turned back. . . . So you're dealing with mental problems—kind of like the Oswald deal.† . . . We talk too damn much about civil liberties and the constitutional rights of the individual, and not enough about the rights of the masses. I think your government is in trouble, General. . . . We're in more danger from left-wing influences now than we've ever been in the thirty-seven years since I've been here.‡

Johnson told Ike, "I wouldn't tell this to any other Republican," but "I've been suffering a terrific onslaught by Bobby Kennedy." He claimed that the Senator had created a group that paid Martin Luther King Jr. to foment urban unrest, "and that's caused me a lot of problems in the cities this year."§ Of King, the President said, "The damn fellow went out to Chicago [last] week and announced that he was trying to destroy Johnson."

The President warned that "Bobby thinks he's going to get the

---

* Following his habit of mangling the name of people who angered him, Johnson actually meant not the 1930s Chicago gangster but David Dellinger, chair of the "New Mobe." Stokely Carmichael was the radical champion of "Black Power."

† Perhaps referring to the accused assassin's emotional problems or anger about his dishonorable discharge by the Marines.

‡ After Johnson shared Hoover's findings with the congressional leadership, Gerald Ford of Michigan publicly called on him to reveal the "Communist participation" in the Pentagon march so Americans "may judge just how deep or widespread anti-Vietnam War sentiment is in this country." But Rusk and Ramsey Clark persuaded the President that doing so might unleash a new McCarthyism. Dellinger told the press that although he had met with Communist Vietnamese, it was "ridiculous to think that a message from Hanoi could get 200,000 people to demonstrate in the United States."

§ Newark and Detroit had been rocked by riots in the summer of 1967.

nomination" in 1968. Eisenhower harrumphed, "If ever they want that little pipsqueak as President of the United States, I'm really going to get on the hustings." Johnson warned, "This boy is awfully vicious." The General agreed: "Absolutely ruthless." Johnson went on, "Old Joe was pretty rough, and this boy is rougher than any of them. He's much different from what Jack Kennedy was. Jack was not a vindictive person." "No, he wasn't," said Eisenhower. Referring to Robert, whom he disdained as beyond his depth, Ike assured the President, "I think you can take care of him." Johnson replied, "I'm going to do my best."

Although he prided himself on his tough exterior, Johnson confessed to Eisenhower on another occasion that he was "terrified" of Kennedy: "I never know what he's going to do, where he is going to strike." Believing that politics should stop at the water's edge, Ike promised Johnson that although he considered himself a "mean Republican," he would not be "partisan on the war" during the 1968 campaign.

Smarting from the Pentagon protest, Johnson explored how to escalate further in Vietnam, asking Rusk and McNamara, "Are we now ready to take the wraps off the bombing? I asked the Joint Chiefs of Staff . . . how to shorten the war, but all of their proposals related to . . . outside South Vietnam.* . . . We've almost lost the war in the last two months in the court of public opinion. . . . The hawks are throwing in the towel. . . . San Antonio did not get through. . . . If we cannot get negotiations, why don't we hit all the military targets, short of provoking Russia and China?"

Citing his intelligence findings, Johnson warned congressional leaders that Hanoi would soon push for "a significant military victory, probably meaning in the DMZ area," which Ho's generals envisaged as "another Dien Bien Phu." McNamara cautioned, "The great danger is to lead our people to think we can win the war overnight with bombing—we cannot." Mansfield replied that "we could bomb North Vietnam into the stone age," but it would not stop "the flow of men and materiel into the South." Dirksen assured the President, "I'm still

---

* Johnson meant the urgings to strike enemy strongholds in Cambodia, which he had turned down.

in your corner. Do not lose this leverage of bombing. Remember how many casualties resulted from the talks during the Korean War." Senator Robert Byrd, Democrat from West Virginia, gave Johnson similar advice about the bombing: "You may lose next year's election because of it, but I believe that history will vindicate you."

By now McNamara felt tortured and disillusioned about the conflict of which he had been a central architect. Over a Halloween lunch at the White House, he told the President it was now "impossible to win the war militarily," and that persevering without change in Vietnam "would be dangerous, costly in lives and unsatisfactory to the American people." As McNamara much later recalled, this apostasy raised his tension with Johnson "to the breaking point." Johnson soon announced that he would nominate McNamara as president of the World Bank. McNamara later told friends he did not know "if I resigned or was fired." (Apprised of this later, some of his nonadmirers from the Johnson White House staff joked that they would be glad to resolve his confusion.) The President now privately deprecated his onetime fair-haired boy by explaining he had feared that McNamara's hand-wringing over Vietnam would make him "pull a Forrestal" and kill himself.*

Johnson solicited advice about Vietnam in November from a band of "Wise Men," including General Omar Bradley and Henry Cabot Lodge. With Senators deserting his war, Johnson told the elders that he felt "like the steering wheel of a car without any control." Dean Acheson, the ex–Secretary of State, said that "the cross you have to bear" was a "lousy" Foreign Relations Committee, chaired by Fulbright, "a dilettante fool." Having made signal mistakes in 1941 and 1950 that had hastened the wars with Japan and Korea, Acheson now gave Johnson a spectacular piece of bad advice during another major war: "I would not talk about negotiations anymore. . . . That isn't the Communist method. If they can't win, they just quit after a while."

Just before Christmas, during a quick world tour, the President stopped once more at Cam Ranh Bay, this time for less than two hours,

---

* In 1949, the deeply troubled first Secretary of Defense, James Forrestal, had jumped from the sixteenth floor of Bethesda Naval Hospital to his death.

telling senior commanders, "I wish I had things in as good shape at home as you have here." He promised them, "We're not going to yield. We're not going to shimmy." Referring to Lynda's new husband, Chuck Robb, he told one Marine, "You know, I'm sending my son-in-law over here in a few weeks." Then, reboarding Air Force One, Johnson was off for Vatican City, where he gave Pope Paul VI a bust of himself.

* * *

IN JANUARY 1968, the President told Congress in his State of the Union that the enemy in Vietnam had been defeated "in battle after battle." But he privately warned House and Senate leaders that "a full-scale attack on Khe Sanh is imminent." Westmoreland formed what he called "a small secret group" to consider the use of tactical nuclear weapons, should the "highest national authority" find it necessary to save US troops at Khe Sanh.* This possibility was code-named Operation Fracture Jaw. When told of this gambit, Johnson was appalled and had Walt Rostow, now his National Security Adviser, ensure that the Joint Chiefs would present him with no such request. Rejecting Eisenhower's earlier advice, Johnson had decided that use of nuclear weapons should only be considered in the event of a terrible showdown with the Soviet Union.

At the end of the month, during the Vietnamese holiday of Tet, came a surprise assault against five of the South's biggest cities, including Saigon, with Viet Cong overrunning the US embassy and presidential palace. "A kamikaze-type thing," Johnson told the congressional leadership. Four years into this war, he was still asking his advisers why

---

* The commander cabled Wheeler that "should the situation in the DMZ area change dramatically," they should weigh using "either tactical nuclear weapons or chemical agents." Admiral Sharp advised Wheeler that "military prudence alone" required "some very closely held planning for employment of tactical nuclear weapons," such as "units to be employed, delivery vehicles, weapon availability, preferred weapons by type and yield, constraints, preferred delivery means." He sent Westmoreland a message relating "step by step the procedures for requesting the selective release of nuclear weapons," along with information on where they were located. In a memo declassified in 2015, Rostow reminded Johnson that "there are no nuclear weapons in South Vietnam" and "Presidential authority would be required to put them there."

Hanoi's soldiers fought "with so much more determination" than those of the South. Richard Helms of the CIA explained, "There is a certain heroism about dying for the cause."

On a Saturday night in February, at El Toro Marine Corps Air Station in California, Johnson said good-bye to a thousand members, in combat gear, of Camp Pendleton's Twenty-Seventh Regimental Landing Team, who were boarding the transports to Vietnam. He later told his aides that "a boy from Ohio" who had served four times in Vietnam told him that he "had a little baby boy born yesterday." Noting that "there wasn't a tear in his eye" and "no bitterness showed in his face," the President confessed that the encounter "really melted me and brought me to my knees."

Johnson knew that if he wanted the 1968 Democratic nomination, he would have to fight for it. In November, Senator Eugene McCarthy had decided to challenge the President after Robert Kennedy had turned down antiwar leaders. McCarthy was outraged not only by Johnson's escalation in Vietnam but by what he considered to be the President's grandiose conception of his constitutional power to make war. The Minnesotan had bristled in August 1967, when Katzenbach, by then Under Secretary of State, told the Senate Foreign Relations Committee that "'declaring a war'" had become "an outmoded expression." As for Kennedy, the head of the nation's most famous political dynasty did not want to spoil his future chances with a quixotic campaign in 1968, but he remained deeply troubled about the war and Johnson's emotional stability.

In the New Hampshire Democratic primary, on March 12, the little-known McCarthy surprised the nation when he almost defeated a Johnson write-in campaign, with 42 percent of the vote. Kennedy, who privately thought McCarthy "vain and lazy," now told reporters that he was "actively" reassessing his position. He assured the new Secretary of Defense, Clark Clifford, that he would not challenge the President if Johnson would agree to appoint an independent commission to reconsider the war, with Kennedy and other doves among its members.* By now,

---

* The President later recalled that Kennedy also insisted that he fire Dean Rusk in favor of Bill Moyers, Johnson's longtime aide and former White House press secretary, who had resigned in

Mayor Daley, whose influence among Democrats extended far beyond Chicago, had quietly come to oppose the war; he nudged Johnson to accept a commission, insisting in a telephone call that it would not "take any power away from the President," just "analyze and review" the conflict. But to Johnson, accepting Kennedy's idea would mean putting his command of the war effort in receivership. Turning it down, he told Clifford that a commission would "appear to be a political deal." Thus on March 16, Kennedy went to the Senate Caucus Room and announced that he would run—not "to oppose any man but to propose new policies."*

His competitive juices flowing, Johnson told Clifford, "What we've got to do is get out of the posture of just being the war candidate that McCarthy . . . and Bobby [have put] us in. We're the true peace candidate. We're not the Chamberlain peace. We're the Churchill peace." Clifford, who himself by now had profound doubts about the war, replied, "We would frighten the people if we just said we are going to win. They would think, 'Well, hell, it just means we are going to keep pouring men in until we win militarily.'" Johnson scoffed: "We're not going to get these doves." On March 22, the President warned Senator Russell, "Bobby is storming these states and those governors [to] switch the bosses all over the country in a pretty ruthless blitz operation. . . . They are going to beat hell out of us in Wisconsin." Recalling the state's isolationist tradition, he went on, "You know the La Follettes, don't you? Well, it's still there—pretty deep, they tell me. . . . They're against any war."

Westmoreland was asking him to send 206,000 more troops to Vietnam and to call up 400,000 reserves. Reconvening his Wise Men, Johnson was staggered when they now almost unanimously advised him to wind down the war. Even the once-belligerent Acheson told him, "We can no longer do the job we set out to do in the time we have left." Meeting with the Joint Chiefs the next day, Johnson wailed,

---

December 1966. The New York Senator's suggestion no doubt deepened Johnson's suspicions that his circle included Kennedy double agents. So did McNamara, later that spring, when he made a television ad touting Robert for President.

* One Kennedy supporter was Bill Clinton, of the Georgetown University class of 1968, who told me in 1997, "I was never a Johnson hater. I just wanted to end the war."

There has been a panic in the last three weeks. The country is demoralized. . . . I will have overwhelming disapproval in the polls and elections. I will go down the drain. . . . I wouldn't be surprised if they repealed the Tonkin Gulf Resolution. Senator Russell wants us to go in and take out Haiphong. Senator McCarthy and Senator Kennedy and the left wing have informers in the departments. . . . Most of the press is against us. . . . We have no support for the war.

The President told the Chiefs, "I don't give a damn about the election. I will be happy just to keep doing what is right, and lose the election."

Unwilling to give in to his political enemies, Johnson worked his telephone, soliciting support for a 1968 campaign. Knowing that, under existing rules, an incumbent President had great power to bend the party to his will, he assured allies that he had the nomination locked up: "Somebody may try, but they can't take it away. I've got my votes already." He implored the Indiana Governor Roger Branigin, who was running in his state's primary as a Johnson stand-in, "Let's don't have a damn New Hampshire thing. . . . Just let us know what you need now. . . . We'll go right after them, hammer and tong."

Johnson reminded Walter Reuther, the United Auto Workers chief, that "when you've got your back to the wall," he came to Reuther's aid, and pooh-poohed McCarthy and Kennedy:

These boys can't get this nomination. . . . They'll win some primaries because I don't have much time to make calls like this. . . . I'm no Goddamn fascist. I'm trying to settle this thing. . . . Anybody can get a Chamberlain peace for thirty days—I could do that. . . . But it just moves right into Thailand, Laos and Cambodia immediately. . . . Roosevelt couldn't end the war with Hitler, by God, just on a chosen day, and I can't end it either. . . . I've been fighting it out there for four long years, without involving Russia and China—and that's some little feat in itself—and without invading North Vietnam or Cambodia. . . . If I was bloodthirsty and went in and took Hanoi and Haiphong and just flattened 'em out, I think we could bring North Vietnam to their knees pretty damn quick. . . . Stand up and bear with me. . . . Walter, I want to depend on you.

But Reuther refused to commit himself, explaining, "I've always done the right thing, because I have to feel that way inside of me." Calling Mayor Daley, Johnson said, "Well, Dick, I appreciate *your* staying with me." Daley's response was underwhelming: "I'm an old-timer that says, 'I'm with my President, right or wrong.'"

Undaunted, Johnson asked Terry Sanford, the liberal ex-Governor of North Carolina, to manage his 1968 campaign. On Wednesday, March 27, Sanford told him, "I'm ready to go to work for you." Johnson replied, "That's wonderful, Terry. . . . God bless you. . . . That's a great comfort to me. . . . We'll make this a better country." But that same day, O'Brien wrote the President that Democratic loyalists were "fearful of the end result" if he maintained his "present Vietnam posture." Johnson scrawled, "Get Larry over here at once and explain." When they spoke, he asked O'Brien to manage "Citizens for Johnson," at double his Post Office salary: "You're the one I want. . . . I'm not pressuring you."

Despite his exertions for another campaign, Johnson had ruminated to family, close friends, and a few advisers about pulling out of the race, noting that "my Daddy" and other Johnson men had not lived past sixty. He feared another coronary or a stroke like those that Woodrow Wilson and Franklin Roosevelt had suffered after leading the nation through major wars. From childhood, Johnson had "horrible memories" of his wheelchair-bound grandmother, who had been paralyzed by a stroke and "couldn't even move her hands." As he later recalled, "I would walk out in the Rose Garden and I would think about it. That was constant with me, all the time."

A few days before his State of the Union in January, he had summoned Horace Busby, his longtime aide and now outside speechwriter, to his bedroom. With his head on the pillows, he told Busby, "I have made up my mind. I can't get peace in Vietnam and be President too." Pointing his thumb at the Capitol, he said, "That bunch up there doesn't want me to have either." He went on, "I've always prayed I'd have sense enough to get out when the time came, before they had to carry me out." He asked Busby to draft a peroration to his speech, announcing his withdrawal from the race: "That ought to surprise the living hell out of them." But when he spoke in the House chamber, he kept the slip of paper in his pocket, convinced that he could not credibly ask Congress for audacious new laws and then tell the members he was departing. Busby concluded that Johnson's renunciation exercise "must have been for purposes of therapy."

Worried about his health, Lady Bird wanted him to retire but also feared that inactivity on their ranch might be enervating. The impassioned Lynda and Luci warned him that his departure from power would endanger their husbands, who had both signed up to fight in Vietnam. Emotionally the President swung back and forth. Recalling that Truman had withdrawn after losing New Hampshire during a detested war, he vowed to make some kind of announcement before the end of March. If this was to be his swan song, he did not want to deliver it before an audience, as Truman had, because the crowd might applaud and cheer the news. Thus Johnson planned a televised speech for Sunday night, March 31, which would be the only time he ever spoke to Americans about the war from the Oval Office.

He summoned Busby that Sunday morning and asked him for a new closing for his address. His guest found the presidential bedroom bursting with doctors, Johnson's valet, aides, friends, and family, including his squealing baby grandson Lyndon. The President told Busby, "I won't know whether I'm going to do this or not until I get to the last line of my speech." Busby asked him what the odds were on pulling out. Johnson replied, "Eighty-twenty against it."

That evening, before his nine o'clock address, Lady Bird told her husband, "Remember—pacing and drama." As she sat nearby, off-camera, Johnson informed the nation that he would halt the bombing if Ho Chi Minh agreed to "serious talks" and declined to exploit America's restraint. The President closed by saying that "with America's sons in the fields far away," he did not believe he should "devote an hour or a day of my time to any personal partisan causes. . . . Accordingly, I shall not seek, and I will not accept, the nomination of my party for another term as your President."

After his speech, with his daughters in tears, Johnson changed into a turtleneck. Upstairs in the Mansion, speaking by telephone with friends and others put through to him, he sounded gracious, modest, even noble:

> We've been a long time trying to figure it out. . . . Now we can try to get along and heal some of these wounds. . . . These primaries and all the hatreds and the divisions and the selfishness—you can't take on everybody and get this done there too. I just know it's the thing to do. . . . I have 525,000 men whose very lives depend on what I do, and I can't worry about the primaries. Now I will be working full time for those men out there.

McCarthy's wife, Abigail, called the President from Milwaukee, where she and Gene had been campaigning against him in the Wisconsin primary: "I don't see how you could have done that." Cordially he replied, "One little person like me—I've got nine months now. . . . I won't spend one moment doing anything except trying to find peace. I just thought I had to do it. Everything will be better. . . . After thirty-seven years, you learn what is important."* Cooler toward the wife of the man who had just helped force Lyndon out of the race, Lady Bird told Abigail, her onetime friend, "When you have boys out there—when you feel pretty darn close to all five hundred thousand of them, and you're just about to get two out there yourself, you don't think much about politics." The next day, boosted by public praise of a kind he had not heard for years, Johnson was feeling so mellow that he even told Fulbright, "I'm sure I've goofed and made a lot of errors, but I've done the best I know how."

---

* Among Johnson's recorded calls that evening, only one suggests the anger beneath the surface of his renunciation. Senator John Sparkman told him it was "the best speech you have ever made." The President—evidently under the misapprehension that the Alabaman was glad he had quit—sharply cut him off, spitting out, "Lady Bird wants to say hello to you" before Sparkman could add "except the last fifteen seconds."

Johnson's worry about his physical condition had certainly influenced his decision not to run, but his chief motive was that he felt he had no serious alternative. Later, in retirement, he insisted to aides that he had "not the slightest doubt" he would defeat the likely Republican nominee, Richard Nixon, "by a substantial margin," although he knew that the fight would have been tough and expensive.* But Westmoreland had asked for hundreds of thousands more troops and still would not guarantee that such a surge would let America prevail.

Johnson knew that during another term, with an increasingly obstreperous Congress, he might become, as he always swore not to be, the first President to lose a war. By pulling out of the campaign, he was trying to seize control of his political predicament by trying to settle what he privately called "this goddamn war." He also knew that if a deal with the enemy seemed to be near before the August Democratic convention, he might be reembraced by Americans as a peacemaker, and the delegates just might be prompted to demand that he serve as President for another four years.

* * *

SEEKING TO WEAKEN Johnson's opposition, Robert Kennedy asked to see him. At first, the President hotly refused an audience with "that grandstanding little runt," but on Wednesday morning, April 3, in the Cabinet Room, the two rivals had what proved to be their final encounter.

Kennedy told Johnson that he was "a brave and dedicated man." The President made him repeat the statement, which caused Kennedy to wonder whether Johnson was secretly taping their conversation. The President assured Robert that he didn't hate or dislike him and was still "carrying out the Kennedy-Johnson partnership." He confessed that it had been "very difficult" to be "under attack every day" from

---

* Johnson told Busby that merely running for the nomination would cost about $10 million, which would mean "I'll never be a free man again. I don't know these people that the money comes from. . . . With my luck, they will probably turn out to be crooks."

Nixon, Kennedy, McCarthy "and the nation's enemies," but he felt "no bitterness and no vituperation." He was not being "pure or holier than thou," but was "simply scared," because "things are more dangerous than people realize." Recalling "what the Senate did" to Wilson and Truman during their wars, Johnson said he did not think he could now "command the leadership" the country needed. Kennedy asked whether Johnson would "mobilize political forces" against him. The President replied, "If I had thought I could get into the campaign and hold the country together, I would have run myself." He pledged that if he decided to take sides in the primaries, he would try to inform Kennedy in advance.

As it happened, Johnson had indeed tried to make a covert recording of the conversation. He was angry when his aide Larry Temple later reported that the device had failed: their technicians speculated that Kennedy had carried a scrambler. Later Johnson met in that same room with McCarthy. The President vowed not to obstruct any candidate—"even Bobby Kennedy." But as McCarthy recounted to me in 1997, Johnson, while speaking those words, pantomimed slitting Kennedy's throat.

The Hanoi government responded to Johnson's withdrawal speech by agreeing to talk to American officials about an unconditional bombing halt "and all other war acts." Johnson said he would accept "any forum, at any time." The two sides chose Paris as their conference site, but Johnson saw "no evidence that the North Vietnamese will negotiate seriously." He told Daley that "the sons-of-bitches in this country, the Fulbrights and Bobby Kennedys," had the Saigon regime "scared to death that we're going to sell them out and have a coalition and let the Commies take over." Returning to Washington, Westmoreland reminded the President that "many Cambodians are working with Viet Cong" and said, "If we could bomb over there, it would be very disconcerting to him." Johnson refused, insisting, "They would impeach me."

At the start of June, the President watched Kennedy joust with McCarthy on ABC's Sunday *Issues and Answers,* from San Francisco, before the California primary; he later told Dirksen that the program "made a lot of votes for the Republicans." On Tuesday night, the fourth, Kennedy accepted victory at the Ambassador Hotel in Los Angeles, proclaiming that "the country wants to move in a different direction" and "we want peace in Vietnam."

After midnight, while leaving the ballroom through the kitchen, the Senator was shot. At the White House later that day, Joe Califano was unnerved by the fact that the President, within the privacy of the White House, kept asking, "Is he dead yet?" Califano later wrote, "I couldn't tell, because Johnson didn't know, whether he hoped or feared the answer would be yes or no." When Kennedy died, the President and Lady Bird attended his funeral at St. Patrick's Cathedral in New York City. But Johnson remained so angry at his old rival that he refused to sign a directive allowing the government to pay the bill for Robert's burial, alongside his brother, at Arlington National Cemetery.

With Kennedy gone, the clear Democratic front-runner was now Humphrey, who, although he had entered no primaries, was now the rallying point for the Johnson forces. After his early apostasy on Vietnam, the Vice President had bent over backward for years to demonstrate fealty to the President's war policies. One evening in July, Humphrey and his wife, Muriel, had the Johnsons to dinner at their apartment in Southwest Washington. The President lay down on the sofa and, while scratching himself, said he had heard that Hubert was making "the best speeches" about the war. He demanded to hear one on the spot. Humphrey reluctantly began to orate, and the President started for the bathroom, saying, "Keep talking, Hubert—I'm listening." Then Johnson warned him, "Don't go to California—they're just a bunch of kooks out there. Somebody'll kill you, just to even up the situation with Kennedy." Humphrey told him, "You shouldn't be saying that, Mr. President."

Secretary Clifford flew to Saigon and warned Thieu and Ky that "in the absence of visible progress," Americans would "simply not support the war effort much longer." Unless a settlement was reached in Paris, South Vietnam must gradually "take over the war." On his return, Clifford told Johnson he was "absolutely certain" that the Saigon duo did not want the war to end—not while they were "protected by over 500,000 American troops and a golden flow of money." The Defense Secretary advised his chief to stop all bombing, without condition, to jump-start the Paris talks. But the President insisted that first the North

Vietnamese agree to include the South at the table, pledge to respect the DMZ, and stop shelling the cities.

In late July, Humphrey shared with Johnson a draft of a speech that was more dovish than the President's position. Furious, Johnson told him that such an address would jeopardize the lives of his sons-in-law, and threatened to "destroy" him. The next day, the newly nominated Nixon came to the White House. Hoping to undermine Humphrey, he promised Johnson that he would say nothing in public that might make it more difficult for the President to seek peace, so long as Johnson refused to "soften" his stand on the war.*

After flying to the LBJ Ranch in early August, the President feared, in private, that he was near death. A medical checkup in San Antonio had turned up danger signs that he was suffering from intestinal cancer. As his personal lawyer Don Thomas later recalled, Johnson's "ambition of the moment was to prepare to die, whereupon there were more real estate transactions in a short period of time, more codicils to more wills than you can imagine." Then the President learned with relief that the diagnosis had been a mistake.

The Democrats were to descend on Chicago for the final week of that month. On the telephone with Dirksen, the President forecast that "they'll have a big knockdown drag-out, with the pacifists and the fellows that Hanoi has been working on," all broadcast on TV by what he bitterly called the "Kennedy networks" of NBC and CBS. Johnson explained that North Vietnam knew that Nixon wouldn't give them a better peace offer, so it would try to "play this other side." Referring to the last surviving Kennedy brother, he told Dirksen, "They're going to try to nominate Teddy—the peaceniks are going to do that." He told Mayor Daley that "I've got a better-than-even break to get peace" before the November election. If Hanoi were made to understand that none of his possible successors would give them a better peace deal than he would, the enemy would "come and sign up with this government—the

---

* The President had been suspicious of Nixon at least since the Californian's rough-edged 1950 campaign for the US Senate against Congresswoman Helen Gahagan Douglas, who had been one of Johnson's paramours. "She was a fine woman," he once told Califano, "and he destroyed her."

quicker, the better, because after November, it'll be harder than it is now." If the delegates endorsed his tough platform plank on Vietnam, "we will stop that bombing the first moment" Hanoi asked for peace. He told Daley, "Go on and get it done!"

From the ranch, the President asked his close friend and fund-raiser Arthur Krim, chairman of United Artists, to commission a secret survey by his private pollster, Oliver Quayle, showing how well he might run against Nixon that fall; the poll found Nixon eight points ahead of Johnson, with similar results for Humphrey. Although disappointed by the survey, the President asked Krim and Marvin Watson, who both went to Chicago as his eyes and ears, to share it with Daley and "ask him whether there's any support for me to let my name come before the convention."

Johnson knew that by threatening to run himself, he might muscle Humphrey into supporting his platform plank on Vietnam. "Hubert's going to favor stopping the bombing," the President told one aide. "That's what he's going to put in the platform, and when he does, I think he'd get probably a majority. . . . Then God knows what happens." But that was not Johnson's only motivation. As his longtime confidante Texas Governor John Connally later recalled, the President "very much hoped he would be drafted." Johnson may have reasoned that if the delegates chose him, vindicating his war and his presidency, he could decline the prize—or perhaps, by now, he had changed his mind and genuinely intended to seek another term.

The convention opened at Chicago's International Amphitheatre on Monday, August 26. The next day, Johnson would turn sixty. He anticipated flying to the city for a birthday celebration, with fireworks, which Daley had promised. The President asked Marvin Watson by telephone to inform the Mayor "that tentatively we hope to come in. . . . I guess we'd go to the Hilton. . . . Do they have a helicopter roof landing? . . . Better check that." He told Watson that Daley should be informed "that if he wants me" at the convention and if "both of you say there'll be a hell of a demonstration for me, you believe I'll do it." A speech was crafted for Johnson to deliver. Responding from the stage to—so the President fantasized—a long, glorious ovation, he intended to say, referring to his triumphal appearance at the 1964 convention, "For a moment there, I closed my eyes and thought I was back in Atlantic City." Hidden in the cellar beneath the Chicago convention floor, to be handed to the delegates, were more than a thousand placards saying "DRAFT LBJ."

At Johnson's behest, Connally met with fellow Democratic governors from the South to gauge their support for a Johnson draft. But Connally found the Southerners exhausted by this President, his struggles over civil rights, and his war. As Connally recalled, "they said, 'No way!'" On Johnson's behalf, Krim and Watson accosted Daley on the convention floor and showed him the private Quayle survey. They asked how the Mayor might react should the President be willing to be drafted. Unimpressed by the poll, Daley brusquely replied that Johnson "has got to announce or do something to show that he wants it. Otherwise there's nothing I can do."

✳ ✳ ✳

DISHEARTENED BY DALEY's brush-off, the President gave up the notion of a draft. While he watched on TV at the ranch, working the channel-changer from his bed, his convention managers in Chicago successfully whipped the delegates to back his Vietnam plank. On Wednesday evening, with Johnson's quiet acquiescence, Humphrey won the nomination. That same night, the Chicago police took up battle with antiwar demonstrators. Having been warned that coming to the city might endanger his life, the President stayed home, in seclusion, feeling thwarted and shunted aside.

Accepting the nomination on Thursday evening, Humphrey ignored widespread advice to make a sharp break with Johnson and his war, perhaps even quitting the Vice Presidency. Well aware of Johnson's lingering influence over party bosses and donors, Humphrey instead lauded the "greatness" of his chief, who had achieved "more of the unfinished business of America than any of his modern predecessors." On Vietnam, the nominee timidly straddled the party's split by pledging "everything in my power" to "aid the negotiations" and "bring a prompt end to this war." What Johnson heard was that his Vice President had refused to embrace his policies in Vietnam. Arriving at the ranch, Krim found his host "an absolute angry man" who found Humphrey's address a "repudiation" and was "very bitter about it." The President ordered Krim, "I do not want you to work in the Humphrey campaign," adding, "I want Hubert to really taste the fact that he needs our help."

Johnson was asking too much to expect that he could convince Ho Chi Minh that his successor would pursue the war at least as fiercely as he, thus moving the North Vietnamese to make a peace deal before the election. The only candidate he could rely on for unflinching belligerence was ex-Governor George Wallace of Alabama, the segregationist third-party nominee who claimed, along with his running mate, General Curtis LeMay, that Johnson had not fought the war aggressively enough.* The President anticipated that Nixon would opportunistically take whatever position would help him win, and that Humphrey would try to grab the support of millions of antiwar Democrats who were sitting on their hands. Johnson threatened his Vice President to "dry up every Democratic dollar, from Maine to California," if he strayed from the White House position on Vietnam. But even if Humphrey met Johnson's fierce loyalty test, Hanoi knew, from its own sources, that the Vice President was privately inclined to liquidate US involvement in the war and that most of his close counselors were doves.

By late September, the Gallup Poll predicted that Nixon would defeat the money-starved Humphrey by 43 to 28 percent, with Wallace close behind. Humphrey's aides begged him to cut Johnson's taut leash. The Vice President replied that if the polls were correct, "I don't stand a chance." He went on, "I don't give a shit anymore. I'm saying what I want to say." During a paid, prerecorded TV broadcast from Salt Lake City, Humphrey endorsed a bombing halt as "an acceptable risk for peace," conditioned only on the enemy's restoration of the DMZ. So that the President could not try to dissuade or denounce him in advance, Humphrey did not inform him of the speech until just before

---

* At the Pittsburgh press conference announcing his candidacy, LeMay proposed using nuclear weapons to end the war, which shocked so many Americans that public support for Wallace plummeted.

it was broadcast. When Humphrey called and described his message, Johnson, predictably furious, complained that he had dispensed with two of the three official conditions for a bombing halt and abruptly broke off the call: "I'll turn it on. Thank you, Hubert."

To maximize the dovish impact of his address, Humphrey's advisers told reporters, on background, that the Vice President would not even stick to his one mentioned caveat. The President fumed to Rusk, "This just ruins us with the other side. . . . If Humphrey's elected, they're in clover." To make amends, Humphrey went to the White House, arriving slightly late. Johnson pointedly kept him waiting. Under strain, Humphrey told a presidential aide—so loud, he hoped, that Johnson could hear it—"You tell the President he can cram it up his ass!" Later, on the telephone, Johnson told Dirksen that Humphrey's Salt Lake City address had been a severe mistake. He noted a recent poll showing that only 8 percent of the voters were still undecided: "Let's assume all of those are McCarthy people." What Humphrey really needed, he said, was to dislodge people from Nixon or Wallace by showing fortitude on Vietnam.

In early October, North Vietnamese diplomats in Paris agreed to include representatives from Saigon in peace talks if the United States halted the bombing, although they did not conclusively meet Johnson's other demands. The President feared that if he stopped bombing so close to the election, it would seem like a "cheap political trick," but as he told Senator Russell, "I don't want to look bad in history and say I was offered something and I just was hard-headed and obstinate."

Nixon had been hearing predictions of an impending bombing halt. Late on the evening of October 22, in a telephone call with his aide H. R. "Bob" Haldeman, the Republican nominee mentioned Anna Chennault, a wealthy stalwart of the China Lobby that backed Chiang Kai-shek. According to Haldeman's notes, Nixon asked him to keep Mrs. Chennault "working" on South Vietnamese officials, and to have Dirksen complain to Johnson. Haldeman recorded, "Any other way to monkey wrench it? Anything RN can do." Nixon was furious about reports that the President was seeking a bombing halt without obtaining from the enemy all three of his preconditions—and even more so be-cause Nixon knew that the news could help give the presidency to Hum-phrey by persuading Americans that peace might be near. The next day, Dirksen indeed called Johnson to warn that Nixon was "rather upset."

Four days later, Johnson discussed a bombing halt with General Creigh-ton Abrams, who had succeeded Westmoreland. He asked, "Can we return to full-scale bombing easily if they attack?" Abrams replied, "Yes, very eas-ily." Although Johnson had obtained, in advance, President Thieu's com-mitment to negotiate, the latter dragged his heels on sending a delegation to Paris. Johnson angrily ordered his Ambassador in Saigon, Ellsworth Bunker, to threaten Thieu that if he ruined the Paris talks that had "cost so much to obtain," then "God help South Vietnam" because "the people of this country would never forget the man responsible."

Johnson was informed of evidence that Nixon was indirectly trying to convince Thieu that he would get a better deal if he sat out the talks and waited for Nixon to become President—and that a cutout between the Nixon campaign and Saigon's envoy in Washington, Bui Diem, was Mrs. Chennault. Walt Rostow cautioned the President that the clues about meddling were "so explosive that they could gravely damage the country whether Mr. Nixon is elected or not." Johnson asked the FBI to make sure that Bui Diem and Chennault were closely monitored, and Hoover agreed. Nixon much later claimed that his campaign plane was bugged.

The President complained to Dirksen ("I don't want it told to a human") that Nixon's people were clearly "getting a little unbalanced and frightened." The evidence of their tampering with his diplomacy was "despicable, and if it were made public, I think it would rock the nation." Johnson said that while Nixon may not have committed the offense personally, there was "no question but what folks for him are doing it, and, very frankly, we're read-ing some of the things that are happening." Clearly hoping that Dirksen would push Nixon to stop his maneuvering, Johnson went on,

> Now I've been at this five years, and if I'd wanted to sell my coun-try out, I'd have sold it out five months ago and gone on and run

for President and got this war behind us and been overwhelmingly elected. But I'm a conscientious, earnest fellow trying to do a job. . . . I really think it's a little dirty pool for Dick's people to be messing with the South Vietnamese ambassador. . . . And to me, when Nixon's saying, "I want the war stopped," that "I'm supporting Johnson," that "I want him to get peace, if he can," that "I'm not going to pull the rug out of him," I don't see how in the hell it could be helped unless he goes to farting under the cover and getting his hand under somebody's dress. And he better keep Mrs. Chennault and all this crowd just tied up for a few days.

On Thursday night, October 31, looking like a gargoyle on the TV screen, Johnson announced that "all air, naval and artillery bombardment" of the North would cease in order to achieve "prompt, productive, serious and intensive" peace negotiations. Benefiting also from a late-hour endorsement by Eugene McCarthy, Humphrey took the lead, by 43 to 40, in the Harris Poll. Johnson sent his Vice President a message "not to open his damn mouth" on Vietnam until after the election.

Two days later, Thieu announced that he would boycott the Paris talks. Nixon publicly charged that "prospects for peace are not as bright" as they had seemed. His aide Robert Finch told reporters that the President hadn't gotten his "ducks in a row." With rising anger, Johnson read an FBI report that Mrs. Chennault had called Bui Diem with a message from her "boss"—"Hold on, we are gonna win"—asking Thieu not to join the talks. The President called Dirksen: "We're skirting on dangerous ground. . . . This is treason!" Prompted by Dirksen, Nixon called Johnson in an effort to blunt his fury. Lying through his teeth, Nixon assured the President that "any rumblings about somebody trying to sabotage" the peace talks had "absolutely no credibility." Knowing that Nixon was lying to him, Johnson replied, "You just see that your people that are talking to these folks make clear your position."

Now that Johnson's bombing halt had clearly failed to produce peace talks, the major polls showed Americans swinging back from

Humphrey toward Nixon. On Monday, Johnson told Rusk and Clifford he was ready to reveal the evidence of Nixon's perfidy to the voters. Rusk told him that no President should unveil "use of interceptions or telephone taps in any way that would involve politics. The moment we cross over that divide, we're in a different kind of society." Johnson believed that exposing Nixon would probably help Humphrey win the election. In the end, he gave the choice to the Vice President, who declined to exploit the damaging information, suggesting to Johnson, once and for all, that Humphrey was too soft to be President.

On Tuesday, November 5, Nixon won with 301 electoral votes and a margin of less than half a million popular votes. Johnson told his Vice President, during a telephone call, that he should blame the anti-war Democrats, who "created all the problems, all the conditions, and stirred up all the divisiveness." Humphrey replied, "We're not going to cry. Nothing you can do about it."*

Three days after the election, afraid that Johnson might reveal his covert machinations to the public, Nixon slavishly promised him to urge the South Vietnamese to join the Paris talks: "If you want me to do something, you know I'll do anything, because we're not going to let these people stop these peace things." The President frankly replied that Saigon officials were assuming "that folks close to you" wanted them to "just not show up" in Paris, adding, "Mrs. Chennault is very much in there." He went on, "That's the story, Dick, and it's a sordid story." Doing backflips, Nixon assured him, "There's nothing that I want more than to get these people to that table. . . . I'll even go out there [to Saigon],

---

* After his defeat, Humphrey flew to Opa-locka, Florida, to meet with Nixon, who advised him, from his own experience in 1960, "Every guy in the world will be calling you up for a month, telling you what a great fight you fought, how gallant it was, and then in six months, they'll be dancing over your grave." Nixon asked Humphrey to consider joining his administration, saying, "I want you" and observing that "our positions weren't so far apart" during the campaign. Nixon later called him to suggest Ambassador to the United Nations, but Humphrey declined, explaining that his wife, Muriel, could not tolerate the "social strain" of New York City. Eager to procure a name-brand Democrat (and perhaps to help thwart opposition to his prosecution of the Vietnam War), Nixon dangled the same job, without success, before Eugene McCarthy and the Kennedy brother-in-law Sargent Shriver, who was serving as Johnson's Ambassador to France.

if necessary, to get them there."* Johnson, remained so incensed that he asked the FBI to track down evidence that Nixon's running mate, Spiro Agnew, might have called Mrs. Chennault from a campaign stop in Albuquerque, as well as any other clues that her orders came from Nixon.

Johnson remained eager to close out his term as a peacemaker. Even as a lame duck, he pressed the Soviets for a farewell summit meeting in Leningrad—perhaps Nixon could attend at his side—but Nixon's aides asked the Kremlin to stiff-arm the outgoing President.

In January 1969, when Johnson departed Washington, 36,756 Americans had been killed in Vietnam on his watch. No longer President, he lit up a cigarette. Knowing that doctors had told him that smoking would kill him, one of his daughters objected, but Johnson told her, "I've raised you girls, I've been President. Now it's *my* time!" Back on his ranch, the ex-President was heartbroken that so many Americans viewed him as the champion not of equal rights or Medicare but a reviled war. Despite his doctors' warnings, he ate and drank to excess, moving Jack Valenti to fear that his old chief was committing "slow-motion suicide." Almost weeping, Johnson told Arthur Krim in a New York nightclub that his life was "over," with "nothing to look forward to." He liked to listen to Simon and Garfunkel's 1970 hit "Bridge over Troubled Water," which may seem a strange choice (the antiwar singers had also recorded "How I Was Robert McNamara'd into Submission") until one remembers the lyrics: "When you're weary, feeling small, when tears are in your eyes. . . . And friends just can't be found."

In April 1972, Johnson suffered a massive heart attack and was told that his days were probably numbered. That July, in Miami Beach, Democrats nominated George McGovern, who vowed to pull "every

---

* The new President remained fearful that Johnson might one day publicly expose Nixon's role in the Chennault affair. He asked his aide Tom Huston to give him a confidential report on the subject, which was not released until 2015. Playing to his boss, Huston informed Nixon that "the most sensitive—and perhaps most troubling—aspect" of the episode was Johnson's "use of Federal investigatory and intelligence agencies in an operation which had highly political domestic implications," and that "a fine line may have been crossed."

American soldier" out of Vietnam within his first three months as President. Johnson's portrait was displayed inconspicuously in the convention hall.

Although polls showed that a majority of Americans had long ago grown fed up with the conflict, Nixon had expanded it into Cambodia and Laos, and blocked two major efforts by the Democratic Congress to stop it. Knowing that it would help to quell antiwar protests, he closed down conscription of young Americans for what was now called the war in Indochina. In January 1972, Nixon scrawled an angry note to his National Security Adviser, Henry Kissinger: "We have had 10 years of *total* control of the air in Laos and V.Nam. The result = Zilch." That spring, he tried to hasten a peace settlement by bombing Hanoi and Haiphong. He told Haldeman, by now his White House Chief of Staff, that "we've crossed the Rubicon. Instead of the foolish gradual escalation of LBJ, this is cleaner and more defensible."

That fall, a *Washington Star* reporter called Johnson's office in Austin, trying to unearth information about Nixon's secret efforts of 1968 to foil his predecessor's efforts to make peace. Probably employing an FBI leak, the reporter asked whether Johnson had requested surveillance of Nixon's entourage. When Johnson heard about that inquiry, he was furious. As his last White House press secretary, George Christian, told me in 2001, the ex-President called his onetime FBI liaison Deke DeLoach, by then working for PepsiCo, asking, "I never ordered such a thing, did I?" DeLoach frankly told him that he had. According to Christian, who recalled this exchange with a laugh, Johnson's only reply was an uneasy "Oh."

Just before the election, Christian, who had joined "Democrats for Nixon," called Haldeman to work out a joint response to the *Star*. Christian reported that Johnson was willing to describe the Chennault episode "as something foolish that someone did without Nixon's knowledge," and to say that he and Nixon had both been "on board" together in the fall of 1968 to "get the war over." As for the FBI, Christian said that Johnson believed that it was "conceivable" that "someone" had asked for surveillance of Nixon's campaign.

Christian also confided to Haldeman that Johnson was "in very serious physical trouble. The doctors say that if he lives until April, the pain may be relieved and his vessels may be strong enough that he'll be all right. There's some discussion of surgery, but he won't do it. He's spending three fourths of his time in bed." When Nixon's aide General Alexander Haig flew to the LBJ Ranch to brief Johnson on Vietnam, he watched as Lady Bird brought her husband pills and a glass of water. Johnson pretended to take them, then, after she left, threw them into the bushes. Johnson told Haig, "I'm dying and I want to get it over with."

Reelected by a landslide, Nixon ordered what came to be called his "Christmas bombing," devised to pulverize the enemy into pursuing a final peace accord in Paris. On the day after Christmas, Harry Truman died, and the Johnsons paid their respects in Independence. In retirement, Johnson had come to identify more closely than ever with Truman, a fellow President from beyond the Eastern Seaboard who had been consumed by an Asian war. As Lady Bird later told me, "Lyndon hated funerals," and seeing Truman's casket left him desolate, reminding him of his own likely not-too-distant fate.

Nixon was privately casting about for ways to block investigation of his growing Watergate scandal. According to Haldeman's diary, the White House counsel, John Dean, suggested they demand that the forthcoming Senate Watergate hearings be expanded to encompass 1968, including Johnson's request for FBI eavesdropping on Nixon. Haldeman pondered threatening Johnson with embarrassing disclosures on that subject, unless the ex-President would agree to use his authority with Senate Democrats to close down the Watergate probe. As Haldeman told his diary, "The problem in going at LBJ is how he'd react, and we need to find out from DeLoach who did it, and then run a lie detector on him." Nixon and Haldeman also knew that exploring the underside of the 1968 campaign could blow up in the sitting President's own face.

On the day after New Year's 1973, Johnson spoke to Nixon for the last time. The President had called him to find out whether he planned to attend a memorial service for Truman in Washington. At the Cotton Bowl in Austin, the Texas Longhorns had defeated Alabama. Johnson had hollered too much, endangering his heart, and his doctor was called to the ranch. He told Nixon, "I had heart pains all night." "Goodness!" came the reply. "I called you at the wrong time." "Not at all!" said Johnson. "I'm cheered." With sweetness in his voice, he told Nixon, "I just feel the torture you're going through on Vietnam. I wish I could do something to help you." "Don't you worry about it," said Nixon. "It's going to come out all right, all right." After Nixon hung up with Johnson, he told his roughneck aide Charles Colson, "He's a hypochondriac. He's unbelievable!" Colson agreed: "So pathetic!"

Two days after Nixon's inauguration for a second term, on the afternoon of January 22, Johnson suffered a fatal heart attack in his bedroom on the ranch. The next evening, from the Oval Office, Nixon announced an accord "to bring peace with honor"; he recounted how Johnson had "endured the vilification of those who sought to portray him as a man of war."* By then, it had been more than eight years since the Tonkin Gulf attacks. Over fifty-eight thousand Americans and at least a million Vietnamese had been killed.

Johnson had not plunged into Vietnam out of madness or hunger for war. It may be obvious today that defending the South was not essential to protect Southeast Asia from Communism and avoid losing the Cold War, but that was by no means clear in 1963. Johnson knew that the postwar order depended on America's willingness to use its armed forces to fulfill its treaty obligations and worried that if he ignored its SEATO pledge to South Vietnam, other Third World countries might side with the seemingly more steadfast Soviet Union. Affected by the high-pressure, self-certain advice of McNamara, Johnson believed he had inherited a commitment from Kennedy, who had publicly vouched for the domino theory and left military advisers in South Vietnam. As

---

* The previous fall, while Henry Kissinger was negotiating with the North Vietnamese in Paris, Haldeman told his diary that President Thieu would have to accept the result, because it would be "the best Thieu's ever going to get—and unlike '68, when Thieu screwed Johnson. He had then Nixon as an alternative. Now he has McGovern as an alternative, which would be a disaster for him, even worse than the worst possible thing that Nixon could do to him." Haldeman added, "The President feels we have to take the best that North Vietnam offers and stuff it down the South Vietnamese, and that's it."

Johnson's defenders argued, America's years of holding the North Vietnamese at bay may have granted other Southeast Asian nations time and breathing space to strengthen their own democracies.

A more fire-breathing President than Johnson might have taken huge military risks in Vietnam, which, as he correctly warned, could have provoked both China and the Soviet Union to enter the conflict directly, spiraling into nuclear war. Unlike his successor, Johnson did not defer to the Joint Chiefs' demands to expand the war into Cambodia and resisted the advice of Eisenhower and Westmoreland to consider using tactical nuclear weapons. Johnson did not abstract himself from the mass suffering and mounting American death toll that were the result of his decisions. Lady Bird had been correct in her fear, at the start of the war, that her husband might be too emotional to serve as Commander-in-Chief.

When Johnson told McNamara in February 1965 that he saw no way to win the conflict, he should have listened to his own excellent political instincts—and to Senator Russell, who uncannily warned him that a Vietnam war would consume ten years and fifty thousand American lives, provoke mass protest, and end in defeat. When Johnson launched his war, he drew on history, but his history was badly flawed. He convinced himself that Ho Chi Minh was like Hitler before Munich, and that his troops in Vietnam were defending a cause as heroic as that of the Texans at the Alamo. He forgot that with Korea, during the more tranquil early 1950s, Americans had turned quickly against a costly war they did not understand, and he ignored the famous warning by MacArthur—who had learned it the hard way—that anyone seeking a ground war on the Asia mainland "should have his head examined."

Johnson rejected Eisenhower's private counsel to wage the war not by gradualism, which would encourage Ho to match and exceed each escalation, but by confronting the enemy with massive US force from the start. Instead Hanoi quickly concluded that Johnson was hamstrung by his fear of provoking the Soviets and China. They knew that with television sending images of the bloody "living room war" back to the United States every night—a problem that had not faced Truman during

Korea—Americans would grow impatient, domestic protest would rise, and the North Vietnamese could wait the invaders out, just as they had done for centuries.

With his limited oratorical skills, at least on television, and a bad case to make, Johnson could never aspire to persuade Americans, as he expressed it to Russell in 1964, what Vietnam should mean to them. Unlike the best war Presidents, he could never hope to lift his war aims to a high moral plane. He could not rally them behind the regime of Thieu and Ky, which was selfish, corrupt, and loathed by so many of its own people. We now know, from Johnson's secret tapes, that at the start of his escalation, he had crippling private doubts that his and McNamara's strategy of war could ever succeed. But he did not fulfill one of the most basic responsibilities of a wartime President, which is to level with the American people when their sons and daughters are being asked to risk their lives.

Instead he concealed the start of Rolling Thunder and claimed to the public and Congress that he expected to win his war, and soon. Disinclined to display his "mother-in-law with only one eye," he never put the country on a true war footing, as Truman had with Korea, which would have required raising taxes early in the conflict, as well as other sacrifices. For years, he refused to call up the reserves, fearing, as he told aides, that such a step would reach "into every home" and hasten the antiwar movement. Instead for too long he allowed the poor, black, and less-educated Americans to bear too much of the burden.

During Vietnam, Johnson did not embrace Benjamin Franklin's belief that our critic is our friend. His outrage at those in Congress and on campuses who questioned his war drove him instead to demand that the FBI and CIA provide evidence that the protestors were being secretly manipulated by Communists. Feeling isolated, with his conspiratorial tendencies in full throttle, weakened by heart disease and other ailments, Johnson demonized his opposition and, in his increasingly troubled mind, allowed the war to become a titanic test of whether he could conquer those domestic political foes who defied him. A more coolheaded President might, by contrast, have cut his losses years earlier. With a half century's hindsight, it is clear that whatever Johnson gained

for the United States with his war in Vietnam was never worth its ruinous cost in lives, treasure, American self-confidence, or what Thomas
Jefferson called "the good opinion of mankind."

✳ ✳ ✳

A FTER NIXON HAMMERED out his Vietnam peace agreement, in
1973, he reassured President Thieu by pledging that if the North
ever violated it, the United States would retaliate with punishing military force. But Nixon was ousted over Watergate, and his successor,
Gerald Ford, lacked the political strength to act when the compact was
broken. Congress refused Ford's request for new aid to South Vietnam.
In April 1975, Saigon collapsed. The enemy seized the renamed "Ho
Chi Minh City," and the final American helicopters lifted off from the
US embassy compound.

Having definitively lost a war for the first time in their history,
Americans resisted the prospect of entering future conflicts. In 1976,
while running for President, Jimmy Carter promised, during an interview for *Playboy* magazine, that if elected, he would not adopt "the same
frame of mind that Nixon or Johnson did—lying, cheating and distort-
ing the truth." In 1980, during his campaign, Ronald Reagan urged voters to rid themselves of their "Vietnam Syndrome," telling the Veterans
of Foreign Wars, "We dishonor the memory of 50,000 young Americans who died in that cause when we give way to feelings of guilt, as if
we were doing something shameful. . . . Let us tell those who fought in
that war that we will never again ask young men to fight, and possibly
die, in a war our government is afraid to let them win."

Reagan's successor, George H. W. Bush, noted in his 1989 inaugural
that the Vietnam War "cleaves us still" and warned that "no great nation can afford to be sundered by a memory." In August 1990, when
Saddam Hussein's Iraq invaded Kuwait, Bush saw the assault as a test
of the post–Cold War world, showing whether UN members would
be allowed to oppress one another, as well as a danger to Saudi Arabia
and other oil-rich Middle East states. Despite the lingering shadow of

Vietnam, Bush dispatched more than half a million Americans to the region and built an international coalition. When Saddam refused UN demands, Bush asked Congress for a resolution enabling him to unleash war against the Iraqis. Although the Democrats were in control, the House acceded by 250 to 183, and the Senate by 52 to 47.

The Persian Gulf War began in January 1991 and, after a six-week air and ground campaign, ended with victory. In a private congratulatory letter, Richard Nixon wrote Bush that he had "finally exorcized the Vietnam Syndrome from the American psyche."

Epilogue

O N TUESDAY MORNING, September 11, 2001, al-Qaeda terrorists, commanded from afar by Osama bin Laden, seized control of two commercial jets and flew them into both towers of New York's World Trade Center, which soon collapsed. Another plane struck the Pentagon. Still another crashed into a field near Shanksville, Pennsylvania, after its hijackers were foiled in their hope to destroy the US Capitol or White House. The death toll that day was 2,977, which almost matched that of the Civil War's Battle of Antietam. It was the most significant attack against the American mainland by foreign nationals since the British invaded Washington in 1814, chasing James and Dolley Madison from the Capital.

George W. Bush later recalled that he had become "something I did not want to be—a wartime President." The tragedies of September 11 came a decade after the end of the Cold War; during that time, many Americans had grown indifferent to developments beyond North America. This gave way to a new national sense of acute vulnerability. The term "homeland security" dominated the American conversation, more than during the early days of World War II. Some conspiracy theorists charged that Bush and his circle had covertly engineered the attack in order to provoke a war, echoing those who had falsely accused William

McKinley of planning the *Maine* disaster and Franklin Roosevelt of masterminding the assault on Pearl Harbor.

When the Taliban regime of Afghanistan rebuffed Bush's demands to stop protecting al-Qaeda, he prepared for military action.* Shortly after noon on Sunday, October 7, 2001, he announced a ground invasion, by coalition, of Afghanistan, against the Taliban government. A Gallup Poll the following month found that Americans supported the war by 80 to 19 percent.

In his January 2002 State of the Union, Bush decried an "axis of evil"—Iraq, Iran, and North Korea—warning that "by seeking weapons of mass destruction, these regimes pose a grave and growing danger." Iraq had "plotted to develop anthrax, and nerve gas, and nuclear weapons for over a decade" and had "something to hide from the civilized world." The President later warned that if Saddam did not submit to inspections, an American-led alliance might have to launch a new war against him. That October, acting on Bush's request, the House and Senate passed a joint resolution, with considerable Democratic support, empowering the President to deploy the armed forces, "as he determines to be necessary," to defend America's security "against the continuing threat posed by Iraq."†

Speaking to Congress in January 2003, Bush cited evidence acquired from the British government that Saddam had "recently sought significant quantities of uranium from Africa"; this later proved to be incorrect. The following month, his Secretary of State, Colin Powell, argued before the United Nations that Saddam was hiding Iraqi development of weapons of mass destruction. In March 2003, the Iraq War began

---

* In 1973, after Richard Nixon pulled American forces from Southeast Asia, Congress passed the War Powers Act over his veto. Frustrated by the failures of Truman, Johnson, and Nixon to ask for declarations of war on Korea and Vietnam, the House and Senate were now insisting that Presidents could not consign the country to an armed conflict unless they obtained a war declaration or "statutory authorization" or there was "a national emergency created by attack upon the United States, its territories or possessions, or its armed forces." The act demanded that after such an engagement began, a President would have to withdraw the military within sixty days unless Congress approved. Like Nixon, later Presidents called the act unconstitutional.

† Among the Democratic Senators who endorsed the resolution were Hillary Clinton, Joe Biden, and John Kerry.

with the bombing campaign called "shock and awe." Nineteen days later, Baghdad collapsed, and by the end of the month, the coalition had seized Saddam's hometown of Tikrit. One hundred and thirty-nine American and thirty-three British combatants had been killed.

On May 1, Bush donned a flight suit and landed a Navy jet on the USS *Abraham Lincoln,* off San Diego, where he announced that "major combat operations have ended" in Iraq. Behind him was a "MISSION ACCOMPLISHED" banner, inspired by a White House advance team. But soon the occupiers faced a widespread insurgency, and they could not find proof that Saddam had been developing weapons of the kind and magnitude that the coalition had claimed. Critics escalated their charges that Bush and his allies had lied about the weapons caches in order to trick the American people and their foreign partners into a war that the President had sought for other, more nefarious reasons. In December 2003, Saddam was discovered hiding underground near Tikrit, but his capture did little to stop rising American opposition to the conflict in Iraq.

No earlier American President waging a major war had ever been compelled to concede in public, while the troops were still fighting, that his central casus belli had been a misapprehension. (Even McKinley had made sure that his justification for war against Spain was not centered on whatever role the Spanish had in the sinking of the *Maine,* about which he retained at least some private doubt.) While accepting the Republican nomination for reelection at Madison Square Garden in August 2004, Bush defended his decision to go to war: "Do I forget the lessons of September 11th and take the word of a madman, or do I take action to defend our country? Faced with that choice, I will defend America every time."

That same month, the 9/11 Commission, established by Congress in an act signed by Bush, reported that it had found no "collaborative operational relationship" between Saddam's regime and al-Qaeda. Nevertheless a September *Newsweek* poll found that 42 percent of Americans believed that Saddam's government had been "directly involved in planning, financing or carrying out" the 2001 attacks—a conclusion that would have made those who believed it more likely to support the Iraq

War. That November, Bush defeated Senator John Kerry of Massachusetts, taking 50.7 to 48.3 percent of the popular vote, the narrowest popular margin for any reelected President since Wilson in 1916.

In November 2006, with the conflicts in Afghanistan and Iraq still raging, Democrats took control of the House and Senate for the first time in twelve years. The new House Speaker, Nancy Pelosi, insisted that her party's midterm victory had been "about Iraq." Bush announced the departure of his Defense Secretary, Donald Rumsfeld, an advocate of the war, and approved a new troop "surge" into Iraq, which improved coalition prospects. But many Americans were feeling worn down by the two conflicts, which, by 2008, had lasted longer than both the Civil War and World War II. At the start of that election year, according to Gallup, 60 percent of Americans believed that launching the Iraq War had been a mistake. Bush's approval rating had dropped from 90 percent, in the wake of the 2001 attacks, to 32 percent.

That year Barack Obama defeated Hillary Clinton for the Democratic nomination, and beat John McCain in the general election. He was aided by his early opposition, as an Illinois state senator, to the war in Iraq. In the fall of 2002, Obama had proclaimed in Chicago, "What I am opposed to is a dumb war." As President, he withdrew US forces from Iraq by the end of 2011. But the Afghanistan struggle did not end—and in 2017, Donald Trump took office as a wartime President, facing a conflict that was, by more than three times, the longest in American history.

* * *

A T THE DAWN of the American Republic, the framers of the Constitution had dreamt that war would be a last resort under the political system they had invented. Unlike in Great Britain and other monarchies and dictatorships of old, it would be declared by Congress, not by the chief of state. But only sixty years later, opposed to what he viewed as an unnecessary conflict with Mexico, Daniel Webster was warning against what he decried as *a Presidential war.* After World War II, although Presidents requested more modest forms of authorization, they stopped bothering to ask Congress to fulfill its constitutional mandate to declare war before major foreign conflicts, and the House and Senate did not seriously object.

As this book has shown, the notion of presidential war took hold step by step. Although he was one of the creators of the founding document, James Madison allowed himself to become the champion of a war against England—despite the absence of an immediate, overwhelming danger, uneven support from Congress and the American people, and an over-reaching mission that included a grab for Canada. Satisfied that his ends would justify his means, James Polk lied and connived, creating a pretext for a war that, despite his public claims, he designed to allow the United States to seize vast territory from Mexico. With the sinking of the *Maine,* William McKinley showed how an outrageous offense that took American lives could be employed to almost instantly unite the country for war. So did Franklin Roosevelt after Pearl Harbor, in his noble effort to save the world from Hitler and Imperial Japan. The experiences of Woodrow Wilson and FDR demonstrated how a major war could enhance a President's contemporary standing and expand the power of his branch of government. Harry Truman, Lyndon Johnson, and later Presidents proved that the Constitution's demand for congressional war declarations could be ignored without serious penalty. With no military draft, Presidents who consider taking the nation into major conflict in our own time may not feel so constrained as earlier leaders by fear that a widespread antiwar movement might erupt.

Those who wrote the Constitution could not foresee the invention of nuclear weapons that could be delivered by a hostile power's missile, giving a President little more than a moment to respond, allowing no time to seek concurrence from Congress, even if the President should like to obtain it. Nor could the Founders anticipate the possibility of a major war initiated by cyberattack, which would compel a quick response from a President working secretly with the intelligence community. John Adams and other early Americans used the word "terrorism," but they could not foresee the prospect, now always imminent, of a single major terrorist event that, in the tradition of the *Maine* disaster, could galvanize the country behind a President's demand for a war that it might otherwise shun. If there should be an unscrupulous leader in the Oval Office, a terrorist attack might someday even be fabricated as a means of shocking the American people to demand a new war that would lead them and Congress to grant that President new deference and authority.

The Founders would probably be thunderstruck to discover that the option to start a war of a magnitude they would find inconceivable—killing hundreds of millions of human beings in less than an hour—may now rest on the whim of a President. James Madison and his contemporaries never presumed that Americans would be angels, not even in the optimistic atmosphere of their newly fledged nation. But they hoped that all future Presidents would be people of sagacity, self-restraint, honesty, experience, character, and profound respect for democratic ideals. They anticipated that any Chief Executive would strain to avoid taking the nation into conflict, except to confront a genuine, immediate national danger. And they expected that in the absence of such a danger, all future Presidents would resist any temptation—which the Founders saw in the European despots they abhorred—to launch a major war out of lust to expand their own popularity and power.

Acknowledgments

W───HEN I STARTED this book, I did not expect it to take more than a decade to research and write. I soon discovered, however, that coming to understand the leadership of Presidents in times of war required almost the same depth of research as if I were writing an entire book on each of them.

For specific counsel during this book's long journey, I thank Jim and Kate Lehrer, Mary Graham, Susan Dunn, David Sanger, and Evan Thomas. Jon Meacham advised me on all aspects of research, writing, and publication. My Williams College teacher, James MacGregor Burns, died in 2014, at the age of ninety-five. For four decades, he helped me to refine the theme and scope of much of what I have written, all the way back to my first book, which started as my college honors thesis, written under his supervision. Any shortcomings in this volume are in spite of Jim's wise advice and noble example.

Early in this project, Margaret Shannon and Justin Reynolds helped to locate a number of published materials. Milton Djuric examined an archive from the McKinley period. Michael Hill searched several manuscript collections from the Jefferson-Madison era and, at the end of the process, checked my Source Notes. Jack Bales helped to compile the bibliography. Dani Holtz recommended a number of journal articles and helped with endnotes. Julie Tate fact-checked the entire book.

I have performed research in presidential libraries since the mid-1970s, when John Kennedy's aide and friend David Powers kindly showed me through the temporary quarters of the Kennedy Library. For the period I worked on this book, I thank David Ferreiro, Archivist of the United States, Cynthia Koch and Paul Sparrow of the Roosevelt Library, Michael Devine of the Truman Library, and the Johnson Library's Mark Updegrove, Tina Houston, Claudia Anderson, and the late Harry Middleton, as well as LBJ's White House aides Tom Johnson and Larry Temple, both now trustees of the Lyndon B. Johnson Foundation.

I am grateful to historians who generously read chapters of the book in manuscript and proof for errors of fact or interpretation. They include David Mattern, of the University of Virginia, who read the chapters on James Madison; Robert Merry on James Polk and William McKinley; Allen Guelzo, of Gettysburg College, on Abraham Lincoln; John Milton Cooper, of the University of Wisconsin, and Margaret MacMillan, of St. Antony's College, Oxford, on Woodrow Wilson; David Kennedy, of Stanford University, on Franklin Roosevelt; H. W. Brands, of the University of Texas, on Harry Truman; and Fredrik Logevall, of Harvard University, on Lyndon Johnson. John A. Farrell, biographer of Richard Nixon, provided additional advice. Corby Kummer of the *Atlantic* read and commented upon the final proofs of the entire volume.

At Crown Publishing, I thank Molly Stern for her wisdom and strong support for this project, as well as Maya Mavjee for her leadership. David Drake provided important advice. Tim Duggan has been a superb editor, aided by Will Wolfslau and Aubrey Martinson. Julie Cepler, Becca Putnam, Rachel Rokicki, and Gwyneth Stansfield have been a pleasure to work with. Chris Brand and Songhee Kim ensured the aesthetics of the book, inside and out. Cindy Berman, Heather Williamson, and Maureen Clark guided it through production. For their early support, I thank Tina Constable and Sean Desmond.

Esther Newberg has been my friend and literary adviser for twenty-five years, through six books, and brought to this one her intense attention, judgment, and verve. At ICM, I also benefited from the work of John Delaney, Kari Stuart, Zoe Sandler, and Alexandra Heimann. I am grateful to my lawyer and friend Michael Rudell and his colleagues Neil Rosini and Eric Brown. My assistant Sarah Convissor was helpful in many ways.

When I began working on this book, my son Alex was in the ninth grade and my son Cyrus in the sixth. Eleven years later, Alex is now a medical student at the University of Pennsylvania and Cyrus is a history major at Williams College. They are both great guys and, while (usually) tolerating the distractions of their father's labors on this volume, gave me advice of a quality that went far beyond their ages. What their mother, Afsaneh Mashayekhi Beschloss, has brought to the life of this author is inexpressible.

Michael Beschloss
Washington, DC
June 2018

Source Notes

ABBREVIATIONS

ALP	Abraham Lincoln Papers	JMP	James Madison Papers
CG	*Congressional Globe*	LBJL	Lyndon B. Johnson Presidential Library
CR	*Congressional Record*		
CWAL	*Collected Works of Abraham Lincoln*	LBJP	Lyndon B. Johnson Papers
		LBJT	Lyndon B. Johnson Tapes, LBJL
DDEL	Dwight D. Eisenhower Presidential Library	LOC	Library of Congress
ERP	Eleanor Roosevelt Papers	Memcon	Memorandum of conversation
FDRL	Franklin D. Roosevelt Presidential Library	NARA	National Archives
		NYT	*New York Times*
FDRP	Franklin D. Roosevelt Papers	OH	Oral History
		PWW	*Papers of Woodrow Wilson*
HSTL	Harry S. Truman Presidential Library	RNL	Richard Nixon Presidential Library
HSTP	Harry S. Truman Papers		
int	Interview or conversation with author	RNT	Richard Nixon Tapes, RNL
		TJP	Thomas Jefferson Papers
JFKL	John F. Kennedy Presidential Library	WMP	William McKinley Papers
		WP	*Washington Post*
JKPP	James K. Polk Papers	WWP	Woodrow Wilson Papers

MANUSCRIPT COLLECTIONS

Dean G. Acheson, HSTL

John Adams, Massachusetts Historical Society

John Quincy Adams, Massachusetts Historical Society

Robert Anderson, LOC

James Barron, College of William and Mary

James Buchanan, LOC

John Bullus, New-York Historical Society

John C. Calhoun, LOC

Henry Clay, LOC

George B. Cortelyou, LOC

Jefferson Davis, LOC

Dwight D. Eisenhower, DDEL

H. R. Haldeman, RNL

John Hay, LOC

Harry Hopkins, FDRL

Cordell Hull, FDRL

Hubert H. Humphrey, Minnesota Historical Society

Andrew Jackson, LOC

Thomas Jefferson, LOC

Andrew Johnson, LOC

Lady Bird Johnson, LBJL

Lyndon B. Johnson, LBJL

John F. Kennedy, JFKL

Joseph P. Kennedy, JFKL

Husband E. Kimmel, University of Wyoming

Abraham Lincoln, LOC

Dolley Madison, LOC

James Madison, LOC

Mike Mansfield, University of Montana

George McClellan, LOC

William McKinley, LOC

James Monroe, LOC

Henry Morgenthau Jr., FDRL

Richard Nixon, RNL

Timothy Pickering, Massachusetts Historical Society

James K. Polk, LOC

Eleanor Roosevelt, FDRL

Franklin D. Roosevelt, FDRL

Arthur Schlesinger Jr., New York Public Library

Selected Collections, NARA

Charles D. Sigsbee, New York State Library, Albany

Edwin M. Stanton, LOC

Henry L. Stimson, Yale University

Zachary Taylor, LOC

Harry S. Truman, HSTL

John Tyler, LOC

Daniel Webster, LOC

Gideon Welles, LOC

Woodrow Wilson, LOC

INTERVIEWS AND CONVERSATIONS WITH AUTHOR (INCLUDING SOME CONDUCTED FOR EARLIER BOOKS)

McGeorge Bundy, 1988; George H. W. Bush, 1998, 2001, 2003; George W. Bush, 2003, 2006, 2009, 2017; Joseph Califano, 2017; Jimmy Carter, 2007; George Christian,

1994, 2001; Clark Clifford, 1983, 1993; Bill Clinton, 1997, 2003; John Eisenhower, 1983, 1990; Milton Eisenhower, 1983; George Elsey, 2004; Betty Ford, 2002; Gerald Ford, 1990, 1995; J. William Fulbright, 1984; Robert Hardesty, 1994, 2001; Richard Helms, 1983, 1989; Lady Bird Johnson, 1994, 1998, 2000, 2001; Luci Johnson, 2001; Nicholas Katzenbach, 2004; Ethel Kennedy, 2017; Clare Boothe Luce, 1978; Eugene McCarthy, 1997; George McGovern, 1976, 1994; Robert McNamara, 1987; Harry Middleton, 1994, 1996, 2015; Newton Minow, 2016; Richard Nixon, 1992; Nancy Reagan, 2011; Lynda Johnson Robb, 2001; Franklin Roosevelt Jr., 1977; James Roosevelt, 1978; John Roosevelt, 1978; Walt Rostow, 1982; Dean Rusk, 1987; Larry Temple, 2015, 2018; Grace Tully, 1978; Jack Valenti, 1999.

BOOKS

Acheson, Dean. *Present at the Creation: My Years in the State Department.* New York: W. W. Norton, 1969.

Adams, Charles. *When in the Course of Human Events: Arguing the Case for Southern Secession.* Lanham, MD: Rowman & Littlefield, 2000.

Adams, Henry. *History of the United States of America During the Second Administration of James Madison.* New York: Library of America, 1986.

Adams, John Quincy. *Diary of John Quincy Adams.* Edited by David Grayson Allen. 2 vols. Cambridge, MA: Belknap Press of Harvard University Press, 1981.

Aikman, David. *Billy Graham: His Life and Influence.* Nashville, TN: Thomas Nelson, 2007.

Alger, Russell Alexander. *The Spanish-American War.* New York: Harper & Brothers, 1901.

Allen, Felicity. *Jefferson Davis: Unconquerable Heart.* Columbia: University of Missouri Press, 1999.

Alley, Robert S. *James Madison on Religious Liberty.* New York: Prometheus Books, 1985.

Allgor, Catherine. *Dolley Madison: The Problem of National Unity.* Lives of American Women. Boulder, CO: Westview Press, 2012.

———. *A Perfect Union: Dolley Madison and the Creation of the American Nation.* New York: Henry Holt, 2006.

Alterman, Eric. *When Presidents Lie: A History of Official Deception and Its Consequences.* New York: Viking, 2004.

Ambrose, Stephen E. *Eisenhower.* 2 vols. New York: Simon & Schuster, 1983 and 1984.

———. *Eisenhower: Soldier and President.* Rev. ed. New York: Simon & Schuster, 1990.

———. *Halleck: Lincoln's Chief of Staff.* Baton Rouge: Louisiana State University Press, 1996.

———. *Nixon: The Triumph of a Politician, 1962–1972.* New York: Simon & Schuster, 1990.

Ambrosius, Lloyd E. *Wilsonianism: Woodrow Wilson and His Legacy in American Foreign Relations.* New York: Palgrave Macmillan, 2002.

Ammon, Harry. *James Monroe: The Quest for National Identity.* New York: McGraw-Hill, 1971.

Anderson, Robert. *An Artillery Officer in the Mexican War, 1846–7: Letters of Robert Anderson, Captain 3rd Artillery, U.S.A.* New York: G. P. Putnam's Sons, 1911.

Anderson, Thomas McArthur. *The Political Conspiracies Preceding the Rebellion; or, The True Stories of Sumter and Pickens.* New York: G. P. Putnam's Sons, 1882.

Andrew, Christopher. *For the President's Eyes Only: Secret Intelligence and the American Presidency from Washington to Bush.* New York: HarperPerennial, 1996.

Anthony, Carl Sferrazza. *Ida McKinley: The Turn-of-the-Century First Lady Through War, Assassination, and Secret Disability.* Kent, OH: Kent State University Press, 2013.

Armstrong, Thom M. *Politics, Diplomacy, and Intrigue in the Early Republic: The Cabinet Career of Robert Smith, 1801–1811.* Dubuque, IA: Kendall/Hunt Publishing, 1991.

Armstrong, William H. *Major McKinley: William McKinley and the Civil War.* Kent, OH: Kent State University Press, 2000.

Ashworth, John. *The Republic in Crisis, 1848–1861.* New York: Cambridge University Press, 2012.

Atkins, Jonathan M. *Parties, Politics, and the Sectional Conflict in Tennessee, 1832–1861.* Knoxville: University of Tennessee Press, 1997.

Atkinson, Rick. *The Day of Battle: The War in Sicily and Italy, 1943–1944.* New York: Henry Holt, 2007.

Auchinleck, Gilbert. *A History of the War Between Great Britain and the United States of America.* Toronto: Maclear & Company, 1855.

Auerbach, Jonathan. *Weapons of Democracy: Propaganda, Progressivism, and American Public Opinion.* Baltimore: John Hopkins University Press, 2015.

Ayers, Eben A. *Truman in the White House: The Diary of Eben A. Ayers.* Edited by Robert H. Ferrell. Columbia: University of Missouri Press, 1991.

Badeau, Adam. *Grant in Peace: From Appomattox to Mount McGregor. A Personal Memoir.* Hartford, CT: S. S. Scranton, 1887.

Baker, Jean H. *James Buchanan.* New York: Times Books, 2004.

———. *Mary Todd Lincoln: A Biography.* New York: W. W. Norton, 1987.

Baker, Peter. *Days of Fire: Bush and Cheney in the White House.* New York: Doubleday, 2013.

Baker, Ray Stannard. *Woodrow Wilson: Life and Letters.* 8 vols. Garden City, NY: Doubleday, Page, 1927–1939.

Barbour, Philip Norbourne. *Journals.* New York: G. P. Putnam's Sons, 1936.

Barker, Jacob. *Incidents in the Life of Jacob Barker, of New Orleans, Louisiana: With Historical Facts, His Financial Transactions with the Government and His Course on Important Political Questions, from 1800 to 1855.* Washington, DC, 1855.

Barnard, Ellsworth. *Wendell Willkie: Fighter for Freedom.* Marquette: Northern Michigan University Press, 1966.

Barron, David J. *Waging War: The Clash Between Presidents and Congress, 1776 to ISIS.* New York: Simon & Schuster, 2016.

Barton, William E. *The Life of Abraham Lincoln.* 2 vols. Indianapolis: Bobbs-Merrill, 1925.

———. *The Soul of Abraham Lincoln.* New York: George H. Doran, 1920.

Bates, Edward. *The Diary of Edward Bates, 1859–1866.* Edited by Howard K. Beale. Washington, DC: US Government Printing Office, 1933.

Bauer, K. Jack. *The Mexican War, 1846–1848.* New York: Macmillan, 1974.

———. *Zachary Taylor: Soldier, Planter, Statesman of the Old Southwest.* Baton Rouge: Louisiana State University Press, 1985.

Beach, Edward L. *Scapegoats: A Defense of Kimmel and Short at Pearl Harbor.* Annapolis, MD: Naval Institute Press, 1995.

Beck, Henry Houghton. *Cuba's Fight for Freedom, and the War with Spain: A History of the Spanish Kingdom and the Latest and Fairest Colony.* Philadelphia: Globe Bible Publishing, 1898.

Beer, Thomas. *Hanna, Crane and the Mauve Decade.* New York: Alfred A. Knopf, 1941.

Beesly, Patrick. *Room 40: British Naval Intelligence, 1914–1918.* San Diego: Harcourt Brace Jovanovich, 1982.

Beisner, Robert L. *Dean Acheson: A Life in the Cold War.* Oxford: Oxford University Press, 2006.

Belknap, Michal R. *The Vinson Court: Justices, Rulings, and Legacy.* Santa Barbara, CA: ABC-CLIO, 2004.

Benton, Thomas Hart. *Thirty Years' View; or, A History of the Working of the American Government for Thirty Years from 1820 to 1850.* 2 vols. New York: D. Appleton, 1854–1856.

Berg, A. Scott. *Wilson*. New York: G. P. Putnam's Sons, 2013.

Bergeron, Paul H. *The Presidency of James K. Polk*. Lawrence: University Press of Kansas, 1987.

Berinsky, Adam J. *In Time of War: Understanding American Public Opinion from World War II to Iraq*. Chicago: University of Chicago Press, 2009.

Bernstein, Iver. *The New York City Draft Riots: Their Significance for American Society and Politics in the Age of the Civil War*. New York: Oxford University Press, 1991.

Beschloss, Michael. *The Conquerors: Roosevelt, Truman, and the Destruction of Hitler's Germany, 1941–1945*. New York: Simon & Schuster, 2002.

———. *The Crisis Years: Kennedy and Khrushchev, 1960–1963*. New York: HarperCollins, 1991.

———. *Kennedy and Roosevelt: The Uneasy Alliance*. New York: W. W. Norton, 1980.

———. *Mayday: Eisenhower, Khrushchev, and the U-2 Affair*. New York: Harper & Row, 1986.

———. *Presidential Courage: Brave Leaders and How They Changed America, 1789–1989*. New York: Simon & Schuster, 2007.

———. *Reaching for Glory: Lyndon Johnson's Secret White House Tapes, 1964–1965*. New York: Simon & Schuster, 2001.

———. *Taking Charge: The Johnson White House Tapes, 1963–1964*. New York: Simon & Schuster, 1997.

Beveridge, Albert J. *The Life of John Marshall*. 4 vols. Boston: Houghton Mifflin, 1919.

Bicknell, John. *America 1844: Religious Fervor, Westward Expansion, and the Presidential Election That Transformed the Nation*. Chicago: Chicago Review Press, 2015.

Billingsley, Andrew. *Yearning to Breathe Free: Robert Smalls of South Carolina and His Families*. Columbia: University of South Carolina Press, 2007.

Bird, Kai. *The Chairman: John J. McCloy & the Making of the American Establishment*. New York: Simon & Schuster, 1992.

———. *The Color of Truth: McGeorge Bundy and William Bundy, Brothers in Arms*. New York: Simon & Schuster, 1998.

Bishop, Chip. *The Lion and the Journalist: The Unlikely Friendship of Theodore Roosevelt and Joseph Bucklin Bishop*. Guilford, CT: Lyons Press, 2012.

Bishop, Joseph Bucklin. *Theodore Roosevelt and His Time Shown in His Own Letters*. Vol. 2. New York: Charles Scribner's Sons, 1920.

Blair, William A., and Karen Fisher Younger, eds. *Lincoln's Proclamation: Emancipation Reconsidered*. Chapel Hill: University of North Carolina Press, 2009.

Blomstedt, Larry. *Truman, Congress, and Korea: The Politics of America's First Unde-clared War.* Lexington: University Press of Kentucky, 2016.

Blow, Michael. *A Ship to Remember: The Maine and the Spanish-American War.* New York: William Morrow, 1992.

Blum, John Morton. *Roosevelt and Morgenthau.* Boston: Houghton Mifflin, 1970.

Blumenthal, Sidney. *The Political Life of Abraham Lincoln: A Self-Made Man, 1809–1849.* New York: Simon & Schuster, 2016.

———. *The Political Life of Abraham Lincoln: Wrestling with His Angel, 1849–1856.* New York: Simon & Schuster, 2016.

Boghardt, Thomas. *The Zimmermann Telegram: Intelligence, Diplomacy, and America's Entry into World War I.* Annapolis, MD: Naval Institute Press, 2012.

Boller, Paul F., Jr. *Presidential Wives.* New York: Oxford University Press, 1998.

Borch, Fred, and Daniel Martinez. *Kimmel, Short, and Pearl Harbor: The Final Report Revealed.* Annapolis, MD: Naval Institute Press, 2005.

Boritt, Gabor S. *The Gettysburg Gospel: The Lincoln Speech That Nobody Knows.* New York: Simon & Schuster, 2006.

Boritt, Gabor S., and Norman O. Forness, eds. *The Historian's Lincoln: Pseudohistory, Psychohistory, and History.* Urbana: University of Illinois Press, 1988.

Borneman, Walter R. *1812: The War That Forged a Nation.* New York: HarperCollins, 2004.

———. *Polk: The Man Who Transformed the Presidency and America.* New York: Random House, 2008.

Bostick, Douglas W. *The Union Is Dissolved! Charleston and Fort Sumter in the Civil War.* Charleston, SC: History Press, 2009.

Boyle, David. *Before Enigma: The Room 40 Codebreakers of the First World War.* N.p.: Real Press, 2016.

Bradford, James C., ed. *Admirals of the New Steel Navy: Makers of the American Naval Tradition, 1880–1930.* Annapolis, MD: Naval Institute Press, 2013.

———. *Crucible of Empire: The Spanish-American War & Its Aftermath.* Annapolis, MD: Naval Institute Press, 1993.

Bradlee, Benjamin C. *Conversations with Kennedy.* New York: W. W. Norton, 1975.

Branch, Taylor. *At Canaan's Edge: America in the King Years, 1965–68.* New York: Simon & Schuster, 2006.

Brands, H. W. *The Age of Gold: The California Gold Rush and the New American Dream.* New York: Doubleday, 2002.

——. *The General vs. the President: MacArthur and Truman at the Brink of Nuclear War*. New York: Doubleday, 2016.

——. *Lone Star Nation: How a Ragged Army of Volunteers Won the Battle for Texas Independence, and Changed America*. New York: Doubleday, 2004.

——. *The Man Who Saved the Union: Ulysses Grant in War and Peace*. New York: Doubleday, 2012.

——. *T.R.: The Last Romantic*. New York: Basic Books, 1997.

——. *Traitor to His Class: The Privileged Life and Radical Presidency of Franklin Delano Roosevelt*. New York: Doubleday, 2008.

——. *Woodrow Wilson*. New York: Times Books, 2003.

Brant, Irving. *James Madison*. 6 vols. Indianapolis: Bobbs-Merrill, 1941–1961.

Breyer, Stephen. *The Court and the World: American Law and the New Global Realities*. New York: Alfred A. Knopf, 2015.

Brockmann, R. John. *Commodore Robert F. Stockton: 1795–1866*. Amherst, NY: Cambria Press, 2009.

Brookhiser, Richard. *James Madison*. New York: Basic Books, 2013.

Brooks, Noah. *Lincoln Observed: Civil War Dispatches of Noah Brooks*. Edited by Michael Burlingame. Baltimore: Johns Hopkins University Press, 1998.

Brown, Charles H. *Agents of Manifest Destiny: The Lives and Times of the Filibusters*. Chapel Hill: University of North Carolina Press, 1980.

Browning, Orville Hickman. *The Diary of Orville Hickman Browning*. Vol. 1. Springfield: Illinois State Historical Library, 1925.

Buchanan, James. *The Works of James Buchanan: Comprising His Speeches, State Papers, and Private Correspondence*. 12 vols. Philadelphia: J. B. Lippincott, 1908–1911.

Budiansky, Stephen. *Perilous Fight: America's Intrepid War with Britain on the High Seas, 1812–1815*. New York: Alfred A. Knopf, 2010.

Buel, J. W. *Great Achievements of the Century: An All-Embracing History of War, Conquest, Exploration and Discovery, Recording in Graphic Narrative the Strange Experiences, Thrilling Adventures, and Great Achievements of the Most Famous Travelers*. Philadelphia: Peoples Publishing, 1898.

Buel, Richard, Jr. *America on the Brink: How the Political Struggle over the War of 1812 Almost Destroyed the Young Republic*. New York: Palgrave Macmillan, 2005.

Bulla, David W. *Lincoln's Censor: Milo Hascall and Freedom of the Press in Civil War Indiana*. West Lafayette, IN: Purdue University Press, 2008.

Bumgarner, John R. *Sarah Childress Polk: A Biography of the Remarkable First Lady*. Jefferson, NC: McFarland, 1997.

Bundy, McGeorge. *Danger and Survival: Choices About the Bomb in the First Fifty Years.* New York: Random House, 1988.

Burlingame, Michael. *Abraham Lincoln: A Life.* 2 vols. Baltimore: Johns Hopkins University Press, 2008.

———, ed. *At Lincoln's Side: John Hay's Civil War Correspondence and Selected Writings.* Carbondale: Southern Illinois Press, 2006.

———. *The Inner World of Abraham Lincoln.* Urbana: University of Illinois Press, 1994.

Burns, James MacGregor. *Roosevelt: The Lion and the Fox.* New York: Harcourt, Brace, 1956.

———. *Roosevelt: The Soldier of Freedom.* New York: Harcourt Brace Jovanovich, 1970.

———. *The Workshop of Democracy.* The American Experiment. Vol. 2. New York: Alfred A. Knopf, 1985.

Burns, James MacGregor, and Susan Dunn. *The Three Roosevelts: Patrician Leaders Who Transformed America.* New York: Grove Press, 2001.

Burstein, Andrew, and Nancy Isenberg. *Madison and Jefferson.* New York: Random House, 2010.

Burt, Robert A. *The Constitution in Conflict.* Cambridge, MA: Belknap Press of Harvard University Press, 1992.

Busby, Horace. *The Thirty-First of March: An Intimate Portrait of Lyndon Johnson's Final Days in Office.* New York: Farrar, Straus and Giroux, 2005.

Bush, George W. *Decision Points.* New York: Crown, 2010.

Byrnes, James F. *All in One Lifetime.* New York: Harper & Brothers, 1958.

Califano, Joseph A., Jr. *Governing America: An Insider's Report from the White House and the Cabinet.* New York: Simon & Schuster, 1981.

———. *The Triumph and Tragedy of Lyndon Johnson: The White House Years.* New York: Simon & Schuster, 1991.

Calore, Paul. *The Causes of the Civil War: The Political, Cultural, Economic, and Territorial Disputes Between North and South.* Jefferson, NC: McFarland, 2008.

Cannon, James. *Time and Chance: Gerald Ford's Appointment with History.* New York: HarperCollins, 1994.

Carlson, Elliot. *Joe Rochefort's War: The Odyssey of the Codebreaker Who Outwitted Yamamoto at Midway.* Annapolis, MD: Naval Institute Press, 2011.

Carnahan, Burrus M. *Act of Justice: Lincoln's Emancipation Proclamation and the Law of War.* Lexington: University Press of Kentucky, 2007.

Caro, Robert A. *The Years of Lyndon Johnson: Master of the Senate.* New York: Alfred A. Knopf, 2002.

————. *The Years of Lyndon Johnson: Means of Ascent.* New York: Alfred A. Knopf, 1991.

————. *The Years of Lyndon Johnson: The Passage of Power.* New York: Alfred A. Knopf, 2012.

————. *The Years of Lyndon Johnson: The Path to Power.* New York: Alfred A. Knopf, 1982.

Carpenter, F. B. *Six Months at the White House with Abraham Lincoln: The Story of a Picture.* New York: Hurd & Houghton, 1866.

Carroll, Andrew. *My Fellow Soldiers: General John Pershing and the Americans Who Helped Win the Great War.* New York: Penguin Press, 2017.

Carson, Thomas L. *Lincoln's Ethics.* New York: Cambridge University Press, 2015.

Caruso, A. Brooke. *The Mexican Spy Company: United States Covert Operations in Mexico, 1845–1848.* Jefferson, NC: McFarland, 1991.

Cary, Edward. *The Trip of the Steamer* Oceanus *to Fort Sumter and Charleston, S.C.* Brooklyn: "The Union," 1865.

Casey, Steven. *Cautious Crusade: Franklin D. Roosevelt, American Public Opinion, and the War Against Nazi Germany.* Oxford: Oxford University Press, 2001.

————. *Selling the Korean War: Propaganda, Politics, and Public Opinion in the United States, 1950–1953.* Oxford: Oxford University Press, 2008.

Chace, James. *Acheson: The Secretary of State Who Created the American World.* New York: Simon & Schuster, 1998.

Chadwick, French Ensor. *The Relations of the United States and Spain: The Spanish-American War.* Vol. 2. New York: Charles Scribner's Sons, 1911.

Chafee, Zechariah. *Freedom of Speech.* New York: Harcourt, Brace, 1920.

Chambers, William Nisbet. *Old Bullion Benton, Senator from the New West: Thomas Hart Benton, 1782–1858.* Boston: Little, Brown, 1956.

Chase, Lucien B. *History of the Polk Administration.* New York: G. P. Putnam, 1850.

Cheathem, Mark R. *Old Hickory's Nephew: The Political and Private Struggles of Andrew Jackson Donelson.* Baton Rouge: Louisiana State University Press, 2007.

Cheney, Lynne. *James Madison: A Life Reconsidered.* New York: Viking, 2014.

Chernow, Ron. *Grant.* New York: Penguin Press, 2017.

Chesnut, Mary Boykin. *Mary Chesnut's Civil War.* Edited by C. Vann Woodward. New Haven, CT: Yale University Press, 1981.

Chitwood, Oliver Perry. *John Tyler, Champion of the Old South.* New York: D. Appleton-Century, 1939.

Churchill, Winston. *The Crisis.* New York: Macmillan, 1901.

———. *The Second World War.* 6 vols. Boston: Houghton Mifflin, 1948–1953.

Cirillo, Vincent J. *Bullets and Bacilli: The Spanish-American War and Military Medicine.* New Brunswick, NJ: Rutgers University Press, 2004.

Clarence, C. W. *A Biographical Sketch of the Life of Ralph Farnham, of Acton, Maine; Now in the One Hundred and Fifth Year of His Age, and the Sole Survivor of the Glorious Battle of Bunker Hill.* Boston, 1860.

Clarfield, Gerard H. *Timothy Pickering and the American Republic.* Pittsburgh: University of Pittsburgh Press, 1980.

Clarke, Thurston. *Pearl Harbor Ghosts: A Journey to Hawaii, Then and Now.* New York: William Morrow, 1991.

Clary, David A. *Eagles and Empire: The United States, Mexico, and the Struggle for a Continent.* New York: Bantam, 2009.

Claxton, Jimmie Lou Sparkman. *88 Years with Sarah Polk.* New York: Vantage Press, 1972.

Cleaves, Freeman. *Old Tippecanoe: William Henry Harrison and His Time.* 1939. Reprint, Port Washington, NY: Kennikat Press, 1969.

Clements, Kendrick A. *The Presidency of Woodrow Wilson.* Lawrence: University Press of Kansas, 1992.

Clifford, Clark M., with Richard C. Holbrooke. *Counsel to the President: A Memoir.* New York: Random House, 1991.

Clinton, Catherine. *Mrs. Lincoln: A Life.* New York: HarperCollins, 2009.

Cogliano, Francis D. *Emperor of Liberty: Thomas Jefferson's Foreign Policy.* New Haven, CT: Yale University Press, 2014.

Cohen, Michael J. *Churchill and the Jews.* Oxford: Routledge, 2013.

Cole, Wayne S. *Roosevelt and the Isolationists, 1932–45.* Lincoln: University of Nebraska Press, 1983.

Collier, Peter, and David Horowitz. *The Roosevelts: An American Saga.* New York: Simon & Schuster, 1995.

Collins, Gail. *William Henry Harrison.* New York: Times Books, 2012.

Colman, Edna M. *White House Gossip, from Andrew Johnson to Calvin Coolidge.* Garden City, NY: Doubleday, Page, 1927.

Connally, John B. *In History's Shadow: An American Odyssey.* New York: Hyperion, 1993.

Conyne, G. R. *Woodrow Wilson: British Perspectives, 1912–21.* New York: St. Martin's Press, 1992.

Cook, Adrian. *The Armies of the Streets: The New York City Draft Riots of 1863.* Lexington: University Press of Kentucky, 2015.

Cook, Blanche Wiesen. *Eleanor Roosevelt.* 3 vols. New York: Viking, 1992–2016.

Cook, Jane Hampton. *The Burning of the White House: James and Dolley Madison and the War of 1812.* Washington, DC: Regnery, 2016.

Cooling, Benjamin Franklin, III. *Jubal Early: Robert E. Lee's Bad Old Man.* Lanham, MD: Rowman & Littlefield, 2014.

Cooper, Charles G., with Richard E. Goodspeed. *Cheers and Tears: A Marine's Story of Combat in Peace and War.* Victoria, BC: Trafford, 2002.

Cooper, John Milton, Jr. *Breaking the Heart of the World: Woodrow Wilson and the Fight for the League of Nations.* Cambridge: Cambridge University Press, 2001.

———. *The Warrior and the Priest: Woodrow Wilson and Theodore Roosevelt.* Cambridge, MA: Belknap Press of Harvard University Press, 1983.

———. *Woodrow Wilson: A Biography.* New York: Alfred A. Knopf, 2009.

Cooper, William J., Jr. *Jefferson Davis, American.* New York: Alfred A. Knopf, 2000.

Corry, John A. *1898: Prelude to a Century.* New York: J. A. Corry, 1998.

Côté, Richard N. *Strength and Honor: The Life of Dolley Madison.* Mt. Pleasant, SC: Corinthian Books, 2005.

Crapol, Edward P. *John Tyler: The Accidental President.* Chapel Hill: University of North Carolina Press, 2006.

Crawford, Samuel Wylie. *The Genesis of the Civil War: The Story of Sumter, 1860–1861.* New York: C. L. Webster, 1887.

Creel, George. *How We Advertised America: The First Telling of the Amazing Story of the Committee on Public Information That Carried the Gospel of Americanism to Every Corner of the Globe.* New York: Harper & Brothers, 1920.

Crispell, Kenneth R., and Carlos F. Gomez. *Hidden Illness in the White House.* Durham, NC: Duke University Press, 1988.

Crocker, H. W. *Don't Tread on Me: A 400-Year History of America at War, from Indian Fighting to Terrorist Hunting.* New York: Crown, 2006.

Crofts, Daniel W. *Reluctant Confederates: Upper South Unionists in the Secession Crisis.* Chapel Hill: University of North Carolina Press, 1989.

Cumings, Bruce. *The Korean War: A History.* New York: Modern Library, 2010.

Curtis, George Ticknor. *Life of James Buchanan, Fifteenth President of the United States.* 2 vols. New York: Harper & Brothers, 1883.

Dall, Curtis B. *My Exploited Father-in-Law.* New York: Christian Crusade, 1967.

Dallek, Robert. *Flawed Giant: Lyndon Johnson and His Times, 1961–1973.* New York: Oxford University Press, 1998.

———. *Franklin D. Roosevelt: A Political Life.* New York: Viking, 2017.

———. *Franklin D. Roosevelt and American Foreign Policy, 1932–1945.* New York: Oxford University Press, 1979.

———. *Lone Star Rising: Lyndon Johnson and His Times, 1908–1960.* New York: Oxford University Press, 1991.

Dalton, Kathleen. *Theodore Roosevelt: A Strenuous Life.* New York: Alfred A. Knopf, 2002.

Daniels, Jonathan. *The Man of Independence.* Philadelphia: Lippincott, 1950.

Daniels, Josephus. *Roosevelt and Daniels: A Friendship in Politics.* Edited by Carroll Kilpatrick. Chapel Hill: University of North Carolina Press, 1952.

———. *The Wilson Era: Years of Peace, 1910–1917.* Chapel Hill: University of North Carolina Press, 1944.

Daughan, George C. *1812: The Navy's War.* New York: Basic Books, 2011.

———. *If By Sea: The Forging of the American Navy—from the American Revolution to the War of 1812.* New York: Basic Books, 2008.

Davis, Jefferson. *The Papers of Jefferson Davis.* Edited by Lynda Lasswell Crist and others. 14 vols. Baton Rouge: Louisiana State University Press, 1971–2015.

Davis, Kenneth S. *FDR: The Beckoning of Destiny, 1882–1928.* New York: G. P. Putnam's Sons, 1972.

———. *FDR: Into the Storm, 1937–1940.* New York: Random House, 1993.

———. *FDR: The War President, 1940–1943.* New York: Random House, 2000.

Davis, Michael A. *Politics as Usual: Thomas Dewey, Franklin Roosevelt, and the Wartime Presidential Campaign of 1944.* DeKalb: Northern Illinois University Press, 2014.

Davis, Sheldon E., and Clarence E. McClure. *Our Government: A Textbook of Civics.* Chicago: Laidlaw Brothers, 1922.

Davis, Stephen. *Jim Morrison: Life, Death, Legend.* New York: Gotham Books, 2004.

Davis, William C. *Jefferson Davis: The Man and His Hour.* 1991. Reprint, Baton Rouge: Louisiana State University Press, 1996.

De Kay, James Tertius. *A Rage for Glory: The Life of Commodore Stephen Decatur, USN.* New York: Free Press, 2004.

———. *Roosevelt's Navy: The Education of a Warrior President, 1882–1920.* New York: Pegasus Books, 2012.

Delaplaine, Edward S. *Francis Scott Key: Life and Times.* Berryville, VA: Hess Publications, 2005.

Detzer, David. *Allegiance: Fort Sumter, Charleston, and the Beginning of the Civil War.* New York: Harcourt, 2001.

Dickon, Chris. *The Enduring Journey of the U.S.S. Chesapeake: Navigating the Common History of Three Nations.* Stroud, UK: History Press, 2009.

Divine, Robert A. *Foreign Policy and U.S. Presidential Elections, 1940–1948.* New York: New Viewpoints, 1974.

Doenecke, Justus D. *Nothing Less Than War: A New History of America's Entry into World War I.* Lexington: University Press of Kentucky, 2011.

Doenecke, Justus D., and Mark A. Stoler. *Debating Franklin D. Roosevelt's Foreign Policies, 1933–1945.* Lanham, MD: Rowman & Littlefield, 2005.

Donald, David Herbert. *Lincoln.* New York: Simon & Schuster, 1995.

Donovan, Robert J. *Conflict and Crisis: The Presidency of Harry S. Truman, 1945–1948.* New York: W. W. Norton, 1977.

———. *Tumultuous Years: The Presidency of Harry S. Truman, 1949–1953.* New York: W. W. Norton, 1982.

Downing, Taylor. *Secret Warriors: Key Scientists, Code Breakers and Propagandists of the Great War.* London: Little, Brown, 2014.

Draper, John William. *History of the American Civil War.* Vol. 1. New York: Harper, 1867.

Duffield, Isabel McKenna. *Washington in the 90's: California Eyes Dazzled by the Brilliant Society of the Capitol [sic].* San Francisco: Press of Overland Monthly, 1929.

Duffy, Bernard K., and Ronald H. Carpenter. *Douglas MacArthur: Warrior as Wordsmith.* Great American Orators, no. 24. Westport, CT: Greenwood Press, 1997.

Dunn, Susan. *1940: FDR, Willkie, Lindbergh, Hitler—the Election Amid the Storm.* New Haven, CT: Yale University Press, 2013.

Dusinberre, William. *Slavemaster President: The Double Career of James Polk.* New York: Oxford University Press, 2003.

Dye, Ira. *The Fatal Cruise of the* Argus: *Two Captains in the War of 1812.* Annapolis, MD: Naval Institute Press, 1994.

Eckert, Allan W. *A Sorrow in Our Heart: The Life of Tecumseh.* New York: Bantam, 1992.

Edling, Max M. *A Hercules in the Cradle: War, Money, and the American State, 1783–1867.* Chicago: University of Chicago Press, 2014.

Edmunds, R. David. *Tecumseh and the Quest for Indian Leadership.* Boston: Little, Brown, 1984.

Edwards, George C., III, and Desmond S. King, eds. *The Polarized Presidency of George W. Bush*. New York: Oxford University Press, 2007.

Eicher, George C. *The Longest Night: A Military History of the Civil War*. New York: Simon & Schuster, 2001.

Eisenhower, David, with Julie Nixon Eisenhower. *Going Home to Glory: A Memoir of Life with Dwight D. Eisenhower, 1961–1969*. New York: Simon & Schuster, 2010.

Eisenhower, John S. D. *Agent of Destiny: The Life and Times of General Winfield Scott*. New York: Free Press, 1997.

————. *Intervention! The United States and the Mexican Revolution, 1913–1917*. New York: W. W. Norton, 1993.

————. *So Far from God: The U.S. War with Mexico, 1846–1848*. New York: Random House, 1989.

Eisenhower, John S. D., with Joanne Thompson Eisenhower. *Yanks: The Epic Story of the American Army in World War I*. New York: Simon & Schuster, 2002.

Elliott, Margaret Axson. *My Aunt Louisa and Woodrow Wilson*. Chapel Hill: University of North Carolina Press, 1944.

Ellis, James H. *A Ruinous and Unhappy War: New England and the War of 1812*. New York: Algora, 2009.

Elmore, A. E. *Lincoln's Gettysburg Address: Echoes of the Bible and Book of Common Prayer*. Carbondale: Southern Illinois University Press, 2009.

Elsey, George McKee. *An Unplanned Life: A Memoir*. Columbia: University of Missouri Press, 2005.

Engle, Stephen Douglas. *Don Carlos Buell: Most Promising of All*. Civil War America. Chapel Hill: University of North Carolina Press, 1999.

————. *Gathering to Save a Nation: Lincoln and the Union's War Governors*. Civil War America. Chapel Hill: University of North Carolina Press, 2016.

Epstein, Daniel Mark. *The Lincolns: Portrait of a Marriage*. New York: Ballantine Books, 2008.

Escott, Paul D. *Lincoln's Dilemma: Blair, Sumner, and the Republican Struggle over Racism and Equality in the Civil War Era*. Charlottesville: University of Virginia Press, 2014.

————. *"What Shall We Do with the Negro?": Lincoln, White Racism, and Civil War America*. Charlottesville: University of Virginia Press, 2009.

Evans, Hugh E. *The Hidden Campaign: FDR's Health and the 1944 Election*. Armonk, NY: M. E. Sharpe, 2002.

Farber, Daniel A. *Lincoln's Constitution*. Chicago: University of Chicago Press, 2003.

Farrand, Max, ed. *The Records of the Federal Convention of 1787.* 4 vols. New Haven, CT: Yale University Press, 1937.

Farrell, John A. *Richard Nixon: The Life.* New York: Doubleday, 2017.

Farwell, Byron. *Over There: The United States in the Great War, 1917–1918.* New York: W. W. Norton, 2000.

Fehrenbach, T. R. *Lone Star: A History of Texas and the Texans.* New York: Macmillan, 1968.

Fehrenbacher, Don E., and Virginia Fehrenbacher. *Recollected Words of Abraham Lincoln.* Stanford: Stanford University Press, 1956.

Feldman, Noah. *Scorpions: The Battles and Triumphs of FDR's Great Supreme Court Justices.* New York: Twelve, 2010.

Ferguson, Niall. *Kissinger: The Idealist. Vol. 1, 1923–1968.* New York: Penguin Books, 2015.

Ferrell, Robert H. *The Dying President: Franklin D. Roosevelt, 1944–1945.* Columbia: University of Missouri Press, 1998.

———. *Harry S. Truman: A Life.* Columbia: University of Missouri Press, 1994.

———. *Ill-Advised: Presidential Health and Public Trust.* Columbia: University of Missouri Press, 1992.

———. *Woodrow Wilson and World War I, 1917–1921.* New York: Harper & Row, 1985.

Ferris, Marc. *Star-Spangled Banner: The Unlikely Story of America's National Anthem.* Baltimore: Johns Hopkins University Press, 2014.

Fisher, Louis. *The Law of the Executive Branch: Presidential Power.* Oxford: Oxford University Press, 2014.

———. *Presidential War Power.* Lawrence: University Press of Kansas, 1995.

Fleming, Thomas. *The Illusion of Victory: America in World War I.* New York: Basic Books, 2004.

———. *The New Dealers' War: Franklin D. Roosevelt and the War Within World War II.* New York: Basic Books, 2001.

Flood, Charles Bracelen. *1864: Lincoln at the Gates of History.* New York: Simon & Schuster, 2009.

Folsom, Burton W., Jr. *New Deal or Raw Deal? How FDR's Economic Legacy Has Damaged America.* New York: Threshold Editions, 2008.

Foner, Eric. *The Fiery Trial: Abraham Lincoln and American Slavery.* New York: W. W. Norton, 2010.

Ford, Gerald R. *A Time to Heal: The Autobiography of Gerald R. Ford.* New York: Harper & Row, 1979.

Ford, Lynne E. *Encyclopedia of Women and American Politics.* New York: Facts on File, 2008.

Foreign Relations of the United States. Vol. 3, Vietnam, June–December 1965. Washington, DC: US Government Printing Office, 1996.

Foreign Relations of the United States. Vol. 6, Vietnam, January–August 1968. Washington, DC: US Government Printing Office, 2002.

Foreign Relations of the United States. Vol. 7, Vietnam, September 1968–January 1969. Washington, DC: US Government Printing Office, 2003.

Fornieri, Joseph R. *The Language of Liberty: The Political Speeches and Writings of Abraham Lincoln.* Washington, DC: Regnery, 2009.

Foster, Augustus John. *Jeffersonian America.* San Marino, CA: Huntington Library, 1954.

Fowler, Robert Ludlow. *Our Predecessors and Their Descendants.* Privately printed, 1888.

Franklin, Benjamin. *Poor Richard's Almanack.* New York: Century, 1899.

Freeberg, Ernest. *Democracy's Prisoner: Eugene V. Debs, the Great War, and the Right to Dissent.* Cambridge, MA: Harvard University Press, 2008.

Freehling, William W. *The Road to Disunion. Vol. 2, Secessionists Triumphant, 1854–1861.* New York: Oxford University Press, 2007.

Freidel, Frank Burt. *Franklin D. Roosevelt. Vol. 1, The Apprenticeship.* Boston: Little, Brown, 1952.

Fromkin, David. *In the Time of the Americans: FDR, Truman, Eisenhower, Marshall, MacArthur—the Generation That Changed America's Role in the World.* New York: Alfred A. Knopf, 1995.

Furgurson, Ernest B. *Freedom Rising: Washington in the Civil War.* New York: Alfred A. Knopf, 2004.

Gaddis, John Lewis. *The Cold War: A New History.* New York: Penguin Press, 2005.

———. *We Now Know: Rethinking Cold War History.* New York: Oxford University Press, 1997.

Gallagher, Gary W. *The Union War.* Cambridge, MA: Harvard University Press, 2011.

Gallup, George H. *The Gallup Poll: Public Opinion, 1935–1971.* 3 vols. New York: Random House, 1972.

Gambrell, Herbert Pickens. *Anson Jones: The Last President of Texas.* Garden City, NY: Doubleday, 1948.

Gannon, Michael. *Pearl Harbor Betrayed: The True Story of a Man and a Nation Under Attack.* New York: Henry Holt, 2001.

Garnett, Richard. *Masterpieces of Oratory. Vols. 1–3, Orations of American Orators.* Rev. ed. New York: Fifth Avenue Press, 1900.

Gibbons, William Conrad. *The U.S. Government and the Vietnam War: Executive and Legislative Roles and Relationships. Part 2, 1961–1964.* Princeton, NJ: Princeton University Press, 1986.

———. *The U.S. Government and the Vietnam War: Executive and Legislative Roles and Relationships. Part 3, January–July 1965.* Princeton, NJ: Princeton University Press, 1989.

———. *The U.S. Government and the Vietnam War: Executive and Legislative Roles and Relationships. Part 4, July 1965–January 1968.* Princeton, NJ: Princeton University Press, 1995.

Gillon, Steven M. *Pearl Harbor: FDR Leads the Nation into War.* New York: Basic Books, 2011.

Goldstein, Gordon M. *Lessons in Disaster: McGeorge Bundy and the Path to War in Vietnam.* New York: Times Books, 2008.

Good, Timothy S., ed. *We Saw Lincoln Shot: One Hundred Eyewitness Accounts.* Jackson: University Press of Mississippi, 1995.

Goode, G. Brown. *Virginia Cousins: A Study of the Ancestry and Posterity of John Goode of Whitby.* Richmond, VA: J. W. Randolph & English, 1887.

Goodheart, Adam. *1861: The Civil War Awakening.* New York: Alfred A. Knopf, 2011.

Goodrich, Thomas, and Debra Goodrich. *The Day Dixie Died: Southern Occupation, 1865–1866.* Mechanicsburg, PA: Stackpole Books, 2001.

Goodwin, Doris Kearns. *No Ordinary Time: Franklin and Eleanor Roosevelt; The Home Front in World War II.* New York: Simon & Schuster, 1994.

———. *Team of Rivals: The Political Genius of Abraham Lincoln.* New York: Simon & Schuster, 2005.

Goodwin, Richard N. *Remembering America: A Voice from the Sixties.* Boston: Little, Brown, 1988.

Gosnell, Harold F. *Truman's Crises: A Political Biography of Harry S. Truman.* Westport, CT: Greenwood Press, 1980.

Gould, Lewis L., ed. *American First Ladies: Their Lives and Their Legacy.* New York: Routledge, 2014.

———. *The Most Exclusive Club: A History of the Modern United States Senate.* New York: Basic Books, 2008.

———. *The Presidency of William McKinley.* American Presidency Series. Lawrence: Regents Press of Kansas, 1980.

———. *The Republicans: A History of the Grand Old Party.* Oxford: Oxford University Press, 2014.

———. *The Spanish-American War and President McKinley.* Lawrence: University Press of Kansas, 1982.

Green, Michael S. *Freedom, Union, and Power: Lincoln and His Party During the Civil War.* The North's Civil War, no. 27. New York: Fordham University Press, 2004.

Greenberg, Amy S. *A Wicked War: Polk, Clay, Lincoln, and the 1846 Invasion of Mexico.* New York: Alfred A. Knopf, 2012.

Greenhalgh, Elizabeth. *Foch in Command: The Forging of a First World War General.* Cambridge: Cambridge University Press, 2011.

Gregory, Jim. *World War II Arroyo Grande.* Mt. Pleasant, SC: Arcadia Publishing, 2016.

Guelzo, Allen C. *Abraham Lincoln as a Man of Ideas.* Carbondale: Southern Illinois University Press, 2009.

———. *Abraham Lincoln: Redeemer President.* Grand Rapids, MI: W. B. Eerdmans, 1999.

———. *Fateful Lightning: A New History of the Civil War and Reconstruction.* Oxford: Oxford University Press, 2012.

———. *Lincoln's Emancipation Proclamation: The End of Slavery in America.* New York: Simon & Schuster, 2004.

Guttridge, Leonard F. *Our Country, Right or Wrong: The Life of Stephen Decatur, the U.S. Navy's Most Illustrious Commander.* New York: Forge, 2006.

Guttridge, Leonard F., and Jay D. Smith. *The Commodores.* New York: Harper & Row, 1969.

Hagan, Kenneth J. *The People's Navy: The Making of American Sea Power.* New York: Simon & Schuster, 1992.

Haig, Alexander Meigs, with Charles McCarry. *Inner Circles: How America Changed the World.* New York: Warner Books, 1992.

Halberstam, David. *The Best and the Brightest.* New York: Random House, 1972.

———. *The Coldest Winter: America and the Korean War.* New York: Hyperion, 2007.

Haldeman, H. R. *The Haldeman Diaries: Inside the Nixon White House.* New York: G. P. Putnam's Sons, 1994.

Haley, James L. *Passionate Nation: The Epic History of Texas.* Texas Authors. New York: Free Press, 2006.

Hall, Simon. *Peace and Freedom: The Civil Rights and Antiwar Movements in the 1960s.* Philadelphia: University of Pennsylvania Press, 2011.

Hallett, Brien. *The Lost Art of Declaring War.* Urbana: University of Illinois Press, 1998.

Hamby, Alonzo L. *Man of Destiny: FDR and the Making of the American Century.* New York: Basic Books, 2015.

————. *Man of the People: A Life of Harry S. Truman.* New York: Oxford University Press, 1995.

Hamilton, Nigel. *The Mantle of Command: FDR at War, 1941–1942.* Boston: Houghton Mifflin Harcourt, 2014.

Harbaugh, William Henry. *Power and Responsibility: The Life and Times of Theodore Roosevelt.* New York: Farrar, Straus & Cudahy, 1961.

Harris, Susan K. *God's Arbiters: Americans and the Philippines, 1898–1902.* Oxford: Oxford University Press, 2011.

Harris, William C. *Lincoln and Congress.* Carbondale: Southern Illinois University Press, 2017.

————. *Lincoln and the Union Governors.* Carbondale: Southern Illinois University Press, 2013.

————. *Lincoln's Last Months.* Cambridge, MA: Belknap Press of Harvard University Press, 2004.

Hassett, William D. *Off the Record with F.D.R., 1942–1945.* New Brunswick, NJ: Rutgers University Press, 1958.

Hastings, Max. *The Korean War.* New York: Simon & Schuster, 1987.

Haynes, Stan M. *President-Making in the Gilded Age: The Nominating Conventions of 1876–1900.* Jefferson, NC: McFarland, 2016.

Hazelgrove, William Elliott. *Madam President: The Secret Presidency of Edith Wilson.* Washington, DC: Regnery, 2016.

Hazelton, John Hampden. *The Declaration of Independence: Its History.* New York: Dodd, Mead, 1905.

Heckscher, August. *Woodrow Wilson.* New York: Charles Scribner's Sons, 1991.

Heidler, David S., and Jeanne T. Heidler. *Henry Clay: The Essential American.* New York: Random House, 2010.

Helsing, Jeffrey W. *Johnson's War / Johnson's Great Society: The Guns and Butter Trap.* Westport, CT: Praeger, 2000.

Hendrickson, Kenneth E., Jr. *The Spanish-American War.* Greenwood Guides to Historic Events, 1500–1900. Westport, CT: Greenwood Press, 2003.

Hendrix, Henry J. *Theodore Roosevelt's Naval Diplomacy: The U.S. Navy and the Birth of the American Century.* Annapolis, MD: Naval Institute Press, 2009.

Henry, Robert Selph. *The Story of the Mexican War.* New York: F. Ungar, 1961.

Herman, Arthur. *Douglas MacArthur: American Warrior.* New York: Random House, 2016.

Hickey, Donald R. *The War of 1812: A Forgotten Conflict.* Urbana: University of Illinois Press, 1989.

Hill, Norman Newell, Jr. *History of Knox County, Ohio, Its Past and Present.* Mt. Vernon, OH: A. A. Graham, 1881.

Hodgson, Godfrey. *Woodrow Wilson's Right Hand: The Life of Colonel Edward M. House.* New Haven, CT: Yale University Press, 2006.

Hogan, J. Michael. *Woodrow Wilson's Western Tour: Rhetoric, Public Opinion, and the League of Nations.* College Station: Texas A&M University Press, 2006.

Holloway, Laura Carter. *The Ladies of the White House.* New York: United States Publishing Company, 1870.

Holmes, David L. *The Faiths of the Postwar Presidents: From Truman to Obama.* Athens: University of Georgia Press, 2012.

Holt, Michael F. *The Rise and Fall of the American Whig Party: Jacksonian Politics and the Onset of the Civil War.* New York: Oxford University Press, 1999.

Holzer, Harold. *Emancipating Lincoln: The Proclamation in Text, Context, and Memory.* Cambridge, MA: Harvard University Press, 2012.

———. *Lincoln and the Power of the Press: The War for Public Opinion.* New York: Simon & Schuster, 2014.

———. *Lincoln President-Elect: Abraham Lincoln and the Great Secession, Winter 1860–1861.* New York: Simon & Schuster, 2008.

Holzer, Harold, Edna Greene Medford, and Frank J. Williams. *The Emancipation Proclamation.* Baton Rouge: Louisiana State University Press, 2006.

Hoogenboom, Ari. *Gustavus Vasa Fox of the Union Navy: A Biography.* Baltimore: Johns Hopkins University Press, 2008.

Hoopes, Townsend, and Douglas Brinkley. *FDR and the Creation of the U.N.* New Haven, CT: Yale University Press, 1997.

Hopkins, Jerry, and Daniel Sugerman. *No One Here Gets Out Alive.* New York: Warner Books, 1980.

Hopkins, William B. *The Pacific War: The Strategy, Politics, and Players That Won the War.* Voyageur Press, 2008.

Hormats, Robert D. *The Price of Liberty: Paying for America's Wars.* New York: Times Books, 2007.

Horner, William T. *Ohio's Kingmaker: Mark Hanna, Man and Myth*. Athens: Ohio University Press, 2010.

Horsman, Reginald. *The Causes of the War of 1812*. Philadelphia: University of Pennsylvania Press, 1962.

———. *Expansion and American Indian Policy, 1783–1812*. East Lansing: Michigan State University Press, 1967.

Hough, Richard. *The Greatest Crusade: Roosevelt, Churchill and the Naval Wars*. New York: William Morrow, 1986.

Howard, Hugh. *Mr. and Mrs. Madison's War: America's First Couple and the Second War of Independence*. New York: Bloomsbury Press, 2012.

Howe, Daniel Walker. *What Hath God Wrought: The Transformation of America, 1815–1848*. The Oxford History of the United States. New York: Oxford University Press, 2007.

Hsieh, Wayne Wei-siang. *West Pointers and the Civil War: The Old Army in War and Peace*. Civil War America. Chapel Hill: University of North Carolina Press, 2009.

Hughes, Ken. *Chasing Shadows: The Nixon Tapes, the Chennault Affair, and the Origins of Watergate*. Charlottesville: University of Virginia Press, 2014.

Hughes, Nathaniel Cheairs, Jr. *General William J. Hardee: Old Reliable*. Baton Rouge: Louisiana State University Press, 1965.

Hughes, William W. *Archibald Yell*. Fayetteville: University of Arkansas Press, 1988.

Humphrey, Hubert H. *The Education of a Public Man: My Life and Politics*. Garden City, NY: Doubleday, 1976.

Hunt, Gaillard. *The Life of James Madison*. New York: Doubleday, Page, 1902.

Ingersoll, Charles J. *Historical Sketch of the Second War Between the United States of America and Great Britain*. Philadelphia: Lea & Blanchard, 1849.

Irons, Peter. *The Courage of Their Convictions*. New York: Free Press, 1988.

———. *War Powers: How the Imperial Presidency Hijacked the Constitution*. American Empire Project. New York: Metropolitan Books, 2005.

Irving, Joseph. *The Annals of Our Time: 1837 to 1868*. London: Macmillan, 1872.

Irving, Washington. *The Works of Washington Irving*. Vol. 8. New York: G. P. Putnam, 1859.

Isaacson, Walter, and Evan Thomas. *The Wise Men: Six Friends and the World They Made: Acheson, Bohlen, Harriman, Kennan, Lovett, McCloy*. New York: Simon & Schuster, 1986.

James, William. *The Naval History of Great Britain: From the Declaration of War by France in 1793 to the Accession of George IV*. 6 vols. London: R. Bentley, 1837.

Janeway, Michael. *The Fall of the House of Roosevelt: Brokers of Ideas and Power from FDR to LBJ.* New York: Columbia University Press, 2004.

Jay, William. *A Review of the Causes and Consequences of the Mexican War.* Boston: B. B. Mussey; Philadelphia: U. Hunt, 1849.

Jenkins, John S. *History of the War Between the United States and Mexico.* Auburn, NY: Derby, Miller, 1849.

Jennings, Paul. *A Colored Man's Reminiscences of James Madison.* Brooklyn: G. C. Beadle, 1865.

Johannsen, Robert W. *To the Halls of the Montezumas: The Mexican War in the American Imagination.* New York: Oxford University Press, 1985.

Johnson, Lyndon B. *The Vantage Point: Perspectives of the Presidency, 1963–1969.* New York: Holt, Rinehart & Winston, 1971.

Jones, Ernest Charles. *Notes to the People.* Vol. 1. London: J. Pavey, 1851.

Jones, Howard. *Crucible of Power: A History of American Foreign Relations to 1913.* Lanham, MD: Rowman & Littlefield, 2009.

Jortner, Adam. *The Gods of Prophetstown: The Battle of Tippecanoe and the Holy War for the American Frontier.* Oxford: Oxford University Press, 2012.

Kaiser, David. *American Tragedy: Kennedy, Johnson, and the Origins of the Vietnam War.* Cambridge, MA: Belknap Press of Harvard University Press, 2000.

———. *No End Save Victory: How FDR Led the Nation into War.* New York: Basic Books, 2014.

Kalman, Laura. *Abe Fortas: A Biography.* New Haven, CT: Yale University Press, 1990.

Kaplan, Amy. *The Anarchy of Empire in the Making of U.S. Culture.* Convergences: Inventories of the Present. Cambridge, MA: Harvard University Press, 2005.

Kastenberg, Joshua E., and Eric Merriam. *In a Time of Total War: The Federal Judiciary and the National Defense, 1940–1954.* New York: Routledge, 2016.

Katzenbach, Nicholas deB. *Some of It Was Fun: Working with RFK and LBJ.* New York: W. W. Norton, 2008.

Kazin, Michael. *A Godly Hero: The Life of William Jennings Bryan.* New York: Alfred A. Knopf, 2006.

Keckley, Elizabeth. *Behind the Scenes; or, Thirty Years a Slave and Four Years in the White House.* New York: G. W. Carlton, 1868.

Keene, Jennifer D. *Doughboys, the Great War, and the Remaking of America.* Baltimore: Johns Hopkins University Press, 2003.

Kennedy, David M. *Freedom from Fear: The American People in Depression and*

War, 1929–1945. The Oxford History of the United States, vol. 9. New York: Oxford University Press, 1999.

———. *Over Here: The First World War and American Society.* New York: Oxford University Press, 1980.

Kennedy, Robert F. *Thirteen Days: A Memoir of the Cuban Missile Crisis.* New York: W. W. Norton, 1969.

Kersten, Andrew E. *A. Philip Randolph: A Life in the Vanguard.* Lanham, MD: Rowman & Littlefield, 2007.

Ketcham, Ralph. *James Madison: A Biography.* Charlottesville: University of Virginia Press, 1990.

———. *The Madisons at Montpelier: Reflections on the Founding Couple.* Charlottesville: University of Virginia Press, 2009.

Keyes, E. D. *Fifty Years' Observations of Men and Events, Civil and Military.* New York: Charles Scribner's Sons, 1884.

Kimmel, Husband Edward. *Admiral Kimmel's Story.* Chicago: Henry Regnery, 1955.

King, Horatio. *Turning on the Light: A Dispassionate Survey of President Buchanan's Administration.* Philadelphia: J. B. Lippincott, 1895.

Kirk, Elise K. *Musical Highlights from the White House.* Malabar, FL: Krieger Publishing, 1992.

Kissinger, Henry. *White House Years.* Boston: Little, Brown, 1979.

———. *Years of Renewal.* New York: Simon & Schuster, 1999.

———. *Years of Upheaval.* Boston: Little, Brown, 1982.

Klein, Maury. *Days of Defiance: Sumter, Secession, and the Coming of the Civil War.* New York: Vintage Books, 1999.

Klein, Philip Shriver. *President James Buchanan: A Biography.* University Park: Pennsylvania State University Press, 1962.

Klement, Frank L. *The Limits of Dissent: Clement L. Vallandigham and the Civil War.* Lexington: University Press of Kentucky, 1970.

Koenig, Louis W. *Bryan: A Political Biography of William Jennings Bryan.* New York: G. P. Putnam's Sons, 1971.

Kotz, Nick. *Judgment Days: Lyndon Baines Johnson, Martin Luther King, Jr., and the Laws That Changed America.* Boston: Houghton Mifflin, 2005.

Kramer, Paul A. *The Blood of Government: Race, Empire, the United States, and the Philippines.* Chapel Hill: University of North Carolina Press, 2006.

Labaree, Benjamin. *America and the Sea: A Maritime History.* Mystic, CT: Mystic Seaport, 1998.

LaFeber, Walter. *The Clash: U.S.-Japanese Relations Throughout History.* New York: W. W. Norton, 1998.

————. *The Deadly Bet: LBJ, Vietnam, and the 1968 Election.* Lanham, MD: Rowman & Littlefield, 2005.

Lambert, Andrew. *The Challenge: America, Britain and the War of 1812.* London: Faber and Faber, 2012.

Lambert, John W., and Norman Polmar. *Defenseless: Command Failure at Pearl Harbor.* St. Paul, MN: MBI, 2003.

Lamon, Ward H. *The Life of Abraham Lincoln: From His Birth to His Inauguration as President.* Boston: James R. Osgood, 1872.

Langguth, A. J. *Union 1812: The Americans Who Fought the Second War of Independence.* New York: Simon & Schuster, 2006.

Lash, Joseph P. *Eleanor and Franklin: The Story of Their Relationship, Based on Eleanor Roosevelt's Private Papers.* New York: W. W. Norton, 1971.

————. *Love, Eleanor: Eleanor Roosevelt and Her Friends.* Garden City, NY: Doubleday, 1982.

————. *A World of Love: Eleanor Roosevelt and Her Friends, 1943–1962.* New York: Doubleday, 1987.

Lawrence, Mark Atwood. *The Vietnam War: A Concise International History.* Oxford: Oxford University Press, 2008.

Lawton, Eba Anderson. *Major Robert Anderson and Fort Sumter, 1861.* New York: Knickerbocker Press, 1911.

Layton, Edwin T., with Roger Pineau and John Costello. *"And I Was There": Pearl Harbor and Midway—Breaking the Secrets.* New York: William Morrow, 1985.

Leech, Margaret. *In the Days of McKinley.* New York: Harper, 1959.

Leepson, Marc. *Flag: An American Biography.* New York: St. Martin's Press, 2007.

Leland, Anne, and Mari-Jana Oboroceanu. *American War and Military Operations Casualties: Lists and Statistics.* Washington, DC: Library of Congress, Congressional Research Service, 2010.

Lelyveld, Joseph. *His Final Battle: The Last Months of Franklin Roosevelt.* New York: Alfred A. Knopf, 2016.

Lengel, Edward G. *To Conquer Hell: The Meuse-Argonne, 1918.* New York: Henry Holt, 2008.

Leonard, Elizabeth D. *Lincoln's Forgotten Ally: Judge Advocate General Joseph Holt of Kentucky.* Civil War America. Chapel Hill: University of North Carolina Press, 2011.

Leonard, Thomas M. *James K. Polk: A Clear and Unquestionable Destiny.* Lanham, MD: Rowman & Littlefield, 2000.

Lepa, Jack H. *The Shenandoah Valley Campaign of 1864.* Jefferson, NC: McFarland, 2003.

Levin, Phyllis Lee. *Edith and Woodrow: The Wilson White House.* New York: Scribner, 2001.

Lewis, Felice Flanery. *Trailing Clouds of Glory: Zachary Taylor's Mexican War Campaign and His Emerging Civil War Leaders.* Tuscaloosa: University of Alabama Press, 2010.

Lincoln, Abraham. *The Collected Works of Abraham Lincoln.* Edited by Roy P. Basler. 9 vols. New Brunswick, NJ: Rutgers University Press, 1953–1955.

Link, Arthur S. *Wilson.* 5 vols. Princeton, NJ: Princeton University Press, 1947–1965.

Lloyd, Alan. *The Scorching of Washington: The War of 1812.* Washington, DC: R. B. Luce, 1974.

Lockwood, John, and Charles Lockwood. *The Siege of Washington: The Untold Story of the Twelve Days That Shook the Union.* Oxford: Oxford University Press, 2011.

Logevall, Fredrik. *Choosing War: The Lost Chance for Peace and the Escalation of War in Vietnam.* Berkeley: University of California Press, 1999.

———. *Embers of War: The Fall of an Empire and the Making of America's Vietnam.* New York: Random House, 2012.

Lomazow, Steven, and Eric Fettmann. *FDR's Deadly Secret.* New York: PublicAffairs, 2009.

Long, John Davis. *The Life Story of Abraham Lincoln.* New York: Fleming H. Revell, 1930.

———. *The New American Navy.* 2 vols. New York: Outlook, 1903.

Lord, Walter. *The Dawn's Early Light.* New York: W. W. Norton, 1972.

Lossing, Benson J. *Harpers' Popular Cyclopedia of United States History.* Vol. 6. New York: Harper & Brothers, 1893.

Lower, Richard Coke. *A Bloc of One: The Political Career of Hiram W. Johnson.* Stanford: Stanford University Press, 1993.

MacMillan, Margaret. *Paris 1919: Six Months That Changed the World.* New York: Random House, 2002.

Maddow, Rachel. *Drift: The Unmooring of American Military Power.* New York: Crown, 2012.

Madison, James. *The Papers of James Madison, Presidential Series.* Edited by Robert A. Rutland, et al. 8 vols. Charlottesville: University of Virginia Press, 1984–2015.

————. *The Papers of James Madison, Retirement Series.* Edited by David B. Mattern, et al. 3 vols. Charlottesville: University of Virginia Press, 2009–2016.

Madison, Dolley. *The Selected Letters of Dolley Payne Madison.* Edited by David B. Mattern and Holly C. Shulman. Charlottesville: University of Virginia Press, 2003.

Madison, James. *James Madison on Religious Liberty.* Edited by Robert S. Alley. Buffalo, NY: Prometheus Books, 1985.

————. *The Writings of James Madison.* Edited by Gaillard Hunt. Vols. 7 and 8. New York: G. P. Putnam's Sons, 1908.

Mahan, A. T. *Sea Power in Its Relations to the War of 1812.* Vol. 1. Boston: Little, Brown, 1905.

Mahin, Dean B. *Olive Branch and Sword: The United States and Mexico, 1845–1848.* Jefferson, NC: McFarland, 1997.

Malone, Dumas. *Jefferson and His Time.* 6 vols. Boston: Little, Brown, 1948–1981.

Manchester, William. *American Caesar: 1880–1964.* Boston: Little, Brown, 1978.

————. *The Glory and the Dream: A Narrative History of America, 1932–1972.* Boston: Little, Brown, 1974.

Mapp, Alf J., Jr. *Thomas Jefferson: Passionate Pilgrim; The Presidency, the Founding of the University, and the Private Battle.* Lanham, MD: Rowman & Littlefield, 2009.

Marcus, Maeva. *Truman and the Steel Seizure Case: The Limits of Presidential Power.* New York: Columbia University Press, 1977.

Marolda, Edward J., ed. *Theodore Roosevelt, the U.S. Navy, and the Spanish-American War.* New York: Palgrave, 2001.

Marrin, Albert. *Uprooted: The Japanese American Experience During World War II.* New York: Random House, 2016.

Marsh, Caroline. *Life and Letters of George Perkins Marsh.* Vol. 1. New York: Charles Scribner's Sons, 1888.

Marszalek, John F. *Lincoln and the Military.* Carbondale: Southern Illinois University Press, 2014.

Martin, George. *Madam Secretary, Frances Perkins.* Boston: Houghton Mifflin, 1976.

Martin, John Bartlow. *The Life of Adlai E. Stevenson.* 2 vols. Garden City, NY: Doubleday, 1976 and 1977.

Marvel, William. *Lincoln's Autocrat: The Life of Edwin Stanton.* Chapel Hill: University of North Carolina Press, 2015.

Masterson, William H. *Tories and Democrats: British Diplomats in Pre-Jacksonian America.* College Station: Texas A&M University Press, 1985.

Masur, Louis P. *Lincoln's Last Speech: Wartime Reconstruction and the Crisis of Reunion*. New York: Oxford University Press, 2015.

Mattern, David B., and Holly C. Shulman, eds. *The Selected Letters of Dolley Payne Madison*. Charlottesville: University of Virginia Press, 2003.

Matthews, Chris. *Bobby Kennedy: A Raging Spirit*. New York: Simon & Schuster, 2017.

McCaffrey, James M. *Going for Broke: Japanese American Soldiers in the War Against Nazi Germany*. Norman: University of Oklahoma Press, 2013.

McCartney, Paul T. *Power and Progress: American National Identity, the War of 1898, and the Rise of American Imperialism*. Baton Rouge: Louisiana State University Press, 2006.

McCavitt, John, and Christopher T. George. *The Man Who Captured Washington: Major General Robert Ross and the War of 1812*. Norman: University of Oklahoma Press, 2016.

McClellan, George B. *The Civil War Papers of George B. McClellan: Selected Correspondence, 1860–1865*. Edited by Stephen W. Sears. New York: Ticknor & Fields, 1989.

———. *McClellan's Own Story*. New York: C. L. Webster, 1887.

McClintock, Russell. *Lincoln and the Decision for War: The Northern Response to Secession*. Chapel Hill: University of North Carolina Press, 2008.

McCormac, Eugene Irving. *James K. Polk: A Political Biography*. 2 vols. 1922. Reprint, Newtown, CT: American Political Biography Press, 1995.

McCoy, Donald R. *The Presidency of Harry S. Truman*. Lawrence: University Press of Kansas, 1984.

McCullough, David. *Truman*. New York: Simon & Schuster, 1992.

McGinty, Brian. *The Body of John Merryman: Abraham Lincoln and the Suspension of Habeas Corpus*. Cambridge, MA: Harvard University Press, 2011.

———. *Lincoln and the Court*. Cambridge, MA: Harvard University Press, 2009.

McMaster, John Bach. *Daniel Webster*. New York: Century, 1902.

McNamara, Robert S. *In Retrospect: The Tragedy and Lessons of Vietnam*. New York: Times Books, 1995.

McPherson, James M. *Battle Cry of Freedom: The Civil War Era*. New York: Oxford University Press, 1988.

———. *Crossroads of Freedom: Antietam*. Oxford: Oxford University Press, 2004.

———, ed. *The Most Fearful Ordeal: Original Coverage of the Civil War*. New York: St. Martin's Press, 2004.

———. *Tried by War: Abraham Lincoln as Commander-in-Chief*. New York: Penguin Books, 2008.

Meacham, Jon. *American Lion: Andrew Jackson in the White House.* New York: Random House, 2008.

———. *Franklin and Winston: An Intimate Portrait of an Epic Friendship.* New York: Random House, 2003.

———. *Thomas Jefferson: The Art of Power.* New York: Random House, 2012.

Meagher, Thomas M. *Financing Armed Conflict.* Vol. 1. New York: Palgrave Macmillan, 2016.

Means, Howard. *The Avenger Takes His Place: Andrew Johnson and the 45 Days That Changed the Nation.* Orlando, FL: Harcourt, 2006.

Meiser, Jeffrey W. *Power and Restraint: The Rise of the United States, 1898–1941.* Washington, DC: Georgetown University Press, 2015.

Meisler, Stanley. *United Nations: A History.* New York: Grove Press, 2011.

Melton, Brad, and Dean Smith, eds. *Arizona Goes to War: The Home Front and the Front Lines During World War II.* Tucson: University of Arizona Press, 2003.

Meredith, Roy. *Storm over Sumter: The Opening Engagement of the Civil War.* New York: Simon & Schuster, 1957.

Merrill, Dennis, and Thomas G. Paterson, eds. *Major Problems in American Foreign Relations.* Vol. 2. Belmont, CA: Cengage Learning, 2009.

Merry, Robert W. *A Country of Vast Designs: James K. Polk, the Mexican War, and the Conquest of the American Continent.* New York: Simon & Schuster, 2009.

———. *President McKinley: Architect of the American Century.* New York: Simon & Schuster, 2017.

The Mexican War and Its Heroes. Philadelphia: J. B. Lippincott, 1860.

Meyer, G. J. *The World Remade: America in World War I.* New York: Bantam, 2017.

Meyerson, Michael I. *Liberty's Blueprint: How Madison and Hamilton Wrote the Federalist Papers, Defined the Constitution, and Made Democracy Safe for the World.* New York: Basic Books, 2008.

Miers, Earl Schenck, ed. *Lincoln Day by Day: A Chronology, 1809–1865.* 3 vols. Washington, DC: Lincoln Sesquicentennial Commission, 1960.

Miley, John D. *In Cuba with Shafter.* New York: Charles Scribner's Sons, 1899.

Miller, Merle. *Lyndon: An Oral Biography.* New York: G. P. Putnam's Sons, 1980.

———. *Plain Speaking: An Oral Biography of Harry S. Truman.* New York: G. P. Putnam's Sons, 1973.

Miller, Randall M., Harry S. Stout, and Charles Reagan Wilson, eds. *Religion and the American Civil War.* New York: Oxford University Press, 1998.

Miller, Scott. *The President and the Assassin: McKinley, Terror, and Empire at the Dawn of the American Century.* New York: Random House, 2011.

Miller, William Lee. *Lincoln's Virtues: An Ethical Biography.* New York: Vintage Books, 2003.

————. *President Lincoln: The Duty of a Statesman.* New York: Alfred A. Knopf, 2008.

————. *Two Americans: Truman, Eisenhower, and a Dangerous World.* New York: Alfred A. Knopf, 2012.

Millett, Alan R. *War for Korea, 1945–1950: A House Burning.* Lawrence: University Press of Kansas, 2015.

Milliken, Jennifer. *The Social Construction of the Korean War: Conflict and Its Possibilities.* Manchester, NY: Manchester University Press, 2001.

Moïse, Edwin E. *Tonkin Gulf and the Escalation of the Vietnam War.* Chapel Hill: University of North Carolina Press, 1996.

Monroe, James. *The Writings of James Monroe.* Edited by Stanislaus Murray Hamilton. 7 vols. New York: G. P. Putnam's Sons, 1898–1903.

Moody, Wesley. *The Battle of Fort Sumter: The First Shots of the American Civil War.* New York: Routledge, 2016.

Moore, Frank, ed. *The Rebellion Record.* 11 vols. New York: G. P. Putnam, 1861–1868.

Morgan, H. Wayne. *William McKinley and His America.* Syracuse, NY: Syracuse University Press, 1963.

Morgan, Robert. *Lions of the West: Heroes and Villains of the Westward Expansion.* Chapel Hill, NC: Algonquin Books, 2011.

Morgan, Ted. *FDR: A Biography.* New York: Simon & Schuster, 1985.

Morris, Edmund. *Colonel Roosevelt.* New York: Random House, 2010.

————. *The Rise of Theodore Roosevelt.* New York: Coward, McCann & Geoghegan, 1979.

————. *Theodore Rex.* New York: Random House, 2001.

Morrison, Michael A. *Slavery and the American West: The Eclipse of Manifest Destiny and the Coming of the Civil War.* Chapel Hill: University of North Carolina Press, 1997.

Muller, Charles G. *The Darkest Day: The Washington-Baltimore Campaign During the War of 1812.* Philadelphia: University of Pennsylvania Press, 2003.

Murphy, Bruce Allen. *Wild Bill: The Legend and Life of William O. Douglas.* New York: Random House, 2003.

Murphy, Douglas A. *Two Armies on the Rio Grande: The First Campaign of the US–Mexican War.* College Station: Texas A&M University Press, 2015.

Myer, Dillon S. *Uprooted Americans: The Japanese Americans and the War Relocation Authority During World War II.* Tucson: University of Arizona Press, 1971.

Nagel, Paul C. *John Quincy Adams: A Public Life, A Private Life.* New York: Alfred A. Knopf, 1997.

Neal, Steve. *Harry and Ike: The Partnership That Remade the Postwar World.* New York: Simon & Schuster, 2002.

Neely, Mark E., Jr. *The Abraham Lincoln Encyclopedia.* New York: McGraw-Hill, 1982.

———. *The Fate of Liberty: Abraham Lincoln and Civil Liberties.* New York: Oxford University Press, 1991.

Neff, Jacob K. *The Army and Navy of America.* Philadelphia: J. H. Pearsol, 1845.

Neimeyer, Charles. *War in the Chesapeake: The British Campaigns to Control the Bay, 1813–14.* Annapolis, MD: Naval Institute Press, 2015.

Nelson, Anson, and Fanny Nelson. *Memorials of Sarah Childress Polk.* New York: A. D. F. Randolph, 1892.

Nelson, Craig. *Pearl Harbor: From Infamy to Greatness.* New York: Scribner, 2016.

Nester, William. *The Age of Jackson and the Art of American Power, 1815–1848.* Lincoln, NE: Potomac Books, 2013.

———. *The Age of Lincoln and the Art of American Power, 1848–1876.* Lincoln, NE: Potomac Books, 2014.

Neu, Charles E. *Colonel House: A Biography of Woodrow Wilson's Silent Partner.* New York: Oxford University Press, 2015.

Newman, Angie F. *McKinley Carnations of Memory: The McKinley Button of Two Campaigns.* New York: Mail and Express, 1903.

Newton, Jim. *Justice for All: Earl Warren and the Nation He Made.* New York: Riverhead Books, 2006.

Newton, Joseph F. *Lincoln and Herndon.* Cedar Rapids, IA: Torch Press, 1910.

New York Post: A Century of Journalism: Forward March! Vol. 1. New York: Literary Publishers, 1943.

New York Times Current History of the European War. Vol. 11. New York: New York Times Company, 1917.

Ng, Wendy. *Japanese American Internment During World War II: A History and Reference Guide.* Westport, CT: Greenwood Press, 2002.

Nichols, Christopher McKnight. *Promise and Peril: America at the Dawn of a Global Age*. Cambridge, MA: Harvard University Press, 2011.

Nickles, David Paull. *Under the Wire: How the Telegraph Changed Diplomacy*. Cambridge, MA: Harvard University Press, 2003.

Nicolay, John G., and John Hay. *Abraham Lincoln: A History*. 10 vols. New York: Century, 1914.

Niven, John. *Martin Van Buren: The Romantic Age of American Politics*. New York: Oxford University Press, 1983.

Nojeim, Michael J., and David P. Kilroy. *Days of Decision: Turning Points in U.S. Foreign Policy*. Washington, DC: Potomac Books, 2011.

Oakes, James. *Freedom National: The Destruction of Slavery in the United States, 1861–1865*. New York: W. W. Norton, 2013.

O'Donnell, Lawrence. *Playing with Fire: The 1968 Election and the Transformation of American Politics*. New York: Penguin Press, 2017.

Offner, Arnold A. *Another Such Victory: President Truman and the Cold War, 1945–1953*. Stanford: Stanford University Press, 2002.

Offner, John L. *An Unwanted War: The Diplomacy of the United States and Spain over Cuba, 1895–1898*. Chapel Hill: University of North Carolina Press, 1992.

Ohrt, Wallace. *Defiant Peacemaker: Nicholas Trist in the Mexican War*. College Station: Texas A&M University Press, 1997.

Olcott, Charles S. *The Life of William McKinley*. 2 vols. Boston: Houghton Mifflin, 1916.

Ollier, Edmund. *Cassell's History of the United States*. 3 vols. London: Cassell, Petter & Galpin, 1874–1877.

Olmsted, Kathryn S. *Real Enemies: Conspiracy Theories and American Democracy, World War I to 9/11*. New York: Oxford University Press, 2011.

Onuf, Peter S. *The Mind of Thomas Jefferson*. Charlottesville: University of Virginia Press, 2007.

Oppenheim, Joanne. *Dear Miss Breed: True Stories of the Japanese American Incarceration During World War II and a Librarian Who Made a Difference*. New York: Scholastic, 2006.

Oppermann, Joseph K. *Fort Sumter, Fort Sumter National Monument*. Atlanta: National Park Service, 2015.

O'Toole, G. J. A. *The Spanish War: An American Epic*. New York: W. W. Norton, 1984.

Owens, Robert M. *Mr. Jefferson's Hammer: William Henry Harrison and the Origins of American Indian Policy*. Norman: University of Oklahoma Press, 2007.

Oxford Dictionary of National Biography. Vol. 18. Oxford: Oxford University Press, 2004.

Paludan, Phillip Shaw. *The Presidency of Abraham Lincoln.* Lawrence: University Press of Kansas, 1994.

Park, Bert Edward. *The Impact of Illness on World Leaders.* Philadelphia: University of Pennsylvania Press, 1986.

Parsons, Lynn Hudson. *John Quincy Adams.* Madison, WI: Madison House, 1998.

Parton, James. *Life of Andrew Jackson.* Vol. 3. New York: Mason Brothers, 1861.

Pash, Melinda L. *In the Shadow of the Greatest Generation: The Americans Who Fought the Korean War.* New York: New York University Press, 2014.

Patterson, James T. *Grand Expectations: The United States, 1945–1974.* New York: Oxford University Press, 1996.

Paullin, Charles Oscar. *Commodore John Rodgers, Captain, Commodore, and Senior Officer of the American Navy, 1773–1838.* Cleveland, OH: Arthur H. Clark, 1910.

Pearlman, Michael D. *Truman and MacArthur: Policy, Politics, and the Hunger for Honor and Renown.* Bloomington: Indiana University Press, 2008.

———. *Warmaking and American Democracy: The Struggle over Military Strategy, 1700 to the Present.* Modern War Studies. Lawrence: University Press of Kansas, 1999.

Peifer, Douglas Carl. *Choosing War: Presidential Decisions in the Maine, Lusitania, and Panay Incidents.* New York: Oxford University Press, 2016.

Pell, Edward Leigh, James W. Buel, and James P. Boyd. *A Memorial Volume of American History. McKinley and Men of Our Times.* N.p.: Historical Society of America, 1901.

Pérez, Louis A., Jr. *Cuba Under the Platt Amendment, 1902–1934.* Pittsburgh: University of Pittsburgh Press, 1986.

Perkins, Bradford. *Prologue to War: England and the United States, 1805–1812.* Berkeley: University of California Press, 1961.

Perkins, Frances. *The Roosevelt I Knew.* New York: Viking Press, 1946.

Persico, Joseph E. *Franklin and Lucy: President Roosevelt, Mrs. Rutherfurd, and the Other Remarkable Women in His Life.* New York: Random House, 2008.

———. *Roosevelt's Centurions: FDR and the Commanders He Led to Victory in World War II.* New York: Random House, 2013.

———. *Roosevelt's Secret War: FDR and World War II Espionage.* New York: Random House, 2001.

Peskin, Allan. *Winfield Scott and the Profession of Arms.* Kent, OH: Kent State University Press, 2003.

Peterson, Barbara Bennett. *Sarah Childress Polk, First Lady of Tennessee and Washington*. Huntington, NY: Nova History Publications, 2002.

Peterson, Dennis L. *Confederate Cabinet Departments and Secretaries*. Jefferson, NC: McFarland, 2016.

Peterson, Merrill D. *The Great Triumvirate: Webster, Clay, and Calhoun*. New York: Oxford University Press, 1987.

———. *Lincoln in American Memory*. New York: Oxford University Press, 1995.

Phillips, Christopher. *The Rivers Ran Backward: The Civil War and the Remaking of the American Middle Border*. New York: Oxford University Press, 2016.

Phillips, Kimberley L. *War! What Is It Good For? Black Freedom Struggles and the U.S. Military from World War II to Iraq*. Chapel Hill: University of North Carolina Press, 2012.

Pinheiro, John C. *Manifest Ambition: James K. Polk and Civil-Military Relations During the Mexican War*. Westport, CT: Praeger Security International, 2007.

Pinkley, Virgil, with James F. Scheer. *Eisenhower Declassified*. Old Tappan, NJ: Revell, 1979.

Pinnegar, Charles. *Brand of Infamy: A Biography of John Buchanan Floyd*. Westport, CT: Greenwood Press, 2002.

Pitch, Anthony S. *The Burning of Washington: The British Invasion of 1814*. Annapolis, MD: Naval Institute Press, 1998.

Polk, James K. *The Diary of James K. Polk During His Presidency, 1845 to 1849*. Edited by Milo Milton Quaife. 4 vols. Chicago: A. C. McClurg, 1910.

Poole, Robert M. *On Hallowed Ground: The Story of Arlington National Cemetery*. New York: Bloomsbury, 2010.

Potter, David M. *The Impending Crisis, 1848–1861*. Completed and edited by Don E. Fehrenbacher. New York: Harper & Row, 1976.

Potter, Lou. *Liberators: Fighting on Two Fronts in World War II*. New York: Harcourt, 1992.

Powell, H. Jefferson. *A Community Built on Words: The Constitution in History and Politics*. Chicago: University of Chicago Press, 2005.

Prange, Gordon W., with Donald M. Goldstein and Katherine V. Dillon. *At Dawn We Slept: The Untold Story of Pearl Harbor*. New York: McGraw-Hill, 1981.

———. *Pearl Harbor: The Verdict of History*. New York: McGraw-Hill, 1986.

Preston, Andrew. *Sword of the Spirit, Shield of Faith: Religion in American War and Diplomacy*. New York: Alfred A. Knopf, 2012.

Price, Glenn W. *Origins of the War with Mexico: The Polk-Stockton Intrigue*. Austin: University of Texas Press, 1967.

Proceedings of the General Court Martial Convened for the Trial of Commodore James Barron, Captain Charles Gordon, Mr. William Hook, and Captain John Hall, of the United States' Ship Chesapeake, in the Month of January, 1808. Washington, DC: J. Gideon, Jr., 1822.

Quinn, Camilla A. *Lincoln's Springfield in the Civil War.* Macomb: Western Illinois University, 1991.

Radosh, Ronald, ed. *Debs.* Englewood Cliffs, NJ: Prentice-Hall, 1971.

Ragsdale, Lyn. *Presidential Politics.* Boston: Houghton Mifflin, 1993.

Rakove, Jack N. *The Beginnings of National Politics: An Interpretive History of the Continental Congress.* New York: Alfred A. Knopf, 1979.

Ramsay, David. *"Blinker" Hall, Spymaster: The Man Who Brought America into World War I.* Stroud, Gloucestershire, UK: Spellmount, 2008.

Randall, Ruth Painter. *Mary Lincoln: Biography of a Marriage.* Boston: Little, Brown, 1953.

Randall, Willard Sterne. *Unshackling America: How the War of 1812 Truly Ended the American Revolution.* New York: St. Martin's Press, 2017.

Rawley, James A. *Abraham Lincoln and a Nation Worth Fighting For.* Lincoln: University of Nebraska Press, 2003.

Reck, W. Emerson. *A. Lincoln, His Last 24 Hours.* Jefferson, NC: McFarland, 1987.

Reeves, Richard. *Infamy: The Shocking Story of the Japanese American Internment in World War II.* New York: Henry Holt, 2015.

Reeves, Thomas C. *The Life and Times of Joe McCarthy: A Biography.* New York: Stein & Day, 1982.

Remini, Robert V. *Andrew Jackson and the Course of American Democracy, 1833–1845.* New York: Harper & Row, 1984.

———. *Andrew Jackson and the Course of American Empire, 1767–1821.* New York: Harper & Row, 1977.

———. *Andrew Jackson and the Course of American Freedom, 1822–1832.* New York: Harper & Row, 1981.

———. *Daniel Webster: The Man and His Time.* New York: W. W. Norton, 1997.

———. *Henry Clay: Statesman for the Union.* New York: W. W. Norton, 1991.

Reynolds, Clark G. *Famous American Admirals.* Annapolis, MD: Naval Institute Press, 1978.

Rhodes, James Ford. *The McKinley and Roosevelt Administrations, 1897–1909.* New York: Macmillan, 1922.

Rickover, Hyman G. *How the Battleship Maine Was Destroyed.* Annapolis, MD: Naval Institute Press, 1995.

Riedel, Bruce. *The Search for Al Qaeda: Its Leadership, Ideology, and Future.* Washington, DC: Brookings Institution Press, 2008.

Riley, Russell L. *The Presidency and the Politics of Racial Inequality: Nation-Keeping from 1831 to 1965.* New York: Columbia University Press, 1999.

Robenalt, James. *January 1973: Washington,* Roe v. Wade, *Vietnam, and the Month That Changed America Forever.* Chicago: Chicago Review Press, 2015.

Robinson, Greg. *The Great Unknown: Japanese American Sketches.* Boulder: University Press of Colorado, 2016.

———. *A Tragedy of Democracy: Japanese Confinement in North America.* New York: Columbia University Press, 2009.

Rodenbaugh, Theophilus. *From Everglade to Canyon with the Second Dragoons.* New York: D. Van Nostrand, 1875.

Roman, Alfred. *The Military Operations of General Beauregard in the War Between the States, 1861 to 1865.* 2 vols. New York: Harper & Brothers, 1884.

Roosevelt, Curtis. *Too Close to the Sun: Growing Up in the Shadow of My Grandparents, Franklin and Eleanor.* New York: PublicAffairs, 2008.

Roosevelt, Eleanor. *The Autobiography of Eleanor Roosevelt.* New York: Harper & Brothers, 1961.

Roosevelt, Elliott. *F.D.R.: His Personal Letters.* 4 vols. New York: Duell, Sloan, & Pearce, 1947–1950.

Rove, Karl. *The Triumph of William McKinley: Why the Election of 1896 Still Matters.* New York: Simon & Schuster, 2015.

Rovere, Richard H., and Arthur M. Schlesinger Jr. *The General and the President, and the Future of American Foreign Policy.* New York: Farrar, Straus & Young, 1951.

Rowley, Hazel. *Franklin and Eleanor: An Extraordinary Marriage.* New York: Farrar, Straus & Giroux, 2010.

Rozell, Mark J. *Executive Privilege: Presidential Power, Secrecy, and Accountability.* Lawrence: University Press of Kansas, 2002.

Rusk, Dean, as told to Richard Rusk. *As I Saw It.* New York: W. W. Norton, 1990.

Russell, Jan Jarboe. *The Train to Crystal City: FDR's Secret Prisoner Exchange Program and America's Only Family Internment Camp During World War II.* New York: Scribner, 2015.

Rutland, Robert Allen. *James Madison: The Founding Father.* New York: Macmillan, 1987.

———. *The Presidency of James Madison.* Lawrence: University Press of Kansas, 1990.

Saldin, Robert P. *War, the American State, and Politics Since 1898.* New York: Cambridge University Press, 2010.

Sale, Kirkpatrick. *The Fire of His Genius: Robert Fulton and the American Dream*. New York: Free Press, 2001.

Samito, Christian G. *Lincoln and the Thirteenth Amendment*. Carbondale: Southern Illinois University Press, 2015.

Samuels, Peggy, and Harold Samuels. *Teddy Roosevelt at San Juan: The Making of a President*. College Station: Texas A&M University Press, 1997.

Savage, Sean J. *JFK, LBJ, and the Democratic Party*. Albany: State University of New York Press, 2004.

Scharf, J. Thomas. *History of Philadelphia, 1609–1884*. 3 vols. Philadelphia: L. H. Everts, 1884.

Schlesinger, Arthur M., Jr. *The Crisis of the Old Order, 1919–1933*. The Age of Roosevelt. Boston: Houghton Mifflin, 1957.

———. *The Imperial Presidency*. Boston: Houghton Mifflin, 1973.

———. *Journals, 1952–2000*. Edited by Andrew Schlesinger and Stephen C. Schlesinger. New York: Penguin Press, 2007.

———. *Robert Kennedy and His Times*. Boston: Houghton Mifflin, 1978.

———. *War and the American Presidency*. New York: W. W. Norton, 2004.

Schlesinger, Stephen C. *Act of Creation: The Founding of the United Nations: A Story of Superpowers, Secret Agents, Wartime Allies and Enemies, and Their Quest for a Peaceful World*. Boulder, CO: Westview Press, 2003.

Schroeder, John H. *Mr. Polk's War: American Opposition and Dissent, 1846–1848*. Madison: University of Wisconsin Press, 1973.

Seale, William. *The President's House: A History*. 2 vols. Washington, DC: White House Historical Association, 1986.

Sears, Louis Martin. *Jefferson and the Embargo*. Durham, NC: Duke University Press, 1927.

Sears, Stephen W. *George B. McClellan: The Young Napoleon*. New York: Ticknor & Fields, 1988.

———. *Lincoln's Lieutenants: The High Command of the Army of the Potomac*. Boston: Houghton Mifflin Harcourt, 2017.

Sehat, David. *The Myth of American Religious Freedom*. Oxford: Oxford University Press, 2011.

Sellers, Charles Grier. *James K. Polk*. 2 vols. Princeton, NJ: Princeton University Press, 2015.

Shachtman, Tom. *Edith and Woodrow: A Presidential Romance*. New York: Putnam, 1981.

Shalhope, Robert E. *John Taylor of Caroline: Pastoral Republican.* Columbia: University of South Carolina Press, 1980.

Shen, Zhihua, and Yafeng Xia. *Mao and the Sino-Soviet Partnership, 1945–1959: A New History.* Lanham, MD: Lexington Books, 2015.

Shenk, Joshua Wolf. *Lincoln's Melancholy: How Depression Challenged a President and Fueled His Greatness.* Boston: Houghton Mifflin, 2005.

Sherwood, Robert E. *Roosevelt and Hopkins: An Intimate History.* New York: Harper & Brothers, 1948.

Shesol, Jeff. *Mutual Contempt: Lyndon Johnson, Robert Kennedy, and the Feud That Defined a Decade.* New York: W. W. Norton, 1997.

Shlaes, Amity. *Coolidge.* New York: Harper, 2013.

Shogan, Colleen J. *The President's State of the Union Address: Tradition, Function, and Policy Implications.* Washington, DC: Library of Congress, Congressional Research Service, 2012.

Sibley, Katharine A. S., ed. *A Companion to First Ladies.* Oxford, UK: Wiley Blackwell, 2006.

Siemers, David J. *Presidents and Political Thought.* Columbia: University of Missouri Press, 2009.

Sigsbee, Charles D. *The "Maine": An Account of Her Destruction in Havana Harbor.* New York: Century, 1899.

———. *The United States Navy in the Spanish-American War of 1898: Narratives of the Chief Events.* 2 vols. N.p., 1899.

Silverstone, Scott A. *Divided Union: The Politics of War in the Early American Republic.* Cornell Studies in Security Affairs. Ithaca, NY: Cornell University Press, 2004.

Simon, James F. *Lincoln and Chief Justice Taney: Slavery, Secession, and the President's War Powers.* New York: Simon & Schuster, 2006.

Skeen, C. Edward. *Citizen Soldiers in the War of 1812.* Lexington: University Press of Kentucky, 1999.

———. *John Armstrong, Jr., 1758–1843: A Biography.* Syracuse, NY: Syracuse University Press, 1981.

Smith, Craig R. *Silencing the Opposition: Government Strategies of Suppression.* Albany: State University of New York Press, 1996.

Smith, Derek. *Sumter After the First Shots: The Untold Story of America's Most Famous Fort Until the End of the Civil War.* Mechanicsburg, PA: Stackpole Books, 2015.

Smith, Gary Scott. *Religion in the Oval Office: The Religious Lives of American Presidents.* Oxford: Oxford University Press, 2015.

Smith, Gene. *When the Cheering Stopped: The Last Years of Woodrow Wilson.* New York: William Morrow, 1964.

Smith, Gene A. *For the Purposes of Defense: The Politics of the Jeffersonian Gunboat Program.* Newark: University of Delaware Press, 1995.

Smith, Jean Edward. *Bush.* New York: Simon & Schuster, 2016.

———. *FDR.* New York: Random House, 2007.

Smith, Jeffery Alan. *War and Press Freedom: The Problem of Prerogative Power.* New York: Oxford University Press, 1999.

Smith, Joseph. *The Spanish-American War: Conflict in the Caribbean and the Pacific, 1895–1902.* Oxfordshire, UK: Routledge, 2014.

Smith, Justin H. *The Annexation of Texas.* New York: Barnes & Noble, 1941.

Smith, Margaret Bayard. *The First Forty Years of Washington Society.* Edited by Gaillard Hunt. New York: Charles Scribner's Sons, 1906.

Smith, Norma. *Jeannette Rankin: America's Conscience.* Helena: Montana Historical Society Press, 2002.

Smith, Richard Norton. *Thomas E. Dewey and His Times.* New York: Simon & Schuster, 1982.

Snow, Peter. *When Britain Burned the White House: The 1814 Invasion of Washington.* New York: St. Martin's Press, 2014.

Snow, William Parker. *Lee and His Generals.* New York: Richardson, 1867.

Solberg, Carl. *Hubert Humphrey: A Biography.* New York: W. W. Norton, 1984.

Sondhaus, Lawrence. *German Submarine Warfare in World War I: The Onset of Total War at Sea.* Lanham, MD: Rowman & Littlefield, 2017.

———. *World War One: The Global Revolution.* Cambridge: Cambridge University Press, 2011.

Sorensen, Theodore C. *Kennedy.* New York: Harper & Row, 1965.

Souvenir of the Visit of President McKinley and Members of the Cabinet to Boston, February, 1899. [Boston]: Home Market Club, 1899.

Spann, Edward K. *Gotham at War: New York City, 1860–1865.* Wilmington, DE: Scholarly Resources, 2002.

Speed, Joshua F. *Reminiscences of Abraham Lincoln and Notes of a Visit to California.* Louisville, KY: J. P. Morton, 1884.

Spivak, Burton. *Jefferson's English Crisis: Commerce, Embargo, and the Republican Revolution.* Charlottesville: University Press of Virginia, 1979.

Stagg, J. C. A. *Mr. Madison's War: Politics, Diplomacy, and Warfare in the Early American Republic, 1783–1830.* Princeton, NJ: Princeton University Press, 1983.

Stahr, Walter. *Seward: Lincoln's Indispensable Man.* New York: Simon & Schuster, 2012.

Startt, James D. *Woodrow Wilson, the Great War, and the Fourth Estate.* College Station: Texas A&M University Press, 2017.

Stashower, Daniel. *The Hour of Peril: The Secret Plot to Murder Lincoln Before the Civil War.* New York: Minotaur Books, 2013.

St. Clair, James E., and Linda C. Gugin. *Chief Justice Fred M. Vinson of Kentucky: A Political Biography.* Lexington: University Press of Kentucky, 2002.

Steers, Edward, Jr. *Blood on the Moon: The Assassination of Abraham Lincoln.* Lexington: University Press of Kentucky, 2005.

———. *Lincoln's Assassination.* Carbondale: Southern Illinois University Press, 2014.

Steinberg, Alfred. *Mrs. R: The Life of Eleanor Roosevelt.* New York: G. P. Putnam's Sons, 1958.

Stepp, John W., and I. William Hill, eds. *Mirror of War: "The Washington Star" Reports the Civil War.* Englewood Cliffs, NJ: Prentice-Hall, 1961.

Stevens, William Oliver. *An Affair of Honor: The Biography of Commodore James Barron, U.S.N.* Chesapeake, VA: Norfolk County Historical Society, 1969.

Stevenson, Charles A. *Warriors and Politicians: US Civil-Military Relations Under Stress.* London: Routledge, 2006.

Stinnett, Robert B. *Day of Deceit: The Truth About FDR and Pearl Harbor.* New York: Free Press, 2000.

Stone, Geoffrey R. *Perilous Times: Free Speech in Wartime from the Sedition Act of 1798 to the War on Terrorism.* New York: W. W. Norton, 2004.

———. *War and Liberty: An American Dilemma: 1790 to the Present.* New York: W. W. Norton, 2007.

Stout, Harry S. *Upon the Altar of the Nation: A Moral History of the Civil War.* New York: Penguin Books, 2007.

———. *American Aristocrats: A Family, a Fortune, and the Making of American Capitalism.* New York: Basic Books, 2017.

Striner, Richard. *Lincoln and Race.* Carbondale: Southern Illinois University, 2012.

———. *Woodrow Wilson and World War I: A Burden Too Great to Bear.* Lanham, MD: Rowman & Littlefield, 2014.

Strode, Hudson. *Jefferson Davis.* 3 vols. New York: Harcourt, Brace, 1955–1964.

Sugden, John. *Tecumseh: A Life.* New York: Henry Holt, 1998.

Summers, Anthony, and Robbyn Swan. *A Matter of Honor: Pearl Harbor; Betrayal, Blame, and a Family's Quest for Justice.* New York: Harper, 2016.

Swanberg, W. A. *First Blood: The Story of Fort Sumter.* New York: Charles Scribner's Sons, 1957.

Symonds, Craig L. *Lincoln and His Admirals: Abraham Lincoln, the U.S. Navy, and the Civil War.* Oxford: Oxford University Press, 2010.

Szulc, Tad. *Fidel: A Critical Portrait.* New York: William Morrow, 1986.

Tap, Bruce. *Over Lincoln's Shoulder: The Committee on the Conduct of the War.* Modern War Studies. Lawrence: University Press of Kansas, 1998.

Tarbell, Ida M. *The Life of Abraham Lincoln.* 2 vols. New York: Lincoln Memorial Association, 1900.

Thomas, Benjamin Platt. *Abraham Lincoln: A Biography.* New York: Alfred A. Knopf, 1952.

Thomas, Evan. *Being Nixon: A Man Divided.* New York: Random House, 2015.

———. *Robert Kennedy: His Life.* New York: Simon & Schuster, 2000.

———. *The War Lovers: Roosevelt, Lodge, Hearst, and the Rush to Empire, 1898.* New York: Little, Brown, 2010.

Thomas, Helen. *Dateline: White House.* New York: Macmillan, 1975.

Thompson, J. Lee. *Never Call Retreat: Theodore Roosevelt and the Great War.* New York: Palgrave Macmillan, 2013.

Tilley, John Shipley. *Lincoln Takes Command.* Chapel Hill: University of North Carolina Press, 1941.

Toland, John. *Infamy: Pearl Harbor and Its Aftermath.* Garden City, NY: Doubleday, 1982.

Toll, Ian W. *Pacific Crucible: War at Sea in the Pacific, 1941–1942.* New York: W. W. Norton, 2012.

———. *Six Frigates: The Epic History of the Founding of the U.S. Navy.* New York: W. W. Norton, 2006.

Tone, John Lawrence. *War and Genocide in Cuba, 1895–1898.* Chapel Hill: University of North Carolina Press, 2006.

Trask, David F. *The War with Spain in 1898.* 1981. Reprint, Lincoln: University of Nebraska Press, 1996.

Traxel, David. *1898: The Birth of the American Century.* New York: Vintage Books, 1999.

Trefousse, Hans L. *Andrew Johnson: A Biography.* 1989. Reprint, New York: W. W. Norton, 1997.

———. *Benjamin Franklin Wade, Radical Republican from Ohio.* New York: Twayne, 1963.

———. *The Radical Republicans: Lincoln's Vanguard for Racial Justice*. New York: Alfred A. Knopf, 1968.

Truman, Harry S. *Memoirs. Vol. 1, Year of Decisions*. Garden City, NY: Doubleday, 1955.

———. *Memoirs. Vol. 2, Years of Trial and Hope*. Garden City, NY: Doubleday, 1956.

———. *Strictly Personal and Confidential: The Letters Harry Truman Never Mailed*. Edited by Monte M. Poen. Boston: Little, Brown, 1982.

———. *Where the Buck Stops: The Personal and Private Writings of Harry S. Truman*. Edited by Margaret Truman. New York: Warner Books, 1989.

Truman, Margaret. *Harry S. Truman*. New York: William Morrow, 1973.

———. *Souvenir: Margaret Truman's Own Story*. New York: McGraw-Hill, 1956.

Tuchman, Barbara W. *The Zimmermann Telegram*. New York: Viking, 1958.

Tucker, George Holbert. *Norfolk Highlights, 1584–1881*. Norfolk, VA: W. S. Dawson Company, 1972.

Tucker, Spencer, and Frank T. Reuter. *Injured Honor: The* Chesapeake-Leopard *Affair, June 22, 1807*. Annapolis, MD: Naval Institute Press, 1996.

Tumulty, Joseph P. *Woodrow Wilson as I Know Him*. Garden City, NY: Doubleday, Page, 1921.

Turner, Justin G., and Linda Levitt Turner. *Mary Todd Lincoln: Her Life and Letters*. New York: Alfred A. Knopf, 1972.

Twomey, Steve. *Countdown to Pearl Harbor: The Twelve Days to the Attack*. New York: Simon & Schuster, 2017.

Tyler, John W. *The Life of William McKinley*. Philadelphia: P. W. Ziegler, 1901.

United States Commission on Wartime Relocation and Internment of Civilians. *Personal Justice Denied: Report of the Commission on Wartime Relocation and Internment of Civilians*. Washington, DC: US Government Printing Office, 1983.

Varon, Elizabeth R. *Appomattox: Victory, Defeat, and Freedom at the End of the Civil War*. Oxford: Oxford University Press, 2013.

Vogel, Steve. *The Pentagon: A History*. New York: Random House, 2007.

———. *Through the Perilous Fight: Six Weeks That Saved the Nation*. New York: Random House, 2013.

Wada, Haruki. *The Korean War: An International History*. Lanham, MD: Rowman & Littlefield, 2014.

Wainstock, Dennis D. *Truman, MacArthur, and the Korean War*. Westport, CT: Greenwood Press, 1999.

Walker, Samuel. *Presidents and Civil Liberties from Wilson to Obama: A Story of Poor Custodians.* New York: Cambridge University Press, 2012.

Walpole, Spencer. *The Life of the Rt. Hon. Spencer Perceval.* Vol. 2. London: Hurst and Blackett, 1874.

Walworth, Arthur. *Woodrow Wilson.* 2 vols. New York: Longmans, Green, 1958.

Ward, Geoffrey C. *Before the Trumpet: Young Franklin Roosevelt, 1882–1905.* New York: Harper & Row, 1985.

———, ed. *Closest Companion: The Unknown Story of the Intimate Friendship Between Franklin Roosevelt and Margaret Suckley.* Boston: Houghton Mifflin, 1995.

———. *A First-Class Temperament: The Emergence of Franklin Roosevelt.* New York: Harper & Row, 1989.

Ward, Geoffrey C., and Ken Burns. *The Vietnam War: An Intimate History.* New York: Alfred A. Knopf, 2017.

Warren, Louis Austin. *Lincoln's Youth: Indiana Years, Seven to Twenty-One, 1816–1830.* New York: Appleton, Century, Crofts, 1959.

Watson, Robert P. *America's First Crisis: The War of 1812.* Excelsior Editions. Albany: State University of New York Press, 2014.

Watson, Robert P., and Anthony J. Eksterowicz, eds. *The Presidential Companion: Readings on the First Ladies.* Columbia: University of South Carolina Press, 2003.

Watson, W. Marvin, with Sherwin Markman. *Chief of Staff: Lyndon Johnson and His Presidency.* New York: St. Martin's Press, 2004.

Waugh, John C. *Reelecting Lincoln: The Battle for the 1864 Presidency.* New York: Crown, 1997.

Weber, Jennifer L. *Copperheads: The Rise and Fall of Lincoln's Opponents in the North.* Oxford: Oxford University Press, 2008.

Webster, Daniel. *The Writings and Speeches of Daniel Webster.* New York: J. F. Taylor, 1903.

Weems, John Edward. *The Fate of the Maine.* New York: Henry Holt, 1958.

Weigley, Russell F. *A Great Civil War: A Military and Political History, 1861–1865.* Bloomington: Indiana University Press, 2000.

Weiner, Tim. *Enemies: A History of the FBI.* New York: Random House, 2012.

Weinstein, Edwin A. *Woodrow Wilson: A Medical and Psychological Biography.* Princeton, NJ: Princeton University Press, 1981.

Weintraub, Stanley. *Final Victory: FDR's Extraordinary World War II Presidential Campaign.* Philadelphia: Da Capo Press, 2012.

Welles, Gideon. *The Civil War Diary of Gideon Welles, Lincoln's Secretary of the Navy.*

Edited by William E. Gienapp and Erica L. Gienapp. Urbana: University of Illinois Press, 2014.

Wert, Jeffry D. *The Sword of Lincoln: The Army of the Potomac.* New York: Simon & Schuster, 2005.

Wheelan, Joseph. *Invading Mexico: America's Continental Dream and the Mexican War, 1846–1848.* New York: Carroll & Graf, 2007.

White, Jonathan W. *Abraham Lincoln and Treason in the Civil War: The Trials of John Merryman.* Baton Rouge: Louisiana State University Press, 2011.

White, Richard. *The Republic for Which It Stands: The United States During Reconstruction and the Gilded Age, 1865–1896.* New York: Oxford University Press, 2017.

White, Ronald C., Jr. *A. Lincoln: A Biography.* New York: Random House, 2009.

———. *American Ulysses: A Life of Ulysses S. Grant.* New York: Random House, 2016.

———. *The Eloquent President: A Portrait of Lincoln Through His Words.* New York: Random House, 2005.

———. *Lincoln's Greatest Speech: The Second Inaugural.* New York: Simon & Schuster, 2006.

White, Theodore H. *The Making of the President, 1968.* New York: Atheneum, 1969.

White, William Allen. *The Autobiography of William Allen White.* New York: Macmillan, 1946.

Whyte, Kenneth. *The Uncrowned King: The Sensational Rise of William Randolph Hearst.* Berkeley, CA: Counterpoint, 2009.

Wilcox, Cadmus M. *History of the Mexican War.* Edited by Mary Rachel Wilcox. Washington, DC: Church News Publishing, 1892.

Wilentz, Sean. *The Rise of American Democracy: Jefferson to Lincoln.* New York: W. W. Norton, 2005.

Williams, Frank J. *Judging Lincoln.* Carbondale: Southern Illinois University Press, 2002.

Williams, T. Harry. *Lincoln and His Generals.* New York: Alfred A. Knopf, 1952.

———. *Lincoln and the Radicals.* Madison: University of Wisconsin Press, 1965.

Williford, Glen, and Terrance McGovern. *Defenses of Pearl Harbor and Oahu, 1907–1950.* Oxford, UK: Osprey Publishing, 2003.

Wills, Garry. *Bomb Power: The Modern Presidency and the National Security State.* New York: Penguin Press, 2010.

———. *James Madison.* New York: Times Books, 2002.

Wilson, Douglas L. *Honor's Voice: The Transformation of Abraham Lincoln.* New York: Alfred A. Knopf, 1998.

———. *Lincoln's Sword: The Presidency and the Power of Words.* New York: Alfred A. Knopf, 2006.

Wilson, Edith Bolling. *My Memoir.* Indianapolis: Bobbs-Merrill, 1939.

Wilson, Joseph R. *Mutual Relation of Masters and Slaves as Taught in the Bible: A Discourse Preached in the First Presbyterian Church, Augusta, Georgia, on Sabbath Morning, Jan. 6, 1861.* Augusta, GA: Steam Press of Chronicle & Sentinel, 1861.

Wilson, Woodrow. *Congressional Government: A Study in American Politics.* Boston: Houghton Mifflin, 1901.

———. *Constitutional Government in the United States.* New York: Columbia University Press, 1908.

———. *A History of the American People.* 5 vols. New York: Harper & Brothers, 1901–1902.

———. *The Papers of Woodrow Wilson.* Edited by Arthur S. Link. 69 vols. Princeton, NJ: Princeton University Press, 1966–1994.

Winders, Richard Bruce. *Mr. Polk's Army: The American Military Experience in the Mexican War.* College Station: Texas A&M University Press, 2001.

Winik, Jay. *1944: FDR and the Year That Changed History.* New York: Simon & Schuster, 2015.

Winkle, Kenneth J. *Abraham and Mary Lincoln.* Carbondale: Southern Illinois University Press, 2011.

Witcover, Jules. *The Year the Dream Died: Revisiting 1968 in America.* New York: Warner Books, 1997.

Wood, Gordon S. *Empire of Liberty: A History of the Early Republic, 1789–1815.* Oxford: Oxford University Press, 2009.

Wood, Lamont. *Thornton's Luck: How America Almost Lost the Mexican-American War.* Guilford, CT: Lone Star Books, 2017.

Woods, Randall Bennett. *Fulbright: A Biography.* Cambridge: Cambridge University Press, 1995.

———. *LBJ: Architect of American Ambition.* New York: Free Press, 2006.

Woodward, David R. *The American Army and the First World War.* Armies of the Great War. New York: Cambridge University Press, 2014.

Wooster, Robert. *Nelson A. Miles and the Twilight of the Frontier Army.* Lincoln: University of Nebraska Press, 1996.

Wright, James. *Those Who Have Borne the Battle: A History of America's Wars and Those Who Fought Them.* New York: PublicAffairs, 2012.

Zeitz, Joshua. *Lincoln's Boys: John Hay, John Nicolay, and the War for Lincoln's Image.* New York: Viking, 2014.

JOURNAL ARTICLES

Adler, David Gray. "The Constitution and Presidential Warmaking: The Enduring Debate." *Political Science Quarterly,* Spring 1988.

Allen, Thomas B. "Remember the *Maine?*" *National Geographic,* Feb. 1998.

————. "What Really Sank the *Maine?*" *Naval History,* Mar.–Apr. 1998.

Arnold, James. "The Battle of Bladensburg." *Columbia Historical Society,* 1937.

Boritt, Gabor S. "Lincoln's Opposition to the Mexican War." *Journal of the Illinois State Historical Society,* Feb. 1974.

Calderhead, William. "A Strange Career in a Strange Navy." *Idaho Historical Magazine,* Fall 1977.

Calhoun, Samuel W., and Lucas E. Morel. "Abraham Lincoln's Religion: The Case for His Ultimate Belief in a Personal, Sovereign God." *Journal of the Abraham Lincoln Association,* Winter 2012.

Carwardine, Richard. "'Simply a Theist': Herndon on Lincoln's Religion." *Journal of the Abraham Lincoln Association,* Summer 2014.

Casper, Gerhard. "Executive-Congressional Separation of Power During the Presidency of Thomas Jefferson." *Stanford Law Review,* Feb. 1995.

Chambers, John W. "Decision for the Draft." *OAH Magazine of History,* Oct. 2002.

Cray, Robert E., Jr. "Remembering the USS *Chesapeake:* The Politics of Maritime Death and Impressment." *Journal of the Early Republic,* Fall 2005.

Farrier, Jasmine. "Judicial Restraint and the New War Powers." *Political Science Quarterly,* June 2016.

Gibson, James. "John Bullus: Reading Physician and Naval Surgeon." *Transactions and Studies of the College of Physicians of Philadelphia,* Dec. 1944.

Gilje, Paul A. "The Baltimore Riots of 1812 and the Breakdown of the Anglo-American Mob Tradition." *Journal of Social History,* Summer 1980.

Jones, Stuart E., and William W. Campbell III. "The President's Music Men." *National Geographic,* Dec. 1959.

Latshaw, K. Michael. "Flawed Judgment: The Court-Martial of Commodore James Barron." *Virginia Magazine of History and Biography,* Autumn 1997.

Lofgren, Charles A. "War-Making Under the Constitution: The Original Understanding." *Yale Law Journal*, vol. 81, Mar. 1972.

Mann, Nick. "Sailors Board Me Now: The *Chesapeake* Affair." *Western Illinois Historical Review*, May 2011.

Matray, James I. "Dean Acheson's Press Club Speech Reexamined." *Journal of Conflict Studies*, Spring 2002.

Morison, Samuel Eliot. "Our Most Unpopular War." *Proceedings of the Massachusetts Historical Society*, 3rd ser., vol. 80, 1968.

Neely, Mark E., Jr. "War and Partisanship: What Lincoln Learned from James K. Polk." *Journal of the Illinois State Historical Society*, Autumn 1981.

Nelson, Anna Kasten. "Operation Northwoods and the Covert War Against Cuba, 1961–1963." *Cuban Studies*, vol. 32, 2001.

Noll, Mark A. "Lincoln's God." *Journal of Presbyterian History*, Summer 2004.

Phillips, James Duncan. "Jefferson's 'Wicked, Tyrannical Embargo.'" *New England Quarterly*, Dec. 1945.

Rohrs, Richard C. "Sectionalism, Political Parties, and the Attempt to Relocate the National Capital in 1814." *Historian*, Spring 2000.

Skeen, C. Edward. "Monroe and Armstrong: A Study in Political Rivalry." *New-York Historical Society Quarterly*, Apr. 1973.

Smelser, Marshall. "Tecumseh, Harrison, and the War of 1812." *Indiana Magazine of History*, Mar. 1969.

Teten, Ryan L. "Evolution of the Modern Rhetorical Presidency: Presidential Presentation and Development of the State of the Union Address." *Presidential Studies Quarterly*, June 2003.

Van Ells, Mark D. "Assuming the White Man's Burden: The Seizure of the Philippines, 1898–1902." *Philippine Studies*, Fourth Quarter 1995.

White, Jonathan W. "The Strangely Insignificant Role of the U.S. Supreme Court in the Civil War." *Journal of the Civil War Era*, June 2013.

Yoo, John C. "The Continuation of Politics by Other Means: The Original Understanding of War Powers." *California Law Review*, Mar. 1996.

CHAPTER NOTES

Presidential speeches and messages are in *Public Papers of the Presidents* (Washington, DC: US Government Printing Office), unless otherwise noted. Newspaper and magazine articles and oral histories are cited within each chapter's notes.

PROLOGUE: THE FUGITIVE

Madisons and British invasion of DC: Muller, pp. 167–192; Jane Cook, pp. 3–261; Peter Snow, pp. 67–134; Allgor, *Perfect Union,* pp. 305–330; Lord, pp. 106–108, 116–117, 124–125, 130–131, 146–148, 150–153, 157, 167–179, 191–195, 201, 212–216; Langguth, pp. 291–315; Borneman, *1812,* pp. 216–235; Howard, pp. 132–208; Pitch, pp. 113–126; Brant, vol. 6, pp. 298–315; Cheney, pp. 405–412; Brookhiser, pp. 208–209; *Papers of James Madison, Presidential Series,* vol. 8, pp. 137–141. "Sparkled like stars": Margaret Bayard Smith, p. 236. Madison as Bible student: Ketcham, *Madison,* pp. 29–30. "Mr. Madison's War": *Federal Republican,* July 27, 1812. "Strike a slave" and "military gentlemen": Jennings, pp. 17, 10. "Tell me" and "unwearied anxiety": Dolley Madison to sister, Aug. 23 and 24, 1814, LOC; Howard, p. 165. Use of term "White House": Seale, vol. 1, pp. 160–161, 626. "Save that picture!": Lossing, vol. 6, p. 66. "Humble but safe": Barker, p. 117. Fate of founding documents: Hazelton, p. 287. "Clear out!": Jennings, p. 11. "I hear of much hostility": Holloway, p. 194. "Dagger or poison": *Memoirs and Letters of Dolley Madison,* p. 100.

"If that's you": *Historical Magazine,* Jan. 1863. "Most hellish looking": Pitch, p. 116. "Harlequin of havoc": Ingersoll, p. 189. "Sun-burnt visage": *Museum of Foreign Literature,* vol. 42, p. 279. "Shall this harbor": *History of Committee on the Judiciary, U.S. House of Representatives,* June 23, 1947, p. 4. "If any man" and "you could not" and "left his capital defenseless": *New York Evening Post,* Sept. 2, 1814. "Super-excellent Madeira": *Literary Gazette,* vol. 18, p. 280. "Little Jemmy": Crocker, p. 103. "Wrapt in one": *Salem Gazette,* Sept. 30, 1814. "Coarse luxury": Ingersoll, p. 188. "Ag[ainst] giving the power": Aug. 17, 1787. "Will not hurry": Wilson at Pennsylvania ratifying convention, Dec. 11, 1787. "True nurse": Hallett, p. 32. "Constitution supposes": Madison to Jefferson, Apr. 2, 1798, TJP. Madison-Gerry revision in war-power language: Farrand, p. 319.

CHAPTER ONE: "TORRENT OF PASSION"

"Antient friend": Jefferson to James Maury, Apr. 25, 1812, TJP. Generally on *Chesapeake* and *Leopard* episode and James Barron: *Magazine of American History,* vol. 25, p. 413; Budiansky, pp. 55–71; Stevens, pp. 41–196; *Proceedings of the General Court Martial;* Dickon, pp. 13–72; Meacham, *Jefferson,* pp. 425–427; Dye, pp. 43–70; Spivak, pp. 81–113; Toll, *Frigates,* pp. 61–62, 138–139, 158–160, 164, 172, 286–287, 289–308; Tucker and Reuter, pp. 1–17, 81–82, 90–99, 145; Burstein and Isenberg, pp. 446–449; Gordon Wood, pp. 647–648; Brant, vol. 4, pp. 380–391; Daughan, *If by Sea,* pp. 387–389; Guttridge and Smith, pp. 108–180; Mahan, *Sea Power,* vol. 1, pp. 155, 167, 171; Barron to Secretary Smith, June, 23, 1807, and Barron to John Bullus, und., Barron Papers; Latshaw, *Virginia Magazine of History and Biography,* Autumn 1997; Nick Mann.

"Th: Jefferson presents" and "From that infamous": Jefferson to James Barron, May 23, 1807, Barron Papers; Budiansky, p. 47. "He was very remarkable": James Barron note, Barron Papers. Jefferson and US Navy: Malone, vol. 5, pp. 492–503; Toll, *Frigates,* pp. 280–281; Budiansky, pp. 46–50; Burstein and Isenberg, pp. 438–439, 449–450. *"First Admiral of American Gun-Boats!":* Burstein and Isenberg, p. 450. "Protect our commerce": Secretary of the Navy to Commodore Dale, May 20, 1801, NARA. Congress's refusal to authorize Jefferson to use force after Spanish incursion: Arthur Schlesinger, *Imperial*, p. 23. "In ordinary": Budiansky, p. 55. *Chesapeake* history: Tucker and Reuter, pp. 1–2, 7–8, 81–83, 90–96. Charles Gordon background: Calderhead. "Too much addicted": Tucker and Reuter, p. 89. John Bullus background: Gibson. John Hall and the Carusis: • Jones and Campbell; Kirk, p. 15. "Deserted and entered": *Cobbett's Weekly Political Register*, vol. 12, pp. 319–320. Jenkin Ratford: Tucker and Reuter, pp. 15, 71–72.

"Charge us with making": *Proceedings of the General Court Martial*, p. 121. "I do not understand": *Naval Chronicle (1808)*, vol. 18. "For God's sake" and "be shot at" and "will nobody do" and "Stop firing" and "Sir, I consider": *Proceedings of the General Court Martial*, pp. 180, 150, 85–86, 50, 138. "I regret" and "A few more" and "Better if the *Chesapeake*": Tucker and Reuter, p. 15; *Proceedings of the General Court Martial*, p. 226. "The late U.S. frigate *Chesapeake*": *Proceedings of the General Court Martial*, p. 142. Departure of Gordon and Bullus: Tucker and Reuter, p. 99. Recollection of Charlotte Bullus: *Magazine of American History*, vol. 25; Fowler, pp. 76–77. Demands for "revenge" and destruction: *American Register*, vol. 2 (1807), p. 196; *New York Evening Post*, June 30, 1807. "Blood of our countrymen": Quoted in *Democratic Press*, July 1, 1807. "First blow of war": *Aurora*, July 5, 1807. "NATION INSULTED": *Massachusetts Spy*, July 8, 1807. "In your full strength": *National Intelligencer*, July 1, 1807. "Desperately mad": *Baltimore American*, July 1807.

"Savage outrage": *Democratic Press*, June 29, 1807. "Time is now arrived": *Aurora*, July 2, 1807. Jay's Treaty: Beschloss, *Presidential Courage*, pp. 1–33. "Quondam colonies": Bradford Perkins, p. 6. Anglo-American clashes on Atlantic: Tucker and Reuter, pp. 49, 60. "New and shameful": James Madison to James Monroe, Sept. 24, 1805, JMP. "George the Third is thus": *Democratic Press*, Aug. 14, 1807. "Never since the battle": Jefferson to Marquis de La Fayette, July 14, 1807, TJP. Jefferson's attitude to war: Onuf, pp. 33, 128, 132, 134, 182–196, 244–251. Jefferson and financial consequences of war: Hormats, pp. 30–31. "I am sincerely sorry": Jefferson to Henry Dearborn, June 25, 1807, TJP. "Once a subject": *Southern Literary Messenger*, vol. 8, p. 298. "We shall then determine" and "future insults": Jefferson to William Cabell, June 29, 1807, TJP. "Sick headake": Dolley Madison to Anna Cutts, Mar. 27, 1807, LOC. "Honorable reparation": Jefferson proclamation, July 2, 1807. "Should do no act": Jefferson to Thomas Randolph, July 5, 1807, TJP. "The public sensibility": Draft, Aug. 1807, in TJP. "Ardor of our fellow citizens": Malone, vol. 5, p. 429. Jefferson, Madison and *Melampus* precedent: Latshaw, p. 382; Tucker and Reuter, p. 72; Mapp, p. 141; Cogliano, pp. 205–207; James, pp. 332–334. "Unreflecting part": Quoted in *New-England Palladium*, July 17, 1807.

"O! for a Washington": Malone, vol. 5, p. 429. "King of Economy": *Newburyport Herald*, Aug. 4, 1807. "Your anxiety that the ship" and "Captn Gordon immediately": James Barron to Secretary Smith, July 23, 1807, Barron Papers. Bullus's trip to London: Latshaw, pp. 400–401; Madison, *Writings*, vol. 7, pp. 454–460. Jefferson and Robert Fulton: Malone, vol. 5, pp. 503–506; Sale, pp. 6, 17–18, 28, 34–36, 66, 82, 89, 105, 108, 115–116. "FULTON'S ARTIFICIAL": *Aurora*, Oct. 20, 1807. "I think we may": Dearborn to Madison, July 17, 1807, JMP. Fulton New York demonstration: *New York Evening Post*, July 22, 1807; *New-England Palladium*, July 28, 1807; *Democratic Press*, Sept. 14, 1807. "Was rent in two": Sale, p. 7. "500 men in a Ship" and "Is there any mode" and "One vessel": Fulton to Jefferson, July 28, 1807, TJP. "Not that I go the whole": Jefferson to Fulton, Aug. 16,

1807, TJP. "We should immediately": Jefferson to Dearborn, Aug. 28, 1807, TJP. "Perhaps the narrows": Jefferson to Robert Smith, Sept. 18, 1807, TJP. "Gunboats are the only": Jefferson to Thomas Paine, Sept. 6, 1807, TJP. "A manifesto against Great Britain": Gallatin to Jefferson, Oct. 21, 1807, TJP. "No commentaries are necessary": Jefferson to Congress, Oct. 27, 1807, TJP.

Bullus's return: *Farmer's Cabinet*, Dec. 22, 1807; *New-England Palladium*, Dec. 23, 1807; *Poulson's American Daily Advertiser*, Dec. 21, 1807; *Alexandria Daily Advertiser*, Dec. 17, 1807. "Unfriendly, proud and harsh" and Canning letter: Gordon Wood, p. 648; Spivak, p. 99; Burstein and Isenberg, p. 480. "Haughty" and "whose interest and wish": Malone, vol. 5, p. 466. "As abject and as obsequious": *Aurora*, Dec. 24, 1807. Jefferson's embargo: Louis Sears, pp. 3, 29–30, 59–60; James Duncan Phillips. "Keeping our ships": Jefferson to Governor Cabell, Mar. 13, 1808, TJP. Barron's court-martial: Latshaw, pp. 377–408; Stevens, pp. 75–94. "So many darts": Guttridge, p. 100; Barron to Bullus, Bullus Papers. "An anonymous friend": Anonymous to James Barron, Mar. 5, 1808, Barron Papers. "Fire a few guns": *Proceedings of the General Court Martial*, pp. 233–234. "Prolix and elaborate": Guttridge, p. 104.

"Stain" on the *Chesapeake*'s flag and "My condemnation": *Proceedings of the General Court Martial*, pp. 435, 296. Bulluses in later life: *NYT*, Oct. 8, 1871, and Oct. 7, 1928; *San Francisco Bulletin*, Mar. 23, 1869; *Connecticut Courant*, Feb. 24, 1808. "Earnest entreaties": Tucker and Reuter, p. 238. "One of the dastardly": *New York Herald*, Feb. 26, 1869. Decatur "prejudiced": Budiansky, p. 69. Carusis' fate: U.S. House of Representatives, "On Claim of Gaetano Carusi," Feb. 4, 1831; *National Geographic*, Dec. 1959. "That unfortunate, unhappy ship": Gordon to Bullus, 1811, Bullus Papers. "Treasonous" charge: De Kay, *Rage*, pp. 176–178, 211. Decatur's fate: Guttridge, pp. 119–131, 217, 228–234; De Kay, *Rage*, pp. 1–8, 183–211. Barron on effort to "embroil" Great Britain: De Kay, *Rage*, p. 109. Barron in later life: *Boston Evening Transcript*, Oct. 4, 1857; *Daily Ohio Statesman*, Apr. 29, 1851; *Pittsfield Sun*, Apr. 17, 1851; *New Orleans Times-Picayune*, Apr. 27, 1851; *Alabama Journal*, May 7, 1851; Latshaw, p. 408; Stevens, pp. 145–191. "More than any other": *New Orleans Times-Picayune*, Apr. 27, 1851.

Jefferson, late 1808: Malone, vol. 5, pp. 613–615; Meacham, *Jefferson*, pp. 431–434; Burstein and Isenberg, pp. 451–463; Louis Sears, pp. 62–63, 116; Spivak, pp. 103–108. "All the trade": *New-England Palladium*, Jan. 1, 1808. "Never seen more gloomy": Spivak, p. 171. Canning on helping Jefferson end embargo: *American Statesmen*, vol. 11, p. 312. "Are our sixty thousand seamen": Pickering to James Sullivan, Feb. 16, 1808, Pickering Papers. "We are destroying" and "Are the people happy?": *New York Evening Post*, July 2, 1808. "I can tell him": *Providence Gazette*, Apr. 9, 1808. "You Infernal Villain": John Lane Jones to Jefferson, Aug. 8, 1808, TJP. "Treason" and "parricide": Jefferson to Mr. Letue, Nov. 8, 1808, TJP. "*The* CONSTITUTION *gone!!*": Handbill in LOC, Portfolio 48, Printed Ephemera Collection. "Awful crisis": Burstein and Isenberg, p. 458. "You have heard": Gallatin to Madison, Sept. 9, 1808, TJP. 1808 election: Malone, vol. 5, pp. 613–614; Meacham, *Jefferson*, pp. 329–331; Burstein and Isenberg, pp. 457–465. "Scenes of rural retirement": Jefferson to Charles Wilson Peale, Feb. 6, 1809, TJP. "I think one war enough": Jefferson to John Langdon, Aug. 2, 1808, TJP. "But if ever I was gratified": Jefferson to James Maury, Apr. 25, 1812, TJP.

CHAPTER TWO: "MAN OF STRAW"

Illusory peace with Great Britain: Bradford Perkins, pp. 209–219; Brant, vol. 5, pp. 42–50; Clarfield, p. 243; Ketcham, *Madison,* pp. 492–495; Wills, *Madison,* pp. 80–81; Brookhiser, p. 185. "GLORIOUS NEWS!": *Bee,* Apr. 25, 1809. "Renewal of Intercourse": *New-England Palladium,* May 5, 1809. "Probably no event": Quoted in *Alexandria Gazette,* May 22, 1809. "That through Mr. Madison": Quoted in *Newburyport Herald,* May 18, 1809. "I sincerely congratulate": Jefferson to Madison, Apr. 27, 1809, JMP. "The British Lion to crouch": CG, Aug. 5, 1854. "England has done now": Quoted in *Federal Republican,* May 3, 1809. Erskine background: Bradford Perkins, pp. 103–104; *Dictionary of National Biography* (1889), pp. 401–402. "Without talents or experience": *Anti-Jacobin Review,* vol. 28 (1808), p. 307. "One of the remarkable": Scharf, vol. 2, p. 1581. "Drive up constantly": *Colonial History Society,* vols. 53–56, p. 347. "For God's sake remember": *North American Review,* vol. 157, p. 98. Erskine's negotiation and backlash: Bradford Perkins, pp. 210–220; Brant, vol. 5, pp. 66–76. "Acted in direct contradiction": *Parliamentary Debates* (London), May 15, 1810. "WHO'S THE DUPE?": *Reporter* (Lexington, KY), June 10, 1809. "*Bribed by* BRITISH GOLD!!": Quoted in *Connecticut Herald,* June 27, 1809. "The greatest lawyer": Ernest Jones, vol. 1, p. 239.

Madison's choice of Smith: Brant, vol. 5, pp. 23–25. "Shameful and treacherous manner": *Farmer's Repository,* Aug. 25, 1809. "Is there any government": *Argus of Western America,* Jan. 27, 1810. "When a nation loses": *Sentinel of Freedom,* Aug. 29, 1809. Madison on "crooked" sleight of hand: Madison to Jefferson, June 12, 1809, JMP. Jefferson on British "tricks": Jefferson to Madison, Aug. 17, 1809, JMP. "My blood boils": Rutland, *Presidency,* p. 43. "Affliction and indignation": Paul Hamilton to Madison, Aug. 24, 1809, JMP. Erskine's later fate: *Oxford Dictionary,* vol. 18, p. 524. "Bloody bully of Copenhagen": *Reporter* (Brattleboro, VT), Oct. 7, 1809. "Personally obnoxious": Caesar Rodney to Madison, Sept. 6, 1809, JMP. "Worthy instrument": Madison to Jefferson, Nov. 6, 1809, JMP. "Ruin and dirt": Ketcham, *Madison,* p. 496. "Mass of folly and stupidity": Henry Adams, p. 120. "Astonishes the natives": Hunt, p. 308. "Without distinction either in manners": Ketcham, *Madison,* p. 496. "Fat and forty": Willard Randall, p. 148. "Had more civility and attention": Allgor, *Perfect Union,* p. 241. Smith to Jackson on future exchanges: Masterson, pp. 131, 128.

Jackson's early contact with US government: Bradford Perkins, pp. 220–221; Brant, vol. 5, pp. 71–93; Brookhiser, pp. 185–186. "Gross insinuation": Henry Adams, p. 132. "No further communications": Ketcham, *Madison,* p. 497; Cheney, p. 361. "Insulted the personal feelings": Quoted in *Republican Star,* Dec. 12, 1809. "Political monster": *Richmond Enquirer,* Sept. 14, 1810. Madison to Congress: Nov. 29, 1809. "Must war be prepared": Quoted in *Rhode-Island Republican,* Jan. 10, 1810. Jackson's tour: Brant, vol. 5, p. 255; *New York Evening Post,* Nov. 20, 1809. "British party in America": Ollier, *Cassell's History of the United States,* vol. 2, p. 532. "Where the *Chesapeake* had been assailed": *American Mercury,* Aug. 10, 1810. "Macon's Bill #2": Bradford Perkins, pp. 239–244; Brant, vol. 5, pp. 137–140; Stagg, p. 52; Wills, *Madison,* p. 87; Rutland, *Presidency,* p. 63. "Held up the honor": Bradford Perkins, p. 241. "We have lost our resentment": Tyler to Jefferson, May 12, 1810, TJP. "No man in the nation": Clay speech, Feb. 22, 1810; Remini, *Henry*

Clay, p. 60. "Hurricane of Passion": Bradford Perkins, pp. 243–244. "Will not have any effect" and "bait does not half": Bradford Perkins, pp. 246, 248. Madison on edicts "revoked": Ketcham, *Madison*, p. 504. "But one contest on our hands": Bradford Perkins, p. 251; Cheney, p. 365. "One of the most astonishing": Gordon Wood, p. 666.

Madison-Cadore letter: Bradford Perkins, pp. 246–252; Stagg, pp. 55–58; Rutland, *Presidency*, pp. 63–66; Gordon Wood, pp. 666–667. "Indolent": Bradford Perkins, p. 237. "Old clucking hen" and "man of straw": Rutland, *Madison*, p. 226; Bradford Perkins, p. 260. Clay and War Hawks: Remini, *Henry Clay*, pp. 75–71; Bradford Perkins, pp. 344–347. Jefferson and War Hawks: Jefferson to Madison, June 21, 1798. JMP. "Solemn stillness": Remini, *Henry Clay*, p. 47. "Has it released from galling": Clay speech, Feb. 15, 1811. Appointment of Monroe: Brant, vol. 5, pp. 282–287; Ammon, pp. 286–288; Brookhiser, pp. 188–189; Stagg, pp. 65–75. "His overthrow is my object": Brant, vol. 5, p. 289. "Sagacious in discerning": Beveridge, vol. 4., p. 35. "One of the rare instances": Rutland, *Madison*, p. 217. *"The eyes of the world"* and "Mr. M": Dolley Madison to Anna Cutts, June 20 and July 15, 1811, LOC. *Guerriere* incident: Brant, vol. 5, pp. 315–316; Ellis, p. 64. "Does not *expel*": *Richmond Enquirer*, 1811. "Pitiful imbecility": *New York Evening Post*, 1811. "Indeed the impressments": Bradford Perkins, p. 271. *Little Belt* episode: Guttridge and Smith, pp. 176–177; Toll, *Frigates*, pp. 321–324; Ketcham, *Madison*, p. 507; Paullin, pp. 209–242. "Before I had time": Auchinleck, p. 24. "Vessel of her inferiour force": *Niles' Weekly Register*, Sept. 21, 1811. "Passive spectator of insult": *True Republican*, June 12, 1811.

Madison's "approbation": Brant, vol. 5, p. 320. "Hug him to my bosom": Budiansky, p. 88. "For British vengeance": Toll, *Frigates*, p. 323. "So conspicuous in the British service": Madison to Jefferson, June 7, 1811, JMP. "What can be thought": *Farmer's Repository*, June 21, 1811. "If I can do no more": Quoted in *Reporter* (Brattleboro, VT), June 4, 1811. "Will these federalists ever cease": *New York Columbian*, 1811. Foster's arrival: Ketcham, *Madison*, pp. 507, 518; Foster, p. 20; Allgor, *Perfect Union*, p. 178; Bradford Perkins, p. 275. "Conditional and ambiguous": Bradford Perkins, p. 280. "War, dreadful as the alternative is": Monroe, vol. 5, pp. 191–192. "We passed two Months": Dolley Madison to Mr. and Mrs. Joel Barlow, Nov. 15, 1811, JMP. "Indians on our frontiers": *New-Jersey Journal*, Sept. 3, 1811. Indian challenge and response by US officials: Horsman, *Expansion*, pp. 3–172; Brant, vol. 5, pp. 190–193; Stagg, pp. 177–192; Owens, pp. 135–143; Horsman, *Causes*, pp. 162–166; Smelser.

Tecumseh: Brant, vol. 5, pp. 384–388; Cleaves, pp. 52–53, 59–60, 71–83; Langguth, pp. 157–160. Harrison's early career: Cleaves, pp. 1–97; Langguth, pp. 160–166. "Who does not know": Eckert, p. 926. "Tool of British fears": Wilentz, p. 148. "This Banditti": *Reporter* (Lexington, KY), Aug. 17, 1811. Battle of Tippecanoe: Collins, pp. 36–47; Cleaves, pp. 98–111; Stagg, pp. 185–189; Horsman, *Causes*, pp. 168–169; Jortner, pp. 133–232; Owens, pp. 217–223. "Real *murderers*": *Richmond Enquirer*, Dec. 10, 1811. *"Behold the effects":* Quoted in *Pittsfield Sun*, Dec. 7, 1811. "Citizens of the *Western country*": *Reporter* (Lexington, KY), 1811. "Crisis is at hand": *Baltimore Sun*, 1811. "War has been begun": *Aurora*, 1811. "I would advise the immediate Extermination": Matthew Lyon to Madison, Nov. 28, 1811, JMP. "My Children": Madison to Indian delegations, Aug. 22, 1812.

"It will certainly add": Clay to John Parker, Dec. 7, 1811, Clay Papers. Eagerness to attack Canada: Bradford Perkins, pp. 284–290; Stagg, pp. 4–7, 41–48; Wills, *Madison,* pp. 97–100.

"Most valuable of all her colonies": *Liberty Hall,* 1811. "Mere stock, or block, or statue": *Reporter* (Lexington, KY), 1811. Madison's message to Foster: Bradford Perkins, pp. 380–382. Madison's request for soldiers: Brant, vol. 5, pp. 390–398. "Mixture of good & bad": Madison to Jefferson, Feb. 7, 1812, JMP. "John Henry letters": Brant, vol. 5, pp. 413–420; Bradford Perkins, pp. 369–372; Borneman, *1812,* pp. 42–44; Stagg, pp. 93–99; Rutland, *Madison,* pp. 220–221. "Secret Agent" had been "fomenting disaffection": Madison to Congress, Mar. 9, 1812. "What national evil": *Republican Star,* Apr. 14, 1812. "If this event does not produce": Bradford Perkins, p. 371. "Electioneering trick": Hickey, p. 38. "This Spy and Traitor" and "had no more right" and *"What a national disgrace!":* Quoted in *Salem Gazette,* Apr. 3, 1812. "We espi'ed a *Henry":* Quoted in *Newburyport Herald,* June 26, 1812. Madison and 1812 embargo: Bradford Perkins, pp. 383–387. "Running mad": Dolley Madison to Anna Cutts, Mar. 27 and Mar. 20, 1812, LOC. Foster normalcy: Bradford Perkins, p. 402; Brant, vol. 5, p. 475; Foster, pp. 96–97. "Name of the Orders": Bradford Perkins, p. 381. US Navy weakness and British strength: Bradford Perkins, pp. 361–362; *Military Institute of National Security* (1953), p. 17; Stagg, pp. 120–176; Gordon Wood, pp. 672–674.

"Go to war without money": Toll, *Frigates,* p. 327. "Very large majority": Samuel Harrison to Madison, May 11, 1812, JMP. "Conquest of Lower Canada": Dearborn to Madison, Apr. 6, 1812, JMP. Dearborn as "Granny": Burstein and Isenberg, p. 529. Madison on "triangular" war: Madison to Jefferson, May 25, 1812, JMP. Madison's negotiations of spring 1812: Bradford Perkins, p. 401; Brant, vol. 5, pp. 466–470. "Wicked obstinacy": Madison to John Jackson, May 17, 1812. JMP. "Utter disregard": Madison to Henry Wheaton, Feb. 26, 1827, JMP. "Of all the enemies": Madison, "Political Observations," Apr. 20, 1795, JMP. "Crossing the sea": Madison to Jefferson, Apr. 27, 1785, JMP. Madison, von Pufendorf, and Grotius: Siemers, p. 89. Madison's attitude to war, late spring 1812: Ketcham, *Madison,* pp. 530–533; Brant, vol. 5, pp. 479–483. Clay and war declaration: Remini, *Henry Clay,* pp. 89–93. "On the side of Great Britain" and "injuries and indignities": Madison to Congress, June 1, 1812. "Let us give, in return": Clay to Jesse Bledsoe, June 18, 1812, Clay Papers. Congressional debate and vote on 1812 war: Brant, vol. 5, pp. 474–477; Bradford Perkins, pp. 406–415; Stagg, pp. 110–115; Rutland, *Madison,* pp. 224–225; Rutland, *Presidency,* pp. 100–102; Gordon Wood, pp. 660–661; *Abridgment of the Debates of Congress,* vol. 1, June 1812.

"A state of war has existed": Franklin Roosevelt to Congress, Dec. 8, 1941. "Endeavored to frighten one another": Masterson, p. 165. "Pushing matters to extremes": Bradford Perkins, p. 416. Events in London and Madison's response: Walpole, pp. 295–310; Ketcham, *Madison,* p. 535; Bradford Perkins, pp. 331–338. "Great Champion": Madison to John Jackson, June 21, 1812, JMP. Madison's pallor: Foster, p. 100. Madison signs war declaration: Brant, vol. 6, p. 22. "Hold back yr. ships": Henry Lee to Madison, June 21, 1812, JMP. "Termination of our disputes": *Independent Chronicle,* Aug. 3, 1812.

CHAPTER THREE: "THE MOST GLORIOUS WAR"

Madison after war declaration: Stagg, pp. 3–4. Opening of 1812 war: Langguth, pp. 173–207; Brant, vol. 6, pp. 22–54; Ketcham, *Madison,* pp. 527–533; Stagg, pp. 193–223; Gordon Wood, pp. 676–683. "Glory! Glory!": Quoted in *New-Jersey Journal,* Aug. 4, 1812. "Should the war continue": *Sentinel of Freedom,* Aug. 4, 1812. "IN-HABITANTS of Canada!!": *Farmer's Repository,* Aug. 7, 1812. "Opened the northern hive": *City Gazette,* Charleston, South Carolina, Sept. 26, 1812. "To take Malden": Madison to Jefferson, Aug. 17, 1812, JMP. "HULL has shamefully": *Reporter* (Lexington, KY), Sept. 5, 1812. "Solely" on "those men": *Poulson's American Daily Advertiser,* Aug. 28, 1812. "Chiefs of the Government": *New York Herald,* Sept. 9, 1812. "Surrender'd Detroit": Allgor, *Perfect Union,* p. 291. "Mortifying and humiliating": Monroe to Clay, Aug. 28, 1812, Clay Papers. "This most disgraceful event": Monroe to Jefferson, Sept. 2, 1812, TJP. "Deserves to be shot": Clay to Monroe, Sept. 21, 1812, Monroe Papers. "Erroneous excitements": Madison to Monroe, Sept. 6, 1812, JMP. "It is impossible for me": David Jones to Madison, Aug. 28, 1812, JMP.

"Author of this War": Quoted in *Salem Gazette,* Oct. 13, 1812. "What can we expect": *Rhode-Island American,* Sept. 1, 1812. "Poor Mr. Madison": *Newburyport Herald,* Aug. 25, 1812. "Unnecessary and ruinous": *Boston Gazette,* Oct. 15, 1812. Dearborn armistice: Stagg, pp. 245–246. "Those already impressed": Monroe to Jonathan Russell, June 26, 1812. Early opposition to war: Stagg, pp. 253–269; Buel, pp. 174–179; Rutland, *Madison,* pp. 127–130, 141. "Against the nation": Ketcham, *Madison,* p. 537. "Federalists in Congress": Madison to Jefferson, June 22, 1812, JMP. "Farmers of New England": Quoted in *New-England Palladium,* Aug. 11, 1812. "Surprize" and "pain": Madison to S. Spring, Sept. 6, 1812, JMP. "Were New England to become": *National Intelligencer,* Aug. 20, 1812. Attack on *Federal Republican:* Hickey, p. 57; *Providence Gazette,* July 4, 1812; *Albany Register,* June 30, 1812; *Poulson's American Daily Advertiser,* June 29, 1812.

Baltimore riot: *Newburyport Herald,* Aug. 4, 1812; *Federal Republican,* July 27 and Aug. 3 and 19, 1812; *National Intelligencer,* Aug. 1, 1812; *Alexandria Gazette,* Aug. 6, 1812; *Centinel of Freedom,* Aug. 11, 1812; *Connecticut Herald,* Aug. 18, 1812; Richard Buel, pp. 162–163; Gilje. "Punishment even of such men": Monroe to Madison, Aug. 4, 1812, JMP. "*The United States swarm*": *Lancaster Journal,* 1812. "War is the parent": Madison, "Political Observations," Apr. 20, 1795, JMP. "Hot-headed Executive": Madison to Jefferson, Feb. 18–19, 1798, JMP. "Perhaps it is a universal": Madison to Jefferson, May 13, 1798, JMP. "May terminate in the destruction": Shalhope, p. 123. *Guerriere-Constitution* encounter: Borneman, *1812,* pp. 89–94; Langguth, pp. 205–206; Willard Randall, p. 231. "Her sides are made of iron!": Labaree, p. 214. "Brilliant Naval victory": Quoted in *Rhode-Island American,* Sept. 1, 1812. Queenston Heights defeat: Langguth, pp. 209–218; Borneman, *1812,* pp. 72–75. "Misfortunes" of "our military": Gallatin to Jefferson, Dec. 18, 1812, TJP.

"Wholly unfit for the storms": Clay to Caesar Rodney, Dec. 29, 1812, Clay Papers. "Feeble and timid mind": Quoted in *Connecticut Herald,* Oct. 6, 1812. "History can scarce afford": *New-England Palladium,* Sept. 29, 1812. "Let us take Canada": Quoted in *Poulson's American Daily Advertiser,* Oct. 29, 1812. 1812 election campaign: Brookhiser, pp. 199–200; Stagg, pp. 118–119; Langguth, pp. 222–223; Wills, *Madison,* pp. 115–116.

"Shall it be said": *Constitutionalist*, Oct. 13, 1812. "Our expectation of gaining": Madison to Congress, Nov. 4, 1812. "Lame apology": *Providence Gazette,* Nov. 14, 1812. "Vindictive, ruinous and sanguinary": *Daily Spy,* Nov. 11, 1812. "Evidence of the unpopularity": *Constitutionalist,* Dec. 8, 1812. "Carriage with four spanking greys": *Poulson's American Daily Advertiser,* Mar. 13, 1813. "Means of conducting": Madison inaugural address, Mar. 4, 1813. "Preposterous eulogiem": *Federal Republican,* Mar. 12, 1813. Financing of 1812 war: Hormats, pp. 40–44; Meagher, p. 150; Edling, pp. 126–131. Possible military draft: Stagg, pp. 325–326. "Any thing like a Pledge": Ketcham, *Madison,* p. 592. Battle of Frenchtown: Langguth, pp. 238–242; Robert Watson, pp. 107–113.

"Terrors of the tomahawk": *National Intelligencer,* Mar. 27, 1813. "Many were burned alive": *Alexandria Gazette,* Mar. 8, 1813. Battle of York: Stagg, pp. 331–335; Langguth, pp. 227–235, 295, 306. "Seize your person": *Princeton Alumni Weekly,* Apr. 24, 1942. "Land as many chosen" and "I do not tremble": Brant, vol. 6, p. 169; Allgor, *Perfect Union,* p. 307. "Bilious fever": Monroe to Jefferson, June 28, 1813, TJP. Madison's medical history and illness: Allgor, *Perfect Union,* p. 300; Dolley Madison to Hannah Gallatin, July 29, 1813, LOC. "Lives by laudanum": Adams to William Wells, June 17, 1813. "His recent sickness": *Federal Republican,* Aug. 13, 1813. "Not from an apprehension": *Boston Daily Advertiser,* July 30, 1813. Dolley Madison background: Allgor, *Perfect Union,* pp. 23–26, 28–34; Allgor, *Problem,* pp. 26–27; Côté, pp. 106–125. Madison and Catherine Floyd: Ketcham, *Madison,* pp. 109–110; Cheney, p. 103. "Presidentess": Allgor, *Perfect Union,* p. 437. "Uncultivated mind": Ketcham, *Madison,* p. 428. "Day of Public Humiliation": Madison proclamation, July 23, 1813. Madison and religion: Gary Scott Smith, pp. 48–86; Ketcham, *Madison,* pp. 46–47, 52, 56–58, 667; Brant, vol. 1, pp. 68–71, 85, 111–122, 127–131, 245–250.

"I wish never to see": *Federal Republican,* Aug. 27, 1813. Madison and religious freedom: Alley, p. 189. "Bigotry may introduce": Madison memo, circa 1817. "Extreme repugnance" and "tremendous broadsides": *Works of Washington Irving,* vol. 8, pp. 45, 32, 252. Summer of 1813: Langguth, pp. 237–256; Brant, vol. 6, pp. 164–185, 195–226. "Don't give up the ship!": Toll, *Frigates,* p. 418. Perry on Lake Erie: *Baltimore Patriot,* Oct. 15, 1813; *Lancaster Journal,* Nov. 2, 1813; *Connecticut Herald,* Oct. 5, 1813; Toll, *Frigates,* pp. 418–419. "It hath pleased the Almighty": Ketcham, *Madison,* p. 565. *"Brilliant atchievement"* and "opened a passage" and "best auguries": Madison to William Jones, Sept. 23, 1813, JMP; Madison to Congress, Dec. 7, 1813. Battle of the Thames and Fort Niagara: Langguth, pp. 264–270. "Horrid massacre": *Constitutionalist,* Dec. 31, 1813. "Present war will continue": *National Intelligencer,* Mar. 23, 1813. "Not a boat was left": *Reporter* (Lexington, KY), Oct. 2, 1813. "Be prepared for the worst": Madison to John Armstrong, May 20, 1814, JMP.

"Depredations of the Enemy": Ketcham, *Madison,* p. 573. Madison's and Armstrong's preparations and Battle of Bladensburg: Langguth, pp. 295–306; Brookhiser, pp. 1–6, 205–208; Stagg, pp. 407–417; Rutland, *Presidency,* pp. 155–163; Skeen, *Armstrong,* pp. 189–198; McCavitt and George, pp. 116–138; Vogel, *Perilous,* pp. 34–118; Arnold. "Put his armor on" and "high spirits": Ketcham, *Madison,* pp. 575–576. "Should be ready at a moment's warning": Dolley Madison to Anna Cutts, Aug. 23, 1814, LOC. "Enemy are in full march": Monroe to Madison, Aug. 22, 1814, JMP. "Speediest counsel": Memo,

Aug. 24, 1814. "Thermometer marked blood heat": Ingersoll, p. 173. "Fell down into the road" and "There goes the President!": Madison, *Writings*, vol. 8, p. 297; Barron, p. 93; Lord, p. 150. Madisons' exile from Washington, DC: Ketcham, *Madison*, pp. 578–581; Brant, vol. 6, pp. 298–315; Cheney, pp. 409–411; Allgor, *Perfect Union*, pp. 314–320; *Federal Republican*, Aug. 30, 1814; *Papers of James Madison, Presidential Series*, vol. 8, pp. 137–141; Ingersoll, vol. 2, pp. 206–208. "Panic struck": *Federal Republican*, Sept. 14, 1814. "Thousands of infuriated negroes": Ingersoll, p. 208. "Heaving black clouds": Allgor, *Perfect Union*, p. 318.

"People are heaping curses": *A Century of Journalism*, vol. 1 (1943), p. 151. "If General Mason and suite" and "my house is filled": *Federal Republican*, Aug. 31, 1814. "Kindest and most touching": Ingersoll, p. 209. "Scar of a wound": Meyerson, p. 111. "Thirty miles since breakfast": *Federal Republican*, Aug. 31, 1814. "Disgrace of the President": *Salem Gazette*, Sept. 6, 1814. Madison at dinner: Vogel, *Perilous*, pp. 218–220; Ketcham, *Madison*, p. 580. "Seeming to forget": *Federal Republican*, Aug. 31, 1814. "Remain in your present quarters" and "hide our heads": Madison to Dolley, Aug. 28 and 27, 1814, JMP. "Ever since the Battle of Bladensburg": *Salem Gazette*, Sept. 9, 1814. Liverpool on Cockburn: *Times* (London), Nov. 8, 1814. Madisons return to Washington, DC: Brookhiser, pp. 209–211; Stagg, pp. 419–420; Ketcham, *Madison*, pp. 581–582. "In ashes, not an inch" and "smouldering ruins": Ketcham, *Madison*, p. 581. "Such destruction!": Howard, p. 217. "Sink our enemy": Lord, p. 204. "My heart mourned": Peter Snow, p. 106.

"Tear off his epaulettes": Brookhiser, p. 210. "Humors of a village mob": Neimeyer, p. 170. Armstrong's firing: Skeen, *Armstrong*, pp. 201–203. "Our country disgraced": *American Watchman*, 1814. "JAMES MADISON IS THE CAUSE": *Federal Republican*, Sept. 5, 1814. "Madisonians feel ashamed": *Delaware Gazette*, Sept. 1, 1814. "Constitutionally impeached": *Newport Mercury*, Sept. 10, 1814. "Do you ever blush?": *New-England Palladium*, Sept. 2, 1814. "Elegant scholar": *Boston Gazette*, Sept. 8, 1814. "'Fly, Monroe'": *New York Evening Post*, Sept. 6, 1814. "Armstrong the Traitor": Skeen, *Armstrong*, p. 199; Vogel, *Perilous*, p. 235. Armstrong in later life: Skeen, *Armstrong*, pp. 141, 209–229; Skeen, *New York Historical Society Quarterly*, Apr. 1973. Investors withdraw assets: Hormats, p. 45. Battle of Baltimore: Brookhiser, pp. 211–212; Langguth, pp. 315–321; Vogel, *Perilous*, pp. 287–360. Key during Baltimore conflict: Delaplaine, pp. 129–247. "In some degree, our national character": Quoted in *Bee* (Hudson, NY), Sept. 27, 1814. Struggle over capital site: Rohrs. Madisons in Octagon House: Allgor, *Perfect Union*, p. 328; Henry Adams, p. 231. Key poem becomes national anthem: Ferris, pp. 89–90, 104, 110–111, 127–128, 138, 143, 151, 156, 163–167, 176, 183, 190–192, 233–235, 239; *NYT*, Mar. 4, 1931.

"Put an end to drawing-rooms": Quoted in *New York Evening Post*, Sept. 19, 1814. "Looks miserably shattered": *Magazine of American History*, vol. 14, p. 451. "Source of our greatest difficulties": Madison to Wilson Cary Nicholas, Nov. 26, 1814, JMP. New England opposition: Stagg, pp. 481–485; Richard Buel, pp. 189–244; Gordon Wood, pp. 693–694. "Handsome new British crown": *Republican Star*, Jan. 24, 1815. "Daring, powerful, unprincipled": Brant, vol. 6, p. 200. "*Talk*, mere *talk*": *Richmond Enquirer*, Jan. 14, 1815. "*Mountain* was in labor": *Independent Chronicle*, Feb. 24, 1815. "Not so easy to get up a civil war": *National Intelligencer*, Jan. 13, 1815. "Our anxieties": Langguth, p. 374. Madison and Battle of New Orleans: Stagg, pp. 489–499; Langguth, pp. 343–369; Rutland, *Presidency*, pp. 183–186; Gordon Wood, pp. 695–696. "Glory be to God": Quoted in Neff,

p. 602. "Degrading practice": Remini, *Henry Clay*, p. 104. "They sit after dinner": Nagel, p. 218; Parsons, p. 116. Ghent peace talks: Langguth, pp. 323–342; Gordon Wood, p. 695. Madison receives treaty: Langguth, pp. 375–376; Ketcham, *Madison*, pp. 596–597; Allgor, *Perfect Union*, pp. 332–334. "Crazy with joy": Jennings, p. 17. "No one could doubt": Howard, p. 291.

"Our glorious Peace": Allgor, *Perfect Union*, p. 342. "Handsome . . . national": Ammon, p. 320. Celebrations of peace: *Hallowell Gazette*, Mar. 8, 1815; *Independent Chronicle*, Feb. 27 and Mar. 20, 1815; *Boston Daily Advertiser*, Feb. 24, 1815; *Pittsfield Sun*, Feb. 23, 1815; *Poulson's American Daily Advertiser*, Feb. 23, 1815. "Exulted as an Ox": *Connecticut Journal*, Feb. 27, 1815. "All of Washington is now jumping": Allgor, *Perfect Union*, p. 337. Federal criticism of treaty: *National Advocate*, Feb. 27, 1815; *Hallowell Gazette*, Mar. 1, 1815; *New York Evening Post*, Feb. 24, 1815; *Delaware Gazette*, Feb. 21, 1815; *Newport Mercury*, Mar. 11, 1815. "Yes, a Peace is made": *Rhode-Island Republican*, Feb. 15, 1815. "If ever there was a necessary": *Rutland Herald*, Mar. 1, 1815. Deaths and casualties in 1812 war: Leland and Oberoceanu, p. 2. "Glorious termination of the most glorious war": Annals of the Congress, vol. 28 (1815), p. 1155. "Not an inch *ceded*": Henry Adams, p. 81. "Second war for our independence": *American Whig Review*, vol. 5, p. 93.

"Additional slander": *Niles' Weekly Register*, vol. 7, p. 53. "Most unpopular war": Morison, "Our Most Unpopular War," *Proceedings of the Massachusetts Historical Society*, vol. 80, p. 38. "If our first struggle": Madison to Charles Ingersoll, Jan. 4, 1818, JMP. "Without those large standing armies": Madison to William Wirt, Sept. 30, 1813, JMP. "Looks just as she did" and "never was strong": Ketcham, *Montpelier*, pp. 167–169. Madison's visit with Ingersoll: Brant, vol. 6, pp. 517–518; *Richmond Enquirer*, Aug. 19, 1836; *Washington Globe*, Aug. 6, 1836; Ketcham, *Montpelier*, pp. 165–171. "All are now united in the wisdom": *Niles' Register*, Oct. 7, 1826; *Eastern Argus*, Oct. 6, 1826. "Straining every nerve": *Niles' Register*, Oct. 12, 1839. "Opposers of the war of 1812": *Eastern Argus*, July 15, 1828. "The illustrious Hero": *Providence Patriot*, May 9, 1832. "Diaries have been burned": Ingersoll, p. 171. "Pre-eminent for his patriotism" and "cut on the spot": Polk to John Hennick, Oct. 6, 1845, JKPP. "Curiously wrought Hickory walking cane": Polk diary, Sept. 24, 1845, JKPP.

CHAPTER FOUR: "THE COUNTRY IS NOW VIRTUALLY OURS"

Seth Thornton and confrontation with Mexicans: Jenkins, pp. 87–90; Wilcox, pp. 43–48, 358; Wheelan, pp. 91–92; Lamont Wood, pp. 50–57; Nathaniel Hughes, pp. 24–30; *Court of Inquiry, Captain W. J. Hardee*, May 1846; William J. Hardee to Zachary Taylor, Apr. 26, 1846, Taylor Papers; Goode, pp. 359–361; Rodenbaugh, p. 451; *Journal of the American Military History Foundation*, Autumn 1937; *Niles' Register*, Aug. 22, 1846; *Boston Evening Transcript*, May 14, 1846; *Idaho Daily Statesman*, July 2, 1916; *New Hampshire Patriot*, May 21, 1846; *New Hampshire Gazette*, May 17, 1846; *New Hampshire Sentinel*, May 20, 1846; *Newport Mercury*, May 16, 1846; *Middletown Constitution*, May 27, 1846; *Baltimore Sun*, May 11, 1846; *Milwaukee Sentinel*, May 23, 1846; *Albany Evening Journal*, May 11, 1846; *Farmer's Cabinet*, May 14, 1846; *Hudson River Chronicle*, May 12, 1846. "Comfort and delight": Goode, p. 359. "Braver and more warm-hearted soul": *Niles' National Register*, Oct. 2, 1847. "Too ardent and impetuous": *Mexican War and Its Heroes*, p. 173.

Polk sends Taylor Army: Merry, *Country,* pp. 186–189; Bauer, *Taylor,* pp. 111–129; Borneman, *Polk,* pp. 190–191. "Horribly mutilated" and "full of Mexicans": Jenkins, pp. 87, 84. "Famished and reduced": *Niles' National Register,* Oct. 2, 1847. "Mexicans had not crossed": W. J. Hardee to Polk, Apr. 26, 1846, JKPP. "Blaze of fire": *Mexican War and Its Heroes,* p. 172. "I very much fear": Barbour, Apr. 26, 1846. Taylor's reaction to report of Mexican attack: Fehrenbach, p. 271. "Hostilities may now be" and "We hope soon to avenge": *New York Herald,* May 14, 1846; *Herald* (Somerset, PA), May 26, 1846. "Ample cause of war": Greenberg, p. 103. "It was so agreed": Polk diary, May 9, 1846, JKPP. "Most gracious": Nathaniel Hughes, p. 26. Polk's early life and career: Borneman, *Polk,* pp. 5–66; Sellers, vol. 1, pp. 3–492; McCormac, vol. 1, pp. 1–211. "Possum looking": Sellers, vol. 2, p. 105. Polk and Van Buren in 1844: Borneman, *Polk,* pp. 43–47, 58–60, 86–87.

Early history of Texas: Fehrenbach, pp. 3–267; Haley, pp. 3–260; Brands, *Lone Star Nation,* pp. 3–525. Tyler and Texas annexation: Merry, *Country,* pp. 71–73; Chitwood, pp. 342–356; Crapol, pp. 218–220; Howe, pp. 698–700. Polk and urinary stones: Merry, *Country,* pp. 15–16. Democrats and Whigs in early 1840s: Holt, pp. 122–207. "Who did not squirt": Sellers, vol. 1, p. 490. "Bombshell" appendix: Wilentz, pp. 41–42, 49–50. Van Buren and Texas annexation: Niven, pp. 445–457, 518–531. "Prosperity & permanent happiness": Remini, *Democracy,* vol. 3, p. 493. "Our western boundary": Parton, vol. 3, p. 659. Jackson in 1844 campaign: Sellers, vol. 2, pp. 71–2; Remini, *Democracy,* vol. 3, pp. 505–508. "It's a forgery!": Merrill Peterson, *Great Triumvirate,* p. 360. "I have no hesitation": Polk to Salmon P. Chase, Apr. 23, 1844, JKPP. "If the Union is to break": Sellers, vol. 2, p. 112. "Corrupt bargain": Remini, *Henry Clay,* p. 270. 1844 Democratic Convention: Sellers, vol. 2, pp. 85–100; McCormac, vol. 1, pp. 212–247; Borneman, *Polk,* pp. 94–110. "You should have heard": Sellers, vol. 2, p. 95.

"Earliest practicable" moment: Remini, *Democracy,* vol. 3, p. 503. "Daughter, I will put you": Borneman, *Polk,* p. 111. Clay inquiry if "serious": Bicknell, p. 92. "Expressly for Texas": *Writings and Speeches of Daniel Webster,* p. 247. "Pronounced *Poke*": *New Hampshire Sentinel,* June 5, 1844. "Third rate politician": *Hudson River Chronicle,* June 4, 1844. "Polkats": *Milwaukee Sentinel,* Oct. 12, 1844. "National dishonor": Clay to Thomas Peters, July 27, 1844, Clay Papers. "Have no patriotism": Justin Smith, p. 263. Polk and slavery: Dusinberre, pp. 16–17, 19–22, 62–63, 77–80, 168–169. "Fanatical wicked": Sellers, vol. 1, p. 349. "Traffics in slaves": *Albany Evening Journal,* Sept. 17, 1844. "Has never owned a slave": *Ohio Statesman,* Sept. 25, 1844. "POLK, DALLAS" and "whole locofoco": *Pittsfield Sun,* Nov. 7, 1844; *Vermont Phoenix,* Nov. 1 and Aug. 9, 1844. "With the settled purpose": Borneman, *Polk,* p. 114. Proposed Nashville demonstration: Cheatham, pp. 165–169; Sellers, vol. 2, pp. 114–116; Atkins, pp. 134–138. J. Q. Adams on Polk victory: John Quincy Adams, p. 572.

"Flag means *Texas*": Marsh, vol. 1, p. 71. "Perpetuity of our glorious": Meacham, *American Lion,* p. 351. Tyler's final effort for Texas annexation: Chitwood, pp. 357–366; Merry, *Country,* pp. 120–124; Howe, pp. 698–700. "Texas, Texas, Texas": Remini, *Democracy,* vol. 3, p. 510. "Never had command": *Constitution* (Middletown, CT), Sept. 4, 1844. "YOU have elected": *Barre Patriot,* Nov. 15, 1844. "Deed is done": *Farmer's Cabinet,* Mar. 6, 1845. "Prolific of evil": Benton, vol. 2, p. 638. Polk's inauguration: Polk address, Mar. 4, 1845; *Baltimore Sun,* Mar. 5, 1845; *Milwaukee Sentinel,* Mar. 22, 1845. "A little band of veteran": *Baltimore Sun,* Mar. 5, 1845. "Large assemblage": John Quincy Adams diary, Mar. 4, 1845. "Air of a man profoundly impressed": *Milwaukee Sentinel,* Mar. 22, 1845. "Deeply fringed": Bumgarner, p. 59. Scene at Carusi's Saloon: Budiansky, p. 59; Merry, *Country,* p. 11; Borneman, *Polk,* p. 144. Polk rejects Benton plan: Merry, *Country,* pp. 127–130, 140–141; Borneman, *Polk,* pp. 138–140, 145–147. "Full assurance": Benton, vol. 1, p. 637. "Most speedily" and "well-known justice" and "placed in jeopardy": Merry, *Country,* p. 136. "Cheated" and "fraud": Benton, vol. 2, p. 636. Polk cites executive privilege: Borneman, *Polk,* p. 146. Polk's ambition for new territory: Borneman, *Polk,* p. 150; Sellers, vol. 2, pp. 213–215. "Our manifest destiny": Brown, p. 16; Nester, *Jackson,* p. 226. Anson Jones and negotiation: Gambrell, pp. 361–365, 392–393; Merry, *Country,* pp. 148–150, 157–158. "Magnificent offers": *Niles' National Register,* Mar. 29, 1845. "May never be recovered": Justin Smith, p. 442. Sam Houston's reaction to Polk's actions: Borneman, *Polk,* pp. 145–147. "I knew British gold": Jackson to Polk, May 26, 1845, JKPP. "Bombastically aggressive": Caruso, p. 24. Stockton background and Stockton affair: Brockmann, pp. 7–156; Merry, *Country,* pp. 151–160; Caruso, pp. 26–35; Price, pp. 49–151. "Of an inferior": *United States Magazine and Democratic Review,* July 1845. "Clear and protect": Caruso, p. 27. "So, gentlemen": Price, pp. 112–113.

Texas approves statehood: Fehrenbach, pp. 263–269; Borneman, *Polk,* pp. 147–149; Wheelan, pp. 55–57, 78. "With becoming dignity": Justin Smith, p. 459. "Die is cast": *New Hampshire Gazette,* Aug. 5, 1845. "Mexico will declare": *New Hampshire Sentinel,* Aug. 6, 1845. "Creative disobedience": Brockmann, p. 12. "Deter and prevent": Polk diary, Sept. 1, 1845, JKPP. "Army of occupation" and "so long at peace": Polk diary, Aug, 30 and Sept. 2, 1845, JKPP. "But for the appearance": Silverstone, p. 165. *"Offensive war":* National Intelligencer, Aug. 1845. "Soon our Army": *New Hampshire Sentinel,* Aug. 20, 1845. Decision of Polk cabinet, Aug. 1845: Bergeron, pp. 62–64. Parrott mission: McCormac, vol. 2, pp. 383–385; Merry, *Country,* pp. 193–195; Caruso, pp. 44–60. "Until after we shall": Sellers, vol. 2, pp. 262–263. American officials agreed: McCormac, vol. 2, p. 384. Slidell mission: Bergeron, pp. 69–72; Merry, *Country,* p. 194; Greenberg, pp. 77–79. "For such a boundary": Sellers, vol. 2, p. 264. "Exceedingly desirous": Borneman, *Polk,* p. 196.

"So strong": Buchanan, vol. 6, p. 261. "Full power": Sellers, vol. 2, p. 331. "Mortifying" failure: Borneman, *Polk,* p. 197. Polk talks with Atocha: Borneman, *Polk,* pp. 197–199; Merry, *Country,* pp. 230–232. "Proper remedies": Sellers, vol. 2, p. 338. "If it could be asserted": *Works of James Buchanan,* vol. 6, p. 403. "Unwilling to take a course": *Massachusetts Quarterly Review,* Dec. 1847. "Despoiled": Merry, *Country,* p. 233. "Be assured": Mahin, p. 61. Polk asks for "succinct" case: Polk diary, Apr. 28, 1846, JKPP. Polk and Oregon: Borneman, *Polk,* pp. 160–169; Merry, *Country,* pp. 199–200, 207–208, 264–266. Mexican ultimatum: Merry, *Country,* pp. 240–241; Greenberg, p. 101. "Decided aversion" and "could not permit": Borneman, *Polk,* p. 203. "Hostilities might" and "but one course": Polk diary, May 5, 6, and 8, 1846, JKPP. Polk's reaction to Thornton ambush: Borneman, *Polk,* pp. 201–205; Merry, *Country,* pp. 242–246. "Great anxiety": Polk diary, May 10, 1846, JKPP. "With which Mexico": William Chambers, *Old Bullion,* p. 308. "Spilling American blood": Benton, vol. 2, p. 678.

"Willing to vote men": Polk diary, May 11, 1846, JKPP. "Speedy and successful": Polk to Congress, May 11, 1846. "Breathless silence": CG, May 15, 1846. Members' skepticism about Polk's message: CG, May 11 and 12, 1846. "Magnetic Telegraph": *Baltimore Sun,* May 12, 1846. "I told him" and "in the nineteenth century" and "The Whigs in the

Senate": Polk diary, May 11, 1846, JKPP. Houston, Cass, Mangum, Calhoun statements: CG, May 12, 1846. Thomas and Dean Rusk: Fehrenbach, p. 222. "So bold a falsehood": CG, May 11, 1846. "Ruined man": Sellers, vol. 2, p. 418. "Difficult—perhaps impossible": Benton, vol. 2, p. 679. "Fear of being nicknamed": *Emancipator,* May 27, 1846. "What no previous Congress": *Middletown Constitution,* 1846. "Gross and palpable": *Vermont Phoenix,* 1846. "Into a monarch": *Berkshire County Whig,* June 18, 1846. "Lickspittles and toadeaters" and "excused himself": *Milwaukee Sentinel,* May 30 and June 9, 1846. "Animating and thrilling": Polk diary, May 12, 1846, JKPP. "Last resort": Polk proclamation, May 13, 1846. May 12 Cabinet meeting and Polk's reaction: Polk diary, May 12–13, 1846, JKPP. "Almost got on their knees": Merry, *Country,* p. 251. "Ay, except the preamble": CG, May 12, 1846.

CHAPTER FIVE: "A PRESIDENTIAL WAR"

"MEXICO OR DEATH": *Boston Evening Transcript,* May 14, 1846. "Outrage upon humanity": Quoted in *Baltimore Sun,* May 18, 1846. "We can send out": Quoted in CG, May 15, 1846. "Sustain the country": Merry, *Country,* p. 255. "Glowing with a spirit": *Vicksburg Daily Whig,* May 7, 1846. "To arms, Texans!": *Louisville Daily Courier,* May 11, 1846. "Has not had his harness off": *Evening Journal,* 1846. Polk at start of Mexican War and "harassing": Polk diary, May 17–18, 1846, JKPP. "Fixed and unalterable": Henry, p. 49. "Officers are all whigs": Polk diary, May 22, 1846, JKPP. Polk and early victories: Merry, *Country,* pp. 259–263; Borneman, *Polk,* pp. 210–215. Retreat across Rio Grande: John Eisenhower, *So Far,* pp. 82–84. "Like another Thermopylae": *Macon Weekly Telegraph,* June 23, 1846. "We look in vain": Quoted in *Milwaukee Sentinel,* June 9, 1846. "My friends in Congress" and "occupy the country": Polk diary, May 25 and 16, 1846, JKPP. "Protect our traders" and "expedition be immediately fitted out" and "the more I reflected" and "I stated that if the war": Polk diary, May 26, 29, and 30, 1846, JKPP.

"War was a necessity": Benton, vol. 2, p. 680. Polk and Cabinet on "objects of the War": Polk diary, June 30, 1846, JKPP. Mackenzie mission: Merry, *Country,* pp. 278, 308, 411–412; Borneman, *Polk,* pp. 329–330. "With pleasure" and "present unhappy war": Merry, *Country,* pp. 278–279. "Extraordinary expenses": Howe, p. 766. "Conclude a treaty": Polk annual message to Congress, Dec. 7, 1847. Polk and Wilmot Proviso: Howe, pp. 689–690, 767–770; Borneman, *Polk,* pp. 231–232; Merry, *Country,* pp. 286–292. Financing of war: Hormats, p. 59. "I am confident" and "responsibility will fall": Polk diary, Aug. 10, 1846, JKPP. Polk's health: Polk diary, Aug. 19–25, 1846, JKPP; *Baltimore Sun,* Aug. 26, 1846; Sellers, vol. 2, pp. 304, 484–487; Bergeron, p. 234. "When I think of the labor": Bumgarner, p. 51. Polk and news from California: Borneman, *Polk,* pp. 234–240, 271–279; Merry, *Country,* pp. 296–306. "Same individual": *New Hampshire Patriot,* Sept. 3, 1846. Kearny's clash with Stockton and Frémont: Clary, p. 258. Veracruz and Santa Anna: Merry, *Country,* pp. 307–310. Taylor's complaint and request to Polk: Bauer, *Taylor,* pp. 185–190. Polk's response and "most ungrateful": Polk diary, Sept. 5 and Nov. 21, 1846, JKPP.

Taylor to Monterrey and Polk's reaction to "magnanimity": Bauer, *Taylor,* p. 184. Webster at Faneuil Hall: Remini, *Daniel Webster,* p. 626. "Universally odious": Webster speech, Nov. 6, 1846. "With all due pomp": *Washington Union,* 1846. "Country is at war": *New Hampshire Patriot,* Dec. 3, 1846. "Hope of soon putting a check": *Milwaukee Sentinel,* Nov. 6, 1846. Lincoln's election to House: Donald, pp. 113–115. "Won against greatly superior": Polk annual message to Congress, Dec. 8, 1846. "By G-d, I opposed": Boritt and Forness, p. 26. "Open and burning shame": Merry, *Country*, p. 323. "Treasonable" and "odium upon at least one half": *New Hampshire Sentinel*, Dec. 23, 1846, Jan. 6, 1847. "Taking Mr. Polk's word": *Cleveland Herald*, 1846. Civility breaks down in House: CG, Dec. 21–22, 1846. "Always somebody opposed": Claxton, p. 174. Sarah Polk background: Bumgarner, pp. 16–25; Barbara Peterson, pp. 1–4; Borneman, *Polk*, pp. 12–17, 41–42, 49–50, 61–62. "Moral treason": Merry, *Country*, p. 323.

"Her wealthy family" and "henpecked": Bumgarner, pp. 25, 60. "I never wanted to see you": Sarah Polk to Polk, May 3, 1843, JKPP. "Despondingly": Polk to Sarah Polk, June 9, 1843, JKPP. "I understand you": Claxton, p. 42. "Exactly the look": Bumgarner, p. 34. "She is certainly master": Bumgarner, p. 60. "Sahara Sarah": Sibley, p. 169. "Sweetness of manner" and "a little too formal": Sellers, vol. 2, p. 308. "Whatever sustained": Greenberg, p. 96. Polk faith: Borneman, *Polk*, pp. 166–168, 203–205, 280, 285; Bergeron, pp. 240–242. "Solemn preparation": Chase, p. 474. "Thank God": Polk diary, Oct. 14, 1846, JKPP. "It does strike me" and "I do not think" and "I do not believe": Sarah Polk to Polk, Dec. 31, 1840, Apr. 8 and 10, 1841, JKPP. "We have gotten along": Bumgarner, p. 70. Polk and civil liberties, censorship, military draft: Winders, pp. 195–200; Pinheiro, pp. 44–54; Bulla, p. 66; Jeffery Smith, pp. 94–98. Polk's accusation of "moral treason": Polk diary, Apr. 16, 1847, JKPP. Polk's eagerness to expand war: Borneman, *Polk*, pp. 254–258; Merry, *Country*, pp. 318–322, 335–338.

"Great weakness and folly" and "giddy": Polk diary, Nov. 21, 1846, JKPP. "So much affected": Polk diary, Nov. 19, 1846, JKPP. "Acquisition, by conquest": McCormac, vol. 2, p. 622. "War-register": *Union*, Dec. 24, 1846. "I am not prepared": Taylor to *Morning Signal*, May 18, 1847. "Would force General Taylor": Merry, *Country*, p. 362. "Course of indecision": Polk to Congress, Feb. 17, 1847. "Masterly inactivity": Merry, *Country*, p. 345. "Manner in which it was brought on": *Niles' National Register*, Feb. 20, 1847. "Causes of this Mexican war" and "now he sets up": Benton, pp. 639–640, 646. "Good feeling prevailed": Polk diary, Mar. 3, 1847. Battle of Buena Vista: Borneman, *Polk*, pp. 249–252; Merry, *Country*, pp. 353–355; Wheelan, pp. 273–274, 279–294. "Cut to pieces": Clary, p. 272. Atocha peace offer: Thomas Leonard, pp. 174–175. "Pursue Santa Anna's Army": Polk diary, Mar. 20, 1847, JKPP. "Ours is a go-ahead": Merry, *Country*, p. 317. Henry Clay Jr.'s death: Heidler and Heidler, pp. 413–416. "This most unnecessary" and "Leave me": Remini, *Henry Clay*, pp. 668, 684. "I find it extremely difficult": Clay to William Mercer, Apr. 1, 1847, Clay Papers. "Gave every assurance": Taylor to Clay, Mar. 1, 1847, Clay Papers. "Lock of his hair": Cary Fry to Clay, Mar. 22, 1847, Clay Papers.

Whig press on death of Clay Jr.: *Milwaukee Sentinel*, Apr. 22, 1847, and *Albany Evening Journal*, Apr. 8, 1847. "Why single out young Henry": *Ohio Statesman*, 1847. Polk and Yell and Yell in battle: William Hughes, pp. 28–31, 41–42, 91–92, 149–150. "Gallantly at the head": Taylor report, Mar. 6, 1847. "Brave and good man": Polk diary, Apr. 1, 1847, JKPP. "None of his relatives": William Hughes, p. 149. "The truth is": Polk diary, Mar. 28, 1847, JKPP. "In fine style": Scott dispatch, Mar. 12, 1847, NARA. "Joyous news": Merry, *Country*, p. 358. "Taken the Gibraltar": *Union*, Apr. 10, 1847. Trist and his mission: Wheelan, pp. 362–366, 393–394; Howe, pp. 800–814; Borneman, *Polk*, pp. 261–266, 288–289; Merry, *Country*, pp. 359–362, 383–386; Greenberg, pp. 91–95, 206–207,

218–219; John Eisenhower, *So Far,* pp. 304–308. "Great outrage upon me": Polk diary, Apr. 21, 1847, JKPP. "Directive from the President": Merry, *Country,* p. 366. "Degrade me": McCormac, vol. 2, p. 495. "Too much occupied": Henry, pp. 296–297, 293.

"What any man of plain": Trist to Scott, May 9, 1847, NARA. "Greatest imbecile": McCormac, vol. 2, p. 498. "I entreat to be spared": Scott to Marcy, May 20, 1847, NARA. "Golden moment": Polk diary, June 16, 1847, JKPP. "Many cruel disappointments": McCormac, vol. 2, p. 505. Polk is persuaded not to fire Trist: Merry, *Country,* p. 369. Trist bonds with Scott and "duty to disregard": Merry, *Country,* pp. 372–374. "My reception was everywhere" and "Nothing of a party": Polk diary, July 4, 1847, JKPP. "All constraint & embarrassment": McCormac, vol. 2, p. 509. Thornton's death in battle: *Vermont Gazette,* Sept. 22, 1847; *Ohio Statesman,* Sept. 21, 1847; Wilcox, pp. 48, 358–359; Hill, pp. 756–757; *Mexican War and Its Heroes,* pp. 172–173; Wheelan, pp. 351–352. "Thornton is cut" and "known to the whole": Hill, p. 757. Contreras: Merry, *Country,* pp. 390–391; Wheelan, pp. 355–356; Greenberg, pp. 208–209. "Too much blood": Henry, p. 344. Conquest of Mexico City: Greenberg, pp. 205–211; Borneman, *Polk,* pp. 257–260, 289–303.

Clay Nov. 1847 speech: Remini, *Henry Clay,* pp. 692–696; Greenberg, pp. 230–237; Heidlers, pp. 427–428, 431, 464. "Day is dark and gloomy": *Whig Almanac,* Nov. 13, 1847. Clay renewed presidential hope: Remini, *Henry Clay,* pp. 695–711. Edward Webster and demise: Remini, *Daniel Webster,* 423–424, 482–483, 496–498, 626–627, 642–645. "Pet of the family": McMaster, p. 6. "What had you to do": Webster to Edward Webster, Apr. 22, 1837, Webster Papers. "I hardly know": Webster to Fletcher Webster, Feb. 23, 1848, Webster Papers. "Wicked & cruel war": Julia Webster to Webster, Feb. 23, 1848, Webster Papers. "So deeply moved": Quoted in *Boston Evening Transcript,* Mar. 27, 1848. "Return our friends" CG, Mar. 23, 1848. Lincoln's speeches of Dec. 1847 and Jan. 1848: CG, Dec. 22, 1847, and Jan. 12, 1848; Donald, pp. 123–126; Burlingame, *Lincoln,* vol. 1, pp. 265–273, 277–280, 526–530; Greenberg, pp. 248–255. "Unnecessarily and unconstitutionally": Foner, p. 53. "Spotty Lincoln" and "Benedict Arnold": Benjamin Thomas, p. 120.

"Remaining third": Polk diary, Nov. 2, 1847, JKPP. "History presents": Polk annual message to Congress, Dec. 7, 1847. Lincoln's one-term pledge: Burlingame, *Lincoln,* vol. 1, p. 271. "Bully of the bailiwick": *Hudson River Chronicle,* Dec. 28, 1847. Calhoun's speech: CG, Jan. 4, 1848. House action against Polk and war: Howe, p. 797. "For the express purpose": *Republican Farmer,* Mar. 28, 1848. "Would exhibit me": McCormac, vol. 2, p. 440. "Would ever trust us": Merry, *Country,* p. 412. "Constitutional right": Rozell, pp. 35–36. "This House ought" and "Should it go abroad": Merry, *Country,* p. 412. Polk and Trist recalcitrance: Borneman, *Polk,* pp. 303–308. "Make the treaty" and Trist's response: Ohrt, p. 140. "Lending himself to all": McCormac, vol. 2, p. 532. "Vanity and tyrannical temper": Polk diary, Dec. 30, 1847, JKPP. "Infallability of judgment": Merry, *Country,* p. 410. "Contemptably base": Polk diary, Jan. 15, 1848, JKPP. Trist and treaty: Merry, *Country,* pp. 424–426; Greenberg, pp. 258–261. "Acted very badly" and "total change of opinion" and "No candidate": Polk diary, Feb. 20–21, 1848, JKPP.

"Saw everything upside" and *"maker* of the President": McCormac, vol. 2, p. 526. "Grant either men": Polk diary, Feb. 21, 1848, JKPP. "Infamous" treaty and "illegality and fraud":

New York Herald, Mar. 16, 1848; Merry, *Country,* pp. 431–439. Polk reacts to *Herald* account: Polk diary, Mar. 24, 1848, JKPP. Buchanan as possibly gay: Jean Baker, *Buchanan,* pp. 20–22, 25–26. Polk-Buchanan showdown: Polk diary, Mar. 25, 1848, JKPP. "GOOD NEWS!": *Milwaukee Sentinel,* 1848. "Country demands peace now": *New-York Tribune,* 1848. "Terms of peace": *Trenton State Gazette,* Mar. 13, 1848. Dead and wounded: US Department of Veterans Affairs. "Not worth a dollar": CG, Mar. 23, 1848. "Immense empire": Polk diary, Feb. 28, 1848, JKPP. Ratification of treaty: Merry, *Country,* pp. 434–435. Washington Monument ceremony: *Baltimore Sun,* July 5–8, 1848; *Washington Union,* July 5, 1848. "Waving plumes": *Baltimore Sun,* July 6, 1848. "Wherever you cast": *Pittsfield Sun,* July 13, 1848. Dolley Madison during Polk years: Côté, p. 356. "Many marked and mourned": *Washington Union,* July 8, 1848. "National character abroad": Polk to Congress, July 6, 1848. "Great labour & anxiety" and "exceedingly fatigued": Polk diary, May 30, 1848, JKPP. "Would be attended": Polk diary, Jan. 5, 1847, JKPP.

Taylor's election: Bauer, *Taylor,* pp. 245–247. "Broken down old man": *Baltimore Sun,* June 22, 1849. Polk's journey as ex-President: Borneman, *Polk,* pp. 338–344; Merry, *Country,* pp. 469–470; Bergeron, pp. 257–260. "Greatly fatigued" and "too far on my journey": Polk diary, Mar. 16 and 18, 1849, JKPP. "Arranging my library": Polk diary, June 2, 1849, JKPP. Polk's illness: Claxton, p. 135. "I love you, Sarah": Borneman, *Polk,* p. 44. Polk's burial: Bumgarner, p. 153. "This silence speaks": *Vermont Gazette,* Jan. 17, 1850. "Memory of the wicked": *North Star,* Nov. 10, 1848. "Left his slaves" and "criminal disregard": *Liberator,* Aug. 25 and 18, 1848. "Not only Texas": Jay, p. 270. Gold Rush: Brands, *Age of Gold,* pp. 14–17, 47–48, 70–72. Sarah Polk's last years and "planted laws": Bumgarner, pp. 133, 142, 153. "Against his own country": *Constitution* (Washington, DC), May 26, 1860. "Did more to embarrass": *New Hampshire Patriot,* June 20, 1860. Lincoln to Herndon: Ronald White, *Lincoln,* p. 150. "Force and compel": CG, Feb. 2, 1848. "My old, withered, dry eyes": Burlingame, *Inner World,* p. 74; William Miller, p. 429. Fate of Polk Place: *Tennessean,* Mar. 24, 2017. Lincoln on "rascality": Pearlman, *Warmaking,* p. 134. "Our fences where they are": Lincoln speech, Sept. 12, 1848. "Allow the president to invade" and "kings had always been": Lincoln to Herndon, Feb. 15, 1848, ALP.

CHAPTER SIX: FORT SUMTER

Robert Anderson and his background: Goodheart, pp. 5–6; Detzer, pp. 16–22; Swanberg, pp. 34–37; Lawton, pp. 4–5; Meredith, pp. 35–36; Maury Klein, pp. 106–107; Stout, *Aristocrats,* pp. 213–238. Eba Anderson: Detzer, pp. 22–27; *NYT,* Feb. 28, 1905. "God grant": Stout, *Aristocrats,* p. 259. "I just this moment" and "killing each other": Robert Anderson, pp. 117, 71; Detzer, p. 20. Scott as Anderson's "best friend": Detzer, p. 17. "Cut my tongue" and "I fancy we shall not": Detzer, pp. 20, 26. Scott and Anderson: John Eisenhower, *Agent,* p. 347; Hsieh, pp. 48–49, 95, 107–108; Peskin, pp. 236–240; McClintock, pp. 105–113, 202–203; Detzer, pp. 55–57, 141–142, 150–152, 218–223. "Rich voice": *Harper's Weekly,* Jan. 12, 1861. Lincoln recent history and 1860 election: Donald, pp. 196–256; Burlingame, *Lincoln,* vol. 1, pp. 486–683; David Potter, pp. 328–355; Calore, pp. 207–231, 254; McPherson, *Battle,* pp. 121–130, 170–189. Scott to Buchanan: Peskin, pp. 234–235. "Question of negro equality": *NYT,* Aug 11, 1860. Anderson meets Floyd: Swanberg, pp. 35–36.

"Few men ever lived": Thomas Anderson, p. 7. "Hatred and contempt": Keyes, p. 370. Anderson friendship with Davis: Detzer, p. 25; Felicity Allen, pp. 75, 204, 273–275; William Davis, pp. 50–51; Davis Papers, vol. 4, p. 58. Anderson to Sumter: Swanberg, pp. 33–39; Maury Klein, pp. 105–109. "So weak as to invite" and "storm may break" and "key to the entrance": Nicolay and Hay, vol. 2, pp. 350, 352, 351. South Carolina special session: Freehling, pp. 343–453. "Cause some of the doubting": Detzer, p. 64. Buchanan after 1860 election: Niven, pp. 350–367. Buchanan on federal "property": Buchanan annual message to Congress, Dec. 3, 1860. "Increase of her darkies": Detzer, p. 24. Eba calls on Buchanan: Maury Klein, pp. 132–133; Detzer, p. 77; Swanberg, p. 61. "Defend yourself": Nicolay and Hay, vol. 3, p. 40. "Ought to have written evidence" and "personal advice": Detzer, 81. "Attacked by a force": Pinnegar, p. 95. Scott appeals to Buchanan: Detzer, p. 89; Sears, *Lieutenants,* pp. 2–3. South Carolina becomes "Independent Commonwealth": Detzer, p. 91.

Farnham: Clarence, *Biographical Sketch.* "Do they talk of dissolving": *Harper's Weekly,* Feb. 2, 1861. Fort Sumter history: Detzer, pp. 103–107; Moody, pp. 47–48; Oppermann, pp. 8–10, 31–46. Anderson moves to Sumter: Swanberg, pp. 94–101; Meredith, pp. 57–61; Detzer, pp. 108–160. "Sympathies are entirely": Crawford, p. 111. "Brought on by the faithlessness": Detzer, p. 126. "I cannot and will not": Crawford, p. 111. Flag raising over Sumter: Maury Klein, p. 164; Detzer, pp. 126–130. Davis meets with Buchanan: Detzer, p. 139. Black's warning to Buchanan: Moody, pp. 67–68; Morrison, p. 252. Buchanan agrees to sign statement: Curtis, vol. 2, p. 390. "You have probably rendered": Maury Klein, p. 191. Lincoln's journey from Springfield to Washington, DC: Draper, vol. 1, p. 552; Donald, pp. 273–279; Holzer, *President-Elect,* pp. 276–407; Burlingame, *Lincoln,* vol. 2, pp. 1–39.

"Greater than that which has devolved": Lincoln speech, Springfield, Feb. 11, 1861. Lincoln at Indianapolis: Holzer, *President-Elect,* pp. 307–314; Lincoln speech, Indianapolis, Feb. 11, 1861. "Declaration of war against": *Baltimore Sun,* Feb. 14, 1861. "Sporting with fireballs": Stashower, p. 151. Lincoln in New York City: Holzer, *President-Elect,* pp. 354–367. Astor House reception and Lincolns at opera: *New York Herald,* Feb. 21, 1861; *New York Sun,* Feb. 22, 1861. Reported plot against Lincoln and Lincoln's response: Holzer, *President-Elect,* pp. 390–405; Donald, pp. 277–279; Burlingame, *Lincoln,* vol. 2, pp. 32–24, 36–39; Stashower, pp. 1–329. Wood and "free city": Bernstein, pp. 143–144. "Excellent opportunity": *New York Herald,* Feb. 21, 1861. "Would rather be assassinated": Lincoln speech, Philadelphia, Feb. 22, 1861. "So unwell": Stashower, p. 249. "What may be done": Lincoln speech, Harrisburg, Feb. 22, 1861. "We will all go": Burlingame, *Lincoln,* vol. 2, p. 36. Lincoln skips Baltimore and dons disguise: Lamon, pp. 522–523; Holzer, *President-Elect,* p. 395. "I might not be mighty": Neely, *Lincoln Encyclopedia,* p. 178. "Blench at the first show" and "more than coward": *New York World,* Feb. 25, 1861; Burlingame, *Lincoln,* vol. 2, p. 39. "Humiliating to have" and "absconding felon" and "frightened at his own": Burlingame, *Lincoln,* vol. 2, p. 38.

Davis's installation: Freehling, vol. 2, p. 503; William Cooper, pp. 345–355. "If we must again baptize": *NYT,* Feb. 18, 1861. "We are probably soon" and "The little garrison": Crawford, p. 264. "48 hours hot fire": Pickens to Davis, Jan. 23, 1861, in *Papers of Jefferson Davis,* vol. 1, pp. 23–24. Lincoln and Tyler "Peace Conference": Burlingame, *Lincoln,* vol. 2, pp. 40–44; Donald, pp. 279–280. Lincoln 1861 inaugural: Donald, pp. 282–284;

Burlingame, *Lincoln,* vol. 2, pp. 58–68. Hay's observations: Burlingame, *At Lincoln's Side,* p. 119. Specter of possible murder: *NYT,* Mar. 4 and 5, 1861. "Under great and peculiar" and crowd's response: Lincoln inaugural address, Mar. 4, 1861, and *NYT,* Mar. 5, 1861. "Man is a fool!": Burlingame, *Lincoln,* vol. 2, p. 63. Wigfall cable: *New York Sunday Mercury,* Apr. 21, 1861. "If ignorance could add": Quoted in *Farmer's Cabinet,* Mar. 15, 1861. "Southern people do not": *Macon Telegraph,* Mar. 9, 1861. "Every Border State": Quoted in *Boston Daily Advertiser,* Mar. 7, 1861. "Virginia must fight": *Albany Evening Journal,* Mar. 6, 1861.

"Do the people": Lincoln to Stephens, Dec. 22, 1860, ALP. "Loose, disjointed": *New York Herald,* Mar. 6, 1861. Lincoln handed message from Anderson: Guelzo, *Fateful,* pp. 136–137; Detzer, pp. 214–216, Symonds, pp. 3–4. *Star of the West* resupply attempt: Meredith, pp. 91–94; Maury Klein, pp. 191–204; Detzer, pp. 159–171. Lincoln sees Holt: William Miller, pp. 49–55; Moody, pp. 96–97. "Depend upon it": Ulysses Doubleday to Lincoln, Jan. 15, 1861, ALP. Lincoln visits Mary Doubleday: Maury Klein, p. 332; Detzer, pp. 215–216. Scott vouches for Anderson: Detzer, p. 216. "No alternative": *CWAL,* vol. 4, p. 279. Scott forecast: Donald, p. 286; Burlingame, *Lincoln,* vol. 2, p. 100. "I was astonished": Bates, p. 177. Doubleday and baseball and home plate: Beschloss, "The National Pastime, Amid National Crisis," *NYT,* May 9, 2014; Detzer, pp. 38–39. "All this talk": Goodheart, p. 148. "Assuming it to be possible": Detzer, p. 220. "Any great national interest": Burlingame, *Lincoln,* vol. 2, p. 102. "Virtually a surrender": Donald, p. 286. "May have said things" and "Go on as you seem": Burlingame, *Lincoln,* vol. 2, pp. 101, 109.

Lincoln sends Lamon: Maury Klein, pp. 341–345; Detzer, pp. 222–233. "Forbid it as your commander" and "deeply mortified": Detzer, p. 223. "I must say": Lawton, p. 11. "Whilst no one will question": Nicolay and Hay, vol. 3, p. 432. Lincoln's pessimism about Sumter: Burlingame, *Lincoln,* vol. 2, pp. 98–130. Lincoln sends Fox: Hoogenboom, pp. 59–60, 75; Maury Klein, pp. 341–342; Detzer, pp. 226–231; Goodheart, pp. 155–159; Burlingame, *Lincoln,* vol. 2, pp. 123–125. "Uncle Abe": Detzer, p. 227. Fox's suspicion and reports to Lincoln: Hoogenboom, pp. 62–63. "Played us false": Goodheart, p. 153. "Our bread will last": Detzer, p. 234. Lincoln charged with bungling over Pickens: McClintock, pp. 230–238. "Anderson has been playing a deep game": *New-York Tribune,* Mar. 14, 1861. "You will best": Detzer, p. 230. "Some anxiety to the President": Cameron to Anderson, Apr. 4, 1861, Anderson Papers. Anderson reaction: Detzer, p. 243. Anderson to Thomas: Tilley, p. 223; Strode, vol. 2, p. 36. "Attempt will be made": Calore, p. 278. "Throw the responsibility": *Richmond Dispatch,* Apr. 5, 1861.

"Necessity of being *ready*": Maury Klein, p. 394. "Whether the revolutionists" and "demonstrate their patriotism": Burlingame, *Lincoln,* vol. 2, p. 126. Davis order to Beauregard: William Cooper, pp. 365–366. "Little garrison" as "point of pride": Maury Klein, p. 205. "Lose us every friend": Dennis Peterson, p. 230. "What if Lincoln gain": Detzer, p. 253. "Take Fort Sumter before": Maury Klein, p. 399. Fort Sumter, early Apr.: Maury Klein, pp. 400–401; Detzer, p. 245; Swanberg, pp. 222–223; Goodheart, pp. 161–162. "Shrewdly inviting the secessionists": *Cleveland Plain Dealer,* Apr. 1861. "Cunning hand of the third rate": Burlingame, *Lincoln,* vol. 2, p. 125. "Any post in the United States": Beauregard to Anderson, Apr. 11, 1861, Anderson Papers. "For the fair, manly, and courteous": Anderson to Beauregard, Apr. 11, 1861, Anderson Papers. "Will General Beauregard open": Goodheart, pp. 165–166. "If you do not batter": Calore, p. 279. "If you will state": Weigley, p. 21. "Desire to avoid": Anderson to Beauregard, Apr. 12, 1861, Anderson Papers.

Criticism of Anderson and his response: Moody, pp. 121–123; Rawley, p. 46. "We have the honor": Chesnut to Anderson, Apr. 12, 1861, Anderson Papers. Chesnut to wife: Chesnut, p. 45. Fort Sumter, Apr. 12: Goodheart, p. 166; Maury Klein, pp. 408–416; Swanberg, p. 295; Detzer, p. 281. "Did not expect it" and "anxious but calm" and "do not like it": Burlingame, *Lincoln,* vol. 2, p. 132; *NYT,* Apr. 13, 1861. "Fame is on every one's tongue": *Hartford Courant,* Apr. 15, 1861. "War! War!! War!!!": *Macon Daily Telegraph,* Apr. 13, 1861. Fort Sumter, Apr. 13: Goodheart, pp. 133, 173–181; Maury Klein, pp. 403–420; Detzer, pp. 287–310; Donald, pp. 292–294; Burlingame, *Lincoln,* vol. 2, pp. 125–130. "Rapidly increased their fire": *Union Memorial,* p. 26. "Would have cheapened": *William and Mary Quarterly,* July 1911, p. 78. "You are on fire": Detzer, p. 298. "Upon what terms": Crawford, p. 440. Wigfall in Charleston: Detzer, p. 301. "Return to your batteries": Eicher, p. 41. "Thank God": Detzer, p. 304. "Cheerfully agreed": William Snow, p. 224. Lowering of flag: Swanberg, pp. 326–330; McPherson, *Ordeal,* pp. 55–57.

"Next day the fort is taken": *Reading Times,* Apr. 28, 1896. "If occasion" and "distress and natural mortification": Guelzo, *Fateful,* p. 140; Roman, vol. 1, pp. 48, 52. Anderson anger at Fox and *Baltic:* Hoogenboom, pp. 68–69. "If we do not meet again": *Farmer's Cabinet,* Apr. 19, 1861. Anderson's state of mind after surrender: Meredith, pp. 193–194. Union Square rally: Meredith, pp. 193–195. Largest public gathering: Stout, *Aristocrats,* p. 262. "Brilliant defence" and snuffbox: *New York Herald,* Oct. 31 and July 14, 1861. "When has the world": Derek Smith, p. 18. "The whole Country looks": Lawton, p. 13. "Defense" as "a sham": Quoted in *Philadelphia Inquirer,* Apr. 16, 1861. "Strongly suspected": *Liberator,* Apr. 19, 1861. "Approbation of the Government": Cameron to Anderson, Apr. 20, 1861, Anderson Papers. "Greatly disabled" and "sheer exhaustion": Stepp and Hill, p. 34; *Boston Daily Advertiser,* Apr. 21, 1861. "Purely private and social": Lincoln to Anderson, May 1, 1861, ALP. Lincoln-Anderson meeting: Detzer, p. 316. Anderson flag auctioned: Leepson, p. 187. Lincoln meeting with Anderson: *Idaho Statesman,* Feb. 9, 1919; Long, *Life Story,* p. 127. "He would die rather": Eba Anderson to Lincoln, May 30, 1861, ALP.

"Inhuman treatment": *Liberator,* May 30, 1861. "Did anybody prevent": *Macon Telegraph,* May 1, 1861. Anderson in 1862: Lawton, pp. 15–16; Detzer, pp. 316–317; Meredith, pp. 205–206. Anderson to take post "at once": Lincoln to Anderson, Sept. 16, 1861, Anderson Papers. "Heart was not in it": Detzer, p. 316. "He has not been equal": *Daily Constitutional Union,* Sept. 30, 1863. Anderson "grieved" and "softening of the brain": *Farmer's Cabinet,* Nov. 19, 1863; Detzer, p. 316. Anderson's last years and death: Meredith, p. 206; Detzer, pp. 310–320; *New York Herald,* July 2, 1870, Oct. 28 and Nov. 4, 1871, Feb. 13 and Apr. 3, 1872; *Macon Weekly Telegraph,* Jan. 11, 1870; *Philadelphia Inquirer,* Oct. 4 and 28, 1871. Eba in later life: *Cincinnati Daily Gazette,* Dec. 1, 1879; *Idaho Statesman,* Nov. 27, 1892; *Philadelphia Inquirer,* Nov. 10, 1904. "Dignified silence under ingratitude": Lawton, p. 5. "The plan succeeded": Donald, p. 293. "The effect upon the public mind": Browning to Lincoln, Apr. 18, 1861, ALP. "There is but one opinion": Medill to Lincoln, Apr. 15, 1861, ALP. "It is now for the people": *Philadelphia Inquirer,* Apr. 15, 1861. "Civil war is a dire": *Vermont Phoenix,* Apr. 18, 1861. "Let him send his myrmidons": *Baltimore*

Sun, Apr. 17, 1861. "Supposed to be dreadfully": *Macon Telegraph,* Apr. 15, 1861. "Insolent and braggart": *Philadelphia Inquirer,* Apr. 15, 1861.

Further secessions: Ashworth, pp. 190–191; Crofts, pp. 340–344. Lincoln's education: Guelzo, *Redeemer,* p. 20; Donald, pp. 29–33; Burlingame, *Lincoln,* vol. 1, pp. 9–10. Lincoln expects lunge: Lockwood and Lockwood, pp. 24–30. Federal warnings: Donald, p. 298. Lincoln summons Congress: Donald, p. 296; Lincoln proclamation, Apr. 15, 1861. Lincoln abjures war declaration: Nester, *Lincoln,* pp. 112–115. Lincoln and Whiskey Rebellion: Carnahan, pp. 41–45. Lincoln's study and admiration of George Washington: Donald, p. 31. "By combinations": Lincoln proclamation, Apr. 15, 1861. Lincoln requests militia: Donald, p. 296. "All loyal citizens": Lincoln proclamation, Apr. 15, 1861. "Shortest way to peace": Donald, p. 296. "By what route": William Harris, *Lincoln and the Union Governors,* p. 17. *"Retarding* men": Ellsworth to Lincoln, Apr. 18, 1861, ALP. "Hot air of Rebellion": Holmes to Lincoln, Apr. 20, 1861, ALP. "Gross and flagrant": Quoted in *Nashville Union,* May 4, 1861. "Wicked violation": Donald, p. 297. "Kentucky will furnish": Engle, *Gathering,* p. 42. Lincoln impatience for military: Donald, p. 298.

Lincoln reaches for means not "strictly legal" and "military despotism": Farber, p. 118; McPherson, *Tried by War,* pp. 4–5, 22–24; Arthur Schlesinger, *Imperial,* p. 59. Lincoln and blockade: Hoogenboom, pp. 77–80; Simon, pp. 195–209. "With less bloodshed": McPherson, *Tried by War,* p. 34. Lincoln on blockade: Lincoln proclamation, Apr. 19, 1861. "Pirates of the Confederacy": *NYT,* Apr. 27, 1861. Lincoln expands Army: Nester, *Lincoln,* pp. 112–113; Donald, p. 301. Scott on Lincoln family: Winkle, p. 82. "Central idea": Goodheart, p. 320. Lincoln and habeas corpus: Neely, *Fate,* pp. 4–5, 8–10; McGinty, *Lincoln,* pp. 65–90; Jonathan White, pp. 72–94, 211–238. "Parties of men": *NYT,* Apr. 20, 1861. "Confederate states" and "very sparingly": Lincoln to Congress, July 4, 1861. *Ex parte Merryman:* Neely, *Fate,* pp. 9–13; Farber, pp. 157–162. "When the very existence": Bates to Lincoln, July 5, 1861, ALP. "Excitement is fearful": Donald, p. 297. "Perform his Constitutional duty": Simon, p. 189. Congress reconvenes: Fornieri, p. 554; Green, pp. 183–184.

"Are all the laws": Lincoln to Congress, July 4, 1861. Danger of Lincoln assassination: Steers, *Blood,* pp. 16–21. "If there is any prospect": *Lincoln Herald* (1962), vol. 5, pp. 54–55; Neely, *Lincoln Encyclopedia,* p. 178. "A war, monstrous": CG, July 10–11, 1861; *NYT,* July 11–12, 1861. Congress approves: Marszalek, p. 17; Guelzo, *Redeemer,* p. 381. Polk expelled, joins Confederacy: Christopher Phillips, p. 182. "Short war is the most humane": James Hamilton to Lincoln, May 3, 1861, ALP. "Already been accused": *Vanity Fair,* July 20, 1861. Battle of Bull Run: Benjamin Thomas, pp. 82–91. "Our troops engaged": Associated Press, July 21–22, 1861. "Washington Shrouded": *Macon Telegraph,* July 24, 1861. "Who has inaugurated this war": *New Orleans Times-Picayune,* July 29, 1861. "Upon excellent authority": Quoted in *Albany Evening Journal,* July 24, 1861. "As well as by the bloodthirsty": *New York Herald,* July 29, 1861. Lincoln signs military bills: Burlingame, *Lincoln,* vol. 2, p. 173. "If to be at the head": Burlingame, *Inner World,* p. 104. "I was sorry to find you": Browning to Lincoln: Aug. 19, 1861, ALP. Lincoln despondency over deaths: Donald, pp. 500–501. "Doesn't it strike you as queer": Warren, p. 225.

CHAPTER SEVEN: "BLOOD FLOWING ALL ABOUT ME"

Lincoln frustrations, early 1862: Donald, pp. 323–324; Burlingame, *Lincoln*, vol. 2, pp. 288–290. "My dearest personal friend": Burlingame, *Inner World*, p. 198. Death of Baker: Donald, pp. 107, 153, 319; Burlingame, *Lincoln*, vol. 2, pp. 104. "Heaving with emotion" and "wept": Brooks, p. 278; Burlingame, *Lincoln*, vol. 2, p. 104. Wade and Chandler on Lincoln: Burlingame, *Lincoln*, vol. 2, p. 194. "In view of the late defeat": Tap, p. 18. "Could only come of one": Trefousse, *Wade*, p. 152. Anger over Frémont: T. Harry Williams, *Radicals*, pp. 48–51. "Damned black Republican": Tap, p. 21. "Virus of slavery": Tap, p. 106. Frémont background: John Eisenhower, *Agent*, pp. 359, 373. Lincoln orders military books: Elmore, p. 145. "Infinitely worse" and "we can win": Tap, pp. 20, 19. Lincoln accepts Scott's resignation and "I can do it all": McPherson, *Battle Cry*, p. 360. "Handled humanely": Tap, p. 101. "An idiot": Donald, p. 319. "Original gorilla" and "I will not fight": Stephen Sears, *Young Napoleon*, pp. 132, 117. "Call on me" and "Can see every eye": McClellan to Mary Ellen McClellan, Aug. 9 and 10, and Sept. 11, 1861, McClellan Papers.

"Help me dodge": McPherson, *Tried*, p. 76. "Was not the restoration": McClellan, p. 149. McClellan's rudeness to Lincoln: Burlingame, *Lincoln*, vol. 2, p. 197. "Better at this time": William Miller, *Lincoln*, p. 173. "I will hold": Burlingame, *Lincoln*, vol. 2, p. 197. "With the power to send": Stephen Sears, *Lieutenants*, p. 199. "Let the country know" and "We must satisfy": CG, Dec. 9, 1861. "Rake things fore and aft": *Chicago Tribune*, 1861. "Let the Army": Tap, p. 63. "You are murdering" and "any right to know": Donald, pp. 332, 329. "People are impatient": T. Harry Williams, *Generals*, p. 55. "Sort of a standing joke" and "said of you": Tap, pp. 64, 62. Stone responds to committee, demands of Wade and Chandler, and Bates's position: T. Harry Williams, *Radicals*, pp. 100–102. "A victim": Sears, *Lieutenants*, p. 143. "Chief distinction": *Chicago Tribune*, Dec. 19, 1861. "I do the very best": Burlingame, *Lincoln*, vol. 2, p. 288, and Nixon speech, Apr. 30, 1974. Stone imprisonment: Marvel, pp. 154–156. "Form of government": Tap, p. 72. "I am tired": Trefousse, *Wade*, p. 185. "General authority": Lincoln to US Senate, May 1, 1862.

"Before you strike": Sears, *Young Napoleon*, p. 144. "I don't know much": T. Harry Williams, *Radicals*, p. 88. "My boy is gone": Zeitz, p. 110. "Completely prostrated" and "crepe is hanging": Burlingame, *Lincoln*, vol. 2, pp. 298–299. "Too good": Burlingame, *Inner World*, p. 103. "You've got no equal": Burlingame, *Inner World*, p. 312. "Paroxysms": Ruth Randall, p. 291. "Child-wife": Jean Baker, *Mary Todd Lincoln*, pp. 132, 212–213. Wade and Chandler warn Lincoln and "Wade, anybody": McPherson, *Tried*, p. 76; Guelzo, *Emancipation*, p. 110. Stone restoration to Army and service on Statue of Liberty: Marvel, p. 302; T. Harry Williams, *Radicals*, p. 102. Lincoln's orders to McClellan, Mar. 1862: T. Harry Williams, *Generals*, pp. 71–73. Lincoln and Norfolk: *The Lincoln Log*, May 9, 1862; *Washington Evening Star*, May 12, 1862; *Abraham Lincoln Quarterly*, Mar. 1952; Tucker, pp. 93–95; Allen Guelzo to author, Feb. 18, 2018. "As nearly inconsolable": McPherson, *Tried*, p. 99. "Suffer the extreme": Trefousse, *Radical Republicans*, p. 198. "Beneath my notice": McClellan, *Correspondence*, p. 369. Radicals' impatience: Riley, pp. 96–97. "No lawful right": Lincoln 1861 inaugural speech, Mar. 4, 1861. "Radical and extreme": Lincoln annual message to Congress, Dec. 3, 1861.

"For God's sake": Medill to Lincoln, Feb. 9, 1862, ALP. "May adopt gradual abolishment": Lincoln to Congress, Mar. 6, 1862. "A little uneasy": Lincoln to Horace Greeley, Mar. 24, 1861, ALP. "Families would at once": Browning diary, Apr. 14, 1862, LOC. "First great step": Guelzo, *Emancipation,* p. 88. "Thin end of the wedge" and "nigger on the brain": Burlingame, *Lincoln,* vol. 2, p. 346. "That we must free the slaves": Welles, p. 3. "We had about played": Guelzo, *Redeemer,* p. 335. "Physical force": Isaac Schermerhorn, Sept. 12, 1864. "As a fit and necessary": Lincoln draft, in July 22, 1862, *CWAL,* vol. 5, pp. 43, 97. "Last measure": Stahr, p. 343. "We have between us": Lincoln to "colored men," Aug. 14, 1862, *CWAL,* vol. 5, pp. 370–375. "If I could save the Union": Lincoln to Greeley, Aug. 22, 1862, ALP. "Would produce dangerous": Donald, p. 367. Lincoln appoints Halleck: Ambrose, *Halleck,* p. 61. "Silly and ridiculous": Burlingame, *Lincoln,* vol. 2, p. 390. "Wrung by the bitterest": McPherson, *Tried,* p. 121. "Will of God prevails": Lincoln note, dated Sept. 30, 1862, ALP. Lincoln decisions after Second Bull Run: McPherson, *Battle Cry,* pp. 533–534, 555–556; Burlingame, *Lincoln,* vol. 2, pp. 376–377; Donald, pp. 371–373.

"What *good* would a proclamation": Lincoln to visitors, Sept. 13, 1862, *CWAL,* vol. 5, pp. 419–425. Lincoln and "preliminary" Emancipation Proclamation: Donald, pp. 364–365; Burlingame, *Lincoln,* vol. 2, pp. 333, 360–363, 399–407; McPherson, *Battle Cry,* pp. 557–560; Carnahan, pp. 75, 104–112, 123–141; Holzer et al., *Emancipation,* pp. 16–20, 46–48, 62–72; Blair and Younger, pp. 40–46, 76–77, 111–116, 172–175. "Fixed it up": Donald, p. 374. "Immediate or gradual": Preliminary Emancipation, Sept. 22, 1862, ALP. Antietam as bloodiest confrontation: McPherson, *Crossroads,* pp. 3, 155. Lincoln's motives behind emancipation: Holzer, *Emancipating,* pp. 2–8; Stout, *Altar,* pp. 170–180. Praise for Lincoln announcement: *Daily Green Mountain Freeman,* Sept. 23 and 24, 1862; *Sunbury American,* Oct. 4, 1862. Criticism of Lincoln order: *Buffalo Evening Courier,* Sept. 25, 1862; *Indianapolis Star,* Sept. 24, 1862; *Joliet Signal,* Sept. 30, 1862; *Spectator* (Staunton, VA), Oct. 7, 1862. "Shout for joy": *Douglass' Monthly,* Oct. 1862. "Ill-success of the war": Lincoln to Carl Schurz, Nov. 10, 1862, ALP. "Even if the streets": Donald, p. 382. "Guilty of any disloyal": *NYT,* Sept. 25, 1862.

"Court martial despotism": Burlingame, *Lincoln,* vol. 2, p. 436. "Constitution as it is": Guelzo, *Fateful,* p. 227. "Hands reeking": Carson, p. 96. First income tax and bond sales: Hormats, pp. 65–83. "No use in being blue": Burlingame, *Lincoln,* vol. 2, p. 420. "Want of confidence": *NYT,* Nov. 7, 1862. "Did great harm" and "would leave off": Burlingame, *Lincoln,* vol. 2, pp. 421, 419. "Believed that their sons": Paludan, p. 101. "Great mistake": Burlingame, *Lincoln,* vol. 2, p. 422. "Would be glad to hear": Guelzo, *Redeemer,* p. 353. "High crime against the Constitution": McPherson, *Battle Cry,* p. 562. "Who stubbed his toe": *Frank Leslie's Illustrated,* Nov. 22, 1862. Stevenson quoted Lincoln: Merrill Peterson, *Lincoln,* p. 325. "I am now stronger": Donald, p. 388. "Absolutely broken down": William Miller, *President Lincoln,* p. 188. McClellan's firing as ill-timed: Stevenson, pp. 43–44. "War shall henceforth": Burlingame, *Lincoln,* vol. 2, p. 431. "We cannot escape": Lincoln annual message to Congress, Dec. 1, 1862. "Now hurrah": Burlingame, *Lincoln,* vol. 2, p. 470. "Knocked the bottom": Foner, p. 249. Lincoln depressions: Shenk, pp. 1–243; Burlingame, *Inner World,* pp. 92–113; Guelzo, *Redeemer,* pp. 95, 110–111, 386; Donald, pp. 27, 66–67, 87–88, 94, 97, 163–164.

"Poor, friendless": Donald, p. 151. "Say to him that if we could meet": Lincoln to John Johnston, Jan. 12, 1851, ALP. Lincoln and new cemetery: Poole, pp. 60–61. Mary Lincoln's instability: Jean Baker, *Mary Todd Lincoln*, pp. 212–213, 230, 277; Clinton, pp. 55, 242–243, 267, 277, 297–316; Epstein, pp. 371–372, 404–416. "All imagination!": Keckley, p. 51. "Need to be taught a lesson" and "That was the worst speech": Burlingame, *Inner World*, p. 281. "Constantly under great apprehension": Shenk, p. 180. Mary Lincoln Confederate relatives and Lincoln wires sanction: Jean Baker, *Mary Todd Lincoln*, pp. 67, 187; Clinton, p. 206. Lincoln and syphilis: Wilson, *Honor's Voice*, p. 127.

"My wife and I are in the habit": Goodwin, *Team*, p. 593. "Have all my life": Joseph Newton, p. 38. Lincoln and faith: Guelzo, *Redeemer*, pp. 81, 50–158, 312, 441–412, 462–463; Stout, pp. 75–77, 145–146, 271, 453; Preston, 162–163, 169–170, 173–174; Calhoun and Morel; Carwardine, pp. 18–36; Noll, *Journal of Presbyterian History*, Summer 2004. "Open scoffer": Guelzo, *Redeemer*, p. 117. "Humble instrument": William Miller, *President Lincoln*, p. 110. "Take all of this book": Speed, *Reminiscences*, pp. 32–33. "Utter, disastrous": CG, Jan. 14, 1863. "Unpleasantly conspicuous": *Memphis Daily Appeal*, Feb. 9, 1863. Vallandigham background and Jan. 1863 House speech: Klement, pp. 3–137. "Surrender to the rebels": *Gallipolis Journal*, Jan. 15, 1863. Origin of "Copperheads": Weber, pp. 2–10; McPherson, *Battle Cry*, p. 494n8.

Lincoln and military draft: Donald, pp. 449–450. "Since I have lived": Medill to White, Mar. 5, 1863, ALP. "Fire in the rear": McPherson, *Battle Cry*, p. 591. "Treason, expressed or implied": Burnside order, Apr. 13, 1863. "Wicked, cruel and unnecessary": McPherson, *Battle Cry*, p. 596. "Hurl King Lincoln": Farber, p. 171. Burnside sends soldiers: Holzer, *Press*, pp. 423–431. Clash with Vallandigham's supporters: Stone, *War and Liberty*, p. 32. Vallandigham's arrest and trial: Klement, pp. 156–189. "Hang him!": *NYT*, May 19, 1863. Lincoln commutes sentence: Stone, *Perilous*, pp. 108–110. "Prisoner of war" and "seems to breathe freer": *NYT*, May 28, 1863; *Macon Daily Telegraph*, May 29, 1863. Vallandigham for governor: Klement, pp. 138–155. "We all know that combinations": *NYT*, July 7, 1863. "Illegal and arbitrary": Donald, p. 441. "Clear, flagrant and gigantic": Lincoln to Erastus Corning and others, June 12, 1863, ALP. "Criminal wrong": Donald, p. 421. "Best campaign document": Donald, p. 443. Springfield mass meeting: Quinn, p. 48. Chancellorsville: Donald, pp. 435–437. "Golden opportunity": T. Harry Williams, *Generals*, p. 270.

"Held the war in the hollow": McPherson, *Battle Cry*, p. 667. "If I had gone up there": Brands, *Man Who Saved*, p. 256. "Within your easy grasp": Lincoln to Meade, unsent, July 14, 1863, ALP. New York City riots: *NYT*, July 14–16, 1863; *Washington Evening Star*, July 14, 1863; Bernstein, pp. 3–7, 21–36, 45–72; Adrian Cook, pp. 49–167; Spann, pp. 93–106, 126–129. Seymour to Lincoln: Furgurson, p. 258. "Drives every ablebodied": Lincoln to Seymour, Aug. 7, 1863, ALP. "Will break to pieces": Donald, p. 456. Lincoln's eagerness to go to Springfield: Ronald White, *Eloquent*, pp. 191–196. "We intend to make": Conkling to Lincoln, Aug. 14, 1863, ALP. "To be plain, you are dissatisfied": Lincoln to Conkling, Aug. 26, 1863, ALP. "That Abraham would honor" and "worthless demagogue": *Joliet Signal*, Sept., 8, 1863, and *Liberator*, Sept. 11, 1863. Lincoln and Gettysburg address: Boritt, *Gospel*, pp. 5–203; Paludan, pp. 228–230; Douglas Wilson, *Lincoln's Sword*, pp. 198–237; Burlingame, *Lincoln*, vol. 2, pp. 568–573; Donald, pp. 460–471. "Great many citizens": *Detroit Free Press,* Nov. 23, 1863. "Like fishes in a barrel": Boritt, *Gospel,* p. 103.

"Heaviest blow yet": Brands, *Man Who Saved,* p. 263. "Issued the proclamation": Lincoln to Conkling, Aug. 26, 1863, ALP. "I hope your anxiety": Everett to Lincoln, Nov. 20, 1863, ALP. "Four score": Lincoln speech, Gettysburg, Nov. 19, 1863. "Necropolis": *Harrisburg Patriot,* Nov. 26, 1863. "Is Mr. Lincoln less refined": *Indiana State Sentinel,* Nov. 30, 1863. "Gross ignorance": Charles Adams, p. 198. "Silly remarks": *Wisconsin Daily Patriot,* Dec. 2, 1863. "How dared he": Gallagher, p. 83. "This war is eating": Carpenter, p. 17. "Much more eager" and Lincoln's wish for second term: Burlingame, *Inner World,* pp. 252–253. Mary resumes entertaining: Flood, pp. 43–46. "Vacillation and indecision": Waugh, pp. 115–116. Chase's machinations and withdrawal, Blair's gambit, Grant's abstention: Escott, *Dilemma,* pp. 163–166; Green, pp. 253–289. Union Party convention: Green, pp. 276–278. "Provided he would add strength": Nicolay to Hay, June 6, 1864, Hay Papers. "Wish not to interfere": Lincoln note, June 6, 1864, ALP. Lincoln jokes about Hamlin: Carpenter, p. 66. Rebel attack on Washington, DC: Cooling, pp. 51–95; Brands, *Man Who Saved,* p. 317; Donald, p. 518.

"Get down": Waugh, p. 241. "Haven't taken Washington": Lepa, p. 114. "Actually catch some": Burlingame, *Inner World,* p. 223; Beschloss, *Presidential Courage,* p. 106. Mary's debts: Clinton, pp. 219–221; Epstein, pp. 427–428; Turner and Turner, pp. 162–164; Jean Baker, *Mary Todd Lincoln,* pp. 235–237. Lincoln's pessimism about reelection and Cabinet meeting: Beschloss, *Presidential Courage,* pp. 96–97; Donald, p. 529. 1864 Democratic convention: Klement, pp. 273–287; Donald, pp. 530–547; Burlingame, *Lincoln,* vol. 2, pp. 681–688. "One genuine American": Burlingame, *Lincoln,* vol. 2, p. 565. "Glory to God": Waugh, p. 14. "Watch Vallandigham": Guelzo, *Fateful,* p. 230. "Experiment of war": Weigley, p. 355. "Goodbye, 'little Mac'" and McClellan announcement: Stephen Sears, *Young Napoleon,* pp. 379, 375. "Principal thunder": *Pittsburgh Daily Commercial,* Aug. 31, 1864. Sherman conquers Atlanta: McPherson, *Battle Cry,* pp. 774–776; Guelzo, *Fateful,* pp. 443–444. "So Atlanta is ours": Sherman to Halleck, Sept. 3, 1864, NARA. "Dark days are over": Waugh, p. 297. "People wanted me": Donald, p. 544.

"September victories have changed": Norman Judd to Lincoln, Oct. 5, 1864, ALP. "Will carry on the war": *States and Union,* Nov. 2, 1864. "No man's life or liberty": *Democrat and Sentinel,* Nov. 2, 1864. Lincoln on election night: Benjamin Thomas, p. 452; Lincoln speech, Nov. 8, 1864. Lincoln antislavery amendment: McPherson, *Battle Cry,* pp. 706, 712–713, 823, 838–840; Donald, pp. 503–509, 553–563; Burlingame, *Lincoln,* vol. 2, p. 641. "May we not agree": Lincoln annual message to Congress, Dec. 6, 1864. "Will bring the war" Guelzo, *Redeemer,* p. 401. "Glory to God": *Liberator,* Mar. 10, 1865. "Greatest measure of the nineteenth": Samito, p. 101. Lincoln and Blair's advice: Donald, p. 556. Hampton Roads meeting: Chernow, p. 468; McPherson, *Battle Cry,* pp. 822–824; Donald, pp. 557–561; Burlingame, *Lincoln,* vol. 2, pp. 749–761; Burt, p. 95; Escott, *What Shall,* p. 202. "We are now spending": Donald, pp. 560–561. Lincoln and struggle over postwar South: McPherson, *Battle Cry,* pp. 471–472, 698–713, 843–852; Donald, pp. 471–472, 510, 524–562; Burlingame, *Lincoln,* vol. 2, pp. 594–600, 659–660. "Whether these men": Burlingame, *Lincoln,* vol. 2, p. 663.

Ashley's proposed compromise: Foner, pp. 319–320. "Congress has dwindled": Donald, p. 562. "He hopes to succeed": Samito, p. 100. "Would soon see they could": Stahr, p. 420; William Harris, *Last Months*, p. 130. "Your brother died to save": Samito, p. 77. "Original disturbing cause": Lincoln's response to serenade: Feb. 1, 1865, *CWAL*, vol. 8, pp. 254–255. 1865 inauguration: Burlingame, *Lincoln*, vol. 2, pp. 765–771; Ronald White, *Lincoln's Greatest*, pp. 13–16, 22–23, 41–80, 150–163, 180–200; Guelzo, *Redeemer*, pp. 414–420; William Harris, *Last Months*, pp. 138–149. "With all your fine feathers": Donald, p. 565. "Unutterable sorrow": Means, p. 91. "Disgraced himself": Trefousse, *Andrew Johnson*, p. 190. "Do not let Johnson": Donald, p. 565. "Has been a severe lesson": Barton, *Life*, p. 316. "Expected for the war": Lincoln inaugural address, Mar. 4, 1865. "Anything I have produced": Ronald White, *Lincoln's Greatest*, p. 180. "Thousand jets of gas": *Philadelphia Inquirer*, Mar. 7, 1865. "I almost wish": Keckley, p. 67. "Frightened he may never": Burlingame, *Inner World*, p. 61. "As though I was not President": Ronald White, *Ulysses*, p. 398.

Lincoln at City Point: Burlingame, Chernow, pp. 482–483; *Lincoln*, vol. 2, pp. 778–781; Donald, pp. 571–584. "For God's sake": Fehrenbacher and Fehrenbacher, p. 297. "Let them all go": Wert, p. 399. Grant-Lincoln exchange: Burlingame, *Lincoln*, vol. 2, p. 780. "A butcher" and "I suppose you think": Keckley, p. 64; Epstein, p. 481. "Thank God that I have lived": Fehrenbacher and Fehrenbacher, p. 366. Lincoln in Richmond: Donald, pp. 575–576; Burlingame, *Lincoln*, vol. 2, pp. 788–794. "Great Messiah" and "Don't kneel" and "My poor friends": Donald, p. 576; Fehrenbacher and Fehrenbacher, p. 366. Lincoln on *Malvern:* Fehrenbacher and Fehrenbacher, p. 91; Burlingame, *Lincoln*, vol. 2, p. 800; Donald, p. 576. "I think we are near the end": Stahr, p. 432. Lee's surrender: Varon, pp. 48–78. Lincoln Apr. 11 speech: Masur, pp. xiii–xiv. "No persecution": Reck, p. 37. "Perhaps been too fast": Donald, p. 591. Deaths: *NYT*, Apr. 2, 2012. Lincoln's wish for Fort Sumter ceremony: Goodrich and Goodrich, pp. 16–20. "Old smoke-stained": Cary, p. 52. Sumter ceremony: *NYT*, Apr. 6, 16, and 18, 1865; *Cleveland Daily Leader*, Apr. 14, 1865; Cary, pp. 31–88; Swanberg, pp. 333–339; Detzer, pp. 318–320; Bostick, pp. 121–123. "Coliseum of ruins": *Daily Progress* (Raleigh, NC), May 12, 1865. "Fulfill the cherished wish" and "No sooner": *NYT*, Apr. 18, 1865. "Most exciting moment" and "brave heart beats": *NYT*, Apr. 16, 1865. "No more war": *NYT*, Apr. 18, 1865.

"Negroes of every shade": Cary, pp. 38–39. Lincoln's last day: Guelzo, *Fateful*, pp. 467–482; Donald, pp. 593–596; Burlingame, *Lincoln*, vol. 2, pp. 778–781; Goodwin, *Team*, pp. 731–738; William Harris, *Last Months*, pp. 218–222; Steers, *Assassination*, pp. 92–105. "Almost joyous": Donald, p. 593. "And well I might": Steers, *Assassination*, p. 42. "Last day he lived": Barton, *Soul*, p. 334. "Now that the rebellion": Reck, p. 20. "He might have shared": Good, pp. 39–40. "Overjoyed, excited": Barton, *Soul*, p. 334. "Most heavenly" and "rested his face": Good, pp. 146, 67. Shouts in theater: Good, pp. 21, 178, 130; Joseph Irving, p. 549. Lincoln assassination scene: Good, pp. 5–22; Steers, *Blood*, pp. 113–118; Donald, pp. 586, 594–599; Burlingame, *Lincoln*, vol. 2, pp. 816–817. "He would die as soon": Good, p. 62. "Out of the way": Epstein, p. 506. "It is not probable": Stanton to General Dix, Apr. 15, 1865, Stanton Papers. "Why didn't he kill me?": Jean Baker, *Mary Todd Lincoln*, p. 244. "Take that woman out": Stahr, p. cxiii. "It is all over!": Epstein, p. 509. "*Why did* you not *tell* me?": Burlingame, *Lincoln*, vol. 2, p. 818. Andrew Johnson swearing-in: Trefousse, *Andrew Johnson*, p. 194. "Who did not consider" and "in office as long" and "Mr. Lincoln had too much": Burlingame, *Lincoln,* vol. 2, pp. 820–821. Lincoln's pockets: Photographs and explanatory material, LOC. *Prize Cases,* 1863: Frank Williams, pp. 65–66. "Executive power itself": Guelzo, *Man of Ideas,* p. 168. Argument that Lincoln was murdered at right moment for reputation: Escott, *Dilemma,* pp. 217–221. "This is the night": Robert Kennedy, p. 84.

CHAPTER EIGHT: "MAINE BLOWN UP"

Sigsbee and sinking of *Maine:* Sigsbee, "About the *Maine,*" and "Gleanings and Reminiscences" (1909), Sigsbee Papers; Sigsbee, *"Maine,"* pp. 1–124; Weems, pp. 71–90; Blow, pp. 95–109, 133–135; O'Toole, pp. 19–34; Rickover, pp. 1–6. "Light-hearted colored man": *Los Angeles Herald,* Dec. 11, 1898. McKinley orders *Maine* to Havana: Leech, pp. 163–164; Gould, *McKinley,* pp. 70–72; John Offner, pp. 98–99. "Steam in when the town" and "Yankee pigs": Sigsbee, *"Maine,"* pp. 24, 35. No socks: Material in Sigsbee Papers. Sigsbee background: Material in Sigsbee Papers; O'Toole, pp. 21–22; Blow, pp. 133–135. "Rarely demonstrative": Sigsbee diary, Sept. 3, 1902, Sigsbee Papers. *"My house is not managed":* Sigsbee diary, Sept. 17, 1902. "Mushroom cults": Sigsbee to A. Worthington, Mar. 7, 1911. "Most excellent man" and "always been a 'nagger'": Sigsbee diary, Sept. 7, 1902; "Memorandum B," Apr. 6, 1911, Sigsbee Papers. "Should I submit" and "I wish I could try": Sigsbee diary, Sept. 3 and Aug. 23, 1902. "Stick it out" and "cheerless existence": Material in Sigsbee Papers. Sigsbee and letter suggesting Eliza liaison: Sigsbee to Eliza Sigsbee, Oct. 14, 1911, Sigsbee Papers.

"Equilibrium" and "really hoped" and "My darling Wife": Notes and Sigsbee to Eliza Sigsbee, Mar. 12, 1898, Sigsbee Papers. "Lovingly, C.D.S." and "bursting, rending" and "intense blackness": Material in Sigsbee Papers; Peifer, p. 16. "For a moment": Sigsbee, *Navy,* p. 242. "When the shock occurred": Sigsbee to Eliza Sigsbee, 1898, Sigsbee Papers. "More dignified way": Sigsbee, *Navy,* p. 243. Sigsbee and Anthony: "About the *Maine,*" *Butte Weekly Miner,* Jan. 10, 1901. Anthony's later fate: *NYT,* Nov. 25, 1899; *WP,* Nov. 25, 1899; material in Sigsbee Papers. "White forms on the water": Sigsbee, *"Maine,"* p. 69. "Poor wretches": Blow, p. 95. "Get into the boats": *Proceedings of the U.S. Naval Institute* (1918), p. 246; *Butte Weekly Miner,* Jan. 10, 1901. "As cool as if at a ball": *Chicago Tribune,* Feb. 18, 1898. "Are there any left": J. W. Buel, *Achievements,* p. 578. "Maine blown up": Sigsbee to Long, Feb. 15, 1898, Sigsbee Papers; Blow, pp. 106–109. Final death toll: Nichols, p. 48. "To tell the truth": *Kansas City Gazette,* Jan. 23, 1901. "MAINE BLOWN UP LAST NIGHT": Sigsbee to Eliza Sigsbee, Feb. 16, 1898, Sigsbee Papers.

McKinley informed about *Maine:* H. Wayne Morgan, pp. 273–274; Blow, pp. 109–110; Gould, *McKinley,* pp. 74–75; Leech, pp. 166–167. McKinley in Civil War: William Armstrong, pp. xiii–144; H. Wayne Morgan, pp. 13–27. "Most sacred cause" and "fall in a good cause" and "precious to my soul": William Armstrong, pp. 106, 18, 11. "My whole life was to be spoiled": William Armstrong, p. 5. "To see Uncle Abraham" and "indescribably sad": William Armstrong, pp. 34, 42. "Never thought that soldiers": *Washington Evening Star,* Aug. 21, 1897. McKinley and recent Cuba history: John Offner, pp. 1–77; O'Toole, pp. 46–89; Leech, pp. 148–150; H. Wayne Morgan, pp. 223, 227. Cleveland warning on Spain: O'Toole, p. 83. President McKinley and Cuba: Gould, *Presidency,* pp. 56–72; John Offner, pp. 37–91; H. Wayne Morgan, pp. 248–265; Leech, pp. 151–162. "Wrapped in the stillness" and "every house" and "destitution and suffering": Gould, *McKinley*, p. 67; John Offner, 47. Castro's guerrillas in 1950s: Szulc, pp. 28–29. "Military codes": John Offner, p. 48. "Show that we had spared" and "injury and suffering" and "early decision": Gould, *McKinley*, pp. 68–69, 30. Spanish assassination: John Offner, pp. 51–52. "Righteous peace": McKinley annual message to Congress, Dec. 6, 1897. Long order to squadron: O'Toole, p. 110. "Mobs, led by Spanish": Corry, p. 25. McKinley message to Spain: John Offner, pp. 98–99. "You have no occasion": Gould, *McKinley*, p. 72. "Catering to the rabble": Merry, *McKinley*, p. 256. "Worst Insult": O'Toole, p. 122.

McKinley's reaction to Dupuy letters: O'Toole, pp. 121–123; H. Wayne Morgan, pp. 269–272; Gould, *McKinley*, pp. 73–74; John Offner, pp. 116–122; Leech, pp. 163–166. "Crisis in Cuban affairs": *Washington Evening Times*, Feb. 19, 1898. McKinley informs Ida about *Maine:* Anthony, pp. 142–143. Ida's medical challenges: Anthony, pp. x, 25–26, 31, 36, 41–42, 55, 75–76, 111–114, 118, 137–138, 140, 153, 165, 178, 197–198, 202, 209–210, 267; Leech, pp. 17–22, 27, 58, 111, 119–120, 182. "My husband's arm": *Philadelphia Times*, June 18, 1901. McKinley's worry about epilepsy: Boller, p. 185. "So influenced by the horror": Olcott, vol. 2, pp. 12–13. "Shall never get into a war": Gould, *War*, p. 41. "Noble unselfishness": McKinley speech, Feb. 22, 1898. "Not a sentence": *Washington Sentinel*, Feb. 23, 1898. "MAINE IS A GREAT": Evan Thomas, *War Lovers*, pp. 211–212. "Warship Maine Was Split": *New York Journal*, Feb. 17, 1898. "Whole Country" and "Havana Populace": *New York Journal*, Feb. 18 and 21, 1898. "There have been no mass meetings": *Springfield Republican*, Feb. 18, 1898. "General avoidance": *Baltimore Sun*, Feb. 17, 1898.

"Too serious": *Scranton Republican*, Feb. 17, 1898. Senate floor debate: CR, Feb. 18, 1898; *Baltimore Sun*, Feb. 19, 1898. Weyler on "indolence" and official study: Sigsbee, *"Maine,"* pp. 55, 231–245. Wolcott and Lodge speeches: CR, Feb. 18, 1898; *Idaho Statesman*, Feb. 19, 1898. Court of inquiry: O'Toole, pp. 124–150; Blow, pp. 133–178; Sigsbee, *"Maine,"* pp. 162–179. Theodore Roosevelt's eagerness for battleships and war: Hendrix, pp. 17–21. Cabinet meeting: Leech, p. 170; Blow, pp. 111–120; H. Wayne Morgan, p. 274; O'Toole, pp. 133–150. "Would be with him" and "You may rest assured": *NYT*, Feb. 25, 1898; *Investors Review*, Mar. 4, 1898; *Independent*, Sept. 1, 1898. "As long as the President": *NYT*, Feb. 24, 1898. "Reassuring to contemplate": *New York Journal*, Feb. 1898. "Much excitement" and offer to father children: Luther Sigsbee to Sigsbee, Feb. 18, 1898, note in Sigsbee Papers. "Tears came into" and "I am amazed" and "I knew that my first telegram" and "It seems": Sigsbee to Eliza Sigsbee, Mar. 8 and 12, 1898, Sigsbee Papers. "One body was recovered" and "My pennant still flies" and "I understand": Sigsbee to Eliza Sigsbee, Mar. 1, 8, and 9, 1898, Sigsbee Papers.

Sigsbee's testimony at court of inquiry: Sigsbee, *"Maine,"* pp. 138–192; Blow, pp. 136–137; O'Toole, pp. 132–135; *Report of the Naval Court of Inquiry*, pp. 9–25. "I hope that something": Sigsbee to Eliza Sigsbee, Feb. 1898, Sigsbee Papers. "Least-used buoy" and "yells, whistles" and "I have no means": *Report of the Naval Court of Inquiry*, pp. 10, 13; O'Toole, p. 132. Wolcott's warning on Sigsbee's career "ended forever": *NYT*, Feb. 18, 1898. Sigsbee defends crew: *Report of the Naval Court of Inquiry*, pp. 11–12. "Ordinary precautions": *Louisville Courier-Journal*, Mar. 29, 1898. "Delighted to learn": *Idaho Statesman*, Feb. 24, 1898. Eliza at "Grand Concert": Eliza Sigsbee to Sigsbee, undated, Sigsbee Papers; *Baltimore Sun* and *Boston Journal*, Mar. 9, 1898. McKinley's request and Congress's response: *Washington Evening Star*, Mar. 8, 1898. "They should see" and "I pray God": Woodford to McKinley, Mar. 19, 1898; *Charlotte Observer,* Apr. 1, 1898. Sampson's report goes to McKinley: John Offner, pp. 136–137; Gould, *McKinley,* pp. 78–79; McKinley to Congress, Mar. 28, 1898. 1911 study of *Maine:* US House of Representatives, "Wreck of the 'Maine,'" Dec. 1, 1911. Rickover 1974 study: Rickover, pp. 1–106. National Geographic Society 1998 study: Thomas Allen, "What Really Sank the *Maine?*," *Naval History,* Apr. 1998; Thomas Allen, "Remember the *Maine?*," *National Geographic,* Feb. 1988.

"Some ship" and "you know, sink the *Maine*": Beschloss, *Crisis Years,* p. 444. "Full self-government": John Offner, p. 154. 1962 proposal to sink US ship and blame Castro: Anna Nelson, "Operation Northwoods," *Cuban Studies,* 2001. "Sense of justice": McKinley to Congress, Mar. 28, 1898. "Fell like a wet blanket" and "do something radical" and "President's sanity": *Philadelphia Inquirer* and *Capital Journal,* Mar. 29, 1898; *Anaconda Standard,* Mar. 31, 1898. Arlington Hotel reception: *Dallas Morning News* and *Washington Times,* Apr. 3, 1898; *WP* and *Springfield Republican,* Apr. 4, 1898. "Frequently mentioned": *NYT,* June 12, 1904. "SET-BACK FOR SIGSBEE": *Baltimore Sun,* June 7, 1898. "In any other country": *Argus Patriot,* Apr. 6, 1898; Blow, p. 99. "In the name of humanity": McKinley to Congress, Apr. 11, 1898. Congressional reaction: *Chicago Tribune,* Apr. 13, 1898; *Omaha World-Herald,* Apr. 12, 1898; H. Wayne Morgan, p. 286; Gould, *McKinley,* p. 86. "Lawful government" and McKinley's reply: Olcott, vol. 2, p. 33; Gould, *McKinley,* p. 50. "Remember the *Maine* when": *Palmyra Spectator* (Palmyra, MO), May 5, 1898.

CHAPTER NINE: "WE MUST KEEP WHAT WE WANT"

"National conscience has been wrought": *St. Louis Republic,* May 2, 1898. "Storm broke so suddenly": McKinley speech, Oct. 12, 1898. "Capture vessels" and "greatest single act": Hendrickson, p. 43; *Tennessean,* July 14, 1901. McKinley on Sunday night: *Overland Monthly,* 1929, p. 353; Duffield, pp. 42–46; Anthony, pp. 146–148. McKinley on Monday morning: O'Toole, p. 199; H. Wayne Morgan, p. 71. Dewey on Manila Bay: Dewey to Long, May 4, 1898, NARA. Roosevelt steals thunder: Leech, pp. 205–206. McKinley's telephone and telegraph: Gould, *War,* pp. 55–56. "Magnitude of this victory": McKinley to Congress, May 9, 1898. Interest in proselytism: Nichols, p. 83; Susan Harris, pp. 15, 29; H. Wayne Morgan, pp. 304–305. McKinley expanding war ambitions: Peifer, p. 34; John Offner, p. 223. "While we are conducting": Olcott, vol. 2, p. 165. Congress and Hawaii: Gould, *McKinley,* pp. 49–50. "We need Hawaii": H. Wayne Morgan, p. 225. "Control of the island": CR, June 30, 1898. Sampson in command: Leech, pp. 197–198.

Long, Alger, Miles views: Wooster, pp. 219–221; Tone, pp. 273–274; O'Toole, p. 197; Trask, pp. 165–174. McKinley and Cuba, May 1898: Leech, pp. 202–236; Gould, *War,* pp. 91–99; John Offner, pp. 194–201; O'Toole, pp. 198–221. McKinley's order to Miles: Joseph Smith, pp. 108–109. McKinley and Schley: Leech, pp. 197–198, 220–224; O'Toole, 219–221; Bradford, *Crucible,* pp. 160–162, 217n; Trask, pp. 33, 120–131, 268; Hendrickson, pp. 46–48. "One of the most infelicitous": Long, *Navy,* vol. 1, p. 275. McKinley and Sampson: Cirillo, pp. 11–12. "Bombarded forts": Miley, pp. 31–32. Roosevelt and Rough Riders: Morris, *Rise,* pp. 643–676; Kaplan, pp. 12–141; Samuels and Samuels, pp. 16–20, 55–56, 64–66; Traxel, pp. 148–183. "Pray present": Roosevelt to McKinley, May 25, 1898, WMP. "Put their heads": Collier and Horowitz, p. 94. McKinley and Santiago:

H. Wayne Morgan, pp. 296–300; Leech, pp. 241–259; John Offner, pp. 203–207; O'Toole, pp. 222–297. "I shall hold": Alger, p. 175. "Fleet under my command": Sampson to Long, July 3, 1898, NARA. "You have the gratitude": McKinley message, July 4, 1898. Sampson and Schley: Hagan, pp. 225–226. "Yet fresh remembrance": McKinley statement, July 6, 1898. Sampson report on *Cristobal Colon*: Sampson to Long, July 3, 1898, NARA.

"Went to Santiago": Olcott, vol. 2, p. 50. McKinley and Cuba, July 1898: Joseph Smith, p. 170; Leech, pp. 247–281. Cabinet meeting: Leech, pp. 267–268. Shafter cable traffic from Cuba: Alger to Shafter, Shafter to Alger, Shafter to Corbin, July 15, 1898; Shafter to adjutant general, July 16 and 25, Aug. 3, 1898. McKinley on occupation: Olcott, vol. 2, p. 168. "So weakened and shattered": O'Toole, p. 360. McKinleys and nephews: Anthony, pp. 150–154; William Armstrong, p. 130. McKinley's anger about prospect of disease: Leech, pp. 260–267; H. Wayne Morgan, p. 299; Gould, *War*, pp. 92–93; John Offner, p. 209; Trask, pp. 160, 200, 229, 249, 290–302. "Unnecessarily and at great expense": Trask, p. 590. McKinley under strain: *NYT*, Aug. 14 and Sept. 6, 1898; Gould, *McKinley*, p. 121. "Religion seems to me": William Armstrong, p. 7. "Mightiest factor": Olcott, vol. 2, p. 368. McKinley caring for Ida: Anthony, pp. 255–256; H. Wayne Morgan, p. 36. Ida and daughters: Anthony, pp. 23–70; Gould, *American First Ladies*, pp. 183–194. "Would sit for hours": Beer, p. 475. "No, I mustn't": H. Wayne Morgan, p. 39.

"Ida would have died": Rove, p. 31. "Oh, Major, they will kill you!": Colman, p. 255. "Never went into her presence": Newman, p. 64. "Mrs. McKinley always wins": Merry, *McKinley*, p. 198. McKinley and napkin: Leech, pp. 431–432. Cambon peace feeler: Leech, p. 277; Gould, *McKinley*, p. 113; H. Wayne Morgan, pp. 300–301; John Offner, pp. 210–212; Trask, p. 430. "Humanely Christian" and "in all the points": Chadwick, vol. 2, p. 430. "Questions of race" and "incur our liability": Gould, *McKinley*, pp. 101, 100. "Guiding hand": Bradford, *Crucible*, p. 209. "Judge Day only wants" and "You Scotch favor": Olcott, vol. 2, pp. 62–63. "I was afraid it would be": H. Wayne Morgan, p. 301. "They are very hard": Leech, p. 287. McKinley-Cambon talk: John Offner, pp. 212–222; H. Wayne Morgan, pp. 300–301; Gould, *McKinley*, pp. 118–121; Trask, pp. 430–434; Leech, pp. 286–291. Protocol signing: H. Wayne Morgan, pp. 300–307; Gould, *McKinley*, p. 121; O'Toole, pp. 371–372; Leech, pp. 288–289.

McKinley visits Camp Wikoff: *Dallas Morning News*, Aug. 7, 1898; *NYT*, Aug. 14, 16, 18, 26, 30, 31 and Sept. 3 and 4, 1898; May 17, 1898; Leech, pp. 307–312; H. Wayne Morgan, p. 299. "You have come home": McKinley speech, Sept. 3, 1898. George W. Bush and painting: Bush, p. 183. Peace commission: H. Wayne Morgan, p. 304. "Fish and hunt": Gould, *Most Exclusive*, p. 15. McKinley 1898 railroad tour: Leech, p. 333; H. Wayne Morgan, pp. 309–310; Gould, *McKinley*, pp. 135–138. McKinley's fear of midterm loss and warning to party leaders: Saldin, pp. 48–49; Gould, *McKinley*, p. 127. "This war, that was so speedily": McKinley speech, Oct. 11, 1898. "It has been said": McKinley speech, Oct. 12, 1898; *Lincoln Evening News*, Oct. 13, 1898. "We have pretty much everything" and "There was no malice": McKinley speeches, Oct. 13, 1898. "Liberated a race": McKinley speech, Oct. 15, 1898. Chicago visit: *Chicago Tribune*, Oct. 20, 1898; *NYT*, Oct. 12, 16, 17, 18, 19, 20, and 23, 1898.

"War with Spain was undertaken": McKinley speech and *Atlanta Constitution*, Oct. 20, 1898. Ceremonial toast and Sigsbee's response: *Chicago Tribune, Minneapolis Journal*, and

Daily Times (New Brunswick, NJ), Oct. 20, 1898; *Los Angeles Times,* Nov. 3, 1898. "How could it be possible": *NYT,* July 23, 1898. "No desire for new territory": *Pittsburgh Press,* Oct. 22, 1898. "Flag never seemed": McKinley speech, Oct. 21, 1898. "We have had such": McKinley speech, Oct. 21, 1898. Philadelphia visit: *Philadelphia Inquirer,* Oct. 28, 1898; *NYT,* Oct. 27 and 28, 1898. "With the recklessness" and "not an Army": *NYT,* Oct. 15, 1898. Chanler charge: *NYT,* Oct. 27 and Dec. 10, 1898. "Make their appeal": *Belleville Telescope* (KS), Sept. 1, 1898. "Is New York going to prove": *NYT,* Oct. 20, 1898. "Ardent jingoism": *NYT,* Oct. 9, 1898. 1898 midterms: Traxel, p. 259. Return to Canton: *Washington Evening Star, Topeka Daily Capital,* and *NYT,* Nov. 9, 1898; Gould, *War,* p. 105. "You are the victors" and "no joint occupation": Gould, *McKinley,* pp. 138, 131. McKinley to Methodists: Olcott, vol. 2, pp. 110–111; Gould, *McKinley,* pp. 1401–41; James F. Rusling in *Christian Advocate,* Jan. 22, 1903; McKinley speech, Sep. 6, 1892. As Gould notes, Rusling was a key source for the account of Lincoln praying before Gettysburg.

"Converting" Igorots: McCartney, p. 200. "There they will stay": Scott Miller, p. 237. "Grave as are the responsibilities": Chadwick, vol. 2, pp. 462–463. "Incessant talk": Beer, p. 303. "Cheerful concurrence": Gould, *McKinley,* p. 142. Parchment signed: Beck, p. 593. Deaths: US Department of Veterans Affairs. McKinley southern trip: *NYT,* Dec. 15–20, 1898. "We Are Now One": *Atlanta Constitution,* Dec. 1898. "Nothing has more deeply": *NYT,* Dec. 15, 1898. "As the Republican politicians": *Chattanooga News,* Dec. 1898. "Repudiation of the President": Olcott, vol. 2, p. 138. McKinley and rebel badge: *NYT,* Dec. 20, 1898. "Ratify the treaty and end": Bryan notification speech, Aug. 8, 1900. "Make us a vulgar": *Literary Digest,* Nov. 12, 1898. Philippines insurrection starts: Van Ells, *Philippine Studies,* 1995. "How foolish": Gould, *McKinley,* p. 146. Senate treaty: Meiser, pp. 46–47. Boston trip: *Souvenir of the Visit of President McKinley; NYT,* Feb. 18, 1899. Death in banquet hall: *Omaha Daily Bee* and *Baltimore Sun,* Feb. 17, 1899. "Ode to President McKinley": *Souvenir of the Visit of President McKinley,* p. 52. "More people were fed": *North Adams Transcript,* Feb. 17, 1899.

McKinley felt "strange" and "extended with all possible": Gould, *McKinley,* p. 147; McKinley message, Dec. 21, 1898. "A Philippine republic" and "a dictatorship": Gould, *McKinley,* p. 135. McKinley appoints Taft: Olcott, vol. 2, p. 175. US soldiers to China: LaFeber, *Clash,* pp. 69–70. Anti-Imperialist League: Nichols, pp. 65, 84–92. "Believe that in fighting": *NYT,* May 25, 1900. "That will hurt the President": *NYT,* July 17, 1900. McKinley-Roosevelt campaign: H. Wayne Morgan, pp. 373–377. "I dread": Pell et al., p. 174; Boller, p. 189. "Those who would have this nation": Bryan notification speech, Aug. 8, 1900; *NYT,* Aug. 9, 1900. Bryan recalls Lincoln on Polk: Garnett, vol. 2, pp. 347–352. 1900 election: Haynes, p. 274. "Unquestioned endorsement": McKinley speech, Nov. 24, 1900; *NYT,* Nov. 25, 1900. "You may be sure": Evan Thomas, *War Lovers,* p. 152; Merry, *McKinley,* p. 212. "What nation was ever able": McKinley speech, Feb. 16, 1899.

"Most striking and momentous": Woodrow Wilson, *Congressional,* pp. xi-xii. McKinleys at Pan-American Exposition: Leech, pp. 592–595; H. Wayne Morgan, p. 392; Scott Miller, pp. 586–590; Anthony, pp. 222–244. "Telegraph keeps us advised": McKinley speech, Sept. 5, 1901. McKinley shooting and death: Scott Miller, pp. 290–295; Anthony, pp. 243–259; Leech, pp. 595–601; Rhodes, p. 170. "Have I been shot?": Tyler, p. 406; Rhodes, p. 171. "Poor, brave little woman": Tyler, p. 270. "God's will, not ours" and "that sleep": Tyler, pp. 361, 270. "Constantly on his mind" and "enfeebled constitution":

Anthony, pp. 255–256. Opening of Lincoln coffin: *Life*, Feb. 15, 1963. Roosevelt accession and Philippines war: Morris, *Theodore Rex*, pp. 13–16; Kramer, pp. 154–157. "The Major had planned" and "would go and teach": Anthony, p. 288. Platt Amendment: Pérez, pp. 49–51. Pearl Harbor: Williford and McGovern, pp. 4–25.

CHAPTER TEN: "THE WORLD IS ON FIRE"

Admiral Hall and discovery and handling of Zimmermann telegram: Boghardt, pp. 1–255; Beesly, pp. 1–8, 16–17, 34–39, 123–138, 175–184, 204–224, 235–236, 239–240, 302–304, 312–315; Ramsay, pp. 17–20, 39–42, 48–49, 107–110, 165–223, 283–310; Tuchman, pp. 3–182; Andrew, pp. 96–117; Boyle, pp. 83–93; Downing, pp. 139–140. "Do you want to bring" and "It isn't very clear": Boghardt, p. 96; Beesly, p. 204; Ramsay, p. 177. "Unrestricted submarine": Boghardt, p. 97. "Sat down by myself": Ramsay, p. 183. "Half Machiavelli" and "coldest-blooded" and "energy and dash": Ramsay, pp. 170, 40, 100. "My ambition to sit": Ramsay, p. 42. "Almost frightening": Ramsay, p. 110. German announcement of unrestricted warfare and UK reaction: Sondhaus, *Submarine*, pp. 23–30. "Probably get soused": Beesly, pp. 214, 102. "Try and get copies": Boghardt, p. 104. Telegram over US circuit: Andrew, pp. 40–41; Boghardt, pp. 86–91. House's courtesy title: Nickles, pp. 140–143.

Hall sees Hardinge: Ramsay, pp. 197–204; Boghardt, pp. 115–118; Beesly, pp. 215–218. Hall receives near-duplicate: Beesly, pp. 216, 101–116; Tuchman, pp. 145–148; Ramsay, pp. 200–202; Boyle, pp. 86–88. Hall sees Bell and "Mexico to reconquer": Ramsay, pp. 196–204; Beesly, pp. 216–217, 229–231; Boghardt, pp. 110–111, 117. "Hall is one genius": Walter Hines Page to Woodrow Wilson, Mar. 17, 1918, WWP. Hall conveys telegram to Page: Boghardt, pp. 101–105, 120–125; Beesly, pp. 218–220; Ramsay, pp. 201–205; Tuchman, pp. 145–149; Boyle, pp. 88–90. "Send a telegram": Tuchman, p. 161. Telegram from Page to Wilson conveying translation: Feb. 24, 1917, General Records of Dept. of State, Record Group 59, NARA. "So greatly exercised": Walter Hines Page to Woodrow Wilson, Feb. 24, 1917, WWP. "Threatened invasion" and "Alone I did": Boghardt, p. 128; Beesly, p. 224. Wilson and Frank Polk: Boghardt, pp. 135–136; Link, vol. 5, pp. 345–346. "Mind and spirit": John Cooper, *Breaking*, p. 2. Wilson's early life: John Cooper, *Wilson*, pp. 3–32; Link, vol. 1, pp. 1–5; Berg, pp. 3–49; Heckscher, pp. 1–31. "I know what war": Tumulty, p. 158. "A boy never gets": Ray Baker, vol. 1, p. 49.

"Bible brings human slavery" and "high time": Joseph Wilson. "Very full of" and "To *me* the Civil War": John Cooper, *Wilson*, pp. 24, 18. "*Because* I love the South": Ray Baker, vol. 1, p. 120. Wilson and Spanish War: John Cooper, *Wilson*, pp. 74–75; Link, vol. 1, pp. 27–28; Heckscher, pp. 128–130. "Leaderless" and "he was belligerent" and "romanticized the Army": John Cooper, *Wilson*, p. 75. Wilson on Jefferson and *Chesapeake*: Woodrow Wilson, *History*, vol. 3, p. 191. Wilson on Madison and War of 1812: Woodrow Wilson, *History*, vol. 3, pp. 194, 207. "Tragical but natural": Wilson, *History*, vol. 3, p. 217. Woodrow Wilson on Polk and Mexican War: Woodrow Wilson, *History*, vol. 4, p. 118. "Black people had multiplied": Woodrow Wilson, *History*, vol. 4, p. 192. "A constitutional crisis": Woodrow Wilson, *History*, vol. 4, p. 208. Wilson on McKinley and Spanish War: Woodrow Wilson, *History*, vol. 5, p. 270. "A vague, conjectural" and "irony of fate": Walworth, vol. 1, pp. 241, 342. Wilson and outbreak of world war: John Cooper, *Breaking*, pp. 12–16; Berg, pp. 10–15, 334–336; Link, vol. 3, pp. 2–9.

"Oh, my God": Link, vol. 2, p. 462. "God has stricken me": Ray Baker, vol. 4, p. 480. "Presidency has had to be paid": Berg, p. 337. "Could not help wishing": Link, vol. 2, p. 464. "I am afraid" and "compulsion of necessity": Ray Baker, vol. 5, pp. 74, 54, 79. "Not to give currency": Link, vol. 3, p. 79. "Madison and I": John Cooper, *Warrior*, p. 274. "It will be easy to excite": Wilson proclamation, Aug. 19, 1914. "Fine poise of undisturbed": Wilson proclamation, Aug. 18, 1914. "We have nothing to do" and "Our whole duty": Wilson speeches, Dec. 18, 1914, and Apr. 20, 1915. Wilson and "America First": John Cooper, *Wilson*, p. 278. Wilson's reaction to *Lusitania* sinking: John Cooper, *Wilson*, p. 286; Tumulty, p. 232. Edith Wilson's background: Levin, pp. 58–73; Hazelgrove, pp. 32–62; Edith Wilson, pp. 1–67; John Cooper, *Wilson*, pp. 281–283; Berg, pp. 356–357. "You can't love me" and "I thrill" and "my pitiful inability": Weinstein, p. 280. "With regret" and "partisanship": *NYT*, Aug. 26, 1914. "My happiness" and "a new certitude": *PWW*, vol. 33, pp. 126, 284. "A man being too proud to fight" and "foolish": Wilson speech, May 10, 1915; John Cooper, *Wilson*, p. 287.

"Retain or regain": *Chanute Daily Tribune*, May 12, 1915. "Colonel House has been": *PWW*, vol. 33, p. 449. "Does not seem to realize": Koenig, p. 549. "No stranger man": John Cooper, *Wilson*, p. 293. Wilson approach to Germany, 1915: Link, vol. 3, pp. 564–569; Berg, pp. 368–369, 384–385; John Cooper, *Wilson*, p. 300. "If my reelection" and America "wants action": Tumulty, pp. 249–250. "Pay the price of self-respect" and "reckless commander" and "world is on fire": Wilson speeches, Feb. 1 and 3, Jan. 29, 1916. *Sussex* sinking: Doenecke, pp. 167–172. "Relentless and indiscriminate": Wilson speech, Apr. 19, 1916. Wilson policy on war, 1916: Link, vol. 4, pp. 261–265; John Cooper, *Wilson*, pp. 276–280, 286–289, 300–301, 307–309, 342–343; Berg, pp. 385–387, 390–397, 417–420. "Shifty expedients": 1916 Republican platform. Wilson's 1916 campaign: John Cooper, *Wilson*, pp. 346–350; Link, vol. 4, pp. 319–321, 340–349, and vol. 5, pp. 93–156; Berg, pp. 402–418. "Serve mankind": Wilson speech, Sept. 2, 1916. "Do not want a peace": *Arizona Daily Star*, Oct. 29, 1916.

"Backs and backs": *Pittsburgh Post Gazette*, Oct. 29, 1916. "Insincere and cold-blooded": John Cooper, *Warrior*, p. 253. "Apothecary's clerk": Walworth, vol. 1, p. 247. "Phrase of a coward": Ray Baker, vol. 6, p. 288. "Pontius Pilate–like": Thompson, p. 147. "War has been carried": *eWP*, Oct. 11, 1916. "Men, Women and children were drowned": *Tucson Citizen*, Aug. 25, 1916. "When the sword": *Chicago Tribune*, Oct. 23, 1916. "Spinelessly creep": *Detroit Free Press*, Oct. 31, 1916. 1916 election: John Cooper, *Wilson*, pp. 303–447; Link, vol. 5, p. 160; Berg, pp. 397–399, 404–414. "Boxed his ears": *Kansas City Star*, Nov. 10, 1916. Wilson policy, Nov. 1916 to Jan. 1917: Link, vol. 5, pp. 187–269; John Cooper, *Wilson*, pp. 362–376; Berg, pp. 318–423. "German militarism" and "ready to join": *PWW*, vol. 40, pp. 68, 199. *"Frantic with rage"*: John Cooper, *Wilson*, p. 363. "We must go" and "time is at hand": *PWW*, vol. 40, pp. 310, 197. "The Drawer": Walworth, vol. 1, p. 435. "Profoundly immoral": *New York Herald*, Jan. 14, 1917. "We are drawing nearer": *PWW*, vol. 40, p. 307.

"Not too many ideas": *PWW*, vol. 33, p. 397. "Peace without victory": Wilson speech, Jan. 22, 1917. "Make Don Quixote": John Cooper, *Breaking*, p. 22. "Spiritual forebears": *New York Herald*, Jan. 29, 1917. "A little low": Wilson to Cleveland Dodge, Jan. 25, 1917,

WWP. "Full employment": John Cooper, *Wilson,* 373. New policy: Greenhalgh, p. 221; Sondhaus, *Submarine,* p. 95. Wilson talks with Lansing and House: *PWW,* vol. 41, pp. 121, 87. "Sad and depressed": Striner, *Wilson,* p. 99. "Time for patience": *PWW,* vol. 41, p. 99. Wilson policy, Feb. 1917: Link, vol. 5, pp. 290–301; Berg, pp. 423–426; John Cooper, *Wilson,* pp. 362–380. "White races": Leuchtenburg, *American Presidency,* p. 92. "Fully trust anybody's": *PWW,* vol. 41, p. 94. "No alternative": Wilson speech, Feb. 3, 1917. "Yellow all through": Berg, p. 424. "Much disturbed": Neu, p. 134. "Innocent agents" and *"Good Lord!"* and "profound impression": Boghardt, p. 137; Thompson, p. 168. Wilson reaction to Zimmermann telegram: Tuchman, pp. 153–182; Meyer, pp. 188–189; Neu, p. 284; John Cooper, *Wilson,* pp. 374–379; Berg, pp. 425–427; Link, vol. 5, pp. 345–346. "Government of butchers": Berg, p. 287.

Wilson and Mexico during first term: John Eisenhower, *Intervention!,* pp. 79–82, 185–186, 228–267; Ambrosius, pp. 38–39. "So many things": *PWW,* vol. 41, p. 298. Wilson suspicion of British: Doenecke, p. 185; Conyne, p. 70. "This blacklist business": Striner, *Wilson,* p. 73. "If you knew": *PWW,* vol. 41, p. 305. "Defend our commerce": Wilson speech, Feb. 26, 1917. "Greatest statesman": Ray Baker, vol. 1, p. 57. "Heartily in sympathy": *PWW,* vol. 38, p. 241. Lansing to Hood: Tuchman, p. 159. Newspaper reactions to Zimmermann telegram: all Mar. 1, 1917. La Follette on Senate floor: John Cooper, *Wilson,* p. 379. "Little group of willful" and "We are provincials": *Washington Times* and Wilson speech, Mar. 5, 1917. Wilson collapse: John Cooper, *Wilson,* p. 381; Berg, pp. 429–430. "Most agile pussy-footer": *PWW,* vol. 41, p. 458. Mar. 20 Cabinet meeting and "I want to do right": John Cooper, *Wilson,* p. 383. Vaudeville: Link, vol. 5, p. 420. "To make even the measures of defense": Link, vol. 5, p. 412. "Too intellectual": John Cooper, *Wilson,* p. 383. "Coarser fiber": Hodgson, p. 139. "Perfectability": American Bar Association, Oct. 20, 1914. "God and humanity": John Cooper, *Wilson,* p. 4. Wilson's manner of typing: John Cooper, *Wilson,* p. 41. "I never knew him": *PWW,* vol. 41, p. 515. Wilson speaks to Congress: *NYT* and *WP,* Apr. 3, 1917; John Cooper, *Wilson,* pp. 383–390; Link, vol. 5, pp. 419–426; Berg, pp. 433–439. "Fitz, thank God": John Cooper, *Wilson,* p. 390.

CHAPTER ELEVEN: "SALVATION OF MANKIND"
Senate debate over war declaration: CR and *NYT,* Apr. 4, 1917; *Durham Morning Herald,* Apr. 5, 1917; John Cooper, *Wilson,* pp. 388–389; Berg, p. 439; Heckscher, p. 441. House debate: CR and United Press, Apr. 5, 1917; *NYT* and *Washington Herald,* Apr. 6, 1917. Rankin and House vote: Norma Smith, pp. 110–114; *NYT,* Apr. 7, 1917. House vote and "counterfeit and lying": *NYT,* Apr. 6, 1917; *Chieftain,* Apr. 1917. Wilson signs declaration: Edith Wilson, p. 133; Berg, p. 440; John Cooper, *Wilson,* p. 389; *WP* and *New-York Tribune,* Apr. 7, 1917. McCandless signal and Roosevelt planning: Heckscher, p. 441; Kenneth Davis, *Beckoning,* pp. 431–434, 458–476. "My days are so full" and "It seems hard": *PWW,* vol. 42, pp. 292, 158. "There is not a single selfish": *New York Times Current History,* vol. 11, p. 201. Wilson builds force: John Cooper, *Wilson,* pp. 390–393; Berg, pp. 440–447, 457–458; Sondhaus, *Revolution,* pp. 315–317; Woodward, pp. 48–53, 93, 112; Keene, pp. 3–6, 10, 18–24, 72. "Thoughtful devotion": Wilson proclamation, May 18, 1917. Wilson rejects Theodore Roosevelt: Morris, *Colonel,* pp. 482–487; Thompson, pp. 177–180; John Cooper, *Wilson,* pp. 393–397; Berg, pp. 457–459. "I could arouse": Harbaugh, pp. 471–473.

"Great big boy": Tumulty, p. 288. "Scientific definiteness": De Kay, *Navy*, p. 193. "A bitter blow": Blanche Cook, vol. 1, p. 214. Lodge Amendment: Fleming, *Illusion*, p. 90. "Tenacity and the pluck" and "Roosevelt has no respect" and "trying to force": CR 55, 1917, pp. 2454, 2451, 2434. Draft bill passage and lottery: John Chambers. "In the interest of the colored": Clements, p. 45. "It is absolutely necessary": Wilson statement, May 19, 1917. "A food dictator": *NYT,* May 20, 1917. "Distressed Mr. Lincoln" and "burden of responsibility": *PWW,* vol. 43, p. 246, and vol. 44, p. 117. "Virtual dictator": *Washington Times,* Aug. 5, 1917. "He is already": *NYT,* Aug. 12, 1917. War financing: Hormats, pp. 94–127. Wilson and civil liberties: Walker, pp. 9–44; John Cooper, *Wilson,* pp. 11, 397–411, 432–433, 512; Berg, pp. 452–455, 494–498; Nichols, p. 225; Craig Smith, pp. 151–153; David Kennedy, *Over Here,* pp. 77–89. "Withdrawn when the emergency": Wilson executive order, Apr. 7, 1917. "Tolerate a gag" and "light of liberty": Quoted in *NYT,* May 26, 1917. "Treason, insurrection": Geoffrey Stone, *Perilous,* p. 150. "Disloyal, profane": Sedition Act, May 16, 1918. "Never in the history": Chafee, p. 3. Pursuit of Debs: Freeberg, pp. 67–107. "Line is manifestly hard": Startt, p. 127. "Exceedingly careful": Debs speech, June 16, 1918. Wilson, summer 1917: Edith Wilson, pp. 141–149; Berg, pp. 399, 402–406; John Cooper, *Wilson,* pp. 415–417. "How to do a jig": Shachtman, p. 154.

"Edith and I are on the *Mayflower*": *PWW,* vol. 43, p. 240. George Creel: Auerbach, pp. 49–68. "Passionate belief": Creel, p. 5. Wilson on anxiety before an audience: Heckscher, p. 478. "Succeeded in getting the 'emotional power'": *PWW,* vol. 44, p. 77. "World may unite" and "We have not yet felt" and "You can explain": Wilson speeches, June 14, Aug. 15, and Nov. 12, 1917. "News from France had been bad": Elliott, pp. 288, 283. "German line, although repeatedly": *NYT,* Dec. 30, 1917. "Remaking the map": Neu, p. 331. Writing of Fourteen Points: Hodgson, pp. 160–161; Neu, pp. 331–333; Heckscher, pp. 459; Berg, pp. 468–473; John Cooper, *Wilson,* pp. 420–424. "Moral climax": Wilson speech, Jan. 8, 1918. "Most luminous": *Washington Herald,* Jan. 9, 1918. "War Super-Cabinet": *Pittsburgh Post Gazette,* Jan. 21, 1918. "Astonishing and absolutely unjustifiable": *Baltimore Sun,* Jan. 22, 1918. "Historical struggle": *Topeka Daily Capital,* Jan. 22, 1918. "Nothing but the kindliest": *Atlanta Constitution,* Jan. 25, 1918. "In the first six months": *New York Herald,* Jan. 25, 1918.

"Does not know the real" and "stupid bill": *Abbeville Press,* Feb. 12, 1918. "What do you know": *NYT,* Feb. 5, 1918. "We might as well": CR, Feb. 4, 1918. "Would have been no clash": *NYT,* Feb. 17, 1918. Wilson and Pershing: John Cooper, *Wilson,* pp. 401–402; Carroll, pp. 105–107. "Identity of which": John Cooper, *Wilson,* p. 402. "Too thin-skinned": Elliott, p. 294. "Check every invasion": Wilson speech, July 4, 1918; *NYT* and *WP,* July 5, 1918. German submarine attacks: Farwell, pp. 74–75. "Stupid submarine commanders": *PWW,* vol. 49, p. 167. Final offensive: John Eisenhower, *Yanks,* pp. 197–296; Lengel, pp. 57–359. "Quentin's mother and I": Chip Bishop, p. 260. "Fine gallantry": *Washington Times,* July 21, 1918. "Peoples of our allies": *PWW,* vol. 51, p. 225. Wilson's worry about 1918 midterms: John Cooper, *Wilson,* pp. 435–450; Berg, pp. 503–507. "Not for my own sake": Wilson statement, Oct. 25, 1918. Roosevelt's anger at Wilson: Morris, *Colonel,* pp. 540–548; Thompson, pp. 272–278. "Greedy unscrupulousness" and "We have sent our sons": *NYT,* Oct. 29, 1918. Taft-Roosevelt statement and "never, in peace or war": *NYT,* Nov. 1 and 2, 1918.

"I would do it": Levin, p. 217. Cummings persuasion: *PWW,* vol. 51, p. 355. "Wants only rubber stamps": *St. Louis Post-Dispatch,* Oct. 28, 1918. Prospect of surrender: Sondhaus,

Submarine, p. 436. 1918 returns: Saldin, pp. 83–89; Gould, *Republicans,* p. 156. "Not at all dismayed": *PWW,* vol. 53, p. 68. "In any free country": Brands, *T.R.,* p. 809. "I never expected to hate": Berg, p. 612. "Greatest criminal known": MacMillan, p. 163. Wilson hears armistice signed: Edith Wilson, pp. 170–171. "We stood mute": John Cooper, *Wilson,* p. 451. "Autocracy is dead": House to Wilson, Nov. 11, 1918, WWP. "This tragical war": Wilson speech, Nov. 11, 1918, and *NYT,* Nov. 12, 1918. "Went completely mad": Rowley, p. 83. Press reaction: Quoted in *NYT,* Nov. 15, 1918. Sherman's threat: *NYT,* Dec. 3, 1918. "Would be a mistake": *PWW,* vol. 52, p. 66. Wilson forms peace delega-tion: Hodgson, pp. 192–194; Neu, pp. 279–380; John Cooper, *Wilson,* pp. 430, 440, 456–468; Berg, pp. 515–520. "Crowning ambition": *PWW,* vol. 53, p. 73. "No room big enough" and "never been more surprised": *PWW,* vol. 53, pp. 135, 147. "Mouthpieces": John Cooper, *Breaking,* p. 34. "Supreme moment of history": Wilson speech, Dec. 2, 1918. "Would give him an ice bath": *PWW,* vol. 53, p. 301. Departure for Europe: Edith Wilson, pp. 172–176; Berg, p. 520; John Cooper, *Wilson,* p. 460; *NYT,* Dec. 4, 1918.

"Legally the Republic's President": *New York Sun,* Dec. 3, 1918. "Every whistle valve": *PWW,* vol. 53, p. 315. "These ancient wrongs": Tumulty, pp. 336–337. "What I seem to see": *PWW,* vol. 53, p. 371. "Long live the champion": *NYT,* Dec. 14, 1918. Arrival in Paris: *NYT,* Dec. 15, 1918. "So many emotions": *PWW,* vol. 53, p. 397. "Visibly ner-vous": Neu, p. 382. Hospital visits: Berg, pp. 20–21. "It was an awful trial": *PWW,* vol. 53, p. 501. Royal visit: Edith Wilson, pp. 195–198; Berg, pp. 21–23, 195–198; John Cooper, *Wilson,* pp. 464–465. Wilson to King: Fleming, *Illusion,* p. 321. "Could not bear him": Meyer, p. 469. "Insisted definitely": *PWW,* vol. 53, p. 564. "Has shocked me": Thomp-son, p. 290. Paris conference: MacMillan, pp. 3–483; John Cooper, *Wilson,* pp. 454–504; Berg, pp. 15–20, 522–593; Neu, pp. 379–422; Hodgson, pp. 175–242; Edith Wilson, pp. 175–271. "We have become what we are": MacMillan, p. 23. "If you're the under-taker": Beesly, p. 307. "My life hatred": MacMillan, p. 27. Clemenceau's demand and "a shell hole" and "unconstitutional and also impossible": MacMillan, pp. 22, 93. "Distrust and bitterness": MacMillan, p. 93.

"Talk and talk": MacMillan, p. 94. Cecil warning: *PWW,* vol. 56, p. 165. Atlantic cross-ing: John Cooper, *Wilson,* pp. 460–462; John Cooper, *Breaking,* pp. 10–54; Berg, pp. 3–5, 520. "Very delightful companions": Levin, p. 253. "Would break the heart": *PWW,* vol. 55, p. 224. Wilson's Boston visit and speech: John Cooper, *Wilson,* p. 477; Berg, pp. 547–548; Levin, p. 255; Walworth, vol. 2, p. 269. "Substitute for the British": MacMillan, p. 93. "If the Saviour of mankind": John Cooper, *Breaking,* p. 57. Wilson's refusal: Berg, pp. 507–508. "Very absolute": John Cooper, *Wilson,* p. 97. Dinner at White House: Berg, pp. 548–549; Burns, *Workshop,* p. 454; John Cooper, *Wilson,* pp. 478–479. "Magnificent reception": Walworth, vol. 2, p. 270. Edith's fingernails: John Cooper, *Wilson,* p. 478. Wilson-Taft appearance: *NYT,* Feb. 27, 1919. "Without destroying" and "My husband never failed": Levin, p. 267. "Would simply" and "seemed to have aged": *PWW,* vol. 55, pp. 480, 488. "Grayer & grimmer": MacMillan, p. 199. "Never sign a French" and "bribe" and "who keeps her trunk": MacMillan, p. 200. "If I were a German": John Cooper, *Wil-son,* pp. 494–495. "Suffering peoples": Berg, p. 590.

"Immeasurably harsh": *The Century,* vol. 102 (1921), p. 151. "I did not know": John Cooper, *Wilson,* p. 504. "Severe only because": Wilson statement, June 28, 1919. "Very little respect": *PWW*, vol. 61, p. 360. Wilson feted in New York and Washington: Berg, pp. 604–608; John Cooper, *Wilson*, pp. 508–510; John Cooper, *Breaking*, pp. 116–121. "Not because our material interests": Wilson speech, July 10, 1919. "Wanted red meat": John Cooper, *Wilson*, p. 509. "Utterly lacking": *NYT*, July 10, 1919. "Very tired": *PWW*, vol. 48, p. 550. Lodge hearings: John Cooper, *Wilson*, pp. 513–518; John Cooper, *Breaking*, pp. 126–127, 132–136; Berg, pp. 611–618. "Would have none of it": *PWW*, vol. 62, p. 258. "No disposition to nag": *NYT*, Aug. 18, 1919; Neu, p. 428. Wilson meets Lodge committee: *NYT*, Aug. 20, 1919; John Cooper, *Wilson*, pp. 515–518; John Cooper, *Breaking*, pp. 138–139; Berg, pp. 617–618. "Hard, and cold": Lower, p. 134. Pittman's reservations and Wilson's reaction: Berg, pp. 618–619; John Cooper, *Breaking*, pp. 148–152; John Cooper, *Wilson*, pp. 514–518. "I promised our soldiers": Walworth, vol. 2, p. 361. Wilson's health in 1918: John Cooper, *Wilson*, pp. 440–441, 485, 509, 512–513, 519–520, 531; Berg, pp. 568–570, 573, 613–620, 628; Park, pp. 3–76. Wilsons' western tour: Hogan, pp. 17–173; Gene Smith, pp. 60–85; Levin, pp. 319–334; Edith Wilson, pp. 274–285; John Cooper, *Breaking*, pp. 158–197; John Cooper, *Wilson*, pp. 520–531; Brands, *Wilson*, pp. 120–122; Berg, pp. 620–637.

"A relief": John Cooper, *Breaking*, p. 157. Wilson speeches: Sept. 6, 9, 11, 12, 13, 20, 22, 23, and 25, 1919. Pueblo speech: Hogan, pp. 153–162; John Cooper, *Wilson*, pp. 529–530; Berg, pp. 632–634. "Who have poured": Wilson speech, Dec. 7, 1915. "Hyphenated American": *NYT*, Oct. 13, 1915. "This will have to be a short": Berg, p. 633. Wilson falls ill: Edith Wilson, pp. 284–289; John Cooper, *Wilson*, pp. 529–531; John Cooper, *Breaking*, pp. 187–189; Berg, pp. 633–638. "Unbearable": Hogan, p. 157. "Wandered like a ghost": John Cooper, *Wilson*, p. 532. "Nervous exhaustion": *PWW*, vol. 63, p. 642. Edith and Grayson intervene: Berg, pp. 636–644, 658; John Cooper, *Wilson*, pp. 532–538; Crispell and Gomez, p. 73. Hitchcock visits: *PWW*, vol. 64, pp. 43–45; Berg, p. 653; John Cooper, *Wilson*, pp. 542–544. Wilson's intransigence: Walworth, vol. 2, p. 385; John Cooper, *Wilson*, pp. 545–547; Berg, pp. 656–658. "Still has in mind": John Cooper, *Breaking*, p. 317. "Little girl": Levin, p. 379. "Sharp attack": *PWW*, vol. 64, p. 325. "Better if I had died": John Cooper, *Wilson*, p. 552. Wilson fires Lansing: Glaser, pp. 153–154; John Cooper, *Wilson*, pp. 552–554; Berg, pp. 665–668. "Sounded like a spoiled": John Cooper, *Breaking*, p. 322.

"Time to spike": Tumulty, p. 445. "Rapidly disintegrating": *PWW*, vol. 64, p. 479. "Strikes at the very heart" and "strangled": John Cooper, *Wilson*, p. 558; John Cooper, *Breaking*, p. 347. Senate acts: John Cooper, *Wilson*, pp. 558–559; John Cooper, *Breaking*, pp. 363–370; Berg, p. 677. "Towering ambition": Meyer, p. 557. "If I were not a Christian": John Cooper, *Wilson*, p. 560. Wilson and Harding nomination: *PWW*, vol. 68, p. 46; *NYT*, June 13, 1920; John Cooper, *Wilson*, pp. 569–570; Berg, pp. 690–691. Wilson and 1920 Democratic convention: John Cooper, *Wilson*, pp. 568–569; Berg, pp. 689–691. "Would mar his place": John Cooper, *Wilson*, p. 568. "Deeply resentful": Ward, *First-Class*, p. 515. Wilson meets nominees: Gene Smith, pp. 164–165; Levin, p. 453; Berg, pp. 691–692; John Cooper, *Wilson*, p. 569. "Shock and sympathy": Fleming, *Illusion*, p. 460. "Very grateful": Walworth, vol. 2, p. 403. Wilson to intimates and "We have torn": Ferrell, *Wilson*, p. 229. "I have not lost faith": Ferrell, *Wilson*, p. 300. Wilson refuses Debs: Radosh, p. 139. "Gross and criminal": *PWW*, vol. 68, p. 167. Newsreels: Gene Smith, pp. 171–172; Levin, pp. 457–458; Berg, p. 694; John Cooper, *Wilson*, p. 577. Wilson's retirement: Edith

Wilson, pp. 320–360; Levin, pp. 467–500; Gene Smith, pp. 181–261; John Cooper, *Wilson*, pp. 579–596; Berg, pp. 703–736.

Edith's attitude toward "normalcy": Lynne Ford, p. 496. "Three Senators get together": *PWW*, vol. 68, p. 251. "Best, after all": Gene Smith, p. 219. "Not directly attacked": Wilson speech, Sept. 11, 1919; Thompson, p. 105. "Ten-cent pickled": William Allen White, pp. 292, 479. "Only national voice": Woodrow Wilson, *Constitutional*, p. 68. "No reason" to limit and "bend our every effort" and "delivered the world": Coolidge speeches, Dec. 6, 1923, May 30 and Aug. 15, 1928.

CHAPTER TWELVE: "HOW COULD THIS THING HAPPEN?"

Husband Kimmel background: *Honolulu Star-Bulletin* and *NYT*, May 15, 1968; Kimmel, pp. 1–10; Reynolds, pp. 175–176; Prange, *At Dawn*, pp. 49–52; Carlson, pp. 146–147; Summers and Swan, pp. 28–42. Pearl Harbor under attack: Prange, *At Dawn*, pp. 483–527; Toland, pp. 304–110; Stinnett, pp. 243–252; Layton, pp. 299–324. Kimmel and shoulder boards: Craig Nelson, p. 261. "There's a message": *Pearl Harbor Hearings*, Joint Committee, Congress, 1946, p. 558. "Something terrible" and "lift out of the water": Layton, p. 313; Prange, *At Dawn*, p. 119. "Hostilities with Japan" and "Too bad": *Pearl Harbor Hearings*, p. 935; Prange, *At Dawn*, p. 516; Summers and Swan, p. 14. "Very charming": Dall, p. 117. "Perfectly stunned": Gannon, p. 162. Roosevelt receives news: Jean Smith, *FDR*, pp. 536–537; Brands, *Traitor*, pp. 6–7; Davis, *War President*, pp. 338–340; Gillon, pp. 51–57.

"Find out": Jean Smith, *FDR*, p. 537. Manning Kimmel: Gannon, pp. 55–56. Roosevelt early interest in Navy and war: *Altoona Tribune*, May 5, 1913; De Kay, *Navy*, pp. 1–29; Jean Smith, *FDR*, pp. 23, 33; Kenneth Davis, *Beckoning*, pp. 23, 38, 40–42, 72, 82–83, 88–93; Ward, *Before*, pp. 159–160. "World's largest known": *NYT*, June 25, 1961. FDR and TR: Burns and Dunn, p. 56; Davis, *Beckoning*, pp. 116, 122–128, 137, 144–149; Ward, *Before*, pp. 193–195, 231–233; Ward, *First-Class*, pp. 87–91. "My father spent": Franklin Roosevelt Jr., int 1978. Roosevelt and Navy Department, World War I: Kenneth Davis, *Beckoning*, p. 306; Ward, *First-Class*, pp. 172–335; Jean Smith, *FDR*, pp. 99–116; De Kay, *Navy*, pp. 93–275. "All my life": De Kay, *Navy*, p. 86. "Complete smashup": Steinberg, *Mrs. R*, p. 99. "These are history-making": Elliott Roosevelt, vol. 2, p. 233. "Nobody seemed": Elliott Roosevelt, vol. 2, p. 238. "As much conception": Arthur Schlesinger, *Crisis*, p. 349. "I am *running*": Freidel, vol. 1, p. 239. "We've got to get": De Kay, *Navy*, p. 175. Roosevelt in World War I: Kenneth Davis, *Beckoning*, pp. 431–571; Jean Smith, *FDR*, pp. 119–123, 126–132, 135–144, 158–160; Ward, *First-Class*, pp. 336–433. "Submission too long" and "interestingly parallel": Ray Baker, vol. 5, p. 415.

"Bring the Fleet back" and "unfriendly act": Roosevelt speech, Feb. 4, 1939. "Tried every diplomatic means" and "definitive historian": Hough, *Naval Wars*, p. 103. Listening "breathlessly": Blanche Cook, vol. 1, p. 214. "You must resign": De Kay, *Navy*, p. 191. "Thought actual fighting": Josephus Daniels, *Roosevelt and Daniels*, p. 50. "Neither you nor I": Arthur Schlesinger, *Crisis*, p. 53. Build a "fence": Josephus Daniels, *Wilson Era*, p. 331. Roosevelt in 1920s: Kenneth Davis, *Beckoning*, pp. 622–853; Ward, *First-Class*, pp. 557–799; Jean Smith, *FDR*, pp. 186–241; Brands, *Traitor*, pp. 132–228. 1928 banquet: Roosevelt speech, Dec. 28, 1928. Roosevelt and 1932 campaign: Burns, *Lion*, pp. 123–157; Brands, *Traitor*, pp. 241–265; Jean Smith, *FDR*, pp. 242–287. "Broad Executive power": Roosevelt inaugural address, Mar. 4, 1933. Nye investigation: Cole, pp. 141–162; Jean Smith, *FDR*, pp. 299–304; Burns, *Lion*, pp. 253–254. "Come around": Cole, p. 168. "Acted like a stinker": Beschloss, *Kennedy and Roosevelt*, p. 200. "Mind our own business": *Brooklyn Daily Eagle*, Oct. 27, 1936. "Shun political commitments": Roosevelt speech, Aug. 14, 1936. Roosevelt and Hitler's invasion of Rhineland: Dallek, *Foreign Policy*, p. 124. Roosevelt and Europe, second term: Dallek, *Foreign Policy*, pp. 125–144; Jean Smith, *FDR*, pp. 416–441.

"Innocent nations": Roosevelt speech, Oct. 5, 1937. Press comment on speech: all Oct. 6, 1937. "It's a terrible thing": Burns, *Lion*, pp. 318–319. Reaction to sinking of *Panay*: Kenneth Davis, *Into the Storm*, pp. 154–158; Dallek, *Foreign Policy*, pp. 153–156. "Deeply shocked": Roosevelt statement, Dec. 13, 1937. Ludlow Amendment: Arthur Schlesinger, *Imperial*, pp. 105, 301; Kenneth Davis, *Into the Storm*, pp. 155–156, 189–190. "You can cast": Jean Smith, *FDR*, p. 422. "Such an amendment": Dunn, p. 26. Roosevelt and Munich: Dallek, *Foreign Policy*, p. 166; Jean Smith, *FDR*, pp. 424–425; Brands, *Traitor*, pp. 509–513; Hamby, *Destiny*, pp. 294–296; Kenneth Davis, *Into the Storm*, pp. 324–346. "Chief of police": Roosevelt to Endicott Peabody, May 8, 1938. "Judas Iscariot": Dallek, *Foreign Policy*, p. 164. Roosevelts and *Kristallnacht*: Hamby, *Destiny*, p. 296; Kenneth Davis, *Into the Storm*, pp. 364–366. "Makes me sick": Eleanor Roosevelt to Lorena Hickok, Nov. 14, 1938, ERP. "Hitler would not have dared": Blum, p. 273. "Complete and utter failure": Casey, *Cautious Crusade*, p. 5. Roosevelt warns committee: Jean Smith, *FDR*, p. 431. Roosevelt frustration about repeal: Doenecke and Stoler, pp. 127–128.

"Well, Captain": Sherwood, p. 133. "Even though I did sign": Elliott Roosevelt, vol. 4, p. 900. Roosevelt and start of European war: Kenneth Davis, *Into the Storm*, pp. 460–461; Dallek, *Foreign Policy*, pp. 175, 176–212. "Well, Bill": Burns, *Lion*, p. 394. "I was almost startled": Memcon, Sept. 1, 1939, FDRP. "End of the world": Beschloss, *Kennedy and Roosevelt*, p. 190. "This nation will remain": Roosevelt speech, Sept. 3, 1939. Lindbergh warning: Lindbergh speech, Sept. 15, 1939. Peaceful "citadel": Roosevelt speech, Sept. 2, 1939. "Almost literally walking": Dallek, *Foreign Policy*, p. 202. Joseph Kennedy sees Roosevelt: Beschloss, *Kennedy and Roosevelt*, pp. 198–200. Roosevelt and Hitler's advance: Dallek, *Foreign Policy*, pp. 218–223; Kenneth Davis, *Into the Storm*, pp. 465–562; Jean Smith, *FDR*, pp. 444–448; Brands, *Traitor*, pp. 542–550. "Hand that held the dagger": Roosevelt speech, June 10, 1940. "Fortified by the grand scope": Churchill to Roosevelt, June 11, 1940, FDRP. Roosevelt and Willkie's nomination: Jean Smith, *FDR*, pp. 452–456; Brands, *Traitor*, pp. 552–557. Eleanor's "hunch": Eleanor Roosevelt to Lorena Hickok, June 20, 1940, ERP.

Roosevelt maneuvers toward 1940 nomination: Burns, *Lion*, pp. 422–430; Brands, *Traitor*, pp. 553–558; Jean Smith, *FDR*, pp. 456–463. "Any desire or purpose": Roosevelt statement, July 16, 1940. "Superficial" things: Arthur Schlesinger, *Crisis*, p. 482. "Will not participate": Byrnes, p. 122. 1940 military draft: David Kennedy, *Freedom*, pp. 492–496; Brands, *Traitor*, pp. 555–558; Jean Smith, *FDR*, pp. 466–467. "Slit the throat": *Life*, Aug. 26, 1940. "No conceivable" and "only democratic": Jean Smith, *FDR*, pp. 465–466. Destroyer Deal: David Kennedy, *Freedom*, pp. 469–476; Kaiser, *No End*, pp. 46–58. "Matter of life and death": Churchill to Roosevelt, June 14, 1940, FDRP. "War of European power politics": Cole, p. 374. "Most important action": Roosevelt to Congress, Sept. 3,

1940. "Most arbitrary": *Life*, Sept. 16, 1940. Fall 1940 campaign: Divine, pp. 41–89; Jean Smith, *FDR*, pp. 452–463; Brands, *Traitor*, pp. 572–577; Beschloss, *Kennedy and Roosevelt*, pp. 198–203, 209–222. "Even at the risk": Berinsky, p. 48. "Who really thinks": Beschloss, *Kennedy and Roosevelt*, p. 213. "Our boys shall stay out": Barnard, p. 251. "You may expect war" and "secret Roosevelt pact": *Hartford Courant*, Oct. 31, 1940; Beschloss, *Kennedy and Roosevelt*, p. 15.

"Fighting mad" and "solemn assurance": Jean Smith, *FDR*, p. 475; Roosevelt speech, Oct. 23, 1940. "Within striking distance": *NYT*, Oct. 30, 1940. "I have said this": Roosevelt speech, Oct. 30, 1940. "It's not necessary": Jean Smith, *FDR*, p. 477. "That hypocritical": Barnard, p. 258. "Lied us into a war": Clare Boothe Luce, int 1978; *Arizona Republic*, Oct. 14, 1944. "Adept at evasion": *Bakersfield Californian*, Oct. 31, 1940. "I don't need to tell you": Roosevelt speech, Nov. 5, 1940. Kennedy, *Globe* interview, and showdown with Roosevelt: Beschloss, *Kennedy and Roosevelt*, pp. 224–229. Roosevelt asks for Lend-Lease: Dallek, *Foreign Policy*, pp. 255–273; Brands, *Traitor*, pp. 577–590; Jean Smith, *FDR*, pp. 484–491. "We shall no longer": Churchill to Roosevelt, Dec. 7, 1940, FDRP. "My garden hose" and "Never before": Roosevelt speeches, Dec. 17 and 29, 1940. "Greatest cause in the world": *Pittsburgh Press*, Dec. 2, 1940. Gallup on possible referendum: Gallup Poll, Dec. 1 and 29, 1940, Jan. 3, 1941. "Our national safety": Roosevelt speech, Jan. 6, 1941.

Debate on Lend-Lease: Cole, pp. 409–422; Jean Smith, *FDR*, pp. 489–491; Dallek, *Foreign Policy*, pp. 255–261. "Plow under every fourth": *Chicago Tribune*, Jan. 15, 1941. "Do you still agree": Burns, *Soldier*, p. 49. Battle of North Atlantic: Kaiser, *No End*, pp. 180–201; Jean Smith, *FDR*, p. 491; Dallek, *Foreign Policy*, pp. 160–271; Burns, *Soldier*, pp. 98–131. "Not willing to fire": Dallek, *Foreign Policy*, p. 265. "Shows evidence of waiting": David Kennedy, *Freedom*, p. 494. "Of course, we are": Jean Smith, *FDR*, p. 496. "Practically an act": Burns, *Soldier*, p. 105. "No supplies" and "still technically neutral": Jean Smith, *FDR*, p. 502. Roosevelt edging toward intervention: Dallek, *Foreign Policy*, pp. 276–290; Jean Smith, *FDR*, pp. 498–504; Kaiser, *No End*, pp. 268–275, 291–292. "More and more provocative": Daniels, *Roosevelt and Daniels*, p. 180. Roosevelt and Japan through 1940: Kaiser, *No End*, pp. 25–56; Dallek, *Foreign Policy*, pp. 147–157, 193–195.

Roosevelt's Japan diplomacy, 1941: Kaiser, *No End*, pp. 110–118, 250–258, 279–286, 303–323; Dallek, *Foreign Policy*, pp. 299–310; Jean Smith, *FDR*, pp. 511–513, 521–534; Kenneth Davis, *Into the Storm*, pp. 144–157, 313–338; Brands, *Traitor*, pp. 617–627; Hamby, *Destiny*, pp. 335–338. "Japs are having": Kaiser, *No End*, p. 251. "Inclined to grant": Jean Smith, *FDR*, p. 516. "Rational" Japanese: Acheson, p. 19. Acheson's caprice: Chace, pp. 82–87; Jean Smith, *FDR*, pp. 517–518. "Gratifying to receive" and "vicious circle": Chace, pp. 63, 86. "Time is of the essence": Twomey, p. 126. Prelude to Pearl Harbor: Kaiser, *No End*, pp. 307–322; Prange, *At Dawn*, pp. 364–372, 396–421; Jean Smith, *FDR*, pp. 518–534; Brands, *Traitor*, pp. 617–627. "Precipitate a crisis": Jean Smith, *FDR*, p. 525. "Likely" to be assaulted: Brands, *Traitor*, p. 622. "How to maneuver": Hamby, *Destiny*, p. 337. "Negotiations with Japanese": *Pearl Harbor Hearings*, p. 79.

"This dispatch": Stark to Kimmel and Short, Nov. 27, 1941, NARA. "That was my opportunity" and "Our mission is to protect": Prange, *At Dawn*, pp. 412, 400. "Urgent instructions": Layton, p. 250; Prange, *At Dawn*, p. 447. Roosevelt on Pearl Harbor night: Jean Smith, *FDR*, pp. 536–538; Brands, *Traitor*, pp. 4–9, 630–631; Craig Nelson, pp. 320–327;

Kenneth Davis, *War,* pp. 339–347. "I'm trying to keep": *Pittsburgh Press,* Dec. 6, 1981. "You cannot escape": Eleanor Roosevelt speech, Dec. 7, 1941. "Chin stuck out": Craig Nelson, p. 277. "Most serious Cabinet meeting": Memcon, Dec. 7, 1941, FDRP. "All the planes": Hamilton, p. 73. "Deeply shaken": Twomey, p. 288. "Great change": Gillon, pp. 148–149. "Most terrific shock": Morgenthau diary, Dec. 7, 1941, FDRL. "Great fleet of Japanese": Memorandum, Dec. 7, 1941, FDRP. "Could not understand": Twomey, p. 288. Roosevelt and Pearl Harbor probes: Borch and Martinez, pp. 1–174; Beach, pp. 110–175; Lambert and Polmar, pp. 129–150; Craig Nelson, pp. 437–454; Toland, pp. 28–245; Kimmel, pp. 146–187; Layton, pp. 350–352; Prange, *At Dawn,* pp. 592–604, 623–625, 653–655, 699–714; Stinnett, pp. 254–260; Feldman, pp. 213–214; Summers and Swan, pp. 272–278.

"You would do America": *Arizona Republic,* May 20, 1968. "That you get him alone": Felix Frankfurter to Roosevelt, Jan. 17, 1942, FDRP. "Errors of judgment": Roberts Commission Report, Jan. 24, 1942, FDRL. "It might give the impression": Stimson diary, Jan. 26 and 28, 1942, Stimson Papers. Short's destiny: *Louisville Courier-Journal,* Sept. 4, 1949. "Suspended disgrace": Dall, p. 159. "Smarter than I was": Kimmel to Stark, Feb. 22, 1942, NARA. Kimmel after leaving Navy: Summers and Swan, pp. 260–368; Prange, *At Dawn,* pp. 608–613, 670–671, 728–729; Clarke, pp. 160–164; Beach, p. 183; Layton, pp. 202–203, 342–353. "That son-of-a-bitch": Summers and Swan, p. 342. "Never sent me a damn thing": *Detroit Free Press,* Dec. 4, 1966. "Changed from a very dejected": *Baltimore Sun,* Dec. 7, 1997. "Satisfaction" and "You betrayed": Summers and Swan, pp. 347–348. "Couldn't talk to him": *Bloomington Pantagraph,* May 2, 1982. "So emotionally upset": Summers and Swan, p. 351. "I cannot excuse": *Waukesha Daily Freeman,* May 21, 1968. Kimmel's later reminiscences: *Des Moines Register,* Dec. 7, 1966; *LaCrosse Tribune,* May 15, 1968; *Galveston Daily News,* Dec. 8, 1991; *Detroit Free Press,* Dec. 4, 1966; *Indianapolis Star,* May 15, 1968. "I don't care": Summers and Swan, p. 355. Roosevelt's security precautions: Marrin, p. 176; Persico, *Roosevelt's Secret War,* p. 269; Harry Hopkins memo, Dec. 8, 1941, FDRL; Morgenthau diary, Dec. 8, 1941, FDRL.

"Live in world history": Draft in Hopkins Papers, Dec. 15, 1941. Scene in House chamber: *NYT* and *WP,* Dec. 9, 1941. "Curious sense": Blanche Cook, vol. 3, p. 405. Kimmel descendants take up cause: UPI, May 2, 1982; *Bloomington Pantagraph,* May 3, 1982; Barnes Review Fourth International Conference, June 20 to 22, 2003. Debate on war declaration: CR, Dec. 8, 1941, and *NYT* and *WP,* Dec. 9, 1941. "As a woman" and Rankin hiding in booth: *Philadelphia Inquirer* and *Des Moines Register,* Dec. 9, 1941. Roosevelt signs: *NYT,* Dec. 9, 1941. "Today all of us": Churchill to Roosevelt, Dec. 8, 1941, FDRP.

CHAPTER THIRTEEN: "THE SURVIVAL WAR"

Roosevelt 1942 State of the Union: *NYT, WP, Los Angeles Times, Philadelphia Inquirer,* and *Pottstown Mercury,* Jan. 7, 1942. Early's request: Associated Press, Feb. 20, 1942. "The Survival War": Roosevelt speech, Apr. 14, 1942. Roosevelt and Japanese internment: Robinson, *Tragedy,* pp. 1–258; Richard Reeves, pp. 1–285; Myer, pp. 3–299; Walker, pp. 78–81, 88–90, 110; Stone, *War and Liberty,* pp. 65–84; Irons, *War Powers,* pp. 132–149; Stone, *Perilous,* pp. 289–310; Jean Smith, *FDR,* pp. 549–553; David Kennedy, *Freedom,* pp. 748–760. "We had an anxious": Eleanor Roosevelt to Lorena Hickok,

Dec. 11, 1941, ERP. "May well be the Achilles' Heel": Jim Newton, *Justice*, p. 128. "Under armed guard" and "Lincoln, the mild-mannered": *Los Angeles Times*, Feb. 16 and 13, 1942. "We have to be tough": Marrin, p. 71. "This is a race war": Robinson, *Tragedy*, p. 84. "Out here, a Jap": *Personal Justice Denied*, p. 476. "No Japanese problem": Commission on Wartime Relocation, House Judiciary Committee, Hearing, 1980, p. 64. "Public hysteria": Stone, *Perilous*, p. 293. "Based primarily upon public": Ng, p. 20. "Great potential danger": Walker, p. 84.

"No reason for mass evacuation": Irons, *Courage*, p. 41. "From good farm land": Richard Reeves, p. 53. Eleanor implores husband: Blanche Cook, vol. 3, pp. 405–408. "West Coast matter" and "very vigorous": Robinson, *Tragedy*, p. 91. "If deemed essential": Biddle to Henry Stimson, Feb. 12, 1942, FDRL. "We have carte blanche": Bird, *Chairman*, p. 152. Executive Order 9066: Feb. 19, 1942, FDRL. Eleanor and internment: Blanche Cook, vol. 3, pp. 416–421. "No law-abiding aliens": Stone, *Perilous*, p. 289. "Marked a turning point": Blanche Cook, vol. 3, p. 419. "Both for their own safety": Melton and Smith, p. 51. "Nobody could move" and "The move": *NYT*, Feb. 21, 1942. "One of the great mass exoduses": Richard Reeves, p. 39. "Advance safeguards": *Baltimore Sun*, Feb. 22, 1942. "Only what you can carry": Richard Reeves, p. 66. "It was too terrible": Oppenheim, p. 112. Warren wept and Warren's possible penance: Richard Reeves, p. 281. "Just a leg man" and "Money, money": Bird, *Chairman*, p. 659. "Reasonably undertaken": *Honolulu Star-Bulletin*, Nov. 6, 1981. Eleanor deeply unsettled: Blanche Cook, vol. 3, pp. 408, 420, 423, 428, 483, 508, 534, 536. Supreme Court and Japanese removals: Walker, pp. 88–89; Richard Reeves, pp. 94–97, 232–234, 283.

"Wrapped in mystery": "My Day," Dec. 20, 1941, FDRL. "Atlantic First": Burns, *Soldier*, pp. 188–190. "Defeat of Germany means": Roosevelt to George Marshall, July 16, 1942, FDRL. "Send Ships to Aid": *New York Journal American*, Mar. 10, 1942. "From now on": Elliott Roosevelt, vol. 4, p. 1300. "Will bring a lot": Roosevelt to Glass, May 5, 1942, FDRP. "Since war came to us": *Detroit Free Press*, Nov. 10, 1942. "Centralized execution": Burns, *Soldier*, p. 193. "Totalitarian collectivism" and "to win total war": *NYT*, Feb. 12 and May 21, 1942. War financing: Homats, pp. 134–172. "Our standard of living": Roosevelt to Congress, Apr. 27, 1942. "Blatant piece of demagoguery": Burns, *Soldier*, p. 257. "Inescapable responsibility": Roosevelt to Congress and Roosevelt speech, Sept. 7, 1942; Barron, pp. 266–280. Roosevelt and tax increase: Burns, *Soldier*, pp. 257–262; Hormats, pp. 135–158. "Next year the taxes": Roosevelt to Eleanor, Oct. 7, 1942, FDRP. "Placed a pistol": *Burlington Free Press*, Sept. 8, 1942. "So revolutionary": *Reno Gazette-Journal*, Sept. 7, 1942. "Most powerful body": *NYT*, Jan. 10, 1943. "Most notorious claim": Arthur Schlesinger, *Imperial*, p. 115. Pentagon construction: Vogel, *Pentagon*, pp. xxi–317.

Manhattan Project: David Kennedy, *Freedom*, pp. 663–665, 838–839; Burns, *Soldier*, pp. 455–456; Jean Smith, *FDR*, pp. 580–581; Brands, *Traitor*, pp. 679, 791. "If we get a decent": Vogel, *Pentagon*, p. 334. "Perfectly silly": Burns, *Soldier*, p. 274. Japanese in Aleutians: Toll, *Crucible*, pp. 378–379. "Whatever it takes": *Sioux Falls Argus-Leader*, Aug. 7, 1942. Operation Torch planning: David Kennedy, *Freedom*, pp. 579–581; Brands, *Traitor*, pp. 684–685, 690–694, 699; Dallek, *Foreign Policy*, pp. 351–353, 362, 367; Jean Smith, *FDR*, pp. 560–565. "Please make it before": Kenneth Davis, *War*, p. 793; Brands, *Traitor*, p. 691. Roosevelt inspection tour: Ward, *Closest*, pp. 173–183; Goodwin, *No Ordinary*, pp. 360–371; Burns, *Soldier*, pp. 268–272. "Several hundred negro": *Indianapolis Star*, Oct. 2, 1942. Robert Smalls: Billingsley, pp. 51–82. "Sewing-machine-type": Roosevelt press conference, Oct. 1, 1942. "Making a lot of money": *York Gazette*, Oct. 2, 1942. "God bless you" and "We all get along" and "restful & satisfactory": Suckley diary, Sept. 26 and 30, 1942, FDRL; Ward, *Closest*, pp. 182–183. "Alleged inspection trips": *Cincinnati Enquirer*, Oct. 2, 1942.

"When we drove unannounced": Roosevelt speech, Oct. 12, 1942. 1942 elections: *NYT*, Nov. 4, 1942; Burns, *Soldier*, pp. 273–281. "All the boys": Dallek, *Lone Star*, p. 245. "Exacted revenge": Quoted in *Tennessean*, Nov. 5, 1942. "Dissatisfaction is rife": Beschloss, *Kennedy and Roosevelt*, p. 249. "Why should it" and "I was perfectly delighted": Roosevelt press conference, Nov. 6, 1942. Shangri-La visit: Suckley diary, Nov. 8, 1942, FDRL; Ward, *Closest*, pp. 183–186. "I have made a constant": Roosevelt speech, Nov. 17, 1942. New Year's 1943: Persico, *Centurions*, p. 258. Casablanca conference: Beschloss, *Conquerors*, pp. 13–14, 19; David Kennedy, *Freedom*, pp. 584–588; Burns, *Soldier*, pp. 314–325; Meacham, *Franklin and Winston*, pp. 204–213; Jean Smith, *FDR*, pp. 565–569. "Whole global picture": Roosevelt-Churchill press conference, Jan. 24, 1943. Theodore Roosevelt and unconditional surrender: Dalton, p. 508. "No terms except": Weigley, p. 111. "Turned his usual": Dalton, p. 508. "Perfect!": Beschloss, *Conquerors*, p. 13. "Inherent right": Stimson statement, Jan. 29, 1943, Stimson Papers. Japanese Americans in military: McCaffrey, pp. 59–61, 70. Eleanor's visit to Gila River: Robinson, *Tragedy*, pp. 184–185, 194; Richard Reeves, p. 164; Blanche Cook, vol. 3, p. 11; Goodwin, *No Ordinary*, pp. 427–429.

"Coddling the Japs": John Rankin in CR, Feb. 3, 1943. "It's sour": Gregory, p. 109. "Certainly not luxurious": Robinson, *Unknown*, p. 131. Roosevelt and civil liberties: Walker, pp. 79–124; Burns, *Soldier*, pp. 216–217. "Secure information": Beschloss, *Presidential Courage*, p. 164. "May have been the originator": Folsom, p. 146. "Subversive activities": Weiner, p. 74. "Philosophical understanding": Russell, p. 148. Huston Plan and George W. Bush–era surveillance: Edwards and King, pp. 21, 55, 103; Walker, pp. 305–306, 466–470. German saboteurs: Walker, pp. 80, 87, 100–103; Barron, pp. 258–263; Irons, *War Powers*, pp. 149–156; Feldman, pp. 215–225. "Death penalty is": Persico, *Roosevelt's Secret War*, p. 202. "I won't give them up" and "If a man": Persico, *Roosevelt's Secret War*, pp. 203, 202. Roosevelt and race: Walker, pp. 81, 89, 105–112; Jean Smith, *FDR*, pp. 357, 398–402, 440, 493–494, 507, 528, 540, 549–552, 551, 688, 794. "No matter what" and "much upset" and "Phil, you know" and "no discrimination": Walker, pp. 105–107. Eleanor and African Americans: Blanche Cook, vol. 3, pp. 9–11, 33–36, 93, 127, 155–187, 216, 320–321, 339–345, 358, 419, 439, 450–451, 497, 566–567.

Ex parte Quirin: Walker, pp. 100–101. "Discrimination against": Kersten, p. 54. "Eleanor's niggers": Lou Potter, p. 119. Lash surveillance: Lash, *Love, Eleanor*, pp. 460–493; Blanche Cook, vol. 3, pp. 456, 467–469; Walker, pp. 85, 91, 99–100. "Gigantic conspiracy" and "intimate" and "anybody who knew": Lash, *Love, Eleanor*, pp. 460, 493; Blanche Cook, vol. 3, p. 467. Eleanor's South Pacific trip: Blanche Cook, vol. 3, pp. 479–480; Rowley, pp. 26–261; Lash, *Eleanor and Franklin*, pp. 876–889; Lash, *Love, Eleanor*, pp. 445, 504, 509. "Too old" and "the people here": *Miami News*, Sept. 2, 1943; Eleanor to Lorena Hickok, Sept. 1, 1943, ERP. "Junket" and "So this is": Rowley, pp. 260–261. "Probably the same crowd": Roosevelt to Eleanor, Apr. 6, 1945, FDRL. "Their expressions" and "ashamed": Lash, *Eleanor and Franklin*, p. 883; Blanche Cook, vol. 3, p. 482. "Broken mentally and emotionally": Eleanor Roosevelt, p. 261. "Pa asked me": Blanche Cook, vol. 3, p. 483. Eleanor's depression: Goodwin, *No Ordinary*, p. 467. "Little or no surface": Blanche Cook, vol. 3, p. 493. Roosevelt's early planning for peace organization: Hoopes and Brinkley, pp. 1–82; Stephen Schlesinger, pp. 7, 39–46; Meiser, pp. 1–20; Jean Smith, *FDR*, pp. 547, 626–627, 631–632; Brands, *Traitor*, pp. 642–643, 652, 675, 683, 702, 710, 717, 746, 798.

"It isn't an awful lot" and "sacrilegious": Roosevelt press conference, Jan. 1, 1943, and State of the Union, Jan. 7, 1943. "Four Policemen": Stephen Schlesinger, p. 40. "International W.P.A.": *NYT*, Aug. 27, 1943. "Appropriate international" and "vote against the Ten Commandments": *NYT*, Sept. 22 and 26, 1943. "Would be a very fine thing": Roosevelt press conference, Oct. 29, 1943. "Repeal the Declaration": *Oakland Tribune*, Oct. 17, 1943. Roosevelt to Hull: Beschloss, *Conquerors*, p. 20. Tehran conference: David Kennedy, *Freedom*, pp. 674–686; Meacham, *Franklin and Winston*, pp. 247–259; Beschloss, *Conquerors*, pp. 22–38; Jean Smith, *FDR*, pp. 581–599. "Take me over": Atkinson, p. 268. "Youngest of the three" and Big Three dinner: Beschloss, *Conquerors*, p. 24. Roosevelt's illness: Jean Smith, *FDR*, pp. 602–603. "Second Bill of Rights" and "not even a dictionary": Roosevelt speech, Jan. 11, 1944, and to Congress, Feb. 22, 1944. "Calculated and deliberate": *Pottstown Press*, Feb. 23, 1944. "Alben must be suffering": Hassett, p. 235. "Doing everything": Roosevelt to Pat Drewry, Mar. 7, 1944, FDRP. "I am very angry": Roosevelt to Churchill, Mar. 20, 1944, FDRP. "Cuba is absolutely": Roosevelt press conference, May 6, 1944. "Spend more time": Curtis Roosevelt, p. 274. Roosevelt and Lucy: Persico, *Franklin and Lucy*, pp. 124, 170–172, 298; Meacham, *Franklin and Winston*, pp. 220–221, 276, 290–291, 341–360.

"I realize more": Eleanor to Lorena Hickok, Oct. 1936, ERP. "Might have been happier": Jean Smith, *FDR*, p. 403. "Unselfish devotion" and "does worry": Suckley diary, Jan. 12, 1945, and Dec. 3, 1944, FDRL; Ward, *Closest*, pp. 380, 353. Roosevelt's health: Ferrell, *Dying*, pp. 1, 27, 40–46, 85–86, 111, 138–139, 147, 163; Evans, pp. 43–134; Lelyveld, pp. 22–24, 73, 90–100, 104, 191, 211, 229, 306; Lomazow and Fettmann, pp. 9, 46–47, 106, 111, 150, 155–157, 176. "Definitely better" and "were not telling *him*": Ward, *Closest*, pp. 295–296. "Suddenly F is more": Lash, *Eleanor and Franklin*, p. 900. "Very, very great purpose": Roosevelt press conference, May 30, 1944. Roosevelt awaits D-Day: Lelyveld, pp. 5–7, 80, 124–129; Jean Smith, *FDR*, pp. 569–575, 599, 613–614. "Christian and a Democrat": *Life*, Nov. 3, 1947. "Had something to do": Jean Smith, *FDR*, p. 643. "He had the radio": Suckley diary, June 6, 1944, FDRL; Ward, *Closest*, p. 309. "Overconfidence destroys" and "How I wish" and "Our sons": Roosevelt press conference and to Churchill and prayer, June 6, 1944, FDRL. Roosevelt and Holocaust: Beschloss, *Conquerors*, pp. 40, 59, 65, 281–285; David Kennedy, *Freedom*, pp. 794–797; Jean Smith, *FDR*, pp. 149, 607–613; Lelyveld, p. 94.

"Annihilate the Jewish" and "most overwhelming disaster" and "win the war": Beschloss, *Conquerors*, pp. 38–40. "Probably the greatest": Cohen, p. 291; Beschloss, *Conquerors*, p. 63. "Never talked" and McCloy changes story: Beschloss, *Conquerors*, pp. 329, 66. "If not in heart failure": Lomazow and Fettmann, p. 120. President a "quitter": Lelyveld, p. 103. "Willing to be 'liberal' ": Suckley diary, Nov. 3, 1943, FDRL; Ward, *Closest*,

p. 251. "Grown old in office": Dewey speech, June 28, 1944. GI Bill: Jean Smith, *FDR*, pp. 584–585. "Country gentleman": Beschloss, *Conquerors*, p. 119. "Too much prejudice": Suckley diary, Jan. 17, 1945, FDRL; Ward, *Closest*, p. 384. Roosevelt plans for "United Nations": Beschloss, *Conquerors*, p. 94. Roosevelt maneuvers over vice presidency: Lelyveld, pp. 54, 156, 167, 170, 179; Weintraub, pp. 40–48; Michael Davis, pp. 119–153; Burns, *Soldier*, pp. 504–506; Hamby, *Destiny*, pp. 398–399; McCullough, pp. 298–324; Jean Smith, *FDR*, pp. 391–392, 618–619, 626. "I hardly know Truman": Byrnes, p. 225. "Public appeal": Janeway, p. 51. "Bring real strength to the ticket": John Nicolay to John Hay, June 6, 1864, LOC. "Wants to break up": Donovan, *Conflict*, p. xiii. "Worldwide job": Roosevelt speech, July 20, 1944, and *NYT*, July 21, 1944.

Roosevelt in Hawaii: Weintraub, pp. 89–98; Lelyveld, pp. 168, 182–189, 192; Jean Smith, *FDR*, pp. 620–622. "Looking for character traits": Curtis Roosevelt, p. 357. "A little right": Beschloss, *Conquerors*, p. 82. "It doesn't seem to be": Beschloss, *Conquerors*, p. 82. "I'm afraid I am": Ferrell, *Dying*, p. 175. "By God, that's not": Ferrell, *Ill-Advised*, p. 40. Roosevelt and Pearl Harbor gambit by Dewey: Richard Norton Smith, *Dewey*, pp. 412–430; Jean Smith, *FDR*, pp. 616–628; Weintraub, pp. 157–168; Olmsted, pp. 66–67; William Hopkins, p. 250; Lelyveld, pp. 218–220; Summers and Swan, pp. 316–319; Beschloss, "Fact-Finding and Its Limits," *NYT*, May 26, 2002. "This constant rumor": Fleming, *New Dealers' War*, p. 447. "Really worried about him": Eleanor Roosevelt, p. 272. "If the Republicans were to win": Roosevelt speech, Oct. 21, 1944. McCormick on isolationism: *Decatur Herald*, Oct. 24, 1944. 1944 results: Winik, pp. 491–492. Roosevelt's 1945 inaugural: Burns, *Soldier*, pp. 559–563; Jean Smith, *FDR*, pp. 628–629. "Who is there here": Burns, *Soldier*, pp. 559–563. "Exactly as my husband": George Martin, p. 461. "So very depressed": Eleanor Roosevelt to Lash, Jan. 21, 1945, ERP.

Roosevelt at Yalta: David Kennedy, *Freedom*, pp. 799–806; Jean Smith, *FDR*, pp. 629–633; Beschloss, *Conquerors*, pp. 174–196; Meacham, *Franklin and Winston*, pp. 313–326. "Bunch of incompetent": Arthur Schlesinger, *Imperial*, p. 123. "I can answer that": Roosevelt press conference, Feb. 23, 1945. Roosevelt final speech to Congress: Jean Smith, *FDR*, pp. 632–635; Lelyveld, p. 296. "I say a prayer": Brands, *Traitor*, p. 815. "You sounded cheerful": Eleanor to Roosevelt, Apr. 8, 1945, FDRL. "I get the gruel": Ward, *Closest*, p. 408. "Terribly shocked": Beschloss, *Conquerors*, pp. 209–210. Roosevelt death scene: Suckley diary, Apr. 12, 1945, FDRL; Ward, *Closest*, pp. 416–420; Lelyveld, pp. 323–324; Beschloss, *Conquerors*, pp. 214–215. "Lucy is such a lovely": Ward, *Closest*, p. 415. US World War II death count is from Congressional Research Service and US Department of Veterans Affairs. Final stages of war: David Kennedy, *Freedom*, pp. 808–858; Hamby, *Destiny*, pp. 413–436. "In every possible way": *NYT*, Mar. 21, 1946. "Men will thank God": *NYT*, Apr. 13, 1945. "Tragic mistakes": Lelyveld, p. 55. UN site search: *NYT*, Jan. 10, 1946. "Surrenders the constitutional power": *Chicago Tribune*, Dec. 6, 1945. "Unlimited Presidential use of force": Arthur Schlesinger, *Imperial*, p. 122. Theodore Roosevelt regretted lack of crisis: John Cooper, *Warrior*, pp. 111–112.

CHAPTER FOURTEEN: "I AM GOING TO LET THEM HAVE IT"

Kenneth Shadrick and his death, and family reaction: *Time*, July 17, 1950; *NYT*, July 6, 1950, and June 21, 1951; *Clarksburg Exponent-Telegram* (WV), July 4, 2004; *Beckley*

Post-Herald (WV), July 7, 1950; *Cumberland Evening Times* (MD), June 25, 1951; *Portsmouth Herald* (NH) and *Morning Herald* (Hagerstown, MD), July 7, 1950; *Berkshire Eagle,* July 7, 1950; *Mansfield News-Journal* (OH), Jan. 25, 1951; Wright, pp. 133–134, 138. Leroy Shadrick: *Port Angeles Evening News* (WA) and *Gadsden Times,* Jan. 6, 1957; *Alexandria Times-Tribune,* Jan. 4, 1957; *Raleigh Register* (Beckley, WV), Oct. 21, 1957. "Ban on women correspondents": Brands, *General,* p. 127. "If any nut tries": *NYT* and *Los Angeles Times,* Dec. 28, 1952. Truman's trip to Independence: AP, June 24, 1950; Eben Ayers diary, June 25, 1950, HSTL; McCullough, pp. 773–774; Hamby, *People,* pp. 533–535; Margaret Truman, *Harry S. Truman,* pp. 187–197.

"Order a new roof": Truman to Stanley Woodward, June 24, 1950, HSTP. "Mr. President, I have": Harry S. Truman, *Trial,* p. 332. "Feared this was": Margaret Truman, *Harry S. Truman,* p. 455. *Arizona Republic* headline: June 25, 1950. Truman's Sunday in Independence: Margaret Truman, *Harry S. Truman,* pp. 455–457; McCullough, pp. 775–776; Hamby, *People,* p. 525; Eben Ayers diary, June 25, 1950, HSTL. "Dean, we've got": Hamby, *People,* p. 534. "Everything is extremely tense": Margaret Truman, *Souvenir,* p. 275. "Strong had attacked": Harry S. Truman, *Trial,* pp. 332–333. "That's all" and "By God": *Los Angeles Times,* June 26, 1950; and James Webb recollection, Apr. 25, 1975, HSTL. Truman's early life: Harry S. Truman, *Decisions,* pp. 112–124; Margaret Truman, *Harry S. Truman,* pp. 45–49; McCullough, pp. 37–73; Hamby, *People,* pp. 3–20. "Stole everything" and "You tell Harry": Merle Miller, *Plain Speaking,* p. 73; Harry S. Truman, *Decisions,* p. 200. Truman as early reader: Beschloss, *Presidential Courage,* pp. 211–212. "Romantic adventure": Harry S. Truman, *Decisions,* p. 119.

"Easier for him" and "ignorance": McCullough, p. 558. "Not all readers" and "only thing new": McCullough, p. 463. "Found it difficult to make" and "every strong President" and "saved the Union" and "its intentions" and "stretch": Harry S. Truman, *Buck,* pp. 15, 286, 289, 382, 384. Although posthumously published under Truman's name, this book was assembled by his daughter, Margaret, so she writes, from his dictation, notes, and public utterances and his private comments to her and her mother (p. xi). "They took a gimlet" and "had mean dispositions": Harry S. Truman, *Buck,* pp. 336, 361. Truman in World War I: Harry S. Truman, *Decisions,* pp. 127–132; McCullough, pp. 102–143; Hamby, *People,* pp. 57–82. "Stirred heart and soul" and "I was a Galahad": Truman note, May 1931, HSTL. "Till the War-drum throbb'd": Ferrell, *Truman,* p. 21. "I don't think it would be right": Truman to Bess, July 14, 1917, HSTP. "I do want to be in on the death": Hamby, *People,* pp. 57–82. "There we were watching": McCullough, p. 111. "Great hubbub" and "The men think": Truman to Bess, Nov. 23 and Sept. 18, 1918, HSTP. "So quiet it made your head": William Miller, *Two Americans,* p. 34. "Very anxious that Woodie": Hamby, *People,* p. 79. "One of the greatest": Harry S. Truman, *Buck,* p. 358.

Truman in 1920s and 1930s: Harry S. Truman, *Decisions,* pp. 133–176; Margaret Truman, *Harry S. Truman,* pp. 61–136; McCullough, pp. 159–243; Hamby, *People,* pp. 82–247. Truman during World War II: Margaret Truman, *Harry S. Truman,* pp. 144–285, 337; McCullough, pp. 253–464; Hamby, *People,* pp. 261–337; Ferrell, *Truman,* pp. 153–176. "Does not go on fishing expeditions": McCullough, p. 260. "Magnificent sum": Hamby, *People,* p. 250. "We don't need old stiffs": Jonathan Daniels, p. 228. "He's so damn afraid": Hamby, *People,* p. 253. "The moon, the stars": *NYT,* Apr. 13, 1945. Origins of Korean War:

Gaddis, *We Now Know,* pp. 70–75; Gaddis, *Cold War,* pp. 40–43; Cumings, pp. 3–146; Wada, pp. 1–73; Patterson, pp. 207–210; Millett, pp. 16–253; Hastings, pp. 23–45. Acheson's National Press Club speech: Acheson, pp. 355–358; Donovan, *Tumultuous,* pp. 136–138; Gaddis, *We Now Know,* p. 72–73; Gaddis, *Cold War,* pp. 42; James Matray. "Significantly reshaped": Gaddis, *We Now Know,* p. 72. "Because he is a Communist": Merrill and Paterson, p. 246. "Americans would never participate": Milliken, p. 49.

"First overt military assault" and "only a full-fledged surprise": Gaddis, *We Now Know,* p. 75. "We can't let the U.N. down!": Ferrell, *Truman,* p. 323. "Very hot" and Sunday dinner menu: Truman to Bess, June 26, 1950, HSTP; McCullough, pp. 777–778. Security Council session: Department of State *Bulletin,* vol. 23, 1950, p. 327; *Chicago Tribune,* June 26, 1950. June 25 meeting: Memcon, June 25, 1950, HSTL; Harry S. Truman, *Trial,* pp. 333–336; Acheson, pp. 402–407; Brands, *General,* pp. 75–81; Ferrell, *Truman,* p. 323; Donovan, *Tumultuous,* pp. 199–203; McCullough, pp. 777–779; Hamby, *People,* pp. 535–537. "US force should be used": Dulles to Acheson, June 25, 1950, HSTL. "Haven't been so upset": Truman to Bess, June 26, 1950, HSTP. "Turning-point in world": Beisner, p. 346. "Korea is the Greece": Hamby, *People,* p. 537. "Roosevelt was up in the clouds": *Orange County Register,* Jan. 3, 2013. "Good fighting shape": Telephone memcon, June 26, 1950. Chang meeting: Memcon, June 26, 1950, HSTL. "Will we continue" and "little chance of stopping": Halberstam, *Coldest,* pp. 236–247, 97. "Not going to sell out": CR, June 26, 1950.

Taft and Korea: Patterson, pp. 213–214. June 26 meeting: Memcon and George Elsey notes, HSTL. "Now let's all have": John Hickerson OH, HSTL. June 27 meeting: Memcon, HSTL, and Donovan, *Tumultuous,* pp. 219–220. Truman-Acheson talk: Acheson, pp. 414–415; Blomstedt, pp. 15–17. UN Security Council request: *NYT,* June 29, 1950. Taft speech and responses: CR, June 28, 1950; *NYT,* June 29, 1950; Donovan, *Tumultuous,* pp. 220–222. "We will either": Truman to O'Mahoney, June 28, 1950, HSTP; NSC memcon and Muccio to Acheson, June 28, 1950, HSTL. "Everybody is asking": Truman press conference, June 29, 1950, and Blomstedt, p. 32. "I do not want any implication": NSC memcon, June 29, 1950, HSTL. Truman's history with MacArthur: McCullough, pp. 399–400; Hamby, *People,* pp. 540–541; Halberstam, *Coldest,* pp. 132–137; Brands, *General,* pp. 3–4. "Mr. Prima Donna": Truman note, June 17, 1945, HSTP. "Supreme egotist" and "could not recall": Eben Ayers diary, July 1, 1950, HSTL; Ayers, p. 360. "Does not constitute a decision": Joint Chiefs of Staff to MacArthur, June 29, 1950, HSTL. "Korean Army and coastal forces": MacArthur to Joint Chiefs, June 30, 1950, HSTL; Brands, *General,* pp. 101–102.

"Desperate and rapidly": Sebald to Acheson, June 30, 1950, HSTL. "Time is of the essence": Memcon, June 30, 1950, HSTL. "To be used at Mac's" and "You will be advised": Truman diary and Memcon, June 30, 1950, HSTP. "Since Britain, Australia": Truman diary, June 30, 1950, HSTP. Congressional leadership meeting: Memcon, June 30, 1950, HSTP; Blomstedt, pp. 33–35. Kennedy-Truman visit: Joseph Kennedy diary, June 30, 1950, JFKL. "Harry, what the hell": Merle Miller, *Plain Speaking,* p. 199. Truman early decision making on Korea: McCullough, pp. 775–792; Hamby, *People,* pp. 537–541; Patterson, pp. 210–215; Halberstam, *Coldest,* pp. 89–149. "Kicking around": Elsey, p. 195. "Contingent of troops": Fisher, *Law of the Executive Branch,* p. 330.

CHAPTER FIFTEEN: "I DON'T ASK THEIR PERMISSION"

July 3 meeting: Memcon, HSTL. "Weakens the power": Lucius Battle OH, Jan. 16, 1997, National Security Archive. "Because Polk regularly": Rusk, p. 154. Downturn in Korea: McCullough, pp. 793–795; Hamby, *People,* p. 540; Halberstam, *Coldest,* pp. 15–153, 215–223, 253, 303. "Situation in Korea": MacArthur to Joint Chiefs, July 9, 1950, HSTL. "It looks bad": Truman to Bess, July 12, 1950, HSTP. "Came without provocation": Truman speech, July 19, 1950. Johnson criticism: *Daily Inter Lake,* July 20, 1950; *Corsicana Daily Sun,* July 12, 1950. "Cost of freedom": Kennedy speech, Oct. 22, 1962. "Subject to atomic attack": *Mason City Globe-Gazette,* July 13, 1950. MacArthur to VFW: McCullough, pp. 796–805; Hamby, *People,* pp. 543–544; Brands, *General,* pp. 132–143. "Who is the President": Lucius Battle memo, Aug. 26, 1950, HSTL. "Enemy has been hammering": Truman speech, Sept. 1, 1950. Inchon: Casey, *Selling,* pp. 95–96; Patterson, pp. 216–221; McCullough, pp. 795–799; Hamby, *People,* pp. 540–542; Halberstam, *Coldest,* pp. 306–309.

"Feel unhampered": Marshall to MacArthur, Sept. 29, 1950, HSTL. "Talk to God's right-hand man": McCullough, p. 801. "Public relations stunt": Hamby, *People,* p. 543. "When does the king": Matthew Connelly OH, HSTL. Truman-MacArthur meeting: Herman, pp. 756–761; Donovan, *Tumultuous,* pp. 283–288; Brands, *General,* pp. 172–184; McCullough, pp. 800–808; Hamby, *People,* pp. 510, 543–545; Halberstam, *Coldest,* pp. 364–369; Rusk, pp. 168–169; Arnold Offner, pp. 381–392; Wallace Graham OH, HSTL. "I feel as if I had just whipped": Eben Ayers OH, HSTL. "Outrageous" Hawaiian shirts: Rusk, p. 168. "Japanese ladies": Trip Log, Oct. 1950, HSTL. "Usual picture orgy": Truman note, Nov. 25, 1950, HSTL. "You're working for me": Floyd Boring OH, HSTL. "Do you mind" and "happy and jolly": Robert Landry OH, HSTL. "No political ambitions" and "Orientals prefer" and "puzzling" French struggle: Truman note, Nov. 25, 1950, and Memcon, Oct. 15, 1950, HSTP. "Hell, no!" and "get out of here": Hamby, *People,* p. 545; Rusk, p. 169. Felt "confident": Truman speech, Oct. 17, 1950. MacArthur false optimism: McCullough, p. 807; Hamby, *People,* pp. 544–545; Brands, *General,* pp. 188–196; Halberstam, *Coldest,* pp. 367–368, 370–380; Blomstedt, pp. 93–96. "Disorganized and retreating North Korean": MacArthur statement, Oct. 19, 1950, HSTP. "Definitely coming to an end": *Brooklyn Daily Eagle,* Oct. 20, 1950.

"Now that the fighting": Truman speech, Oct. 24, 1950. "Victory meeting": *Jacksonville Daily Journal,* Oct. 28, 1950. "Come across the Yalu": Brands, *General,* pp. 226–227. Chinese enter war: Brands, *General,* pp. 207–211; McCullough, pp. 808, 814–818; Donovan, *Tumultuous,* pp. 300–308; Hamby, *People,* pp. 551–554; Halberstam, *Coldest,* pp. 380–383. "Deeply concerned" and "thirteen Chinese": *Bend Bulletin,* Nov. 1, 1950; UP, Nov. 3, 1950. "At least six divisions": *NYT,* Nov. 7, 1950. Stalin secret request of Mao: Gaddis, *We Now Know,* p. 87. 1950 elections: Casey, *Selling,* pp. 109–123; Thomas Reeves, pp. 331–346; McCullough, pp. 813–814; Donovan, *Tumultuous,* pp. 296–298; Hamby, *People,* pp. 549–551. "Communists in High Places": DDEL collection. "Korean death-trap": *Decatur Herald,* Aug. 13, 1950. "All the piety": *Louisville Courier-Journal,* Oct. 1, 1950. "Blood of our boys": Donovan, *Tumultuous,* p. 295. "Taxes higher": *NYT,* Nov. 6, 1950. "Antics of McCarthy": Hamby, *People,* p. 550. State Department "clique": Farrell, pp. 150–154, 156. "Dragged our foreign policy": Truman speech, Nov. 4, 1950. "Five years of coddling": *Chicago Tribune*, Nov. 5, 1950.

"Obvious attempt": *NYT*, Nov. 6, 1950. "Doesn't she care": Farrell, p. 156. Truman drunk: Donovan, *Tumultuous*, p. 298. Truman and 1950 election: McCullough, p. 814. "Campaign of vilification": NSC memcon, Nov. 28, 1950, HSTL. "People do not like to be told": Casey, *Selling*, p. 113. Truman on Chinese intervention: Press conference, Nov. 16, 1950. Joint Chiefs' request of MacArthur and his reply: Brands, *General*, pp. 205–208; McCullough, pp. 814–818; Wainstock, p. 83; Duffy and Carpenter, pp. 38–41. "Longest retreat": McCullough, p. 834. "Entirely new war": Chace, p. 303. "Entry of Chinese Communists": MacArthur to Joint Chiefs, Nov. 25, 1950, HSTL. "Lose face": NSC memcon, Nov. 28, 1950, HSTL. "That son-of-a-bitch": Wallace Graham OH, HSTL. "Always been active consideration" and "by law": Truman press conference and White House statement, Nov. 30, 1950, HSTL. Truman ponders Chinese negotiation: Hamby, *People*, pp. 552–553. Truman's attitude to nuclear weapons: Bundy, pp. 231–235; Ferrell, *Truman*, pp. 343–345. "We go south": Memcon, Dec. 2, 1950, HSTL. "Most solemn one": Truman note, Dec. 2, 1950, HSTP. "Satellites of Russia": Memcon, Dec. 4, 1950, HSTL.

"I've worked for peace": Truman diary, Dec. 9, 1950, HSTP. "Thrown up a chicken wire" and "circle of confusion": *Richmond Palladium-Item* and *Abilene Reporter-News*, Dec. 13, 1950. "Never quite trusted": Caro, *Master*, p. 307. "Time is of the essence": Blomstedt, p. 107. "Aggression has won": Truman speech, Dec. 15, 1950; Donovan, *Tumultuous*, pp. 319–320. Truman and taxes: Hormats, pp. 183–206. "Dictatorship and totalitarian": Taft speech, Jan. 5, 1951. "Shred of courage": *Terre Haute Star*, Jan. 9, 1951. "I don't ask their permission": Truman press conference, Jan. 11, 1951. "Constitutional crisis": Blomstedt, p. 116. Truman Gallup ratings: Gallup, vol. 2, pp. 958–962. "Hunkered down": Elsey, p. 203. "Atomic death belt": Blomstedt, p. 136. Truman confronts and fires MacArthur: Brands, *General*, pp. 284–278; Halberstam, *Coldest*, pp. 600–607; Casey, *Selling*, pp. 236–239; Herman, pp. 802–813; Hamby, *People*, pp. 555–556; McCullough, pp. 831–856; Manchester, *Glory*, pp. 545–546, 558–565; Patterson, pp. 226–232; Donovan, *Tumultuous*, pp. 340–362. "Second Asiatic front": *NYT*, Apr. 6, 1951. "Last straw": Truman diary, Apr. 6, 1951, HSTP. Truman recalls Lincoln: McCullough, pp. 837–840. "Son of a bitch": Ferrell, *Truman*, p. 334. Bradley warning: Wainstock, p. 126. "A crime": Manchester, *Glory*, p. 561.

"Bourbon and Benedictine": Thomas Reeves, pp. 370–371. "Unfit, morally and mentally": *Chicago Tribune*, Apr. 12, 1951. "Secret inner coterie": *NYT*, Apr. 11, 1951. "Quite an explosion" and "worse double-crosser": Truman diary, Apr. 10, 1951, HSTP; Pearlman, *Truman and MacArthur*, p. 198. "Undoubtedly cause": *Detroit Free Press*, Mar. 18, 1952. "Cause of world peace": Truman speech, Apr. 11, 1951. Gallup Poll: Manchester, *Glory*, p. 562. "Go put them": Roger Tubby OH, HSTL. "Seems to have lost": Truman to Leslie Skerry, Apr. 18, 1951, HSTP. "Only politics I have": Manchester, *Caesar*, p. 656. Truman sends Vaughan and Vaughan's later life: Rovere and Schlesinger, pp. 11–12; Ayers, p. 4; Donovan, *Tumultuous*, pp. 361, 117–118; Ferrell, *Truman*, p. 361. MacArthur in Congress: Hamby, *People*, p. 562; Manchester, *Glory*, pp. 562–563. "We heard God" and not a dry eye: Patterson, p. 230; McCoy, p. 263. "Damn fool Congressmen": Beisner,

p. 432. "Appeasement on the battlefield": Pearlman, *Truman and MacArthur,* p. 36. "Quit your bickering": Truman speech, May 21, 1951. Truman's private suffering: Truman speech, Jan. 15, 1953. Truman's faith and "if only men": Beschloss, *Presidential Courage,* pp. 221–222; Holmes, pp. 1–23. Truman's physical regimen and health problems: Wallace Graham OH, HSTL; *Prologue,* Fall 2012; Gosnell, p. 542; McCullough, pp. 585, 768, 857–858, 902, 918. "Doc tell's [*sic*] me": Truman diary, Mar. 7, 1947, HSTP. McCarthy speech: CR, June 14, 1951. "Trying to set the people": Truman speech, June 25, 1951.

Possible cease-fire: Shen and Xia, pp. 82–85; Blomstedt, pp. 110–146. "Planned betrayal of 1951": *Chicago Tribune,* June 30, 1951. Gallup on truce: Gallup, vol. 2, pp. 993–994. "Not too optimistic": Blomstedt, p. 146. "We are not sure": Truman to Bess, July 3, 1951, HSTP. "We will not buy an armistice": Truman statement, May 7, 1952. "Dealing with Communist Governments": Truman note, Jan. 27, 1952, HSTP. Truman considers another term: Donovan, *Tumultuous,* p. 396; McCullough, pp. 873–874. "There is a lure": Truman diary, Apr 16, 1950, HSTP. Truman and Vinson: St. Clair and Gugin, pp. 189–197, 334–337. "Believes in me": Truman to Bess, Mar. 24, 1950, HSTP. Truman approaches Stevenson: John Martin, vol. 1, pp. 402–403, 518–528. "Complete idiot" and "duty to save": John Martin, vol. 1, p. 524. "Intellectually dishonest": Truman note, Dec. 25, 1952, HSTP. "What the hell": Truman note, Mar. 4, 1952, HSTP. "Administration was going": Donovan, *Tumultuous,* p. 396. "Have no bearing": Truman press conference, Mar. 20, 1952. "Some Republicans seem": Truman speech, Mar. 29, 1952. "With really macabre": Arthur Schlesinger, *Journals,* p. 4. "I found myself shouting": Schlesinger diary, Mar. 29, 1952, Schlesinger Papers.

Truman and steel seizure: Marcus, pp. 1–259; Breyer, pp. 42–83; Bruce Murphy, pp. 313–314; St. Clair and Gugin, pp. 215–218; Donovan, *Tumultuous,* pp. 382–391, 397–398; Walker, pp. 152–153; Ferrell, *Truman,* pp. 370–375; Feldman, pp. 356–359; Belknap, pp. 95–98; Kastenberg and Merriam, p. 182; Ragsdale, p. 110; Newton Minow, clerk to Chief Justice Vinson, int 2016; Duquesne University symposium, Nov. 22, 2002. "Very great inherent powers": Truman to Casey Jones, Apr. 27, 1952, HSTL. "Recklessly forcing": Truman speech, Apr. 8, 1952. "My heart was in it" and "played out": Donovan, *Tumultuous,* p. 387. "Hitler and Mussolini": *New York Daily News,* Apr. 1953. Johnson on "dictatorship": Dallek, *Lone Star,* p. 405. "Valid case": *NYT,* Apr. 18, 1952. Bender's warning: *NYT,* Apr. 20, 1952. "As great an emergency": Truman press conference, Apr. 24, 1952. "Don't see how a Court": Truman to William O. Douglas, unsent, July 9, 1952, HSTP. "Courage to fight": *Chicago Tribune,* July 8, 1952. "Was a complete flop": Truman to Bess, July 8, 1952, HSTL. Truman's illness: *Prologue,* Fall 2012; Wallace Graham OH, HSTL; McCullough, pp. 902–903. "We agreed that we would support": Truman note, July 11, 1952, HSTP. Truman and Stevenson nomination: John Martin, vol. 1, p. 592. "We have met aggression": Truman speech, July 26, 1952.

Stevenson's distance and "Old Man": Blomstedt, p. 207; Arthur Schlesinger, *Journals,* p. 9. Stevenson cites own record and Truman's fury: *Idaho State Journal,* Aug. 21, 1952; Donovan, *Tumultuous,* pp. 397–398. "Above associating with the lowly" and "makes nice reading": Truman to Stevenson, undated, unsent, HSTL. "Never let anyone tell you": Truman speech, Williston, ND, Sept. 29, 1952. Eisenhower Korea pledge: Donovan, *Tumultuous,* p. 401. "Burial ground": *Baltimore Sun,* Oct. 25, 1952. "If you still desire" and "I sincerely wish": *Time,* Nov. 17, 1952; Truman diary, Nov. 15, 1952, HSTP. "Intolerable": Ambrose, *Soldier and President,* pp. 294–295. "Piece of demagoguery": Truman press conference, Dec. 11, 1952. "First time that the slightest": *New York Sun,* Dec. 10, 1952. "Farewell address": Truman speech, Jan. 15, 1953. Inaugural Day 1953: Chace, p. 362; Ambrose, *Soldier and President,* pp. 295–298. "Have to drop out": Beschloss, *Mayday,* p. 36. Eisenhower wins armistice: Gaddis, *We Now Know,* pp. 107–110; Gaddis, *Cold War,* pp. 59–60; Ambrose, *Eisenhower,* vol. 2, pp. 97–99, 101–106. Eisenhower secret messages: Eisenhower–Lyndon Johnson memcon, Feb. 17, 1965, LBJL.

Eisenhower on Korea truce as achievement: Pinkley, p. 352. "I sincerely hope": *Detroit Free Press,* July 27, 1953. "Ominous threat of a third world war": Harry S. Truman, *Trial,* p. 463. Acheson defends National Press Club speech: Acheson, p. 358. American men drafted: Kimberley Phillips, pp. 147–149; Pash, p. 13. Amnesia over Korea: Patterson, p. 207. "Tragic toll of more than an eighth": 1956 Republican platform. "Today Korea means": *Des Moines Register,* Sept. 20, 1956. "Very famous speech": Kennedy-Nixon debate, Washington DC, Oct. 7, 1960.

CHAPTER SIXTEEN: "WE GOT SLAPPED"

Jim Morrison: *NYT,* Apr. 30, 1965, Dec. 8, 2008; *Coronado Clarion,* Feb. 2, 2001; *Ukiah Daily Journal,* Jan. 24, 1964; *Salt Lake Tribune,* Apr. 10, 1964; Stephen Davis, pp. 5–56; Hopkins and Sugerman, pp. 3–54; Interview with Stephen Morrison, "When You're Strange" (DVD), 2010. Origins of Vietnam War: Logevall, *Embers,* pp. 67–463; Logevall, *Choosing,* pp. 1–192; Kaiser, *Tragedy,* pp. 1–283. Johnson on Aug. 2: Johnson, *Vantage,* pp. 112–113; McNamara, pp. 131–132; Rusk, p. 444; Goldstein, pp. 121–125; Bird, *Color,* pp. 284–286; Moïse, pp. 73–93; Dallek, *Flawed,* pp. 147–149; Logevall, *Choosing,* pp. 196–197. "Where are my Bundys?": Goldstein, pp. 122–125. "Keep them off base": Johnson-Bundy, Mar. 4, 1964, LBJT, in Beschloss, *Taking,* p. 267. Punctuation in some quotations from conversations that appear in Beschloss, *Taking* and *Reaching,* has been slightly revised without changing meaning. "Failures infest": Goldwater acceptance speech, July 16, 1964. "Is it always": Goldstein, p. 124. "There have been some covert": Johnson-Anderson, Aug. 3, 1964, LBJT, in Beschloss, *Taking,* pp. 493–494. "Lyndon, did you ever see": Dallek, *Lone Star,* p. 179.

Johnson's early life: Dallek, *Lone Star,* pp. 1–184; Caro, *Path,* pp. 3–768. "Just had the bed full": Johnson–Isabelle Shelton, Mar. 21, 1964, LBJT, in Beschloss, *Taking,* pp. 294–296. "Remember this": Johnson–Douglass Wynn, Nov. 7, 1964, LBJT, in Beschloss, *Reaching,* pp. 135–136. Sidey tried: Halberstam, *Best,* p. 439. Johnson shows King letter: Kotz, p. 244. "Born on a mountaintop": Johnson speech, Oct. 9, 1964. Johnson and House Naval Affairs: Dallek, *Lone Star,* pp. 160–161. "Though the President cannot declare war": Davis and McClure, pp. 121–122. "Kind of uninhibited": Caro, *Path,* p. 449. "Loved peace so much": Johnson–Gale McGee, Apr. 29, 1965, LBJT, in Beschloss, *Reaching,* pp. 295–296. "If the day ever comes": Caro, *Means,* p. 19. Johnson in Navy: Caro, *Means,* pp. 33–53; Dallek, *Lone Star,* pp. 325–343. "Active duty" and "Sabbath Day": Dallek, *Lone Star,* pp. 230–231. Johnson and *Heckling Hare*: Dallek, *Lone Star,* pp. 225–243; Caro, *Means,* pp. 33–53. "Wants for the sake" and "I'll never wear": Caro, *Means,* pp. 33, 51. "I didn't want to go": Johnson-McCormack, Dec. 20, 1963, LBJT, in Beschloss,

Taking, pp. 110–112. "Admiration of your courageous" and "I remember": Caro, *Master*, p. 307. Johnson and investigating subcommittee: *NYT*, June 17, 1951; Dallek, *Lone Star*, pp. 384–388; Caro, *Master*, pp. 311–350.

Johnson, Eisenhower, Rayburn: Dallek, *Lone Star*, pp. 435–437. "The Catholics": Johnson-Humphrey, Mar. 6, 1965, LBJT, in Beschloss, *Reaching*, pp. 206–210. "Steam really went": Bradlee, p. 226. Johnson during Kennedy councils: Sorensen, p. 266; Dallek, *Flawed*, pp. 16–17, 44–45. "Shaking his head": Robert Kennedy OH, JFKL. "Damn good hand of poker": Beschloss, *Crisis Years*, p. 543. "George Washington of Southeast Asia": *Minneapolis Star-Tribune*, July 15, 1963. "Tragic mistake": Johnson-Russell, May 27, 1964, LBJT, in Beschloss, *Taking*, p. 366. "Divine retribution": Arthur Schlesinger, *Robert Kennedy*, p. 649. Johnsons' White House arrival: Dallek, *Flawed*, p. 57; Caro, *Passage*, pp. 500–502. "Haven't got any Daddy" and "You don't feel": Johnson-Russell, Nov. 29 and Dec. 7, 1963, LBJT, in Beschloss, *Taking*, pp. 66–72, 94–95. Vietnam War, early 1964: Logevall, *Choosing*, pp. 75–133; Kaiser, *Tragedy*, pp. 284–340. "Probably a good thing": Johnson-Ball, Jan. 29, 1964, LBJT, in Beschloss, *Taking*, p. 194. "Toughest one": Johnson–Walker Stone, Jan. 31, 1964, LBJT, in Beschloss, *Taking*, pp. 199–200. "Our boy": Maxwell Taylor memcon, Mar. 4, 1964, LBJL. Rusk on SEATO pact: Rusk, pp. 433–436, 443, 445.

"Preventing the loss": Joint Chiefs to McNamara, Mar. 2, 1964, LBJL. "Tide of deterioration": Beschloss, *Taking*, p. 359. "Still going to hell": NSC memcon, May 24, 1964, LBJL. "Make a presidential decision": Bundy to Johnson memo draft, May 25, 1964, LBJP. "Damn worst mess": Johnson-Russell, May 27, 1964, LBJT, in Beschloss, *Taking*, pp. 363–370. "More that I stayed awake": Johnson-Bundy, May 27, 1964, LBJT, in Beschloss, *Taking*, pp. 370–372. "Those twin commanders": *Chicago Tribune*, May 12, 1964. "Doing well as can be": Gallup, vol. 3, p. 1882. "Defensive war is never": *Cincinnati Enquirer*, May 25, 1964. "Contradictions, confusion": *NYT*, July 3, 1964. "Goddamn, there's not anything": Johnson-Russell, June 11, 1964, LBJT, in Beschloss, *Taking*, pp. 400–403. "To solve Lyndon's dilemma": Lady Bird Johnson diary, June 15, 1964, LBJL. "I was with some folks": Johnson-McNamara, June 16, 1964, and Johnson-Russell, May 27, 1964, LBJT, in Beschloss, *Taking*, pp. 410–411, 368. "Get the same crowd" and "greatest danger" and "falls over": Johnson-Russell, May 27, 1964, Johnson-McNamara, June 18, 1964, and Johnson-McCormack, June 23, 1964, LBJT, in Beschloss, *Taking*, pp. 364, 415, 426. "Conferences ain't gonna": Johnson-Russell, May 27, 1964, LBJT, in Beschloss, *Taking*, p. 367. "When necessary": *WP*, June 29, 1964. "All measures, including": Alterman, p. 195. "Torn his balls off": Dallek, *Flawed*, p. 105. "Crash landing": Ward and Burns, p. 104.

"We had the United Nations": Johnson–Robert Kennedy, June 9, 1964, LBJT, in Beschloss, *Taking*, p. 390. "If we're going": Johnson-McNamara, June 9, 1964, LBJT, in Beschloss, *Taking*, p. 396. "Substantial increase": Alterman, p. 195. Johnson on Aug. 3: Goldstein, pp. 122–125; Rusk, p. 444; McNamara, pp. 131–132; Bird, *Color*, p. 286; Moïse, pp. 94–105; Dallek, *Flawed*, pp. 147–150; Caro, *Passage*, pp. 534–545. "Was nice, didn't ask too many": Johnson-Smathers, Aug. 3, 1964, LBJT. Johnson and Morse: Caro, *Master*, pp. 321, 577. Johnson talks with McNamara, Aug. 4 morning: Beschloss, *Taking*, pp. 495–498. Johnson on Aug. 4: Johnson Daily Diary, Aug. 4, 1964, LBJL; Johnson, *Vantage*, pp. 114–115; Logevall, *Choosing*, pp. 198–204; Moïse, pp. 106–142; Kaiser, *Tragedy*, pp. 333–335; Dallek, *Flawed*, pp. 143, 155–156.

"Exactly what we *have*": Johnson-Rowe, Aug. 4, 1964, LBJT, in Beschloss, *Taking,* p. 499. Johnson generally on Aug. 4: Johnson Daily Diary, Aug. 4, 1964, LBJL; Johnson, *Vantage,* pp. 114–115; Logevall, *Choosing,* pp. 198–204; Moïse, pp. 106–142; Kaiser, *Tragedy,* pp. 333–335; Dallek, *Flawed,* pp. 143, 155–156; Beschloss, *Taking,* pp. 495–496.

"There is a limit": NSC memcon, Aug. 4, 1964, LBJL. "Firm, swift retaliatory strike": Kaiser, *Tragedy,* p. 334. "Marshal the evidence": JCS 7720 to CINCPAC, Aug. 4, 1964, LBJL. "Brief the lawmakers": Beschloss, *Taking,* p. 500. "Story has broken on the AP": Johnson-McNamara, Aug. 4, 1964, 5:09 p.m., LBJT, in Beschloss, *Taking,* p. 500. "I'm for keeping us": Johnson-Johnston, Aug. 4, 1964, LBJT, in Beschloss, *Taking,* p. 501. "Continued their attacks": NSC memcon, Aug. 4, 1964, LBJL. "After we were attacked": Leadership Meeting Notes, June 4, 1964, LBJL. "Bombing the hell": Johnson-O'Brien, Aug. 4, 1964, LBJT, in Beschloss, *Taking,* p. 502. "When they leave the carrier": Johnson-McNamara, Aug. 4, 1964, LBJT, in Beschloss, *Taking,* p. 503. "Barry, I'm going": Johnson-Goldwater, Aug. 4, 1964, LBJT, in Beschloss, *Taking,* p. 504. "Initial attack": Johnson speech, Aug. 4, 1964; *NYT,* Aug. 5, 1964. "Little shitass Foreman": Johnson-McCormack, Aug. 7, 1964, LBJT, in Beschloss, *Taking,* p. 508.

Johnson on Aug. 5: Goldstein, pp. 125–128; Dallek, *Flawed,* pp. 152–156. "We may have to escalate": Goldstein, p. 128. "Deliberate" and "unprovoked": Johnson speech, Aug. 5, 1964. "Count on" and "show business": Goldstein, pp. 128. Johnson and McNamara for Vice President: Dallek, *Flawed,* p. 137. "Most uncomfortable experience": Johnson-McCormack, Apr. 28, 1964, LBJT, in Beschloss, *Taking,* p. 330. "Trying to satisfy": Beschloss, *Taking,* p. 314. McNamara on "no knowledge": Senate Foreign Relations and Armed Services Committees hearing, Aug. 6, 1964; Beschloss, *Taking,* p. 506. Herter lying to Congress: Beschloss, *Mayday,* p. 314. "Absolutely no connection": McNamara testimony, House Armed Services Committee, Jan. 30, 1963. "Hell of a time": Johnson-McNamara, Aug. 6, 1964, LBJT, in Beschloss, *Taking,* p. 506. Debate over Gulf of Tonkin Resolution: CR, Aug. 6, 1964. "To seal the lips": *WP,* Aug. 8, 1964. "Undependable and erratic": Johnson-McCormack, Aug. 7, 1964, LBJT, in Beschloss, *Taking,* p. 506.

"Only three weeks ago": *NYT,* Aug. 26, 1964. Only half a dozen: *Public Papers of the Presidents: Lyndon B. Johnson, 1964* (Washington, DC: US Government Printing Office). Tonkin Resolution in Johnson's wallet: CR, 117 (1971), p. 698. "I would keep those 502": Johnson-Rusk, Feb. 25, 1965, LBJT, in Beschloss, *Reaching,* p. 193. "Bob, I think if you do": Johnson-McNamara, Feb. 22, 1965, LBJT, in Beschloss, *Reaching,* p. 191. "I've got a vote": Johnson-Mahon, May 5, 1965, LBJT, in Beschloss, *Reaching,* p. 311. "Congress gave us": CBS interview, aired Feb. 6, 1970. "I did lousy": Leo Janos, "The Last Days of the President," *Atlantic,* July 1973. "If you let a bully": Beschloss, *Reaching,* p. 445. Later Tonkin evidence: Moïse, pp. 143–225. "Hell, those dumb": Gibbons, part 2, p. 355. "Now, Bob, I have found": Johnson-McNamara, Sept. 18, 1964, LBJT, in Beschloss, *Reaching,* pp. 38–39. "Just confusion": *The Fog of War,* McNamara interview transcript. Fulbright and Foreign Relations colleagues' secret discussion in 1968: *Executive Sessions of the Senate Foreign Relations Committee (Historical Series), 1968,* vol. 20, made public in 2010.

CHAPTER SEVENTEEN: "I DO NOT HAVE A PARACHUTE"

Johnson and 1964 election: Dallek, *Flawed,* pp. 177–185. Johnson's illness: Beschloss, *Reaching,* pp. 168–169. "Just patted him" and black dress: Lady Bird Johnson diary, Jan. 23 and July 16, 1965, LBJL. "Washed out" and "slough of despond": Lady Bird Johnson diary, Jan. 29, 1965, LBJL. Pleiku: Johnson, *Vantage,* p. 124; Dallek, *Flawed,* p. 247; McNamara, pp. 170–171; Goldstein, pp. 97–99; Kaiser, *Tragedy,* pp. 398–404, 417, 440. Feb. 6 meeting: Memcon, Feb. 6, 1965, LBJL; Beschloss, *Reaching,* pp. 172–173; Dallek, *Flawed,* pp. 247–248. "Ring of the phone": Lady Bird Johnson diary, Feb. 7, 1965, LBJL. Qhy Nhon attack: Beschloss, *Reaching,* pp. 176–177. "Get in a position" and "Let's just get them": Johnson-Bundy, Feb. 10, 1965, LBJL, in Beschloss, *Reaching,* pp. 175–177. "I'm not temperamentally": Lady Bird Johnson diary, Feb. 11, 1965, LBJL. "I don't want to put it up": Johnson-Eisenhower, Feb. 15, 1965, LBJT, in Beschloss, *Reaching,* pp. 178–179. "Campaign of pressure": Memcon, Feb. 17, 1965, LBJL. "The General would bitch": David Eisenhower, p. 166. "I'm having hell!": Johnson-Truman, Feb. 15, 1965, LBJT, in Beschloss, *Reaching,* pp. 179–180.

McGovern-Church call to negotiate: Beschloss, *Reaching,* p. 181. "Neither one of them really": Johnson-Bundy, Feb. 18, 1965, LBJT, in Beschloss, *Reaching,* pp. 184–185, 373. "Can't come bomb us": Johnson-Dirksen, Feb. 17, 1965, LBJT, in Beschloss, *Reaching,* pp. 181–183. Johnson's outrage at Humphrey on Vietnam and "limbo": Humphrey, pp. 319–327; Solberg, pp. 272–273. "Involvement in a full scale": Humphrey to Johnson, Feb. 17, 1965, Humphrey Papers. "Desperate and dramatic": Johnson-Rusk, Feb. 25, 1965, LBJT, in Beschloss, *Reaching,* pp. 192–193. Rolling Thunder: Dallek, *Flawed,* pp. 247–257; Kaiser, *Tragedy,* pp. 417–418; McNamara, pp. 174–176; Goldstein, p. 163. "Decided to open": *NYT,* Mar. 1, 1965. "I don't know how": Johnson-McNamara, Mar. 1, 1965, LBJT, in Beschloss, *Reaching,* pp. 195–196. "They can't hit an outhouse": Helen Thomas, p. 291. "Want to be called" and "can't separate himself": Lady Bird Johnson diary, Apr. 18, 1965, LBJL.

"What's it look like": Johnson–Situation Room, Mar. 2, 1965, LBJT, in Beschloss, *Reaching,* pp. 199–200. "Now, the Marines!": Johnson-Bundy, Mar. 5, 1965, LBJT, in Beschloss, *Reaching,* pp. 204–205. "I guess we've got": Johnson-Russell, Mar. 6, 1965, LBJT, in Beschloss, *Reaching,* pp. 210–213. "My answer is yes": Johnson-McNamara, Mar. 6, 1965, LBJT, in Beschloss, *Reaching,* pp. 213–216. "I can't get out": Lady Bird Johnson diary, Mar. 7, 1965, LBJL. Mekong offer: Johnson, *Vantage,* pp. 132–134; Dallek, *Flawed,* pp. 260–262. "Meet mounting military requirements": Beschloss, *Reaching,* p. 309. "Being frank and candid" and "that we got the money": Johnson-Mahon, May 5, 1965, and Johnson-Stennis, May 4, 1965, LBJT, in Beschloss, *Reaching,* pp. 310–312. "Blank check" and "wider war": Robert Kennedy speech, May 6, 1965. "Little snide remarks": Johnson-McNamara, June 21, 1965, LBJT, in Beschloss, *Reaching,* pp. 364–366. Ky coup: Dallek, *Flawed,* p. 270. "Four or five Hitlers": Drew Pearson column, *WP,* Aug. 13, 1965. "Absolutely the bottom": Lawrence, p. 96. "Very dangerous situation": Johnson-McNamara, June 5, 1965, LBJT, in Beschloss, *Reaching,* pp. 343–344.

"Will probably be necessary": US Embassy Saigon to Department of State, June 5, 1965, LBJL. "Stalled them off" and "We may have to face" and "very pessimistic": Mike

Mansfield memo, June 3, 1965, Mansfield Papers. "If you'd see what": Johnson-Hartke, May 27, 1965, LBJT, in Beschloss, *Reaching*, pp. 341–342. "Awfully irresponsible": Johnson-Russell, July 26, 1965, in Beschloss, *Reaching*, pp. 407–411. "Defensive posture" and "bombshell": Westmoreland to McNamara, June 7, 1965, LBJL, and McNamara, pp. 187–188. "Unless we're really willing": Johnson-McNamara, June 10, 1965, LBJT, in Beschloss, *Reaching*, pp. 348–353. "Doesn't want to give up": Johnson-McNamara, July 2, 1965, LBJT, in Beschloss, *Reaching*, pp. 381–383. "Our 75,000 men": Johnson-Mansfield, June 8, 1965, LBJT, in Beschloss, *Reaching*, pp. 344–348. "We almost got a Civil War": Johnson-Eisenhower, July 23, 1965, LBJT, in Beschloss, *Reaching*, pp. 403–405. "Short of decision": Westmoreland to Wheeler, June 24, 1965, NARA. "Ho Chi Minh said": Johnson-Eisenhower, July 23, 1965, LBJT, in Beschloss, *Reaching*, pp. 403–404. "Last longer": Johnson-Bayh, June 15, 1965, LBJT, in Beschloss, *Reaching*, pp. 354–356.

"I'm very depressed": Johnson-McNamara, June 21, 1965, LBJT, in Beschloss, *Reaching*, pp. 364–365. "Thought I might invite": Johnson-Truman-Goldberg, June 22, 1965, LBJT. "We know ourselves": Johnson-McNamara, July 2, 1965, LBJT, in Beschloss, *Reaching*, pp. 381–383. "Vietnam is getting worse": Lady Bird Johnson diary, July 8, 1965, LBJL. Johnson July escalation decision: Memcon, July 20, 1965, LBJL; Johnson, *Vantage*, pp. 144–153; Rusk, pp. 450–454; McNamara, pp. 169–206; Clifford, p. 414; Goldstein, pp. 113–116, 164–184; Beschloss, *Reaching*, pp. 402–403; Dallek, *Flawed*, pp. 246–296, 340–373. "We are in a new war": Memcon, July 22, 1965, LBJL; Gibbons, part 3, p. 410. "Low-key manner": Helsing, p. 175. "If you have a mother-in-law": Dallek, *Flawed*, p. 277. "Old South Carolina boy": Johnson-Russell, July 26, 1965, LBJT, in Beschloss, *Reaching*, pp. 407–411. Johnson persuades Goldberg: Kalman, pp. 240–241; Beschloss, *Reaching*, pp. 394–400. "Young Americans" must "toil and suffer": Johnson press conference, July 28, 1965; *NYT*, July 29, 1965. "America wins the wars": Johnson speech, Aug. 3, 1965.

"No one ever knows": Johnson–Robert Kennedy, Oct. 5, 1965, LBJT. Johnson's 1937 and 1948 illnesses: Caro, *Means*, pp. 194, 204–208. Johnson's slow recovery: Beschloss, *Reaching*, pp. 425–426; Califano, *Triumph*, p. 121. "Using specific numbers": Memcon, Meeting with Eisenhower, Aug. 3, 1965, LBJL. JCS Nov. request: Dallek, *Flawed*, p. 341. "Shitheads": Charles Cooper, pp. 1–5. "Cautioned that boy": Ferguson, p. 675. "Where the hell we are going": Johnson-Clifford, Dec. 1965, LBJT. "I've had little real sympathy": Memcon, Dec. 7, 1965, LBJL. "Running wild" and "pious priest" and "not going to withdraw": Johnson-O'Brien, Jan. 1966, LBJT. Morse request to rescind and "before we can approve": *Tampa Bay Times*, Jan. 29 and 30, 1966. "Interested only in the *New York Times*": Johnson-O'Brien, Feb. 5, 1966, LBJT. "Going through a menopause": Johnson-Humphrey, Mar. 2, 1966, LBJT.

Johnson and Robert Kennedy, 1966: Arthur Schlesinger, *Robert Kennedy*, pp. 725–742; Shesol, pp. 286–356. "If we regard bombing": Johnson-Russell, Mar. 2, 1966, LBJT. "Has greatly weakened": Johnson-Rusk, Feb. 22, 1966, LBJT. "In a hell of a shape": Johnson-Mansfield, 1966, LBJT. "Architect of surrender": Johnson-McCarthy, Feb. 1, 1966, LBJL. "Since George Washington came down": Johnson-Long, Feb. 26, 1966, LBJT. "Bobby is sniping": Johnson-Luce, Feb. 21, 1966, LBJT. Johnson's suspicions: Richard Goodwin, pp. 584–590. "Very upset": Johnson-McGee, Mar. 1, 1966, LBJT. Clare Boothe Luce and Johnson: Caro, *Means*, p. 134. Johnson and civil liberties: Walker, pp. 260–278; Califano,

Triumph, pp. 186–188. "Red-hot, one-million-two": Johnson-Katzenbach, Mar. 29, 1965, LBJT, in Beschloss, *Reaching*, pp. 251–266. "Contacts with opinion-molders": Johnson-DeLoach, Mar. 14, 1966, LBJT. Johnson pushes CIA and Army: Stone, *Perilous*, pp. 491–492. "Don't kid yourself": Memcon, Mar. 12, 1966, LBJL; Califano, *Triumph*, pp. 173–174. "Foreign Communists": Richard Helms, int 1989. "Put a surveillance": Dallek, *Flawed*, p. 369. Lady Bird on files: Richard Goodwin, p. 590.

"Why Americans who dissent": Memcon, Feb. 24, 1966, LBJL. "Nervous Nellies": Johnson speech, May 17, 1966. Lippmann and "Credibility Gap": *WP*, Mar. 28, 1967. "What might I be asked next?": Memcon, June 17, 1966, LBJL. "I'm trying to win": Johnson-Eisenhower, Oct. 3, 1966, LBJT. Johnson 1966 Vietnam visit: Johnson speech, Oct. 26, 1966; *Life*, Nov. 4, 1966; *NYT* and *Minneapolis Star-Tribune*, Oct. 27, 1966; AP dispatch, Oct. 26, 1966. 1966 campaign and results: Dallek, *Flawed*, p. 335–339. Nixon in campaign: Ambrose, *Nixon*, p. 84. "Chronic campaigner": Johnson press conference, Nov. 4, 1966. "Wants to escalate the war": Johnson-Fulbright, Nov. 5, 1966, LBJT. "Sharpest rebuff" and "pendulum swings": *Indianapolis Star*, Nov. 10, 1966; Johnson press conference, Nov. 10, 1966. Sept. 1966 Gallup Poll: Gibbons, part 4, p. 24. Johnson and draft unfairness: Califano, *Triumph*, pp. 196–198. Johnson–Robert Kennedy Feb. 1967 confrontation: Johnson–Walt Rostow, Feb. 15, 1967, LBJT; *NYT*, Feb. 12, 1967; Shesol, pp. 363–369; Arthur Schlesinger, *Robert Kennedy*, p. 768; Katzenbach, pp. 261–263. "Ready to negotiate": *NYT*, Mar. 3, 1967. "Didn't select these folks": Johnson-Rostow, Feb. 15, 1967, LBJT.

Martin Luther King opposes war: Branch, pp. 591–595. "Almost a declaration": *Pittsburgh Post-Gazette*, Mar. 1, 1967. "Other men of goodwill": Johnson-Mansfield, Mar. 1, 1967, LBJT. "Just spit in your face": Johnson-Russell, Mar. 2, 1967, LBJT. Johnson and Robert Kennedy, 1967: Shesol, pp. 325–336; Arthur Schlesinger, *Robert Kennedy*, pp. 783–803, 820–822. "I think he'd be President": Johnson-O'Brien, Mar. 30, 1967, LBJT. "Being used" and "hurting our country": Johnson-Dirksen, Oct. 4, 1967, LBJT. "We may wake up": Woods, *LBJ*, p. 758. Johnson and taxes and spending: Hormats, pp. 207–226. "San Antonio formula": Johnson speech, Sept. 29, 1967; Dallek, *Flawed*, pp. 481–482; Marvin Watson, pp. 134–136. "Have no idea": Memcon, Oct. 16, 1967, LBJL. Johnson's faith and "Protestant with a capital": Sorensen, p. 163. Praying with Billy Graham: Aikman, p. 197. "My little monks": Califano, *Triumph*, p. 336. Complaint about knee pads: *Life*, Aug. 11, 1967. "During that time" and coffins and "wine and roses": Lady Bird Johnson, int 1998; Luci Johnson, Lynda Johnson Robb, ints 2001; Califano, *Triumph*, pp. 334–335; Holmes, pp. 76–98.

Oct. 1967 Pentagon march: Hall, pp. 120–127; Savage, p. 267; *NYT*, Oct. 21–22, 1967; Califano, *Triumph*, pp. 198–203. "Not going to run me out": Memcon, Oct. 3, 1967, LBJL. "Was curious": Marvin Watson, p. 216. "That the right": Califano, *Triumph*, p. 201. "We've just had hell": Johnson-Eisenhower, Nov. 3, 1967, LBJT. "Communist participation": *NYT*, Nov. 23, 1967. "Terrified" of Kennedy: David Eisenhower, p. 205. "Mean Republican": Johnson-Eisenhower, Feb. 20, 1968, LBJT. "Are we now ready" and "The great danger": Memcon, Oct. 23, 1967, LBJL. McNamara's torment and Johnson's reaction: Califano, *Triumph*, p. 249; Dallek, *Flawed*, pp. 494–495; McNamara draft memo to Johnson, Nov. 1, 1967, LBJL; McNamara, p. 311. "If I resigned": George Christian, int 2001. "Pull a Forrestal": Dallek, *Flawed*, p. 495; Califano, *Triumph*, p. 249. "Wise Men":

Isaacson and Thomas, pp. 683–684; Dallek, *Flawed,* pp. 493–496. "Like the steering wheel": Memcon, Nov. 2, 1967, LBJL. Johnson's 1967 Vietnam visit: *NYT* and AP dispatch, Dec. 23, 1967; UPI dispatch, Dec. 22, 1967. "Battle after battle": Johnson State of the Union, Jan. 17, 1968. Johnson and Khe Sanh: Dallek, *Flawed,* pp. 502–503; *Foreign Relations of the United States,* vol. 6, p. 58; Rostow to Johnson, Feb. 10, 1968, LBJL.

Johnson and nuclear weapons in Vietnam: Westmoreland to Wheeler, Feb. 3, 1968; Sharp to Wheeler, Feb. 1968; Rostow to Johnson, Feb. 10, 1968, LBJP; Bundy, pp. 535–538. Tet Offensive: Dallek, *Flawed,* pp. 502–513. "Kamikaze-type thing" and "certain heroism": Memcons, Feb. 2 and 11, 1968, LBJL. "A boy from Ohio": Memcon, Feb. 20, 1968, LBJL. Katzenbach on war declaration and McCarthy reaction: Katzenbach testimony, Aug. 17, 1967; O'Donnell, p. 15. New Hampshire primary: Witcover, pp. 42–102; Theodore White, pp. 88–90. Robert Kennedy and possible commission: Evan Thomas, *Robert Kennedy,* p. 359; Arthur Schlesinger, *Robert Kennedy,* pp. 851–852. "Vain and lazy": Theodore White, p. 158. "Take any power away": Johnson-Daley, Mar. 13, 1968, LBJT. "Appear to be a political deal": Shesol, p. 546. Not "to oppose any man": Robert Kennedy speech, Mar. 16, 1968. Johnson's 1968 campaign planning: Marvin Watson, pp. 272–282; Witcover, pp. 131–132; Theodore White, pp. 66–68. "What we've got to do": Johnson-Clifford, Mar. 20, 1968, LBJT. "Bobby is storming": Johnson-Russell, Mar. 22, 1968, LBJT. "Wise Men" return: Johnson, *Vantage,* pp. 416–418; Dallek, *Flawed,* pp. 511–512. "We can no longer" and "There has been a panic": Memcons, Mar. 26, 1968, LBJL. "Somebody may try": Johnson memcon, Jan. 19, 1968, LBJL. "Never a Johnson hater": Bill Clinton int 1997.

"Let's don't have a damn": Johnson-Branigin, Mar. 17, 1968, LBJT. "These boys can't get": Johnson-Reuther, Mar. 20, 1968, LBJT. "Well, Dick, I appreciate": Johnson-Daley, Mar. 1968, LBJT. "Ready to go": Johnson-Sanford, Mar. 27, 1968, LBJT. "Fearful of the end result": O'Brien to Johnson, Mar. 27, 1968, LBJL. "You're the one I want": Johnson-O'Brien, Mar. 1968, LBJT. Johnson's fear of dying: Beschloss, *Reaching,* p. 445; Harry Middleton and Larry Temple, ints 2015. Johnson's possible withdrawal in State of the Union: Busby, pp. 172–180. Lady Bird worries: Lady Bird Johnson, int 1998. Johnson on Mar. 31: Lady Bird Johnson diary and Johnson speech, Mar. 31, 1968, LBJL; Watson, pp. 282–287; Califano, *Triumph,* pp. 253–272; Busby, pp. 3–12, 181–225; Dallek, *Flawed,* pp. 530–538, 568–70; Witcover, pp. 139–144; O'Donnell, pp. 225–230. "I'll never be a free man": Busby, pp. 193–194. "We've been a long time trying": Johnson conversations with John Sparkman, Frank Stanton, Arthur Krim, Mar. 31, 1968, LBJT. "I don't see how": Johnson–Abigail McCarthy, Mar. 31, 1968, LBJT.

"I'm sure I've goofed": Johnson-Fulbright, Apr. 1, 1968, LBJT. "Not the slightest doubt": Joseph Califano, int 2017; Califano, *Triumph,* pp. 291–292. "This goddamn war": Memcon, July 12, 1967, LBJL. Johnson–Robert Kennedy final meeting: Larry Temple int 2018; Rostow memcon, Apr. 3, 1968, LBJL; Shesol, pp. 3, 441–444; Arthur Schlesinger, *Robert Kennedy,* p. 868; Evan Thomas, *Robert Kennedy,* pp. 365–366. Johnson pantomimed: Eugene McCarthy, int 1997. "All other war acts": Maxwell Taylor to Johnson, Mar. 4, 1968, LBJL. "Any forum" and "no evidence": Dallek, *Flawed,* pp. 538, 541. "Scared to death": Johnson-Daley, Apr. 19, 1968, LBJT. Plea to bomb Cambodia: Memcon, Apr. 6, 1968, LBJL. "Made a lot of votes": Johnson-Dirksen, June 1968, LBJT. "Country wants to move": Robert Kennedy speech, June 4, 1968. Johnson and Robert Kennedy assassination: Califano, *Triumph,* pp. 294–306; Joseph Califano, int 2017; Arthur Schlesinger, *Robert Kennedy,* pp. 900–916. "Best speeches" and "Keep talking" and "Don't go to California": Solberg, pp. 302, 347. "Absence of visible progress": Clifford, pp. 550–551. "Protected by over 500,000": Dallek, *Flawed,* p. 566; Clifford, p. 551. Johnson's threat to Humphrey: O'Donnell, p. 335. Nixon's July visit with Johnson: Dallek, *Flawed,* p. 571; O'Donnell, pp. 335–336. "Fine woman, and he destroyed her": Califano, *Governing,* p. 216. Johnson's sudden death fear: Don Thomas remarks at symposium, May 7, 1990, LBJL. "Big knock-down drag-out": Johnson-Dirksen, Aug. 1968, LBJT.

Johnson and 1968 Democratic convention: Larry Temple, int 2015; Arthur Krim OH, LBJL; Marvin Watson, pp. 294–301; Califano, *Triumph,* pp. 318–329; Connally, pp. 203, 214; Dallek, *Flawed,* pp. 572–574, 617; Theodore White, pp. 269–311; Justin Nelson. "Kennedy networks": Johnson-Dirksen, Aug. 27, 1968, LBJT. "Better-than-even break to get peace": Johnson-Daley, Aug. 1968, LBJT. "Very much hoped": John Connally remarks at symposium, May 7, 1990, LBJL. "Hubert's going to favor": Aug. 1968, LBJT. Johnson's possible plan to decline draft: Califano, *Triumph,* p. 320. "Tentatively we hope": Johnson-Watson, Aug. 26, 1968, LBJT. "For a moment": Califano, *Triumph,* p. 321. " 'No way!' ": John Connally remarks at symposium, May 7, 1990, LBJL. Fall 1968 campaign: Witcover, pp. 346–419; O'Donnell, pp. 377–409; Solberg, pp. 372–402; Theodore White, pp. 324–343, 348–384; LaFeber, *Deadly Bet,* pp. 164–179. "Dry up every Democratic": LaFeber, *Deadly Bet,* p. 158. "An absolute angry" and "I do not want you": Arthur Krim OH, LBJL. Sept. Gallup Poll: Gallup, vol. 3, p. 2162. "I don't stand": Solberg, p. 380.

"Acceptable risk": Humphrey speech, Sept. 30, 1968. "I'll turn it on": Johnson-Humphrey, Sept. 30, 1968, LBJT. "This just ruins us": Johnson-Rusk, Sept. 1968, LBJT. "He can cram it": Solberg, p. 392. "Let's assume all of those": Johnson-Dirksen, Oct. 1968, LBJT. Johnson's peace efforts and Nixon's maneuvering: Farrell, pp. 340–344; Evan Thomas, *Being,* pp. 172–181; Ken Hughes, pp. 26–29; O'Donnell, pp. 392–404; Nixon Foundation, "Misunderstanding a Monkey Wrench," June 2, 2017. "Don't want to look bad in history" and Nixon "rather upset": Johnson-Russell, Oct. 23, 1968, LBJT. "Can we return to full-scale bombing": *Foreign Relations of the United States,* vol. 7, p. 404. "So explosive": Rostow to Johnson, Oct. 29, 1968, LBJP. "Cost so much to obtain": Department of State to US Embassy Saigon, Oct. 30, 1968, LBJL. Nixon on bugging of his plane: Ken Hughes, p. 156. "Getting a little unbalanced": Johnson-Dirksen, Oct. 31, 1968, LBJT. "All air, naval and artillery": Johnson speech, Oct. 31, 1968. "Not to open his damn mouth": Johnson–James Rowe, Nov. 1, 1968, LBJT. "Prospects for peace are not as bright" and "ducks in a row": *Philadelphia Inquirer,* Nov. 3, 1968.

"Skirting on dangerous ground": Johnson-Dirksen, Nov. 2, 1968, LBJT. "Any rumblings" and "You just see": Johnson-Nixon, Nov. 2, 1968, LBJT. Preelection polls: Theodore White, pp. 364–382; Farrell, pp. 339–340; Witcover, pp. 425–426. Johnson thinks Humphrey too soft: Harry Middleton, int 1996. 1968 election results: Dallek, *Flawed,* pp. 589–596; Solberg, pp. 403–408. "Created all the problems": Johnson-Humphrey, Nov. 6, 1968, LBJT. "If you want me to do something": Johnson-Nixon, Nov. 8, 1968, LBJT. Johnson asks FBI about Agnew and other possible clues: Dallek, *Flawed,* pp. 596–587; Farrell, p. 343. "Most sensitive—and perhaps most troubling": Tom Huston to Nixon, Feb. 25, 1970, RNL.

Johnson's postpresidential depression and 1972 heart attack: ints with Robert Hardesty, 1994, Jack Valenti, 1999, Harry Middleton, 2015, and Larry Temple, 2015; Arthur Krim OH, LBJL; Dallek, *Flawed*, pp. 602, 604, 617; Merle Miller, *Lyndon*, pp. 544–545; *Atlantic*, July 1973. Nixon conducts war and ends draft: Farrell, pp. 347–370; O'Donnell, p. 427. "We have had 10 years": Nixon handwriting on Jan. 3, 1972, memo from Kissinger, RNL. "I never ordered": George Christian, int 1994. Johnson to Haig: Haig, p. 141. "Lyndon hated funerals": Lady Bird Johnson, int 1998. Johnson and Watergate: Farrell, pp. 517–518, 546; Haldeman, pp. 12–14, 493–494; Haldeman diary, RNL.

"I had heart pains all night": Johnson-Nixon, Jan. 2, 1973, RNT. "He's a hypochondriac": Robenalt, p. 266. "Endured the vilification": Nixon speech, Jan. 22, 1973. Fall of Saigon: Cannon, pp. 272, 397–398, 415–420; Kissinger, *Renewal*, pp. 520–546; Gerald Ford, pp. 250–258; Maddow, pp. 25–27. "Same frame of mind": *WP*, Sept. 23, 1976. "We dishonor the memory": Reagan speech, Aug. 18, 1980. "No great nation can afford": George H. W. Bush inaugural address, Jan. 20, 1989. "Finally exorcized": Nixon to Bush, Feb. 24, 1991, RNL.

EPILOGUE

2001 most injurious attack since 1814: Riedel, p. 1. George W. Bush, 2001 attacks, Afghanistan and Iraq Wars: Bush, pp. 126–271; Peter Baker, pp. 120–303; Jean Smith, *Bush*, pp. 217–243, 292, 300. 9/11 Commission finding: National Commission on Terrorist Attacks Against the United States, *The 9/11 Commission Report* (2004), p. 504. *Newsweek* poll: Sept. 4, 2004. "Dumb war": Obama speech, Oct. 2, 2002. War powers legislation: Fisher, *Presidential*, pp. 144–153; Irons, *War Powers*, pp. 197–199; Maddow, pp. 22–25; Barron, p. 344. Changes in presidential war power from time of Constitution: Fisher, *Presidential*, pp. 1–281; Arthur Schlesinger, *Imperial*, pp. 1–419; Arthur Schlesinger, *War*, pp. 44–48; Barron, pp. 388–389; Wills, *Bomb Power*, pp. 187–196; Stevenson, pp. 1–80; Irons, *War Powers*, pp. 1–273.

Photo Credits

PAGE 6

Top: Public domain
Bottom: Lithograph by Adolphe Jean-Baptiste-Bayot after a drawing by Carl Nebel

PAGE 7

Top: Public domain
Bottom: Library of Congress

PAGE 8

Top: Public domain
Bottom: Public domain

PAGE 9

Top: Library of Congress
Bottom: Public domain

PAGE 10

Top: Public domain
Bottom: North Wind Picture Archives/Alamy Stock Photo

PAGE 11

Top: Public domain
Bottom: Public domain

PAGE 12

Top: Library of Congress
Bottom: Public domain

PAGE 13

Top: Public domain
Bottom: Public domain

PAGE 14

Top: Public domain
Bottom: GRANGER/GRANGER—All rights reserved.

PAGE 15

Top: Public domain
Bottom: Courtesy of the State Archives of Florida

PAGE 16
Top: Public domain
Bottom: Public domain

INSERT 2

PAGE 1
Top: Deutsches Bundesarchiv
Bottom: Public domain

PAGE 2
Top: Public domain
Bottom: Library of Congress/Corbis Historical/Getty Images

PAGE 3
Top: Public domain
Bottom: Woodrow Wilson Presidential Library

PAGE 4
Top: Bettmann/Getty Images
Bottom: Library of Congress

PAGE 5
Top: Public domain
Middle: Bettmann/Getty Images
Bottom: Popperfoto/Getty Images

PAGE 6
Top: Public domain
Bottom: Lt. Lotzof/IWM via Getty Images

PAGE 7
Top: Public domain
Bottom: Bettmann/Getty Images

PAGE 8
Top: Public domain
Bottom: Courtesy of Harry S. Truman Library

PAGE 9

Top: George Skadding/The LIFE Picture Collection/Getty Images
Bottom: Bettmann/Getty Images

PAGE 10

Top: Corbis/Getty Images
Middle: George Skadding/The LIFE Picture Collection/Getty Images
Bottom: Public domain

PAGE 11

Top: John Rous/AP
Bottom: Bob Schutz/AP

PAGE 12

Top: PhotoQuest/Getty Images
Bottom: Rick Merron/AP

PAGE 13

Top: Bill Eppridge/Getty Images
Bottom: Henry Burroughs/AP

PAGE 14

Top: Bettmann/Getty Images
Bottom: Bettmann/Getty Images

PAGE 15

Top: Yoichi Okamoto—Lyndon Baines Johnson Library
Bottom: Lyndon Baines Johnson Library

PAGE 16

Top: Robert Clark
Middle: National Archives
Bottom: Trinity Mirror/Mirrorpix/Alamy Stock Photo

Index

About the Author

Michael Beschloss was born in Chicago in 1955 and attended Phillips Academy (Andover), Williams College, and Harvard Business School. He has served as a historian at the Smithsonian Institution, a Senior Associate Member at St. Antony's College (Oxford), and a Senior Fellow of the Annenberg Foundation.

His first book, *Kennedy and Roosevelt: The Uneasy Alliance* (1980), originated as his Williams College honors thesis. *Mayday: Eisenhower, Khrushchev, and the U-2 Affair* (1986) argued that the spring of 1960 was a turning point in the US confrontation with the Soviet Union. *The Crisis Years: Kennedy and Khrushchev, 1960–1963* (1991) was praised by David Remnick in the *New Yorker* as the "definitive" history of John F. Kennedy and the Cold War. Beschloss was the first historian to write books based on Lyndon Johnson's newly opened White House tapes— *Taking Charge* (1997) and *Reaching for Glory* (2001). These volumes were followed by *The Conquerors: Roosevelt, Truman, and the Destruction of Hitler's Germany* (2002) and *Presidential Courage: Brave Leaders and How They Changed America, 1789–1989* (2007), both *New York Times* bestsellers.

Beschloss serves as the NBC News Presidential Historian and a contributor to the *PBS NewsHour*. He has won an Emmy and six honorary degrees. He has also been awarded the State of Illinois's Order of Lincoln, the Ambassador Book Prize, the Harry S. Truman Public Service Award, the Founders Award of the Historical Society of Pennsylvania, the New York State Archives Award, and the Rutgers University Living History Award. He is a trustee of the White House Historical Association and the National Archives Foundation, and a former trustee of the Thomas Jefferson Foundation. He is on Twitter at @BeschlossDC.